Encyclopedia of Barbarian Europe

Encyclopedia of Barbarian Europe

Society in Transformation

Michael Frassetto

A B C CLIO

Santa Barbara, California
Denver, Colorado   Oxford, England

Library of Congress Cataloging-in-Publication Data

Frassetto, Michael.
    Encyclopedia of barbarian Europe : society in transformation / Michael Frassetto.
        p. cm.
Includes bibliographical references and index.
    ISBN 1-57607-263-0 (hardcover : alk. paper) ISBN 1-85109-586-1 (e-book)
    1. Europe—History—392-814—Encyclopedias. 2. Germanic peoples—Europe—Influence—Encyclopedias. 3. Migrations of nations—Encyclopedias. 4. Germanic peoples—Encyclopedias. 5. Civilization, Medieval—Encyclopedias. 6. Military history, Medieval—Encyclopedias.
I. Title.
    D135.F73 2003
    940.1'03—dc21
                                        2003000302

07 06 05 04 03   10 9 8 7 6 5 4 3 2 1

This book is also available on the World Wide Web as an e-book.
Visit http://www.abc-clio.com for details.

ABC-CLIO, Inc.
130 Cremona Drive, P.O. Box 1911
Santa Barbara, California 93116-1911

This book is printed on acid-free paper ∞.

Contents

Encyclopedia of Barbarian Europe

Acknowledgments

The completion of this volume has been a long but often pleasant task, and any merit the book may claim is the result of the help that I have received along the way from many sources. I would like to recognize those especially without whom this work would not have appeared. I would like to thank Joyce Salisbury, who introduced me to the editors at ABC-CLIO and encouraged me to take on the project. I received further encouragement and great support from my original editor, Vince Tobin, and from his successor, Simon Mason, who inherited the unenviable task of bringing the volume to its conclusion when Vince left for greener pastures. It has been a great pleasure working with them and the entire staff of editors and researchers at ABC-CLIO who have helped bring this project to a timely end. I should thank especially and dedicate this volume to Jill and Olivia, who have helped me in more ways than they know.

Introduction

Once regarded as a period of unending savagery and ignorance, the age of barbarian Europe has come to be recognized as a time of important social and cultural transformation Although the great civilization of the ancient Mediterranean gradually faded away during this time, it was replaced by a new and dynamic culture. Despite the very real decline in population, literacy, city life, and economic strength, the leaders of government and society from the fourth to the tenth centuries created a unique culture that drew on a legacy that was at once Christian, German, and Roman. This emerging world laid the foundation for later medieval and modern civilization. Indeed, great leaders refashioned ideas about law and kingship and provided a model of Christian government that remained influential into the modern age. (See Alfred the Great, Justinian, Charlemagne.) Early medieval rulers also established the basic outlines of the later medieval and modern nation states (see Verdun, Treaty of) as they created new kingdoms out of the former Western Empire. Although plagued by invasion and civil and international war, barbarian Europe enjoyed important cultural achievements. During late antiquity and the early Middle Ages, influential thinkers and writers (see Alcuin, Augustine of Hippo, Bede, Boethius) preserved the literary and intellectual traditions of ancient Rome and shaped the theological traditions of the church. Moreover, important church institutions, including monasticism and the papacy (see Benedict of Nursia, Gregory I the Great), underwent significant growth in this period. The age of barbarian Europe, therefore, was a period of important transformation from the ancient to the medieval world, and an age that laid the foundation for later medieval and modern civilization.

Overview of the Historiography of Barbarian Europe

Writing in the late eighteenth century, the great historian Edward Gibbon observed, "If a man were called to fix the period of the history of the world during which the condition of the human race was most happy and prosperous, he would, without hesitation, name that which elapsed from the death of Domitian to the accession of Commodus. The vast extent of the Roman Empire was governed by absolute power, under the guidance of virtue and wisdom" (*The Decline and Fall of the Roman Empire,* vol. 1, p. 70). Gibbon then proceeded to outline the subsequent collapse of the Roman Empire, which he believed was the greatest political structure in human history. Beyond the moral corruption that afflicted Rome in the period following what he saw as the golden age, he identified two major causes for the collapse of the empire. One was an internal revolution brought on by the gradual growth of Christianity and its adoption by the emperor and people of Rome. No longer were the Romans willing to fight for the empire because of their adoption of a pacifistic religion that drew them away from their traditional devotion to the service of the empire.

The other significant factor contributing to the collapse of this most magnificent empire, according to Gibbon, was the invasion of the barbarians. Large numbers of uncivilized peoples began to put pressure on and then cross over the imperial frontiers. These barbarians entered the empire and destroyed ancient civilization because of their illiteracy and hatred of all things Roman. (See FRANKS, HUNS, VANDALS, VISIGOTHS.) Moreover, the Romans' inability to provide for their own defense made it necessary that they enroll large numbers of the same barbarians that were invading the empire in the defense of the empire. Internal weakness and the end of traditional civic virtue, along with the invasion of the barbarian peoples, for Gibbon were the main factors in the fall of the Roman Empire and the emergence of the Dark Ages.

As a result of Gibbon's remarkable prose, wide knowledge of the original sources in Latin and Greek, and compelling argument, his view of the end of the ancient world and the Middle Ages remained the standard understanding of this period well into the twentieth century. Indeed, generations of scholars built upon his fundamental assumption in their studies of Romans and barbarians. In the early twentieth century, for example, the English scholar J. B. Bury and the French historian Ferdinand Lot refined and elaborated on the principle arguments of Gibbon. They offered meticulous studies of the movements and character of the various barbarian peoples and the great social and political changes that accompanied the end of the ancient world. The end of the Roman Empire for Gibbon and his successors signaled not only the end of a political entity, but also all of ancient civilization. The causes for this collapse came to be seen as more varied and complex, involving a broad range of factors (economic, social, political, and military), but the consensus remained that the combination of internal Roman weakness and the invasion or migration of peoples led to the demise of the Roman Empire and ancient civilization in the year 476. (See ODOVACAR.)

During the course of the twentieth century and into the twenty-first, the view once established by Gibbon was gradually eroded, as scholars brought new methodologies and new insights to the study of ancient and early medieval civilization. One of the most obvious observations was that the Roman Empire did not cease to exist in 476; only the Western Empire succumbed to the movements of the barbarian peoples. The Eastern Empire (now known as the Byzantine Empire, from its capital of Byzantium, rechristened Constantinople) survived for another thousand years and fell to the Turks only in 1453. The Byzantine Empire clearly enjoyed a long and prosperous life after the "fall" in 476, and Constantinople even ruled again, for a time, over parts of the Western Empire, thanks to the conquests of Justinian and his generals. (See BELISARIUS and NARSES.) Moreover, Roman traditions were preserved by the Byzantine state even after the so-called fall of Rome, as they were in the former Western Empire. Indeed, historians have emphasized continuity in a number of areas in the Germanic successor states that emerged after the end of Roman political organization in the West. As the language of law and government, Latin continued, as did economic structures, the machinery of taxation, administrative organization, the religion of the empire—Christianity—and a variety of other social and cultural traditions.

Rather than a time marked by an abrupt and dramatic end of one civilization and appearance of another, historians now regard the period as one of transformation. The end of the ancient world came gradually, and its continuation can be seen in a number of areas. In the early part of the twentieth century, the great economic historian, Henri Pirenne, argued that the ancient world survived until the time of the expansion of Islam in the eighth century. Later in the century, Peter Brown also demonstrated the survival of ancient civilization into the eighth century, but went beyond Pirenne to consider broader social and cultural developments. Some scholars have even argued that ancient civilization survived until the year 1000, when slavery, the last vestige of classical culture, finally disappeared. Although the exact date remains uncertain, ancient civilization clearly lingered on past the traditional date of its end in 476 in the form of a number of social, cultural, and economic trends that shaped the lives and governments of the Germanic successor kings who ruled over the former Western Empire.

The picture of the "barbarians" also has evolved since the time that Gibbon wrote his classic work. The traditional understanding of the peoples who succeeded the Romans was that they were savages and barbarians. Drawing from ancient works by Tacitus, Jordanes, and others, Gibbon and the historians who followed him saw the Germans and other peoples who entered the empire as uncivilized—the noble savage of Tacitus or the barbaric and ugly Hun of Jordanes. The barbarians were seen only as invaders bent on the destruction of the Roman Empire and classical civilization. Citing the examples of Alaric and Gaiseric, who sacked and pillaged the city of Rome in 410 and 455 respectively, the older generation of scholars argued that the intent of the barbarians was destruction of the old order and its replacement with new barbarian kingdoms. Indeed, they saw the great movement of peoples that took place in the fourth and fifth centuries as an invasion of the empire by the barbarians, who then created new kingdoms out of the old political order. Moreover, this negative view of Rome's successors influenced the assessment of their cultural contributions, which were regarded as nonexistent or inferior. The term *Gothic* was applied to the architecture of the twelfth and thirteenth centuries because it was deemed crude and barbaric, like the barbarian tribe of the Goths.

Scholarship in the twentieth century, especially the work of Walter Goffart, has provided a new perspective on the "barbarians" and their relations with the Roman Empire. Although the argument that the increased numbers of barbarians or Germans in the imperial army still carries weight with some scholars, the association of German/barbarian and Roman is seen in a much more positive light. Longstanding contacts between Romans and the peoples outside the empire reshaped both the Romans and barbarians. There was a gradual transformation on each side, as the Romans and their neighbors traded with each other and intermarried. Many Germans did enter the military and imbibed a better appreciation for the empire, and the leaders came to identify with the empire. (See THEODORIC THE GREAT.) Although some Germanic and barbarian peoples invaded the empire for spoil and territory, others petitioned for entry into a greater political entity and sought to become part of that entity. (See ATTILA THE HUN and GAISERIC.) Furthermore, the traditional identification of the Germans and barbarians with national or tribal groups has been eroded in the new understanding of them. The groups are now seen as less nationally distinct, and there is clear historical discontinuity between the earliest manifestations of the various tribal groups and the groups that established kingdoms in the former Western Empire.

The period of late antiquity and the early Middle Ages has also traditionally been recognized as the "Dark Ages." Indeed, the entire period from the fall of Rome to the start of the Renaissance was once understood as a period of little or no cultural achievement, with the possible exception of the Carolingian Renaissance, which was deemed the one shining moment of the nearly thousand-year period. (See CAROLINGIAN RENAISSANCE.) As the twentieth century progressed, this view came to be revised, so that a smaller and smaller portion of the Middle Ages was deemed "dark." But the notion that the early Middle Ages (c. 400 to c. 1000) was a period of cultural stagnation persisted for a longer time, even though the period of "darkness" was narrowed to circa 500 to circa 750. Whatever the chronological limits, the "Dark Ages" that followed the fall of Rome in the West have been traditionally understood as a period of limited intellectual and cultural productivity. Both city life and the overall population of Europe had diminished. The great monuments of sculpture and architecture were no longer produced in the cities, and there was also a decline in literacy among the general population. Related to the decline in literacy was the near disappearance of the use of writing in government administration and other public activities. The cultural decline was, it had been argued, related to the general disdain for ancient civilization that many of barbarians held, as well as to their own cultural backwardness.

Just as the understanding of the barbarians has undergone a revision, so too has the view of the period as the "Dark Ages. Although the term itself continues to be used, the period after the fall of the Roman Empire is seen less as a dark age. Indeed, even in the period of 500 to 750, important cultural developments took place and artistic activity continued. Even though the scale and focus of artistic activity was reduced, it nevertheless continued, as the metalwork of early medieval artisans reveals. Moreover, the barbarians are better understood as the heirs of the ancient Roman tradition, and in the early Middle Ages the various social and cultural trends that characterized later medieval civilization were taking shape. Important Roman cultural traditions, particularly in law and language, continued into the so-called "Dark Ages" and influenced the shape of government and society after 476. Furthermore, the traditions of learning and letters were preserved by the church, especially in the monasteries. Late antique and early medieval churchmen produced poetry, literature, history, and theology in Latin and preserved the works of the ancient Romans. Clearly, Europe of the early Middle Ages was not the equal of Athens in the fifth century B.C. or of Florence in the fifteenth century, but historians have come to recognize the important cultural developments of the period. And although the Carolingian Renaissance continues to be seen as a great cultural milestone, it is no longer seen as the lone example of early medieval brilliance, and its roots in the sixth and seventh centuries have been identified.

A Brief History of Late Antiquity and the Early Middle Ages

The Later Roman Empire

Although the Roman Empire did not "fall" until the late fifth century, it had undergone a profound change already in the third century, a change that in some ways foreshadowed the transformation of the early Middle Ages. Indeed, during the crisis of the third century, as it is often called, the empire endured many of the difficulties it faced again in the fourth and fifth centuries. The empire suffered a dramatic economic collapse, decline in population and urban life, military disasters, and foreign invasions. The essential strength of Roman civilization and the emergence of several highly talented and determined emperors, however, enabled the empire to survive the crisis. The empire that emerged at the end of the third century and the beginning of the fourth was fundamentally different from the empire of the second century, which was so highly praised by Gibbon.

The empire of the fourth century was shaped by the reforms of two of the greatest rulers in Roman history, Diocletian and Constantine. (See CONSTANTINE.) Although in one sense they saved the empire, establishing a foundation upon which the Western Empire survived nearly two hundred years and the Eastern Empire survived over one thousand years, in another sense Diocletian and Constantine forged a new empire, one that looked forward to the religious and political structures that characterized the early medieval world. Building on the work of his immediate predecessors, who managed to stop the advance of the Goths and stabilize the imperial government, Diocletian reformed the Roman government and military. Organizing imperial administration into four main divisions and establishing a plan of succession, Diocletian saved the empire from ruin and foreshadowed the divisions in the empire that came later, as well as the structure of government and society. He also launched the last major persecution of the Christian church, which failed to destroy it. His religious policy, and much of his imperial settlement, was undermined by his ultimate successor, Constantine.

The first Christian emperor, Constantine seized power in a civil war that followed Diocletian's retirement in 305. Although he accepted baptism only on his deathbed in 337, Constantine legalized the Christian faith and was the church's greatest benefactor. He granted privileges to bishops, allowed the church to inherit money and property, and made many pious donations of his own. In this way, Constantine helped ensure the success of Christianity, the major religion of late antique and early medieval society. The emperor's other reforms also paved the way for the future of the Mediterranean basin. His reform of the coinage stabilized the economy and provided the basic unit of money, the *solidus,* for generations to come. (See COINS AND COINAGE.) He also established a new imperial capital at Constantinople, the new Christian city that remained the capital of a "Roman" empire for more than a thousand years.

The reforms of Diocletian and Constantine secured the survival of the empire, and the fourth century appears, on the surface, to have been a time of renewed vitality. Indeed, some emperors resumed wars of expansion, and despite the usual turmoil and dissension in the imperial household, the empire was ably run by Constantine's successors. The house of Constantine maintained united rule of the empire for several generations, and even in the later fourth century cooperation between the emperors in the Eastern and Western Empire was the rule rather than the exception. Indeed, Theodosius ruled over the entire empire for a time before his death in 395; he also protected the empire from the increasing threat from the barbarians and made Christianity the official religion of the empire.

At the same time, however, the fundamental weaknesses of ancient civilization became increasingly evident, especially in the Western Empire. There was clear evidence in the decline of city life in the West, most notably the demise of the original heart of the empire, as Rome was abandoned as the imperial capital and replaced by Milan. Moreover, the increasingly heavy burden of taxation caused the aristocrats to flee the cities for their large plantations, where they could avoid the long arm of government. Flight from paying taxes paralleled the flight from honoring their traditional participation in government. The aristocrats and their plantations also prefigured the estates, or manors, of the Middle Ages, where servile labor farmed as tenants of the lord. (See AGRICULTURE.)

These important social changes were accompanied, in the Western Empire, by population and economic decline. The economy remained an agricultural one that failed to develop an industrial component, and as the soils became exhausted, agricultural and economic life collapsed. Unlike the Eastern Empire, the Western did not have long established urban and commercial traditions to save it in the face of agricultural decline. As a result of economic and demographic decline as well as the widespread reluctance to serve the state, the Romans enrolled more and more Germans in the army. They would defend imperial borders and then retire to farm imperial lands. The underlying weakness of the Western Empire, therefore, was already evident in the fourth century and prepared the way for the so-called fall of Rome in the fifth century.

The Migrations of Peoples
The fall of Rome, or gradual transformation from late antique to early medieval society, was the result of the internal weaknesses of the Western Empire and the empire's inability to respond to the influx of large numbers of Germanic and other barbarian peoples. These peoples, whose origins are obscure, but who are traditionally held to have come from Scandinavia, had long existed along the frontiers of the Roman Empire. They had frequent contact with the empire and as early as the first century had scored great victories against Roman armies, and in the second century the emperor Marcus Aurelius spent much of his reign fighting the Germans along the Danube River. In the third century again

these peoples threatened the empire and violated its frontiers. But the empire survived these repeated threats until the late fourth century, and the Germans saw the empire as a great power whose peace and prosperity they desired to share. Indeed, most Germanic peoples sought not to destroy the empire but to join it, and some did. Germans were enrolled in the army, and significant numbers of them became Roman soldiers by the reforms of Constantine. They often sought entry into the empire to enjoy the better climate and farmlands and the strength and stability of Rome.

In the late fourth century, the traditional relationship that existed between Rome and the peoples on her frontiers was profoundly altered by the entry of a new power, the Huns (see HUNS). These East Asian peoples, for reasons still unknown, began an aggressive movement west in the fourth century. Their great skill on horseback and ferociousness in battle enabled them to create a great empire that stretched across large parts of Europe and Asia. As they moved westward, they absorbed or displaced the peoples settled in their way and initiated a general westward migration of peoples. As a result, the tribes long settled along the imperial frontiers now exerted increasing pressure on the frontiers, in the hopes of entering the empire to find protection against the Huns. Notably, the Hunnish assault on one group of Goths caused another group, traditionally known as the Visigoths, to move toward the empire in the hopes of protection from the Huns. (See OSTROGOTHS and VISIGOTHS.) The Goths, like other so-called barbarians, came not as conquerors or invaders, but almost as refugees who sought to join the empire, not to destroy it.

Although many of the tribal groups that entered the empire had great respect for it and did not seek to destroy it, their movements led to the gradual demise of an independent Roman state in the West. Fearing the advance of the Huns and with the permission of the emperor Valens, some 80,000 Goths entered the empire in 376. The failure of the Romans to accommodate this large body of people led to increasing difficulties for both the Goths and Romans. In 378, war broke out between the Goths and Romans, a war that led to the destruction of Roman armies and the death of the emperor and gave free reign to the Goths, whose movements within the empire further destabilized the situation. (See ADRIANOPLE, BATTLE OF.) Their independence was cut short by the emperor Theodosius, who settled them in the Balkans, where they remained until the death of the emperor in 395. They resumed the warpath in 395 under a new king, Alaric, who assumed a more aggressive stance toward the empire. (See ALARIC.) His movements were restricted somewhat by the general Stilicho, whose murder in 406 opened the way for Alaric. (See STILICHO.) In 410 the unthinkable occurred, when Alaric and his followers sacked the city of Rome, the first time it had been sacked in eight hundred years. This event was a profound shock to the people of the empire and prefigured worse events to come.

The Fall of Rome and the
Germanic Successor States

In the fifth century, the pressures on the Roman frontiers increased even more, and the internal weakness of the Western Empire made it almost impossible to prevent gradual dismemberment of the Western Empire. Indeed, the Huns, Visigoths, and other peoples continued to pose a threat to the integrity of the empire, as a series of weak emperors were propped up by their generals, some of whom were Germans themselves. (See AËTIUS, RICIMER, and STILICHO.) The Visigoths, for example, continued their wanderings in the western Roman world after the sack of the city, eventually settling in Spain and southern France and creating the first of the Germanic successor states.

The Visigoths, however, were not the only people to undermine the imperial order in the West. The Huns also continued to plague the Romans and barbarians alike, especially under their greatest leader, Attila the Hun. Forging a massive empire across parts of Europe and Asia, Attila forced disparate peoples to come under his authority and repeatedly challenged the power of the empire. Although he was unable to replace it, Attila seriously weakened the empire, fighting several major battles against an alliance of Romans and barbarians and threatening to sack the city of Rome in 453. (See CATALAUNIAN PLAINS, BATTLE OF, and LEO THE GREAT, POPE.) At his death, however, the Hunnish empire collapsed, as the various subject peoples revolted against the Huns. While the Huns and Visigoths assaulted the empire, large numbers of other German peoples entered the empire seeking territory, and the empire gradually abandoned its authority in England and elsewhere.

Among the other peoples to enter the empire in the fifth century were the Anglo-Saxons and Vandals, who established important successor kingdoms at opposite ends of the Western Empire. (See ANGLO-SAXONS, VANDALS.) As the Romans fled England, the native population sought aid against raids from the tribes to the north and invited the leaders of the Saxons to defend them, an invitation that led to the Anglo-Saxon conquest of the country. (See HENGIST AND HORSA, KING ARTHUR, and VORTIGERN.) The Vandals also carved a successor kingdom in the Western Empire, settling in much of North Africa, which remained the base for subsequent harassment of the empire by the Vandals and their leader Gaiseric, who sacked Rome for a second time in 455.

The Western Empire was gradually dismembered during the course of the fifth century, as one province after another was transformed into a Germanic successor kingdom. For most of the century, however, Italy remained protected from the onslaught. Indeed, the policy of many of the imperial military commanders was to protect the old heart of the empire. In 476, however, Italy, too, fell to a Germanic conqueror. Leading a mixed band of Germans, the barbarian general Odovacar deposed the reigning emperor, Romulus Augustulus, and killed the power behind the throne, the general Orestes. (See ORESTES and ROMULUS AUGUSTULUS.) Instead of promoting a puppet emperor as Orestes and others had done, Odovacar sent the imperial insignia and other official seals and symbols back to Zeno, the emperor in Constantinople, and established an independent kingdom in Italy, which lasted until 493 and established the framework for later Italian successor kingdoms. (See ZENO.) The deposition of Romulus Augustulus by Odovacar thus is traditionally recognized as the end of the Western Empire, and no emperor reigned in the West again until the ninth century.

The Post-Roman World: Theodoric the Great, Justinian, and the Lombards

Although independent imperial rule was brought to a close by Odovacar in 476, Rome and its influence continued well into the early Middle Ages. Indeed, Odovacar recognized at least the nominal authority of the emperor in Constantinople over Italy, and other Germanic leaders respected the empire and its leaders. Furthermore, Roman traditions were maintained in a number of other areas, including law, religion, and language. Social, economic, and cultural trends that began as early as the fourth century were preserved into the sixth century, as city life was gradually replaced by a more rural society. The institutions of the church that took shape in late antiquity also continued to evolve in the early Middle Ages. Throughout much of the former Western Empire, the bishops, especially the bishop of Rome, assumed many of the administrative duties of the old Roman establishment, as well as the responsibility for social welfare. The traditions of monasticism continued to spread throughout the old Western Empire, and the various Germanic peoples either converted to Christianity or continued in their adherence to it.

The abolition of the imperial office in the Western Empire in 476 did not, moreover, end the interest of the emperor in Constantinople in Italian affairs. Indeed, even though he did not recognize Odovacar's usurpation, Zeno granted the German the title of Patricius and remained in uneasy correspondence with him. Zeno also used the uncertain situation in Italy to his advantage when the great

Ostrogothic leader, Theodoric, became an increasingly difficult figure in the Eastern Empire. In 488, the emperor commissioned Theodoric to invade Italy and depose Odovacar, thus resolving two problematic issues for the emperor. Theodoric accepted the emperor's offer and led the Ostrogoths to Italy, where they faced strong resistance from Odovacar. In the early 490s, the two leaders fought to a standstill, and in 493 the two came to terms, which were to be celebrated at a banquet held by Theodoric. Upon his arrival, Odovacar was murdered by Theodoric's men, and the Ostrogoth became the sole ruler in Italy.

Theodoric's Italian realm was one of the most dynamic and important of the immediate post-Roman kingdoms, and the king himself was the greatest power in the former Western Empire. Despite his Arian faith, Theodoric enjoyed good relations with the majority Catholic Italian population. Although a "barbarian," Theodoric remained on good terms with the descendants of the Roman citizens in Italy because of his respect for Roman traditions and his promotion of them. He was a patron of the arts and culture, and promoted two of the leading late Roman writers, Boethius and Cassiodorus, to important court positions. (See BOETHIUS and CASSIODORUS.) He supported Roman traditions in law and education and was a great builder—as all Roman rulers were. Even though Theodoric created a successful kingdom and left an important legacy, the last years of his reign were troubled, as relations with the senatorial aristocracy worsened. His increasing brutality, seen for example in his execution of Boethius, soured relations with the Italian population and revived the desire for imperial rule. His death in 526, moreover, left the kingdom in an even more difficult situation for his heir, Athalaric, whose mother, Amalaswintha, was Theodoric's daughter. Internal political disputes, in part involving relations with the Eastern Empire, led to the murder of Amalaswintha, which opened the door for the invasion of the emperor Justinian.

The legacy of Rome weighed heavily on Justinian, who was born in a Latin-speaking region of the Eastern Empire. He was also filled with the traditional ideas of the former united empire and felt it his responsibility to rule over both the eastern and western halves of the empire. His conquest of Italy brought about the reunification of the empire, but at great cost to both the Eastern Empire and Italy. The Gothic Wars devastated the Italian countryside, as Justinian's generals fought great battles against the Ostrogoths for over two decades, from 535 to the late 550s. Although able to bring the Ostrogothic kingdom to an end, Justinian was not able to restore long-term authority over Italy. Byzantine influence in Italy continued into the eighth century, but the Eastern Empire's control of the peninsula was curtailed within a few years of the emperor's death. Indeed, just as the Byzantines under Justinian ended Ostrogthic rule in Italy, so the Lombards ended Byzantine control of much of Italy. (See LOMBARDS.) Indeed, they too were replaced in the eighth century by the greatest of the Germanic successors of Rome, the Franks (see FRANKS).

The Kingdom of the Franks

Unlike most of the other Germanic peoples, the Franks established a lasting kingdom and came to include Gaul and much of post-Roman Europe from the late fifth to the late tenth century. In two great dynasties, the Franks created a great and powerful kingdom, and triumphed over several of the other successor peoples to the Romans, and established numerous precedents for later medieval society. (See MEROVINGIAN DYNASTY and CAROLINGIAN DYNASTY.) The first of the dynasties, the Merovingian, was founded by the great king Clovis, who was an effective warrior and the first of the barbarian kings to accept Catholic Christianity. (See CLOVIS.) Although none of his heirs were his equal, many of them were colorful and effective rulers, especially Chlotar II and Dagobert (see CHLOTAR II and DAGOBERT). Others were involved in bitter civil wars that nearly destroyed the kingdom, and the last of Clovis's heirs were increasingly less effective rulers. (See BRUNHILD, FREDEGUND, and ROIS FAINÉANTS.) The dynasty, despite its ultimate demise, managed to secure good relations with the church, protected and promoted important missionaries, and enjoyed the production of important works of history and literature. (See GREGORY OF TOURS.)

The Carolingian dynasty, which replaced the Merovingians in 751, was perhaps the most important family in the early Middle Ages. Their rise to power is often seen as a great triumphal march, but neither their success nor Merovingian failure was foreordained. Indeed, they faced numerous setbacks in the seventh and eighth centuries, and even once they secured the royal throne, they were beset by revolts and turmoil. Nonetheless, the great Carolingian kings Pippin and Charlemagne, and to a lesser extent Louis the Pious and Charles the Bald, guided the kingdom and empire of the Franks to great political, military, and cultural heights. (See CHARLEMAGNE, CHARLES THE BALD, LOUIS THE PIOUS, and PIPPIN III, CALLED THE SHORT.) Under the Carolingian kings, the Frankish state reached its greatest extent, without peer in the former Western Empire and the rival of the Eastern Empire in territorial size. The Carolingians were great conquerors, who expanded the boundaries of the realm into Saxony, Italy, and beyond, and who also spread Christianity into new regions. They also revived imperial rule in the west when Charlemagne, their greatest king, was crowned emperor by Pope Leo III. (See LEO III, POPE.) And even though Charlemagne is the king most associated with the Carolingian Renaissance, all the Carolingian kings and emperors promoted learning and religious reform throughout their vast realms. Although the empire forged by Charlemagne collapsed in the two generations following his death, it remained one of the great accomplishments of the early Middle Ages and provided important precedents for the later history of Europe.

The Importance of Barbarian Europe

Although long recognized as a backward period politically and culturally, the age of barbarian Europe was an important period in history and a critical period in the transition from ancient Roman civilization to medieval and modern civilization. Long associated with the "fall" of the Roman Empire, barbarian Europe accomplished more than the destruction of ancient civilization. Rather, it adopted aspects of classical culture and mixed them with Christian and Germanic traditions to create a unique and impressive new culture. The various barbarian kings of the early Middle Ages provided a variety of legal and governmental precedents for the future. Indeed, the greatest of them, Charlemagne, was a model for kings for centuries after his death, and his empire also provided the highest ideal of government into the nineteenth century. The church continued to evolve in this period, and key ecclesiastical institutions took shape in this period. Many kings also promoted cultural life, and most monasteries remained centers of education and learning. Far from being the Dark Ages, the early Middle Ages were a pivotal period in the history of civilization.

Select Bibliography

Bois, Guy. *The Transformation of the Year One Thousand: The Village of Lournand from Antiquity to Feudalism.* Trans. Jean Birrell. Manchester, UK: Manchester University Press, 1992.

Brown, Peter. *The World of Late Antiquity,* A.D. *150–750.* London: Thames and Hudson, 1971.

———. *The Rise of Western Christendom: Triumph and Adversity,* A.D. *200–1000.* Cambridge, MA: Blackwell, 1996.

Bury, John B. *The Invasions of Europe by the Barbarians.* 1928. Reprint, New York: W. W. Norton, 1967.

Ferrill, Arther. *The Fall of the Roman Empire: The Military Explanation.* New York: Thames and Hudson, 1986.

Fossier, Robert, ed. *The Cambridge Illustrated History of the Middle Ages, 350–950.* Vol. 1. Trans. Janet Sondheimer. Cambridge: Cambridge University Press, 1989.

Geary, Patrick. *Before France and Germany: The Creation and Transformation of the Merovingian World.* Oxford: Oxford University Press, 1988.

Gibbon, Edward. *The Decline and Fall of the Roman Empire.* 1776. 3 vols. Reprint, New York: Modern Library, 1983.

Goffart, Walter. *Barbarians and Romans, A.D. 418–584.* Princeton: Princeton University Press, 1981.

———. *The Narrators of Barbarian History (A.D. 500–800): Jordanes, Gregory of Tours, Bede, and Paul the Deacon.* Princeton: Princeton University Press, 1988.

Herrin, Judith. *The Formation of Christendom.* Princeton: Princeton University Press, 1989.

Jones, Arnold Hugh Martin. *The Later Roman Empire, 284–602: A Social, Economic, and Administrative Survey.* Norman: University of Oklahoma Press, 1964.

Laistner, Max Ludwig Wolfram. *Thought and Letters in Western Europe, A.D. 500 to 900.* 2d ed. Ithaca, NY: Cornell University Press, 1976.

Lot, Ferdinand. *The End of the Ancient World and the Beginnings of the Middle Ages.* 1931. Reprint, New York: Harper and Row, 1961.

McKitterick, Rosamond. *The Uses of Literacy in Early Medieval Europe.* Cambridge: Cambridge University Press, 1992.

Murray, Alexander Callander, ed. *After Rome's Fall: Narrators and Sources of Early Medieval History.* Toronto: University of Toronto Press, 1998.

Pirenne, Henri. *Mohammed and Charlemagne.* Trans. Bernard Miall. New York: Barnes and Noble, 1992.

Riché, Pierre. *Education and Culture in the Barbarian West: From the Sixth through the Eighth Century.* Trans. John Contreni. Columbia: University of South Carolina Press, 1978.

Sullivan, Richard. *Heirs of the Roman Empire.* Ithaca, NY: Cornell University Press, 1974.

Wallace-Hadrill, John Michael. *The Barbarian West, A.D. 400–1000.* New York: Harper and Row, 1962.

Wolfram, Herwig. *The Roman Empire and Its Germanic Peoples.* Trans. Thomas J. Dunlap. Berkeley: University of California Press, 1997.

Chronology of the Late Antique and Early Medieval World

305 With the retirement of the emperors Diocletian and Maximian, the Roman Empire falls again into civil war, which leads to the eventual triumph of Constantine the Great.

313 The emperors Constantine and Licinius issue the Edict of Milan, which legalizes Christianity and establishes religious toleration in the Roman Empire.

325 In the year following a victory over Licinius and reunification of the empire under one ruler, Constantine calls the Council of Nicaea to resolve the great dispute over the nature of Christ's relationship to God the Father. The council accepts the Athanasian definition and rejects the teachings of Arius. Although the former lays the foundation for later Christian belief, the latter continues to exercise great influence in the empire and on the barbarians who eventually settle in much of the Roman world.

330 Constantine founds the new imperial capital of Constantinople on the straits of the Bosporus. The city will stand as the capital of the Roman Empire, and its successor the Byzantine Empire for more than 1,000 years before falling to the Ottoman Turks in 1453. Constantine's city will be a Christian city and the political and religious heart of the empire.

337 The great emperor Constantine converts to Christianity, accepting baptism, and dies shortly after on May 22, 337.

341 Ulfilas is consecrated bishop. He will later translate the Bible into the Gothic language and spread an Arian form of Christianity among the Goths.

370 First appearance of the Huns in southeastern Europe. Their arrival forces further movement of the peoples living along the empire's frontier, including movement into the empire.

376 Emperor Valens welcomes a large number of Visigoths into the empire to settle a frontier area, which they will cultivate and help defend.

378   After failing to settle the Visigoths, Emperor Valens leads a major Roman army against them and is defeated and killed at the Battle of Hadrianople. The Visigoths are then able to move freely about the empire until forced to settle by Theodosius the Great.

380   Theodosius the Great issues a decree declaring Catholic Christianity the official religion of the Roman Empire.

382   Death of Ulfilas, Gothic missionary, bishop, and translator of the Bible.

391   Alaric I becomes king of the Visigoths.

394   Defeat of Arbogast and the pretender Eugenius by Stilicho, the Roman military commander.

395   Death of Emperor Theodosius the Great, the last ruler of a united Roman Empire. He has divided the realm between his two sons, Honorius and Arcadius. Death of the great Roman historian Ammianus Marcellinus.

402   Stilicho wins major victories over the Visigothic leader Alaric at Pollentia and Verona.

405/406   Major crossing of the Rhine by large numbers of Alans, Franks, Visigoths, and other Germanic peoples. The removal of Roman frontier troops to protect the imperial heartland more effectively has led to this serious breach of the frontier.

406   Burgundians establish kingdom along the Rhine.

408   Murder of Stilicho by Emperor Honorius. Despite questionable relations with the Gothic king Alaric, Stilicho has managed to keep the Goths at bay and preserve the well-being of Italy. After his death, Alaric and the Visigoths invade Italy.

409   Vandals and other barbarian peoples settle in Spain.

410   Sack of the city of Rome by Alaric and the Visigoths. The first major attack on the city in 800 years, the event profoundly shocks both pagan and Christian Romans across the Mediterranean. Pagan Romans blame the Christians for the event, and St. Jerome is so dismayed that he cannot speak. The sack of Rome, however, will contribute to the composition of one of the great works of Christian literature, Augustine's *City of God,* a response to pagan criticisms of Christianity. Roman armies make final withdrawal from Britain. Death of Alaric.

414   Marriage of the Visigoth king Ataulf and the emperor's sister Galla Placidia, who was captured by the Goths during the sack of Rome.

428   Gaiseric becomes king of the Vandals.

429   Picts and Scots raid British territory. Vandals leave Spain and enter Africa.

430   Death of St. Augustine of Hippo, the year before the city is to fall to the onslaught of the Vandals.

432   St. Patrick begins the mission to Ireland, where he will remain until 461.

433   Attila the Hun takes the throne.

439   Vandals capture Carthage and strengthen their hold on North Africa.

440   Huns begin raiding in the Balkans.

449/450   Traditional date of first Saxon invasions of England at the invitation of the British leader Vortigern. The invasions will provide the context for the origins of the legend of King Arthur.

451   Aëtius and an army of Roman and barbarian troops win the Battle of the Catalaunian Plains over Attila and the Huns. Council of Chalcedon is held to determine important matters of faith and ecclesiastical organization.

452   Attila the Hun threatens Rome but is persuaded not to sack the city by Pope Leo I.

453   Attila dies, and by 455 his great empire will collapse.

454   Death of Aëtius.

455   The city of Rome is sacked by Gaiseric and the Vandals. Defeat of the Huns at the Battle of Nedao and collapse of their empire.

456   Ricimer, Roman military leader of Germanic descent, defeats Vandal fleet off the coast of Italy.

459   The future Ostrogothic king of Italy, Theodoric, to be known as Theodoric the Great, arrives in Constantinople as a hostage and remains there for ten years.

461   Ricimer becomes master of the Western Empire and remains so, ruling in the name of puppet emperors of his creation, until his death in 472.

475   Traditional date of the issuance of one of the most influential barbarian law codes, the *Codex Euricianus* ("Code of Euric"), by the Visigothic king Euric, ruler of a large territory in France and northern Spain.

476   Traditional date of the fall of the Roman Empire. Odovacar, Germanic leader serving in the Roman army, deposes the last Roman emperor in the west, Romulus Augustulus, and rules as king in Italy until his murder by the Ostrogoth Theodoric the Great.

481   Clovis becomes king the Franks and establishes the Merovingian dynasty, which will rule the Franks until 751.

486/7   Victory of Clovis and the Franks over the Roman Syagrius, ruler of the kingdom of Soissons.

488   Theodoric the Great, after long being a thorn in the side of the eastern emperor Zeno, invades Italy at the emperor's behest to deal with the Germanic king Odovacar.

493   Murder of Odovacar by Theodoric, whose reign in Italy begins.

496   Traditional date of Clovis's victory over the Alemanni. According to Gregory of Tours, Clovis swore that he would abandon the traditional gods and convert to Christianity if God would grant him victory.

498   Traditional date of the baptism of Clovis as a Catholic Christian by Archbishop Remigius and subsequent conversion of the king's followers. Clovis is the first of the Germanic successor kings to accept Catholic Christianity.

506   On February 2, the Visigothic king Alaric II issues the *Breviarium Alaricianum* (Breviary of Alaric) as a complement to the *Codex Euricianius* issued by his father Euric. The Breviary, also called *Lex Romana Visigothorum* (Roman Law of the Visigoths), covers the Romans living under Visigothic rule.

507   Clovis defeats the Visigoths at the Battle of Vouillé, fought, according to Gregory of Tours, by the Catholic king Clovis to expel the Arian Visigoths from Gaul.

511   Clovis provides for the succession, dividing the kingdom of the Franks among his four sons, and dies on November 27.

516   Traditional date of the Battle of Badon Hill, in which King Arthur turns back the invading Anglo-Saxons.

517   Codification and publication of the *Lex Gundobada* or *Liber constitutionem*, which probably appeared in some form already around the year 500, and the *Lex Romana Burgundionum* by the Burgundian king Sigismund.

524   Boethius, the Roman writer and statesman who has served Theodoric the Great, is executed, having written his great work, *The Consolation of Philosophy,* while in prison, suspected of having conspired against Theodoric, during his last year of life.

526   Death of Theodoric the Great, after which the Ostrogothic kingdom in Italy enters a period of unrest caused by conflict concerning the succession and the course of royal policy. His daughter, Amalaswintha, becomes regent and focus of discontent.

527   Justinian becomes Byzantine emperor and begins one of the most important reigns in Byzantine history. During his long reign, which will last until 565, he will rebuild Constantinople, reconquer much of the former Western Empire, and codify Roman law.

529	St. Benedict of Nursia founds the great monastery at Monte Cassino.
531	Franks destroy the kingdom of the Thuringians.
532	Justinian, thanks to his empress Theodora, survives the Nika Revolt and begins construction of the great church, Hagia Sophia.
533	Conquest of the North African kingdom of the Vandals by the great Byzantine general Belisarius, which will be completed in 534. Justinian's codification of Roman law, begun in 527, is completed.
534	Franks, according to Gregory of Tours at the suggestion of Chlotild, destroy the Burgundian kingdom.
535	Murder of Amalaswintha. Her death provides Justinian the pretext for invading Italy, and he begins what will later be known as the Gothic Wars in Italy.
540	Belisarius captures Ravenna in the war against the Ostrogoths in Italy.
548	Death of the empress Theodora.
550	Death of St. Benedict of Nursia, the father of Western monasticism. Approximate time of the appearance of the writings of Gildas, an important writer on the conquest of England by the Anglo-Saxons.
552	Byzantine armies under Narses win the Battle of Busta Gallorum, defeating the Gothic armies and essentially ending the power of the Ostrogoths in Italy, and even their independent existence.
555	Last of the Ostrogoths in Italy surrender to the Byzantines.
565	Death of the great Byzantine emperor, Justinian, who is succeeded by his nephew Justin II.
567	Division of the Frankish kingdom into Austrasia, Neustria, and Burgundy.
568	The Lombards begin the invasion of Italy; according to one tradition, they come at the invitation of the disgruntled Byzantine general, Narses. The Merovingian queen Radegund founds the monastery of the Holy Cross at Poitiers.
575	Murder of the Merovingian king of the Franks, Sigebert, by Chilperic I and Fredegund. Brunhilde assumes the regency and continues her rivalry with Fredegund.
579	Hermenegild revolts against his father, Leovigild, the king of Visigothic Spain, and converts to Catholic Christianity. The revolt will fail, and Hermenegild will die shortly after it ends in 584.
580	Lombards sack Benedict of Nursia's famed monastery of Monte Cassino.

584   Assassination of King Chilperic I, possibly by his wife Fredegund.

587   Reccared, king of Visigothic Spain, converts to Catholic Christianity and renounces his former adherence to Arian Christianity.

590   Gregory I, called the Great, becomes pope; he will reign until 604.

594   Death of Gregory of Tours, Frankish bishop and author of an important history of the Franks.

589   Marriage of the Lombard king Authari with the Bavarian princess Theudelinde on May 15, which forms an important alliance against the Franks. Theudelinde will remain an important figure in the Lombard kingdom until her death in 628. A Catholic in an Arian kingdom, she will maintain good relations with Pope Gregory the Great.

591   Death of King Authari. Theudelinde chooses Agilulf as her new husband and successor to Authari.

595   Gregory the Great sends Augustine of Canterbury on a mission to England to convert the Anglo-Saxons. Augustine will successfully introduce Christianity to England two years later.

597   Death of the Merovingian queen Fredegund. Æthelberht, king of Kent, accepts baptism at the hands of Augustine, whom the king had granted land in Canterbury. According to tradition, thousands of the king's subjects accept baptism on Christmas day in this year.

613   Brunhilde, queen of the Franks, is overthrown and brutally executed by Chlotar II, who will reign alone until 622, and with his son Dagobert until 629. He will then be succeeded by Dagobert, who will rule until 638. The two kings will represent the high point of Merovingian kingship after Clovis. At some point following the overthrow, Pippin of Landen and St. Arnulf of Metz will form a marriage alliance that lays the foundation for the later Carolingian dynasty.

614   The Irish missionary St. Columban founds the celebrated monastery of Bobbio. Columban dies the following year.

616   The Lombard king Agilulf dies, and his son, Adaloald, succeeds to the throne. Theudelinde, Adaloald's mother, acts as regent.

629   Visigoths expel the last of the Byzantine armies from Spain.

636   Death of the Spanish prelate and scholar Isidore of Seville, a man of great learning and the historian of the Visigoths.

643   Edict of Rothari, an important Lombard legal code, is issued.

652   Benedict Biscop, Anglo-Saxon churchman from the kingdom of Northumbria in northern England, makes his first trip to Rome, where he acquires many important religious manuscripts. The founder of monasteries at Jarrow and Wearmouth, Benedict exercises great influence on the religious and cultural life of northern England, and his trips to Rome will be important in the formation of Northumbrian culture and learning.

656   Death of the Carolingian mayor of the palace, Grimoald, who attempted to usurp the throne but failed.

657   Death of the Merovingian king Clovis II, who is suceeded by his young son Chlotar III. Balthild, Chlothar's mother, assumes the regency and provides wise rule for the kingdom.

664   Synod of Whitby is held, presided over by Oswy, a powerful king in the north of England, and the Anglo-Saxon church accepts Roman Christianity over Irish Christianity. Chlotar III assumes his majority and ends the regency of his mother Balthild, who will die c. 680.

674   Benedict Biscop founds the monastery at Wearmouth.

681   Benedict Biscop founds the important and influential monastery at Jarrow.

687   The mayor of the palace, Pippin of Herstal, wins the Battle of Tertry and establishes Carolingian hegemony in the Frankish kingdom.

711   Muslims from North Africa invade and begin the conquest of the Visigothic kingdom of Spain, which will fall in 725.

712   Liutprand becomes king of the Lombards and rules until his death in 744.

714   Death of Pippin of Herstal. After some conflict over who will assume the Carolingian mantle, Charles Martel succeeds his father Pippin as mayor of the palace.

717   Leo III, called the Isaurian, ascends the imperial throne in Constantinople and defends the city against an Arab assault that nearly succeeds.

722   The Anglo-Saxon missionary, Boniface, begins his preaching in Germany. Early in his mission, he destroys the sacred oak of the thunder god Thor at Geismar.

730   Leo III officially introduces the policy of iconoclasm in the Byzantine Empire, a policy that will be condemned by Pope Gregory III in the following year.

731   Anglo-Saxon scholar, theologian, and historian Bede, the most famous beneficiary of the revival of letters in Northumbria started by Benedict Biscop, completes his important and influential *History of the English Church and People*.

732   Charles Martel defeats Muslim invaders from Spain at the Battle of Poitiers.

735	The great Anglo-Saxon scholar and monk Bede dies.
737	The Merovingian king, Thierry IV, dies, and no new Merovingian ruler is placed on the throne by Charles Martel, who will rule alone as mayor of the palace until his death in 741.
739	Liutprand, king of the Lombards, lays siege to the city of Rome, and Pope Gregory III appeals to the Carolingian mayor of the palace, Charles Martel, for assistance. Charles is unable to assist because of an alliance with the Lombards that was necessary to protect the southwestern part of the Frankish realm from Muslim raids from Spain.
741	Death of Charles Martel and ascension of Pippin III and Carloman to the office of mayor of the palace. They will rule without a Merovingian figurehead until 743, when they will be forced to raise Childeric III to the throne.
747	The Carolingian mayor, Carloman, retires to the monastery of Monte Cassino, leaving his brother Pippin as the de facto ruler of the Frankish kingdom.
749	Aistulf becomes king of the Lombards and takes up an aggressive policy against the papacy, which will lead to an alliance between the papacy and the Franks.
750	Pippin III, called the Short, writes Pope Zachary asking whether the person with the title or the person with the real power should be king. The pope answers as Pippin hoped.
751	Deposition of Childeric III, the last Merovingian king, by Pippin, who is crowned king of the Franks by the bishops of his realm and founds the Carolingian dynasty. The Lombards, under their king Aistulf, capture the imperial capital in Italy, Ravenna.
753	Pippin welcomes Pope Stephen II to his court and begins negotiations with the pope, which possibly lead to the Donation of Pippin.
754	Pope Stephen II crowns Pippin king of the Franks. Byzantine Emperor Constantine V holds the Council of Hiereia, which supports his iconoclastic policies. Martyrdom of the Anglo-Saxon missionary Boniface while evangelizing in Frisia on June 5. The Donation of Constantine, a forged document giving the papacy great power, appears around this time.
755	Aistulf, king of the Lombards, lays siege to Rome. Pippin undertakes his first Italian campaign to protect the papacy against Lombard advances. Pippin holds an important reform council at Ver.
756	Pippin's second Lombard campaign. Pippin deposits the so-called Donation of Pippin on the altar of St. Peter in Rome, helping to create the Papal States.
757	Offa becomes king of Mercia and rules until 796. His reign will be remembered for the famed dyke he ordered built to protect his kingdom from the Welsh.

763   Publication of the revised version of the Salic Law, a collection of the laws of the Franks first published under the great Merovingian king Clovis.

768   Death of Pippin and succession to the throne of his sons Carloman and Charlemagne.

771   Death of Carloman, whose reign was characterized by strife with his brother that nearly led to a disastrous civil war.

772   Charlemagne's first campaign to punish Saxon raiders. Within the next few years, the campaign will turn into a full-scale effort to conquer and convert the Saxons that will last until 804. Hadrian becomes pope and will reign until 795.

774   Pavia falls to Charlemagne, and the Lombard kingdom is incorporated into the growing Carolingian empire.

778   Charlemagne invades Spain but returns to settle unrest in his own kingdom. While crossing back into his kingdom, his rear guard, led by Roland, is attacked and destroyed by the Basques. The incident will be the foundation for one of the great epics of the Middle Ages, the *Song of Roland.*

782   Charlemagne orders the massacre of 4,500 Saxons at Verdun in retaliation for Saxon defeat of his armies and harassment of the church.

785   Saxon revolt of Widukind, which is put down by Charlemagne, though only with the greatest difficulty. Widukind converts to Christianity, and Charlemagne issues the first Saxon capitulary, a law intended to impose Christianity on the Saxons.

787   Irene and her son Emperor Constantine VI hold the Second Council of Nicaea, the seventh ecumenical council, to resolve the iconoclastic dispute that has raged throughout much of the century in the Byzantine Empire. Deposition of Tassilo, duke of Bavaria, by Charlemagne. The *Royal Frankish Annals* are first written in this year or in 788.

789   Charlemagne issues the capitulary *Admonitio Generalis,* which lays the foundation for the religious and cultural revival known as the Carolingian Renaissance. Around the same time, certainly by 800, Charlemagne issues the Letter to Baugulf, which also encourages learning and the establishment of schools in his realm.

793   First Viking raid on England.

794   Charlemagne holds the Synod of Frankfurt to address the great questions facing the Frankish church, including the issues of Adoptionism and Iconoclasm.

795   Pope Hadrian I dies and is succeeded by Pope Leo III.

796   Charlemagne's armies destroy the Avar kingdom. King Offa of Mercia dies.

797	Irene deposes and blinds her son Constantine VI and assumes the imperial throne. Charlemagne issues the second Saxon capitulary, a Carolingian law that encouraged conversion to Christianity.
799	Pope Leo III is attacked while on procession in Rome and is rescued by Charlemagne's representatives in Rome. Leo goes to Charlemagne's court to explain the situation.
800	Charlemagne visits Rome to resolve the dispute involving Pope Leo III and presides over a council at which the pope swears his innocence. On December 25, Leo crowns Charlemagne emperor of the Romans during Christmas mass. First Viking raids on the continent of Europe.
802	Empress Irene is overthrown by Nikephoros I. Charlemagne issues important reform capitulary and uses his official imperial title.
804	Death of the Anglo-Saxon Alcuin of York, one of Charlemagne's most important advisors and court scholars.
806	Charlemagne introduces succession plan that divides the realm among his sons but does not pass on the imperial title.
811	Charlemagne completes creation of the Spanish March, a militarized border region including territory on the Spanish side of the Pyrenees.
813	Coronation of Louis the Pious as emperor by Charlemagne at a great assembly in Aix-la-Chapelle (modern Aachen, Germany).
814	Death of Charlemagne on January 28 and succession to the throne of his son Louis the Pious.
816	Louis the Pious crowned emperor by Pope Stephen IV. Agobard, a Carolingian scholar and ecclesiastic from Spain, made archbishop of Lyons.
817	Louis the Pious nearly killed in an accident while crossing a bridge. Louis holds a great council and issues his *Ordinatio Imperii,* which provides for the succession to the imperial title by Louis's oldest son, Lothar, and settlement of the other two, Louis the German and Pippin, as kings under the emperor's authority. Louis also issues the *Pactum Ludovicianum,* prepared the previous year, codifying Carolingian relations with the papacy. He promulgates important religious reforms, with the advice of the Visigothic monk and reformer Benedict of Aniane. Revolt of Louis's nephew, Bernard, king of Italy.
823	Birth of Charles the Bald to Louis and his second wife, Judith.
824	Lothar issues the *Constitutio Romana,* which further defines Carolingian relations with Rome.

827   Louis the Pious alters his succession plan to include his son Charles the Bald, to the dismay of his older sons.

830   Revolt of Lothar, Louis the German, and Pippin against their father Louis the Pious. Einhard writes *Life of Charlemagne,* though some historians think it appeared as early as 817. Nennius writes the *Historia Brittonum* (History of the Britons), though it may have appeared as early as 800.

833   Meeting at the "Field of Lies," between Louis the Pious and his sons at which Louis's troops dessert, and beginning of second revolt against Louis the Pious, who is deposed and imprisoned.

834   Restoration of Louis the Pious and disgrace of Lothar, the leader of the revolt.

840   Death of Louis the Pious, succession of Charles the Bald, Lothar, and Louis the German, and beginning of civil war between the three sons of Louis.

841   Battle of Fontenoy on June 25 between Lothar and his brothers Louis the German and Charles the Bald.

842   Louis the German, Charles the Bald, and their followers subscribe to the Oath of Strasbourg, which makes the two leaders allies and which contains the first written examples of early Romance languages and of early Germanic languages.

843   Restoration of the practice of the veneration of icons in the Byzantine Empire. The Carolingian rulers, Charles the Bald, Lothar, and Louis the German, agree to the Treaty of Verdun, which divides the empire equally between them.

845   Vikings attack Paris.

848   Gottschalk of Orbais called before a council at Mainz to defend his views on predestination, starting a controversy that will involve Hincmar of Rheims, John the Scot Eriugena, and other leading Carolingian ecclesiastics.

853   Alfred the Great of England makes his first pilgrimage to Rome.

855   Alfred the Great makes his second pilgrimage to Rome and on the return marries Judith, the daughter of Charles the Bald. Emperor Lothar dies and his realm is divided between his two sons.

871   Alfred the Great ascends the throne in the kingdom of Wessex.

875   Death of Emperor Louis II on August 12; imperial coronation of Charles the Bald on December 25.

876   Death of Louis the German on August 28.

877   Death of Charles the Bald on October 6.

878   Danes force Alfred the Great from the kingdom of Wessex to the island of Athelney. Alfred marshals his forces and is able to win a major victory over the Danes at the Battle of Eddington. The Danes withdraw from England.

882   Death of Hincmar of Rheims on December 21.

884   Charles the Fat reunites the Carolingian empire under one ruler.

885   Alfred the Great takes London from the Danes.

888   Death of Charles the Fat, the last Carolingian to rule a united empire, who was deposed from the throne in 887.

890   The *Anglo-Saxon Chronicle* first appears in or around this year.

892   Danes invade England again.

896   Alfred finally expels the Danes after four years of fighting.

899   Death of Alfred the Great on October 26.

909   Death of Asser, biographer of Alfred the Great.

911   Charles the Simple grants Normandy to the Viking Rollo. Death of Louis the Child, the last Carolingian to rule in the East Frankish kingdom.

987   Carolingian dynasty replaced by the Capetian dynasty in France.

1000   The sole surviving manuscript of the Anglo-Saxon epic *Beowulf* is written.

MEROVINGIAN
KINGDOMS

SAXONS

THURINGIA

N

• Tournai

Soissons •

• Trier

Paris •

LOMBARDS

Vienne •

ITALY

ILLYRICUM

• Pavia

Toulouse •

Arles •

• Ravenna

SEPTIMANIA

VISIGOTHIC
KINGDOM

• Rome

OSTROGOTHIC
KINGDOM

0   100   200   300 mi

0 100 200 300 400 500 km

• Palermo

	Merovingian kingdom under Clovis		Maximum extent of the Merovingian kingdom in the seventeenth century
	Ostrogothic kingdom under Theodoric	- - - -	Boundaries of Roman dioceses

Barbarian kingdoms, early sixth century. Reprinted with the permission of Cambridge University Press.

Ordinatio imperii. *Reprinted with the permission of Cambridge University Press.*

Partition of the Empire. *Reproduced from W. Hollister, Medieval Europe, with permission of the McGraw-Hill Companies.*

British Isles in the eighth and ninth centuries. Reprinted with the permission of Cambridge University Press.

The Frankish Kingdoms, 751–768. Reprinted with the permission of Cambridge University Press.

Admonitio Generalis

The capitulary promulgated by Charlemagne in 789 that established the foundation for the Carolingian Renaissance by announcing the educational and religious goals and ideals of the great Frankish ruler. The *Admonitio Generalis* (General Admonition) consists of eighty-two chapters. Although fifty-nine of the chapters borrow heavily from the canon law collection, the *Dionysio-Hadriana,* that Charlemagne received from Pope Hadrian I, the capitulary is truly a creation of the king and his advisors. Its extensive use of quotations from Holy Scripture reveals the level of cultural sophistication achieved at Charlemagne's court and points to the greater goals the court sought to achieve.

In this capitulary, Charlemagne asserted his belief that he was a new Josiah, the ancient Hebrew king who reformed Jewish belief and practice, with the responsibility to rule over God's new chosen people and the duty to reform their moral and spiritual lives so that they would be able to achieve salvation. To fulfill his role as the new Josiah, and to create peace and harmony among the Christian people, Charlemagne included chapters concerning the moral reform and discipline of the priesthood in the *Admonitio.* The capitulary also emphasizes the responsibility of the priests in Charlemagne's kingdom to preach "rightly and honestly" and to avoid innovation and teachings contrary to the laws of the church. Priests are expected to live moral lives; they are to teach their flocks to follow the example they set. The priests themselves are to be guided in the performance of their duties by the bishops, who are instructed to obey the accepted beliefs and practices of the church.

Perhaps the most important section of the *Admonitio* is chapter seventy-two, which lays out Charlemagne's program of education. This chapter asserts the responsibility of the bishops and monks of his kingdom to establish schools to teach the psalms, music and singing, and grammar. The schools, in other words, are to teach boys to read and write so that they can help spread the Christian faith. The chapter calls on the leaders of the church to set up schools so that those who wish to pray may do so in the proper fashion. Indeed, it was one of Charlemagne's great hopes that all his people would be able to recite the Lord's Prayer and the Apostle's Creed. The *Admonitio* was intended to contribute to that goal by mandating that the schools be established; another purpose was to provide for the correction of books important to the faith. The *Admonitio Generalis* established the religious reform program of Charlemagne's reign, and, with the Letter to Baugulf (*Epistola de litteris colendis*) it promoted the revival of learning associated with his broader reform program.

See also Capitularies; Carolingian Dynasty; Carolingian Renaissance; Charlemagne

Bibliography
Brown, Giles. "Introduction: the Carolingian Renaissance." In *Carolingian Culture: Emulation and Innovation,* ed. Rosamond McKitterick. Cambridge: Cambridge University Press, 1994.
McKitterick, Rosamond. *The Frankish Church and the Carolingian Reforms, 789–895.* London: Longman, 1977.

Aethelberht I of Kent (d. 616)

A powerful and important king of Kent, in southern England. Although he was recognized by his English contemporaries as the leading power in the south, his marriage to a Frankish princess brought little excitement from continental chroniclers. Although of little note to the chroniclers, he was recognized as important enough to marry a Merovingian princess and received attention from Pope Gregory I. Aethelberht is important as the first king in England to convert to Christianity. He was also the first Anglo-Saxon king to issue a legal code. Even if Frankish chroniclers did not notice it, Aethelberht had an important impact on early medieval England.

Aethelberht was king of the most sophisticated and most populous kingdom of England in the late sixth and early seventh century. Although Bede says that he ruled from 560 to 616, it is more likely that he assumed the throne at some time between 589 and 593 and was born in 560. He was the most powerful ruler of his time, extending his authority across most of southern England, and is identified by Bede as the third king to rule all of England south of the Humber. Perhaps in recognition of his status in England or possibly as a result of his own desires to associate himself with the most powerful family of the continent, Aethelberht married at some point before 588 Bertha, the niece of the Merovingian king Chilperic and the daughter of Charipert, king of Paris. Even though Frankish chroniclers made little of the marriage, it was an important alliance for Aethelberht, and his association with the Frankish dynasty shaped the remainder of his reign.

The closeness of Aethelberht's ties with the Merovingians is, perhaps, revealed in the two great accomplishments of his reign. His most important achievement was his conversion to Christianity. In 595, after having seen angelic boys from England sold as slaves in the market place at Rome, Pope Gregory the Great—who bought and freed them—sent an evangelical mission to England led by St. Augustine of Canterbury. Aethelberht welcomed the mission, although with some hesitation at first, since he feared that they were practitioners of the magical arts who would try to deceive and control him. But after meeting the missionaries, the king gave them permission to preach in his kingdom, and, as Bede notes, Aethelberht was so impressed by their preaching and miracles that he converted and accepted baptism from them. Although he would not compel his subjects to convert, the king did favor Christians in his kingdom and built a number of churches for the missionaries, including St. Paul's Cathedral in London and a church in Rochester. He also allowed them to settle in Canterbury, which later became the most important episcopal see in England.

The king's conversion restored the connection with Rome that had been severed by the invasions of the fifth century. This connection was further confirmed by letters that Aethelberht received from the pope, including one in which Gregory praised the king, compared him with Constantine, and encouraged him to spread the faith throughout his kingdom. Although his son Eadbald (616–640) at first turned his back on Christianity, giving it a temporary setback, Eadbald later converted to the faith and furthered the process of conversion of his people.

Aethelberht's other great achievement was the codification of the law. Although the codification may not have been a thorough one, the king's legal reforms were important nonetheless. His publication of Anglo-Saxon laws reveals the influence of the Merovingians once again, because it recalls the famous codification of the Salic law by Clovis (r. 481–511), the first great Merovingian king. It also suggests Christian or Roman influence, because the great Christian emperor Justinian had codified Roman law a generation before Aethelberht's code. Indeed, the king not only demonstrated the importance he attached to his continental connections with the code, but revealed the sophistication his kingdom had achieved. The code was unique in one regard: Unlike the codes of Clovis and the other Germanic kings, which were in Latin, Aethelberht's code was in the Anglo-Saxon tongue. As a result, it was the earliest code written in any Germanic language.

The code did not reflect any advanced legal theory, but it did define the laws of the land and relations among the king's subjects. The code, among other things, established the scale of payment owed for injury, such as the payments (called wergeld) due for killing men and women of various social ranks and for other violations of person and property. The code also established the preeminent place of the king in Kentish society, as well as the important place of the bishops in the kingdom. The laws also established the legal rights and status of the clergy in the kingdom. Although Aethelberht is less well known than some other Anglo-Saxon kings, his importance is no less than theirs, since he was the first to reform the law and the first to convert to Christianity.

See also Anglo-Saxons; Augustine of Canterbury, St.; Bede; Chilperic I; Clovis; Constantine; Gregory the Great; Justinian; Merovingian Dynasty

Bibliography

Attenborough, Frederick L., ed. and trans. *The Laws of the Earliest English Kings.* Felinfach, Wales: Llanerch Publishers, 2000.

Bede, *Ecclesiastical History of the English Church and People,* trans. Leo Sherley-Price. Revised edition. London: Penguin Classics, 1968.

Kirby, David P. *The Earliest English Kings.* London: Unwin Hyman, 1991.

Sawyer, Peter H. *From Roman Britain to Norman England.* 2d ed. London and New York, 1998.

Stenton, Frank M. *Anglo-Saxon England.* 3d ed. Oxford: Clarendon, 1971.

Yorke, Barbara. *Kings and Kingdoms of Early Anglo-Saxon England.* London: Seaby, 1990.

Æthelflæd, Lady of the Mercians (d. 918)

Daughter of King Alfred, traditionally known as the Great, and wife of the powerful ealdorman (or lord) of Mercia, Ethelred. Although she was described by later historians as too weak to endure the pains of childbirth more than once, despite the powerful motivation of having borne no male heir, Æthelflæd was a strong partner for her husband while he lived and a leader against Viking attacks after his death. After 911, she was recognized as "queen," or "lady," of the Mercians and ruled the kingdom in her own name. Her marriage forged an important alliance between her native Wessex and Mercia during the critical period of the Viking invasions.

Æthelflæd's career in Mercia began by the end of 889, with her marriage to Ethelred to solidify an alliance between her father and her new husband, an alliance that was to be important in the face of increased Viking pressure. During her entire married life, Æthelflæd exerted influence on her husband's rule, and at least by 900 her name was associated with his in charters confirming grants of land. But it was after her husband's death in 911 that Æthelflæd left her greatest mark as a warrior queen. She assumed control of the kingdom in 911 and was able to keep the loyalty of her husband's vassals. Joining with her brother, King Edward, she led the campaign against the Vikings and enabled her brother to make significant progress against the Danish Vikings in the south. She led her armies personally and achieved smashing victories over the Vikings, victories that enabled her to retake Derby and Leicester. Her victories forced Viking settlers and Welsh kings to recognize her authority. She also built a number of important fortifications, inspired perhaps by her father's example. With her husband, she fortified Worcester. After 911, she embarked on a deliberate program of building to strengthen the defenses of Mercia. She built as many as ten fortresses, which limited the effectiveness of Viking attacks and allowed her to send out armies against her enemies with increasing effectiveness.

She ruled in her own name until her death in 919. She had one daughter, Ælfwyn, who inherited the loyalty of the Mercian nobility. Unfortunately, family ties were not so strong, and her uncle, King Edward, marched into Mercia, seized his niece, and took control of Mercia. Edward thus unified Mercia and Wessex. Despite the absorption of Mercia by Wessex, Æthelflæd left an important legacy to Anglo-Saxon England and had a great impact on the struggle against the Vikings.

See also Alfred the Great; Anglo-Saxons

Bibliography
Jewell, Helen. *Women in Medieval England.* Manchester and New York: Manchester University Press, 1996.
Leyser, Henrietta. *Medieval Women: A Social History of Women in England, 450–1500.* New York: St. Martin's, 1995.
Stafford, Pauline. *Queens, Concubines, and Dowagers: The King's Wife in the Early Middle Ages.* Athens: University of Georgia Press, 1983.
Stenton, Frank M. *Anglo-Saxon England.* 3d ed. Oxford: Clarendon, 1971.
Whitelock, Dorothy, ed. *The Anglo-Saxon Chronicle.* Westport, CT: Greenwood, 1986.

Adoptionism
See Alcuin of York

Aelfric
See Anglo-Saxons

Aëtius (d. 454)

Called "the last of the Romans" by the sixth-century Byzantine historian Procopius, Aëtius was the servant of the emperor Valentinian III, the rival of the empress Galla Placidia, and the military commander who preserved Roman control over Gaul but lost Africa. Like Stilicho before him and Orestes after, Aëtius was the power behind the throne; he maintained the integrity of Western Roman imperial authority in the face of the turmoil and tumult brought on by the Hunnish invasions and movement of various Germanic tribes. A contemporary chronicler called him "the great safety of the western republic," (Macellinus, *Chronicle,* quoted in Bury 1959, 300) and Aëtius's death was a grave misfortune for the Western Empire.

Born in Lower Moesia, a Roman territory in the Balkans, to an Italian mother and to Gaudentius, a Roman military commander who served Theodosius, Aëtius was sent as a hostage to Alaric and also to the Huns. His family background and experiences among the Visigoths and Huns were to be of great importance for his future. He learned important military techniques from the barbarians and found an ally in the Huns, who helped him gain and hold power once he was an adult. According to Gregory of Tours, Aëtius was described by one contemporary in a panegyric as being of "middle height, of manly condition, well shaped, so that his body was neither too weak nor too weighty, active in mind, vigorous in limb" (Gregory of Tours 1974, 119). The panegyrist notes that he was a skilled horseman and deadly with both an arrow and spear. An "excellent warrior and famous in the arts of peace" (119), Aëtius, our panegyrist continues, was hardworking, able to endure the hardships of the military life, free from greed, and intellectually gifted. Even though it was intended to praise Aëtius, the panegyric offers a good assessment of the Roman leader, as his career would prove.

Aëtius first came to prominence in the 420s during the usurpation of the imperial throne in Ravenna by the civil servant John.

At the death of the emperor Honorius in 423, John was elevated to the throne but was opposed by the emperor in Constantinople, Theodosius II, as well as by the widow and son of Honorius, Galla Placidia, and Valentinian III. Aëtius, a rising soldier, recognized the authority of John and went to recruit an army from the Huns to support John. The pretender, however, was captured and executed before Aëtius could return with an army numbering 60,000 Hunnish soldiers. The army was an important bargaining chip for Aëtius, who was able to avoid the fate of John and demand a position of authority. Reluctantly, Galla Placidia came to terms with Aëtius and his army. Aëtius was pardoned by the empress and given the title of count and military command in Gaul.

Although he rose to prominence in an act of rebellion against the Western Empire, Aëtius spent much of his career defending the empire against its various barbarian foes. His command in Gaul brought him great prestige, and the continued enmity of Galla Placidia and her allies. Aëtius's prestige came from his great success in Gaul against the barbarian armies that threatened the empire's hold on the province. He fought a series of successful battles against the Franks, including one in 428 against one of the first known kings of the Franks, Chlodio. He also engaged the Visigoths during his time in Gaul and prevented them from taking the important city of Arles, often using both Frankish and Hunnish allies against the Visigoths. His success brought Aëtius the enthusiastic support of the Roman nobility in Gaul and promotion to the high rank of Master of Both Services (*magister utriusque militum*).

Aëtius's success also brought him the increasing hostility of Galla Placidia, especially after he orchestrated the deposition of her favorite Felix. With her support, Boniface, the military commander of Africa and count, challenged Aëtius in a great battle in Ariminum in 432. Although Aëtius lost the battle and returned to his allies the Huns, he won the war because Boniface died shortly after the battle, possibly from wounds he received in the battle. Once again with support from the Huns, Aëtius was able to reestablish his authority in 433 and remained the most important figure in the Western Empire until his death in 454. The empress now resigned herself to the success of Aëtius, who had defeated her favorites, held important military and civilian rank, and gained great influence over her son Valentinian.

As the real power in the Western Empire, Aëtius took charge of its defense and waged a series of successful and unsuccessful struggles with various barbarian peoples. One of his greatest failures was the loss of Africa to Gaiseric and the Vandals in the early 430s. The loss of Africa occurred for several reasons: Aëtius's distaste for the region as the base of power of his vanquished rival Boniface, his lack of an adequate fleet to defeat the Vandals, and his strategic decision to put his efforts toward preserving control of Gaul, an area equally under pressure from barbarian armies. In 436, Aëtius sent an army of Huns against the Burgundian kingdom of Worms. In an event celebrated in the German medieval epic poem the *Nibelungenlied,* the kingdom was destroyed, and as many as 20,000 Burgundians were killed, including the king Gundahar. But the Burgundians themselves were not wiped out and were resettled near modern Geneva, where they remained important allies of the empire. Aëtius also continued his struggle against the Visigoths, who sought to extend their influence into Gaul. In the late 430s he stopped them at Toulouse, preserving the imperial hold on southern Gaul.

Perhaps his most disappointing struggle with a barbarian people was his war with his long-time allies the Huns and their new king Attila. The invasion of Attila forced Aëtius to respond in the 440s and 450s. Attila's drive into the Western Empire was of great concern to Aëtius, who needed to find new allies to stop his old allies. Somewhat surprised by the Hunnish king's assault, Aëtius mobilized an army of Franks, Burgundians, and Romans and negotiated an alliance with his former enemies, the Visigoths. It was this mixed army that stopped Attila at Orléans and limited his success at Troyes. It was also this army that Aëtius led against Attila at the Battle of the Catalaunian Plains (somewhere between Châlons and Troyes, France). This bloody battle was a near disaster for Attila, who prepared for his own suicide during the fight. Although he defeated them, Aëtius allowed the Huns to leave the battlefield without destroying them because of their important service as his allies. Aëtius was less successful at stopping Attila when he invaded Italy, but the death of the king of the Huns ended their threat to the empire and allowed Aëtius to turn his attention to other problems.

Aëtius, however, had little time to attend to the remaining problems of the empire. Although he faithfully defended the Western Empire and its emperor, Aëtius fell under the suspicion of that emperor, Valentinian III. Perhaps angered by Aëtius's success and attempt to marry his family into the imperial line or influenced by one of Aëtius's rivals, Valentinian ordered the murder of his faithful general. Whatever the case, Aëtius fell to imperial treachery on September 24, 454, when Valentinian accused him of treason and had him killed immediately. After the murder a contemporary is supposed to have said to the emperor, "You have caught off your right hand with your left" (Bury 1959, 299). In fact, the emperor signed his own death warrant, for the following March, loyal followers of Aëtius murdered the emperor. These murders left the Western Empire without a legitimate successor to the throne and, perhaps even worse, without one of its greatest defenders and one who deserved the title of "last of the Romans," at a time when his talents were needed more than ever.

See also Alans; Alaric; Attila the Hun; Catalaunian Plains, Battle of the; Gaiseric; Galla Placidia; Huns; Procopius; Stilicho, Flavius; Theodosius; Vandals; Visigoths

Bibliography

Bury, John B. *History of the Later Roman Empire: From the Death of Theodosius I to the Death of Justinian*. Vol. 1. 1923. Reprint, New York: Dover, 1959.

Gregory of Tours. *The History of the Franks*. Trans. Lewis Thorpe. Harmondsworth, UK: Penguin, 1974.

Lot, Ferdinand. *The End of the Ancient World and the Beginnings of the Middle Ages*. New York: Harper and Row, 1961.

Randers-Pehrson, Justine Davis. *Barbarians and Romans: The Birth Struggle of Europe, A.D. 400–700*. Norman: University of Oklahoma Press, 1983.

Agobard of Lyons, St. (769–840)

Carolingian bishop and religious leader. Agobard's life and career reflects the importance of ecclesiastics in the Frankish kingdom, as well as the tumult that occurred there in the ninth century. As bishop he struggled against clerical abuse and ignorance as well as against the ignorance of the laity. He also strove to enforce clerical discipline and criticized royal abuse of power over the church. Agobard further rejected a number of pious practices approved by the Carolingian church and was a vocal critic of Louis the Pious's policy toward the Jews. He played an important role in the civil wars that shook the reign of Louis, supporting Louis's sons against the emperor, whom he denounced for opposing God's will by violating the *Ordinatio Imperii* (Disposition of the Empire) of 817. His support for the rebels led to his removal from involvement in the daily affairs of his bishopric, although he was eventually restored to his full authority as bishop and resumed his duties for the emperor.

Agobard was probably born in Spain and moved into the Frankish kingdom in 782 at the age of thirteen. Upon his arrival in Lyons, if not before, Agobard began his ecclesiastical career by joining a monastery near Narbonne. He later moved to Lyons, where he received holy orders and, in 804, was consecrated as a suffragan bishop. In 816 he was elevated to the position of archbishop of Lyons, where he remained, with the exception of a period of exile in the 830s, until his death. As archbishop, he played an important role in the religious and political life of the empire and challenged the emperor, Louis the Pious, on several occasions. He also supported the general reform initiatives of Louis, and he transformed Lyons into one of the centers of learning in the Carolingian world.

In the realm of politics, Agobard remained a staunch supporter of the unity of the empire and believed in its sacrosanct nature. He was an ardent proponent of the *Ordinatio Imperii* of 817, which was Louis's plan of succession. The *Ordinatio* was seen by some, especially in the church, as establishing the essential unity of the empire under God and his divinely appointed ruler. The plan also enhanced the power and status of the church, which could be seen as a guarantor of God's blessings on the realm. Agobard was one of the most adamant supporters of this plan and challenged the emperor for his efforts to undermine the *Ordinatio,* especially when Louis restructured the plan to include Charles the Bald, his youngest son, who was born in 823. Gradually, a group of churchman came to form a sort of "imperialist" party, which advocated the preservation of the original settlement and came to oppose the emperor to the point of rebellion. Indeed, in 830 many churchmen joined the rebellion against the emperor led by his sons. Agobard, however, did not participate in the revolt but remained neutral, even though he had written a letter to Louis the previous year in support of the *Ordinatio* and against Louis's violation of it.

In the mid-830s, however, Agobard underwent a change of heart in regard to Louis. In 833, when Lothar again revolted against his father, Agobard joined with the rebellion. He was among the bishops who called for Louis's abdication, and he wrote in defense of the rebellion. He criticized Judith, the emperor's second wife and the mother of Charles the Bald, and denounced Louis for abandoning his obligations as a Christian emperor and for allowing war and injustice to occur in the empire. Unlike Lothar, Agobard did not flee the empire when Louis was restored to power. He

was subsequently stripped of his responsibilities as bishop by a church council in 835. He regained the emperor's favor and was restored to his position in Lyons in 838. He was able to return, in part, because of the unorthodox reforms implemented by his successor. Agobard remained loyal to the empire in his remaining years and died while performing a diplomatic mission for the emperor.

Agobard was also an influential critic of contemporary religious policy and practice. In the Carolingian Empire religion and politics were often mixed, as Louis's succession plan demonstrates, and Agobard frequently called for the proper administration of justice. He criticized secular and religious judges for taking bribes and bending justice to favor the rich over the poor. He was also a harsh critic of the practice of trial by ordeal and the judicial duel. As archbishop, Agobard ruled on more traditional religious issues and participated in debate over religious policy in the empire. He was an active crusader against corruptions of the faith, including ignorance and impiety among the clergy and superstition and pagan practices among the laity. He supported the iconoclastic thinker, Claudius of Turin (d. 827), who rejected the veneration of images in the church. Agobard, Claudius's bishop, wrote a rebuttal to Carolingian thinkers who had attacked Claudius. Agobard also wrote a series of treatises criticizing Louis's Jewish policy. The emperor had favored and protected the Jews, which Agobard thought undermined the unity and integrity of the Christian empire of the Carolingians. Indeed, as with so many other things, Agobard's hostility to the Jews was part of a broader agenda that sought the proper ordering of Christian society.

See also Carolingian Dynasty; Charles the Bald; Franks; Judith; Lothar; Louis the German; Louis the Pious; *Ordinatio Imperii*

Bibliography

Cabaniss, Allen. *Agobard of Lyons: Churchman and Critic.* Syracuse, NY: Syracuse University Press, 1953.

Cohen, Jeremy. *Living Letters of the Law: Ideas of the Jew in Medieval Christianity.* Berkeley: University of California Press, 1999.

Halphen, Louis. *Charlemagne and the Carolingian Empire.* Trans. Giselle de Nie. Amsterdam and New York: North-Holland, 1977.

Laistner, Max Ludwig Wolfram. *Thought and Letters in Western Europe,* A.D. *500 to 900.* 2d ed. Ithaca, NY: Cornell University Press, 1976.

McKitterick, Rosamond. *The Frankish Kingdoms under the Carolingians, 951–987.* London: Longman, 1983.

Riché, Pierre. *The Carolingians: A Family Who Forged Europe.* Trans. Michael Idomir Allen. Philadelphia: University of Pennsylvania Press, 1993.

Agriculture

In the early Middle Ages the vast majority of the population of Europe was dedicated in some fashion or other to food production, which invariably involved agriculture. In early medieval Europe, as well as in later medieval and modern Europe, agriculture involved both crop farming and animal husbandry—a unique combination compared with agriculture in other parts of the world. In the economy of barbarian Europe, farming and animal husbandry existed in a symbiotic arrangement, in which specific crops were cultivated for animals, which in turn provided food and fertilizer. Despite the attention to agriculture, and the labor put into it, crop yields were generally small—the result of limited technology—and thus the vast majority of the population lived barely at the subsistence level.

In the agricultural villages of early medieval Europe the agricultural practices of the ancient Romans and their barbarian invaders came together to form the uniquely European agricultural tradition. One aspect of this, perhaps the result of the more pastoral nature of the barbarians who settled in much of the old Western Roman Empire, was animal husbandry. A number of different animals were bred, although not selectively as they were in Roman times, by early medieval peasants. The animals—including cows, oxen, horses, and pigs—provided a supply of both food and ready labor. Although little meat was eaten by the peasants, it was a welcome addition to an otherwise meager diet. But perhaps more important was the labor animals provided in the fields where various cereals were grown. Oxen and, eventually, horses were used to pull the plows that tilled the soil in early medieval villages. Peasants also grew oats specifically for the horses when the horse came into widespread use as a draught animal at the very end of the early medieval period. Cattle were often allowed to graze on the stubble found in the fields after the harvest, and their manure helped revitalize the fields. Also, hay and various grasses grew in the meadows of the villages, and the animals were allowed to wander in those meadows to eat the grasses.

Although animal husbandry was a significant practice of the peasants in barbarian Europe, it was far less important, and provided a much smaller amount of food, than farming. Some distinctive crops were produced in different parts of Europe because of climatic differences. Notably, grapes were grown in the warmer climates but were seldom found in the cooler climate of northern Europe. Despite this variety, the fundamental food crop was some type of cereal, which was often consumed in the form of bread and beer. Various types of wheat were grown in the village fields, as were barley, oats, rye, and spelt. The crop yields were quite poor, averaging a yield of between 2.5 to 1 to 3 to 1 to seeds planted. There were often times when this meager yield was even smaller, and thus famine was not an uncommon phenomenon; hunger was almost constant for the peasants. One means to make up for the poor production of the grains in the fields, however, was to plant small gardens near the home. These gardens often supplied foods that added valuable vitamins and minerals to the diet; the peasants grew root vegetables, peas, beans, and other legumes in their gar-

Peasant farmers ploughing, sowing, and pruning in January and February. Print from Strutts, "Manners and Customs,"
ca. 1250. (Hulton/Archive)

dens. Thus even though early medieval peasants spent much of their time cultivating grain, they also found time to grow a variety of vegetables to bring to the table.

Along with hunger, the greatest problem the peasant farmers of the early Middle Ages faced was soil depletion. In order to produce even the minimal yields they did, the peasants had to find some way to revitalize the fields they planted. One solution, of course, was to manure the fields, which they accomplished by allowing their livestock to graze in the fields and fertilize it while feeding. The early medieval peasant also collected manure from stables and spread it on the fields. But dependence on manure for fertilizer was an inadequate solution because of the smaller size of most farm animals during this period and because most animals were sold or slaughtered every fall (since the peasants did not have enough food to keep the animals

through the winter). The most effective way to allow the soil to replenish itself was to let it lie fallow. Peasants in barbarian Europe were forced to leave part of their fields unplanted each year so that the soil could be revitalized and continue to return at least the small harvests that the peasants needed to survive.

Because of the need to let some fields lie fallow each year, the peasants practiced a regimen of crop rotation as well as rotation of fields to be planted. In the drier climates and even in the wetter north the standard practice until the ninth century was a two-field system of crop rotation. In this approach, half of the available land was plowed and half was left fallow, and in the following year the situation was reversed. Although this practice enabled the soil to replenish itself, it did leave much of the farmland uncultivated, which worsened the already difficult problem of food production. A series of Carolingian documents from around the time of Charlemagne (surveys of the great estates called polyptychs) reveal a new three-field rotation system emerging at that time. Even before then, and even in the drier regions, a second planting sometimes occurred; beginning in the ninth century, the new practice of dividing the fields into thirds became more widespread.

The most obvious advantage of this system was that it brought more land under cultivation each year, thus increasing the productivity of the fields; it also enabled the peasants to plant different crops. In this approach one third of the field was left fallow, another third was planted with winter wheat, and the other third was planted with a spring crop, generally oats or barley and sometimes legumes. The new system of planting did not completely replace the old two-field practice and was used mostly in northern Europe, where the soil was moister and the climate wetter. Although it was not introduced universally, the new three-field planting regimen was a great benefit to those who used it, and they enjoyed better yields of seed to crop than those who did not.

Peasants used a variety of tools in their daily farm labors, but for much of the period were hindered by the simplicity of design and the materials used to make them. The farmer's tools were often made of wood, which was a less durable material than metal. Iron came into more general use only later in the early medieval period; when it did, it offered a great improvement in the quality of farming tools. The most important of all farm implements was perhaps the plow. The most common plow used by peasants in the post-Roman world of western Europe was the Roman or scratch plow. This was a simple, light tool that could be easily operated by the farmer with a small team of oxen, generally two. The scratch plow, as the name suggests, did little more than break the surface of the soil without turning it over. In areas like Italy where the soil is dry or sandy, this plow was often sufficient for the farmer's needs, but in northern Europe where the soil is moist and heavy, this plow alone was inadequate. Often digging by hand was necessary to supplement the furrow made by the scratch plow.

Probably in the Carolingian age, a new more efficient plow appeared, better suited to till the soil in northern Europe. This plow, known as the *carruca* in contemporary documents, was a wheeled plow that was fitted with a moldboard and needed as many as eight oxen to work it. It was a more complex and expensive tool, but it also was furrowed and turned the soil over, thus aerating the soil and making it more fertile. Although a technological improvement, the *carruca* did not immediately replace the scratch plow even in the north; nevertheless, its gradual spread improved agricultural productivity.

The peasant farmers of early medieval Europe used a number of other tools as well. By the Carolingian period, water and wind mills were coming into more general use to grind the grain that was such an important part of the diet. Even before these mills appeared, hand-operated mills, which were much more labor intensive to operate, enjoyed widespread use by early medieval farmers. Finally, there were several handheld tools that were generally found on early medieval farms, including spades (a useful supplement to the plow for digging in the fields), axes, hoes, sickles, and scythes.

The tools and practices medieval farmers used, especially the plow, dictated the way they farmed and the shape of their fields. Most fields in early medieval villages were long narrow strips because of the difficulty of plowing them, especially when the *carruca* came into more widespread use. It was a difficult and time-consuming job to turn the team of oxen and plow around and so, to accommodate the new plow, the fields were long and narrow instead of short and wide. Also, medieval farmers fenced in their fields or sometimes built wide ditches to manage the livestock that were allowed to graze on the fields. The fences and ditches were intended both to keep livestock in and out so that they would not overgraze some fields or wander off to another village.

Agriculture in the early Middle Ages, therefore, was focused primarily on farming various grains. Peasants also practiced animal husbandry and planted small gardens where they grew beans and leafy vegetables. The level of farming was barely above subsistence and hunger was not unknown. The early medieval peasant, nonetheless, survived in the face of various difficulties through cooperation with other peasants and various techniques developed during that time. Use of animal fertilizer was not uncommon as was the use of animals, especially horses and oxen, as draft animals. Early medieval farmers also gradually developed a heavy plow for the rich soils of northern Europe, and they also practiced crop and field rotation.

See also Animals; Carolingian Dynasty; Charlemagne; Diet and Nutrition

Bibliography

Bloch, Marc. *French Rural History: An Essay on Its Basic Characteristics.* Trans. Janet Sondheimer. Berkeley: University of California Press, 1966.

Duby, Georges. *Rural Economy and Country Life in the Medieval West.* Trans. Cynthia Postan. Columbia: University of South Carolina Press, 1968.

————. *The Early Growth of the European Economy: Warriors and Peasants from the Seventh to the Twelfth Century.* Ithaca, NY: Cornell University Press, 1979.

Finberg, Herbert P. R., ed. *Agrarian History of England and Wales.* Vol. 1. Cambridge: Cambridge University Press, 1972.

Harvey, John. *Mediaeval Gardens.* Beaverton, OR: Timber, 1981.

Lewit, Tamara. *Agricultural Production in the Roman Economy, A.D. 200–400.* Oxford: Tempus Reparatum, 1991.

Riché, Pierre. *Daily Life in the World of Charlemagne.* 1978. Trans. Jo Ann McNamara. 4th Reprint, Philadelphia: University of Pennsylvania Press, 1983.

Slicher van Bath, Bernard H. *The Agrarian History of Western Europe: A.D. 500–1850.* Trans. Olive Ordish. London: Arnold, 1963.

White, Lynn, Jr. *Medieval Technology and Social Change.* Oxford: Oxford University Press, 1964.

Aistulf (d. 756)

Penultimate Lombard king (r. 749–756), and one of the most ruthless and bloodthirsty to wear the iron crown of the Lombard monarchy. Like all the Lombard kings, Aistulf sought to extend his authority over the important central Italian possessions of the papacy and the Byzantine Empire and thereby establish Lombard power over the entire Italian peninsula. Successful against the Byzantines, Aistulf met his match in the protector of the pope, Pippin, king of the Franks. Indeed, it was Aistulf's aggression and repeated violation of diplomatic agreements that forced Pope Stephen II to seek aid from the great power in the north. Stephen's revolutionary act led to the final split between Rome and Constantinople, which in turn led to the formation of the independent papal state, and also brought about the important alliance of the papacy and the kings and, eventually, emperors of the Franks. Aistulf's threats and Stephen's response also provided the conditions in Rome that led to the creation of the greatest forgery of the Middle Ages, the Donation of Constantine.

Aistulf's reign was a difficult time for the papacy because he was determined to unify the Italian peninsula under his authority. Italian unity, however, could be accomplished only at the expense of the pope's vast estates in central Italy, and therefore the official biography of Pope Stephen II contains a very negative picture of the Lombard king. According to the *Book of the Popes* (*Liber Pontificalis*), Aistulf was a "shameless Lombard king" who was "contaminated by the Ancient Enemy's cunning" (Davis 1992, 94.6, 55). He was accused of "pernicious savagery" (Davis 1992, 94.5, 55) and cruelty. Stephen's biographer describes him as an "atrocious king . . . [who] boiled over with mighty rage and, roaring like a lion, kept sending pestilential threats to the Romans" (Davis 1992, 94.10, 56–62). Clearly this account is biased, but other contemporary accounts reveal that Aistulf was a treacherous and ambitious ruler who was not unwilling to violate treaties in pursuit of his goal. And although he was a Catholic king, Aistulf did not let his religion get in the way of conquest.

Aistulf became king in 749 after the death of Liutprand, whose threats to Roman territory and security had already caused the pope to seek Frankish aid. Liutprand, however, was respectful of St. Peter and a less ruthless and duplicitous adversary than Aistulf. From the very outset of his short and terrible reign, Aistulf took the initiative against his rivals in Italy. Within two years of his ascension to the throne, Aistulf captured Ravenna, the imperial stronghold in Italy and seat of the Byzantine emperor's representative in the Latin West, and had begun to issue royal proclamations from the city. The exarch of Ravenna, as the emperor's representative, had been the protector of the pope, and the loss of the imperial city was a blow not only to Constantinople's prestige but to the safety of Rome and its estates in central Italy.

The Lombard king's success against imperial Italy encouraged him to increase the pressure on papal Italy. Rome was now without its protector and powerless to prevent the expansion of Aistulf, who, according to the *Book of the Popes* (*Liber Pontificalis*), instituted "a great persecution" of Rome (Davis 1992, 94.5, 54). He invaded Roman territory, capturing cities in the northern part of the duchy and increasing pressure on Rome itself. Pope Stephen, following the practice his predecessors had used with other Lombard kings, sought to negotiate a peace with Aistulf. Stephen sent his brother and other high-ranking papal officials, along with many gifts, to Aistulf to sign a peace treaty in June 752. Although Aistulf agreed to a peace of forty years, he violated the treaty in only four

months. Tearing up the treaty, Aistulf imposed a heavy tribute on Rome, piled insults on the pope, threatened the Roman people, and claimed that the city was under his jurisdiction.

The difficult position Stephen faced was further complicated by imperial demands that the pope negotiate the return of Ravenna and other imperial territories seized by Aistulf. Shortly after the Lombard resumed hostilities toward Rome, Stephen received an envoy form Emperor Constantine V ordering the pope to secure the return of imperial territory. Stephen now faced the prospect of pleading for his safety and that of the emperor's lands in Italy in the face of a most unfriendly foe. In the summer and fall of 753, Stephen sought come to terms with his enemy. He had also contacted Pippin, the recently crowned king of the Franks, who had sent his own ambassadors to meet with the pope. Aistulf refused to meet with the pope or begin discussions over lands he had conquered.

In October 753 Stephen began a journey that was to have revolutionary consequences for the papacy, Franks, and Lombards. Contemporary accounts note that his departure was marked by heavenly signs, including a fireball that rose in the sky from the north— over the Frankish kingdom—and set to the south—over the Lombard kingdom. He met Aistulf at the king's residence in the royal capital of Pavia, but the pope's advances were rejected by the king, who demanded that the pope return to Rome rather than continue his trip north. Nevertheless, protection from Frankish allies guaranteed that Stephen could continue to meet the Frankish king in his residence in Ponthion. The meeting was decisive for Frankish-papal relations and was the beginning of the end of Aistulf's dream to unite Italy under his authority.

The fall and winter of 753–754 was spent forging an alliance between Pippin and Stephen. The creation of the alliance was quickened by Aistulf's miscalculation. He sent Pippin's brother, Carloman, who had retired to the monastery of Monte Cassino, to intervene on Aistulf's behalf and convince Pippin not to ally with the pope. Carloman's pleas were rejected, and he was not allowed to return to Italy. At the same time, Pippin grew closer to the pope, who may have used the claims of the Donation of Constantine to support his position. Although it is unlikely that the Donation had been written (most scholars believe it was composed sometime after 755), the basic ideas of the forgery were in evidence in Rome and may have played a role in the negotiations. Stephen confirmed the alliance by crowning Pippin king of the Franks for a second time and bestowing on him the imperial title of Patrician, thus providing the king with the right to intervene in Italy. The discussions between the king and pope did yield a donation from Pippin, one that promised that the lands of St. Peter would be returned to the pope. Pippin agreed to guarantee the return of the lands by an invasion of Italy if necessary and sent repeated demands to Aistulf to return St. Peter's patrimony.

Aistulf refused to submit to Pippin's demands and forced the Frankish king to invade Italy. After convincing the Frankish nobility of the wisdom of his policy, Pippin invaded in the spring of 755 to defend the interests of St. Peter—a focus of Carolingian devotion—and his representative, the pope. Aistulf moved north to stop the advancing Frankish armies, but he was defeated and his army put in disarray. Pippin then laid siege to the Lombard capital of Pavia, and Aistulf sued for peace. He agreed to send hostages to the Frankish court, return cities seized from Rome and Ravenna, and keep the peace, an agreement he broke shortly after Pippin left Italy. Once again Aistulf invaded Roman territory and with three separate armies laid siege to the city of Rome. He violated the cemeteries outside the city by digging up the graves and threatened to kill all the Romans by a single sword if they failed to submit to his authority.

Stephen again sent a letter to the king of the Franks seeking aid in the name of St. Peter. Upon learning of the pope's appeal, Aistulf remarked, "Let the Franks come and get you out of my hands now." In the spring of 756 Pippin did just that, invading Italy, with little of the difficulty from Frankish nobles his first invasion occasioned, and overwhelming Aistulf. The Lombard king was forced to lift his siege and to accept another treaty at the hands of the Frankish king. A list of twenty-two cities was compiled that were to be returned to the pope, and Pippin's representatives, including Abbot Fulrad, were sent to each of these cities to ensure that Aistulf honored the terms of the treaty. Fulrad accepted the keys of the cities and symbolically laid them on the altar of St. Peter in Rome as a sign of Rome's power.

It is likely that Aistulf would have violated the treaty yet again had he not died in a hunting accident in December 756. He was succeeded by Desiderius, the duke of Tuscany. His repeated assaults on Rome and treaty violations played an important role in the revolution of the eighth century. Aistulf's aggression forced the pope finally to sever ties with the emperor in Constantinople and find a more reliable protector. Stephen's alliance with Pippin and his dynasty had far-reaching repercussions throughout the rest of the Middle Ages and laid the foundation for the creation of a new Western empire. Aistulf's reign was important too because his attempted conquest of Rome helped create the papal states and established the conditions that contributed to the composition of the Donation of Constantine.

> ***See also*** Carloman, Mayor of the Palace;
> Carolingian Dynasty; Desiderius; Donation of
> Constantine; Liutprand; Lombards; Pippin III,
> Called Pippin the Short

Bibliography
Christie, Neil. *The Lombards: The Ancient Langobards.* Oxford: Blackwell, 1998.
Davis, Raymond, trans. *The Lives of the Eighth-Century Popes* (Liber Pontificalis): *The Ancient Biographies of Nine Popes from* A.D. *715 to* A.D.

817. Liverpool, UK: Liverpool University Press, 1992.

Herrin, Judith. *The Formation of Christendom.* Princeton: Princeton University Press, 1987.

Llewellyn, Peter. *Rome in the Dark Ages.* New York: Barnes and Noble, 1996.

Noble, Thomas F. X. *The Republic of St. Peter: The Birth of the Papal State, 680–825.* Philadelphia: University of Pennsylvania Press, 1984.

Riché, Pierre. *The Carolingians: A Family Who Forged Europe.* Trans. Michael Idomir Allen. Philadelphia: University of Pennsylvania Press, 1993.

Aix-la-Chapelle

See Charlemagne

Alans

A central Asian people who moved into southern Russia, the Alans participated in the migrations of peoples of the fourth and fifth centuries. Unlike other barbarian groups such as the Huns, the Alans never formed a united hoard, and therefore their impact was felt in various places in the Roman Empire. They were also associated with a number of other groups, including Huns, Vandals, and Visigoths, as well as serving the Roman military commanders Aëtius and Stilicho. Groups of Alans settled in Gaul, Italy, and Spain, with the Spanish contingent joining the Vandals who conquered the empire's North African province. Although active during the fourth and fifth centuries as both allies and enemies of the Roman Empire, the Alans disappeared as an independent people during the sixth century. They were defeated with the Vandals by Justinian's armies in North Africa and gradually absorbed by the surrounding population in both Africa and Europe. Despite their assimilation, the Alans did influence artistic styles in southern France and were known for a special breed of hunting dogs, now extinct, the *canis Alani.*

The Alans were first identified by Roman writers in the first century of the Common Era, but had only limited and minor contact with the Romans until the fourth century. There was, however, one major confrontation before then, and the Alans were often used by the Romans as interpreters. In the late fourth century the Alans, like other peoples of the central steppes of Asia, were forced to move westward by the onslaught of the Huns. Some groups of Alans were defeated by the Huns and incorporated into their army, and one group of Alans joined with the Visigoths who sought entry into the Roman Empire in the 370s. This alliance proved beneficial for the Alans but nearly fatal to the empire. The Alans joined with the Visigoths at the Battle of Hadrianople in 378, having been promised substantial rewards by the Visigoths for their assistance. After the battle, at which the Roman armies were destroyed and the emperor killed, groups of Alans settled in northern Italy and parts of southeastern Europe. Moreover, many Alans remained with the main Visigothic force and served them into the fifth century. They were part of the force that Alaric led during his rampage in Italy and sack of Rome in 410. They migrated into Gaul with Alaric's successor, where they broke ranks with the Visigoths in exchange for an alliance with the empire and lands from Narbonne to Toulouse.

The greatest number of Alans, however, entered the empire during the mass barbarian crossing of the Rhine River in 406. Led by their kings Goar and Rependial, the Alans entered imperial territory with the Vandals and fought a battle against the Franks, a Germanic people allied with the empire, who attacked the Vandals. After defeating the Franks, the Alans marched across Roman territory and sacked Trier and other cities. The group led by King Goar became an ally of Rome after the king was promised land and gold. His followers were settled around Worms, later supported a rebel Roman general, and were ultimately settled near Orléans by Aëtius. They remained important but untrustworthy allies of the Roman commander during the mid-fifth century and played a significant role in the struggle with Attila. In 451, when the great Hun decided to invade the Western Empire, he hoped to regain control over the Alans. But the Alans of Orléans, led by their King Sangiban, stood with the imperial forces in defense of the Gaul. The king's opposition to Attila slowed his advance. The king also joined with Aëtius in the great Battle of the Catalaunian Plains, but the Roman general placed the Alans between Gothic and Roman troops because of his fear that Sangiban would go over to Attila's side.

Although one group of Alani settled in Gaul, another group remained with the Vandals and entered Spain in 409. After pillaging Gaul, the Alans carved out small kingdoms in Spain and shared land with the native Roman population. Their independent existence in Spain, however, was short-lived because the Visigoths, under imperial direction, conquered the Alans, who then joined with the Vandals, losing their political independence at the same time. Although now subject to the Vandals, the Alans continued to play an important role in late imperial history. They joined with the Vandals under King Gaiseric, who was officially styled *rex Vandalorum et Alanorum* (king of the Vandals and Alans), when he led an invasion of North Africa in 429. They were part of the force that gradually displaced Roman rule in the region and established an independent kingdom ruled by Gaiseric and his successors for more than a century. The kingdom fell, however, before the armies of Justinian, led by the great general Belisarius in 533. This defeat, along with the easy assimilation of other Alan tribal units in the old Western Empire and the Alans' conversion to Christianity, brought about the disappearance of the group as an independent people in the sixth century.

See also Aëtius; Alaric; Attila the Hun; Belisarius; Catalaunian Plains, Battle of the; Gaiseric; Hadrianople, Battle of; Justinian; Vandals; Visigoths

Bibliography

Bachrach, Bernard S. "The Alans in Gaul." *Traditio* 23 (1967): 476–89.

————. *A History of the Alans in the West, from Their First Appearance in the Sources of Classical Antiquity through the Early Middle Ages.* Minneapolis: University of Minnesota Press, 1973.

Bury, John B. *History of the Later Roman Empire: From the Death of Theodosius I to the Death of Justinian.* 2 vols. 1923. Reprint, New York: Dover, 1959.

Wolfram, Herwig. *The Roman Empire and Its Germanic Peoples.* Trans. Thomas J. Dunlap. Berkeley: University of California Press, 1997.

Alaric (c. 370–410)

Great Visigothic king and warrior whose sack of the ancient capital city of Rome in 410, following the assassination of his rival Stilicho, profoundly shocked and dismayed the people of the Roman Empire, a shock from which the Western Empire never fully recovered. Alaric's sack of the city was a signal of the declining fortunes of the Western Empire, which finally fell in 476. As king, Alaric revived the challenge the Visigoths had posed for Rome since their entry into the empire in 376 and subsequent stinging defeat of imperial armies at the Battle of Hadrianople, during which the emperor, Valens, died. Ambitious and talented, an Arian Christian who could be most ruthless when necessary, a skilled general who could not achieve a decisive victory over the Romans, Alaric attempted to create a barbarian kingship to rival Roman imperial power and an independent barbarian kingdom in the empire. Although he ultimately failed in his grand design, Alaric's challenge to Roman authorities did set the tone for the way the Romans dealt with other barbarian leaders and the political, military, and territorial arrangements they made with the barbarians in the coming century.

Born around 370, Alaric is first mentioned in the early 390s, and most likely was involved in Gothic actions in the late 380s. In 376, his fellow tribesmen had entered the empire to avoid the westward movement of the Huns—whose activities also shaped the subsequent history of the Goths—defeated imperial armies, killed the emperor in battle in 378, and signed a treaty with the empire in 382 that Alaric spent his career attempting to undo. Alaric's first appearance was as the king of a mixed band of Goths and allied peoples who crossed the Balkans into Thrace in 391. Alaric's advance was stopped by the recently promoted general, Stilicho. It was the first meeting between the two barbarian leaders and the beginning of a long rivalry between them. Stilicho defeated and encircled Alaric at their first meeting but at the order of the emperor, Theodosius, allowed him to go free. Alaric managed to establish the first independent Gothic kingdom on Roman soil on this occasion and was the first barbarian king to be made a general in the Roman army. In this way Alaric broke with tradition, and the empire established important precedents for its future dealings with other barbarian kings. Despite some gains, Alaric was forced to renew the terms of the treaty of 382, which, among other things, required the Goths to serve the Roman military.

In 394 Theodosius called on Alaric to honor the terms of the treaty, as he faced the challenge of the usurper, Eugenius, who had been elevated to the imperial throne in the West after the death of Valentinian II. Failed negotiations between the pretender and the emperor led to open warfare, and although he received a subordinate command and directed no Roman troops, Alaric supplied a sizeable contingent to the imperial army and distinguished himself in battle. The usurper was put down, but only after a terrible battle in which many Goths were killed. To many Goths, it appeared that they had been sacrificed by the imperial generals to secure victory over Eugenius and to reduce the power of the Goths. Indeed, the treatment Alaric received led him to revolt, even though he received a high imperial post.

Alaric's actions were probably motivated by several factors: dissatisfaction over treatment in the suppression of Eugenius; the Hunnish advance in 394–395; and the death of Theodosius in 395, which ended the treaty of 382 because the major party to the treaty dropped out. Of course, the movements of other Goths and the turmoil within the empire allowed Alaric more freedom of action. Whatever the case, he revolted in 395 and spent the next two years on the move throughout the empire. Once again he was opposed by Stilicho, who managed to surround the Goth on occasion but was prohibited from crushing his rival because of imperial restrictions and because of court politics that undermined Stilicho's effectiveness and also threatened his life and position. Alaric plundered Greece during this period, entered into secret negotiations with Stilicho, and, in 397, extracted significant concessions from the empire. He received a new command that gave him regional authority as the *magister militum* for the region of Illyricum, and he also received important territorial concessions. In this way, the empire set further precedents by incorporating a barbarian people more fully into the administrative structure of the empire and placing authority in the hands of that people's king.

Turmoil among some of Alaric's fellow Goths, and their desire to emulate his success, led to a Gothic attempt to take Constantinople, which was suppressed with the aid of the Huns and their leader Uldin. Alaric remained aloof from the struggle, but he did not remain quiet long. In 401, while his rival Stilicho was active against a Vandal force, Alaric invaded Italy and threatened the imperial capital of Milan, an action that so dismayed the emperor, Honorius, that he transferred his residence to Ravenna. Stilicho quickly moved to Italy; he met Alaric in battle at Pollentia, where he inflicted serious damage on the Gothic army, though not able to defeat it outright. Alaric was allowed to return to his lands in the east, but for unknown reasons he stopped at Verona in 402. Stilicho struck at Alaric with great force and handed Alaric his worst defeat. And this time Alaric left Italy for his Balkan homelands.

Having once again escaped destruction,

Alaric once again waited for the opportunity to arise to allow him to strike again. It was presented as a result of further turmoil between the Eastern and Western imperial courts and by further pressure from the frontiers. In 404–405, Stilicho fell out with the Eastern authority and may have negotiated with Alaric, making him *magister militum* of Illyricum again. (Alaric received this rank by 407 and may have held it as early as 405, but the record is unclear.) This was a clear violation of relations between East and West because Illyricum was the possession of the Eastern emperor. Stilicho's difficulties were increased by the invasion of the Gothic king Radagaisus, barbarian invasions over the Rhine, and the appearance of the usurper Constantine in Britain. Although he was able to overcome these threats, Stilicho was forced to attempt reconciliation with the Eastern Roman Empire, and he broke the treaty with the Goths. In 408, Alaric rose up in rebellion, occupying important territories and threatening to invade Italy unless he received payment of 4,000 pounds of gold. Alaric's long-time rival, Stilicho, was willing to grant these demands, but he fell from favor and was executed, along with thousands of barbarians living in Italy.

The death of Stilicho opened the final chapter in the life of Alaric. The massacre of so many barbarians caused thousands of Stilicho's supporters to join Alaric, who took the opportunity to invade Italy with a substantially larger army. He reached Rome in 409 and camped outside the city until the following year, threatening to sack it unless Emperor Honorius yielded to his demands. But Honorius refused Alaric's offer of alliance in exchange for the grant of a generalship, payments of gold and grain, and land for the troops. Alaric offered a different arrangement in which he would make an alliance in exchange for land and grain. The emperor again refused, and thus Alaric's attempt to prop up an emperor who would meet his demands failed.

Exasperated with his failure to move Honorius, Alaric ordered the sack of the city on August 24, 410. A Roman noblewoman, according to tradition, opened the city gates for Alaric, and for three days the Goths plundered and burned the city, leaving the churches in peace. The Goths came away with great spoils, including the booty the emperor Titus brought back from the First Jewish War and the destruction of Jerusalem in the first century and Galla Placidia, the sister of the emperor, who was kidnapped by her future husband Ataulf. The sack, the first in 800 years, profoundly shocked the people of the empire, including St. Jerome, who was rendered speechless by the tears he cried, and St. Augustine, who wrote his great work, *On the City of God,* in response to the sack.

Alaric, however, did not long enjoy the spoils of his victory. After the sack of the city, he moved south with his armies and attempted to cross to Sicily as a first step toward seizing the grain-producing regions of Africa. His fleet was wrecked, and he then turned north, perhaps with designs on Naples or some other city. Along the way he became ill and died in Bruttium. According to tradition, he was buried in the bed of the Busento River while it was temporarily diverted, and the slaves who buried him were killed so that the whereabouts of the tomb would remain unknown. Alaric was succeeded by his brother-in-law, Ataulf.

Although he died shortly after his epoch-making sack of the city of Rome, Alaric had a long-lasting impact on the empire. Indeed, the events of 410 profoundly altered the way the Romans, Christian and pagan, saw themselves. The aura of invincibility and permanence associated with *Roma aeterna* (eternal Rome) had been shattered, and the city suffered further assaults in the course of the fifth century. By the century's end, the Western Roman Empire had disappeared. Alaric also forced the empire to reevaluate its relations with the barbarians and led them to create precedents that affected their dealings with other barbarian tribes that moved into the empire in the coming decades.

See also Hadrianople, Battle of; Huns; Stilicho, Flavius; Theodosius; Visigoths

Bibliography

Burns, Thomas S. *Barbarians within the Gates of Rome: A Study of Roman Military Policy and the Barbarians, ca. 375–425 A.D.* Bloomington: University of Indiana Press, 1994.

Heather, Peter. *The Goths.* Oxford: Blackwell, 1996.

Lot, Ferdinand. *The End of the Ancient World and the Beginning of the Middle Ages.* New York: Harper and Row, 1961.

Wolfram, Herwig. *History of the Goths.* Trans. Thomas J. Dunlap. Berkeley: University of California Press, 1988.

———. *The Roman Empire and Its Germanic Peoples.* Trans. Thomas J. Dunlap. Berkeley: University of California Press, 1997.

Alaric II (d. 507)

Visigothic king of Toulouse (484–507) who traditionally has been seen as a weak and unworthy successor to his great father Euric, but who more recently has been seen as an important and innovative king. Even by traditional estimates, Alaric is worthy of better treatment than he has received because of his successful military alliance with the most powerful Germanic king of his age, Theodoric the Great. He introduced important legislation during his reign and prepared an important legal codification. He also instituted a new and farsighted religious policy, which laid the foundations for an important church council and would have established an important institutional framework for church-state relations in the Visigothic kingdom had the kingdom not been smashed by the great Frankish king Clovis (r. 481–511). Indeed, it is Alaric's defeat by Clovis that has, most unfairly, shaped his modern reputation.

Although overshadowed by his Ostrogothic father-in-law Theodoric and his Frankish rival Clovis, Alaric was an ambitious and, for much of his reign, successful king. He oversaw the expansion and consolidation of the kingdom of Toulouse that his father Euric may have intended in his attempts to extend the kingdom's boundaries. During Alaric's reign, Visigoths from his kingdom began to migrate in significant numbers into Spain and often fought the local inhabitants to gain control of large estates, military campaigns supported by Alaric.

In the early 490s, Alaric joined Theodoric in his struggles in Italy against the Germanic king Odovacar. Upon Theodoric's victory over Odovacar in 493, Alaric was rewarded by marriage to one of Theodoric's daughters. At the same time Theodoric married one of his daughters to Clovis, so that the new king in Italy could gain the support of the powerful Frank. It is possible that it was for the same reason—to gain the friendship of Clovis—that Alaric handed over Syagrius, the former king of Soissons who had earlier been defeated by Clovis and fled to Toulouse. Although Gregory of Tours in his history places this act earlier and sees it as a sign of weakness, it most likely happened in 493 as part of the broader political strategy involving Theodoric. Indeed, in the early sixth century, when the Franks sought to expand into his territory, Alaric defeated Clovis, who then sought to reestablish their previous amity. But once again the relationship between the two kings changed.

According to Gregory of Tours, Clovis attacked Alaric because the Visigothic king was an Arian Christian and Clovis could not stand the thought of a heretic living as his neighbor. Clovis ignored the warning of Theodoric that he would defend Alaric, and war broke out between Clovis and Alaric in 507. At this point, Alaric may have overextended his resources, and Theodoric himself was concerned about the strength of Alaric's army. In late summer of that year, Alaric and Clovis met in battle at Vouillé, near Poitiers. Alaric was outnumbered by his rival and was defeated. Clovis supposedly killed Alaric himself and then absorbed the kingdom of Toulouse.

Although defeated and killed in battle, Alaric was still a noteworthy king. His success in battle against Clovis, Odovacar, and others before his final defeat testifies to his martial abilities. But more important than his military prowess are the legal and religious reforms he instituted. He promulgated a new legal code, the *Breviarium Alaricianum* (*Breviary of Alaric*), in 506, which had been compiled by a commission of legal experts under the direction of a high-ranking royal official. The code was based upon earlier Roman legal codes and their commentaries and became the official law for the Roman subjects of the kingdom.

The participation of the Roman bishops in the codification of the law laid the foundation for the Council of Agde in 506. The council was Alaric's means to integrate the Roman Catholic bishops and church into the governmental framework of the kingdom ruled by an Arian Christian. His father had been more hostile to the church, but Alaric, recognizing perhaps the wave of the future, sought to incorporate the church into his kingdom. The council at Agde was an important first step in that process, and plans were made at the council to hold a national council in the following year at Toulouse. Although the council was never held because of Alaric's defeat by Clovis, preparation for it foreshadowed church councils in the future. Alaric established an important precedent for later church-state relations with the council at Agde and the proposed council at Toulouse. Although known best for his defeat at Vouillé, Alaric was a successful and innovative king for much of his reign.

See also Clovis; Euric; Gregory of Tours; Merovingian Dynasty; Odovacar; Ostrogoths; Theodoric the Great; Visigoths

Bibliography

Gregory of Tours. *History of the Franks.* Trans. Lewis Thorpe. Harmondsworth, UK: Penguin, 1974.

Bury, John B. *History of the Later Roman Empire: From the Death of Theodosius I to the Death of Justinian.* Vol. 1. 1923. Reprint, New York: Dover, 1958.

Heather, Peter. *The Goths.* Oxford: Blackwell, 1996.

Wolfram, Herwig. *History of the Goths.* Trans. Thomas J. Dunlap. Berkeley: University of California Press, 1988.

———. *The Roman Empire and Its Germanic Peoples.* Trans. Thomas J. Dunlap. Berkeley: University of California Press, 1997.

Alboin (d. 572)

According to Paul the Deacon, Alboin was the tenth of the Lombard kings (r. 560/561–574) and the first to rule in Italy. A successful warrior, who defeated a number of rival peoples, including the Gepids, he was also a successful diplomat and enjoyed good relations with the Franks, even marrying a daughter of one of the Merovingian kings. Alboin also enjoyed fairly good relations with the bishops of Italy, even though he and his people were pagans and Arians and the bishops and people of Italy Catholic. Although neither he nor his successors ruled a united Italy, Alboin laid the foundation for an important kingdom in Italy, which survived until it was absorbed by Charlemagne in 774.

Alboin, according to Paul the Deacon, was "a man fitted for wars and energehz in all things" (49). And he spent much of his career after succeeding his father Audoin in 560/561 in waging wars. Alboin ascended the throne in traditional Lombard fashion—by election. As proved to be the case throughout Lombard history, Alboin was elected by his people, who usually chose the heir of the former king. He had distinguished himself already during the reign of his father, when he led the Lombards in battle against the Gepids and, according to tradition, killed the Gepid king. Three years after the battle, in 555, Alboin was rewarded with marriage to the daughter of the Merovingian king Chlotar I (r. 511–561), and he maintained good relations with the Franks ever after.

Upon succeeding his father, Alboin led the Lombards against the Gepids and into Italy. His struggles with the Gepids were not always successful, and in 565 he lost a battle against them. Two years later, after forging an alliance with the Avars, Alboin destroyed the Gepids. In the battle, Alboin killed the king and made a drinking cup of his skull, and also seized and married the king's daughter, Rosamund. In 568, according to tradition, Alboin accepted an invitation from the general Narses, who felt slighted by the emperor Justin II, to invade Italy. In thanks for their help, Alboin arranged a treaty with the Avars that gave them control of the old Lombard homeland.

See also Arianism; Avars; Charlemagne; Franks; Justinian; Lombards; Merovingian Dynasty; Narses; Ostrogoths; Paul the Deacon; Totila

Bibliography

Paul the Deacon. *History of the Lombards.* Trans. William Dudley Foulke. Philadelphia: University of Pennsylvania Press, 1974.

Christie, Neil. *The Lombards: The Ancient Langobards.* Oxford: Blackwell, 1998.

Llewellyn, Peter. *Rome in the Dark Ages.* New York: Barnes and Noble, 1993.

Wolfram, Herwig. *The Roman Empire and Its Germanic Peoples.* Trans. Thomas J. Dunlap. Berkeley: University of California Press, 1997.

Alcuin of York (c. 730/735–804)

An Anglo-Saxon scholar, trained in the tradition of the Venerable Bede, Alcuin was the most important and influential of Charlemagne's court scholars. As one of Charlemagne's most trusted advisors, Alcuin participated in important church councils and guided Charlemagne through some of his more important political decisions. Although he was not an original thinker, he was widely respected for his encyclopedic knowledge. His influence is perhaps demonstrated by the importance and number of his students, including Louis the Pious and Rabanus Maurus, and the warm regard they had for him because of his incomparable talent as a teacher. Indeed Einhard, Charlemagne's biographer and possibly one of Alcuin's students, described him as "the greatest scholar of the day." He is no longer recognized as the author of the *Libri Carolini* or the creator of the form of writing called Carolingian minuscule. Nevertheless, he remains one of the most important figures in the Carolingian Renaissance because of his teaching and because of his numerous writings, including commentaries on various books of the Bible (Genesis, Psalms, Ecclesiastes, the Song of Songs, and the Gospel of John), a new edition of the Bible, hagiography, poems, letters, and works on grammar, rhetoric, and dialectic (the trivium, the three most basic disciplines of the seven liberal arts).

Little is known for certain of Alcuin's early years. He was born in 730/735 to a noble family of York and was a kinsman of the great missionary saint, Willibrord. He entered the cathedral school at York, where he received an education that eventually brought him to the attention of Charlemagne, having prepared him to help shape a renaissance in the great king's realm. The school had recently been founded by Bede's friend and student, Egbert, who introduced the great Anglo-Saxon's love of learning there and invited Aethelberht (or Aelberht) to oversee the creation of a library. It was Aethelberht who taught Alcuin and instilled the love of books and learning that Alcuin bore with him through the rest of his life, an affection that had a strong effect on the Franks and was the foundation of their cultural revival.

Aethelberht evidently recognized Alcuin's talents, for he took his student with him to the continent on two occasions. On these trips Alcuin collected books and met other scholars; he met Charlemagne for the first time on a trip in 768. When Aethelberht succeeded to the position of archbishop of York, Alcuin took over the cathedral school of York, and when Aethelberht retired in 780, Alcuin also took over direction of the library. The new archbishop, Eanbald, had such confidence in Alcuin that he sent the scholar to Rome to collect the pallium (liturgical vestment granted by the pope to bishops with metropolitan authority), and on Alcuin's return he met Charlemagne at Parma and was invited to take charge of the king's court school. After gaining permission from Eanbald, Alcuin returned to France and spent the rest of his life in the Frankish kingdom, with the exception of two periods, 786 and 790–793, when he returned to his native land.

It was in the service of Charlemagne that Alcuin made his mark on history. From 781 until his retirement in 794, Alcuin was a member of Charlemagne's peripatetic court. At court, he participated in the cultural and religious revival that Charlemagne promoted and was, no doubt, important in the direction that the revival took. He also led the court school, teaching a broad range of subjects, including astronomy, to Charlemagne, his children, and many others who went on to contribute to the Carolingian Renaissance. He brought the great Anglo-Saxon tradition with him to create, as he once wrote, a new, and better, Athens in the Frankish kingdom, one that honored learning in devotion to God. He was rewarded by Charlemagne with the revenues from several abbeys, and at his retirement was made abbot of the important monastery of St. Martin of Tours, even though he may never have taken monastic vows and took orders no higher than the level of deacon. Even in retirement he continued to influence the cultural and religious life of his adopted homeland. He contributed to and promoted the handwriting reform at Tours, even though he did not create Carolingianminuscule. He wrote treatises on a variety of religious and secular subjects and produced a new edition of the Bible, now lost, which he presented to Charlemagne on Christmas day 800. On May 19, 804, Alcuin died at Tours, having composed his own epitaph: "Alcuin was my name and wisdom always my love."

A scholar and teacher, Alcuin's influence was felt in many areas during his lifetime, not the least of which was education. He wrote a treatise on the liberal arts and resurrected the system of the seven liberal arts devised by Cassiodorus. He taught a number of topics, including chant, grammar, rhetoric, dialectic (logic), mathematics, and astronomy. His method of teaching is preserved in a dialogue with one of Charlemagne's sons that reveals Alcuin's extraordinary pedagogical talents. It is a dialogue in which student and teacher alternate asking and answering questions. He brought encyclopedic learning, which he dispensed to his many students who, in turn, passed it along to their students, including Rabanus Maurus, the preceptor of Germany. Indeed, his active and energetic mind, his comprehensive (though derivative) knowledge, was precisely what was needed for the first generation of the Carolingian Renaissance.

Alcuin was more, however, than the teacher to the renaissance, he was an important contributor. He supplied the scholars in the Frankish kingdom with numerous books from his native England. He wrote over 300 letters and over 220 poems that reveal his ability with Latin, his religious and intellectual concerns, and his own attractive personality. His poetry included light verse to students, for example the *Lament for the Cuckoo* with its echoes of the great Roman poet Virgil, hymns, and acrostic poems to Charlemagne. He also wrote longer, more serious poems, including one on the Viking destruction of Lindisfarne abbey in 793, a life of St. Willibrord, and *The Bishops, Knights, and Saints of York*. He also wrote works of hagiography and treatises on the virtues and vices, the nature of the soul, and confession.

He was a great influence on Carolingian religious life and a staunch defender of religious orthodoxy. He reformed the liturgy of the Frankish church to bring it into line with Roman usage, revised the mass book, and composed a series of masses drawn from the Anglo-Irish tradition of piety. He advised Charlemagne on religious policy and criticized the king's brutal Saxon policy and forced baptisms. Indeed, Alcuin's influence is clearly evident in Charlemagne's second Saxon capitulary of 797. He was an ardent foe of Felix of Urgel and the Adoptionist heresy, which denied that Jesus Christ in his humanity was the natural son of God. Alcuin presented the case against it at the Synod of Frankfurt in 794 and wrote a number of treatises against it, including a longer commentary on the Trinity. It is likely that he also participated in the debate on the decisions of the Second Council of Nicaea, 787, approving veneration of icons, which were misunderstood in the Frankish world because of a faulty translation. Although it is now believed that Theodulf of Orléans, not Alcuin, wrote the official work, the *Libri Carolini* (the *Caroline Books*), he influenced their content and may have had an editorial hand in their preparation.

Finally, it should be noted that Alcuin also influenced political life in the Frankish kingdom. He was used by Charlemagne as an ambassador to King Offa of Mercia in 790, and frequently served on the king's council. Alcuin sent numerous letters to Charlemagne on a wide variety of subjects, including Frankish relations with the Saxons and the duties of kings and nobles. His most famous letter, however, was written in 799 and concerned the great powers of the world. After noting that the imperial throne in Constantinople was vacant, and the holder of the throne of Peter had been attacked and depended on Charlemagne's protection, Alcuin wrote:

> Third, there is the Royal Dignity . . . in power a ruler more excellent than the aforementioned ones, in wisdom more radiant, and in grandeur more sublime. Behold, now in you alone lies the salvation of the churches of Christ. You are the avenger of crimes, the guide of those who err, the consoler of the afflicted, the uplifter of the righteous. (Riché, p. 120)

This letter clearly reveals Alcuin's understanding of Charlemagne's power, and it is generally recognized as Alcuin's endorsement of Charlemagne's acceptance of the imperial crown in the following year. Indeed, through-

out the 790s, Alcuin and Charlemagne's other advisors had begun to speak of the king in imperial terms. It is most likely that Alcuin himself actively encouraged his friend to accept the imperial dignity because it would be a means of resolving the crisis in Italy and also because Charlemagne surely had earned the right to be called emperor.

See also Anglo-Saxons; Bede; Carolingian Dynasty; Carolingian Renaissance; Charlemagne; Einhard; Felix of Urgel; Louis the Pious; Saxon Capitularies; Theodulf of Orléans

Bibliography
Bullough, Donald. "Alcuin and the Kingdom of Heaven: Liturgy, Theology, and the Carolingian Age." In *Carolingian Essays,* ed. Uta-Renate Blumenthal. Washington, DC: Catholic University Press, 1983, pp. 1–69.
Duckett, Eleanor Shipley. *Alcuin, Friend of Charlemagne: His World and His Work.* New York: Macmillan, 1951.
Dutton, Paul Edward, ed. *Carolingian Civilization: A Reader.* Peterborough, Ont.: Broadview, 1993.
Laistner, Max L. W. *Thought and Letters in Western Europe, A.D. 500–900,* 2d ed. Ithaca, NY: Cornell University Press, 1957.
Mayvaert, Paul. "The Authorship of the 'Libri Carolini': Observations Prompted by a Recent Book." *Revue bénédictine* 89 (1979): 29–57.
Riché, Pierre. *The Carolingians: A Family Who Forged Europe.* Trans. Michael Idomir Allen. Philadelphia: University of Pennsylvania Press, 1993.
Wallach, Luitpold, *Alcuin and Charlemagne: Studies in Carolingian History and Literature.* Ithaca, NY: Cornell University Press, 1959.

Alemanni

A confederation of Germanic tribes or warrior bands, which may have included the Bucinobantes, Juthungi, Lentienses, and Suevi. The Alemanni first appeared in the third century in a conflict with the Roman Empire. Their name, which they may not have used, means "all men" or "all of mankind" and indicates that they were composed of many different peoples. It was also understood in a pejorative sense by their enemies to mean "half-breeds" or "newcomers." They were distinguished by their long heads, which they created by artificially deforming the skull of newborns with bandages around the head. They were often in conflict with the Roman Empire in the third century and sought to carve out settlements in imperial territory in the fourth. In the fifth century they were able to exploit imperial weakness and enter the empire, but they faced a greater challenge as the century went on from the Franks and their Merovingian dynasty. The Alemanni were ultimately absorbed by their Merovingian rivals, and despite a short period of independence, were subject also to the Carolingian dynasty.

The Alemanni first appeared, according to the Roman historian Cassius Dio, in a conflict with the Roman emperor Caracalla (r. 211–217) in 213. The Alemanni were able to take advantage of the empire during its period of crisis from 234 to 284. They were most likely part of the group of barbarians who crossed the Rhine River and other parts of the imperial frontier in the mid-third century. They were among the first groups of barbarians to take control of Roman territory and settle in parts of the empire. Throughout the mid-third century, even after some settled in the empire, the Alemanni continued to make plundering raids on imperial territory, often reaching Italy. Despite occasional success against them, the Romans were unable to stop the raids of the Alamanni because of their loose organization. They had no central king, but various warlords who led raids of plunder and pillage with loyal war bands. By the late third century, however, the Romans restored order to the empire, and the Alamanni became more settled, acting as more traditional opponents of Rome or as servants of the empire.

In the fourth and fifth centuries, the Alemanni continued their efforts to secure Roman territory. They fought actively along the Rhine and Danube frontiers of the empire, and, on occasion, enjoyed some success. But several emperors during the fourth century inflicted stunning defeats on the Alemanni, including Constantine, Julian the Apostate, and Valentinian I. In fact, Valentinian drove deep into Alemanni territory in 368 to turn back Alemanni advances into the empire. Although the emperors enjoyed victories over the Alemanni in the fourth century, they suffered defeats by their rivals in the fifth century. In 406, a large body of barbarians crossed the Rhine River during a winter freeze, and it is most likely that the Alemanni were part of that group. Their success was limited, however, by the Franks, another Germanic people, which later produced the Merovingian and Carolingian dynasties, and by imperial diplomacy. But with the movement of the Huns under Attila, the Rhine defenses were sufficiently undermined to allow the further incursion of the Alemanni.

The westward movement of the Alemanni into imperial territory was not without negative consequences for these tribes. Although they managed to settle on Roman territory, the Alemanni once again came into contact with the rising power of northern Europe, the Merovingian Franks. The conflict between these two peoples led to the eventual subjugation of the Alemanni by the Merovingians and to the conversion to Christianity of the Merovingians. According to the historian Gregory of Tours, the Alemanni fought a great battle against the Frankish Merovingian king Clovis at Tolbiac (modern Zülpich, Switzerland), which is traditionally dated 495. Gregory informs us that Clovis was losing the battle and promised to convert to Christianity if the Christian God allowed him to win the battle. Clovis won the battle and then converted to Catholic Christianity. Although the date of the battle remains controversial and the entire story of Clovis's conversion is problematic, it is certain that he incorporated the Alemanni into his ever growing kingdom. From the time of Clovis, therefore, the Alemanni were subject to the Franks.

During the sixth and seventh centuries, the Alemanni remained part of the Merovingian kingdom. The exact course of their history, however, remains uncertain because of the lack of written records about them and because of the unclear archeological record. It is likely that they participated in Merovingian military activities, including campaigns in northern Italy. The Alemanni also continued to be ruled by dukes rather than kings, and although loosely organized, codified their laws. They were able to expand their territories of settlement into southern Germany and parts of Switzerland during this period. They also, finally and only gradually, converted to Christianity. This conversion was the result of the missionary activities of St. Columban and his disciples in the later sixth century.

In the later seventh and early eighth centuries, the Alemanni regained their independence from the Merovingians. The Alemanni were able to throw off the Merovingian rule because of the turmoil in the Merovingian kingdom brought on by the decline of Merovingian power and the rise of Carolingian power. Although the Carolingian mayors of the palace Pippin of Herstal and Charles Martel were able to restore Frankish authority over the Alemanni for short periods, the Alemanni remained independent for most of the first half of the eighth century. It was only during the reign of Pippin the Short that the Alemanni were forced once again to submit, permanently this time, to Frankish power. Pippin defeated the Alemanni in two great battles in 744 and 748 and thereby reincorporated them into the kingdom. They remained subjects of the Carolingians thereafter.

See also Attila the Hun; Carolingian Dynasty; Charles Martel; Clovis; Gregory of Tours; Huns; Merovingian Dynasty; Pippin II, Called Pippin of Herstal; Pippin III, Called Pippin the Short; Vandals

Bibliography

Bachrach, Bernard S. *Merovingian Military Organization, 481–751.* Minneapolis: University of Minnesota Press, 1972.

Bury, John B. *History of the Later Roman Empire: From the Death of Theodosius I to the Death of Justinian.* 2 Vols. 1923. Reprint, New York: Dover, 1959.

Gregory of Tours. *The History of the Franks.* Trans. Lewis Thorpe. Harmondsworth, UK: Penguin, 1974.

Wood, Ian. *The Merovingian Kingdoms, 450–751.* London: Longman, 1994.

Wolfram, Herwig. *The Roman Empire and Its Peoples.* Trans. Thomas J. Dunlap. Berkeley: University of California Press, 1997.

Alfred the Great (849–899)

The most important and influential of the Saxon kings of England, Alfred has been known as "the Great" since the sixteenth century. As king of Wessex he was involved in a prolonged struggle with the Danes, who invaded England almost annually until the end of Alfred's reign. His victories over the invaders, as well as the navy he created, the network of fortifications he built to defend the country, and his various military reforms greatly curtailed the threat of invasion. He also reformed the law and promoted learning in his kingdom. As the patron of learning in his kingdom, Alfred sponsored the translation of many important Christian texts and even translated some of them himself. As a warrior, legal reformer, and educator, Alfred left an important legacy for his successors.

The youngest of the five sons of the deeply religious but not very effective King Æthelwulf of Wessex—who also had one daughter—and his queen, the noble woman Osburh, Alfred was born in 849 in Wantage, Oxfordshire. Although little is known about his earliest years, it is likely that they were not marked by preparation to succeed to the throne, since Alfred's older brothers would surely have been expect to succeed to the throne before Alfred could. Asser, Alfred's biographer, does offer some information on his hero's earliest years. He says that Alfred was the most beloved of all the children of Æthelwulf and Osburh and was raised at court. In chapter 22 of his life, Asser notes that as a child Alfred was "fairer in all forms than all his brothers, and more pleasing in his looks, his words and ways." He was a skilled hunter who practiced as often as he could, and continued to enjoy hunting as an adult, even though he was afflicted with illness his whole life.

Asser notes too that Alfred was deeply religious and, as a boy and an adult, attended mass daily, prayed often, and gave alms generously. But the most remarkable thing Alfred demonstrated as a youth, and as king, was his great desire for learning. Although he did not learn to read until he was twelve and read Latin when he was older still, Alfred possessed "from his cradle a longing for wisdom." Although he learned to read only in later life, Alfred, according to Asser, "listened attentively" to Saxon poems until he could recite them from memory. Alfred's devotion to learning is revealed in a story his biographer tells of his boyhood. His mother, Osburh, promised her sons that whichever one of them could learn a book of Saxon poetry would receive the book as a prize. Alfred asked if she really meant to give one of them the book, and she replied that she would. Alfred had his master read the book to him and then he repeated it to his mother.

Alfred's zeal for learning may have been inspired by two trips to Rome that he took early in his life. In 853 Alfred paid his first visit to the Holy See, where he was received by Pope Leo IV and underwent a special ceremony of investiture. According to both Asser's life and the *Anglo-Saxon Chronicle,* Alfred was anointed with the kingship by the pope—a most unlikely occurrence because of Alfred's older sons. It is more likely that Alfred was anointed as Leo's godson. In 855 Alfred made a pilgrimage to Rome with his father, who stayed a year. The journey to Rome and back went, as had the previous trip, through the Carolingian realm. On the return during the second trip, Æthelwulf, whose first wife had died, married Judith, the daughter of Charles the Bald, at whose court

Alfred the Great (Perry-Castaneda Library)

the pilgrims stayed. Alfred certainly came into contact with the dazzling culture of the court of Charles the Bald on this trip, which most likely left a lasting impression on a young boy who had a great thirst for knowledge. He may also have become aware of the great legacy of Charlemagne during this visit to the court of the great king's grandson. Charles the Bald had sought to revive the glories of the Carolingian Renaissance, and Alfred's exposure to those glories would surely have reinforced his own interests in learning. When he became king, Alfred attempted to revive learning and letters in his kingdom as the great Frankish rulers had in theirs.

Alfred's path to the kingship was a most indirect one, because his older brothers had precedence over him to the throne. In fact, one of his brothers, Æthelbald, claimed his

Alfred Jewel, with King Alfred, 849–899, King of Wessex, late ninth century A.D., *Somerset (The Art Archive/Ashmolean Museum Oxford/Eileen Tweedy)*

right to the succession while Æthelwulf was on pilgrimage in 855–856. Æthelwulf submitted to his son's demands by dividing the kingdom and ruling with his eldest son until Æthelwulf died in 858. Two other brothers preceded Alfred to the throne in the 860s. In that decade the Danish threat became increasingly serious and was the major focus of the king's activities. In 868, for example, Alfred joined his brother King Ethelred in support of the king of Mercia, Buhred, in a battle against invading Danes at Nottingham. The Danes continued their raids and had great success against various Saxon rulers, killing Edmund, king of East Anglia, in one engagement.

Alfred succeeded his brother Æthelred on the throne in 871 and began the difficult struggle with Danish invaders that lasted most of his reign. In the first year of his kingship, according to the *Anglo-Saxon Chronicle,* Alfred fought numerous battles against various Danish warrior bands and although he won an important victory at Wilton against a much larger force, in all likelihood he lost most of the battles. In 872, to stem the tide of invasion, Alfred purchased a truce from the Danes, which allowed him time to strengthen his hold on the kingdom and prepare for future attacks. Alfred's truce kept the Danes away from his kingdom for several years, but the surrounding kingdoms were not as fortunate. In the 870s East Anglia, Mercia, and

Northumbria were overrun by Danish armies, and at one point the Mercian king was forced to flee to Rome in the face of the onslaught.

The Danes mounted a renewed challenge on Alfred's kingdom in 876. The next few years were the most difficult of Alfred's entire reign, and the Danes nearly took over his kingdom of Wessex. Indeed, in 878 the Danes drove Alfred from his kingdom to the island of Athelney. This was a dark time for Alfred and the English, but it was also the moment (but not the last) that Alfred showed his true greatness. Marshaling his forces from his base on Athelney, Alfred began to attack Danish forces over the course of seven weeks. These attacks culminated in a major victory over the Danes at the Battle of Eddington, breaking their army and driving them from the field. The Danes and their king, Guthrum, agreed to leave Wessex and convert to Christianity. Alfred's great victory saved his kingdom from occupation by the Danes, but it did not end the Danish threat. Guthrum merely turned his attention to other parts of England, and Alfred himself faced further challenges later in his reign.

During the 880s Alfred strengthened his position in England. He extended his authority over other English kingdoms, most importantly Mercia. In 886 Alfred took control of London, an event of such importance to the English that, as the *Anglo-Saxon Chronicle* notes, "all the English people not under subjection to the Danes submitted to him" (Whitelock). Alfred also reorganized his military, so that he would be better prepared for future attacks by the Danes from land or sea. He reformed the fyrd, the traditional peasant militia of Anglo-Saxon England that was essential for local defense. Useful as the fyrd was for local defense, its greatest weakness was the unwillingness of peasant soldiers to serve outside their county or for significant lengths of time. Alfred could not resolve the problem of distance, but he was able to keep the fyrd in the field by dividing service into six-month terms and mobilizing half the peasantry for each term. He also built a series of

burghs, fortified settlements throughout the kingdom that could serve as defensive positions or as bases of further operation and counterattack. Situated at key points throughout the realm, the burghs were primarily military garrisons, but some had administrative and financial functions, roles that became more important as time went on. Alfred also built a fleet of ships to meet the Danes on the open sea. The ships were larger than anything the Danes had and were certainly a match for the Danish ships.

Alfred's military reforms were an important precaution, because he faced further attacks in the 890s. In 892 an invasion force crossed the channel from Francia in 250 ships, followed by a second fleet of 80 ships. Over the next several years, Alfred once again was forced to defend his kingdom and once again was successful. From 893 to 896 Alfred waged a series of offensives against the invading Danes, on occasion capturing their camps and forcing them to flee before being totally destroyed. In 896 Alfred's various military reforms served him to good end when he trapped a large Danish navy on the Lea River. Building fortifications and thereby cutting off their escape route, Alfred forced the Danes to abandon their ships and scatter. Although this victory did not end the Danish threat, which continued into the tenth and eleventh centuries, it did provide a degree of peace and stability in the kingdom, which Alfred was able to enjoy until his death on October 26, 899.

Alfred's legacy, however, is not limited to his defense against the Danes and military reforms. Indeed, in some ways, his legal and literary contributions are more important than his other achievements. It was probably in the 890s that Alfred issued his compilation of the law. Building on the precedents of kings of Wessex, Kent, and Mercia, Alfred issued a legal code that was intended to cover all the English, even though Alfred referred to himself only as the king of the West Saxons. His use of oaths of loyalty in the code suggests Carolingian influence as well, but it was his genius that gave the code its final shape. He clearly borrowed from his predecessors, but introduced restrictions on the feud, the duty of subjects to their lords, and, as fitting a deeply religious king like Alfred, legislation protecting the church. His religious convictions were evident also in his concerns with learning and literacy in his kingdom. Alfred, lamenting the extreme poverty of learning in his kingdom, undertook the effort to translate a series of important Christian works into the Anglo-Saxon tongue, because many people in his kingdom could read their native tongue but could not read Latin, the language of learning. With his support translations of various works appeared, including Bede's *History of the English Church and People,* Pope Gregory the Great's *Dialogues,* a martyrology, and a work by St. Augustine of Hippo's supporter, Orosius, *Seven Books against the Pagans.* Alfred himself was responsible for a number of translations, including Pope Gregory's *Pastoral Rule* (*Regula pastoralis*), which Alfred translated as the *Pastoral Care,* Boethius's *Consolation of Philosophy,* and Augustine's *Soliloquies.* The translations by Alfred vary in their loyalty to the original. The work of Gregory was closely translated, but for the works of Boethius and Augustine Alfred took great liberty with the text. He introduced new ideas and questions in the translation of Boethius, and he added material from the Bible, Gregory the Great, and other works by Augustine to the *Soliloquies.* These works reveal the breadth of Alfred's interests, and they continued to be copied into the twelfth century. It was also during Alfred's reign that the first compilation of the *Anglo-Saxon Chronicle* was made.

Alfred's contributions to the history of Anglo-Saxon England were numerous and varied. Even though his efforts to revive learning among the people were modest, his translations remain of interest today and had an important impact on scholars long after his death. His defense of the kingdom against the Danes provided England important infrastructure to continue the struggle after his death, even though it was to be nearly two centuries before the Danes were finally expelled from England and the threat of invasion ended. Alfred truly was one of the great kings of England.

See also Anglo-Saxon Chronicle; Anglo-Saxons; Bede; Boethius; Carolingian Dynasty; Charlemagne; Charles the Bald; Offa of Mercia

Bibliography

Hodges, Richard. *The Anglo-Saxon Achievement: Archeology and the Beginnings of English Society.* London: Duckworth, 1989.

Keynes, Simon. "The British Isles: England, 700–900." In *The New Cambridge Medieval History,* vol. 2, ed. Rosamond McKitterick. Cambridge: Cambridge University Press, 1995.

Keynes, Simon, and Michael Lapidge, trans. *Alfred the Great: Asser's Life of King Alfred and Other Contemporary Sources.* Harmondsworth, UK: Penguin, 1983.

Sawyer, Peter H. *From Roman Britain to Norman England,* 2d ed. London and New York: Routledge, 1998.

Smyth, Alfred P. *King Alfred the Great.* Oxford: Oxford University Press, 1995.

Stenton, Frank M. *Anglo-Saxon England.* 3d ed. Oxford: Clarendon, 1971.

Sturdy, David J. *Alfred the Great.* London: Constable, 1995.

Whitelock, Dorothy, ed. *The Anglo-Saxon Chronicle.* Westport, CT: Greenwood, 1986.

Amalaswintha (d. 535)

Gothic princess and daughter of the important Ostrogothic king of Italy, Theodoric the Great. As regent, Amalaswintha was active in the political life of Italy after Theodoric's death, and she promoted her personal interests and those of her immediate family against enemies in her extended family and among the Gothic nobility in Italy. Her rivalry with other Gothic leaders over control of her son, Athalaric, and then for control of the kingdom after Athalaric's death brought her great difficulties and increased her longstanding pro-Roman political sensibilities. Her relationship with the Byzantine emperor Justinian brought her support in Italy but, if the sixth-century Byzantine historian Procopius is to be believed, the enmity of the great empress Theodora. A possible pawn in Justinian's grand political designs, Amalaswintha drew Justinian further into Italian affairs, and her death led to the Byzantine invasion of the peninsula and the Gothic Wars of Justinian.

The daughter of Theodoric, the most powerful barbarian king of the early sixth century, Amalaswintha was an important figure in Italian political life even before her father's death in 526. Her marriage in 515 to the Spanish Visigoth, Eutharic, was part of Theodoric's efforts to preserve and extend his control over the Goths and in Italy. Eutharic's marriage to Amalaswintha made him part of Theodoric's family and allowed the great king to appoint his son-in-law as his successor, thus eliminating Theodoric's own nephew from the succession and from power in general. Although it caused problems after 526 for Amalaswintha, Eutharic's death in 522/523 hindered Theodoric's plans little, because Eutharic had provided an heir, Athalaric, who, jointly with Amalaswintha, was designated successor to the throne. Moreover, although it was not apparently political, Amalaswintha's first-rate education served her well during her father's lifetime and after. And in fact her education did have political overtones because it was a traditional Roman education; Theodoric may have provided her with a Roman education because of his interest in establishing harmonious Roman-Gothic relations.

Before his death, Theodoric appointed Athalaric as his successor. In 526 Athalaric was still a minor, and his mother assumed the regency. The opening years of Amalaswintha's regency were relatively peaceful, and her abilities were recognized by many, including Procopius, who spoke highly of her courage and intelligence. She sought to restore good relations between Goths and Romans, which had broken down in the last years of her father's reign, especially over Theodoric's imprison-

ment and execution of Boethius. She restored the confiscated estates of Boethius to his family and sought the counsel of the Roman Senate. To promote good relations with the Romans, she sent a letter to the emperor in Constantinople, seeking to bury old hatreds, and provided her son with a Roman education. To placate the Gothic nobility, she sought to improve relations with other barbarian peoples in the former Western Roman Empire. Ostrogothic armies enjoyed success in 530 against a mixed barbarian force on the northeastern frontier, and Amalaswintha pursued improved relations with the Burgundians. The alliance collapsed, however, in the early 530s as a result of her failure to send the army against the Merovingian Franks when they invaded and conquered the Burgundians. The situation on the kingdom's northern frontier worsened as a result of this failure, and it may also have contributed to her problems with the Gothic nobility in the early 530s.

Despite her early successes and the peace in the kingdom in the opening years of the regency, Amalaswintha faced a grave crisis in 532/533 that nearly ended her power. As her son approached his majority, a rival, possibly anti-Roman, faction in the kingdom attempted to take control of her son and the kingdom. One of the criticisms her enemies raised was that Athalaric was being made "too Roman" and needed to learn good Gothic values. The young king was persuaded by the rebels and supported them against his mother. In the face of this crisis, Amalaswintha sent a letter to Justinian seeking political asylum. The emperor invited the queen to Constantinople and sent a ship with 40,000 pounds of gold to rescue her. Amalaswintha sent the royal treasury to a palace provided by Justinian, but decided to stay and fight for control of her kingdom. The Frankish threat to the frontier provided the queen with the pretext to send the three leaders of the revolt to the frontier. Once they were away from court, she had them killed and as a result saved her position.

Although she secured her hold on power,

Amalaswintha faced continued difficulties over the next few years, worsened perhaps by the death of her son in 534. She hoped to resolve the crisis by remarrying, and in 534 she married her hostile family rival, Theodohad, made him coregent, and declared herself queen. Allowed to mint coins and to assume the royal title, Theodohad had to recognize the authority of Amalaswintha and follow her commands. But Theodohad, along with the families of the murdered rebels of 532, had other ideas. They plotted together against Amalaswintha, and in April 535 she was captured and imprisoned on an island in Lake Bolsena.

The rough treatment of the queen brought strong protests from the imperial court at Constantinople, because she had remained neutral during Justinian's invasion of the Vandal kingdom in North Africa and had allowed the Byzantine commander, Belisarius, to use Sicily as a staging ground for his armies. Certainly, too, Justinian's earlier support for Amalaswintha and the long-standing good relations between the two reinforced the emperor's desire to protect her. Moreover, according to Procopius, the emperor had tired of his wife, Theodora, and was highly attracted to the young and intelligent Gothic queen, who would have provided the emperor with great wealth and access to Italy, which he hoped to reattach to imperial control. Procopius further suggested that although Justinian publicly demanded the release of the queen, Theodora secretly plotted her murder with agents in Italy. Although Procopius's version of events is unlikely, Justinian did support the queen against her rivals, and her murder was a public affront to the emperor, especially after Theodohad assured him that no harm would come to her. Her murder provided Justinian with the justification he needed to invade Italy, defeat the Goths, and reunite the old heartland of the empire with the Eastern Empire.

See also Belisarius; Boethius; Justinian; Ostrogoths; Procopius; Theodora; Theodoric the Great

Bibliography

Bury, John B. *History of the Later Roman Empire: From the Death of Theodosius I to the Death of Justinian.* Vol. 2. 1923. Reprint, New York: Dover, 1959

Heather, Peter. *The Goths.* Oxford: Blackwell, 1996.

Llewellyn, Peter. *Rome in the Dark Ages.* New York: Barnes and Noble, 1993.

Procopius. *The History of the Wars; Secret History,* 4 vols. Trans. Henry Bronson Dewing. Cambridge, MA: Harvard University Press, 1914–1924.

Thiébaux, Marcelle, ed. and trans. *The Writings of Medieval Women: An Anthology.* 2d ed. New York: Garland, 1994.

Wolfram, Herwig. *The Roman Empire and its Germanic Peoples.* Trans. Thomas J. Dunlap. Berkeley: University of California Press, 1997.

Ammianus Marcellinus (c. 330–395)

Last important pagan historian of Rome, and the first to write a major history since Tacitus (c. 56–c. 120). Although nearly half of his work, the *Res gestae* (Deeds done), has been lost, Ammianus remains one of the most important writers for the history of the Roman Empire and the movement of the Germanic peoples in the fourth century. Inspired by Tacitus, whose work he emulated, Ammianus provides a unique view, especially compared with Christian historians of the time, of the late Roman Empire. In some ways unlike his Christian contemporaries, Ammianus believed that "Rome will last as long as mankind shall endure." Indeed, even though he chronicled the crises of the late fourth century, including the catastrophic defeat of imperial armies by the Visigoths led by Alaric, Ammianus preserved the characteristic faith of the Romans in the empire.

Little is known precisely about Ammianus other than what is revealed in his work of history. He describes himself as a "former soldier and a Greek" in the pages of a history that was written in Latin. He was probably born in Antioch in Syria around 330. He served in the 350s as an officer in both Gaul and Persia under the emperor Constantius II (r. 337–361); his military background enabled him to write effectively about military matters in his history. He later joined the campaigns of the emperor Julian the Apostate (r. 361–363), the nephew of Constantine the Great, against Persia in 363. Julian was raised as a Christian by his uncle but rejected that upbringing in favor of traditional Roman religion, which he actively promoted to the detriment of the Christian church. Although he had earlier enjoyed military success, Julian failed in his attack on Persia and was killed near Baghdad while retreating. Ammianus retired from military service after the failed Persian campaign and traveled widely across the Mediterranean, spending time especially in Egypt and Greece. Sometime in the 380s, he settled in Rome, where he wrote his history, probably in 390.

Written in the last decade of the fourth century, the history of Ammianus began in 96, where Tacitus left off, and covered events down to 378. The work was composed in thirty-one books, but only books fourteen to thirty-one have survived. This section, however, covered the years 354–378, the period of the author's active military career, and contains much eyewitness reporting. The work is both a personal memoir and testimony and a defense of the career of Emperor Julian. The history contains not only personal observations but many important observations on military and political affairs, as well as the reflections of a tolerant late Roman pagan. The work of Ammianus is often colorful; it contains numerous details of daily life and scathing accounts of the flaws of Christian and pagan leaders of Rome. Like Tacitus before him, Ammianus criticized the moral weaknesses and political foolishness of his contemporaries and wrote in a highly rhetorical style. His work reflects the attitudes of a late Roman soldier and noble who valued the traditional Roman virtues of moderation and who believed in the permanence of Roman power. Indeed, his account of the terrible Roman defeat by the Visigoths at Hadrianople in 378 reveals his belief that the empire would recover from this defeat and eventually triumph over its enemies, just as earlier Romans had defeated their great rival Hannibal after his victory at Cannae (216 B.C.).

Ammianus not only left important information about the Romans and their defeat by the Visigoths but also about the barbarian invaders themselves. He describes the origins and background of the Goths and the extent of their territory. He also describes the origins of the Huns, their nomadic lifestyle, their customs and manners, and their success against the Goths. Although the surviving portion of the history covers only a short period, Ammianus's work is an important source of information on Romans and barbarians in the later fourth century.

See also Alaric; Hadrianople, Battle of; Huns; Visigoths

Bibliography

Ammianus Marcellinus. *Ammianus Marcellinus.* Trans. John C. Rolfe. Cambridge, MA: Harvard University Press, 1971–1972.

Barnes, Timothy D. *Ammianus Marcellinus and the Representation of Historical Reality.* Ithaca, NY: Cornell University Press, 1998.

Cameron, Averil, and Peter Garnsey, eds. *The Late Empire, A.D. 337–425. Cambridge Ancient History,* vol. 13. Cambridge: Cambridge University Press, 1998.

Hunt, David, and Jan Willem Drijvers, eds. *The Late Roman World and Its Historian: Interpreting Ammianus Marcellinus.* London: Routledge, 1999.

Matthews, John. *The Roman Empire of Ammianus Marcellinus.* Baltimore: Johns Hopkins University Press, 1989.

Wolfram, Herwig. *The Roman Empire and Its Germanic Peoples.* Trans. Thomas J. Dunlap. Berkeley: University of California Press, 1997.

Angilbert, St. (c. 740–814)

An important figure during the reign of Charlemagne, Angilbert was one of the great king's court scholars and was a central figure in what is called the Carolingian Renaissance. He was given the nickname Homer by Charlemagne and the other court scholars because of his talents as a poet. He also served as an ambassador for the king and was the lay abbot of St. Riquier, which he received from Charlemagne and where he introduced important liturgical reforms. He was also the lover of Charlemagne's daughter, Bertha, with whom he had two sons, Hartnid and the historian Nithard.

Angilbert was a Frank of noble parentage, and he and his family, according to Nithard, were held in high esteem by Charlemagne. Nithard's view is confirmed by Angilbert's place at Charlemagne's court. Angilbert obtained an excellent education and may have been a student of Alcuin, the leading Carolingian court scholar and close advisor to Charlemagne, at one point. His poetry and liturgical reforms, along with his gift of over 200 manuscripts to the library at St. Riquier, indicate his interest in learning and support for the religious and educational reforms of Charlemagne. His later activities at St. Riquier further demonstrate his concern for learning; he seems to have established, in conformity with Charlemagne's capitulary *Admonitio Generalis,* a school to educate the local boys. He also served as Charlemagne's ambassador to Rome on two occasions. In 792, he was sent to Rome with copies of one of the Saxon capitularies, sections of the *Libri Carolini* (Caroline Books), and the heretical bishop Felix of Urgel, all of which he was to submit to Pope Hadrian I for papal consideration. Angilbert went to Rome a second time in 796 to deliver a great portion of the spoils of the Avar Ring, the Avar capital captured by Carolingian armies in 796, to St. Peter and his representative, Pope Leo III.

As court scholar and abbot of an important monastery, Angilbert assumed a key position in Charlemagne's kingdom and promoted the great ruler's educational and religious ideals. He was a poet of great talent, whose work provides a glimpse into the "court school" of Charlemagne. His poem to the king (*Ad Carolum regem*) portrays the king and his courtiers in discussion with the king, who bestows favors on those around him, especially to his children. The poem also reveals the hustle and bustle of the court, as well as giving sketches of the court's members. Angilbert's poetry could also be quite personal and touching, as in one short poem sent to the court to inquire about his young son.

Angilbert's activities as abbot of St. Riquier were designed to further the religious goals of Charlemagne. The abbot introduced new wrinkles to the liturgy at the monastery, organized elaborate religious processions, and formed the monks into three shifts to pray continuously for the salvation of the emperor. His support for the literary, educational, and religious reforms of Charlemagne make Angilbert an important example of the success of the Carolingian Renaissance.

See also Admonitio Generalis; Alcuin of York; Capitularies; Carolingian Dynasty; Carolingian Renaissance; Charlemagne; Franks; Hadrian I, Pope; Leo III, Pope; Nithard

Bibliography

Laistner, Max L. W. *Thought and Letters in Western Europe,* A.D. 500 to 900. 2d ed. Ithaca, NY: Cornell University Press, 1976.

McKitterick, Rosamond. *The Frankish Kingdoms under the Carolingians, 751–987.* London: Longman, 1983.

Riché, Pierre. *The Carolingians: A Family Who Forged Europe.* Trans. Michael Idomir Allen. Philadelphia: University of Pennsylvania Press, 1993.

Scholz, Bernhard Walter, trans. *Carolingian Chronicles: Royal Frankish Annals and Nithard's History.* Ann Arbor: University of Michigan Press, 1972.

Sullivan, Richard. *Aix-La-Chapelle in the Age of Charlemagne.* Norman: University of Oklahoma Press, 1974.

Anglo-Saxon Chronicle

The most important source for the history of Anglo-Saxon England, especially for the period from the mid-ninth century until the fall of the Anglo-Saxons to William the Conqueror in 1066, the *Anglo-Saxon Chronicle* also provides useful information on the development of the English language. It survives in seven manuscripts, some of which include both Old English and Latin entries, and its accounts are arranged as annals, or year-by-year summaries of events.

The *Chronicle,* including both its earliest versions and most complete later versions, covers the history of England and the Anglo-Saxons from the first century B.C. until 1154. Events covered by the *Chronicle* include Julius Caesar's invasion of England, the Anglo-Saxon invasions, and the deeds of the Anglo-Saxon kings. Although called the *Anglo-Saxon Chronicle,* the focus of the annals is the West Saxon kings, with occasional mention of events in Mercia and on the European continent. The first version, which appeared during the reign of Alfred the Great in the late ninth century and was known to Asser, the biographer of Alfred, focuses on the history of the West Saxon kings, beginning with the fifth-century King Cerdic and ending with King Aethelwulf and his sons. Although the work covers a broad span of time, the period that receives the best and fullest treatment is that after 850.

After the first version, the manuscript tradition divided into several versions, which do not always treat events in the same fashion, some versions of the *Chronicle* treating events more fully than others. Major events, like Alfred's campaigns against invading Vikings, however, often receive similar coverage in all the versions. The continuations of the *Chronicle* lasted until 1154, covering the events of the tenth and early eleventh century with little detail but offering more depth for the later eleventh and twelfth century. It provides useful discussion of William's conquest in 1066, and one version offers a brief and bitter summary of events of the year.

The sources used by the compilers of the *Chronicle* vary. Works by Jerome and Isidore of Seville were used in the preparation of the early material covered by the annals; also useful for the early period was a Latin translation of the *Ecclesiastical History* of Eusebius. Other sources used for the preparation of the *Chronicle* were the *Liber Pontificalis* (Book of the Popes), genealogies, northern and West Saxon annals, Frankish annals, lists of kings and bishops, and, most probably, oral material. The most important source, and one that helped shape the organizational structure of the annals, was Bede's *History of the English Church and People.*

See also Alfred the Great; Anglo-Saxons; Bede; Isidore of Seville

Bibliography
Whitelock, Dorothy, ed. *The Anglo-Saxon Chronicle.* Westport, CT: Greenwood, 1986.

Anglo-Saxons

Germanic peoples who invaded England in the fifth century, the Anglo-Saxons formed enduring institutions and cultural and religious traditions that remained an important part of English society even after their ultimate defeat by William the Conqueror in 1066. Coming from various points on the European continent, the bands that formed the Anglo-Saxon people entered England during the mid-fifth century. The exact details of the invasions and conquest of England by the Anglo-Saxons, however, remain uncertain and shrouded in legend. Indeed, one of the greatest legends of English history, the legend of King Arthur, is rooted in the history of the invasions. Although the details of the origins of the Anglo-Saxons in England are unclear, the later details of their history are not. In brief, they formed a number of smaller kingdoms that gradually coalesced into a more unified realm. They welcomed Christianity, developed sophisticated political and cultural traditions, faced the challenge from the Danes, and, finally, submitted to the Normans.

According to the Anglo-Saxon historian and monk Bede who wrote in the eighth century, the origins of the Anglo-Saxons are to be found in northern Europe. Bede identifies three main groups of invaders in his history of the English church and people: Angles, Jutes, and Saxons. He notes that the Jutes came from parts of modern Denmark and inhabited the kingdom of Kent and the Isle of Wight. The Saxons were from lands between the Elbe and Ems Rivers and established kingdoms in Essex, Sussex, and Wessex. The Angles settled in the kingdoms of East Anglia, Mercia, and Northumbria and came originally from lands lying between those of the Jutes and Saxons. Although these three groups are traditionally recognized as the conquerors of Roman Britain, they were most likely accompanied by other Germanic peoples. The Frisians, who lived along the coast of northern Europe, were probably among those who joined the invaders. Indeed, it is likely that many people living along the coast from the modern Netherlands to Denmark were involved in the invasions, a group that may have even included the Swedes.

The invasion of Britain began in the confusion that attended the Roman withdrawal from the island and the collapse of the Western Empire. According to the earliest accounts, those of Gildas (d. mid-sixth century) and, especially, Bede, the invasions were part of the religious history of the island. For Gildas the invaders were ignorant barbarians who were to be opposed by faithful Christians, but for Bede, they were punishment sent by God to chastise the natives of Britain. In any event, the invasions most likely began in the mid-fifth century, about a generation after the withdrawal of imperial troops from England in 410. Shortly after that withdrawal, the people of England had become subject to raids by Scots and Picts to the north. In order to deal with these raids, according to the traditional account, the British leader Vortigern invited groups of Angles or Saxons to come to England to serve as mercenaries in defense of the region from outsiders. But once having expelled the raiders, the Angles and Saxons, led by the brothers Hengist and Horsa, turned against their masters and began the conquest of England.

Over the course of the next century, Angles, Saxons, and other groups gradually took control of the island, despite the possible appearance of a leader of resistance, later to be known as King Arthur. Indeed, by the late fifth century the various tribes had established themselves throughout most of the eastern half of the island, from the Humber River in the north to the Thames in the south. It was at this point that "King Arthur" may have appeared and slowed down the process of Anglo-Saxon penetration of the island. But this was at most a temporary setback for the Anglo-Saxons, who were not only successful warriors but also farmers and shepherds who laid claim to the land and slowly colonized England at the same time that they fought the native population. During the sixth century the various groups of Anglo-Saxons formed what is traditionally termed the heptarchy. The famed seven kingdoms of Anglo-Saxon England—Kent, Sussex, Essex, Wessex, East Anglia, Mercia, and Northumbria—struggled for predominance throughout the Anglo-Saxon period, and from time to time a ruler of one of these kingdoms managed to establish hegemony over the other six. For a time the kingdom of Mercia predominated, and later the kingdom of Wessex provided leadership and unified much of the island, in part due to its most important ruler, Alfred the Great.

Although the traditional designation of heptarchy suggests a degree of equality among the seven kingdoms, such equality seldom existed, and there were smaller units, like the subkingdom of Deira, which formed part of Northumbria, that were greater than some of the kingdoms of the heptarchy. Moreover, the kingdoms of Essex and Sussex were negligible powers, and already in the seventh century, the kingdom of Mercia had become the leading power of the south. Indeed, under its great king, Penda, Mercia undertook a belligerent and expansive policy that culminated in Mercian hegemony in England. He successfully extended Mercian power over parts of central England and even exacted tribute from the king of Northumbria, Oswy. His death in battle against Oswy slowed, but did not stop, the expansion of the kingdom. In the generation after his death, Christianity was established in Mercia, and Northumbrian overlordship was ended.

In the eighth century, Mercia reached its greatest heights of power under the kings Æthelbald (r. 716–757) and, especially, Offa. Although he only gradually established his control in Mercia and the rest of England after the murder of Æthelbald, Offa created the most impressive realm before Alfred. He brought much of England from the Humber River to the English Channel under his control, subjugated lesser kings to his authority, and married daughters to kings in Northumbria and Wessex. He built an extensive dyke along the frontier with Wales, reformed the coinage, issued laws, and enjoyed good relations with and the respect of Charlemagne and Pope Hadrian I. Following his death in 796, however, the kingdom fell into gradual decline under the assault of the Vikings and the rise of the power of Wessex.

As Mercian power declined in the wake of Offa's death, the ascendancy of Wessex began. In the early ninth century, Egbert (r. 802–839) ended Mercian dominance of Wessex and expelled the Mercians from parts of Wessex. He defeated the Mercian king Beornwulf in battle in 825 and broke the power of the rival kingdom. He managed to extend his authority over Essex, Sussex, and Kent, and even conquered and controlled Mercia for a short time. His successors, however, faced an even greater challenge than that posed by the kings of Mercia. Indeed, even before Egbert's death, Danes began raiding the English countryside. Over the next several generations the raids turned into large-scale invasions, and the Danes conquered large sections of England. Wessex withstood the onslaught, and its kings forged marriage pacts with their defeated rivals in Mercia to better withstand the assault. In 865, the situation became critical, as Danish pressure increased and Danish armies seized much of England outside Wessex.

The efforts of Æthelred I (r. 865–871) and, especially, Alfred halted the Danish advance. Indeed, after some initial setbacks, Alfred took back control of much of England below the Humber from the Danes and was recognized as king of all the English not subject to the Danes. In the early tenth century, Edward the Elder completed his father's struggle with the Danes and rid the island of their influence for much of the tenth century. Alfred not only enjoyed success against the Danes but also restructured English defense and military organization. He was a great patron of learning and personally translated a number of important religious texts. He also worked closely with the church and elevated the ideal of kingship. One of the greatest of all English kings, Alfred unified England under the authority of the kingdom of Wessex, and his dynasty ruled England until the Anglo-Saxon defeat at the Battle of Hastings in 1066 and the conquest of England by the Normans.

Political division and eventual unification characterized Anglo-Saxon history before the Norman conquest, and it was matched by division and unification in religion. Like many of the peoples who established kingdoms in the former Roman Empire, the Anglo-Saxons converted to Christianity, but only after an internal struggle between traditional religion and the new faith. They also faced divisions within Christianity, although their division was between Irish and Roman Catholic Christianity instead of the struggle faced by the Franks and Goths between Arian and Catholic Christianity. Although the island had received Christianity while under imperial rule, its loss of contact with the continent contributed to the breakdown of the church. During the sixth and seventh centuries, efforts to Christianize the island were launched from both Rome and Ireland.

The conversion of the Anglo-Saxons was begun in earnest at the end of the sixth century by St. Augustine of Canterbury, who had been sent on his mission by Pope Gregory I, traditionally referred to as the Great. Augustine established himself in Canterbury in 597, where he became archbishop and introduced Roman institutional structures. His greatest success came with the conversion of Aethelberht, the king of Kent, whose wife, Bertha, was a Merovingian Frank and a Christian. In a great outdoor ceremony, Aethelberht, who was greeted by a procession of monks singing psalms and carrying the cross, accepted Christianity and allowed the mission to continue. Bede notes that more churches were built, including one at Canterbury by Aethelberht, and that the king's subjects also came to the faith. The conversion of Aethelberht aided in the conversion of other parts of Anglo-Saxon England, including the northern kingdom of Northumbria, whose king, Edwin, married a daughter of Aethelberht.

Edwin only gradually came to the faith and needed the approval of a royal council before accepting baptism. Although there was a pagan reaction in the generation after Edwin's death, his conversion brought Christianity to the north, and it survived both his death and the pagan reaction. The conversion of Northumbria, however, was further complicated by the influence of Irish Catholic Christianity, which maintained a unique organizational structure; Irish Catholics also calculated the date of Easter and tonsured their clergy in their own way, rather than following the practice of the Roman church. Irish missionaries were active in England and the continent in the seventh century and offered an attractive alternative to Roman Christianity. At the great Synod of Whitby in 664, however, King Oswy accepted the teachings and organization of the Roman church. His decision had a great impact on the church and people of England in the generations to come.

The conversion of Northumbria, which completed the conversion of all of Anglo-Saxon England, was of great and lasting significance. Indeed, until the Reformation England and Rome maintained a special relationship. The Anglo-Saxon church promoted this tie, and as a result the tie greatly influenced cultural and political events in the eighth and ninth centuries. One of the more significant results of the conversion of England was the development of literary culture that followed it. The greatest expression of this culture was the so-called Northumbrian Renaissance of the seventh and eighth century. Associated with the monasteries of Wearmouth and Jarrow and their founder, Benedict Biscop, the revival had as its most important figure was the man known as the Venerable Bede, one of the most influential historians of the Middle Ages as well as a noted Christian scholar. Bede's work on time was very popular among Christian scholars in the Middle Ages; his history of the English church and people was one of the first great national histories and remained an influential work throughout the Middle Ages. The renaissance influenced Carolingian culture because of the numerous books collected by Benedict Biscop, Bede, and others for their monasteries, many of which found their way to the Frankish kingdom through Alcuin. Alcuin also introduced many of the ideals of the renaissance to his fellow Carolingian scholars and ecclesiastics.

The Latin literary tradition of Bede, Alcuin, and others is matched by an equally impressive and important literary tradition in the Anglo-Saxon tongue, which includes both secular and religious material. The most famous example of Old English literature, of course, is *Beowulf,* which is preserved in a single manuscript from around the year 1000. It is a 3,182-line epic poem that recounts the heroic life and death of its main character, Beowulf, the great king of the Geats, who defeated three terrible monsters and ruled his people wisely after rescuing the king of the Danes from Grendel and his mother. Although Christianized, the poem reveals many of the traditional virtues of the pre-Christian Anglo-Saxons. Other important Old English literary works include *The Battle of Brunanburh* and *The Battle of Maldon*. *The Battle of Brunanburh* includes dramatic battle scenes and a panegyric to King Æthelstan (r. 924–939); it concerns an important battle in the unification of England. *The Battle of Maldon* exists only as a fragment, but it is celebrated for its depiction of warrior virtues maintained in adversity in its tale of an English loss to Viking invaders. Along with the secular verse tradition, there exists a body of Old English religious poetry. The most important example is *The Dream of the Rood,* in which the Rood, the Cross on which Christ was crucified, speaks of the importance of the crucifixion and of its own role and describes Jesus as a traditional Anglo-Saxon hero.

The Anglo-Saxon literary corpus also contains a number of prose works. The most significant of these is the *Anglo-Saxon Chronicle*. The chronicle, first compiled in the late ninth century, is one of the most valuable sources for the early history of England; it covers the entire period from the arrival of the Anglo-Saxons in England to their defeat by William the Conqueror. Some manuscript traditions of the chronicle continue into the Norman period, extending into the 1120s. Other prose works include the many translations made by King Alfred or his court. Alfred was responsible for translations into English of Boethius's *Consolation of Philosophy,* as well as of various works by St. Augustine of Hippo and Pope Gregory I, known as the Great. He also sponsored translations of Gregory's *Dialogues* and Bede's history. Alfred himself was the subject of a biography, in Latin, by Asser, which is an important part of the Anglo-Saxon tradition of writing history and biography. Finally, in the late Anglo-Saxon period, the ecclesiastics Ælfric and Wulfstan composed a number of sermons in English that advocated reform, lamented the moral decay of the Anglo-Saxons, and expressed the belief that they were living in the Last Days.

See also Aethelberht; Alcuin of York; Alfred the Great; *Anglo-Saxon Chronicle;* Arianism;

Augustine of Canterbury, St.; Augustine of Hippo, St.; Bede; *Beowulf;* Boethius; Franks; Hengist and Horsa; Heptarchy; King Arthur; Merovingian Dynasty; Offa of Mercia; Penda; Sutton Hoo; Thegn; Vortigern

Bibliography

Arnold, Christopher J. *Roman Britain to Saxon Shore.* Bloomington: Indiana University Press, 1984.

Bassett, Steven, ed. *The Origins of Anglo-Saxon Kingdoms.* Leicester, UK: Leicester University Press, 1989.

Bede. *Ecclesiastical History of the English People with Bede's Letter to Egbert and Cuthbert's Letter on the Death of Bede.* Trans. Leo Sherley-Price. Harmondsworth, UK: Penguin, 1991.

Blair, Peter Hunter. *The World of Bede.* Cambridge: Cambridge University Press, 1990.

Gildas. *The Ruin of Britain and Other Works.* Ed. and trans. Michael Winterbottom. London: Phillimore, 1978.

Heaney, Seamus, trans. *Beowulf: A New Verse Translation.* New York: Farrar Straus and Giroux, 2000.

Higham, Nicholas J. *The Convert Kings: Power and Religious Affiliation in Early Anglo-Saxon England.* Manchester, UK: Manchester University Press, 1997.

Howe, Nicholas. *Migration and Mythmaking in Anglo-Saxon England.* New Haven: Yale University Press, 1989.

Keynes, Simon, and Michael Lapidge, trans. *Alfred the Great: Asser's Life of King Alfred and Other Contemporary Sources.* Harmondsworth, UK: Penguin, 1983.

Myres, John N. L. *The English Settlements.* Oxford: Clarendon, 1986.

Sawyer, Peter H. *From Roman Britain to Norman England.* 2d ed. London and New York: Routledge, 1998.

Stenton, Frank M. *Anglo-Saxon England.* 3d ed. Oxford: Clarendon, 1971.

Whitelock, Dorothy, ed. *The Anglo-Saxon Chronicle.* Westport, CT: Greenwood, 1986.

Yorke, Barbara. *Kings and Kingdoms of Early Anglo-Saxon England.* London: Seaby, 1990.

Animals

Domestic animals served a variety of purposes in the early Middle Ages, including farmwork and fieldwork, and were also an important source of food. Among the more important and useful animals was the horse, which was used not only as a draft animal but also for transportation and in war. The other animals used in early medieval society were cattle, sheep, dogs, pigs, geese, and chickens. They provided material for food and clothing, but they were generally smaller than their modern counterparts.

The horse played an important role in daily life in the early Middle Ages and was known to both the ancient Romans and the barbarians who migrated into the empire. There were various breeds of horse bred either by the Romans or the barbarians, and the importance of the horse is revealed in early medieval legislation. The famous Carolingian Capitulary de Villis, which regulated management of the royal estates, contains precise regulations for maintenance of horses, including instructions for overseeing stud horses, mares, and foals. It also rules that foals be brought to the king's palace each year on St. Martin's Day (November 11). Moreover, after the conversion of the barbarians to Christianity, prohibitions against eating horseflesh were enacted by various bishops and popes, including Theodore of Tarsus, archbishop of Canterbury. And in 732, Pope Gregory III ordered Boniface, the missionary and papal legate in Germany, to prohibit consumption of horseflesh.

One of the primary purposes of horses, in peace or war, was transportation. The horse, unlike other large domesticated animals, had a much faster pace than humans and thus provided a fast and reliable source of transportation. The use of horses as riding animals, however, was generally limited to kings and nobles, who could afford them. (Estimates place the cost of a horse as equal to that of four to ten oxen or forty to one hundred sheep.) Horses were used more generally as draft animals because of their strength and

speed and were often used to pull carriages of passengers and heavy loads of produce or other material on wagons. Although they may have been used in Anglo-Saxon England to plow the fields, horses were seldom used for agricultural work in the early Middle Ages. As the result of technological change around the year 1000, however, horses came into more widespread use in agricultural work as plow animals.

The other major use for the horse was in war, and many barbarian peoples used the horse to good effect in war. The Huns were most famous for their use of the horse in war, and the horse was also used in the preparation of food for the Huns and was used in the ceremonies to bury great leaders like Attila. The Lombards and Visigoths were also known for their use of the horse. Among the Franks, both the Merovingian and Carolingian dynasties employed the horse and cavalry in their armies. It must be noted that these horses were not the great warhorses of the later Middle Ages, which could carry a knight in full armor and operate as a sort of premodern tank. Indeed, the horses of barbarian Europe were smaller and lighter, as were most animals, and bore light-armored bowmen. Moreover, Carolingian horses were not used to carry mounted shock troops, as some scholars have suggested. There is no evidence to prove that the Carolingians had the stirrup, which would have been necessary to allow the use of mounted shock troops.

Cattle, both oxen and cows, were important for labor and food. With the arrival of the barbarians and the end of Roman civilization in the old Western Empire, however, the practice of selective breeding—except in the case of horses and dogs—came to an end, and cattle, as well as most other domestic animals, decreased in size. Despite their smaller size, cows and oxen remained vital in daily life. Before the so-called agricultural revolution of the year 1000, the ox was the most important agricultural draft animal. Its size, strength, and docility made the ox an ideal source of power to drive the plows used in cereal production and farm wagons. Although slower than horses, oxen were the preferred draft animal because they were less expensive to feed and keep than horses.

Cows and bulls, although prevalent, were rarely used as draft animals and were used primarily as a food source. Not only was beef the main source of meat for those who could afford it, but cows also provided milk, cheese, and butter, which were prominent in much of the northern European diet. Although the end of selective breeding and the practice of mating before maturity limited the size of the animals and their milk production, cows continued to be a significant part of agricultural life and diet. Cattle had one further use. In the summer they were put out to pasture to graze in farmland left fallow (land that was left unplanted so that it could replenish itself), which they would fertilize naturally with their manure. Most extra animals were sold before winter because of the scarcity of food to feed them and their human owners.

Along with horses and cattle, a number of other animals were commonplace in early medieval daily life and diet. Sheep provided a source of food and clothing, and pigs also formed a valuable food source. Pigs were raised nearly in the wild, being left in the forest to forage for food, mostly nuts and berries. Written records, such as Charlemagne's capitularies, and archeological evidence reveal the existence of chickens and geese, useful for both eggs and meat, on early medieval farms. Along with these domesticated animals, wild game—including deer, rabbit, and swine—was hunted and made part of the diet. Finally, dogs were a common feature in society. They were selectively bred and used in hunting and to shepherd flocks of animals.

See also Agriculture; Attila the Hun; *Capitulare de Villis;* Capitularies; Carolingian Dynasty; Charlemagne; Clothing; Diet and Nutrition; Lombards; Merovingian Dynasty; Visigoths

Bibliography
Bachrach, Bernard S. *Merovingian Military Organization, 481–751.* Minneapolis: University of Minnesota Press, 1972.
Contamine, Philippe. *War in the Middle Ages.* Trans. Michael Jones. Oxford: Basil Blackwell, 1984.
Duby, Georges. *Rural Economy and Country Life in the Medieval West.* Trans. Cynthia Postan. Columbia: University of South Carolina Press, 1968.
Gladitz, Charles. *Horse Breeding in the Medieval World.* Dublin: Four Courts Press, 1997.
Riché, Pierre. *Daily Life in the World of Charlemagne.* Trans. Jo Ann McNamara. Philadelphia: University of Pennsylvania Press, 1983.
Slicher van Bath, Bernard H. *The Agrarian History of Western Europe: A.D. 500–1850.* Trans. Olive Ordish. London: Arnold, 1963.

Arbogast (d. 394)

A Germanic general of Frankish descent, Arbogast was the first in a series of military leaders in the Roman Empire, a list that later included Stilicho, Aëtius, and Ricimer, to appoint a puppet emperor. Although his efforts established a dangerous and important precedent, Arbogast's career as the power behind the throne in the Western Empire was cut short by the arrival of Theodosius the Great. Nonetheless, Arbogast's career foreshadowed many of the events to come and revealed one of the weaknesses of the Western Empire.

Arbogast rose through the military ranks to assume an important leadership position in the Roman army and the Western Empire. He earned the rank of *magister equitum* (master of the horse) in the army of the Western Empire, and, from 380 to 388, served the emperor Theodosius in the east in his struggles against the Goths. In 388 he was sent back to the Western Empire to serve the young emperor Valentinian II (r. 375–392), who had recently been restored to the throne following a period of civil war. Arbogast served Valentinian well and recovered Gaul and strengthened the Rhine frontier. He also imposed a treaty on his fellow Franks who had invaded Gaul. His successes and the death of Bauto, another Frank sent as an adviser by

Theodosius, emboldened him to assume the office of *magister militum* (master of the soldiers) without the emperor's consent. Valentinian was outraged and sent his general a letter of dismissal, to which Arbogast replied that since Valentinian had not appointed him the emperor could not dismiss him. Shortly thereafter, in May 392, Valentinian was found dead, and some contemporaries suggested that he was killed by Arbogast.

The death of Valentinian presented Arbogast an opportunity to seize command, but as a barbarian he could not do it personally. He then appointed the teacher of rhetoric Flavius Eugenius emperor, a move that found little favor with Theodosius. Although Theodosius did not strike immediately at Eugenius and Arbogast, he clearly resented the move. Arbogast, a supporter of the pagans of Rome, had hoped to find favor with the Christian Theodosius by his promotion of another Christian. He also attempted to gain Theodosius's support by issuing new coins with the image of Theodosius on them. But these attempts bore little fruit, and Theodosius designated his son Honorius as the heir to the throne in the west. Arbogast and his emperor then promoted the pagan cause more strenuously and restored the famed Altar of Victory to its traditional place in the senate. To further secure his grip on the Western Empire, Arbogast again waged successful campaigns in Gaul during the winter of 393–394. But his efforts proved of little avail when Theodosius led a large force, which included Stilicho and many Germans, against Arbogast and his emperor. In a two-day battle on September 6–8, 394, Arbogast suffered a crushing defeat near the river Frigidus. Eugenius was executed following the defeat, and Arbogast committed suicide.

Although Arbogast was short-lived, his career was still significant. His rise to power in the military demonstrated one way to success in the empire, and his use of that power provided a precedent for later military commanders. Indeed, the Western Empire in the fifth century was ruled by several military commanders who had established figureheads on the imperial throne. Arbogast's example was especially important to the many Germans in the military, who could not hold the highest civil office in the empire. His virtual removal of the emperor from military command also had long-lasting consequences by further dividing the civil and military offices in the empire. It also distanced the Western emperors from the army, their most important constituency. The struggles between Theodosius and Arbogast and Eugenius brought further unrest to the empire and drew troops from the frontiers, thus weakening Rome's defense of its borders, which were seriously breached early in the fifth century.

See also Aëtius; Franks; Ricimer; Stilicho, Flavius; Visigoths

Bibliography
Bury, John B. *The Invasions of Europe by the Barbarians.* New York: W. W. Norton, 1967.
Cameron, Averil, and Peter Garnsey, eds. *The Late Empire, A.D. 337–425. Cambridge Ancient History,* vol. 13. Cambridge: Cambridge University Press, 1998.
Matthews, John. *Western Aristocracies and Imperial Court, A.D. 364–425.* Oxford: Clarendon, 1998.
Zosimus. *New History.* Trans. Ronald T. Ridley. Canberra: Australian Association for Byzantine Studies, 1982.

Arianism

Religious heresy associated with the Alexandrian presbyter Arius (c. 260–336). Arianism offered a concept of the relationship between God the Father and God the Son different from that of the Catholic tradition in the late Roman and early medieval period. It was popular throughout the fourth century with several Roman emperors, including Valens (d. 378), as well as with much of the Eastern Roman aristocracy. Although eventually outlawed by the devout Catholic Christian and emperor Theodosius the Great who declared

Ceiling mosaic from Arian baptistry, Ravenna (Vanni Archive / Corbis)

the Catholic faith the official religion of the empire, Arianism had great influence among the barbarian peoples who migrated into the empire. In fact, Arianism had adherents among the Franks, Goths, Lombards, and others into the late seventh century, and was often part of the political and military policies of these peoples. An attractive and in some ways simpler doctrine than Catholic Christianity, Arianism nonetheless was eventually abandoned by its Germanic adherents in favor of the predominant faith of the church of Rome.

Arianism took shape in the early fourth century, after Christianity was legalized in the Roman Empire and supported by the emperor Constantine. It formed in opposition to the Catholic faith, and as a result a great controversy erupted in the empire between supporters of each teaching. Unlike the Catholic faith, which stressed the essential unity of the godhead, the faith of Arius emphasized the superiority of God the Father. Arius taught that God the Son was subordinate and poste-

rior to the Father. According to Arius, the Son, rather than existing from before the beginning of time, was created in time; he argued further that God the Father created the Son as a mediator between himself and fallen humankind. He was divine by grace of the Father, and since he had become like God the Father, others had hope to become like the Father.

The teachings of Arius divided the church in the fourth century. To resolve this controversy Constantine held the first ecumenical council at Nicaea in 325, which was attended by 318 bishops and presided over by the emperor himself. The council upheld the Catholic view of the essential unity of the godhead, embodying it in the summary of the faith that formed the basis of what is traditionally called the Nicene Creed, but the controversy continued for the next several decades. Even Constantine, in the 330s, became more inclined to the Arian view. His successors often adopted Arianism as the preferred expression of Christianity.

During the reign of Constantius (337–361), the emperor adopted an Arian creed, which became the foundation for the Arianism of the Germanic peoples in the generations to come. The faith of Arius continued to have supporters among the emperors for the next few decades, but it faced a terrible setback under the Arian emperor Valens. His defeat by the Visigoths at the Battle of Hadrianople in 378 was understood as the judgment of God against a heretical ruler. His successor, Theodosius, was a staunch advocate of the Nicene Creed and promoted Catholic Christianity to the rank of state religion at the expense of Arian Christianity, as well as traditional paganism.

The triumph of Catholic Christianity in the empire did not spell the end of Arian Christianity, however. The missionary activities of the Arian Goth Ulfilas from the early 340s until his death in 382/383 and his translation of the Bible into the Gothic language contributed to the acceptance of Arian Christianity by large numbers of Goths. In the 370s, the Gothic leader Fritigern, possibly an ally of Ulfilas, converted to the Arian faith as part of his pro-Roman policy and his rivalry with Athanaric. Of course Fritigern's Arianism did not prevent him from defeating his fellow Arian, the emperor Valens, at the Battle of Hadrianople in 378. It did, however, complicate things for the Visigoths who settled in Spain and other parts of the old Roman Empire where the Roman population was predominantly Catholic. The Arian Visigoths also faced an established Catholic infrastructure of churches, monasteries, and most importantly, bishops, who wielded great power and influence. Ultimately, the Spanish Visigoths converted to Catholic Christianity in 587 when their great king, Reccared I, converted.

Not all Arian Goths had difficulty with their Catholic subjects, however. The Ostrogothic king of Italy, Theodoric the Great, ruled effectively despite religious differences with the majority of his subject population. He benefited from the resistance of the church in Italy to domination by the Eastern church centered in Constantinople, a resistance that made Catholics in Italy more willing to accept local control even if by an Arian. Moreover, Theodoric was a tolerant ruler and took few steps aimed at restricting the rights of Catholics. He was most respectful of the pope during a visit to Rome in 500 and, according to one contemporary, honored the pope just as any Catholic Christian would. As king, Theodoric also presided over a great cultural flourishing. His capital at Ravenna was the beneficiary of a building program that created great monuments of Arian architecture in a baptistery, palace church, and other churches throughout the city. Theodoric also built beautiful Arian churches in other Italian cities. Only late in his reign, when Theodoric had brutally crushed an alleged conspiracy, did he lose favor among the Italian population, so that his Arianism became a problem.

Other peoples, including the Burgundians and Vandals, accepted Arian Christianity, and the Lombards in particular used it as part of a grander political scheme. Invading Italy in 568, the Lombards attempted to unify the entire peninsula under their king. This policy met the opposition of various popes, who presided over significant territories in central Italy. Consequently, the Arianism of the Lombards took on political, especially antipapal, and to a lesser extent, anti-imperial connotations. Although the Lombards converted to Catholic Christianity in the late seventh century, their political agenda remained unchanged, although some kings did take a softer stance in relation to the popes.

Arianism had a very different career among the Merovingian Franks under their greatest leader, Clovis (r. 481–511). According to the sixth-century historian Gregory of Tours, Clovis favored Catholic Christianity long before his conversion. His wife, Clotilda, was a Catholic Christian who repeatedly sought to convert her husband to her faith. When Clovis did convert, according to Gregory, he chose Catholic Christianity, and was described as a new Constantine. Indeed, his conversion during a great battle recalls Constantine's conversion prior to the Battle of the Milvian Bridge. Gregory also describes Clovis's wars against the Visigoths as a sort of crusade, launched because the great Merovingian king could not tolerate Arian heretics living in Gaul. Of course, the situation is not so clear-cut as Gregory presents it. Clovis did ultimately convert to Catholic Christianity, but there is evidence that his conversion may not have been directly from paganism to Catholic faith. Clovis, at the very least, had sympathies with the Arian tradition and may have been an Arian Christian for a time before his final conversion to the Catholic faith.

See also Athanaric; Clotilda; Clovis; Constantine; Fritigern; Gregory of Tours; Hadrianople, Battle of; Lombards; Merovingian Dynasty; Ostrogoths; Reccared I; Theodoric the Great; Ulfilas; Visigoths

Bibliography

Geary, Patrick. *Before France and Germany: The Creation and Transformation of the Merovingian World.* Oxford: 1988.

Gregory of Tours. *History of the Franks.* Trans. Lewis Thorpe. Harmondsworth, UK: Penguin, 1974.

Hanson, Richard P. C. *The Search for the Christian Doctrine of God: The Arian Controversy, 318–381.* Edinburgh: 1988.

Herrin, Judith. *The Formation of Christendom.* Princeton: Princeton University Press, 1987.

Pelikan, Jaroslav. *The Emergence of the Catholic Tradition.* Vol. 2 of *The Christian Tradition: A History of the Development of Doctrine.* Chicago: University of Chicago Press, 1978.

Randers-Pehrson, Justine Davis. *Barbarians and Romans: The Birth Struggle of Europe,* A.D. *400–700.* Norman: University of Oklahoma Press, 1993.

Wolfram, Herwig. *The Roman Empire and Its Germanic Peoples.* Trans. Thomas Dunlap. Berkeley: University of California Press, 1997.

Arnulf of Metz, St. (580–643/647)

Bishop, saint, and traditionally the founder, with Pippin I, called Pippin of Landen, of the Carolingian family, Arnulf is generally thought to have been an important figure in the political life of the Frankish kingdoms in the seventh century. The marriage of Arnulf's son to one of Pippin's daughters is traditionally thought to have joined two of the most powerful aristocratic factions in Austrasia, the eastern realm of the Merovingian Franks, and Pippin II of Herstal was the product of this marriage. Arnulf's reputation for sanctity, no doubt, strengthened the family's position, and, according to the early ninth-century *Annals of Metz,* Arnulf of "all the Franks is held before God and men to be a special patron" (Fouracre and Gerberding 19976, 352). Much of what is known of Arnulf's life, however, is shrouded in mystery and myth created by later Carolingian writers, and the exact relationship between Arnulf and the two Pippins is uncertain.

According to the traditional account, Arnulf was born in 580 to an aristocratic family with extensive land holding between the Mosel and Meuse Rivers. He early on showed an inclination toward the religious life, possibly inspired by Irish missionaries who established a monastery nearby, and was taught to read and write. He later joined the court of the mayor of the palace (major domo) and then the court of the Merovingian king, Theudebert II. He assumed important administrative duties over royal domains and rose to prominence at court. His youth and early years at court occurred during a time of unrest and often brutal civil war between the queens Fredegund and Brunhilde. After Fredegund died, Brunhilde was the real power in the Merovingian kingdoms, even though she ruled through her sons and grandsons. In 613, Arnulf, along with Pippin and other Austrasian nobles, joined Chlotar II in a revolt that overthrew and savagely executed Brunhilde.

During the reign of Chlotar (613–629), both Arnulf and Pippin played influential roles and were rewarded for their service to the king. Indeed, the alliance they had forged during the revolt had drawn the fortunes of the two ancestral Carolingian leaders closer together. Joined by rebellion, they also were joined by the marriage of Arnulf's son, Ansegisel, and Pippin's daughter, Begga. Moreover, as the *Annals of Metz* note, Arnulf "very often strengthened [Pippin] with sacred admonitions and divine and human learning so that he would be strengthened for more important matters" (Fouracre and Gerberding 1996, 352). Pippin became mayor of the palace, thus acquiring the office that provided the foundation for later Carolingian success. Arnulf was rewarded by Chlotar with the office of bishop of Metz, perhaps as a result of Arnulf's religious inclinations as well as of his administrative talents. As bishop he controlled sizable estates and wealth that would have been important to the king, who allowed Arnulf to retain possession of his administrative posts at the royal court. He was also entrusted with the responsibility of tutor to Chlotar's young son, the future Dagobert I.

In his later years Arnulf yearned to resign from his official religious and secular duties to take up the life of a monk. He was prohibited from doing so by Chlotar, who valued Arnulf's talents. On the death of Chlotar, however, Arnulf was allowed to retire to a monastery, where he died some time between 643 and 647 after years of pious service. The pious life he led at the monastery contributed to his reputation as a saint, and his feast day is celebrated on August 16 or 19 at his former monastery. Although Arnulf's life may have been subject to Carolingian mythologizing, which makes some of the exact details of his life certain, he was surely an important figure in the early years of the Carolingian family and in the Frankish kingdoms of the seventh century.

See also Brunhilde; Carolingian Dynasty; Chlotar II; Fredegund; Merovingian Dynasty; Pippin I, Called Pippin of Landen; Pippin II, Called Pippin of Herstal

Bibliography
Fouracre, Paul, and Richard A. Gerberding. *Late Merovingian France: History and Hagiography, 640–720.* Manchester, UK: University of Manchester Press, 1996.
Fouracre, Paul. *The Age of Charles Martel.* 1996.
Riché, Pierre. *The Carolingians: A Family Who Forged Europe.* Trans. Michael Idomir Allen. Philadelphia: University of Pennsylvania Press, 1993.
Wood, Ian. *The Merovingian Kingdoms, 450–751.* London: Longman, 1994.

Arthur, King
See King Arthur

Asser
See Alfred the Great

Athalaric
See Ostrogoths

Athanaric (d. 381)
Gothic warrior leader or judge from 365 to 381, whose reign was marked by prolonged struggles against the Romans and the Huns as well as against other groups of Goths. His reign was later recognized by the Visigoths as the moment of the beginning of that people, and he was deemed their founder king. It was as a result of the pressure of the advancing Huns that Gothic followers of Athanaric abandoned their leader and, with rival Gothic groups, petitioned the Roman emperor Valens for entry into the Roman Empire. The entry of the Visigoths in 376 led to the Battle of Hadrianople, but Athanaric was not involved in that battle and was eventually welcomed to Constantinople and honored there shortly before his death. His reign was characterized also by the indiscriminate persecution of Christians, Catholic and non-Catholic, living in his territory, which led later Christian historians to blacken his name.

Athanaric was a member of a royal clan among the Gothic Tervingi, and from his youth he had strained relations with the empire. His father, after an apparent failed diplomatic contact with Constantine the Great (r. 306–337), made Athanaric swear an oath never to step foot in the empire. Moreover, although the empire supported Athanaric's dynasty, Goths fought with Rome against Persia, and trade went on between the Goths and Rome, these good relations followed a crushing defeat by Rome and rested on Gothic hostages at the Roman court. In the 360s, when he had come to rule in his own name, Athanaric supported the pretender to the Roman throne, Procopius, against the legitimate emperor, Valens (r. 364–378). Valens massacred the warriors Athanaric sent to support Procopius and prepared for open war against Athanaric.

The Roman campaign against the Goths in the late 360s brought great devastation and suffering to Athanaric's people. From 367 to 369 Valens prosecuted war against Athanaric but, despite considerable advantages, could not defeat the Goth. Athanaric was no match for Roman power and lost battles against Rome, but he managed to avoid the severe defeats his predecessors suffered. In 369, with a growing Persian threat, Valens accepted Athanaric's offer of peace. The treaty was settled, much to the chagrin of Valens, on an island in the Danube, because Athanaric refused to set foot in Roman territory. The treaty freed Athanaric's Goths from Roman hegemony and ended tribute payments to the Romans.

After settling with the Romans, Athanaric turned his attention to affairs in his realm. From 369 to 372 Athanaric, fearing that Christianity would undermine the traditions of Gothic society, conducted a systematic persecution of Christians in his realm, many of whom had converted as a result of the missionary activities of Ulfilas. He forced Christians in his realm to honor a tribal idol and make sacrifices to it, and if they refused they were punished and their houses burned. The idols were probably images of important ancestors or tribal founders, and those who failed to honor them denied the tribe and its divine origins. In other words, they violated the integrity of the community to which they otherwise belonged. In a sense Athanaric, much like the Roman emperors before the conversion of Constantine, was trying to preserve the unity of his realm by forcing Gothic Christians to adhere to the traditional religion. Athanaric's persecutions were also part of his anti-imperial policy, because of the close association of Christianity with the Roman Empire, which had sponsored missionaries north of the Danube River. But Athanaric's efforts backfired because they failed to unite the Goths. In fact, his persecutions led to a division within the community when his rival, Fritigern, agreed to convert to Christianity in exchange for the support of the Roman emperor Valens. Fritigern also challenged Athanaric's authority in the mid-370s, but Athanaric managed to keep control as a greater threat emerged on the horizon.

The Huns' advance followed in the wake of the Gothic war with the Romans and the internal struggle between Athanaric and Fritigern. Although at first modest, the pressure of the Huns became increasingly intense and caused a dramatic realignment of barbarian settlements inside and outside the frontier of the empire. As the Huns moved eastward, various Gothic groups faced them, with generally disastrous consequences. One tribe of Ostrogoths was smashed by the Huns, even though a small group managed to make their way to Athanaric's territory. In the summer of 376, Athanaric was ambushed by an advance force of Huns, from which he managed to escape with his army intact.

In response to the threat of the Huns, Athanaric began a program of building defensive fortifications similar to Roman fortresses along his frontier. Unfortunately for Athanaric and his Goths, this policy of wall building proved ineffective, as Hunnish raiding parties once again fell on him and defeated the Goths in battle near the Danube River.

His ability to retreat successfully and regroup failed him after his defeat by the Huns, in part because the Huns took control of important territory and managed to cut off Athanaric's supply lines. As a result of his losses to the Huns and the devastation it caused, Fritigern, Athanaric's old rival, established himself as a leader and, with a majority of the Tervingi, withdrew from Athanaric and received the right from Emperor Valens to settle in the Roman Empire. The division of the Goths had serious consequences for both Athanaric, who had lost most of his followers, and Valens, who was defeated by Fritigern and killed at the Battle of Hadrianople in 378.

Athanaric and his remaining followers did not follow Fritigern into the Roman Empire, but he could not remain where he was because of continued pressure from the Huns. Just as the Huns advanced at Athanaric's expense, Athanaric's successful withdrawal came at the expense of other barbarian peoples. He advanced against another barbarian people who lived across the Carpathian Mountains and settled there for the next four years with his remaining followers. In late 380, Athanaric was forced out in a coup engineered by Fritigern. Despite his long-standing hostility toward the empire, Athanaric sought asylum in Constantinople in January 381. He was welcomed by the emperor Theodosius, who met him at the gates of the city and offered him a lavish reception. The welcome afforded Athanaric was outdone only by the funeral Theodosius provided him two weeks later, after the Goth's death on January 25, 381.

See also Fritigern; Hadrianople, Battle of; Huns; Ulfilas; Visigoths

Bibliography

Heather, Peter. *The Goths.* Oxford: Blackwell, 1996.

Randers-Pehrson, Justine Davis. *Barbarians and Romans: The Birth Struggle of Europe, A.D. 40–700.* Norman: University of Oklahoma Press, 1983.

Wolfram, Herwig. *History of the Goths.* Trans. Thomas J. Dunlap. Berkeley: University of California Press, 1988.

———. *The Roman Empire and Its Germanic Peoples.* Trans. Thomas J. Dunlap. Berkeley: University of California Press, 1997.

Attila the Hun (d. 453)

The fifth century king of the Huns, called the scourge of God. Attila was a mighty warrior who extracted great wealth from the Roman Empire and posed a threat to the peace of the late ancient world during his reign from 435 to 453. Although he did not pose a direct challenge to the existence of the Roman Empire, Attila invaded the empire on several occasions and inflicted serious damage on the empire and its armies. His armies threatened both the new Rome, Constantinople, and the original city of Rome. His empire was a rival to the Roman Empire, but despite its size and military power, the empire of the Huns did not long survive Attila, its greatest king.

Several late ancient writers have left descriptions of Attila's physical appearance and personality. The sixth-century historian of the Goths, Jordanes, describes Attila as short of stature but of mighty bearing. Attila had a swarthy complexion, a broad chest, a large head with small eyes, a thin beard, and a flat nose. In his history, Jordanes observes that Attila had a haughty walk, which revealed his proud spirit and abundant self-confidence. A lover of war, he terrified all the world but was gracious to suppliants. The Roman ambassador to Attila's court, Priscus, left an account of diplomacy at the court that complements the account of Jordanes. Priscus describes the favorable treatment he received from the king, who spoke "friendly words" to him and sent warm greetings to the emperor. He also describes a banquet he was invited to by Attila. The king sat on a couch in the middle of the room, surrounded by couches for his guests. The guests were served lavish dishes on silver platters and wine in goblets of silver and gold, but Attila ate meat on a wooden plate and wine from a wooden goblet. His clothing, Priscus notes, was plain but clean. His sword, boots, and bridle were without elaborate ornamentation. Attila had numerous wives and an even larger number of children.

In the year 435, Attila and his brother Bleda ascended to the throne of the Huns, succeeding their uncle Ruga. It was Ruga who enjoyed the first successes against the Roman Empire, invading the empire, threatening the capital, and extracting tribute from the emperor. Ruga, in the 420s, brought cohesion to the disparate bands that made up the Hunnish confederation and imposed unity of purpose on these tribes. Ruga also imposed a treaty on the empire, demanding not only tribute but also the return of Huns who had deserted and joined the imperial army. This was a most serious demand for the empire, which had come to rely on the service of Hunnish soldiers. It also proved critical to Attila, who exploited the terms to his advantage.

As king, Attila immediately took the offensive and negotiated a new treaty—the Treaty of Margus—with the empire, which became the cornerstone for relations with the empire for the rest of his reign. According to the new treaty, the amount of tribute paid to the Huns was doubled from 350 pounds of gold a year to 700 pounds. Huns who had deserted were to be returned to Attila or ransomed at the value of a Roman solider. (The fate of returned deserters was not pleasant, as the example of two royal deserters who were sent back by the Romans and crucified by Attila suggests.) Constantinople was not to make treaties with the enemies of the Huns and had to guarantee that fairs be held along the frontier between the two powers. Attila also extended the size of the empire he inherited by waging war on the barbarian tribes on his northern and eastern frontier during the later 430s.

In response to the refusal of the emperor, Theodosius II, to honor the terms of the Treaty of Margus—he suddenly ceased the payment of tribute—Attila invaded the empire. Seizing the opportunity to harass the empire while Theodosius II was engaged with the Persians, Attila inflicted great damage on imperial territory. He razed a number of important cities, including Singidunum (Belgrade) and Serdica (Sofia). Another city, Naissus (Nis), was badly devastated; the stench of death was so great that no one could enter the city, and human bones filled the Danube River. He won a series of battles in 443 and threatened the city of Constantinople itself. His numerous victories forced the empire to renegotiate its treaty with the Huns. The annual subsidy was raised to 2,100 pounds of gold, with a one-time payment of 6,000 pounds of gold to cover the missed payments.

The early successes of Attila, however, were suddenly interrupted. The terror inspired by the great Hunnish horsemen no longer seemed so great, and they no longer acquired the spoils of war they once did. Epidemic or rebellion may have struck the empire of the Huns. The armies were no longer successful in battle. And the emperor once again refused to make the tribute payments to the Huns. Following these setbacks, Attila murdered his brother Bleda in 444. It may have been an assassination motivated solely by the lust for power, but it is also possible that Bleda was blamed for the misfortunes that had struck the Huns. Bleda's incompetence may have caused the military setbacks. He was clearly a *rex inutilis,* a "useless king," or even worse, a king who had lost the favor of the gods. Whatever the reason for the assassination, Bleda's murder left Attila in sole control of the empire.

Shortly after the murder of his brother, Attila once again took the offensive and invaded the Eastern Empire a second time. This invasion was even greater than the previous campaign and led to even greater devastation. Although suffering heavy losses himself, Attila inflicted severe defeats on imperial armies. He laid waste to large sections of the Balkans and had led his armies to Thermopylae by 447 when the emperor pleaded for peace. The treaty renewed the terms of the earlier treaties. The Empire was to renew annual payments of 2,100 pounds of gold. It was forced to ransom Roman captives and to promise to return Huns who had deserted and to stop accepting them into the empire and its army. The empire also ceded a significant portion of its Danubian province to Attila.

In 450 Attila was once again on the warpath, but this time it was the Western Empire that felt the wrath of God's scourge. There are several factors that inspired Attila to attack the imperial West, not the least of which was its military weakness. The Vandal king, Gaiseric, fearful of the power of the Visigoths, encouraged Attila's western focus. The death of Theodosius II in 450 also contributed to Attila's decision to attack the empire again, because the new emperor, Marcian, refused to pay the tribute or make any other concessions to the Huns. Finally, there is the interesting case of Honoria, daughter of Galla Placidia and sister of the emperor Valentinian. She had led a dissolute life and was caught with a servant. He was executed, and she was betrothed to a trustworthy senator—that is, one who posed no threat to the emperor. To avoid marrying a senator she detested and to acquire a protector, Honoria sent a ring to Attila. The great king interpreted this as a proposal of marriage and demanded that Honoria be turned over and that she be given half of the territory of the Western Empire. Although there was some interest in turning Honoria over to the king of the Huns, Marcian's refusal to pay the tribute pushed Attila to take his bride by force.

The preparations for the invasion were extensive, and Attila entered Gaul in the Western Empire with a massive army, counted at between 300,000 and 700,000 men by contemporary sources. Although these numbers are probably exaggerated, it is certain that Attila led an army of great size into the Western Empire. His army contained a large number of allied and subject peoples, including Alans, Burgundians, Heruls, Ostrogoths, Ripuarian Franks, Sarmatians, Suevi, and Vandals led by Gaiseric, as well as his own Huns. He faced a great alliance of Romans and Burgundians,

Celts, Salian Franks, and Visigoths, all led by the Roman military commander, Aëtius, who had long relied on the Huns for the imperial army. Despite the great alliance against him, Attila enjoyed success early in the campaign and sacked the important cities of Rheims, Metz, Strasbourg, Cologne, and Trier. His efforts to seize Orléans in the summer of 451, however, failed. Aëtius managed to secure the city before Attila's arrival, and rather than waste time and men on a prolonged siege, Attila withdrew. Although a wise tactical move, Attila's withdrawal provided the Romans with a victory and raised their morale.

Attila's own morale was undermined by the loss at Orléans, as well as by a soothsayer who predicted that the impending battle would prove disastrous for the Huns, even though a great rival would die. Nonetheless, Attila prepared for a showdown with his enemy, and on June 20 on the plains between Troyes and Châlons, the two armies fought a great battle that some have seen as one of the decisive battles of world history. The Battle of the Catalaunian Plains (also known as the Battle of Maurica, or of Châlons) was a terrible, bloody battle in which, according to Jordanes, 165,000 men died. The fighting was so ferocious in this battle of nations that the ancients report that a small stream near the field grew to a raging torrent from the blood of the combatants.

The battle for a time went so poorly for the Huns that Attila prepared a funeral pyre for himself should it come to that. But the death of the Visigoth Theodoric staved off the destruction of the Huns, and Attila was able to withdraw from the field of battle and leave Gaul. Aëtius, victorious, decided not to pursue his foe, perhaps because he did not wish to destroy the Huns, who were an important counterbalance to Rome's other barbarian rivals. Aëtius's use of the Huns in his army no doubt also kept him from destroying his rival's army. Attila was like a wounded animal at this point, more ferocious because of his own injury, and any pursuit could have led to a devastating counterattack that would have destroyed the army of Aëtius and opened the Western Empire to Attila.

Attila may have been beaten near Châlons, but he was a determined enemy and planned an even greater invasion in 452. Attila crossed the Alps and led his armies on a grand invasion of Italy that brought devastation to the north of the peninsula and threatened the ancient capital, Rome. Aëtius was unable to rally his allies among the Alans and Visigoths and thus had insufficient forces to challenge the great army of the Huns. As a result much of northern Italy suffered heavy damage from the Huns. Many cities were pillaged and destroyed. The city of Aquileia was razed to the ground, and its inhabitants, according to tradition, fled into the lagoons of the Adriatic and founded Venice. According to one early account, the cities of Milan and Pavia were completely destroyed and left depopulated. Attila's armies sacked Verona and Vicentia as well and extorted a ransom from the people of Ticinum to spare that city. Unchecked by imperial armies, Attila set up court in northern Italy, probably at Milan. He was met there by two Roman senators and Pope Leo I, known as the Great; the eloquence and prestige of the elderly pontiff is alleged to have convinced Attila to withdraw from Italy. According to papal tradition, it was not Leo alone who persuaded the king to leave the peninsula; the heavenly hosts, led by the apostles Peter and Paul, threatened Attila with death if he disobeyed the papal commands. The plague afflicting the army of the Huns and the threat of an imperial army from the east no doubt also influenced Attila's decision to withdraw.

Once again, despite military setbacks, Attila planned further campaigns against the empire, including a massive invasion of the Eastern Empire in 453. His plans, however, were cut short by his own death. He was found dead with his new wife the morning after his wedding. There were rumors that his wife had poisoned him. He may have celebrated his marriage too enthusiastically and, in a drunken stupor, drowned in his own nosebleed. Or he may have suffered a fatal stroke. Whatever the cause, the mighty king was dead, and he was buried in great state. His body was borne by the best horsemen of the Huns into an open field, where it was laid to rest. The body was placed in a tent of the finest Chinese silk, and a great revel, the *strava,* took place around it. The Huns rode around the tent, chanting a dirge, tearing out their hair, and gashing their faces. The body was then placed in three nested coffins bound with gold, silver, and iron. It was buried with great wealth, including gem-encrusted weapons, and the slaves who prepared Attila's tomb were killed so that its whereabouts would remain unknown.

The empire of the Huns did not long survive its greatest king. None of Attila's many sons had the abilities of their father, and fraternal squabbling worsened a bad situation. The many subject peoples revolted and brought down the empire. Rome surely rejoiced. Despite its rapid demise, the empire of Attila had posed a grave threat to the empire of Rome. His ambition and military prowess challenged Rome, and he nearly succeeded in taking control of the Western Empire. His untimely death cut short even greater plans of conquest that could have proved devastating to the Roman Empire, and despite his ultimate failure Attila remains one of the best known and greatest of Rome's foes.

See also Aëtius; Gaiseric; Galla Placidia; Huns; Visigoths

Bibliography

Baüml, Franz H., and Marianna Birnbaum. *Attila: The Man and His Image.* Budapest: Corvina, 1993.

Bury, John B. *History of the Later Roman Empire: From the Death of Theodosius I to the Death of Justinian.* Vol. 1. 1923. Reprint, New York: Dover, 1959.

Thompson, Edward A. *A History of Attila and the Huns.* Oxford: Clarendon, 1948.

———. *The Huns.* Oxford: Blackwell, 1995.

Wolfram, Herwig. *The Roman Empire and Its Germanic Peoples.* Trans. Thomas J. Dunlap. Berkeley: University of California Press, 1997.

Augustine of Canterbury, St. (d. 604)

Missionary to the Anglo-Saxon people, Augustine was sent to England by Pope Gregory I, called the Great, with forty other missionaries. Much of our knowledge of his evangelical mission comes from two primary sources: the letters sent to Augustine from Gregory, which were preserved, in part, by Bede in *A History of the English Church and People,* and Bede's history itself. Augustine successfully introduced Christianity to the kingdom of Kent, converted the Kentish king, built or restored churches, and introduced monastic life to England. Augustine was not only a successful evangelist, but he was also the first archbishop of Canterbury. Although there was a period of apostasy after the deaths of Augustine and Æthelberht, the Anglo-Saxon king, Augustine can be recognized as restoring contacts between England and Rome that had been broken during the barbarian invasions and also as reestablishing Christianity in Anglo-Saxon England.

According to Bede, the inspiration to evangelize England was the result of an experience Gregory had before he became pope. One day while in the marketplace in Rome, Gregory came upon some merchants who had recently arrived with young boys to sell as slaves. Remarking on their attractive features, Gregory asked the name of their race. He was told they were Angels, and he said that was appropriate because "They have angelic faces" (Bede 1981, 100). He learned too that they were pagan and from the land of Deira, and he hoped to rescue them from the wrath of God (*de ira*). He approached the pope, asking to be sent as a missionary but was refused this request. According to the tradition recorded by Bede, however, he did not forget his hope and as pope sent a mission to England. Although the tale may be apocryphal, it does reveal Gregory's desire to convert the English as well as his possible awareness of the importance of western Europe for the papacy.

Whatever the truth of Bede's tale, Gregory did send an evangelical mission to England, which was led by Augustine. Little is known of Augustine's life before he was chosen to lead the mission to England, other than that he was probably a student of Felix, bishop of Messana, and was a monk and prior of St. Andrew's monastery in Rome. In 596 Augustine was appointed to lead roughly forty monks to England to preach the Christian faith or at least to learn if the people would be receptive to hearing the word. It was a mission of some uncertainty and setbacks but one that ultimately proved successful.

Leaving Rome sometime before July 596, Augustine and his fellow missionaries arrived first in Gaul, bearing letters from Gregory asking the bishops of Gaul to support the missionaries on their way. Augustine's route through Gaul possibly took him to the cities of Arles, Lyons, Marseilles, and Tours. As the letters of Gregory reveal, the missionaries also visited the powerful Merovingian queen Brunhilde and possibly also her grandsons Theudebert, later Theudebert II, and Theuderic, later Theuderic II. The queen was, no doubt, interested in the mission because her niece Bertha was married to the English king Æthelberht. A letter from Gregory in 597 suggests that she was most helpful; the pope thanks her for her efforts and praises her as a new Helena, the mother of the first Christian emperor Constantine. The journey through Gaul, however, was not without incident. At either Lérins or, more likely, Arles, the missionaries sent Augustine back to Rome to ask the pope to reconsider sending the mission because of their fears of going to a barbarous, pagan nation. Gregory promoted Augustine to the rank of abbot and returned him with a letter encouraging the missionaries to proceed to England and another letter seeking support for the missionaries from the bishop of Arles.

The exact date of the arrival of the missionaries in England remains uncertain, but it was probably sometime during the summer of 597. They arrived first on the island of Thanet near the coast of Kent and brought with them Frankish interpreters. Augustine, now a bishop, having been consecrated at Arles, made contact with the king, Æthelberht. Although his wife was a Christian, the king remained a pagan, but he informed Augustine that he would welcome them, even though Augustine was to stay on the island. The king feared that Augustine would use magic to deceive him and ordered an open-air audience to be held, rather than one in a house where Augustine would more easily be able to use magic. The bishop arrived at the head of a procession bearing a silver cross and an icon of Jesus Christ. Although he did not convert, the king welcomed Augustine and offered him a dwelling in the capital of Canterbury, where Augustine settled and restored the ancient church of St. Martin. He thus began the mission, and then his prayers and the miracles he performed convinced the king to convert. This was Augustine's greatest accomplishment, and even though the king did not compel his subjects to convert, many did, and Gregory reported in a letter to the patriarch of Alexandria that Augustine baptized 10,000 people on Christmas Day, 597.

Augustine set about establishing the infrastructure needed for the church in England. In 601 he received the pallium, symbol of full episcopal authority, from Gregory and permission to establish a number of new bishoprics under his authority as archbishop. He was to promote London to the status of archbishopric and also create a new archiepiscopal see in York and twelve new episcopal sees under the authority of York. Augustine's see at Canterbury, was to remain the primatial see in England. Augustine also repaired the cathedral in Canterbury, Christ Church, which was consecrated on June 9, 603, and established a monastery near the cathedral, which served as the burial site for Augustine and his successors as archbishop as well as for the kings of Kent. He received aid from further missionaries in 601, who brought a number of items necessary for worship, including altar covers, books, church ornaments, relics, and vestments. He corre-

sponded often with Gregory in Rome and received instructions on various matters, including an order not to destroy the pagan temples of the English. Gregory approved destruction of pagan idols but recommended purifying existing pagan temples and consecrating them as churches so that the English would flock "more readily to their accustomed resorts, [and] come to know and adore the true God." (Bede 1981, 87) Augustine also received a letter from Gregory cautioning the archbishop against taking pride in the miracles that God was performing through the archbishop in England.

Augustine also organized a council at Augustine Oak in 603, between the church he had established and the British churches that existed outside the Anglo-Saxon kingdoms. These churches had fallen out of communication with Rome, and Augustine hoped to reconcile with them and introduce Roman practices to them. The conference was a failure because the British churches refused to accept his, and Rome's, teaching on the date of Easter and other matters. Even though Augustine miraculously cured a man of blindness as a test of whom God favored, while the British clerics failed at the task, the conference ended without reconciliation between the two churches. A second council was held sometime later, and again the two sides failed to agree. The British priests refused to accept Augustine's compromise of allowing them to continue their traditional practices but requiring them to conform to Roman usage on Easter and baptism because Augustine did not rise from his seat when they approached. Bede records Augustine's prophecy of strife afflicting the British churches, which, Bede notes, was fulfilled.

Despite this failure and the period of apostasy after his death on May 26, 604, and the death of Æthelberht, Augustine's mission was of great importance for the history of Christianity in England. He successfully restored connections between England and Rome. He baptized many Anglo-Saxons, including the king of Kent, established a network of bishops, built a monastery, and restored many churches that had fallen into disuse and disrepair. Indeed, as the epitaph on his tomb notes, the first archbishop of Canterbury "supported by God with miracles guided King Æthelberht and his people from the worship of idols to the faith of Christ." (Bede 1981, 105)

See also Æthelberht; Anglo-Saxons; Bede; Brunhilde; Constantine; Gregory the Great; Merovingian Dynasty

Bibliography

Bede. *Ecclesiastical History of the English People with Bede's Letter to Egbert and Cuthbert's Letter on the Death of Bede.* Trans. Leo Sherley-Price. Harmondsworth, UK: Penguin, 1991.

Blair, Peter Hunter. *The World of Bede.* Cambridge: Cambridge University Press, 1991.

Mayr-Harting, Henry. *The Coming of Christianity to Anglo-Saxon England,* 3d ed. University Park: Pennsylvania State University Press, 1991.

Stenton, Frank M. *Anglo-Saxon England.* 3d ed. Oxford: Clarendon, 1971.

Augustine of Hippo, St. (354–430)

The greatest of the Latin church fathers. Augustine's influence extended from late antiquity into the early Middle Ages and beyond. His voluminous writings, of more than 5 million words, shaped much of the intellectual culture of barbarian Europe. His autobiography, polemical and theological works, sermons, and other treatises shaped how early medieval ecclesiastics from Caesarius of Arles to Alcuin understood the faith. Early medieval writers also looked to Augustine for instruction on how to interpret and teach Scripture. It was not only learned ecclesiastics, but also the barbarian kings of the early Middle Ages who were influenced by Augustine's ideas. If Charlemagne's biographer, Einhard, is to be believed, one of the great king's favorite books was the *City of God,* which, for the king and his advisors, may have offered a model of the just earthly society.

Augustine was born in Thagaste in North

Augustine of Hippo (Perry-Castaneda Library)

Africa (now Souk Ahras, Algeria) in 354 to parents, Patricius and Monnica, who belonged to the lower aristocracy, and was probably their only child. He was educated in the traditional Roman fashion, and was sent to the best schools his father could afford, including those in the great city of the province, Carthage. There was little remarkable about his youth, except, as Augustine notes in his autobiographical work *Confessions,* for his theft of some pears with his friends. As a young adult he acquired a mistress who bore him a son, Adeodatus, and, much to his Christian mother's dismay, he converted to Manichaeanism, a religion that taught the belief in a good god and a bad god and held that the material world was evil because it was created by the bad god. He remained a Manichaean until his conversion to Christianity in Milan in 386.

Having developed a reputation as a teacher in Thagaste and Carthage, Augustine had moved to Milan in 384 to find a position at the imperial court. While there he met the archbishop, Ambrose, and converted to Christianity. After his conversion, he returned to Africa, without his mistress or the woman to whom he had become engaged while in Milan, and hoped to live the quiet life of a Christian scholar. He was ordained a priest in 391 and in 395 made bishop of Hippo, a promotion that forced him to consider the meaning of his new faith and write *On Christian Doctrine* and *Confessions.* As bishop he was involved with fighting a number of religious heresies, administering the diocese, and preaching. Over his long career, he wrote numerous sermons, which provided an important outlet to develop his theology.

In 413, he began his greatest work, *The City of God,* a Christian apology inspired by the Visigoths' sack of Rome in 410. This massive work contains philosophies of history and politics, a defense of Christian belief, and profound Christian theology. It tells, among other things, the history of the tragedies that befell the Roman Empire before the sack of Rome, which the pagans blamed on Christianity, to prove that the pagans were wrong and to comfort Christians who questioned their belief in the face of disaster. Augustine spent his last years administering his diocese, struggling against one final heresy, and reexamining his many written works. He died on August 28, 430, as the Vandals began to threaten Augustine's city of Hippo, which they sacked in 431.

Shortly after his death, Augustine's writings, together with his relics, were moved from his native Africa to Italy and from there continued to shape intellectual life for centuries after. His influence on the cultural life of Europe can be measured by the many ecclesiastics who borrowed from his writings and the libraries where his works were found. Isidore of Seville (c. 560–636), the late Roman bishop and encyclopedist, who was influential in the Visigothic courts of Spain, borrowed heavily from the principles Augustine laid out in his work *On Christian Doctrine,* which advocated the use of classical learning in the service of the Christian faith.

In the seventh century, the works of Augustine were deposited in numerous monasteries in the Merovingian kingdom of the Franks. And in the eighth century, the Anglo-Saxon missionary, Boniface, recognized the authority of Augustine as a biblical commentator, and the bishop of Hippo's influence can be detected in the work of the great Anglo-Saxon scholar Bede. But the extent of Augustine's influence is perhaps best revealed in the Carolingian Renaissance.

Manuscript copies of his works were found in most Carolingian libraries, and of particular importance was the library at Lyons, which was a virtual Augustine research center. Augustine's treatise on Christian doctrine was the foundation for Carolingian educational ideas, and his influence can be seen on the works of the greatest Carolingian teacher, the Anglo-Saxon scholar Alcuin. Finally, the great debate over predestination begun by Gottschalk of Orbais in the mid-ninth century involved competing interpretations of Augustine's works.

Augustine's influence was felt beyond the intellectual realm, however, since his ideas also affected the political realm, especially during the Carolingian age. Einhard, in his biography of Charlemagne, noted that the great king of the Franks enjoyed hearing excerpts from the *City of God* read during his banquets. Indeed, it has been suggested that Charlemagne's, or at least his advisors', ideas of government were inspired by a reading of Augustine's works. Although the question of whether Augustine intended to provide a blueprint for the just Christian society in his great work remains open, many of his readers saw such a blueprint and worked to establish it. Political Augustinianism was an important influence in early medieval society and involved a number of key concepts touched on by the great bishop in the *City of God.* The *City of God* describes the existence of two "cities" on earth—the city of God, whose members are virtuous, and the earthly city, whose members are corrupt. Augustine explains that the two societies coexist but that the only true and just city is the heavenly one. Implicit, however, in his discussion is the notion that a society could be just if it were ruled by a Christian monarch, and it is this implication that may have inspired Charlemagne and his advisors, such as Alcuin.

See also Alaric; Alcuin of York; Bede; Boniface, St.; Caesarius of Arles; Carolingian Renaissance; Charlemagne; Einhard; Gottschalk of Orbais; Isidore of Seville; Merovingian Dynasty; Vandals; Visigoths

Bibliography

Augustine. *Confessions: Books I-XIII.* Trans. Francis J. Sheed. Indianapolis: Hackett, 1993.

———. *Concerning the City of God against the Pagans.* Trans. Henry Bettenson. Harmondsworth, UK: Penguin, 1981.

———. *On Christian Doctrine.* Trans. Donald W. Robertson, Jr. New York: Macmillan, 1958.

Brown, Peter. *Augustine of Hippo: A Biography.* Berkeley: University of California Press, 1967.

Deane, Herbert. *The Political and Social Ideas of Saint Augustine.* New York: Columbia University Press, 1964.

Laistner, Max L. W. *Thought and Letters in Western Europe, A.D. 500 to 900.* 2d ed. Ithaca, NY: Cornell University Press, 1976.

O'Donnell, James J. *Augustine.* Boston: Twayne, 1985.

Wills, Gary. *Saint Augustine.* New York: Penguin, 1999.

Avars

An amalgamation of peoples from the central steppes of Europe, the Avars were a late arrival among the barbarian peoples who were the successors of the Western Roman Empire. They were skilled horsemen, who may have had an important impact on the development of military technology in the early Middle Ages, and successful warriors. Although less well known than their relatives the Huns, they had similar success in threatening the established kingdoms of their day and greater success in creating a permanent kingdom. They were seen as a threat by the Byzantine Empire and caused difficulty for the Franks before their great capital was destroyed by Charlemagne's armies.

The exact origins of the Avars remain uncertain. They have been identified with the Juan-Juan, a group of tribes in Mongolia, and with a tribal group of Afghanistan, the Ephthalites. There is, however, general agreement that at some time in the mid-sixth century, the Avars were pushed out of their homeland by the Turks. They appear in the historical record in 558, when an Avar embassy arrived in Constantinople and met with the emperor Justinian. They settled not long after that in the region of modern Hungary.

On their arrival, the Avars were welcomed by the Byzantines, who needed allies along their eastern frontier, but they quickly wore out their welcome. They demanded land and other privileges from Emperor Justinian, who offered them some gifts but insisted they prove themselves before he made any major concessions. They very quickly subdued several nomadic steppe tribes and thus demonstrated their abilities. By 562 they made further demands for territory from Justinian, who agreed to give them land west of modern Belgrade. They had wanted other territory, and the two powers were on the verge of war when the Avars turned their attention for the first time to the Franks. For the next generation they continued their westward efforts. By the 580s, with Slavic subjects and allies, the Avars turned their attention to Byzantine territory in the Balkans. They extended their influence into the Balkans and posed a serious threat to the empire, which they forced out of the region of the Danube River in 602. In 626, with the Slavs and new Persian allies, the Avars pressed on and threatened the city of Constantinople. The siege failed, and the Avars lost ground to the Byzantines, as well as to the Bulgars and other Slavs who were supported by the empire. The Avars showed their first sign of decline in the face of their defeat and the Slavic rebellions. These losses of ground were the first sign of decline for the Avars. They subsequently posed less of a problem for the Byzantines, even though occasional battles took place for decades to come.

The Avars made their mark not only on the Byzantine Empire but also on the kingdom of the Franks and other powers in the former Western Roman Empire. In 562, rather than launch an attack on the Byzantine Empire, the Avars turned their attention westward to make their strength known in that region. They attacked the Merovingian kingdom of Austrasia in 562 but were turned back by the king Sigebert (r. 560/561–575). But in 565 or 566, the Avars attacked Sigebert's kingdom again and defeated him. According to Gregory of Tours, the Avars won the second battle because they "made a number of phantom figures dance before [the Franks'] eyes and so beat them easily" (29). Sigebert gave them many gifts and agreed to a treaty with them. Following this success, the Avars, in 567, joined with the Lombards to destroy the Gepid kingdom. The Lombards, uncertain of Avar intentions, moved into Italy, leaving the Avars the main power along the Danube River.

Although they turned their attention elsewhere, the Avars returned to their struggle with the Franks in the early seventh century. They had some success in the early seventh century, but an alliance of Franks and Saxons led by King Dagobert pushed them out of eastern Frankish territory in the Rhineland. Again in the eighth century, the Avars and the Franks were at war when the Avars invaded the kingdom and destroyed the city of Lorch and its surrounding territory in 711. They launched another campaign into Frankish territories in 740 and were decisively defeated. This marked the end of their period of aggression and the beginning of the end of their kingdom. They now faced the expansionistic policies of the Carolingian dynasty and its greatest member, Charlemagne. He directed an eight-year war against the Avars from 788 to 796 that led to the destruction of the kingdom and its great capital. According to Einhard, the entire Avar "nobility died in this war, all their glory departed" (67). He noted further that the Avars had unjustly acquired their wealth and that Charlemagne justly took it from them in a war that brought the Franks more wealth than any other war.

Although the Avars disappeared in the face of the Carolingian attack, they left an important legacy. According to some historians, the Avars introduced important military technology to Europe. The Avars may have used an iron stirrup. The stirrup improved the fighting ability of soldiers on horseback by making them more secure and steady in the saddle. With the stirrup, they could more effectively wield their lances. The Byzantines, who made contact with them before other peoples around the Mediterranean, adopted the iron stirrup for their cavalry by 600, but the stirrup only gradually made its appearance in the barbarian kingdoms. The Avars also used a composite bow in battle that was more effective than other bows, and skilled Avar riders at full gallop could shoot up to twenty arrows a minute. The arrows had heavy three-winged heads and could be fired up to 1500 feet. The bow was shorter than most other simple bows and was made of layers of horn, sinew, and wood that were glued together and reinforced with bone. Although very effective for the Avars, the bows were not widely used by other peoples because they were difficult to produce.

See also Carolingian Dynasty; Charlemagne; Dagobert; Einhard; Franks; Gregory of Tours; Huns; Justinian; Lombards; Merovingian Dynasty

Bibliography

Bury, John B. *History of the Later Roman Empire: From the Death of Theodosius I to the Death of Justinian.* 2 vols. 1923. Reprint, New York: Dover, 1959.

Einhard and Notker the Stammerer. *Two Lives of Charlemagne.* Trans. Lewis Thorpe. Harmondsworth, UK: Penguin, 1981.

Gregory of Tours. *The History of the Franks.* Trans. Lewis Thorpe. Harmondsworth, UK: Penguin, 1982.

Herrin, Judith. *The Formation of Christendom.*
  Princeton: Princeton University Press, 1989.
Wallace-Hadrill, John M. *The Barbarian West, A.D.
  400–1000.* New York: Harper and Row, 1962.

Wolfram, Herwig. *The Roman Empire and Its
  Germanic Peoples.* Trans. Thomas J. Dunlap.
  Berkeley: University of California Press, 1997.

B

Balthild, St. (d. 680)

Wife of King Clovis II (639–657) and regent of Chlotar III (657–683), Balthild was an important figure in the Merovingian kingdom of the second half of the seventh century. A saint, whose feast is celebrated on January 30, Balthild was also a shrewd political leader who successfully guided her son's regency and implemented important political and religious reforms. Often compared with the Merovingian queen Brunhilde (d. 613), Balthild could be as ruthless as her predecessor could when family interests were at stake, but Balthild was not quite so brutal as the earlier Merovingian queen. Indeed, even when their policies seem most similar, Balthild seems to have been motivated less by simple power politics than Brunhilde. Balthild also seemed genuinely committed to the reform of the Frankish church and, according to her biographer, was a devout and pious member of the convent where she spent her last years. Her biography, or saint's life, *The Life of Saint Balthild* or *The Life of the Lady Balthild,* written by a member of her community at Chelles, is the primary source for our knowledge of Balthild's life.

Little is known of Balthild's early life. Her biographer notes that before her marriage to Clovis II she had an "admirable and pious religious way of life" and that she was "kind in her heart, temperate and prudent" (*Vita Dom-nae Balthildis,* 119). She was described as an Anglo-Saxon slave, who was purchased by a Frankish noble to serve at his court. Indeed, so attractive were her personality and appearance that, as her biographer tell us, the noble desired to marry her, but she resisted. "By the true will of God," (120) she eventually married Clovis, son of the great king Dagobert I, and bore him the future kings Chlotar II (584–629) and Childeric II (662–675). She apparently had little direct influence during her husband's reign and lived a life of piety and religious devotion. Her husband recognized this and granted her as a servant Abbot Genisius, who assisted her in works of charity, including donations of food and clothing to the poor as well as grants of money to churches and monasteries.

After Clovis's death in 657, however, Balthild assumed the regency for her son Chlotar III and exercised much power and influence throughout the kingdom. She may also have been instrumental in the reunification of the three parts of the Merovingian kingdom, Austrasia, Neustria, and Burgundy. Under his mother's regency, Chlotar assumed authority over Neustria, and Balthild's close ties with important abbots and bishops in Burgundy strengthened the connection between Neustria and Burgundy. She also appointed a new mayor of the palace for Neustria, further extending her authority in the realm. She also arranged the marriage of her son Childeric with an important noblewoman in Austrasia in 622. The marriage and Balthild's connection with Austrasian nobles paved the way for Childeric's ascension to the Austrasian throne.

Balthild's political success was due in part to the good relationship she had with the clergy in the Merovingian kingdom. She was by all accounts pious and deeply committed to the reform of the Frankish church. She was an ardent supporter of the cult of the saints, and she also actively collected the relics of the saints, perhaps to gain the saints' support for her family. As regent, Balthild was actively involved in the daily affairs of the church and its hierarchy. She appointed bishops to their sees and to important positions in the regency government.

Although she has been blamed for the death of nine bishops, Balthild should not be compared too closely with Brunhilde in this matter. As regent, Balthild was responsible for executions, but only after the letter of the law had been followed; apparently, she never acted arbitrarily. Indeed, any executions she ordered were to preserve the peace and order of the kingdom. Moreover, despite the suggestion that some of these bishops were martyred, Balthild's relations with the bishops were not that bad, and the appointments she made were uniformly good bishops. She also, unlike Brunhilde, was an active opponent of simony and a strong supporter of religious reform. She promoted the more stringent monasticism of the Irish missionaries and founded monasteries, including one at Chelles that followed the pattern of Luxeuil, which had been founded by the great Irish saint Columban. To strengthen monasticism in the kingdom, she ordered that certain monasteries be exempted from episcopal jurisdiction, an act that surely alienated some bishops in her kingdom but also found much support from the bishops as a whole.

By the mid-660s, Balthild had ruled effectively and proved a successful regent for her son, Chlotar, who reached his majority in

664. In that year or the year after, 665, Balthild fell from power. According to the author of the saint's life, Balthild lost power because of her opposition to the murder of the bishop of Paris, Sigobrand. Her struggle against the nobles responsible for the murder proved unsuccessful, however, and she was deposed and allowed to enter the woman's monastery she founded at Chelles. She stayed at Chelles until her death in circa 680. Although she may have felt the convent to be a prison, Balthild's hagiographer assures the reader that the queen was a model of pious devotion at the monastery. She exhibited "great humility," "joy," and a "cheerful heart" even when cleaning the kitchen or the latrines (127). Her piety was so great that as her death approached, according to the author of *The Life of Saint Balthild,* she received a vision in which she ascended a stairway leading to Mary. Although she lived her final years secluded in a monastery in a sort of internal exile, Balthild left an important mark on the Merovingian kingdom, its ruling dynasty, and its church.

See also Anglo-Saxons; Brunhilde; Columban, St.; Dagobert; Merovingian Dynasty

Bibliography

Vita Domnai Balthildis (The Life of Lady Balthild, Queen of the Franks). In *Late Merovingian France: History and Hagiography, 640–720.* By Paul Fouracre and Richard A. Gerberding. Manchester, UK: University of Manchester Press, 1996. Pp. 47–132.

Nelson, Janet L. "Queens as Jezebels: The Careers of Brunhild and Balthild in Merovingian History." In *Medieval Women,* ed. Derek Baker. Oxford: Blackwell, 1978, pp. 31–77.

Schulenburg, Jane Tibbetts. *Forgetful of their Sex: Female Sanctity and Society, ca. 500–1100.* Chicago: University of Chicago Press, 1998.

Wemple, Suzanne. *Women in Frankish Society: Marriage and the Cloister, 500 to 900.* Philadelphia: University of Pennsylvania Press, 1981.

Wood, Ian. *The Merovingian Kingdoms, 451–751.* London: Longman, 1994.

Barbarian Art

The product of the various peoples who entered the Roman world in late antiquity and then established successor kingdoms during the early Middle Ages, barbarian art was often highly stylized and quite accomplished. Indeed, the label *barbarian* or *barbarian art* in some ways demeans the quality of the works that Germanic and other peoples created from the fourth to ninth centuries. Works of art were produced in various media. These artists produced works in ivory and precious metals and gems, creating beautiful book covers of carved ivory or metalwork and jewelry of gold and silver. Weapons, too, were created as works of art. Some of the most impressive examples of barbarian or early medieval art, however, are found in the manuscript illuminations that were produced in monasteries throughout Europe. Both the covers and illustrations of early medieval manuscripts reveal a high level of skill and a well-developed aesthetic sensibility. Barbarian art drew its inspiration from various sources and, especially after the initial period of contact and conversion, mixed Christian, Germanic, and Roman influences to create a distinctive and often beautiful artistic style.

The most predominant form of artistic expression of the migration period and into the early post-Roman period was in metalwork. Artists and artisans created exquisite pieces of jewelry—earrings, rings, bracelets, and brooches—and other things, such as belt buckles, to adorn clothing and the body. There were several categories of the design of metalwork during the migration period. Some pieces were simply abstract and geometric in design; other styles were more clearly representational, and the decoration of the jewelry and other metalwork included animal patterns. The representational, animal style is generally classified in one of two categories, Style I or Style II. Style I, which originated in northern Europe and spread into France by the sixth century, arranged parts of animals or complete but compact animals in a decorative pattern in the metalwork. The ribbon animal style, Style II, was a Lombard innovation that spread to other peoples, and it placed animal figures in elongated, intertwined, continuous, and symmetrical patterns in the metalwork. These traditional designs mixed and mingled with Roman influences, especially among the Visigoths and Lombards, as the various Germanic peoples settled in the former Western Empire and came into fuller contact with Roman artistic traditions.

Other forms of metalwork include that done in bronze and other base metals, used for adorning soldiers. A polychrome cloisonné style, which developed by the fourth century and employed gold and precious gems, was also popular. The polychrome style was used in brooches and to decorate the swords and other weapons of kings and nobles. Gold was also employed by late antique and early medieval artisans to decorate book covers, especially of the more important manuscripts in a monastic, cathedral, or royal library. Borrowing the techniques and styles used for jewelry and other metalwork, craftsmen decorated book covers with figures in gold and other metals, and incorporated precious gems to further enhance the beauty and value of the book and its cover. Because many of the covers were for books of the Bible and other religious texts, the scenes on the covers were often drawn from the history of the church and from the religious texts themselves. Especially popular were decorations portraying Christ in majesty, with the four Evangelists represented by their symbols.

Another medium in which early medieval artists were skilled is ivory, which was used for decoration of book covers as well as liturgical objects. The style of the carved miniatures that adorned important books in the early Middle Ages was at first a continuation of ancient Roman styles. The artists borrowed both technique and subject matter from their Roman predecessors, but as time went on, they began to develop their own unique styles. The carvings often displayed scenes from the Gospels, Psalms, and other

Brooch earrings, bracelets, and Visigothic jewelry, 621–672 A.D. (The Art Archive / Archaeological Museum Madrid / Album / Joseph Martin)

books of the Bible. The carvings themselves reveal variation in style, technique, and talent. Some ivory carvings are noteworthy for their monumental quality, even though they were done on a miniature scale, and others are characterized by more animated figures that recall the illuminations found inside the books. They also reveal the mingling of Christian, Roman, and Germanic influences. The covers often included scenes from the Christian Scriptures or history that were modeled on Roman or Byzantine precedents. The artists also often included decorative borders with geometric or floral patterns. Ivory carvings also adorned reliquaries and other small containers, various liturgical objects such as

crosiers, and even larger architectural items, such as the doors of Santa Sabina in Rome.

Among the most characteristic and magnificent products of early medieval artists are the manuscript illuminations that decorated many of the great books of the period. Although mural painting was practiced, few examples survive—one important exception is the mural from the church of Theodulf of Orléans, which portrays the story of the Ark of the Covenant and reveals Theodulf's sophisticated theory of art—to allow us to judge them, in contrast to the manuscript illuminations. Particularly by the Carolingian period, manuscript illuminators had achieved a highly developed style that merged Christian,

Ark of the Covenant from the Oratory of Theodulf (mosaic), Germigny-des-Pres (Gianni Dagli Orti/Corbis)

Roman, and German traditions, just as the artists in ivory had. Numerous psalters, gospels, and other important texts received luxurious illuminations.

Subjects included Jesus, Mary, the saints and apostles, and other important figures in the history of the church such as the popes. By the Carolingian age, subjects included kings and emperors, including Louis the Pious, Charles the Bald, and Lothar. The illustrations portraying the monarchs stressed key political ideas, emphasizing the religious nature and divine origin of kingship. The illustrations often borrowed from classical models, and some clearly repeat their Roman predecessors, but others reveal a more unique and individual spirit. The illuminations, in many colors and sometimes highlighted with gold, are often dramatic and stately.

Individual letters in the text were some-

times decorated. These letters, the so-called historiated capitals, included images that captured a brief incident or scene or were decorated with abstract designs or floral patterns. The miniatures also included the kind of abstract or geometric ornamentation in the borders and throughout the main image that had been popular in the migration period. Some images as well include the dramatic movement and expression that the migration-period peoples seemed to favor. But Roman styles also shaped the illuminations and defined the way individuals like Louis the Pious or the Evangelist Matthew were portrayed: the former as a Roman ruler, the latter as a classical scribe.

See also Carolingian Renaissance; Charlemagne; Charles the Bald; Clothing; Franks; Ivories; Jewelry and Gems; Lombards; Lothar; Louis the Pious; Weapons and Armor; Visigoths

Bibliography

Beckwith, John. *Early Medieval Art.* London: Thames and Hudson, 1969.

Grabar, André. *Early Medieval Painting from the Fourth to the Eleventh Century.* Lausanne: Skira, 1957.

Hubert, Jean, Jean Porcher, and Wolfgang Fritz Volbach. *The Carolingian Renaissance.* New York: George Braziller, 1970.

Lasko, Peter. *Ars Sacra 800–1200.* 2d ed. New Haven: Yale University Press, 1994.

———. *The Kingdom of the Franks: Northwest Europe before Charlemagne.* London: Thames and Hudson, 1971.

Mütherich, Florentine, and Joachim E. Gaehde. *Carolingian Painting.* New York: George Braziller, 1976.

Ross, Marvin, and Philippe Verdier. *Arts of the Migration Period in the Walters Art Gallery.* Baltimore: Walters Art Gallery, 1961.

Snyder, James. *Medieval Art: Painting, Sculpture, Architecture, 4th–14th Century.* New York: Harry Abrams, 1989.

Bede (c. 673–735)

Traditionally known as the Venerable Bede, Bede is the most important and influential Anglo-Saxon scholar and the most important scholar of the period from the death of Pope Gregory I, called the Great, to the coronation of Charlemagne in 800, a period sometimes known as the Age of Bede. He was a monk at the communities of Wearmouth and Jarrow, which were founded by Benedict Biscop. He was a devout monk who seldom traveled far from his Northumbrian monastery. He was also an accomplished writer and teacher, whose values were transmitted to the Carolingian world by his most famous admirer, Alcuin. He popularized the *anno Domini* dating system and had great influence on the practice of biblical exegesis and history writing. He wrote numerous commentaries on Scripture and other works, but his most famous work is *A History of the English Church and People.*

Much of what is known of Bede comes from an autobiographical note at the end of his history. Born probably in 673 on lands that later belonged to the monastery of Wearmouth, Bede tells us that he was sent to that monastery at the age of seven. He later joined Abbot Ceolfrith at the monastery of Jarrow, which he ruled, together with nearby Wearmouth, after its founder, Benedict Biscop, died. In the anonymous life of Abbot Ceolfrith, we learn that a young boy, generally believed to be Bede, was one of the only survivors, with the abbot, of a plague that struck Jarrow in 686. Bede helped the abbot sing the canonical hours after the disaster and retained a great love for the hours throughout the rest of his life. In a story told by Alcuin, Bede is once supposed to have said, "I know that angels visit the congregation of brethren at the canonical hours, and what if they should not find me among the brethren? Would they not say, 'Where is Bede?'"

Bede himself tells us that he spent his entire life in the monastery, although he did visit the abbey of Lindisfarne and other monasteries, as well as the archbishop of York and King Ceolwulf of Northumbria, who was a patron of learning and who became a monk shortly after Bede's death. He also notes that he became a deacon at age nineteen and a priest at age thirty and that he "observed the regular discipline [of a monk] and sung the choir offices daily in church" (Bede 1981, 336). Although devoted to the monastic life, he explains that his greatest pleasure came from "study, teaching, and writing" (336). From the age of thirty until the age of fifty-nine he "worked, both for my own benefit and that of my brethren, to compile short extracts from the works of the venerable Fathers on Holy Scripture and to comment on their meaning and interpretation" (336). He lists these works in his autobiographical note, and they include commentaries on the books of the Hebrew Bible and Christian Scriptures, letters, saints lives, a history, a martyrology, and a book on hymns.

He continued writing and teaching until his death, four years after writing his autobiographical note. His last work, which he left unfinished when he died on May 25, 735, was an Old English translation of the Gospel of John. He was buried in the south porch of the monastery church but later moved to the main altar. His fame continued long after his death and was the cause of the theft of his relics in 1020. His bones were stolen by a monk of Durham, who buried them at the shrine to St. Cuthbert in Durham. They were later encased in a gold and silver reliquary, and during the Reformation, when the monasteries were pillaged and closed by Henry VIII, his relics were allegedly transferred to the Holy Land.

Bede's fame rests on his talents as biblical commentator, teacher, and historian. He left a great legacy to the generations that followed and had a marked influence on the Carolingian Renaissance because of his writing and teaching. In the Middle Ages, he was perhaps best known for his biblical commentaries. He wrote some twenty-four commentaries on the books of the Bible in an elegant, almost classical Latin, mainly line-by-line explanations of biblical texts, which were commissioned by Bishop Acca of Hexham. Most of his exegetical work is on the books of the Hebrew Bible, including commentaries on Genesis, Song of Songs, Isaiah, Daniel, and Job. He wrote commentaries on the Gospels of Mark and John as well as works on the Epistles and Apocalypse of John. His commentaries on the books of the Bible employed allegorical interpretation of the literal events recorded in Scripture. He borrowed from numerous Christian fathers, including St. Augustine of Hippo, St. Ambrose, and Pope Gregory the Great. Although he often read his sources in compendia rather than the original texts, Bede was very familiar with Jerome's Latin translation of the Bible, the Vulgate.

His talents as a teacher are revealed in two ways. First, they are demonstrated in the importance of his students and the students of his students, such as Alcuin. His talents, along with his interest in teaching, are also revealed in numerous works written as instructional aids. In fact, all his work, including the lives of St. Cuthbert and of the abbots of Wearmouth and Jarrow, have a didactic purpose. He wrote three little books designed specifically for teaching students in monastic schools, one book on spelling and two books on poetry. The books on poetry include a collection of commentaries on an ancient Latin book of grammar and a book in which Bede discusses the language of the Bible. He wrote a book on natural phenomena, influenced by Isidore of Seville, which discusses earthquakes, storms, the planets, stars, and the heavens. He was also a master of the important monastic art of *computus,* the science of calculating dates in the calendar, most importantly Easter. His first attempt to explain this science, written in 703, led to charges of heresy against Bede, which he vigorously denounced in a letter to another monk. A second work, *De temporum ratione,* was much less controversial and much more successful. It became the standard introduction to the science of computus, and through it the practice of dating from the birth of Jesus Christ, rather than from the beginning of the world, became commonplace in medieval Europe.

Bede's most important and well-known work, however, is his *History of the English Church and People,* which he completed in 731. True to his concerns as a teacher, Bede wrote his history so that his reader could follow the good examples therein and act in ways pleasing to God. Organized in five books, the *History* traces the events from the time of Roman Britain, through the period of invasions, the deeds of the Anglo-Saxon kings, and the establishment of Roman Christianity in England. The arrival and triumph of Roman Christianity is one of the important themes of the book and includes some of his more memorable stories, including the tale of Gregory the Great's decision to evangelize England, and the tale of the Synod of Whitby in 664.

The work itself is a true history and not a simple chronicle of events, of the kind his predecessors and contemporaries had compiled. It was an immensely popular work throughout the Middle Ages because of

Bede's powerful style and command of the Latin language. He also was most skilled at handling his sources, and although he included miraculous events, he was a critical reader of his sources. He sifted through a variety of eyewitness, oral, and written traditions and borrowed from writers such as Orosius and Pliny. His *History* was so popular that it was translated into Old English during the reign of King Alfred the Great, and his talents as a historian so great that he has been called the father of English history.

Bede was truly one of the great teachers and writers of the early Middle Ages. A devout monk and ardent supporter of Roman Christianity, Bede was venerated in his own time and is still venerated in ours for his many talents and faith. In 1899 he was declared a Doctor of the Church, and in 1935 he was declared a saint. His tomb in Durham, pillaged in 1541, remains a site of veneration.

See also Alcuin of York; Alfred the Great; Anglo-Saxons; Augustine of Hippo, St.; Benedict Biscop; Carolingian Renaissance; Charlemagne; Gregory the Great; Isidore of Seville

Bibliography

Bede. *Commentary on the Acts of the Apostles.* Trans. Lawrence Martin. Kalamazoo, MI: Cistercian Publications, 1989.

———. *Ecclesiastical History of the English People with Bede's Letter to Egbert and Cuthbert's Letter on the Death of Bede.* Trans. Leo Sherley-Price. Harmondsworth, UK: Penguin, 1991.

Blair, Peter Hunter. *The World of Bede.* Cambridge: Cambridge University Press, 1990.

Brown, George Hardin. *Bede the Venerable.* Boston: Twayne, 1987.

Farmer, David H. *The Age of Bede.* Harmondsworth, UK: Penguin, 1998.

Laistner, Max L. W. *Thought and Letters in Western Europe, A.D. 500–900.* 2d ed. Ithaca, NY: Cornell University Press, 1976.

Lapidge, Michael. *Bede and His World: The Jarrow Lectures, 1958–1993.* 2 vols. Aldershot, UK: Variorum, 1994.

Riché, Pierre. *Education and Culture in the Barbarian West: From the Sixth to the Eighth Century.* Trans. John Contreni. Columbia: University of South Carolina Press, 1978.

Stenton, Frank M. *Anglo-Saxon England.* 3d ed. Oxford: Clarendon, 1971.

Belisarius (c. 500–c. 565)

Leading general and loyal supporter of Justinian for more than forty years, Belisarius fought numerous campaigns against the Persians, the Vandals in Africa, and the Goths in Italy. Completely loyal to Justinian throughout his life, despite the suspicions held by the emperor that sent Belisarius into disgrace, the general helped save Justinian during the Nika Revolt and was critical to Justinian's efforts to reconquer Italy and other sections of the Western Empire that were governed at that time by barbarian kings. His successes, however, sometimes worsened Justinian's fears about his powerful and popular general. Indeed, the respect contemporaries felt for Belisarius is best illustrated in the pages of the sixth-century Byzantine historian Procopius, the general's military secretary. Best known for his scandalous accounts of Justinian and Theodora, Procopius portrayed Belisarius in the least unfavorable light in the *Secret History* and in some ways made Belisarius the great hero of *The History of the Wars*.

Born in a village in modern western Bulgaria in circa 500, perhaps as late as 505, Belisarius was a Romanized Thracian, with possible Gothic ancestry, of modest, but not peasant, circumstances. He entered the military as an officer, and his talents and dazzling personality must have quickly come to the attention of Justinian, then Master of Soldiers, who appointed him to his staff. In the mid-520s, Belisarius, still in his early or mid-twenties, was given a military command against Rome's great eastern rival, Persia. His early command met with little success, but in 529, Justinian, now emperor, appointed Belisarius Master of Soldiers with a command over the eastern frontier. Further campaigns in the east met with little success, but Belisarius demonstrated great personal courage and saved an important imperial city from conquest by the Persians. Recognizing his value, Justinian had Belisarius marry Antonina, an old friend of Justinian's wife Theodora. His greatest early accomplishment, however, was the part he played in the Nika Revolt in 532. Belisarius remained loyal to the emperor during this moment of great crisis. He volunteered to lead a garrison to capture the rival emperor, Hypatius, an enterprise that failed because he met some imperial bodyguards. Despite this setback, Belisarius played a part in the final suppression of the revolt and commanded a group of Germanic mercenary soldiers who massacred the rebels in the capital of Constantinople. Belisarius's demonstration of loyalty and military ability revealed his full worth to the emperor.

His presence in Constantinople in 532 was a lucky accident; Justinian had recalled him from the east to give him charge of the forces to be sent against the Vandals of North Africa. The Vandals, previously thought to be a potential ally in Justinian's efforts to recover Italy, were to be the first step in a grand scheme of conquest. In 533 Belisarius invaded the Vandal kingdom and quickly smashed it. In two great battles, Belisarius and his well-trained imperial armies and cohort of Hunnish auxiliaries overwhelmed their Vandal opponents. At the second battle, Belisarius displayed his abilities for strategy and tactics. By forcing battle he managed to retake the initiative, and his assault forced the Vandals from the field, their camp, and the pages of history. Indeed, the Vandals as a people disappeared after their defeat by Belisarius, and imperial authority was restored in North Africa. His achievement was so highly regarded in Constantinople that he was awarded a triumph— the ancient Roman ceremonial parade accorded to victorious generals—through the capital's streets.

Belisarius provided further service for Justinian's great plan to reconquer the Western Empire, leading imperial armies, although sometimes with inadequate support, into Italy. In the early 530s the Gothic kingdom of the late Theodoric the Great was rent by conflict between his daughter Amalaswintha and much of the Gothic nobility over the management of her regency of her son Athalaric and of relations with Constantinople. Amalaswintha had much support from Justinian, and her murder, accomplished according to Procopius with the complicity of Theodora, provided the emperor with the justification he needed to invade Italy.

In 535, in the midst of the turmoil among the Goths of Italy, Justinian ordered Belisarius to invade. His opening campaigns in Sicily and southern Italy were surprisingly easy, as Roman militias welcomed the imperial armies and Gothic commanders were eager to negotiate. Belisarius reached Rome by the end of 536; in the following year he faced stiffer resistance, from the new Gothic king, Witigis, who had begun to rally the Goths in 536. Witigis laid siege to Rome in 537 and 538, and despite great hardship and starvation Belisarius was able to hold the city. His troops were able to kill many of the besiegers, and their spirits were revived by reinforcements, which allowed Belisarius to take the offensive against Witigis in 538. By 540, after his efforts to attract support from the Franks and Lombards failed, Witigis was forced to submit to Belisarius, who had surrounded and besieged his rival at Ravenna. There is also the suggestion that Belisarius was offered royal and imperial titles at this point by the Goths and his own soldiers, a possibility supported by Justinian's cool reception of his victorious commander. Nonetheless, Belisarius returned to Constantinople after successfully establishing the imperial presence once again.

The Gothic Wars, however, did not end in 540, even if Belisarius decreed that they had. Another new Gothic king, Totila, took the offensive against Justinian, and his successes forced the emperor to recall his loyal general. From 544 to 548, Belisarius was once again leading Roman armies, with only limited support from Constantinople, against the enemy Goths in Italy. Despite Justinian's limited support of his general, Belisarius managed some success against Totila and even took Rome back from the Gothic king and managed to tilt the struggle back in Constantinople's favor. Achieving some few victories, Belisarius left Italy in late 548 with the conquest incomplete, leaving it to Narses the Eunuch to ultimately complete the task.

Belisarius had one final moment of glory in the service of Justinian and the empire. In 559 an army of Huns invaded from the north and came within thirty miles of Constantinople. Justinian called on Belisarius to save the city, and, with only a small army, he did just that. Persuading the Huns that his army was much larger than it was, Belisarius convinced them to depart. After that victory Belisarius resumed his retirement, only to fall into disgrace again in 562 for alleged involvement in a plot against Justinian. He was restored to favor the following year and died two years later, after a long career in defense of the empire, still loyal to an emperor who did not always appreciate him.

See also Amalaswintha; Gothic Wars; Huns; Justinian; Narses the Eunuch; Ostrogoths; Procopius; Theodora; Theodoric the Great; Vandals; Witigis

Bibliography
Browning, Robert. *Justinian and Theodora,* rev. ed. London: Thames and Hudson, 1987.
Bury, John B. *History of the Later Roman Empire: From the Death of Theodosius I to the Death of Justinian.* Vol. 2. 1923. Reprint, New York: Dover, 1959.
Heather, Peter. *The Goths.* Oxford: Blackwell Publisher, 1996.
Llewellyn, Peter. *Rome in the Dark Ages.* New York: Barnes and Noble, 1993.
Procopius. *The History of the Wars; Secret History,* 4 vols. Trans. H. B. Dewing. Cambridge, MA: Harvard University Press, 1914–1924.
Randers-Pehrson, Justine Davis. *Barbarians and Romans: The Birth Struggle of Europe,* A.D. 400–700. Norman: University of Oklahoma Press, 1983.
Wolfram, Herwig. *History of the Goths.* Trans. Thomas J. Dunlap. Berkeley: University of California Press, 1988.
———. *The Roman Empire and Its Germanic Peoples.* Trans. Thomas J. Dunlap. Berkeley: University of California Press, 1997.

Benedict Biscop (d. 689)

Founder of the two great Northumbrian monasteries of Wearmouth and Jarrow, Benedict Biscop was a leading intellectual and monastic leader of the later seventh century, who laid the foundation for the so-called Northumbrian Renaissance. A frequent pilgrim to Rome, where he collected relics and other treasures and, most importantly, books, Benedict, known as Biscop Baducing before his monastic conversion, left an important legacy for Anglo-Saxon learning. The libraries he established at the monasteries of Wearmouth and Jarrow provided the books necessary for the work of numerous scholars, including Alcuin, who transferred this great learning—and the desire for books—to the empire of Charlemagne and created the basis for the Carolingian Renaissance.

A Northumbrian noble in the service of King Oswy, Benedict Biscop received numerous estates appropriate to his rank and service, estates that were of great importance later in his life. The kingdom of Northumbria was a meeting place of Celtic and Roman Christianity and the site of the important Synod of Whitby in 664, at which Roman Christianity triumphed. Benedict's experience in Northumbria exposed him to important influences from both forms of Christianity. He was a lifelong supporter of Roman Christianity, as witnessed by his numerous trips to Rome, and he looked to Rome for books, relics, and the proper rule of religious life. But he also was probably influenced by elements of Celtic Christianity, especially the tradition of *peregrinatio,* the tradition of pilgrimage or missionary activity far from home. This influence would help to explain his numerous trips to the Continent, the first of which was a trip to Rome with Wilfrid of Ripon in 652–653, when Benedict was roughly twenty-five years old.

Although the first trip was not without significance—or controversy, as Wilfrid and Benedict separated at Lyons—Benedict's second trip to Rome was even more critical for the life of Benedict. Sometime after 657, in the company of Alchfirth, son of King Oswy and friend of Wilfrid, Benedict journeyed to the Continent. From Rome he went to the important monastery of Lérins, where he received the tonsure and learned the monastic life. When Benedict later founded his own monasteries, he drew from his experience at Lérins, a place where many of the great ancient and early medieval Irish monastic leaders had stayed and shaped the monastic life. But as important and influential as Lérins was, it could not hold Benedict permanently; he again heard the call of Rome, after probably two years at the monastery. While in Rome, Benedict was sent back to England. He accompanied the new archbishop of Canterbury, Theodore of Tarsus. Departing Rome in the spring of 668 and arriving about a year later, Theodore and Benedict took up residence in Canterbury. Benedict resided in the monastery founded by Augustine of Canterbury in the early years of the century for the next two years, until the arrival of the community's new abbot.

In 671–672 Benedict made another trip to Rome, but this trip may have been taken with the purpose of acquiring the materials necessary to found a new monastic community. Earlier trips to Rome had been taken so that Benedict could improve his understanding of the faith at its capital. But in the early 670s Benedict had absorbed a great deal from his earlier trips and had also had extensive monastic experience at Lérins and Canterbury. While in Rome Benedict collected books of all sorts that would be useful for the monastic library, and also collected books at Vienne and in the Rhone Valley. The books, along with relics and other materials collected, provided the foundation for his first great monastic community, Wearmouth.

The foundation at Wearmouth was the first of two important monasteries Benedict established. He founded the monastery on land he had received from his old friend King Ecgfrith, who had succeeded Oswy in 671, and with the collaboration of Ceolfrith, a Northumbrian noble who like Benedict had left the secular life for the monastic. Benedict's many trips and connections on the continent continued to serve him in the construction of the monastery, which began in the year 674. Leaving Ceolfrith in charge, Benedict returned to the continent, where he hired builders and masons from a friend in Francia. He also recruited glassmakers to put windows in the church and other monastic buildings at Wearmouth. When the buildings of the monastery were completed or well on their way, Benedict, joined by Ceolfrith and most likely a large group, returned to Rome yet again to acquire even greater learning in the faith so that he could better prepare a rule for his new community. He also accumulated more books for the library at Wearmouth and received an exemption from the pope that allowed the monks to elect their abbots without outside interference. He was joined on his return to the monastery by Abbot John, the archcantor of the church of St. Peter in Rome, who taught the monks of Wearmouth the Roman method of singing and, possibly, the Roman style of handwriting.

The success of Wearmouth inspired Ecgfrith to grant Benedict more territory at Jarrow, which was some seven miles distant from the original foundation; the new house was established in 681. It was colonized by a group of monks from Wearmouth, possibly including the great historian and scholar Bede, which was led by Ceolfrith, who became the abbot of the new community. Benedict again went to Rome and appointed a relative as abbot of Wearmouth, but Ceolfrith assumed the superior position in Benedict's absence and oversaw the election of a new abbot for Wearmouth when Benedict's relative died. The two communities were ruled separately at first, but they remained very closely connected. After the second abbot of Wearmouth died, Ceolfrith was elected as abbot and thus ruled both houses, and Benedict declared that the two communities should be ruled by one abbot.

Benedict took one final trip to Rome in the mid-680s to acquire still more books for the monasteries of Wearmouth and Jarrow. He died on January 12, 689, sometime after returning from his final Roman pilgrimage. His legacy in England was a great one. He strengthened English ties to Rome and the continent and passed his devotion to Rome on to his many disciples. He established two of the great monastic communities of medieval England and created a library at Wearmouth and Jarrow that inspired generations of Anglo-Saxons scholars, including the greatest of all, Bede. Benedict's monastic foundations influenced cultural developments in England and, through Alcuin, on the continent for generations to come and contributed to renaissances in Northumbria and the Carolingian kingdom.

See also Alcuin of York; Anglo-Saxons; Bede; Augustine of Canterbury, St.; Carolingian Renaissance; Synod of Whitby; Wilfrid of Ripon

Bibliography

Bede. *Ecclesiastical History of the English People with Bede's Letter to Egbert and Cuthbert's Letter on the Death of Bede.* Trans. Leo Sherley-Price. Harmondsworth, UK: Penguin, 1991.

Blair, Peter Hunter. *The World of Bede.* Cambridge: Cambridge University Press, 1990.

Laistner, Max L. W. *Thought and Letters in Western Europe, A.D. 500 to 900,* 2d ed. Ithaca, NY: Cornell University Press, 1976.

Riché, Pierre. *Education and Culture in the Barbarian West: From the Sixth through the Eighth Century.* Trans. John Contreni. Columbia: University of South Carolina Press, 1976.

Stenton, Frank M. *Anglo-Saxon England.* 3d ed. Oxford: Clarendon, 1971.

Benedict of Aniane (c. 750–821)

A Visigothic monk and reformer, Benedict of Aniane was a close advisor of the Carolingian emperor Louis the Pious. He helped establish the Rule of Benedict of Nursia as the official rule of monastic life in the Carolingian Empire in the early years of the reign of Louis. His implementation and interpretation of the Rule, moreover, involved a reform of monastic life that is traditionally seen as the precursor to the great monastic reform movement of Cluny in the tenth and eleventh centuries.

The son of a Gothic count of southern Gaul, Benedict, or Witiza as he was originally known, was sent to the court of the Frankish king Charlemagne to be educated and taught the use of arms. While on campaign in Italy with Charlemagne, however, Benedict nearly drowned, and the incident forced him to examine himself. His soul-searching led him to abandon the world for the monastic life, and in 774 he joined the monastery of Saint-Seine, near Dijon, France. His life there was unsatisfactory, and his extreme asceticism led the abbot to criticize him, to which Benedict, according to his biographer, responded, "the Rule of blessed Benedict as for beginners and weak persons, he strove to climb up to the precepts of blessed Basil and the rule of blessed Pachomius" (Ardo 220). Indeed, Benedict revealed his single-minded determination early in his monastic career, as well as his desire for a better, purer monastic life than existed in the "mixed rule" communities of the Carolingian realm. In 780, Benedict left the community of Saint-Seine to found a new monastery on his father's property in Aniane, near Montpellier, France, and probably about that same time changed his name to Benedict. Despite his earlier interest in the great eremitic monks, Benedict established the Rule of Benedict of Nursia at his monastery, but, true to his earlier zeal, strictly followed the rule of his namesake. With his dedication to Benedict's rule, he broke with the contemporary mixed rule traditions of Carolingian monasticism; nevertheless, the devotion and discipline of his house attracted numerous followers. Over the next few decades, Benedict and his followers spread the strict observance of the rule to many monasteries throughout Aquitaine and Septimania in southwestern France. Moreover, in 802 Benedict participated in a council of bishops and abbots meeting at Aachen to discuss the Rule of Benedict, and in fact the later Benedict was the most important discussant at the council. His activities surely brought him to the attention of the king of Aquitaine, Louis the Pious, whose mentor Benedict became.

Shortly after Louis became sole emperor following his father's death in 814, he called Benedict from Aquitaine because of "the fame of his life and saintliness," according to a contemporary chronicle. Benedict was to be the emperor's religious advisor and was to introduce throughout the entire empire the reforms implemented in Aquitaine. Benedict was installed in a new monastery, which Louis built for him at Inde, near the imperial palace at Aachen. The monastery, consecrated in 817, was not only the residence of Louis's chief religious advisor but also the model for monastic life in the empire. Benedict welcomed monks and abbots from throughout the realm and instructed them on the Rule of Benedict. Perhaps of even greater importance was Benedict's role at two councils at Aachen in 816 and 817, at which monastic life in the Carolingian Empire underwent dramatic reform. Under Benedict's direction, and with the support of the emperor, the council reformed the life of all religious in the empire and established the Rule of Benedict as the standard for all monasteries in the empire, ending the long-standing tradition of the mixed rule.

Benedict's career is important for two reasons. First, Benedict successfully imposed the Rule of Benedict of Nursia on all the monasteries (with a few exceptions) in the Carolingian Empire. His activities are important also because the original Benedictine rule was reformed by Benedict, a reform that foreshadowed the reforms at Cluny in the next century. Among other things, Benedict of Aniane's reforms altered the relationship between the abbot and his monks. On the one hand, the reforms limited the abbot's authority, as well as the community's independence, by subjecting both to an overall "abbot-general," whose authority superseded that of the local abbot. The reforms also granted the abbot certain privileges that the original rule had not.

The reforms of 816 and 817 also enforced a stricter rule of cloister, which not only limited the monks' access to the outside world but also severely restricted the access of the outside world to the monastery. Most notably, the reforms eliminated access to the monastery school for the laity or secular clergy. But the most important reform involved the increase in the liturgical duties of the monks. The original Benedict had sought to establish a balance in the lives of the monks between labor and prayer, but Benedict of Aniane dramatically increased the amount of time the monks were expected to pray, chant the Psalms, and perform divine services. Benedict's death in 821 and the civil war and division in the Carolingian Empire beginning in the 830s limited the impact of his reforms, but he remains important for his efforts on behalf of the Rule of Benedict and the foundation he put in place for later monastic reform movements.

See also Benedict of Nursia, St.; Carolingian Dynasty; Charlemagne; Louis the Pious; Visigoths

Bibliography
Ardo. "The Life of Saint Benedict, Abbot of Aniane and of Inde." Trans. Allen Cabaniss. In *Soldiers of Christ: Saints and Saints' Lives from Late Antiquity to the Early Middle Ages,* edited by Thomas F. X. Noble and Thomas Head. University Park: Pennsylvania State University Press, 1995, pp. 213–254.
Knowles, David. *Christian Monasticism.* New York: McGraw Hill, 1969.
Lawrence, Clifford H. *Medieval Monasticism: Forms of Religious Life in Western Europe in the Middle Ages,* 2d ed. London: Longman, 1989.

Riché, Pierre. *The Carolingians: A Family Who Forged Europe.* Trans. Michael Idomir Allen. Philadelphia: University of Pennsylvania Press, 1993.

———. *Education and Culture in the Barbarian West: From the Sixth through the Eighth Century.* Trans. John Contreni. Columbia: University of South Carolina Press, 1976.

Sullivan, Richard. "What Was Carolingian Monasticism? The Plan of St. Gall and the History of Monasticism." In *After Rome's Fall: Narrators and Sources of Early Medieval History,* ed. Alexander Callander Murray. Toronto: University of Toronto Press, 1998, pp. 251–287.

Wallace-Hadrill, John M. *The Frankish Church.* Oxford: Clarendon, 1983.

Benedict of Nursia, St. (c. 480–c. 547)

Founder of Western monasticism, whose Rule (code of behavior, spiritual life, and monastic organization) was the most influential rule in the early Middle Ages. Little is known of his life, except what is found in the pages of Pope Gregory the Great's *Dialogues,* which were written nearly a half-century after Benedict's death. Gregory's life was a model of hagiography and remained an important source for later monastic writers. Benedict's personality, however, can best be discerned from his Rule, which reveals the intelligence and humanity of the saint, who made allowances in his code for human weakness. His monastic foundation at Monte Cassino, roughly eighty miles south of Rome, was an influential house until its destruction by the Lombards in 589 (the community was reestablished in 720), but Benedict's influence continued, as his Rule became the basic rule for most monks in the post-Roman world. Indeed, during the reign of the Carolingian dynasty and under their direction, the Benedictine Rule became the primary rule for monks.

Born, according to tradition, in 480 in Nursia, about seventy miles north of Rome,

Benedict, according to Gregory the Great, was "blessed also with God's grace [and] in boyhood he showed mature understanding, for he kept his heart detached from every pleasure with a strength of character far beyond his years" (Geary 1989, 215). Gregory also tells us that Benedict's family sent him to Rome for a liberal education, which suggests that Benedict was from a fairly prosperous family. In Rome, however, Benedict saw that the other students had fallen into vice, and fearing that he might do the same and offend God, he turned his back on worldly learning. He also renounced his family and wealth and took up the religious life in a cave in Subiaco, about thirty-five miles outside Rome, in circa 500. He was assisted during his stay at Subiaco by a monk from a nearby monastery named Romanus, who brought Benedict some food on occasion. Moreover, Benedict began to attract the attention of others and gathered numerous disciples. And he was elected abbot by the monks of a nearby abbey. Although called unanimously by the monks, he soon left the community because the monks found his rule too strenuous and tried to poison him. According to Gregory, Benedict was saved by a miracle when the pitcher with the poisoned wine shattered after Benedict made the sign of the cross over it.

After the attempted poisoning, Benedict left the community and took up the path that led to the establishment of his famous rule and community at Monte Cassino. He returned to Subiaco with several companions to establish a new community. He was again the target of poisoning, this time by a jealous local priest, and he also attracted a great number of followers. After the second attempt on his life, Benedict founded his famous monastery on a mountain some 1,500 feet high. He had great success at this monastery, which he built on top of an old pagan shrine, attracting many monks and preaching to the people in the surrounding region. According to Gregory the Great, Benedict performed more than a few miracles while at the monastery, including saving one the monks of Monte Cassino from drowning. He also sent a group of monks to found another monastery, and he met once a year with his sister Scholastica, who was a nun in a nearby community. After establishing his house and laying the foundation for Western monasticism, Benedict died, according to tradition on March 21, 547.

Benedict's greatest accomplishment was the composition of the Rule of Benedict, a code guiding the life of the monks and the organization and government of the monastery. The Rule evolved over time and was probably composed in its final from, a prologue and seventy-three chapters, in the later 530s. Although the Rule was once thought to have been an independent creation by Benedict, it is now recognized that he borrowed heavily from the Rule of the Master, the anonymously written monastic rule composed around 500. But comparison of the two demonstrates Benedict's practical wisdom, humanity, and organizational ability. The Rule of the Master is a long and often rambling blueprint for monastic life, but Benedict's Rule is much briefer and more focused. Benedict's Rule opens with a discussion promoting the ascetic life and outlining the virtues a monk should cultivate, particularly obedience and humility. The next section outlines the daily routine of divine service, prayer, and readings of Scripture. There are chapters on the election of the abbot and other officers of the community in the next section of the Rule. Benedict also regulated hours of sleep, manual labor, and reading for the monks in his community, and provided guidelines for meals and for monastic discipline.

The daily routine for the monks was clearly outlined by Benedict and was all focused on service to God. But the Rule is important not only for its religious devotionalism but also for its flexibility and humanity. Indeed, it is these last two characteristics that help explain the success of the Rule. Benedict not only included guidelines for the recruitment and training of monks, but also provided guidelines for the duties of the abbot. Benedict's

St. Benedict of Nursia (ca. 480–543), the founder of Western monasticism, ca. 510 (Hulton Archive)

abbot was to be a father figure, who could be stern and demanding when the situation required, but who was also to be consoling and encouraging as circumstances dictated. Benedict intended that the abbot respond to the needs of the monks as well as rule over them. He also recognized that not all monks were on the same level and established different guidelines for different monks. For example, he allowed different measures of wine and food for those who were sick or elderly, as compared to those who were in better physical or spiritual condition.

The wisdom and humanity of the Rule of Benedict account for its ultimate triumph in Western monasticism, but in the first two centuries of its existence it competed with other monastic rules or was used in combination with them. Indeed, there are few references to Benedict and his Rule in the sixth century beyond the important account by Gregory the Great. Benedict surely had influence in the sixth century, however, because Gregory composed part of his life of Benedict with the aid of four monks who knew the saint, and it is possible that St. Columban knew Benedict's Rule. But in general in the seventh and eighth centuries, Benedict shared influence with Columban and other monastic lawgivers such as Caesarius of Arles. It was commonplace to combine elements from the Benedictine, Celtic, and other monastic traditions in the so-called *regula mixta* (mixed rule) in the monasteries of barbarian Europe.

It is possible that Benedictine monasticism was exported to England by the mission Gregory sent under the direction of St. Augustine of Canterbury, but this is widely disputed by scholars today. But even if Augustine did not bring the Rule, it did arrive by the mid-seventh century; there is evidence for its introduction to Northumbria in 660, and both Benedict Biscop, founder of Wearmouth and Jarrow, and the Venerable Bede, the great Anglo-Saxon scholar, were greatly influenced by the Rule of Benedict. The Anglo-Saxon missionaries of the eighth century, especially St. Boniface, brought the Rule with them on their evangelical missions to the continent. The reform activities of these missionaries greatly influenced the Frankish church and the leaders of Frankish society, especially the great rulers Charlemagne and Louis the Pious.

Under Charlemagne, the Benedictine Rule was increasingly important in the empire he established, and it was recognized by the great ruler as the best rule for the monastic life. His esteem for the Rule was so great that he sent an abbot from the realm to Monte Cassino in 787 to obtain an authentic copy. Although important to Charlemagne, the Rule of Benedict was established throughout the realm as the official monastic rule only by his son Louis the Pious. With the help of his close friend and advisor, Benedict of Aniane, Louis imposed the Rule on all monasteries of the empire by the decrees of two councils held in Aachen in 816 and 817. Over the next several centuries, the Rule of Benedict was the official standard of all monasteries, and it was the foundation for major monastic reforms at Cluny in the tenth century and at Cîteaux in the twelfth.

See also Anglo-Saxons; Augustine of Canterbury, St.; Bede; Benedict of Aniane; Benedict Biscop; Boniface, St.; Caesarius of Arles; Carolingian Dynasty; Charlemagne; Columban, St.; Gregory the Great; Lombards; Louis the Pious

Bibliography

Fry, Timothy, ed. and trans. *RB 1980: The Rule of Benedict in Latin and English with Notes.* Collegeville, MN: Liturgical Press, 1981.

Gregory the Great. *Life and Miracles of St. Benedict (Book Two of the Dialogues).* Trans. Odo J. Zimmerman and Benedict Avery. Collegeville, MN: St. John's Abbey Press, 1949.

Farmer, David Hugh, ed. *Benedict's Disciples.* Leominster, UK: Fowler Wright, 1980.

Geary, Patrick J., ed. *Readings in Medieval History.* Peterborough, Ontario: Broadview Press, 1989.

Knowles, David. *Christian Monasticism.* New York: McGraw Hill, 1969.

Lawrence, Clifford H. *Medieval Monasticism: Forms of Religious Life in Western Europe in the Middle Ages.* 2d ed. London: Longman, 1989.

Riché, Pierre. *The Carolingians: A Family Who Forged Europe.* Trans. Michael Idomir Allen. Philadelphia: University of Pennsylvania Press, 1993.

————. *Education and Culture in the Barbarian West: From the Sixth through the Eighth Century.* Trans. John Contreni. Columbia: University of South Carolina Press, 1976.

Sullivan, Richard. "What Was Carolingian Monasticism? The Plan of St. Gall and the History of Monasticism." In *After Rome's Fall: Narrators and Sources of Early Medieval History,* ed. Alexander Callander Murray Toronto: University of Toronto Press, 1998, pp. 251–287.

Wallace-Hadrill, John M. *The Frankish Church.* Oxford: Clarendon, 1983.

Beowulf

The greatest literary work of Anglo-Saxon literature, *Beowulf* is a heroic epic poem of 3182 lines that contains a mixture of history, legend, and myth. The poem, the earliest extant long poem written in English, describes the legendary feats of the great hero, Beowulf, who, unlike other characters in the poem, is known only from this poem. Divided into two parts, *Beowulf* describes the title character's great victories over Grendel, his mother, and a fire-breathing dragon. The poem addresses the great heroic ideals of courage, loyalty, and service, and also matters of life and death. Although the poem conveys the values of pagan Germanic culture, it was probably written at a Christian court; it expresses belief in the Christian God and upholds the Christian ideals of good against evil.

The events of the poem take place in the fifth and sixth century—Gregory of Tours, the sixth-century historian, describes the raid into Francia by Hygelac, Beowulf's uncle, in his *History of the Franks*—and begins at the court of the Danish king Hrothgar. The poem opens with the genealogy of Hrothgar, the great and good king of the Danes who brought peace and prosperity to the kingdom and built the great hall Heorot. In his mead hall, Hrothgar and his warriors celebrate the good things that Hrothgar has brought, and the king gives his warriors gifts of gold. The good times at Heorot are suddenly disrupted by the monster Grendel, who is of the line of Cain, which has been cursed by God and exiled from humanity. Hearing the sounds of revelry at Heorot, Grendel is enraged and attacks the hall, killing and eating Hrothgar's warriors. Grendel's reign of terror lasts twelve years before the arrival of the great hero Beowulf, who offers his services to the king. Although his talents are questioned by Unferth, one of the king's counselors, Hrothgar welcomes Beowulf as his hero. That evening Grendel returns and devours one of Beowulf's men before reaching for Beowulf himself. But the monster meets the unexpected—a hero whose grip is greater than any man's. A terrible struggle follows, as the two enemies fight each other with their bare hands. Heorot suffers great damage, and the Danes fear for their hero. But Grendel cannot overcome Beowulf. The great warrior's grip holds firm, and Grendel is able to get away only by having his arm torn off. The monster then flees to his home, where he bleeds to death.

Beowulf's victory is welcomed by Hrothgar, who rewards his hero handsomely, and a great celebration ensues in Heorot, in which Beowulf is praised and songs are sung that foreshadow the dark events to come. Not everyone rejoices at the death of Grendel, however. Upon learning of her son's death, Grendel's mother is enraged and moves quickly to avenge her son's death. She too attacks the great hall of Heorot, and, although she is not as powerful or ferocious as her son, brings great destruction with her and manages to kill and eat one of the Danes before being driven back to her home in a lake. Beowulf is then asked to defend Hrothgar once again.

This time, uncertain of what he will face, Beowulf dons full battle armor and carries a sword offered by Unferth. Beowulf has to dive into a lake and swim a full day to reach his enemy's lair. Before he arrives, the she-monster senses his coming and reaches out to take him, beginning to fight him underwater. She drags him into her lair, where he now can fight without the weight of the water. A mighty struggle again takes place, and Beowulf strikes his foe with the sword from Unferth, but it proves of no use against the monster. Beowulf is in dire straits, as Grendel's mother nearly overwhelms him. He manages to take hold of the giant's sword he sees on the wall and slays Grendel's mother with it. Although the sword kills his enemy, it melts like thawing ice because of the great heat of the monster's blood, which then bubbles up to the surface.

The sight of the blood greatly dismays Beowulf's men, who fear the worst. But these fears are quickly laid to rest by the return of Beowulf, who bears the head of Grendel, which he cut off after his victory over the monster's mother. Once again Beowulf returns to Heorot to receive the thanks and praise of Hrothgar, whose speech carries a warning for the future. After the celebration Beowulf takes leave, in a moving scene with Hrothgar, and departs for his home in Geatland. Once he arrives in his homeland he is warmly received by his king, Hygelac, who learns of Beowulf's great success in Denmark.

The second part of the poem begins some time later, after Beowulf has ruled the Geats for fifty years. Although Beowulf has ruled the Geats well, his path to the throne was marked by the tragic deaths of Hygelac and his son and by bitter wars with the Frisians and Swedes. Under Beowulf there is peace, but that peace is suddenly interrupted by the appearance of a fire-breathing dragon, who terrorizes the kingdom and brings great destruction, burning houses, forts, and Beowulf's own great hall. The dragon has risen in anger because a slave of one of Beowulf's warriors stole a cup of gold from the dragon's great treasure hoard. Once again, the great hero Beowulf prepares to do battle with a powerful foe. Dressing in a suit of armor and bearing a mighty sword and a shield of iron—instead of the traditional shield of wood—Beowulf marches out to meet the dragon. He is joined by twelve warriors, and then by one more (the warrior who forced the slave to steal the cup). After declaring that it is his duty alone to fight the dragon, Beowulf begins his terrible and final battle with the dragon.

Beowulf has finally met his match and is overwhelmed by the dragon, whose breath of fire greatly wounds Beowulf. In the heat of the battle, all but one of his warriors, Wiglaf, abandon Beowulf in his hour of need. Wiglaf denounces the cowardice of his fellow warriors and enters the struggle with the dragon. Together, Beowulf and Wiglaf are able to defeat the horrible creature, but only after Beowulf has been fatally wounded. Beowulf then offers a final speech and looks over the fantastic treasure hoard of the dead dragon. After his death, prophecies are made about the impending destruction of the Geats by their rivals, who will take advantage of the Geats after the death of their great king. The poem concludes with the funeral of Beowulf, whose warriors ride around his tomb singing a dirge and lamenting their loss.

The poem was preserved in one manuscript from about the year 1000, and was first published in a modern edition in 1815. The original composition of the poem is uncertain, but most scholars believe that it was composed in the early eighth century at a court in Bede's Northumbria, although there are those who argue for a late eighth-century composition at the court of King Offa of Mercia. Those who support an early date argue that a Scandinavian hero would not have appeared in an English poem at a time when Viking warriors were invading the island. Of course, others suggest that the poet may have hoped to appeal to the invaders. The date of composition is important for both the understanding of the poet and the poem, but once again there is little agreement among scholars on those matters. Most *Beowulf* scholars are split between those who believe that the poem was composed in a predominantly oral culture or those who believe it was composed in a literate culture.

The values embodied in the poem and its hero provide support for both sides. The nature of the language of the poem, the interest in material wealth—helmets, swords, jewelry—these suggest the possibility of an oral environment. The expression of belief in a creator God, references to the Hebrew Bible, especially the line of Cain, and Christian values of good and evil suggest composition in a literate culture. The answer is probably a mixture of both: The poem may well have been composed at a Christian court in an oral culture, which had absorbed the values of the literate culture by the time the poem was committed to parchment. Finally, interpretation of the poem is complicated by its uncertain origins. Despite variety of opinion, it is certain that the meaning of *Beowulf* is shaped by its origins in a superficially Christianized environment. The poem advocates the epic values of bravery, honor, and fidelity, but within the framework of belief in the Christian God and the importance of the struggle against evil.

See also Anglo-Saxons; Bede; Gregory of Tours; Offa of Mercia

Bibliography
Alexander, Michael, trans. *Beowulf.* Harmondsworth, UK: Penguin, 1983.
Heaney, Seamus, trans. *Beowulf: A New Verse Translation.* New York: Farrar Straus and Giroux, 2000.
Baker, Peter S., ed. *Beowulf: Basic Readings.* New York: Garland, 1995.
Bjork, Robert E., and John D. Niles, eds. *A Beowulf Handbook.* Lincoln: University of Nebraska Press, 1997.
Chambers, Raymond W. *Beowulf: An Introduction to the Study the Poem with a Discussion of the Stories of Offa and Finn.* 3d ed., supplement by C.L. Wrenn. Cambridge: Cambridge University Press, 1959.
Hasenfratz, Robert J. *Beowulf Scholarship: An Annotated Bibliography, 1979–1990.* New York: Garland, 1993.
Tolkien, J. R. R. "*Beowulf*: The Monsters and the Critics." *Proceedings of the British Academy 22* (1936): 245–295.

Bertrada (d. 783)

The wife of Pippin the Short, the first Carolingian king, and mother of Charlemagne, the first Carolingian emperor, Bertrada surely played an important role in the Carolingian kingdom. At the very least, she fulfilled the traditional role of royal wives by producing an heir; she bore Pippin three sons, two of whom survived, and a daughter. Her activities may well have stretched beyond the traditional to include support for Pippin's religious reforms. She also was involved in diplomacy after her husband's death and strove to maintain peace between her two sons, Charlemagne and Carloman. Her intervention had limited success, but she remained, according to Einhard, the beloved mother of the greatest Carolingian ruler, Charlemagne.

Pippin and Bertrada were married in 744, but the nature of their relationship, at least at the outset, is confused, in part because of the changing marriage traditions of the realm in the mid-eighth century. It was thought at one time that the two were not legitimately married, but that Pippin took Bertrada as a concubine or in the old Frankish marriage practice of *friedelehe*. The marriage was only legitimate, according to this view, once Charlemagne was born, in either 742 or 748. It is now generally recognized that in fact the two were formally married and that Charles was not illegitimate. Even though the marriage is now recognized as legitimate, it was not the most stable one. Pippin married Bertrada, as was often the case, for her connections with a powerful noble family, connections that would allow Pippin, as mayor of the palace, to strengthen his hold on the kingdom after the death of his father, Charles Martel. At some point during their marriage Pippin tried to repudiate Bertrada in order to marry another woman, but his efforts were stopped by Pope Stephen II (752–757), and the marriage continued until Pippin's death in 768. Despite his attempt to divorce her, Pippin brought Bertrada along with his entourage when he went to meet Stephen on the latter's visit to the kingdom. And Stephen bestowed a special blessing on Bertrada when he crowned and anointed Pippin and his sons in 754.

After Pippin's death, Bertrada continued to influence affairs in the kingdom, and her most important moment came early in the reigns of her sons Charlemagne and Carloman. On the death of their father, tensions between the two brothers broke out that threatened the peace and stability of the realm. The strain was worsened by Carloman's refusal to help his older brother suppress a rebellion in Aquitaine. At this point Bertrada intervened in the hopes of preventing civil war and also to strengthen Carolingian power and her sons' diplomatic ties in Bavaria and Italy. In 770, according to the *Royal Frankish Annals,* Bertrada met with her son Carloman before proceeding to Italy "in the interests of peace" (Scholz 1972, 48). It is possible that she hoped to allay any fears Carloman may have had about his brother or, on the other hand, to upbraid him for his lack of support for his brother. In either event, she went to Italy through Bavaria, where she met with Duke Tassilo.

The duke had commended himself into vassalage to Pippin in 757, but had failed to honor his oath in 763. Bertrada may have attempted to reconcile Tassilo, and his important and powerful duchy, to her two sons. After meeting with Tassilo, Bertrada went to Lombard Italy to meet with King Desiderius. Allies of the Franks before Pippin's campaigns to protect the pope, the Lombards remained a powerful force in Italy and a potential threat to both the pope and, to a lesser extent, the Carolingians. Bertrada arranged a marriage between the king's daughter, Desiderata, and her son Charlemagne. The apparent success of Bertrada's trip was shattered in the following year with the death of Carloman and the disinheritance of his children, as well as Charlemagne's repudiation of Desiderata.

The rejection of Bertrada's diplomatic initiative, however, according to Einhard, was the only example of tension between Bertrada and Charlemagne. Einhard notes that Bertrada lived to a "very great age," was honored by Charlemagne, with whom she lived, and was "treated with every respect" by her son (Einhard 1981, 74). She lived to see the birth of three grandsons and three granddaughters to Charlemagne. She died in 783 and, Einhard notes, was buried by her son "with great honor in the church of Saint Denis, where his father lay" (74).

See also Carloman, King of the Franks; Carolingian Dynasty; Charlemagne; Charles Martel; Desiderius; Einhard; Lombards; Pippin the III, Called Pippin the Short; *Royal Frankish Annals;* Tassilo

Bibliography

Einhard and Notker the Stammerer. Two Lives of Charlemagne. Trans. Lewis Thorpe. Harmondsworth, UK: Penguin, 1981.

McKitterick, Rosamond. *The Frankish Kingdoms under the Carolingians, 751–987.* London: Longman, 1983.

Riché, Pierre, *The Carolingians: A Family Who Forged Europe.* Trans. Michael Idomir Allen. Philadelphia: University of Pennsylvania Press, 1993.

Scholz, Bernhard Walter, trans. *Carolingian Chronicles: Royal Frankish Annals and Nithard's History.* Ann Arbor: University of Michigan Press, 1972.

Wemple, Suzanne. *Women in Frankish Society: Marriage and the Cloister, 500 to 900.* Philadelphia: University of Pennsylvania Press, 1981.

Bleda

See Attila the Hun

Boethius, Anicius Manlius Severinus (c. 480–c. 525)

Roman senator and noble, whose family boasted an emperor in its lineage and strong Christian credentials, Boethius was one of the last great philosophers of antiquity. Like most Romans of his class, he also served in government, in his case as advisor of the great Ostrogothic king of Italy, Theodoric. A talented philosopher, theologian, and orator, Boethius is best known for his *Consolation of Philosophy (De consolatione philosophiae),* which he wrote while in prison awaiting his execution at the order of Theodoric. Despite this tragic ending, Boethius's memory lived on long after his death, and his greatest work influenced many, including the ninth-century Anglo-Saxon king Alfred the Great, who translated it.

Like many traditional Romans, Boethius enjoyed a good education and was set on the path to holding public office. His later writings suggest that he was a particularly good student, who may have traveled to the great schools at Athens and Alexandria to study for a time, and his talents as an orator stood him in good stead in his political career. His father had served as consul, but had died in 487 while Boethius was quite young. The early death of his father, however, had one beneficial result—the important Christian senator Quintus Aurelius Memmius Symmachus assumed Boethius's father's place and raised and educated him. His family background and education prepared him for a career in public service, which he accepted, as he notes in the *Consolation,* in accordance with Plato's endorsement of philosophers serving in government. In 510, he was made consul, and in 522 his two sons were elevated to the consulship, a great honor that suggests Boethius held favor with the imperial government in Constantinople. He was also highly favored by the Ostrogothic king in Italy, Theodoric, who made Boethius his Master of Offices *(magister officiorum)* in 522.

Boethius's career in public service and his relationship with Theodoric are complex, celebrated, and tragic. His focus was plainly on serving the interests of Italy and its people, and at one point he helped resolve an economic crisis in southern Italy. He was also willing to work with the Arian Theodoric. Although an Arian ruler of a Catholic population, Theodoric was generally a wise and tolerant king, with whom educated and public-minded senators like Boethius could work. Indeed, Theodoric often called Boethius to his service, and not only in 522 when he was made chief of staff. Theodoric had often requested Boethius to employ his great mathematical and mechanical talents to create objects that the king could use in diplomacy as gifts. At the same time, there is evidence that Boethius was interested in bridging the gap between the eastern and western parts of the Roman Empire. During the Middle Ages his intellectual work remained an important conduit of the teachings of Plato and, to a lesser extent, Aristotle, to the Latin West. The theological treatises he wrote in the 510s were designed to reconcile Eastern and Western theology—an attempt, perhaps, to draw Constantinople and Italy closer together at a time when Theodoric's policy was to keep the two far apart. Indeed, Boethius's efforts were appreciated by the imperial government at Constantinople, which rewarded him and his sons with the consulship. Clearly, Boethius was involved in a complex web of competing political and religious interests.

His political involvement came to a bad end not long after his promotion to Master of the Offices. The aging Theodoric faced serious difficulties in Italy in his last years, which included tensions at his own court over relations with Constantinople, an aggressive and ambitious emperor in Constantinople, and an uncertain succession because of the death of one son-in-law and the conversion to Catholicism of the other. In the early 520s, Theodoric cracked down hard on anti-Semitic rioters and ordered all Romans disarmed. In 522, he learned of a conspiracy headed by the leading senator, Albinus, who was implicated in corresponding with Constantinople against Theodoric. The king quickly ordered Albinus arrested, and Boethius came to his fellow senator's defense. Despite his good service to Theodoric, Boethius had also made enemies of the king's advisors for his promotion of Catholic orthodoxy against Arianism and for exposing corruption in the king's administration.

Standing before the king, Boethius declared "If Albinus is guilty, then so am I, and so is the whole senate" (Wolfram 1997, 224). Although modern scholarship remains divided on whether Boethius was involved in the conspiracy or not, Theodoric had Boethius arrested. Several senators, in need of money, brought evidence against Boethius, who was found guilty of witchcraft and treason. He was imprisoned in Pavia where he wrote his masterpiece, *The Consolation of Philosophy,* and suffered a gruesome execution, most likely after torture, probably in 525.

Revered as a martyr throughout the Middle Ages because of his brutal execution by Theodoric, Boethius is best known for his theological work and the *Consolation*. His earlier treatises included works on mathematics and music, which preserved elements of earlier Greek works on the subjects. Boethius also translated Aristotle's works on logic, and his theological treatises were heavily influenced by Neoplatonic thought. His *Consolation of Philosophy,* which some interpret as a Christian philosophical work and others do not, was written as a dialogue between Boethius himself depicted as rebelling against his unjust fate and Lady Philosophy; it reflects on the great questions of human happiness and suffering, and vindicates divine providence and human freedom. It may have been an effort by Boethius to reconcile Greek philosophy with Christian theology, and whatever the intent it was an important source for the preservation of Greek thought for medieval Latin thinkers.

See also Alfred the Great; Arianism; Ostrogoths; Theodoric the Great

Bibliography
Boethius. *The Consolation of Philosophy.* Trans.
    Richard Green. New York: Bobbs-Merrill, 1962.
Chadwick, Henry. *Boethius: The Consolations of Music, Logic, Theology, and Philosophy.* Oxford: Clarendon, 1981.
Gibson, Margaret, ed. *Boethius: His Life, Thought, and Influence.* Oxford: Blackwell, 1981.
Laistner, Max L. W. *Thought and Letters in Western Europe, A.D. 500–900.* 2d ed. Ithaca, NY: Cornell University Press, 1976.
Wolfram, Herwig. *The Roman Empire and Its Germanic Peoples.* Trans. Thomas Dunlap. Los Angelos and Berkeley: University of California Press, 1997.

Boniface, St. (c. 675–754)

Most famous and influential of all the Irish and Anglo-Saxon missionaries to the continent in the seventh and eighth centuries, Boniface spread the Christian faith to pagan Saxons and other Germanic peoples. He also founded several bishoprics and the important monastery at Fulda and reorganized numerous dioceses during his career as a missionary and reformer. He was supported early in his missionary work by the Carolingian mayor of the palace, Charles Martel, and also by the pope. His support from the pope was perhaps most important to Boniface, because, like all Anglo-Saxons, he felt a special devotion to the papacy and structured his reforms along models established at Rome. He later played a role in the reform of the Frankish church and was supported by Charles Martel's sons, Pippin the Short and, especially, Carloman. Martyred on June 5, 754, Boniface has been recognized as the Apostle to Germany because of his successful missionary activity, and his feast day is celebrated on June 5.

Born in circa 675 to a noble family in Devonshire, England, and originally called Winfrith (Pope Gregory II gave him the name Boniface in 719), Boniface, according to his biographer, demonstrated great piety and zeal for the monastic life from an early age. While still a boy, according to his biographer, Boniface "subdued the flesh to the spirit and meditated on things eternal" and discussed spiritual matters with priests who visited his father's house (Talbot 1995, 111). Although reluctant to allow his son to take up the monastic life, Boniface's father eventually relented, after a serious illness, and sent him to a Benedictine community near Exeter. He received an excellent education at the community, was ordained a priest at age thirty, and developed a reputation as a scholar. Indeed, in 705 he was called on by the archbishop of Canterbury to help resolve a number of issues facing the king of Wessex, which Boniface did successfully.

Despite his success and the possibility of ecclesiastical advancement, Boniface, like many Irish and Anglo-Saxon monks, felt the call to take up missionary work. In 716 he joined his fellow Anglo-Saxon missionary, Willibrord, on the continent and traveled to the region called Frisia (in the modern Low Countries), whose inhabitants had slid back into paganism during the turmoil after the death of the mayor of the palace Pippin of Herstal. His efforts, however, proved unsuccessful because he found no support from the Frisian leader, Radbod. Boniface then returned to England, but would not stay there for long, even though he was elected abbot of his monastery, an honor he declined in favor of further missionary activity.

In 719, Boniface began his second evangelical mission on the continent. He visited Rome first this time and received both a new name and a commission from Gregory II to preach to the pagan Saxons east of the Rhine River and to spread the Roman method of baptism and the Roman liturgy. Returning north, he joined Willibrord again in Frisia and spent three years evangelizing the Frisians, where the death of Radbod, the Frisian king who opposed the Franks, and the rise of Charles Martel offered the opportunity for success. Indeed, in 723 Charles Martel sent an official letter to the ecclesiastical and lay nobility proclaiming Martel's protection of and support for the activities of Boniface. In the previous year, Boniface had been called

back to Rome, where Gregory consecrated him bishop, provided him the mandate to preach to the pagan Saxons, and sent a letter to the Carolingian mayor of the palace requesting his support. Boniface returned to the north and began his mission in most aggressive fashion by chopping down one of the pagan Saxons sacred oaks near Fritzlar. This event had great significance, because Boniface suffered no vengeance from the pagan gods and demonstrated that the power of his God was far greater.

Over the next several decades, Boniface continued his missionary activities and remained in frequent contact with the pope in Rome. From 725 to 735 he spent most of his time in Thuringia, where he converted pagans and struggled against rival missionaries whose methods he disliked and termed heretical. As with all things, Boniface sought the support of Rome in his struggles with rival missionaries. His devotion to Rome, his efforts to spread Roman traditions, and his frequent reports to the pope attracted the attention of the new pope, Gregory III, during his years in Thuringia. Gregory welcomed his efforts and raised him to the rank of archbishop, which increased Boniface's authority and reinforced his power and prestige as the official representative of the pope in Germany.

In 735, Boniface was sent to the duchy of Bavaria to reorganize and reform the church, activities that turned out to be important when the duchy was absorbed by the Frankish kingdom. Although supported by the duke, Boniface was often opposed by the bishops and other church leaders in Bavaria, especially after his trip to Rome in 737. There he had been welcomed by Gregory III, who supported his efforts in Germany. Returning to Bavaria, Boniface wholeheartedly began reorganization of the church of Germany, despite frequent opposition. He established numerous new bishoprics, including those at Erfurt, Freising, Regensburg, and Würzburg. He also, in 744, established a monastery at Fulda, which he placed under the protection of the pope and entrusted to his Bavarian convert Sturmi. His activities in Bavaria were an important prelude to his activities in the Frankish kingdom after the death of his patron, Charles Martel.

Until the rise to power of Pippin and Carloman, Boniface had done little with the Frankish church, which was much in need of reform. Indeed, it is from Boniface that we learn of the sorry shape of the Frankish church. Certainly there is some exaggeration, but Boniface complained that there had been no church council in the kingdom in eighty years and that the bishops were "greedy laymen" or "adulterous, undedicated clerical carousers." Moreover, he lamented that the bishops also shed blood and that the lower clergy were often ignorant and had "four, five, or more concubines in their bed each night." With the support of the Carolingian mayors of the palace, particularly Carloman, Boniface instituted reform of the Frankish church. The German Council of 742 or 743 held by Carloman implemented the reform ideas of Boniface, declaring that priests and other clergy must wear distinctive and simple clothes and must not keep arms, hunting dogs, or women in their house. Monks were encouraged to follow the Rule of St. Benedict and were to live chaste and stable lives. Carloman, inspired by Boniface, also established new episcopal sees, which he put under Boniface's authority as archbishop. Finally, Boniface reinforced the pro-Roman tendencies in the Frankish church, inadvertently laying the foundation for a political alliance between the Carolingians and the pope.

After Carloman's retirement to a monastery Boniface's influence at the Carolingian court declined, particularly because of Pippin's close relationship with Chrodegang of Metz, an important bishop and religious reformer, and Boniface returned to missionary work. His influence continued in the kingdom, and he did not completely separate himself from Pippin's affairs, at least according to the *Royal Frankish Annals,* which declare that Boniface anointed Pippin king in 751. There is more than a little uncertainty about his presence at the ceremony, but his impor-

tance in the realm even after Carloman's retirement is attested by the assertion that he participated in the coronation. It is certain that Boniface resumed his evangelical activity and remained dedicated to it during the last year of his life. Retiring from his duties as archbishop, he turned the office over to one of his disciples and began preaching to the pagan Frisians. He was attacked on the morning of June 5, 754, and suffered martyrdom, and, according to his biographer, Boniface encouraged his followers not to fear the attackers but to "endure with steadfast mind the sudden onslaught of death, that you may be able to reign evermore with Christ" (Talbot 1995, 136). Boniface's biographer notes further that within a few years great miracles occurred at the spot of the martyrdom.

See also Anglo-Saxons; Carloman, Mayor of the Palace; Carolingian Dynasty; Charles Martel; Chrodegang of Metz; Gregory II, Pope; Gregory III, Pope; Pippin II, Called Pippin of Herstal; Pippin III, Called Pippin the Short; *Royal Frankish Annals*

Bibliography

Duckett, Eleanor Shipley. *Anglo-Saxon Saints and Scholars.* New York: Macmillan, 1947.

Emerton, Ephraim, ed. and trans. *The Letters of Saint Boniface.* New York: Columbia University Press, 2000.

Lawrence, Clifford H. *Medieval Monasticism: Forms of Religious Life in Western Europe in the Middle Ages,* 2d ed. London: Longman, 1984.

Levison, Wilhelm. *England and the Continent in the Eighth Century.* New York: Oxford University Press, 1998.

Reuter, Timothy, ed. *The Greatest Englishman: Essays on St. Boniface and the Church at Crediton.* Exeter: Paternoster Press, 1980.

Riché, Pierre, *The Carolingians: A Family Who Forged Europe.* Trans. Michael Idomir Allen. Philadelphia: University of Pennsylvania Press, 1993.

Scholz, Bernhard Walter, trans. *Carolingian Chronicles: Royal Frankish Annals and Nithard's History.* Ann Arbor: University of Michigan Press, 1972.

Talbot, C. H., trans. "Willibald: The Life of Saint Boniface." In *Soldiers of Christ: Saints and Saints' Lives from Late Antiquity to the Early Middle Ages,* ed. Thomas F. X. Noble and Thomas Head. University Park: Pennsylvania State University Press, 1995.

Wallace-Hadrill, John M. *The Frankish Church.* Oxford: Clarendon, 1983.

Bretwalda

Term used to designate any Anglo-Saxon king who exercised power over all of southern England, *bretwalda,* or *bretwald,* was probably a scribal correction of the Old English term *Brytenwealda,* which probably meant "Britain ruler" or "ruler of the Britons."

Although often used in modern scholarship, the term *bretwalda* appears only in one manuscript copy of the *Anglo-Saxon Chronicle.* In the year 829, according to the *Chronicle,* King Egbert of Wessex conquered "the kingdom of Mercia and all that was south of the Humber, and he was the eighth king who was Bretwalda." Other manuscripts reporting the event use the Old English word *Brytenwealda,* but even that version of the term was not widely used. However, echoes of the term bretwalda can be heard in a charter of Æthelbald of Mercia from 736, in which the king is called "rex Britanniae," the Latin version of "king of Britain." The *Chronicle* also lists Egbert's predecessors as bretwalda: Aelle of Sussex, Ceawlin of Wessex, Æthelberht of Kent, Raedwald of East Anglia, and Edwin, Oswald, and Oswy of Northumbria. This list of kings is taken from Bede's history, which identifies the kings as ruling over all the lands south of the Humber and thus reinforces the notion that the term meant "Britain ruler."

Although a clear definition of the term seems to have existed among Anglo-Saxon writers, bretwalda was probably not a regular institution. The appearance of bretwalda in the *Chronicle* may reveal the memory of an overall leader of the combined regions of the south from early Anglo-Saxon history. It may also be of poetical origin, emerging in the banquet halls of the kings and used as a term of praise and honor. It may also have emerged from church ideology, and the writing of the church's most famous representative, Bede, to testify to the unity of the English people.

See also Æthelberht I of Kent; *Anglo-Saxon Chronicle;* Anglo-Saxons; Bede; Heptarchy

Bibliography

Bede, *Ecclesiastical History of the English Church and People.* Trans. Leo Sherley-Price. Revised edition. London: Penguin Classics, 1968.

Loyn, Henry R. *Anglo-Saxon England and the Norman Conquest,* 2d ed. London: Longmans, 1991.

Sawyer, Peter H. *From Roman Britain to Norman England,* 2d ed. London and New York: Routledge, 1998.

Stenton, Frank M. *Anglo-Saxon England.* 3d ed. Oxford: Clarendon, 1971.

Whitelock, Dorothy, ed. *The Anglo-Saxon Chronicle.* Westport, CT: Greenwood, 1986.

Breviarum Alaricianum

See Alaric II

Brunhilde (d. 613)

Visigothic princess, Merovingian queen, and rival of the queen Fregedund, Brunhilde had great influence on politics in the Frankish kingdoms in the late sixth century and the early seventh. Her struggle with Fredegund contributed to the instability and civil war in the Frankish kingdoms in the late sixth century. Despite frequent attempts on her life by her rival, Brunhilde survived Fredegund and was the power behind the throne in the last decade of the sixth century and the first decade of the seventh. She worked consistently during her reign of more than thirty years to promote the interests of her family, especially her sons and grandsons. Her efforts, however, provoked opposition and led to a revolt that ended in her death and contributed to the rise of the Carolingian dynasty.

According to the sixth-century bishop and

historian, Gregory of Tours, Brunhilde was "elegant in all that she did, lovely to look at, chaste and decorous in her behavior, wise in her generation and of good address" (221). Although Gregory may have been biased toward the queen, since there is good evidence to suggest that she secured his appointment as bishop, his opinion seems born out by Brunhilde's successes while a queen of the Franks. She came to the kingdom, again according to Gregory, to marry the Merovingian king Sigebert I (r. 560/561–575), who saw that his brothers were marrying their servants and decided to seek the hand of a princess. Brunhilde was the daughter of the Visigothic king of Spain, Athanagild, and she was also an Arian Christian, who converted to Catholic Christianity shortly after her arrival in the Frankish kingdoms. She arrived, therefore, with wealth and pedigree unrivaled by any of the other Merovingian queens.

Her arrival inspired jealousy in Sigebert's half-brother, King Chilperic I (560/561–584), who arranged to marry Brunhilde's sister, the princess Galswintha. She too arrived with great wealth and prestige, but not so much that Chilperic hesitated to murder her shortly after her arrival, refusing to return the dowry. He then married, or remarried, the former servant Fredegund, who may have been behind the murder. The murder of Galswintha and promotion of Fredegund surely embittered relations between the two Merovingian queens. Some scholars argue that a blood feud followed the murder of Galswintha, but others maintain that the strife between Brunhilde and Fredegund was simply an example of the violent politics that occasionally plagued the Merovingian dynasty. Whatever the case, the relationship between the two was hostile and led to great civil strife.

In 575 tragedy again struck Brunhilde when Chilperic had Sigebert murdered and then took control of his kingdom and treasure. Brunhilde was captured and exiled to Rouen from her husband's capital at Paris, and her son Childebert was taken from her.

Despite this setback, Brunhilde returned to power in the 580s and became increasingly powerful thereafter. The first step in her return was her marriage to Merovech, son of her rival Chilperic. The marriage provided her with supporters and access to power once again, and Merovech had access to control of a kingdom. But Chilperic separated the two and returned Brunhilde to her eastern Frankish kingdom. When Merovech attempted to return to Brunhilde she rebuffed him, and shortly afterward he was captured and killed, possibly, as Gregory suggests, at Fredegund's orders. Although Merovech met a sad fate, his former wife's fortunes climbed in the 580s. This occurred, in part, because of the death of Chilperic and the subsequent weakness of Fredegund, who may have killed him and certainly made attempts to kill Brunhilde. The murders, possibly at the queen's order, of an abbot and a bishop who opposed her strengthened her hand as well. But the most important factor in her improved circumstances was that her son, Childebert, reached his majority and was recognized as a legitimate king by other Merovingian kings.

For the next three decades, Brunhilde dominated the scene in the Frankish kingdoms. Although first her son and then grandsons were the titular rulers, she held the real power in the kingdom and exercised it in both church and state. She arranged important political marriages for her children, alliances with Visigoth rulers in Spain which included the marriage of her daughter, Ingunde, to the prince Hermenegild. She also corresponded with the Byzantine emperor, who had captured her daughter and grandson after Hermenegild revolted. She also conspired to break up marriages of her son and grandsons to limit threats to her position at court.

Within the kingdom, she strengthened her position further by arranging treaties with other Merovingian kings and orchestrating the murders of her rivals. Moreover, she corresponded with Pope Gregory I, known as the Great (590–604), and oversaw the administration of the church and appointment of bishops in the realm. Her relationship with the pope was an important one, for Gregory who hoped that the queen would help reform the Frankish church and aid Augustine of Canterbury's mission to England. In both regards Gregory was not disappointed, and in return he supported the queen's request to elevate one of her favorites to the rank of metropolitan bishop. Her relations with the church, however, were not always happy. She may have ordered the murder of Bishop Desiderius of Vienne and certainly exiled St. Columban because they both questioned the behavior and right to rule of members of her family.

The difficulties she faced with Desiderius and Columban reveal the problems that arose for Brunhilde after the death of her son Childebert in 596. She continued to rule as regent for her grandsons, Theudebert II (596–612) and Theuderic II (596–613), but she faced growing opposition in the kingdoms, especially among the nobility in Austrasia, where Theudebert ruled, and among the clergy who opposed her heavy-handed control of the church. She took up residence with Theuderic, whom she set against his brother, claiming that Theudebert was the son of a gardener. These first efforts failed, but Brunhilde would not be stopped. She broke the engagement of Theuderic, and worked to maintain her influence at court. In 612 she convinced Theuderic to attack his brother's kingdom, and this time Theudebert was defeated, captured, and killed.

In 612, Brunhilde remained at the pinnacle of power, and threatened Fredegund's son, Chlotar. But her fortunes quickly changed when Theuderic died of dysentery in 613. Although she made her great-grandson, Sigebert II, king, she could not put down the successful revolt Chlotar led against her. She was captured by her former rival's son and tried for the murder of ten kings, including her husband, children, grandchildren, Merovech, and Chilperic. She was found guilty and condemned to death in a most gruesome fashion, tied to the back of a wild horse and dragged to her death. Although she met a most unfortunate end, Brunhilde ruled effectively for over thirty years, acting as any Merovingian queen would to defend the rights of herself and her family against their rivals.

See also Augustine of Canterbury, St.; Carolingian Dynasty; Chilperic I; Chlotar II; Columban, St.; Fredegund; Gregory the Great, Pope; Gregory of Tours; Merovingian Dynasty; Visigoths

Bibliography

Gregory of Tours, *The History of the Franks.* Trans. Lewis Thorpe. Harmondsworth, UK: Penguin, 1974.

Nelson, Janet L. "Queens as Jezebels: The Careers of Brunhild and Balthild in Merovingian History." In *Medieval Women,* ed. Derek Baker. Oxford: Blackwell, 1978, pp. 31–77.

Wallace-Hadrill, John M. *The Long-Haired Kings.* Toronto: Toronto University Press, 1982.

Wemple, Suzanne. *Women in Frankish Society: Marriage and the Cloister, 500 to 900.* Philadelphia: University of Pennsylvania Press, 1985.

Wood, Ian. *The Merovingian Kingdoms, 450–751.* London: Longman, 1994.

C

Caedwalla (c. 659–689)

According to the historian Bede, Caedwalla was "a daring mad young man of the royal house of Gewissae" (232) who began his career as a pagan but converted to Christianity. He was king of the West Saxons for only a few years but initiated the tradition among West Saxon kings, down to Alfred the Great in the ninth century, of attempting to rule all of southeastern England.

Caedwalla was a member of the royal line but had been sent into exile during the reign of his predecessor, King Æthelwalh. In 685, Caedwalla began his struggle for the kingdom, and leaving exile, he attacked and killed Æthelwalh. He was turned away by his dead rival's retainers but managed to return and assume the throne. As king, he was involved in incessant warfare and conquest. He extended his power throughout southeastern England. Almost immediately after becoming king, Caedwalla invaded the Isle of Wight, where he was seriously wounded, and sought to kill all its inhabitants and replace them with people from Wessex. He took control of Sussex and killed one of its leaders and one of his chief rivals there. In 686, he invaded Kent and managed to secure recognition as king there as well. Although he was able to establish his power in several kingdoms, Caedwalla was unable to keep permanent hold on any of them, with the exception of the Isle of Wight.

Although he was a ferocious warrior king and pagan, Caedwalla remained on good terms with the bishops of his kingdom and eventually converted to Christianity. He was a patron of the church in England and may have founded a monastery at Hoo, in Kent between the Thames and Medway estuaries. According to Bede, Caedwalla abdicated the throne after roughly two years as king, 688, "for the sake of our Lord and his eternal kingdom" (279). Although accepting the faith in 688, the king desired the great honor of baptism in Rome and hoped to die shortly after baptism so that he could pass to "everlasting happiness" (279). In the summer of 688, Caedwalla left England. He stopped at Calais and donated money for the building of a church, and he also spent time at the court of the king of the Lombards, Cunipert. He reached Rome by the spring of 689 and was baptized by Pope Sergius on Holy Saturday before Easter, April 10, in that year, and was given the name Peter. As he wished, Caedwalla fell ill and died in Rome ten days later on April 20, 689. Although his reign and life were short, Caedwalla left an important legacy for his kingdom as king and Christian convert.

See also Alfred the Great; Anglo-Saxons; Bede; Lombards

Bibliography

Bede. *Ecclesiastical History of the English People with Bede's Letter to Egbert and Cuthbert's Letter on the Death of Bede.* Trans. Leo Sherley-Price. Harmondsworth, UK: Penguin, 1991.

Blair, Peter Hunter. *The World of Bede.* Cambridge: Cambridge University Press, 1970.

Stenton, Frank M. *Anglo-Saxon England.* 3d ed. Oxford: Clarendon, 1971.

Whitelock, Dorothy, ed. *The Anglo-Saxon Chronicle.* Westport, CT: Greenwood, 1986.

Caesarius of Arles (c. 470–542)

An important bishop and monk whose influence on the later barbarian churches was great, Caesarius ruled as bishop during a critical period in the transition from the Roman to barbarian world. During his reign his city of Arles was controlled by several different barbarian kingdoms, ultimately becoming part of the Merovingian kingdom of the Franks. Although he carefully guided his diocese through troubled times, Caesarius is best known for his pastoral efforts and simple but elegant sermons. A talented preacher, Caesarius introduced the ideas of Augustine of Hippo to a broader audience. He was also very much interested in monastic life and composed two monastic rules, one for women and the other for men.

Born to a noble family near Chalon-sur-Saône in circa 470, Caesarius's relatives included his predecessor as archbishop of Arles. Although he later dedicated his life to the church, Caesarius showed interest in classical culture and the arts of rhetoric as a youth. He studied with an acclaimed teacher of rhetoric but, like St. Jerome and others, experienced a dream that persuaded him to devote himself solely to the church. His later sermons revealed the consequences of his decision by their lack of classical allusions. His decision led him to the monastery of Lérins, one of the great centers of monastic life, in 490. He remained there until 497, but was forced to abandon the rigors of the monastic life because of ill health. He left the monastery for the city of Arles, where he was made a deacon and then ordained priest. He later became an abbot of a local monastery and, in 504, archbishop of Arles, a position he held until his death in 542.

His career as archbishop was an important one for the church in Arles and Gaul. He was confirmed in his position as archbishop by the Visigothic king, Alaric II, and in 505 was summoned to the king's court on charges of conspiring with Alaric's enemies. Caesarius was acquitted, but he was forced to deal with the Ostrogothic king Theodoric after Alaric was defeated by the Merovingian king Clovis (r. 481–511). Although the city was to be ceded to Clovis's descendants in 536, in the meantime it remained subject to the Ostrogoths, and Caesarius was called to appear at Theodoric's court in 513 on suspicion of conspiracy. While visiting Theodoric, Caesarius met with the pope, who named him papal vicar to Spain and Gaul. As archbishop and papal legate, Caesarius assumed important duties in the church, including convening church councils. He held six councils during his reign, councils that shaped religious practice and doctrine. The most important council, at Orange in 529, established the interpretation of Augustine's teachings on salvation.

Archbishop in a critical time for the church and society in Gaul (now France), Caesarius is remembered best for his preaching and monastic rules. His sermons, which reveal Caesarius as a theologian of no great originality, are models of elegant simplicity and instruction. He abandoned the rhetoric he had once studied for a simpler style of delivery, using a less studied manner to comment on the Scriptures. His style of delivery made his sermons, of which some 238 still exist, more comprehensible to his flock. The sermons, however, were not overly simplistic but contained important lessons. They disseminated the ideas of Augustine, as well as other church fathers, to the faithful and included admonitions against superstition and immorality. He encouraged his listeners to read the Scriptures at home during dinner and throughout the evening and suggested that those who could not read should have the Scriptures read to them. He also called on his listeners to ponder the message of the sermon and to sing the psalms to reinforce the teachings of the faith.

Caesarius is also known for his monastic rule. Although unable because of health reasons to live as a monk, Caesarius remained dedicated to the monastic ideal during his life. An archbishop, he was also an abbot and the founder of a community of nuns at Arles. It was for this community that he wrote his famous monastic rule. This important rule seems to have been influenced by the Rule of the Master, and Benedict of Nursia seems to have borrowed from Caesarius when composing his monastic rule. Moreover, according to Gregory of Tours, a version of the rule of Caesarius was adopted by the royal nun Radegund for the convent she founded. The rule legislated on such matters as the length of the novitiate, personal property, and stability in the monastery, and set the precedent for monastic life in Gaul for generations to come.

See also Augustine of Hippo, St.; Benedict of
Nursia, St.; Clovis; Franks; Gregory of Tours;
Merovingian Dynasty; Ostrogoths; Radegund;
Theodoric the Great; Visigoths

Bibliography

Caesarius of Arles. *Caesarius of Arles: Sermons.* Trans.
Mary Magdeleine Mueller. 3 vols. New York:
Fathers of the Church, 1956–1973.

Klingshirn, William E. *Caesarius of Arles: The Making
of a Christian Community in Late Antique Gaul.*
Cambridge: Cambridge University Press,
1994.

Laistner, Max L. W. *Thought and Letters in Western
Europe, A.D. 500 to 900.* 2d ed. Ithaca, NY:
Cornell University Press, 1976.

Lawrence, Clifford H. *Medieval Monasticism: Forms
of Religious Life in Western Europe in the Middle
Ages.* 2d ed. London: Longman, 1989.

McCarthy, Maria Caritas. *The Rule for Nuns of St.
Caesarius of Arles: A Translation with Critical
Introduction.* Washington, DC: Catholic
University of America Press, 1960.

Riché, Pierre. *Education and Culture in the Barbarian
West: From the Sixth through the Eighth Century.*
Trans. John Contreni. Columbia: University of
South Carolina Press, 1976.

Wood, Ian. *The Merovingian Kingdoms, 450–751.*
London: Longman, 1994.

Capitulare de Villis

One of the most famous and significant of Charlemagne's capitularies, the *Capitulare de Villis* (capitulary on the royal estates) provides important insights into Carolingian government and economic life. The capitulary reveals Charlemagne's interest in governing local affairs as well as the need for Carolingian kings to attend to such matters. It also shows the economic resources available to Carolingian kings and the obligations of royal servants to their king.

The *Capitulare de Villis* is traditionally held to have been issued sometime between 771 and 800, and most likely closer to the year 800. A later date, of 807, for the issuance of the capitulary has also been proposed. It was issued by Charlemagne to improve administration in the kingdom and to end the abuses of the royal treasury and of the king's residences throughout his vast realm. The capitulary was also designed to guarantee that certain basic necessities would be found in each of the residences, so that the king and his court could be well provided for when he and his retinue visited the various estates in the kingdom. Indeed, the capitulary was intended to establish the standards by which Charlemagne wanted his estates maintained and was, thus, an important part of his reform of Carolingian government and administration. It was, in fact, one of a number of rulings by the king to improve administration, and it laid the foundation for similar rulings by his son, Louis the Pious. The depth of detail in the rulings in the capitulary reveal both the king's interest in government and the rudimentary nature of the administration in Charlemagne's day.

The capitulary legislated the day-to-day workings of the royal estates throughout the realm, regulating the materials and laborers found on these estates. In fact, the capitulary laid out instructions for all economic life in the royal estates. It provided rules for making wine, salting food, maintaining buildings, and taking care of animals, as well as a list of the agricultural products to be raised on the estates. The steward of the palace was to provide an annual statement of the revenues derived from the fields farmed by royal plowmen and from tenant farmers, as well as from the number of piglets born, various fines, and payments from mills, forests, fields, boats, and bridges. The steward was also to keep a record of fruits, vegetables, honey, wax, oil, soap, vinegar, beer, wine, wheat, chickens, eggs, geese, and other farm products raised each year. The capitulary also mandated an account of fishermen, smiths, shield makers, and cobblers who worked on the estates as well as the number of workshops in which they worked. The number of tools on each estate was also given, and this account reveals that most of the tools were wood and not iron. Although the *Capitulare de Villis* is no longer used as a tool to understand the entire economic and social structure of the Carolingian world, since it applied only to the royal estates, it remains an important document for understanding Carolingian material culture and political administration.

See also Capitularies; Carolingian Dynasty; Charlemagne; Louis the Pious

Bibliography

Dutton, Paul. *Carolingian Civilization: A Reader.* Peterborough, Ont.: Broadview, 1993.

Ganshof, François Louis. *Frankish Institutions under Charlemagne.* Trans. Bryce Lyon and Mary Lyon. Providence, RI: Brown University Press, 1968.

Halphen, Louis. *Charlemagne and the Carolingian Empire.* Trans. Giselle de Nie. Amsterdam: North-Holland, 1977.

McKitterick, Rosamond. *The Carolingians and the Written Word.* Cambridge: Cambridge University Press, 1989.

Riché, Pierre. *The Carolingians: A Family Who Forged Europe.* Trans. Michael Idomir Allen. Philadelphia: University of Pennsylvania Press, 1993.

Capitularies

Carolingian legislative documents, the capitularies were an important tool of government and administration for all Carolingian kings, especially Charlemagne. The capitularies covered a wide range of topics, from economics and estate management to religious and political reforms. The term comes from contemporary usage, which refers to this kind of document as a *capitulare* or in the plural *capitularia,* because the documents were organized into short sections or chapters (in Latin, *capitula*). The capitularies demonstrate the growing importance of writing and the written word for Charlemagne and all Carolingians; even though the documents did not replace the word of the king as the rule or law, they did make known the king's word. The capitularies were sent to the special agents of the king called *missi dominici,* or messengers of the lord king, who were charged with circulating them throughout the realm (unless the capitularies contained specific instructions for the missi).

The earliest of the capitularies were issued by Carloman and Pippin the Short in the 740s, 750s, and 760s, but they were used to a much greater degree under Charlemagne. Indeed, Charlemagne issued a large number of capitularies as part of his broader reform of the Carolingian church and state. Some of the most famous and important Carolingian capitularies were issued by Charlemagne. The Capitulary of Herstal (779) aimed at general reform of society, and the programmatic *Admonitio Generalis* (789) announced the religious goals and ideals of the Frankish king and laid the foundation for the Carolingian Renaissance by mandating teaching and the establishment of schools. Charlemagne also issued a capitulary shortly after his coronation as emperor of the Romans in 800, restating the goals he pursued throughout his reign, as well as capitularies that addressed images, monastic life, and the law. Either Charlemagne issued the *Capitulare de Villis,* which regulated management of the royal estates. Charlemagne's successors Louis the Pious and Charles the Bald continued to issue capitularies throughout their reigns, but the documents were not used in other parts of the divided empire. The last capitulary was issued in 877.

See also *Admonitio Generalis; Capitulare de Villis;*
Carloman, Mayor of the Palace; Carolingian
Dynasty; Charlemagne; Charles the Bald; Louis
the Pious; Pippin III, Called Pippin the Short

Bibliography

Loyn, Henry R., and John Percival. *The Reign of
Charlemagne: Documents on Carolingian
Government and Administration.* New York: St.
Martin's Press, 1975.

McKitterick, Rosamond. *The Carolingians and the
Written Word.* Cambridge: Cambridge
University Press, 1989.

Riché, Pierre. *The Carolingians: A Family Who Forged
Europe.* Trans. Michael Idomir Allen.
Philadelphia: University of Pennsylvania Press,
1993.

Carloman, King of the Franks (d. 771)

Son of Pippin III the Short and brother of Charlemagne, Carloman ruled with his brother as king of the Franks from their father's death in 768 until his own death in 771. Although short, his reign was marked by controversy with his brother, which could have led to a destructive civil war had not Carloman suddenly died. His death saved the kingdom from disaster and allowed Charlemagne to rule with a free hand and subsequently forge one of the great empires of the Middle Ages.

The younger son of Pippin—he was about four years younger than Charlemagne—Carloman first appears in the *Royal Frankish Annals* in 754. With his older brother, Carloman received royal unction from Pope Stephen II when the pope traveled to the Frankish kingdom to crown Pippin king of the Franks. He was elevated to joint kingship of the Franks with his brother on their father's death. Pippin had passed the royal crown to his two sons and divided the realm between them. Carloman received a compact and contiguous territory that included Alsace, part of Aquitaine, Burgundy, Provence, and other neighboring regions, and he was crowned king at Soissons in October 768. As king Carloman followed policies similar to those of his father, especially in regard to monastic policy.

Carloman's short reign is best known, however, for the strife that existed between the two brothers. In 769, Charlemagne sought aid from Carloman in the face of a revolt in Aquitaine led by Count Hunald. Only with great difficulty, made worse by Carloman's unwillingness to help, was Charlemagne able to suppress the revolt. Carloman's refusal to help may have been part of his strategy to undermine his brother's authority; certainly it is likely to have contributed to the strains of an already tense relationship. In 770, Carloman met with his mother, Bertrada, who then went to Italy to help establish peace between the two brothers. Arranging a marriage with the Lombard king, Desiderius, for Charlemagne, Bertrada hoped to establish an alliance with the Lombards as a means to promote harmony in the Frankish kingdom. But Charlemagne repudiated his wife within a year, and the situation between the Franks and Lombards, as well as that between Charlemagne and Carloman, worsened. The potentially explosive situation was resolved by the sudden death of Carloman on December 4, 771. Charlemagne, with the approval of Carloman's supporters, dispossessed Carloman's widow, Gerberga, and two sons, who fled to the Lombard court of Desiderius. They received Desiderius's protection until Charlemagne conquered Italy in 774, and they were then turned over to Charlemagne and disappeared from the records at that point.

See also Carolingian Dynasty; Charlemagne;
Desiderius; Lombards; Pippin III, Called
Pippin the Short; *Royal Frankish Annals*

Bibliography

Davis, Raymond, trans. *The Lives of the Eighth-Century Popes (Liber Pontificalis): The Ancient Biographies of Nine Popes from A.D. 715 to A.D. 817.* Liverpool, UK: Liverpool University Press, 1992.

Einhard and Notker the Stammerer. *Two Lives of Charlemagne.* Trans. Lewis Thorpe. Harmondsworth, UK: Penguin, 1981.

Fichtenau, Heinrich. *The Carolingian Empire.* Trans. Peter Munz. Toronto: University of Toronto Press, 1979.

Halphen, Louis. *Charlemagne and the Carolingian Empire.* Trans. Giselle de Nie. Amsterdam: North-Holland, 1977.

McKitterick, Rosamond. *The Frankish Kingdoms under the Carolingians, 751–987.* London: Longman, 1983.

Riché, Pierre. *The Carolingians: A Family Who Forged Europe.* Trans. Michael Idomir Allen. Philadelphia: University of Pennsylvania Press, 1993.

Scholz, Bernhard Walter, trans. *Carolingian Chronicles: Royal Frankish Annals and Nithard's History.* Ann Arbor: University of Michigan Press, 1972.

Carloman, Mayor of the Palace (d. 754)

Son of the Carolingian Mayor of the Palace, Charles Martel, Carloman inherited control of the Frankish kingdoms with his brother, Pippin the Short, on his father's death in 741. Together as mayors of the palace, Carloman and Pippin built upon the legacy of their father and strengthened the position of the Carolingian family in the Frankish kingdoms at the expense of the Merovingian dynasty. Although they placed a Merovingian on the throne, Carloman and Pippin were the real powers in the kingdoms. Carloman was also active in reform of the church, supporting the activities of the Anglo-Saxon missionary Boniface and promoting reform in the Frankish church. Indeed, his interest in the church and religious life was so great that he left worldly power for the monastic life. His ab-dication paved the way for the establishment of Carolingian royal power by his brother and eventually for the establishment of imperial power by his nephew Charlemagne.

Although perhaps best known for his retirement to a monastery in 747, Carloman was an active and vigorous mayor (r. 741–747), who helped his brother Pippin suppress the many revolts they faced at the outset of their joint rule. Together they squashed the revolt of their half-brother Grifo, who sought to lay claim to part of his father's legacy. They laid siege to Laon and captured Grifo, who was kept in custody by Carloman until his retirement. The two mayors also faced difficulties from their sister, Chiltrude, who fled to the court of the Bavarian duke, Odilo. They eventually defeated Odilo in 743 but were not able to force him from the duchy. Carloman and Pippin also enforced their authority on subject peoples in Aquitaine and Alemannia, where Carloman imposed Carolingian authority with a terror campaign. The new mayors were ultimately able to establish themselves in the kingdom, but only with much difficulty.

The revolts Carloman and his brother faced led them to an important step. Their father had ruled during the last four years of his life without a Merovingian king on the throne. It became apparent to Carloman and Pippin, however, that in order to secure their position in the Frankish kingdoms, they needed to place a Merovingian monarch on the throne. In 743 they discovered a member of the dynasty in the monastery of St. Bertin, whom they established as King Childeric III. It is likely that Carloman was the prime mover in the reestablishment of the Merovingian dynasty. And although portrayed as a poor and powerless do-nothing king by Einhard, the last Merovingian provided the legitimization that the brothers needed to maintain their control in the kingdoms.

Carloman, and to a lesser extent his brother Pippin, were active supporters of Boniface, and both mayors were equally strong supporters of the reform of the Frankish church, particularly the reform of clerical behavior and education. Boniface, who had been protected by Charles Martel, found particularly strong support for his missionary and reform efforts from Carloman. At one point, the Carolingian mayor granted him the Anglo-Saxon missionary lands around Fulda so that Boniface could establish a monastery. Carloman also worked with Boniface to reform ecclesiastical organization in the Frankish kingdoms, in order to bring it more fully into cooperation with the papacy. Carloman also presided at several reform councils in the 740s, with, at times, Boniface and Pippin, to improve the life of the church in the Frankish kingdoms. Carloman, among other things, promised to protect the churches from impoverishment and to protect ecclesiastical property rights.

Carloman's religious inclinations, revealed by his active support for Boniface and church reform, were fully displayed in 747 when he announced to Pippin that he had decided to withdraw from his position of power and retire to a monastery. He settled his affairs and made donations to a monastery in his domain before departing for Rome. He received the tonsure from Pope Zachary and then built a monastery in honor of St. Sylvester on Mt. Soracte. In 754, perhaps because too many pilgrims visited him at his monastery, Carloman moved to the monastery at Monte Cassino. Contemporary sources make clear that Carloman departed voluntarily, but his decision did not bode well for his immediate family, especially his son Drogo, who was disposed of by his uncle.

Carloman's public career, however, did not end with his retirement in 747. In fact, his decision indirectly had a profound influence on the fate of his dynasty and of the Frankish kingdoms. As a result of Carloman's abdication, Pippin was left the sole mayor, and for all intents and purposes, the sole power in the realm. In 751, after deposing Childeric III, Pippin assumed the throne of the king of the Franks and founded the Carolingian royal dynasty. In 754, Carloman directly participated in the public affairs of the kingdom. At the request of the Lombard king Aistulf, Carloman left his monastery at Monte Cassino to take part in the debate among Pippin and the Frankish nobility concerning a possible invasion of Italy. Aistulf had been threatening the pope, Stephen II, who had requested aid from the Frankish king. In order to prevent an invasion by Pippin, Aistulf sent Carloman to oppose the invasion by his brother. Aistulf's plan failed, however, and the invasion followed shortly after the debate. Carloman was not allowed to return to Italy but was sent to a monastery in Vienne, where he died sometime later in the year 754.

See also Aistulf; Boniface, St.; Carolingian Dynasty; Charlemagne; Charles Martel; Childeric III; Merovingian Dynasty; Pippin III, Called Pippin the Short

Bibliography

McKitterick, Rosamond. *The Frankish Kingdoms under the Carolingians, 751–987.* London: Longman, 1983.

Riché, Pierre. *The Carolingians: A Family Who Forged Europe.* Trans. Michael Idomir Allen. Philadelphia: University of Pennsylvania Press, 1993.

Scholz, Bernhard Walter, trans. *Carolingian Chronicles: Royal Frankish Annals and Nithard's History.* Ann Arbor: University of Michigan Press, 1972.

Wood, Ian. *The Merovingian Kingdoms, 450–751.* London: Longman, 1994.

Caroline Books
See Theodulf of Orléans

Carolingian Dynasty
Ruling nearly all of Christian Europe from the eighth to the tenth century, the Carolingians, as they were known from their greatest member, Charles the Great, in Latin Carolus Magnus, known as Charlemagne, established a great empire, presided over an important religious reform, and laid the foundation for

Illustration from a ninth-century manuscript of Emperor Charlemagne and his son presiding over a tribunal (The Art Archive/Biblioteca del Duomo Modena/Dagli Orti)

many of the cultural and political achievements of later medieval civilization. The Carolingian tradition of coronation and their governmental ideas served as the model for medieval rulers long after the demise of the dynasty and the breakup of the Carolingian Empire had led to the emergence of the medieval kingdoms of France and Germany. Their reign witnessed, too, a great cultural flowering traditionally called the Carolingian Renaissance.

The dynasty's origins can be traced to the mid-seventh century, when the Austrasian nobles St. Arnulf, bishop of Metz (d. c. 645), and Pippin I of Landen (d. 640) joined together in a marriage alliance. The fortunes of the family came from its control of the office of mayor of the palace *(major domus)*, a reward that Pippin earned after helping the Merovingian king Chlotar II (584–629) overthrow Queen Brunhilde and assume the Frankish throne in 613. Pippin exploited his position and became one of the most powerful figures in the kingdom. Although his fortunes ebbed and flowed as the throne passed between various Merovingian kings, Pippin was able to establish a secure base of power and wealth, and to pass it on to his son Grimoald (d. 657), who succeeded his father as mayor when the latter suddenly died.

Grimoald's career turned out to be an instructive one for generations to come and a reminder of the vagaries of political power. Grimoald was a popular and ambitious figure, but the family suffered an almost fatal setback as a result of his political ambitions and his effort to replace the reigning Merovingian with his own son. His own success in some ways laid the foundation of his ultimate demise. Shortly after his elevation to power, Grimoald accompanied the Merovingian king ruling Austrasia, Sigebert III (r. 633/634–656), on a military expedition to suppress the revolt of one of the dukes of the kingdom. The campaign was a disaster, and the king survived only because of the actions of Grimoald, who thus was now closer to Sigebert and able to impose his will on the king.

Grimoald next expanded his own base of power by acquiring territory and, in what was to become good Carolingian fashion, forging alliances with monasteries and their monks. The mayor also persuaded the king to adopt his son as heir because Sigebert was without a son. Sigebert, however, did have a son, Dagobert, who was to be his heir, but who was entrusted to Grimoald at the king's death. Making the best of this opportunity, Grimoald deposed Dagobert, sent him to a monastery in distant Ireland, and placed his own son, Childebert the Adopted, on the throne. Unfortunately for Grimoald, his coup failed. The Merovingian king in Neustria, Clovis II, who may have assisted in the deposition but was surprised by Grimoald's enthronement of his son, invited the mayor and his son to Neustria where he captured and executed them—a most unhappy end for Grimoald and his family.

The fortunes of the family were revived by Pippin II, of Herstal (r. 687–714). Pippin, the nephew of Grimoald and grandson of Arnulf and Pippin I, recovered the office of mayor. The mayor of Neustria, Ebroin, was most tyrannical and harbored ambitions of unifying the realm under his own authority. His ambition and tyranny brought him enemies, which unsettled the kingdom even more at a time when the Merovingian kings were rapidly losing power. Many Austrasian nobles who had supported Grimoald rallied to Pippin, who united the Frankish kingdom when he defeated Ebroin at the Battle of Tertry in 687. As sole mayor, Pippin ruled in the name of several Merovingian kings, including Theuderic III, Clovis IV, Childebert III, and Dagobert III. He strengthened his family's hold on power by improving relations with the church and gaining control of monasteries. He also enforced royal authority over the various parts of the kingdom and expanded the eastern boundaries of the kingdom. For both his family and the kingdom, Pippin's reign was most beneficial.

Despite his successes, the kingdom fell into civil strife after Pippin's death. Desirous that her descendants should assume the office of mayor, Pippin's widow, Plectrude, imprisoned Charles Martel (the Hammer; r. 714–741), Pippin's son with his second wife or concubine. But her plans were undermined by a rebellion of Neustrian nobles and Charles's escape from prison. Although suffering setbacks of his own, Charles, the first of his family to be so named, laid claim to his inheritance as mayor, seized much treasure held by Plectrude, and forced her from power.

Charles Martel's term as mayor brought increasing prestige and power to the family. A ferocious warrior, Charles managed to take control of the kingdom in the 720s when he forced the Neustrians to accept his authority, and he won numerous victories against foreign foes, as his father had done before him. His most important and famous victory took place near Poitiers in 732, when he defeated a Muslim army from Spain. Although more battles were necessary to expel the Muslims from the Frankish kingdom, the Battle of Poitiers confirmed Martel's reputation as a great warrior. The victory was understood by contemporaries as the demonstration of God's favor on the Carolingian mayor.

Charles's successes were not limited to the military arena, however, because he further strengthened the alliance between his family and the Frankish church. Although he alienated much church land to compensate the nobility and ensure their loyalty, thus seriously weakening the church, Charles supported the church and its missionary activities. He established strong ties with the royal abbey of St. Denis, an important political as well as religious act, because the abbey had long supported the Merovingian dynasty. He promoted the activities of Anglo-Saxon missionaries, including St. Boniface, and received a proposal from Pope Gregory III for an alliance against the Lombards in Italy. So great was Charles's power in the kingdom by the end of his life that he ruled without a Merovingian king from 737 on and, following Frankish royal tradition, divided the succession between his two sons, Pippin III, called Pippin the Short (d. 768) and Carloman (d. 754).

The new mayors faced much opposition at the outset of their reign. They faced resistance from various sections of the nobility and also from their half-brother, Grifo, who had been granted a number of estates by their father and who desired to rule with his half-brothers. Carloman and Pippin, however, dispossessed Grifo from his legacy and imprisoned him. They also suppressed the dissension they faced and extended their power over Aquitaine and Bavaria. One step they thought necessary to take was to appoint a new Merovingian king, Childeric III, as a means to legitimize their rule and restore confidence in the government among the nobility. At the same time, it was the mayors who held the reigns of government and who asserted their authority over the kingdom. They led military campaigns, supported the activities of Boniface, held councils attended by nobles and bishops to address matters concerning the kingdom and the church, and promoted needed religious and political reform—until Carloman withdrew to a monastery in 747, an action that left Pippin as sole mayor.

Pippin next took the fateful steps once taken without success by Grimoald. Secure in his power, Pippin sent two trusted and powerful advisors with a letter to the pope, Zachary (r. 741–752), asking if he who had the power or he who had the title should be king. Zachary responded as Pippin had hoped. Pippin deposed Childeric, the last Merovingian king, and sent him to a monastery for the rest of his life. In November, 751, Pippin, following traditional Germanic practice, was elected king by the Frankish nobles, and, to demonstrate the new and more powerful charisma he possessed, he was crowned and anointed by the bishops of the realm, possibly including the pope's representative Boniface. Coronation and unction were repeated in 754 by Pope Stephen, which led to the establishment of a firm alliance between Rome and the kingdom of the Franks and the grant of what is called the Donation of Pippin to the pope.

Pippin's reign as king (751–768) was a critical time in the history of the dynasty; it was Pippin who established the foundation of Carolingian royal policy. He continued the program of reform of the church that had begun during his shared rule with Carloman. His efforts included the introduction of Roman liturgical practices to the churches in his kingdom, the reform of religious life, and the reinforcement of ties with the influential monastery of St. Denis. He also strengthened ties with Rome. The papacy and its extensive holdings were under constant threat from the Lombards, who sought to unify the Italian peninsula under their authority. Pippin received requests for aid from the pope, and therefore he undertook two invasions to protect the pope from his Lombard enemies. He also undertook the vigorous expansion of the realm and promoted the idea of sacral kingship, the idea that the king is chosen by God to rule and is God's representative on earth. Despite his many achievements, Pippin's reign is often overshadowed by that of his illustrious son, Charlemagne.

When Pippin died in 768 he left the kingdom to his sons Carloman and Charlemagne. Tensions existed between the two brothers, and civil war nearly broke out, but Carloman's death in 771 prevented this and opened the way for the sole rule of his brother, as king until 800 and then as emperor until 814. Charlemagne's success was, in part, the result of his abilities as a warrior, and during his reign the kingdom enjoyed a dramatic expansion of its territory. This expansion began almost from the death of Carloman, when Charles began a campaign to conquer and convert the Saxons, which lasted from 772 to 804. This process saw nearly annual campaigns into Saxony, the mass execution of 4,500 Saxons at Verdun, the destruction of pagan shrines, and the deportation of large numbers of Saxons. Reviving the efforts of his father Pippin, but with far greater enthusiasm, Charles invaded Italy, defeated the Lombards, and became king of the Lombards in 774. He overcame Tassilo, the duke of Bavaria, in 787, and smashed the Avar capital, or ring, in the early 790s. His first campaign into Muslim Spain in 778 led to the disastrous attack at Roncesvalles, after which Roland and the entire rear guard were massacred, but Charlemagne returned undaunted to create the Spanish March, a militarized border region that includes territory in Spain beyond the Pyrenees.

A successful empire-builder, Charlemagne was also an innovator in government. The county was the primary administrative governmental unit and was ruled in the king's name by local nobles called counts. The responsibilities of the counts included maintaining peace and order, implementing royal law, and dispensing justice. A new class of judicial officers (called *scabini*) was established to adjudicate local disputes. Special representatives of the king, the *missi dominici,* or messengers of the lord king, were responsible for overseeing the activities of the local officials. Two missi, a noble and a churchman, were generally sent out together to ensure the proper administration of justice, hear oaths of loyalty, and publish new laws. Moreover, Charles issued a new kind of law, the capitulary, and increased the use of writing as a tool of administration and government. The capitularies, so-called because they were arranged in chapters *(capitula),* addressed a broad number of issues, including administration of royal palaces, education, and religious reform. The most famous of the capitularies was the *Admonitio Generalis* of 789, which laid the foundation for the cultural revival known as the Carolingian Renaissance. Charles himself invited scholars from throughout Europe, including Alcuin, Theodulf of Orléans, and Paul the Deacon, to participate in his court, his reforms, and the cultural revival.

Charlemagne was also responsible for reestablishing the imperial dignity in the former Western Empire, a restoration that occurred when Charles visited Rome to investigate an attack on Pope Leo III (r. 795–816).

On December 25, 800, Charles attended Christmas mass, and as he rose from prayer, Leo crowned him emperor, and those in the church hailed him as emperor and augustus. Although doubts about Charlemagne's interest in the imperial title were raised by his biographer, Einhard, who declared that Charles would not have entered the church that day had he known what was to happen, many of the court scholars had already asserted Charlemagne's imperial stature in the 790s. They no doubt noted that the imperial authority was vacant in the Byzantine Empire because a woman, Irene, claimed to be emperor. Charlemagne's building program, especially the church and palace complex at Aachen, which was influenced by similar structures in the former Byzantine imperial capital in Ravenna, Italy, suggests that he was not unaware of his imperial stature. His dismay was likely over the way the imperial crown was bestowed; certainly Charles employed the title in his last years and rededicated himself to his program of renewal with a new "imperial" capitulary in 802.

Charles first understood the title as a special honor for himself alone, but in 813 he passed on the office of emperor to his surviving son, Louis the Pious (778–840). Louis's reign was characterized by continued cultural and religious reform but also by civil war. Louis made the imperial authority the foundation of his power and thus emphasized it in ways that his father, who preserved his royal titles, had not. He also sought to maintain the empire's permanent integrity by implementing a well-thought-out succession plan in 817, shortly after a near-fatal accident. The *Ordinatio Imperii,* as the capitulary that laid out the succession was called, provided a place in the succession for each of Louis's sons; the younger sons, Pippin and Louis the German, were assigned authority over subkingdoms, and imperial and sovereign authority was granted to his eldest son, Lothar (795–855), who was to be associated with his father as emperor during his father's life and then become his successor as emperor. Dis-

satisfaction with the plan emerged almost immediately and led to the revolt of Louis's nephew, Bernard, in 817; Bernard was blinded and died in the forceful suppression of the revolt. Despite this rebellion, Louis's reign during the 810s and 820s saw important achievements, including monastic reform, which was a precursor of later monastic reform, and governmental reform that provided legal and constitutional grounds for Carolingian power in Italy.

Despite these positive developments, Louis faced a number of crises in the late 820s and 830s. The birth of a son, Charles the Bald (823–877), to his second wife Judith, and the reorganization of the succession plan to include Charles, provided the other sons, and many nobles and bishops, reason to revolt against Louis's authority. The 830s was plagued by much turmoil in the empire, brought on by the revolts of Lothar and Pippin and Louis. In 834 Louis was deposed by Lothar, and Charles and Judith were placed in religious houses. But Louis, despite his ill-deserved reputation for weakness, regained his throne and ruled until his death in 840, when he was succeeded by Lothar, Charles, and Louis the German.

Civil war intensified in the years after Louis's death, as his surviving sons struggled for preeminence in the empire. After several battles, including an especially bloody one at Fontenoy, the brothers agreed to the Treaty of Verdun in 843, which divided the realm between them, with Charles getting western Francia, Louis eastern Francia, and Lothar central Francia and Italy as well as the imperial title. Lothar's territory was the least defensible, a problem not only because of the threats he faced from his brothers but also because of the growing threat of Viking, Muslim, and Magyar invasions. His acceptance of the tradition of dividing the inheritance among his own sons further undermined the territorial integrity of the central kingdom. Indeed, the weaknesses of Lothar's portion were revealed in the treaty of Meerssen, 870, which divided the northern parts of Lothar's territory between his brothers Charles the Bald and Louis. Charles survived the wars of the 830s and 840s to establish a strong kingship and resurrect the dynamic court culture of his grandfather. He also assumed the imperial crown and captured Aachen before his death in 877.

Although the kings of West Francia preserved the line the longest, until 987 when death and betrayal brought an end to the line, the power and authority of the Carolingian line underwent a process of decline beginning in the generation after the death of Charles the Bald. From the time of Louis II, the Stammerer (r. 877–879), until the time of the last Carolingian, Louis V (r. 986–987), the dynasty faced a series of great problems that eroded their power base. The west Frankish kingdom faced repeated Viking incursions, which the traditional Frankish military was unable to stop. Instead, local leaders, dukes and counts, began to exercise their authority and took steps to protect their territories from these invaders. Their ability to provide some protection offered them greater political authority, and their gradual acquisition of territory made them increasingly powerful. The civil strife of the later Carolingians also contributed to their decline, as various kings gave away significant amounts of land from the royal treasury to ensure the loyalty of the nobility. This effort accomplished little more than the gradual impoverishment of the dynasty, and by its fall in 987 it could only command a small region around Paris, where it held its last important estates.

In East Francia, the dynasty was replaced much sooner, but it nevertheless left an important legacy to its successors and to the medieval empire. After the wars of the 840s, Louis the German continued the Carolingian line in East Francia, but he was faced with many challenges. He ruled over a diverse kingdom, comprising Bavaria, Franconia, Saxony, Swabia, and Thuringia. He was plagued by attacks from Slavs and Vikings and faced the rising power of the nobility, especially the Liudolfings, and suffered revolts

from within his family, including two by his son Carloman (d. 880). His dependence on the church, especially the monasteries of his realm, was in part the result of the special problems of his kingdom. He divided the realm between his three sons, who succeeded him on his death on August, 28, 876, but it was Louis's son, Charles the Fat (r. 876–887, d. 888), who received the imperial title and, for a short time, reunited the empire.

Despite a strong start to his reign and early success against invaders, Charles's ill health and the growing success of Viking raiders led to his deposition in 887. He was succeeded in East Francia by his brother's illegitimate son, Arnulf of Carinthia (r. 887–899), who ruled with much early success and was crowned emperor in Rome. But Arnulf too was plagued by ill health in his later years, and he was succeeded after his death by his six-year-old son, Louis the Child (r. 899–911). Louis was the last of the Carolingians to rule in East Francia. His reign was marked by destructive Magyar invasions and the deaths of powerful nobles who were critical to the defense of the realm. On the death of Louis, the nobles of East Francia elected Conrad I (r. 911–918) king. Conrad and his successors inherited a realm divided into numerous duchies and threatened by foreign invaders, but they also inherited Carolingian traditions in government and the Carolingian tradition of strong ties with the church, which laid the foundation for the restoration of the empire by Otto I in 962.

See also Boniface, St.; Brunhilde; Carolingian Renaissance; Charlemagne; Charles the Bald; Charles Martel; Childeric III; Chlotar II; Dagobert; Louis the German; Louis the Pious; Merovingian Dynasty; Pippin I, Called Pippin of Landen; Pippin II, Called Pippin of Herstal; Pippin III, Called Pippin the Short; Plectrude; Tertry, Battle of

Bibliography
Bachrach, Bernard. *Early Carolingian Warfare: Prelude to Empire.* Philadelphia: University of Pennsylvania Press, 2001.

Einhard and Notker the Stammerer. *Two Lives of Charlemagne*. Trans. Lewis Thorpe. Harmondsworth, UK: Penguin, 1981.

Fichtenau, Heinrich. *The Carolingian Empire*. Trans. Peter Munz. Toronto: University of Toronto Press, 1979.

Ganshof, François L. *The Carolingians and the Frankish Monarchy: Studies in Carolingian History*. Trans. Janet L. Sondheimer. London: Longman, 1971.

Halphen, Louis. *Charlemagne and the Carolingian Empire*. Trans. Giselle de Nie. Amsterdam: North-Holland, 1977.

McKitterick, Rosamond. *The Frankish Kingdoms under the Carolingians, 751–987*. London: Longman, 1983.

Odegaard, Charles E. *Vassi et Fideles in the Carolingian Empire*. Cambridge, MA: Harvard University Press, 1945.

Riché, Pierre. *The Carolingians: A Family Who Forged Europe*. Trans. Michael Idomir Allen. Philadelphia: University of Pennsylvania Press, 1993.

Scholz, Bernhard Walter, trans. *Carolingian Chronicles: Royal Frankish Annals and Nithard's History*. Ann Arbor: University of Michigan Press, 1972.

Sullivan, Richard E. "The Carolingian Age: Reflections on Its Place in the History of the Middle Ages." *Speculum* 64 (1989): 257–306.

Carolingian Renaissance

An intellectual and cultural revival of the eighth and ninth centuries, the Carolingian Renaissance was a movement initiated by the Carolingian kings, especially Charlemagne, who sought not only to improve learning in the kingdom but to improve religious life and practice. Although once understood as an isolated, shining beacon in an otherwise dark age, the Carolingian Renaissance, or *renovatio* (renewal, or renovation) as it is sometimes called, is now understood to have roots in the Merovingian world and influence on later developments. Despite its foundations in an early period, the real impetus for the movement came from Charlemagne, who sought to reform learning and literacy, improve the education of the clergy, and provide at least a basic understanding of the faith to all his subjects. Toward this end, he attracted a large number of scholars from across Europe to assist him. They laid the foundation for even greater accomplishments in the two generations following Charlemagne's death. Indeed, during the reign of Louis the Pious, as well as in that of Charles the Bald, who consciously modeled his reign on his grandfather's, Carolingian scholars produced beautiful manuscript illuminations, copied and wrote numerous books and poems, and involved themselves in theological controversies. Although the renaissance never accomplished the goals Charlemagne intended and reached only the upper levels of society, it did provide an important foundation for cultural and intellectual growth in the centuries to come.

Although the roots of the renaissance can be traced to the reign of Pippin the Short and even back into the seventh century, the movement was inspired by the reforms of Charlemagne. Indeed, the program of reform and renewal that brought about the emergence of the renaissance was one of the fundamental concerns of the great Carolingian ruler. In two pieces of legislation, the capitulary *Admonitio Generalis* (General Admonition) of 789 and the Letter to Baugulf written between 780 and 800, established the foundation for the Carolingian Renaissance. In the *Admonitio* Charlemagne announced the educational and religious goals and ideals of his reign, which involved the improvement of Christian society in his realm and, at the very least, providing all people in the kingdom knowledge of the Lord's Prayer and Apostle's Creed. He sought to improve the moral behavior and knowledge of the Christian faith among both the clergy and laity, and he believed that for people to live good Christian lives they must have an understanding of the faith.

In chapter seventy-two of the *Admonitio* Charlemagne asserted the responsibility of the bishops and monks of his kingdom to establish schools to teach the psalms, music and

Codex Aureus of St. Emmeram (Bayerische Staatsbibliothek, Munich)

singing, and grammar, so that the boys of the kingdom could learn to read and write and so that those who wished to pray could do so properly. This program of religious and educational reform was restated in the circular let-

ter on learning to the abbot Baugulf of Fulda, or *De litteris colendis*. In the letter Charlemagne emphasized the importance of learning and proper knowledge of the faith for living a good Christian life. The letter proclaims the need for the creation of more books and calls on the higher clergy of the realm to establish schools at churches and monasteries to educate young boys. The Carolingian Renaissance thus grew out of Charlemagne's desire to improve the religious life of the clergy and laity of his kingdom.

To accomplish this end, Charlemagne needed scholars and books, and he managed to acquire both with little difficulty. Indeed, his wealth and power and program of religious reform attracted many of the greatest scholars of his age, many of whom received important positions in the Carolingian church. Among the more noteworthy scholars to join the Carolingian court were the grammarian Peter of Pisa and the Lombard Paul the Deacon, who wrote an important history of the Lombards. Theodulf of Orléans was another important figure, who joined the court from Spain and became a bishop and the author of significant theological treatises and legislation.

Perhaps the greatest of the foreign scholars to join the court was Alcuin of York, whose importance was recognized in his own day. Alcuin brought the great Anglo-Saxon tradition of Bede and the Northumbrian revival of learning to the Carolingian realm. His was not an original mind, but his contribution to learning was exactly what Charlemagne needed; Alcuin's knowledge was encyclopedic, and his talents as a teacher were widely recognized. Indeed, his learning and pedagogy are revealed by the number of great students, such as Rabanus Maurus, the preceptor of Germany, who followed in Alcuin's tradition. Moreover, Alcuin brought books to the continent from England and remained in contact with his homeland throughout his life, which allowed him to import more books needed for the growth of learning under Charlemagne and his descendants. Alcuin also has long been associated with an important reform, the creation of the elegant and highly readable writing style known as Carolingian minuscule. Although his role is now recognized as less central in the creation of the script, he and his monastery at Tours did play some role in the development of Carolingian minuscule, which was to be admired and copied during the Italian Renaissance centuries later.

The arrival of numerous scholars with their books stimulated learning throughout the realm, especially at the highest levels of society, where the renaissance had its greatest impact, as Alcuin and others began to teach and establish schools associated with cathedrals and monasteries. The new emphasis on learning contributed to the increased production of books, so central to the renaissance, and numerous books of Christian and pagan antiquity were copied in Carolingian monasteries. Indeed, one of the great achievements of the renaissance is the preservation of ancient Latin literature, and the earliest versions of many ancient Latin works survive from copies done by the Carolingians. Among the ancient Roman writers whose works were preserved by the Carolingians are Ammianus Marcellinus, Cicero, Pliny the Younger, Tacitus, Suetonius, Ovid, and Sallust. There were also important works of grammar and rhetoric copied in Carolingian scriptoria (writing rooms). But most important to the Carolingian rulers and scholars and central to their reform effort were the works of Christian authors, many of which were copied in the scriptoria.

The most important book copied by the Carolingian scribes was the Bible, which was often divided into different volumes (e.g., collections of the Prophets, historical books, or Gospels), and a new edition of the Bible was one of Alcuin's many achievements. The scribes also copied the works of the great Christian writers of antiquity and the early Middle Ages, including Bede, Isidore of Seville, Cassiodorus, Pope Gregory the Great, St. Jerome, and others. Of course, St. Augustine of Hippo was also copied extensively, and the monastery at Lyons became a great center of Augustine studies.

As important as the preservation of ancient manuscripts was, Carolingian scholars did much more than just have books copied. Indeed, the renaissance was marked by the production of many new books in a variety of disciplines. One noteworthy area of production was in the writing of history, biography, and hagiography. Carolingian authors wrote numerous saints' lives, as well as more traditional works of history and biography. One of the most famous contributions of the renaissance was the life of Charlemagne, written by his friend and advisor Einhard. The biography provides a somewhat idealized portrait of the great ruler, one that borrows heavily from the ancient Roman biographer Suetonius, but still provides important insights into the personality, appearance, and achievements of its subject. A later ninth-century writer, Notker the Stammerer, also wrote a life of Charlemagne for one his descendants that offers an even more idealized version of the great emperor's life. Charlemagne was not the only Carolingian to be immortalized in a biography, however. Louis the Pious was the subject of three biographies written in his own lifetime, including one in verse. Numerous annals were also written at the monasteries throughout the Carolingian realm, along with the semiofficial *Royal Frankish Annals* and the famous history of the civil wars of the mid-ninth century by Nithard.

Carolingian Renaissance authors also wrote numerous commentaries on the books of the Bible, as well as treatises on proper Christian behavior. Alcuin, Theodulf of Orléans, and others wrote a number of treatises defending the Carolingian understanding of the faith against Adoptionists (Christian heretics who taught that Jesus was the son by adoption) in Spain, icon worshippers in the Byzantine Empire, and others who went astray. Manuals of education and Christian learning, an encyclopedic work by Rabanus Maurus, works of law and political practice by Hincmar of Rheims, and epistles of almost classical elegance by Lupus of Ferrieres were among other noteworthy works of Carolingian writers. Carolingian scholars also wrote Latin poetry. Their work may not be the most

original or inspired, but it demonstrates the degree of sophistication they achieved, as well as providing great insights into the court of Charlemagne and its values.

Although initiated by Charlemagne, the renaissance enjoyed its greatest achievements in the generations following his death. And there is perhaps no better witness of the intellectual confidence and maturity reached by the Carolingian scholars than the doctrinal controversies that took place in the mid-ninth century. One dispute, which concerned the exact nature of the Eucharist, involved the theologians Paschasius Radbertus and Ratramnus of Corbie. An even greater controversy involved the reluctant monk, Gottschalk of Orbais, and a great number of Carolingian theologians. The dispute revolved around Gottschalk's doctrine of predestination and his interpretation of the teachings of St. Augustine of Hippo. Gottschalk's teachings, which promoted the doctrine of double predestination (that is, both to hell and heaven), caused concern among the clergy, especially his bishop, Rabanus Maurus. The dispute attracted the attention of Hincmar of Rheims and the court royal of Charles the Bald. The king himself called upon the brilliant theologian, also the only Carolingian scholar with an understanding of Greek, John Scotus Erigena. His response to Gottschalk, however, was misunderstood by those around him and even further complicated the situation. That notwithstanding, the ability of the Carolingians to carry on high-level doctrinal debates demonstrates the maturity and sophistication of the Carolingian Renaissance.

The achievements of the Carolingian Renaissance were not, however, limited to literary and theological works and book production. Carolingian artists and architects created a great number of brilliant works in the plastic arts. The most notable architectural monument of the Carolingian age, and one of the few remaining (because most buildings were made of wood), was the palace complex that Charlemagne, with the help of his chief architect, Einhard, built at Aix-la-Chapelle (modern Aachen, Germany). The palace was a magnificent structure, as the remaining portion, an octagonal chapel inspired by late Roman imperial models in Italy, suggests. Carolingian artists were skilled jewelers and goldsmiths and created beautiful works in ivory, often used as covers for manuscripts. But perhaps the most remarkable Carolingian works of art are the miniatures that illuminated numerous manuscripts of the late eighth and ninth centuries.

Carolingian painting drew from a varied legacy of Roman, Christian, and Germanic influences. It clearly borrowed from ancient Roman models, its themes were often related to Christian themes and scenes from the Scriptures, and it incorporated the geometric designs and animal figures popular in Germanic traditions. Illustrations based on the Gospels and the Book of Revelation were popular, as were scenes depicting King David, an important figure in Carolingian political thought. Carolingian artists also left stunning depictions of the Evangelists, renderings of various Carolingian kings, and numerous representations of Christ in majesty, an image that had both religious and political connotations for the Carolingians. As with all aspects of the renaissance, Carolingian kings promoted painting, and the courts of Charlemagne and Charles the Bald were especially noteworthy for their support of art.

See also Admonitio Generalis; Agobard of Lyons; Alcuin of York; Ammianus Marcellinus; Anglo-Saxons; Augustine of Hippo, St.; Barbarian Art; Bede; Capitularies; Carolingian Dynasty; Cassiodorus; Charlemagne; Charles the Bald; Dhuoda; Einhard; Gottschalk of Orbais; Gregory I the Great; Hincmar of Rheims; Isidore of Seville; Ivories; John Scotus Erigena; Letter to Baugulf; Louis the Pious; Nithard; Pippin III, Called Pippin the Short; *Royal Frankish Annals;* Theodulf of Orléans

Bibliography
Beckwith, John. *Early Medieval Art.* London: Thames and Hudson, 1969.

Brown, Giles. "Introduction: The Carolingian Renaissance." In *Carolingian Culture: Emulation and Innovation,* ed. Rosamond McKitterick. Cambridge: Cambridge University Press, 1994, pp. 1–51.

Cabaniss, Allen, trans. *Son of Charlemagne: A Contemporary Life of Louis the Pious.* Syracuse, NY: Syracuse University Press, 1961.

Contreni, John J. "The Carolingian Renaissance: Education and Literary Culture." In *The New Cambridge Medieval History,* vol. 2, ed. Rosamond McKitterick. Cambridge: Cambridge University Press, 1995, pp. 709–757.

Dutton, Paul. *Carolingian Civilization: A Reader.* Peterborough, Ont.: Broadview, 1993.

Einhard and Notker the Stammerer. *Two Lives of Charlemagne.* Trans Lewis Thorpe. Harmondsworth, UK: Penguin, 1981.

Henderson, George. "Emulation and Invention in Carolingian Art." In *The New Cambridge Medieval History,* vol. 2, edited by Rosamond McKitterick. Cambridge: Cambridge University Press, 1995, pp. 248–273.

Hubert, Jean, Jean Porcher, and Wolfgang Fritz Volbach. *The Carolingian Renaissance.* New York: George Braziller, 1970.

Laistner, Max L. W. *Thought and Letters in Western Europe, A.D. 500 to 900.* 2d ed. Ithaca, NY: Cornell University Press, 1976.

McKitterick, Rosamond. *The Carolingians and the Written Word.* Cambridge: Cambridge University Press, 1989.

———. *The Frankish Kingdoms under the Carolingians, 751–987.* London: Longman, 1983.

Mütherich, Florentine, and Joachim E. Gaehde. *Carolingian Painting.* New York: George Braziller, 1976.

Nelson, Janet. *Charles the Bald.* London: Longman, 1992.

Riché, Pierre. *Education and Culture in the Barbarian West: From the Sixth to the Eighth Century.* Trans. John Contreni. Columbia: University of South Carolina Press, 1976.

———. *The Carolingians: A Family Who Forged Europe.* Trans Michael Idomir Allen.

Philadelphia: University of Pennsylvania Press, 1993.

Scholz, Bernhard Walter, trans. *Carolingian Chronicles: Royal Frankish Annals and Nithard's History.* Ann Arbor: University of Michigan Press, 1972.

Cassiodorus (c. 490–c. 585)

One of the great scholars of late antiquity, Cassiodorus, in full Flavius Magnus Aurelius Cassiodorus, wrote one of the most influential works on later barbarian Europe and, like, the senator and scholar Boethius, was an important advisor to the Ostrogothic king of Italy, Theodoric the Great. Like Boethius, Cassiodorus came from a prominent noble family and rose through the ranks of government. He held numerous high offices and was secretary to Theodoric. Unlike Boethius, he left government service to dedicate himself to letters and the religious life. He founded a monastery, Vivarium, where he spent the end of his life quietly and wrote one of the great classics of sacred learning. He also wrote works of history and theology and encouraged his monks to copy important manuscripts. His influence lasted long beyond his long life; his great library was dispersed, benefiting many later scholars, including the great Anglo-Saxon scholar of the eighth century, the Venerable Bede, who used a Bible once owned by Cassiodorus.

Born to a noble family of southern Italy, Cassiodorus enjoyed a long and active life. In the footsteps of his grandfather, who served the emperor and was sent on an embassy to Attila the Hun, and his father, who served the king Odovacar, Cassiodorus followed the traditional path of Roman families and devoted himself to service to the state. By his time, however, it was no longer the ancient Roman emperors that he served, but a series of Ostrogothic rulers, most importantly Theodoric the Great and then his daughter Amalswintha. Before joining the royal court, Cassiodorus served in various imperial offices, including the prestigious office of consul. He was Theodoric's secretary and wrote many of the king's letters to popes, emperors, and kings. He later served as the praetorian prefect of Amalswintha, whose death precipitated the invasion of Italy by Justinian.

His services throughout his long career were highly valued, and, unlike Boethius, he never lost the confidence of his masters. He also conducted a personal correspondence with various popes in Rome, including Pope Agapetus I (r. 535–536), to whom he suggested establishing a school of higher Christian learning. His service lasted into the 530s at least, and he appears to have retired to his ancestral estates around 538. There is, however, evidence that he was in Constantinople in 550, possibly in the service of the pope. His retirement from government service, whenever it finally occurred, found him at the monastic community he founded in 540 or 553 on his family land, which was called Vivarium because of the fish ponds (in Latin, *vivaria*) that decorated the estate.

While loyally serving the Gothic rulers of Italy, Cassiodorus began his other lifelong career, the pursuit of learning, especially learning in the service of the faith. It was in this endeavor, which was demonstrated in his letter to Agapetus and in the foundation of his monastery, that Cassiodorus left his greatest legacy.

See also Amalswintha; Attila the Hun; Boethius; Huns; Jordanes; Justinian; Odovacar; Ostrogoths; Theodoric the Great

Bibliography

Amory, Patrick. *People and Identity in Ostrogothic Italy, 489–554.* Cambridge: Cambridge University Press, 1997.

Bury, John B. *History of the Later Roman Empire: From the Death of Theodosius I to the Death of Justinian.* 2 vols. 1923. Reprint, New York: Dover, 1959.

Cassiodorus. *The Variae of Magnus Aurelius Cassiodorus.* Trans. S. J. B. Barnish. Liverpool, UK: Liverpool University Press, 1992.

Heather, Peter. *The Goths.* Oxford: Blackwell, 1996.

Hodgkin, Thomas. *Theodoric the Goth: The Barbarian Champion of Civilization*. New York: G. P. Putnam, 1983.

Laistner, Max L. W. *Thought and Letters in Western Europe, A.D. 500 to 900*. 2d ed. Ithaca, NY: Cornell University Press, 1976.

Llewellyn, Peter. *Rome in the Dark Ages*. New York: Barnes and Noble, 1993.

O'Donnell, James J. *Cassiodorus*. Berkeley: University of California Press, 1979.

Riché, Pierre. *Education and Culture in the Barbarian West: From the Sixth through the Eighth Century*. Trans. John Contreni. Columbia: University of South Carolina Press, 1976.

Wolfram, Herwig. *The Roman Empire and Its Germanic Peoples*. Trans. Thomas J. Dunlap. Berkeley: University of California Press, 1997.

Catalaunian Plains, Battle of the (451)

Major battle in June 451 between Attila the Hun and his Hunnish and allied armies against the Roman imperial forces and their allies, led by the great general Aëtius. Although it is traditionally known at the Battle of the Catalaunian Plains or Battle of Châlons, J. B. Bury has argued that because of the battlefield's proximity to Troyes it should be known as the Battle of Troyes. Whatever the name should be, the battle was the most important of several that Attila fought as part of his invasion of the Western Empire in the early 450s. Although the battle ended in a draw, Attila himself was on the verge of suicide during the fighting and survived only because Aëtius allowed him to escape.

The battle itself was part of Attila's campaign in the Western Empire after several years harassing the Eastern Empire and extracting significant wealth and political concessions from Constantinople. The invasion of 451 may have been brought on by the emperor's sister, Honoria, who, like her aunt Galla Placidia, may have offered her hand in marriage to the barbarian king. Attila's demands for Honoria and other things were rejected, and therefore he invaded Gaul, seizing Metz, Rheims, and numerous other cities before being repulsed at the important city of Orléans. Despite that setback, Attila caused great destruction and bloodshed and threatened Visigothic power in Gaul. The Goths were compelled to assist the imperial armies in defense of Gaul because of the ferocity of Attila's assault.

After leaving Orléans, Attila moved toward Troyes, where he met the imperial armies of Aëtius, which included Alans, Bretons, Franks, Burgundians, and Visigoths. Attila's army was also made up of peoples of numerous nations, including his own Huns, Alans, Franks, Gepids, Heruls, and Ostrogoths. On the eve of the battle, Attila consulted a priest who examined bones of a sheep. The priest proclaimed that the Huns would lose the battle but that a great enemy leader would fall; Attila desired the death of the leader and therefore risked battle. On the day of the battle, Attila arranged his Huns in the center of his lines and the subject peoples on both flanks. On the opposite side, Aëtius, with his Romans, commanded the left flank; Theodoric commanded his Visigoths on the right flank; and the center was held by the Alans. After major skirmishing on the previous night, the battle began at three o'clock in the afternoon and went on into the evening.

It was a ferocious battle, which, according to one contemporary, ended with 165,000 dead, including the Visigothic king Theodoric. The battle went so badly for Attila that he fortified himself in a circle of wagons, preparing for the final assault that would have left him dead from battle or from suicide. But the Roman commander, Aëtius, recognized the value of having Attila's Huns as a legitimate threat to other barbarian peoples in order to preserve the balance of power. Consequently, Attila was allowed to withdraw from the battlefield without being annihilated by the armies of Aëtius. Although the battle ended technically as a draw, Aëtius could claim victory because he stopped Attila's advance and killed a large number of his enemy's troops.

The battle was a major setback for Attila, who was forced to withdraw from his invasion following the contest on the Catalaunian Plains. Although he again invaded Italy in the following year, Attila's aura of invincibility was damaged and his army seriously depleted by the near disaster on the battlefield between Châlons and Troyes. Although the importance of the battle is overstated when it is described as one of the great battles of history, it was an important moment in late imperial history because Attila's virtual defeat left him much less of a threat to the Roman empire. Never a serious threat to the life of the empire, Attila nonetheless demanded significant tribute from the empire, and anything that weakened his challenge was a benefit to the emperors.

See also Aëtius; Attila the Hun; Galla Placidia; Huns; Visigoths

Bibliography
Bury, John B. *History of the Later Roman Empire: From the Death of Theodosius I to the Death of Justinian.* Vol. 1. 1923. Reprint, New York: Dover, 1959.
———. *The Invasions of Europe by the Barbarians.* New York and London: W. W. Norton, 1967.
Randers-Pehrson, Justine Davis. *Barbarians and Romans: The Birth Struggle of Europe,* A.D. *400–700.* Norman: University of Oklahoma Press, 1983.
Thompson, Edward A. *A History of Attila and the Huns.* Oxford: Clarendon, 1948.
———. *The Huns.* Oxford: Blackwell, 1995.
Wolfram, Herwig. *The Roman Empire and Its Germanic Peoples.* Trans. Thomas J. Dunlap. Berkeley: University of California Press, 1997.

Charlemagne (742–814)

The greatest king of the Middle Ages, Charlemagne forged a powerful empire during his long reign from 768 to 814 and left an indelible mark on his age and the generations to come. The son of Pippin the Short, the first Carolingian king, Charles (called Charles the Great, in Latin Carolus Magnus, whence his commonly used name) inherited an important political and military legacy from his father. He used that inheritance and expanded upon it, creating a political ideal that would influence European history for the next thousand years.

The great king was physically and personally imposing as well. A full seven times the length of his foot in height, according to his biographer Einhard, Charlemagne towered over his contemporaries, of lofty stature and of regal bearing whether seated or standing. Although his neck was thick, his stomach rather pronounced, and his voice a bit higher than his size would suggest, Charles carried himself in such a way as to make these defects unnoticeable. His health was excellent until old age, but even then he refused to eat boiled meat as his doctors recommended. He had long hair, large eyes, and his face was cheerful and full of laughter.

In his biography Einhard describes a monarch who was most personable and who loved company. He often had many guests to dinner, where he indulged in food but drank only in moderation, while German epic tales were told or pages from the works of St. Augustine of Hippo were read. Moreover, he built a great palace over a hot spring, where he would swim with many fellow bathers. He seldom went anywhere without his daughters, whom he loved so much that he could not bear to be apart from them. His daughters never married, but they did bear Charles several grandchildren he loved as dearly as he loved his own children. He took great pains to educate his children and often took them riding and hunting, pastimes at which he excelled and which he enjoyed greatly. He was also deeply religious, according to the climate of the age, attended mass regularly, and honored the pope, bishops, and abbots. For Einhard, Charlemagne was as great a person as he was a ruler.

The early part of his reign, however, was a time of crisis. In accordance with Frankish tradition, at his death in 768 Pippin divided the realm between his two sons, Charles and

Equestrian statue of Charlemagne or another Carolingian ruler (The Art Archive / Musée du Louvre Paris / Dagli Orti)

Carloman. In some ways the division was more favorable to the younger Carloman, whose kingdom was compact and easier to manage than the territory given to Charles. Moreover, Charles received territory that had only recently been fully incorporated into the kingdom and was more susceptible to revolt at the change of leadership. And in the opening years of his reign Charles did face a serious revolt in his territory, which was suppressed only with difficulty. The situation was made all the worse by Carloman's unwillingness to come to his brother's aid. Despite efforts to prevent civil war by their mother, Bertrada, who had recently arranged a marriage for her older son with the daughter of the Lombard king, tensions ran high between her two sons. The two were on the point of war when Carloman suddenly died, leaving Charles as the sole Carolingian king, a situation he exploited by dispossessing his nephews and repudiating his Lombard wife.

Having survived his brother and a potentially disastrous civil war, Charlemagne was now able to make his mark as king. His success as king rested on his indomitable will and his ability as a warrior, a fact recognized by Einhard, who dedicated much of his tale of the great king to his military campaigns. One of Charlemagne's first actions after Carloman's death was the conquest of Saxony, a process that lasted thirty years and had important consequences for later medieval history. The wars began in 772 as punitive expeditions against Saxon raiders who plundered Frankish territory, but soon after took on a crusading character. Perhaps inspired by the support the Anglo-Saxon missionary St. Boniface received from his father, Pippin the Short, and uncle, Carloman, Charlemagne was determined to convert the pagan Saxons to Christianity. The great king not only sent armies of warriors into Saxony to impose Frankish political authority over the inhabitants but also sent armies of priests to spread the Christian faith. The Saxons, however, refused to accept the great privilege of being subject to the political and

religious power of the Franks and resisted mightily.

One contemporary lamented that the Saxons revolted against Carolingian rule annually, and Frankish armies had to return to put down the revolts. Charlemagne would not be refused, however, and he met force with force. He imposed the death penalty for Saxons who harmed priests or practiced pagan religion, as well as for those who violated Christian fasts or burned their dead. His warriors destroyed pagan shrines, massacred 4,500 Saxons at Verdun, and moved many Saxons from their homeland into Frankish territory; his priests imposed baptism before teaching the Saxons the Christian faith and built churches on destroyed pagan shrines. Even the great revolt of Widukind (782–785) did not stop the process of conversion and subjugation of the Saxons. Charles's brutality was tempered by the time of the second Saxon capitulary of 797, which provided the milk and honey of the faith instead of Frankish iron. Charlemagne's conquest and conversion of the Saxons was completed by the early ninth century, a process that bore great fruit in the tenth century.

Charlemagne's activities as a warrior found other theaters as well. He annexed Bavaria after its duke, Tassilo, failed to honor an oath he had sworn to attend the court of the Frankish king. Breaking an oath was seen as a violation of God's will, and thus again Charlemagne could be seen doing God's work and ensuring God's justice. In the early 790s, in part as a result of the annexation of Bavaria, he was forced to secure his southeastern frontier. He sent his armies against the remnants of the Hunnish tribes that had plundered Europe savagely and smashed the central stronghold of the Huns. Huge wagonloads of treasures were taken from the Huns, and a good portion was diverted to the pope in Rome.

Great conqueror though he was, Charlemagne's military record is not without failure. In the last years of his reign he was unable to respond successfully to the attacks of the Danes, whose lands abutted the Carolingian Empire as a result of the conquest of the Saxons. He also suffered a serious defeat in 778. In that year, responding to the invitation of the Muslim leader of Barcelona to assist him in a struggle against the Spanish emir, Charlemagne invaded Spain. He found his allies in disarray and was able to accomplish little in Spain, but worse was to come. As he crossed the Pyrenees back into France his rearguard was attacked, and it and its commander, Roland, were destroyed. The memory of the event later provided the foundation for one of the most enduring epics of the Middle Ages, the *Song of Roland,* but this could provide little consolation for Charlemagne, who left Spain early to respond to unrest in the kingdom and to another in the series of Saxon revolts. Indeed, the great king not only faced the occasional military setback, he also faced a number of revolts during his long reign, including one led by his favorite illegitimate son, Pippin the Hunchback.

Despite the occasional failure and revolt, Charlemagne was a warlord to be reckoned with. He did suppress the revolts he faced, and he extended the boundaries of the empire with the creation of the Spanish March, a militarized border region that included territory on the Spanish side of the Pyrenees. But his most important military campaign, after the conquest of Saxony, was his conquest of the kingdom of the Lombards in Italy. This was also one of his earliest victories (773–774), following shortly after the death of his brother Carloman in 771. It signaled a dramatic reversal of a Carolingian policy of close ties with the Lombards that had been in effect, in some ways, since the time of Charlemagne's grandfather, Charles Martel. Even though his father, Pippin the Younger, invaded Italy twice, he did so without the force or the desire that Charlemagne had. Moreover, it was also a dramatic change in the personal life of the king himself. His mother, hoping to keep the peace among her sons and with traditional Frankish allies, had arranged a marriage between her older son and Desiderata, the daughter of the Lombard

king in Italy, Desiderius. But Charles repudiated his wife and broke with the Lombards, preferring to ally himself with a far greater power, the pope in Rome. His invasion quickly brought about the defeat of the Lombards and the capture of their capital at Pavia. His invasion also brought much new territory to the growing empire, as Charles not only defeated Desiderius but deposed him and usurped his crown.

The conquest of the Lombards was important for a number of reasons. It brought Charlemagne into close contact with Rome, provided him the legal right to exercise authority in Italy as the king of the Lombards, brought under his control the heartland of the old Roman Empire, and gave him the opportunity to visit Rome as a pilgrim. The first of several visits to the city, his pilgrimage in 774 strengthened the devotion that Charles and his line had for St. Peter and reinforced the family's relationship with Peter's successor, the pope. Although relations with the reigning pope, Hadrian, were sometimes strained, they were of great importance to Charles, who wept openly when Hadrian died. Rome supplied Carolingian ecclesiastics and their king with a great deal of material essential to Carolingian church reform, including numerous legal and liturgical texts. But more than a source for religious reform and spiritual inspiration, Rome provided Charles with the political justification of his power as an anointed ruler.

One of his most important legacies was his idea of kingship. His father before him had been crowned and anointed by the pope, an act that consciously recalled the ceremonies at the crowning of the ancient kings of Israel. The influence of the Hebrew Bible on the Carolingians was great, and the biblical king David was the model king for the new Frankish dynasty. Charlemagne himself, inspired by his court scholars, saw himself as a "new David" ruling a new chosen people and was given the nickname of David by those at court. He saw himself as God's anointed, with responsibilities over God's church and people, a belief that manifested itself in his relations with the church in his kingdom and in Rome. In his capitularies, he instituted moral reform of the clergy, encouraging them to know the mass, to live a chaste life, and to avoid frequenting taverns. He also reformed the organization of the Frankish church. He introduced liturgical reforms, appointed bishops and abbots, and employed ecclesiastics in the highest levels of his government. He felt an obligation to defend the faith from heresy and moral corruption and to extend the boundaries of Christendom. His conquests accomplished the goal of extending the faith, and he presided over church councils to protect the faith from internal enemies. At his most famous council, at Frankfurt in 794, he and the assembled clerics denounced the Spanish heresy of Adoptionism (teaching that Jesus was the son of God by adoption), struggled to find the appropriate response to the Iconoclastic Controversy in the Byzantine Empire, and instituted a series of organizational and disciplinary reforms.

As an anointed Christian king, Charles felt obligated to ensure justice throughout his realm, and to accomplish this end he implemented several new administrative practices and reformed existing ones. The use of writing in government increased dramatically during Charlemagne's reign, and the most important instrument in his administration was the capitulary, a written decree divided into chapters (*capitula*). These laws addressed a broad range of topics, and the greatest of them, the *Admonitio Generalis* of 789, outlined Charlemagne's program of government. Other capitularies addressed matters of secular and ecclesiastical administration, religious reform, religious belief and orthodoxy, legal jurisdiction, the price of bread, weights and measures, and general economic matters. The capitularies were issued, often orally (to be afterward written down), from the effective center of government, Charlemagne's court, which moved from place to place and was attended by the leading religious and secular figures of the kingdom.

On the local level Charlemagne's will and desire for justice was implemented by a number of officers. The most important regional officer was the count, who ruled over a specific territorial unit. The count was the king's deputy and received the authority to govern from the king. He was responsible for protecting the interests of the king and disseminating his laws. The count had the right to punish criminals and was expected to maintain peace and order. He also owed military and court service to the king, and could be called on to serve as the king's special envoy. Another area of comital responsibility was the administration of justice, and included in that was the appointment of the *scabini*. The *scabini* were a new class of permanent judges established by Charlemagne to render judgment of legal disputes at the local level. The most important of the royal officials, however, were the *missi dominici,* or messengers of the lord king. These officials, eventually sent out in pairs of one secular and one ecclesiastical noble, were charged with ensuring the proper application of royal laws and justice. They were to guarantee that legal cases were resolved without corruption and that the king's other representatives—counts, judges, and the like—enforced the law honorably.

Charlemagne's sense of responsibility as an anointed Christian king was perhaps the source of inspiration for his promotion of what is called Carolingian Renaissance. Although not the decisive break with an earlier "dark age" it has traditionally been considered, the renaissance did see a quickening of intellectual pace and a dramatic increase in the use of writing in government and the church. Charlemagne's goal was to create an educated clergy that could properly say the mass and teach the fundamentals of the faith to his people. As God's chosen king, he felt responsible for the salvation of his people and desired that all his subjects know the Lord's Prayer and the Apostles' Creed. To do this he needed learned priests and books. He attracted some of the best minds of his day, including Theodulf of Orléans, Paul the Deacon, Peter of Pisa, and, most importantly, the great Anglo-Saxon scholar and teacher, Alcuin of York. These scholars brought with them a devotion to Charlemagne's reforms and a devotion to Christian learning, which they shared with their students, who then contributed to the increasing sophistication of Carolingian government and society. They brought great learning with them, as well as numerous books, especially books of the Bible, and they oversaw the production of new copies of these books. And, beginning in Charlemagne's day, his efforts at cultural reform led to the production of a new edition of the Bible, heightened theological discussion, works of history and poetry, and numerous magnificently illuminated manuscripts.

By the last decade of the eighth century, Charlemagne was the preeminent figure of Western Europe. He ruled over the greatest kingdom, presided over councils and governmental and religious reform, and in many ways rivaled the Byzantine emperor in status and prestige. Indeed, there was the sense among some of his court scholars that Charles was more than a king. A letter from Charlemagne to the pope in 795, a letter from Alcuin to Charlemagne in 799, and the palace complex at Aachen, which was modeled on an imperial palace in Ravenna, all suggest that Charlemagne, or at least those around him, had imperial pretensions. Whether Charles did harbor the desire to be recognized as an emperor in the 790s is unknowable, but the opportunity to become an emperor presented itself shortly after the ascension of Leo III to the papal throne.

The chain of events that led to Charlemagne's elevation to the imperial dignity began in a crisis early in the reign of Pope Leo III. Elected pope in 795 after the death of the powerful and well-connected Hadrian, Leo faced the challenge of ruling the church with significant enemies in Rome, especially relatives of the former pope who were dissatisfied by the election of Leo. Although Charlemagne supported the new pope and called on him to raise his arms in prayer like

Moses to support the success in battle of the king, Leo's position remained tenuous. On April 25, 799, Leo was attacked by Hadrian's nephews, Paschal and Campulus, while leading a religious procession through the streets of Rome. He was dragged from his horse and, according to some reports, was blinded and had his tongue cut out. He was then imprisoned in the monastery of St. Erasmus, and his attackers alleged that he was corrupt and guilty of adultery and perjury. He escaped from the monastery and was escorted to the Frankish court by one of Charlemagne's dukes in Italy, where he regained the powers of sight and speech. He was welcomed by the king and returned to Rome, where he awaited the arrival of the king to resolve the dispute.

In November 800, Charles and a sizeable entourage ventured to Rome to determine the fate of the rebels and the pope. After several weeks of meeting with the pope and the nobility, a great council was held on December 23 where the rebels were found guilty and condemned to death, a sentence which was commuted to exile at Leo's request. Leo himself swore an oath of his innocence, which was accepted by all. On Christmas day, Charles attended a mass presided over by the pope, who placed a crown on the king's head when he rose from kneeling at the altar. The assembled crowd then arose and proclaimed Charles emperor and augustus.

The empire had been revived and a new emperor crowned, but according to Einhard, had Charlemagne known what was going to happen he would not have attended mass that day. Einhard's remark has troubled historians ever since. It is most unlikely that Charles did not know and approve of what was going to happen. Although the imperial crown offered him little real new power, it surely brought great prestige. His conquests, his creation of an empire, and his protection of the church qualified him for the position in the eyes of his contemporaries and most likely in his own eyes. The construction of the palace and church in Aachen demonstrated his sense of his imperial authority, and his court scholars had spoken of him in imperial terms throughout the decade. Moreover, a letter from his most important advisor, Alcuin of York, identified Charlemagne as the greatest power in Christendom, given the attack on Leo and the vacancy of the imperial throne in Constantinople (vacant in eighth-century eyes because it was held by a woman). Indeed, it is quite likely that Charlemagne knew that he was to be crowned emperor and welcomed the imperial crown, but perhaps he was troubled by the way the coronation itself took place.

The coronation opened the final phase of Charlemagne's career, a period of diminished activity for the emperor, during which the strains of empire began to show. The emperor was less active on the military front and faced an increasing Viking threat, one that his armies had difficulty stopping. He was also less peripatetic than he had been earlier in his reign, settling primarily at the palace at Aachen. He continued to pass new laws, however, including a capitulary in 802 that restated the religious and political program he had long promoted, now presented as the program of an emperor. By 802 he had also decided on his official title and had come to accept and appreciate the honor bestowed on Christmas day 800. In 806 he issued a succession decree, in which he divided the empire among his three sons but did not bestow the imperial title, which he may have regarded as a personal honor, on any of them. In 813 he altered the decree because two of his sons had died, leaving only his son Louis as his eventual successor. Charlemagne crowned Louis emperor in a great ceremony at Aachen, which was attended by members of the secular and religious aristocracy but not the pope. Having settled his affairs, dividing his wealth among his children and the church, Charlemagne died on January 28, 814.

Although the empire dissolved in little more than a generation after his death, Charlemagne left an indelible mark on his age and the later Middle Ages. His model of Christian kingship remained the ideal for much of the rest of the Middle Ages, and the imperial dignity he created was regarded as the ultimate expression of political power into the modern era. The close ties he forged with the popes in Rome influenced political events long after his death, and his reform of the church in his kingdom revived a sagging institution. The efforts at cultural and religious renewal that created the Carolingian Renaissance established an important foundation for later cultural growth in the Middle Ages. Indeed, Charlemagne's achievement was unsurpassed in the early Middle Ages, and he was the greatest king of the entire Middle Ages.

See also Admonitio Generalis; Capitularies; Carolingian Dynasty; Louis the Pious; Pippin III, Called Pippin the Short

Bibliography

Bullough, Donald. "*Europae Pater:* Charlemagne and His Achievement in the Light of Recent Scholarship." *English Historical Review* 75 (1970): 59–105.

Collins, Roger. *Charlemagne.* Toronto: University of Toronto Press, 1998.

Davis, Raymond, trans. *The Lives of the Eighth-Century Popes* (Liber Pontificalis): *The Ancient Biographies of Nine Popes from* A.D. *715 to* A.D. *817.* Liverpool, UK: Liverpool University Press, 1992.

Dutton, Paul. *Carolingian Civilization: A Reader.* Peterborough, Ont.: Broadview, 1993.

Einhard and Notker the Stammerer. *Two Lives of Charlemagne.* Trans. Lewis Thorpe. Harmondsworth, UK: Penguin, 1981.

Fichtenau, Heinrich. *The Carolingian Empire.* Trans. Peter Munz. Toronto: University of Toronto Press, 1979.

Ganshof, François Louis. *The Carolingians and the Frankish Monarchy: Studies in Carolingian History.* Trans. Janet Sondheimer. London: Longman, 1971.

———. *Frankish Institutions under Charlemagne.* Trans. Bryce Lyon and Mary Lyon. Providence, RI: Brown University Press, 1968.

Halphen, Louis. *Charlemagne and the Carolingian*

Empire. Trans. Giselle de Nie. Amsterdam: North-Holland, 1977.

McKitterick, Rosamond. *The Frankish Kingdoms under the Carolingians, 751–987.* London: Longman, 1983.

McKitterick, Rosamond, ed. *Carolingian Culture: Emulation and Innovation.* Cambridge: Cambridge University Press, 1994.

Riché, Pierre. *The Carolingians: A Family Who Forged Europe.* Trans. Michael Idomir Allen. Philadelphia: University of Pennsylvania Press, 1993.

Scholz, Bernhard Walter, trans. *Carolingian Chronicles: Royal Frankish Annals and Nithard's History.* Ann Arbor: University of Michigan Press, 1972.

Sullivan, Richard E. *Aix-la-Chapelle in the Age of Charlemagne.* Norman: University of Oklahoma Press, 1963.

Charles Martel (d. 741)

Son of Pippin II of Herstal and father of Pippin III the Short, Charles, later known as Martel (the Hammer), was an important Carolingian mayor of the palace, whose reign, after a difficult beginning, marked a significant step in the growth of his family's power and the erosion of the power of the Merovingian dynasty. His reign as mayor witnessed important changes in relations between his line and the Frankish church, not all of which were positive from the church's point of view. He did, however, support the activities of missionaries, including the great Anglo-Saxon St. Boniface, in the kingdom and along the realm's frontier, and was seen as a champion of the church by the pope in Rome, who sought his aid. Charles is best known for his victory over invading Muslims from Spain at the Battle of Poitiers, a significant, although generally overemphasized, military victory.

Although he eventually came to command the entire Frankish kingdom and was able to pass this power on to his sons Carloman and Pippin, Charles Martel had few advantages at the time of the death of his own father, Pippin

II, in December 714. Overlooked in the plan of succession to the office of mayor of the palace, which had come to rival the authority of the office of king in the early eighth century, Charles was in fact imprisoned by Pippin's widow, Plectrude. Charles, whose mother was one of Pippin's mistresses and so despised by Plectrude, was rejected for the office of mayor of the palace in Neustria by Plectrude in favor of her young grandson, Theodoald, whose father had been designated heir but who was murdered while praying at a religious shrine several months before Pippin's death. Despite these disadvantages, Charles managed to break out of prison and organize a warrior band to support his claims to power.

The next few years were critical for Charles, who faced rivals from within his own family and from other Frankish nobles. His first attempt to acquire power, in fact, was a failure. He was defeated by the mayor, Ragamfred, who had defeated and deposed Theodoald, and the Frisian ruler, Radbod, in 715, and forced to withdraw to his private estates. In the following year Ragamfred, who was supported by the newly crowned Merovingian king Chilperic II, turned against Plectrude, who had retired to Cologne and seized a large part of the treasure of Pippin. Charles, in the meanwhile, had organized a new band of soldiers and fell on Ragamfred as he left Cologne, inflicting heavy losses on his rival. In 717, Ragamfred and Charles again met in battle at Vinchy, where Charles again won a major victory over his rival. At this point Charles felt secure enough to promote his own Merovingian king, Chlotar IV (d. 718), and he seized Pippin's fortune from Plectrude. He next faced battle in 719 from Ragamfred and Duke Eudo of Aquitaine, and once again emerged victorious, pushing the Aquitainians out of the kingdom and taking control of Ragamfred's king. Clearly, Charles was now the dominant figure in the kingdom and was able to appoint a true do-nothing king (as the last Merovingian kings are often called). Theuderic IV, on Chilperic's death in 721.

Although he had secured his position as mayor of the palace by the early 720s, Charles's authority was not guaranteed, and he continued to expand his power in the kingdom throughout the 720s and 730s. During the next two decades, Charles imposed his authority over his fellow Franks and over tributary peoples along the frontier of the kingdom. In 723 he fought and defeated Ragamfred again, but Ragamfred remained in control of Angers until his death in 731. In the following years, Charles defeated the Saxons, Alemanni, Bavarians, and, in the later 730s, the Burundians, whose territory he subjugated all the way to the Mediterranean. His personal resolve and military skill enabled Charles to assume such great stature in the kingdom that he was able to rule without a Merovingian puppet after the death of Theuderic in 737.

Charles also extended Carolingian power into Aquitaine, where his former rival, Eudo, continued to rule until his death in 735. Charles was able to take over Aquitaine after Eudo's death, in part because the duke had sought Charles's aid against the Muslim invaders from Spain. Indeed, Eudo faced not only the growing power of his rival to the north in the 720s but also the encroachment of the Muslims. Eudo managed, on occasion, to beat back the Muslim invaders with a mixed army of Aquitainians and Franks, but was clearly on the defensive in the face of successive successful raids in the early 730s. He had little choice but to seek aid from Charles, whose willingness to join with Eudo occasioned his most famous military victory. The raids of the Spanish Muslims had become so serious in the early 730s that they had begun to enter Frankish territory. One raid reached especially deep into Frankish territory, and on October 25, 732, somewhere between Tours and Poitiers, Charles and his ally fought a great battle that stopped the Saracen advance. Although perhaps a bit exaggerated because it was merely a victory over a raiding party and not an invading army, Charles's victory at the Battle of Poitiers was an important

victory and was followed by his continued action against the Muslims, whom he pushed from Aquitaine by the end of the 730s. His victory and continued success against Muslim raiders were central to his subsequent reputation and his acquisition of Aquitaine.

Charles established his control in the Frankish kingdom by his military victories, but he was able to maintain that control by introducing new means to rule, including the appointment of family members to key positions in the church and the establishment of important new ties between his family and the church. He made numerous appointments to episcopal and abbatial office, sometimes deposing the supporter of a rival from the offices in order to make his appointment. He deposed one of Ragamfred's supporters as abbot of Fontanelle and replaced him with his nephew Hugo, who was later made bishop of Rouen and Paris. He appointed his lay supporter, Carivius, as bishop of Le Mans, and made another noble follower bishop of Redon. These appointments were made repeatedly throughout Charles's reign, and were made in both the heartland of the kingdom and regions like Aquitaine that were a new or restored part of the realm.

Many of the appointments were secular nobles with little training or inclination for the job, who often did more harm than good to the church. Indeed, by the ninth century, his reputation for secularizing church lands found him consigned to hell by religious writers. They did, however, strengthen Charles's position in the kingdom, improve his ties with noble families in newly acquired territories, and, ironically considering the lack of concern for things spiritual the appointments showed, strengthened his ties with the church. At the very least, appointment of lay followers to important ecclesiastical offices brought access to the church's wealth and lands to Charles.

Despite a poor record of appointments, Charles was not completely neglectful of the church, and his reputation for secularizing church property is generally exaggerated. Perhaps his most important connection with the church was his support and protection of the Anglo-Saxon missionary Boniface. The great apostle to the Germans, Boniface was allowed to introduce reform to the Frankish church and was afforded protection by Charles during his evangelical missions among the pagan Saxons. Boniface also reinforced Frankish attention to Rome and St. Peter. The Anglo-Saxon missionary visited Rome, received approval to preach from the pope, and was made the pope's representative in the Frankish kingdom. Boniface's devotion to Rome was reflected by the Franks, who came to the attention of the papacy during the time of Charles Martel. So great had Charles's reputation become that when Pope Gregory III needed help against the Lombards in the 730s he turned to Charles. The Carolingian mayor could not help the pope at the time, but the invitation foreshadowed similar communication between Pippin the Short and Pope Stephen II in the 750s. Indeed, the connection between Rome and the Carolingians that began to form during the reign of Charles was to be essential to the ultimate triumph of the dynasty.

By the end of his life Charles was clearly the dominant figure in the Frankish kingdom, and he could afford to rule without a Merovingian figurehead during the last four years of his life. Like a traditional Frankish king, he divided the realm between his two sons, who both ascended to the office of mayor on their father's death in 741. Charles's reign was critical to the ultimate success of his family. His military victories and ability to attract supporters from the aristocracy strengthened his family, and his recognition by the pope elevated Charles and his dynasty above the other families of the realm. Although the achievement of the kingship had to wait a generation, the groundwork for Carolingian succession to the throne was laid by Charles Martel.

See also Boniface, St.; Carolingian Dynasty; Charlemagne; Gregory III; Lombards; Merovingian Dynasty; Pippin II, Called Pippin of Herstal; Pippin III, Called Pippin the Short; Plectrude; Poitiers, Battle of

Bibliography

Wallace-Hadrill, John M., ed. and trans. *The Fourth Book of the Chronicle of Fredegar with Its Continuations.* London: Nelson, 1960.

Bachrach, Bernard S. *Merovingian Military Organization, 481–751.* Minneapolis: University of Minnesota Press, 1972.

Fouracre, Paul, and Richard A. Gerberding. *Late Merovingian France: History and Hagiography, 640–720.* Manchester, UK: University of Manchester Press, 1996.

Riché, Pierre. *The Carolingians: A Family Who Forged Europe.* Trans. Michael Idomir Allen. Philadelphia: University of Pennsylvania Press, 1993.

Wood, Ian. *The Merovingian Kingdoms, 450–751.* London: Longman, 1994.

Charles the Bald (823–877)

Carolingian king and emperor, Charles the Bald reigned during a time of great unrest for the Carolingian Empire. As fourth son of Louis the Pious and only son of Louis with his second wife Judith, Charles was forced to endure the challenges of his brothers to his father's authority and to his own legitimate rights of inheritance. After his father's death, Charles faced the rivalry of his brothers and participated in a terrible civil war that led to the division of the empire among Louis's three surviving sons. Charles came to rule the western part of the kingdom, the region that later became France. Although Charles did not receive the imperial title at the division of the empire, he actively sought after it and laid claim to it in 875. His pursuit of the imperial title was, in part, the result of his devotion to the memory of his grandfather, Charlemagne, and the greatness of his reign. Charles, like his grandfather, actively promoted cultural life in the kingdom and was the friend and patron of some of the most important scholars of the Carolingian Renaissance, including Hincmar of Rheims, Rabanus Maurus, and John Scotus Erigena.

Iluminated manuscript page of Charles the Bald enthroned (Bayerische Staatsbibliothek, Munich)

The birth of Charles the Bald in 823 was met with great joy, but also with some consternation because of the questions it raised about the succession to the throne after his father's death. Several years earlier, in 817, Louis the Pious had held a great council of the leading churchmen and nobles of the empire to determine the matter of the succession. He devised a system in which the realm was divided between his three sons, with the eldest, Lothar, recognized as co-emperor and, eventually, sole emperor. Louis's other two sons, Louis the German and Pippin, were made sub-kings and were granted authority within their own kingdoms but were subject to Louis and then Lothar. The birth of Charles complicated this settlement, a problem made worse because many believed that the settlement was divinely inspired and to undo it would be an offense against God. But this is precisely, under the influence of his wife Judith, what Louis did in the late 820s, with the consequence being revolts of his older sons in 830 and 833–834. During both revolts, Charles was packed off to a monastery, where he was to remain without claim to his inheritance. Charles was rescued both times by his father, who managed to regain, after some difficulty, control of the empire on both occasions. In 837 Charles was granted as his inheritance a sizeable kingdom that included much of modern France. In the following year, after the death of Charles's brother Pippin, Louis disinherited Pippin's sons and granted Aquitaine to his youngest son. Charles also benefited from the reconciliation his father made with Lothar, who had been Charles's godfather, and as a result Lothar and Charles forged an alliance in their father's last year.

After the death of Louis the Pious in 840, the alliances forged by Louis broke down, and the empire fell into civil war. Lothar, who had promised to protect Charles, now turned against him in an effort to take control of the entire empire. Charles quickly turned to his other brother, Louis the German, to forge an alliance against their mutual foe, and for the next three years the three brothers fought for control of the empire. In 841, Charles and Louis inflicted a stinging defeat on Lothar at the Battle of Fontenoy, which Nithard, the chronicler of the civil wars, notes was interpreted as God's judgment against Lothar, delivered by Charles and Louis. Firm in their conviction that God was on their side, and in the face of Lothar's continuing attempts to draw Charles away from Louis, Charles and Louis swore an oath to one another in 842. The so-called Oath of Strasbourg was an important moment in the civil wars, but important also because it contains the first recorded examples of the Romance and Germanic languages. The alliance held, and in 843, Lothar submitted and the three brothers accepted the Treaty of Verdun, which assigned the western kingdom to Charles; the eastern kingdom to Louis; and the central kingdom, Italy, and the imperial title to Lothar.

Over the next two decades and more Charles was involved in continued conflict with his brothers for preeminence in the empire and with the sons of Pippin for control of the west Frankish kingdom. In an effort to safeguard his position in his kingdom, Charles held a council in Coulaines, near Le Mans, in 843, in which he promised to protect the property of the church and the nobility and to secure peace and justice in the realm in exchange for the aid and counsel of the nobility. This was an important step in the relations of the king and nobles, in which Charles sought to establish a reciprocal working relationship. Although he was not always successful, Charles restructured government and administration in his kingdom in meaningful ways. Of course, he did not always have the support of the nobility, but Charles did manage to secure some support for his authority despite the nobility's ambitions. Notably, in Aquitaine he managed to find support despite local patriotism and support for the heirs of Pippin. Indeed, one of Louis the Pious's former allies now struggled against Charles, but because of some local support Charles was able to defeat him and also Pippin's heir. But, like his grandfather before him,

Charles was forced to recognize Aquitainian uniqueness, and he appointed his son, Charles the Child, king of Aquitaine. Moreover, although he had only mixed support from the nobility, Charles could count on the full support of the church in his kingdom, particularly from the indomitable bishop, Hincmar of Rheims. The church and bishops played a critical role in preserving Charles's authority in the face of invasion by his brother Louis the German in 858.

Relations with his brothers ebbed and flowed after the treaty of Verdun. At times, relations were better with Lothar and at others better with Louis the German. Indeed, warming relations between Lothar and Charles may have precipitated the invasion by Louis in 858. There were also examples, however, of cooperation between the three, best exemplified in the meeting at Meerssen in 847 to respond to the assaults by the Northmen. But as Charles became increasingly secure in his kingdom, and his brothers and nephews became less of a threat, Charles turned his attention to the kingdom of his nephew Lothar II, son of the emperor Lothar. Particularly after 860, Charles was in a position to expand his authority at the expense of his brothers. He was interested in the dynastic problems of his older brother's son and successor, who was unable to provide an heir or to gain the divorce he desired, and in 862, Charles and Louis agreed to share their nephew's territory, Lotharingian, on Lothar II's death. In 870, the year after Lothar's death, Louis and Charles signed the Treaty of Meerssen, in which they agreed to share their nephew's kingdom and ignored the claims of Louis II, the emperor who ruled in Italy. In 872, Pope Hadrian II wrote to Charles and expressed his support for the king's claim to the imperial title. Indeed, Charles's ambitions grew as his control of the west Frankish kingdom increased.

Seeking to expand his authority and resurrect the glory of his grandfather Charlemagne, Charles awaited the proper moment. When Louis II died without an heir in 875,

Charles seized the opportunity to become emperor, and on Christmas day of that year he was crowned by the pope, John VIII, in Rome. He was opposed by Louis the German, who sent troops to impede Charles's progress in Italy and invaded the western Frankish kingdom. Once again, Charles was saved by Hincmar and returned secure in his kingdom. Charles clearly intended to rule the entire empire, not just his kingdom, after the coronation. After the death of Louis the German in 876, Charles marched into Lothar's old kingdom to take control of Aachen, the imperial capital. He also threatened to invade the eastern Frankish kingdom of his late brother Louis, but became ill and was easily repulsed by the new king, his nephew Louis the Younger. Despite this setback, Charles remained dedicated to the imperial ideal and his responsibilities as emperor, and thus willingly accepted a call by the pope to come to the defense of Rome.

Preparing for his departure, Charles held a council at Quierzy in 877, and his proclamations at the council have long been seen as a concession to the nobility and the confirmation of the rights of hereditary succession. The capitulary of Quierzy, however, was intended to strengthen royal authority by reinforcing the king's right to recognize the successor to the office of count. He departed for Italy soon after the council but was forced to return when he learned of a revolt by the nobility and the invasion by Carloman, the eldest son of Louis the German. Worn out by overexertion, Charles died on his return to the kingdom on October 6, 877. Although his reign as emperor was short and tumultuous, Charles was one of the great Carolingian kings and a worthy heir of his namesake Charlemagne.

See also Carolingian Dynasty; Charlemagne; Fontenoy, Battle of; Judith; Lothar; Louis the German; Louis the Pious; Nithard; Strasbourg, Oath of; Verdun, Treaty of

Bibliography
Gibson, Margaret, and Janet Nelson, eds. *Charles*

the Bald: Court and Kingdom. Oxford: British Archaeological Reports, 1981.

Laistner, Max L. W. *Thought and Letters in Western Europe,* A.D. *500 to 900.* 2d ed. Ithaca, NY: Cornell University Press, 1976.

McKitterick, Rosamond. *The Frankish Kingdoms under the Carolingians, 751–987.* London: Longman, 1983.

Nelson, Janet. *Charles the Bald* London: Longman, 1992.

Riché, Pierre. *The Carolingians: A Family Who Forged Europe.* Trans Michael Idomir Allen. Philadelphia: University of Pennsylvania Press, 1993.

Scholz, Bernhard Walter, trans. *Carolingian Chronicles: Royal Frankish Annals and Nithard's History.* Ann Arbor: University of Michigan Press, 1972.

Childeric III (d. 754)

The last ruler of the Merovingian dynasty, Childeric was king from 743 to 751, but the real power in the Frankish kingdom was held by the Carolingian mayors of the palace, Pippin the Short and Carloman. Drawn from obscurity and hailed as the heir to the dynasty after a six-year interregnum, Childeric was a "do-nothing king" (one of the *rois fainéants,* as the later Merovingians are traditionally called), the puppet of the real rulers of Francia. In a memorable passage by Charlemagne's biographer, Einhard, Childeric is portrayed in most unsympathetic, almost ridiculous, terms. According to the biography, Childeric had little more than the empty title of king and had no influence on government beyond his annual visits to court. Arriving in a rustic oxcart led by a peasant, Childeric would play the role of king, sitting on his throne with his beard and long flowing hair (long hair was the symbol of Merovingian royal power), where he would receive ambassadors from other kingdoms. The answers he gave these ambassadors had been thoroughly rehearsed with the Carolingian mayors. Childeric was not only without political power but he was also without economic power. He owned only a single estate with a house and few servants. The estate itself brought him a meager income, and he was dependent upon the good graces of the mayors of the palace for his economic support. Childeric, thus, was a mere shadow of his illustrious ancestor Clovis (r. 481–511), the first Merovingian king.

Despite his alleged economic and political weakness, Childeric was not a completely useless king. It is likely, first of all, that Einhard exaggerated Childeric's inadequacies to enhance the reputation of the new Carolingian dynasty, and there is evidence that he issued charters and possessed more than a single estate. Clearly, the Merovingian monarch was highly dependent on his Carolingian patrons, but at his enthronement he declared that he was pleased to be restored to the kingship and pleased to allow the Carolingians help rule the kingdom. Moreover, he possessed a certain charisma as a member of the royal line that Pippin and Carloman did not possess. Indeed, it was that very charisma that the Carolingian mayors needed to secure their positions in the kingdom. Childeric was raised to the throne to establish continuity in the kingdom, or at least give the appearance that the traditional dynasty remained in control of the kingdom and that the good fortune of the dynasty would preserve the kingdom. The Carolingian mayors had faced widespread opposition within the Frankish kingdom that was, perhaps, worsened by the absence of a legitimate king. Their father, Charles Martel, had ruled as mayor without a king on the throne during his last years, and Pippin and Carloman inherited this situation To reduce internal opposition, they put Childeric on the throne, and thus he performed an important political function.

Childeric's utility, however, came to an end by the close of the 740s. In 747 Carloman withdrew from the world and retired to a monastery. Pippin was thus the sole mayor of the Frankish kingdom and much more secure in that role than he had been at the beginning of the 740s. In 750 he sent messengers to the pope in Rome asking if the person with the title or the person with the power should rule as king. The pope answered as Pippin had hoped, and in the following year Childeric was deposed, and Pippin assumed the throne. Childeric was tonsured and placed in a monastery, where he quietly lived out his days.

See also Carolingian Dynasty; Charlemagne; Charles Martel; Einhard; Merovingian Dynasty; Pippin III, Called Pippin the Short

Bibliography

Einhard and Notker the Stammerer. *Two Lives of Charlemagne.* Trans. Lewis Thorpe. Harmondsworth, UK: Penguin, 1981.

Wallace-Hadrill, J. M. *The Long-Haired Kings.* Toronto: University of Toronto Press, 1982.

Wood, Ian. *The Merovingian Kings, 450–751.* London: Longman, 1994.

Chilperic I (c. 537–584)

Merovingian king from 561 to 584, Chilperic was the son of Chlotar I (d. 561) and grandson of the great king Clovis (r. 481–511). His reign as king was marred by almost constant warfare with his brothers, especially Sigebert, for control of the kingdom. The relationship between Sigebert and Chilperic was further complicated by their marriage practices and the enmity between Sigebert's wife, Brunhilde, and Chilperic's wife, Fredegund. Indeed, after the death of the two kings, Brunhilde and Fredegund continued the feud until Fredegund's death in 597. Chilperic's ambition, brutality, and corrupt ways are highlighted by his contemporary Gregory of Tours in Gregory's *History of the Franks.*

Chilperic, according to Gregory of Tours, was "the Nero and Herod of our time" (379), and it is from Gregory that Chilperic's reputation for violence and deceit comes. Gregory notes that Chilperic destroyed many villages and brought many unjust charges against his subjects in order to seize their wealth. The king persecuted the bishops, whom he accused of taking all the wealth of the kingdom. According to Gregory, Chil-

peric's "god was in his belly" (380), and the king practiced all forms of vice and debauchery. Chilperic declared to his judges, "If anyone disobeys my orders, he must be punished by having his eyes torn out" (380–381). Although Gregory provides a memorable portrait of Chilperic, he was not the only one to do so, and other evidence provides a less brutal image of the king. The great poet Venantius Fortunatus wrote a panegyric praising the king for his authority and intellectual talents. Indeed, even Gregory recognizes that Chilperic had some literary talent and notes that the king wrote two books of poetry and composed hymns and other pieces for the mass. Chilperic also wrote a book of theology on the doctrine of Christ, added several Greek letters to the alphabet to reflect pronunciation of Frankish better, and added to the Salic law.

Although he was more than the brutal king portrayed by Gregory, Chilperic is best known for the civil wars with his brothers, particularly the blood feud involving his wife, Fredegund, and his brother Sigebert and his brother's wife, Brunhilde. Hostilities did, however, precede his marriage with Fredegund, when Chilperic, who had inherited part of the kingdom with its capital at Soissons, attacked Sigebert's kingdom in 562. The attack began thirteen years of war between the two brothers, war that nearly led to the defeat and destruction of Chilperic. He was aided throughout the struggle by his ambitious and ruthless wife, Fredegund. She was not Chilperic's first wife, however. Indeed, Chilperic had previously married the Visigothic princess Galswintha. This had constituted a break with the usual practice of the Merovingian kings, who had married lowborn women. Indeed, even before his marriage to Galswintha, Chilperic took the serving maid Fredegund as a concubine and, possibly, wife. His marriage to Galswintha was inspired by Sigebert, who had previously married Galswintha's sister Brunhilde. Shortly after the marriage to Galswintha, who brought a sizeable dowry to the marriage, Chilperic had her murdered, possibly at Fredegund's request, and then married Fredegund. The murder of Galswintha may have worsened an already difficult situation between Sigebert and Chilperic.

The civil wars between the two brothers were quite fierce; they may have been the worst wars in Merovingian history. After Chilperic's initial attack, Sigebert was able to counterattack and seize Chilperic's capital of Soissons. Chilperic was driven from his kingdom and eventually took refuge with his brother Guntram, who also faced invasion by Sigebert. In the mid-570s, Chilperic, allied with Guntram, and Sigebert once again came to blows. The situation was quite grave for Chilperic, because Guntram had made peace with Sigebert and Chilperic's son had been killed in battle by supporters of Sigibert. On the point of destruction, Chilperic learned that Sigebert had been killed. It is generally held that the murder was committed by agents of Chilperic's queen, Fredegund.

Chilperic exploited his opportunity after the death of Sigebert and invaded his late brother's territory. He seized several cities formerly ruled by Sigebert and nearly disinherited Sigebert's heir, Childebert (d. 596). But the intervention of Guntram saved Childebert and stopped Chilperic's advance. At the same time, Chilperic faced the ambitions of Merovech, his son by one of his concubines. Merovech, having reached his majority and eager to rule as king, sought out and married Chilperic's rival Brunhilde. The marriage gave Merovech claim to a kingdom and returned Brunhilde to the game of Merovingian power politics. But the couple were no match for the ruthlessness of Chilperic and Fredegund, and Merovech, failing to secure power, asked a servant to kill him. Gregory, however, suggests that Merovech was murdered by Fredegund. Whatever the case, Chilperic survived the challenge and was now, in 581, bereft of any heirs. At that point, he made peace with Childebert, adopted him, and named him as heir. For the next three years, Childebert, Chilperic, and Gun-

tram were involved in a complicated diplomatic and military struggle for predominance in the kingdom. Although Chilperic acquired the largest share of the kingdom, he was abandoned by Childebert, who once again allied with Guntram, putting Chilperic on the defensive. Before much further turmoil between the three occurred, Chilperic was murdered while hunting. He was succeeded by an infant son, Chlotar II, who was protected by his mother Fredegund and supported by an important segment of the nobility. It was in fact Chlotar II who ended the civil strife that had existed since the beginning of his father's reign when he overthrew Brunhilde in 613 and unified the kingdom.

See also Brunhilde; Chlotar II; Clovis; Fredegund; Galswintha; Gregory of Tours; Guntram; Merovingian Dynasty; Salic Law

Bibliography

Gregory of Tours. *History of the Franks.* Trans. Lewis Thorpe. Harmondsworth, UK: Penguin, 1974.

James, Edward. *The Franks.* Oxford: Blackwell, 1988.

Lasko, Peter. *The Kingdom of the Franks: North-West Europe before Charlemagne.* New York: McGraw-Hill, 1971.

Wallace-Hadrill, J. M. *The Long-Haired Kings.* Toronto: University of Toronto Press, 1982.

Wemple, Suzanne. *Women in Frankish Society: Marriage and the Cloister, 500 to 900.* Philadelphia: University of Pennsylvania Press, 1985.

Wood, Ian. *The Merovingian Kingdoms, 450–751.* London: Longman, 1994.

Chlotar II (584–629)

Merovingian king from 613 to 629 and the first monarch to rule a united kingdom since the first Merovingian king of the Franks, Clovis, in the late fifth and early sixth century, Chlotar was a successful king who restored the integrity of the dynasty and laid the foundation for the high point in the dynasty's history. The son of Chilperic I and Fredegund,

Chlotar established a period of peace and prosperity for the kingdom and ended generations of civil strife and fraternal violence that had plagued the realm since the early sixth century. Chlotar improved relations with the nobility and the church, reformed the law, established a rudimentary chancery that was to develop in the generations to follow, and emphasized the king's stature as a sacred figure. The peace and prosperity enjoyed by the kingdom during his reign continued during that of the reign of his son, Dagobert, because of important foundation laid by Chlotar and because of the talents of his successor.

Chlotar was born during a time of great civil strife in the kingdom that was the result of the competition between his parents, Chilperic and Fredegund, and their rivals King Sigebert (r. 560/561–575) and his queen Brunhilde. He ascended to the throne in 584 when his father was murdered by his mother and immediately faced numerous difficulties that threatened his claim to the throne. One of the most serious problems was the question of his legitimacy and right to inherit. Many leaders in the kingdom, including the historian Gregory of Tours and King Guntram, the pious and highly respected Merovingian ruler, expressed doubts about his parentage. Only after Fredegund gathered the sworn oaths of three bishops and three hundred nobles was Chlotar's claim preserved, with the aid of his uncle, King Guntram. He faced further challenges, however, in the 590s, including the ascendancy of his mother's rival, Brunhilde, attacks on his own part of the kingdom, and the loss of important territories. Growing dissatisfaction among the nobility with Brunhilde and her sons, however, provided Chlotar with the opportunity not only to secure his place in his own part of the kingdom but to establish his authority over the entire Frankish realm. He led a revolt against Brunhilde that led to her deposition and brutal execution in 613.

The opening years of Chlotar's reign, known mainly from the garbled pages of the chronicle of Fredegar, were marked by an attack on the reign of his predecessor. The condemnation and savage execution of Brunhilde for numerous murders were only the start of Chlotar's war on his predecessor's memory. To further denigrate the reputation of his predecessor, Chlotar promoted the memory and saint's cult of one of the bishops that Brunhilde had murdered. He also made contact with the Irish missionary St. Columban, who had been exiled by the queen. Although Columban did not return, his foundation at Luxeuil received protection from Chlotar. These actions not only worsened Brunhilde's reputation, they also improved Chlotar's relationship with the church in his realm.

Chlotar made significant overtures to the nobility during the early years of his reign. His success against Brunhilde was due to the support of the nobility, particularly to the founders of what later became the Carolingian dynasty, Arnulf of Metz and Pippin of Landen. They were made important advisors of the king and rewarded with prominent religious and political office, Arnulf with the see of Metz and Pippin with the office of mayor of the palace (*major domus*). The support of the Frankish nobility was essential for the success of the king, particularly because of the shifting alliances of various noble families. During his entire reign and that of his son Dagobert, Chlotar sought to manage these unstable alliances. His creation of a subkingdom in Austrasia in 622 for Dagobert may have been an attempt to appease regional interests and draw powerful families in the region closer to the ruling dynasty. Marriage alliances were also made to maintain good relations with various noble factions. Dagobert's mother, Berthetrude, may have been Burgundian, which would have preserved ties between Chlotar and that part of the kingdom. After Berthetrude's death, Chlotar married again, and Dagobert married Chlotar's new wife's sister, both marriages attempted to gain the support of the wives' family for the two kings.

Chlotar throughout his entire reign introduced significant legal reforms and issued numerous charters and diplomas. One of his most important pieces of legislation came very early in his reign, when he pronounced the Edict of Paris of 614. Once seen as a concession to the nobility, the edict bound the king and nobility closer together and provided them the shared purpose of ruling a great kingdom and maintaining peace and order throughout the realm. The edict also addressed tolls, ecclesiastical property, and the restitution of property lost under Chlotar's predecessor Brunhilde; in this way Chlotar further denigrated Brunhilde's memory and enhanced his own image before the nobility. His activity as a lawgiver had two further consequences. It forced him to establish a writing office, which in generations to come evolved into an official chancery, an office that attracted skilled men, often from the church, who would support his power. The office also enhanced his reputation as king and reinforced his image as an almost sacred figure, a result that distinguished him from the nobles who served him and needed him to continue to act as lawgiver.

By the end of his reign in 629, Chlotar had reestablished the authority of the Merovingian dynasty and laid the foundation for even greater successes by his son Dagobert. Chlotar had reunited the kingdom under his sole authority and maintained good relations with the nobility. He reordered and improved relations with the church in his kingdom, which offered a valuable counterweight to the nobility should he need it. He reformed the law and enhanced his reputation as king through his role as lawgiver. Chlotar also redefined the status of the king in the Merovingian realm—all of which aided his son and established an era of prosperity for the dynasty.

See also Arnulf of Metz, St.; Brunhilde; Carolingian Dynasty; Clovis; Columban, St.; Dagobert; Fredegund; Gregory of Tours; Guntram; Merovingian Dynasty; Pippin of Landen

Bibliography
Bachrach, Bernard S. *Merovingian Military Organization, 481–751.* Minneapolis: University of Minnesota Press, 1972.
Geary, Patrick. *Before France and Germany: The Creation and Transformation of the Merovingian World.* Oxford: Oxford University Press, 1988.
Gregory of Tours. *The History of the Franks.* Trans. Lewis Thorpe. Harmondsworth, UK: Penguin, 1974.
James, Edward. *The Franks.* Oxford: Blackwell, 1991.
Lasko, Peter. *The Kingdom of the Franks: North-West Europe before Charlemagne.* New York: McGraw Hill, 1971.
———. *The Frankish Church.* Oxford: Clarendon, 1983.
Wallace-Hadrill, J. M. *The Long-Haired Kings.* Toronto: Toronto University Press, 1982.
Wallace-Hadrill, J. M., ed. and trans. *The Fourth Book of the Chronicle of Fredegar with Its Continuations.* London: Nelson, 1960.
Wemple, Suzanne. *Women in Frankish Society: Marriage and the Cloister, 500 to 900.* Philadelphia: University of Pennsylvania Press, 1985.
Wood, Ian. *The Merovingian Kingdoms, 450–751.* London: Longman, 1994.

Chrodegang of Metz (c. 712–766)

Perhaps the most important ecclesiastic in the Carolingian kingdom in the first half of the eighth century, after the Anglo-Saxon missionary Boniface, Chrodegang was a committed church reformer and a close ally of the Carolingian mayor of the palace and later king, Pippin the Short. He assumed the important see of Metz, which one of the founders of the Carolingian line, Arnulf of Metz, once held. Although not as zealous in his commitment to Roman-focused reform as Boniface, Chrodegang nonetheless became papal legate, introduced Roman liturgical forms to the kingdom, visited Rome, and collected important relics from Rome. He helped Pippin with his reforms of the Frankish church and composed an important rule for canons.

Born into a noble family, Chrodegang had many important family connections throughout the kingdom, including prominent ecclesiastics and aristocrats. His uncle may have been a supporter of the mayor of the palace, Charles Martel, and Chrodegang himself served in the chancery at Martel's court. In 742, the year after Pippin and his brother Carloman succeeded their father, Chrodegang was made bishop of Metz by Pippin and with the Carolingian mayor began the reform of the Frankish church. Over the next several decades, in association with Pippin, Chrodegang introduced improvements to religious life and practice at Metz. He also expanded the size of his church at Metz and built several new episcopal buildings, which could accommodate the Roman liturgical practices and chant that he introduced to the church in the Frankish kingdom. In 748, with Pippin's help, Chrodegang founded the monastery of Gorze near his see of Metz; the new monastery was guided by the bishop's reform principles, and monks from Gorze helped to found new monasteries. While on a trip to Rome sometime between 753 and 755, Chrodegang was made archbishop and papal legate by Pope Stephen II to replace the recently martyred Boniface. He also participated in several church councils held by Pippin that implemented spiritual and institutional reform of church life in the kingdom.

Chrodegang is best known, however, for the rule of canons (*Regula canonicorum*) he wrote between 754 and 756. The rule, inspired by and based on the monastic rule of St. Benedict of Nursia, was intended to improve the religious life of the canons at the cathedral church in Metz and was widely adopted throughout the Frankish kingdom in the coming years. The rule, which received official sanction at the Council of Aachen in 816, reflected Chrodegang's monastic temperament. Chrodegang's rule ordered that the canons, clergy serving at a bishop's cathedral church, live in a community with a common place to eat and sleep. They were to care for the sick, possess no personal wealth, and

perform the daily round of prayers. The canons were also expected to spend time reading and studying so that they could better perform their preaching duties. Chrodegang's rule was widely copied in his day and remained the most important rule for canons for several centuries after his death.

See also Anglo-Saxons; Arnulf of Metz, St.; Benedict of Aniane; Benedict of Nursia, St.; Boniface, St.; Carolingian Dynasty; Charles Martel; Louis the Pious; Pippin III, Called Pippin the Short

Bibliography
Knowles, David. *Christian Monasticism.* New York: McGraw Hill, 1969.
Lawrence, Clifford H. *Medieval Monasticism: Forms of Religious Life in Western Europe in the Middle Ages,* 2d ed. London: Longman, 1989.
McKitterick, Rosamond. *The Frankish Kingdoms under the Carolingians, 751–987.* London: Longman, 1983.
Riché, Pierre. *The Carolingians: A Family Who Forged Europe.* Trans. Michael Idomir Allen. Philadelphia: University of Pennsylvania Press, 1993.
———. *Education and Culture in the Barbarian West: From the Sixth through the Eighth Century.* Trans. John Contreni. Columbia: University of South Carolina Press, 1976.
Wallace-Hadrill, J. M. *The Frankish Church.* Oxford: Clarendon, 1983.

Clothing

The dress in barbarian Europe was most likely a combination of traditional Germanic clothing and imported Roman fashions. Clothing was relatively uniform throughout the Roman and post-Roman world, although there was variation in style and fabric across Europe. There was also some variation, especially in quality, between the peasantry and upper classes; the latter were obviously able to afford higher quality clothing and often adorned themselves with jewelry. In general, though, clothing was simple and functional and was adapted to the prevailing climate, with people in colder regions wearing warmer, heavier clothing.

As with many things, the Roman historian and moralist Tacitus (c. 56–c. 120) provides a useful description of the clothing of pre-migration Germans. Although Tacitus's *Germania* must be treated carefully since its praise of the Germans is often simply a means of veiled criticism, its treatment of dress seems relatively accurate, especially when the information it gives is compared with what is known of some later barbarian practices. Tacitus notes that the Germans wear a cloak fastened with a clasp, and the wealthiest wear a close-fitting garment underneath that is "tight and exhibits each limb" (115) (in other words, trousers, never worn by the Romans). They also wear the skins of animals, which are carefully chosen and include, among others, the skins of spotted beasts. He says that they wear animal skins, a practice disdained in Roman society, because they cannot acquire other material through trade. Women, according to Tacitus, dress in the same fashion as men, except that they wear linen garments embroidered in purple and do not extend the garment into sleeves, leaving the lower arm bare.

Under the influence of their contact with Rome, various barbarian peoples wore more loose-fitting and flowing clothes along with their furs and tight-fitting garments. The peasants, whose fashions changed little throughout the Middle Ages, wore heavy shoes, often of wood, a leather belt, and a simple, short tunic with narrow sleeves. The wealthier classes wore more elaborate and expensive versions of this basic outfit, and Carolingian princes and possibly other nobles changed their clothes every Saturday. Perhaps the best-known literary depiction of barbarian dress is Einhard's description of Charlemagne's clothing. He notes that the great king wore "a linen shirt and linen breeches, and above these a tunic fringed with silk" (77). Charlemagne covered his legs with hose and wore shoes on his feet. He also wore an otter or ermine coat to protect against the cold and covered everything with a blue cloak. Einhard

explains that this was traditional Frankish dress, which differed little from that of the common people. A similar outfit was given to King Harold the Dane by Louis the Pious and included white gloves, a cloak set with a pin, and a tunic with straight sleeves and jewels.

The standard dress of men during much of the early Middle Ages, therefore, included a tunic that reached to the knees and could be gathered with a belt. More than one tunic was often worn, with the sleeves of the undertunic extending the full length of the arm and the sleeves of the outer tunic extending only part way down the arm. The Franks and other barbarian folk wrapped their legs with hose or pants, and they wore shoes of wood or boots of leather to cover their feet. A full-length cloak covered their clothes; the cloak was open in the front and held together by a brooch. The primary fabrics were linen and wool, but silk was popular with those who could afford it. The garments were also trimmed with embroidery. In the cold weather, a coat of animal fur was worn, with the fur side turned inward to insulate better and to keep from appearing too animal-like. Women's dress was similar. They too wore tunics, but covered theirs with a full-length gown, which was either held up by chains or open in front to make walking easier. They also wore necklaces, rings, bracelets, brooches, and jewels with their clothing. By the Carolingian era, women generally wore long veils, but, as they had earlier, they wore their hair long and braided, laced with gold thread or ribbon.

Even though a standard form of dress existed throughout most of the early Middle Ages, there was some variety among peoples. As Einhard again demonstrates, there were differences in fashion preferences between various peoples. Indeed, he notes that Charlemagne hated foreign clothing, but wore it twice out of his respect for Popes Hadrian and Leo III. On two occasions in Rome, Charlemagne wore Roman dress, including local styles of shoes and tunic and the Greek chlamys. The great king also wore more elaborate clothes on feast days and other occasions of state that included embroidered clothes and shoes along with a bejeweled sword.

See also Animals; Carolingian Dynasty; Charlemagne; Einhard; Franks; Hadrian I, Pope; Jewelry and Gems; Leo III, Pope; Women

Bibliography

Einhard and Notker the Stammerer. *Two Lives of Charlemagne.* Trans. Lewis Thorpe. Harmondsworth, UK: Penguin, 1981.

Riché, Pierre. *Daily Life in the World of Charlemagne.* Trans. Jo Ann McNamara. Philadelphia: University of Pennsylvania Press, 1983.

Tacitus, Cornelius. *Agricola and Germany.* Trans. Anthony R. Birley. Oxford: Oxford University Press, 1999.

Veyne, Paul. *A History of Private Life.* Vol. 1, *From Pagan Rome to Byzantium.* Trans. Arthur Goldhammer. Cambridge, MA: Harvard University Press, 1987.

Clotilda, St. (d. 544)

The wife of the great Merovingian king Clovis, Clotilda is traditionally thought to have played a key role in the conversion of her husband to Catholic Christianity. She may also have influenced his foreign policy by encouraging a war of conquest against her uncle in Burgundy. She fulfilled her primary obligation as a Merovingian queen by providing Clovis with four sons, three of whom survived their father (Chlodomer, Childebert I, and Chlothar I), and a daughter, Clotilda. After the death of Clovis, Clotilda took the veil and entered a convent. She was later recognized as a saint because of her religious life and her influence on her husband.

Clotilda was the daughter of the king of Burgundy, Chilperic, and his Gallo-Roman Catholic wife, Caretena. As a result of her mother's influence, Clotilda was raised as a Catholic Christian, even though most of the Burgundian royal family was Arian Christian. It is possible that Clotilda's Catholic faith attracted Clovis to her because he hoped it would smooth relations with the powerful Catholic bishops of his kingdom. Late sixth and early seventh century sources, however, offer a less mundane picture of the courtship. Clotilda was orphaned and in exile by the time she came to Clovis's attention, her mother and father having been murdered by her uncle Gundobad. Clovis sent his envoys to secretly observe the exiled princess, and they informed him of her beauty, elegance, and intelligence. He then sent her a ring inscribed with his name, a portrait of himself, and a proposal of marriage. She hesitated because Clovis was still a pagan, but the following year, when he approached Gundobad to ask for her hand, Clotilda's uncle would not refuse the powerful Frank, and she married Clovis.

As queen, Clotilda desired nothing more than the conversion of her husband to Catholic Christianity, and according to the late sixth-century bishop and historian Gregory of Tours, she was pivotal to that conversion. She encouraged Clovis to accept Christianity and denounced the immorality and belief in the pagan gods. She argued that her God was the creator of all things and that her husband's gods were nothing more than idols of wood or metal. When their first son, Ingomer, was born Clotilda had him baptized. The child died shortly after the baptism, which angered Clovis, who claimed the baptism caused his son's death. But Clotilda held firm and thanked God that he chose to take Ingomer after baptism, ensuring the child's entry into heaven. Clotilda baptized their second son, Chlodomer, who became ill shortly after the baptism. Clovis blamed Christ again, but Clotilda prayed for her son's recovery, and Chlodomer regained his health. She continued to urge Clovis to convert, and when faced with certain defeat against the Alemanni, Clovis agreed to accept baptism should he emerge victorious. Winning the battle, he accepted instruction and baptism from St. Remigius, bishop of Rheims, who had been ordered to the court by Clotilda. Although it is a wonderful story, most historians generally discount Gregory's version of events and note that Clovis probably converted to Arian Christianity before finally accepting the Catholic faith. It is still likely, however, that his decision was influenced by Clotilda and her domestic proselytizing.

Clotilda's influence on Merovingian affairs extended beyond her likely influence on the conversion of Clovis. According to work praising her sanctity, Clothild encouraged Clovis to destroy pagan shrines and to build churches, and also to support the poor, widows and orphans. She also influenced affairs in the kingdom during the reigns of her sons. Gregory of Tours notes that she called on her sons to make war against the Burgundians, allegedly to avenge the murder of her parents. Her son Chlodomer led the war, which ended with the defeat of the Burgundians and the death of Chlodomer, whose children were then raised by Clotilda.

See also Alemanni; Clovis; Gregory of Tours; Merovingian Dynasty

Bibliography

Gregory of Tours, *History of the Franks.* Trans. Lewis Thorpe. Harmondsworth, UK: Penguin, 1974.

Schulenburg, Jane Tibbetts. *Forgetful of Their Sex: Female Sanctity and Society, ca. 500–1100.* Chicago: University of Chicago Press, 1998.

Wemple, Suzanne. *Women in Frankish Society: Marriage and the Cloister, 500 to 900.* Philadelphia: University of Pennsylvania Press, 1985.

Wood, Ian. *The Merovingian Kingdoms, 450–751.* London: Longman, 1994.

Clovis (c. 466–511)

The most important king (r. 481–511) and founder of the Merovingian dynasty, Clovis was a "magnus et egregius pugnator" (a great and distinguished warrior) according to the bishop and historian Gregory of Tours. At times a brutal and treacherous warrior, he unified the Frankish kingdoms and laid a foundation for later Frankish power and influence that was in part drawn from the more advanced traditions of the late Roman Empire. He cultivated good relations with the bishops in his realm and was the first Frankish king to convert to Christianity.

Clovis waged a series of wars to expand the boundaries of his realm. Although there exists much debate over the exact chronology of these events and even over the extent of Clovis's war making, it is likely that he pursued an aggressive policy against other Germanic tribes and other Frankish groups that led to the enlargement of his kingdom. One of his most famous battles was his victory over Syagrius, the late Roman ruler of the kingdom of Soissons, in 486. He also enjoyed a series of other victories during his reign over other foes, including the Alemanni at the Battle of Tolbiac in 496, the Burgundians in 500, the Visigoths in 507, and various lesser Frankish kings in his last years.

Although Clovis fought a great number of wars during his reign, he was careful, even before his conversion, to maintain the support of the Catholic bishops of Gaul that he had enjoyed from the beginning of his reign. He took great care to guarantee the support of the bishops by ruling that his soldiers should not harm the clergy or despoil the lands of the bishops, the tombs of the saints, or other sacred or church ground. An even greater example of the importance of the Catholic bishops to Clovis can be found in the story of the chalice of Soissons. According to Gregory, Clovis was approached after his victory by the bishop of Soissons, who asked that a precious chalice used for Mass be returned to him. Clovis promised he would return the chalice should it come to him during the division of spoils, and when he requested it all his warriors, save one, proclaimed he should have it. The lone warrior refused and cut the chalice in half, offering the king his share. Later, while Clovis was reviewing the troops, he came upon this same warrior. Clovis denounced the warrior as a bad example and threw the latter's sword to the ground. As the warrior bent to pick up, Clovis brought his great axe down

Baptism of Clovis by St. Remigius, fourteenth century (Archivo Iconografico, S.A. / Corbis)

on the soldier's head, reminding him that he had done the same thing to the chalice at Soissons. Although it is a most unlikely story, the tale of the chalice of Soissons reveals the importance of the Catholic bishops to Clovis.

The wars against Syagrius, the Alemanni, and the Visigoths were given religious significance by Gregory, and, although an unlikely interpretation, it reveals the importance of the conversion of Clovis to this Gallo-Roman bishop. Moreover, there may have been some truth to Gregory's view of the king, because Clovis did convert to Christianity. Traditionally, the king's conversion was due to the influence of his wife Clotilda, who was a Catholic from the kingdom of Burgundy. In fact, as Gregory tells us, Clotilda baptized their first son, who shortly thereafter died. For Clovis this was a sign of the power of the traditional Frankish gods, but Clotilda remained undaunted. She baptized the second child as well, who in turn became deathly ill, but her prayers saved the child. Clovis remained devoted to his traditional gods, nonetheless, until the Battle of Tolbiac. According to Gregory, the battle was going poorly for Clovis and the king feared defeat. He vowed to the Christian god that should he win the battle he would then convert to the Christian faith. And, of course, he won the battle and, eventually, accepted baptism, along with 3,000 of his followers, at the hands of St. Remigius, the bishop of Rheims.

Both of these stories are probably little more than pious legend, but Clovis did convert to Catholic Christianity at some point between 496 and 508. It is no longer generally held that Clovis converted directly to Catholic Christianity from paganism but that he converted first to Arian Christianity or at least was sympathetic to the Arian confession. His conversion did not greatly influence Frankish belief, nor should Clovis's Christianity be understood in very sophisticated terms. Clovis's conversion remains, however, one of his great accomplishments, because he was the first German ruler to adopt Catholic Christianity rather than the Arian form. Thus his conver-

sion solidified relations with the Catholic hierarchy in his realm and provided his dynasty with an important source of political and religious support for generations to come.

In his last years his power came to be recognized by the emperor in Constantinople, who may have granted Clovis an honorary consulship—perhaps as part of diplomatic struggles with the Ostrogoth, Theodoric—and even in Theodoric's kingdom in Italy. Also in his last years, he focused more on domestic policy by holding a church council at Orléans and by issuing the Salic law. This codification of the law—putting it into organized, written form rather than simply expecting people to follow the unwritten, customary law—was an act of some sophistication, one that reveals the influence of Roman legal and administrative traditions on the king and suggests that Clovis was a more "civilized" ruler than the traditional understanding of him implies. Roman influence can also be seen in Clovis's adoption of several imperial administrative structures, including the system of tax collection.

At his death, the kingdom was divided among Clovis's sons, Theuderic I, Chlodomer, Childebert I, and Chlotar I. Traditionally, the partition of the realm has been seen as a consequence of the Frankish patrimonial view of kingship, in which the kingdom was understood as the king's personal possession to be shared among his family. The division, however, followed the established administrative boundaries of the Roman Empire, suggesting further Roman influence on Clovis. Whatever the precise meaning of the partition of the realm, it established a tradition that continued throughout Merovingian history.

See also Alaric II; Clotilda, St.; Merovingian Dynasty; Salic Law; Theodoric the Great

Bibliography

Bachrach, Bernard S. *Merovingian Military Organization, 481–751.* Minneapolis: University of Minnesota Press, 1972.

Daly, William M. "Clovis: How Barbaric, How Pagan?" *Speculum* 69 (1994): 619–664.

Gregory of Tours. *History of the Franks.* Trans. Lewis Thorpe. Harmondsworth, UK: Penguin, 1974.

Geary, Patrick. *Before France and Germany.* New York: 1988.

Wallace-Hadrill, J. M. *The Long-Haired Kings.* Toronto: Medieval Academy Reprints, 1982.

Wood, Ian. *The Merovingian Kingdoms, 450–751.* London: Longman, 1994.

Coins and Coinage

An important method of exchange, coins were minted by the Roman emperors and the various barbarian kings that succeeded them. Coins were minted in gold, silver, and bronze, and their values and uses varied from time to time and place to place. They were used as a medium of exchange between kingdoms, bishoprics, duchies, and counties. Control of the coinage was a great concern for the barbarian rulers of the early Middle Ages, as it had been of the emperors, but the successor kings had less success that their imperial predecessors. Later kings, however, did manage to assume greater control of the coinage and instituted important reforms to make their coins more stable and useful. The gold coin continued to be the standard, but its use was limited to large-scale exchange; it was not used for local commerce. The introduction of the silver coin by Carolingian monarchs and others facilitated local trade and contributed to, and reveals the existence of, economic growth.

The Romans, as in many other areas, established important precedents for the Germanic successor kingdoms in terms of coins and coinage. The Germanic successor kings learned much from the Romans about coinage, which underwent important reforms during the reigns of Diocletian (284–305) and Constantine. Although he met with little success in his efforts to institute a major reform of the coin because of a lack of precious metals, Diocletian did introduced new copper and silver coins. He also established a significant change in the production of coins by bringing a number of regional mints under imperial control. His reforms strengthened the coin and made its value, which had suffered a dramatic political and economic collapse in the generations before Diocletian's reign, more uniform across the empire.

Even more significant for the future of Roman, Byzantine, and German coinage was the reform of Constantine, who introduced a coin that became the standard for centuries to come. Building upon Diocletian's efforts, Constantine produced a new gold coin, the solidus, which retained its value and purity well into the Middle Ages; it was minted at 72 coins to the pound of gold. This coin was an important tool of the government, which used it to pay the soldiers' salaries, and archeological discoveries reveal that it was widely circulated. Another popular and commonly used coin was the *triens* or *tremissis,* which was based on the solidus. The triens valued at one third of the solidus and was originally minted in gold and later minted in a mixture of gold and silver. The Romans also used coins of bronze and, for a time in the second half of the fourth century, silver. The bronze coins were plentiful, but often debased in value. Roman coinage is noted for its symbolism, consisting of striking images of the emperors as well as Christian symbols, which thus conveyed the central political and religious ideologies of the empire.

The various Germanic kings who assumed control over parts of the Western Empire inherited the tradition of coinage from the Romans, even though their coins lacked the stability and uniformity of the Roman precedents. These kings not only inherited the practice of coinage from the Romans, but until the sixth century they continued to mint coins in the name of the emperor, now resident in Constantinople. Among the various peoples that took control of the Western Empire, the Vandals and Ostrogoths most closely adhered to imperial traditions, minting in gold, silver, and bronze, and issuing their version of the *triens.* The Vandal kings who issued coins include Gunthamund (r. 484–496) and Hilderic (r. 523–530), who issued silver and bronze coins with their own names on the coins but using imperial models, and the greatest of Vandal kings, Gaiseric (428–477), who may have issued gold coins.

The Ostrogoths of Italy minted coins that imitated imperial models most closely, and Theodoric issued some fine coins based on Roman models. Other Germanic rulers of Italy also minted coins in imitation of their imperial predecessors. Odovacar minted coins in silver and bronze, and the Lombards issued highly imitative coins until the reforms of Cuncipert (r. 680–688 coruler, 688–700) established a uniquely Lombard version. In Spain, Visigothic kings, beginning with Leovigild, minted coins, issuing a thin, gold version of the triens, and they came to include their own names and the name of the town in which the coin was struck. The most important Spanish mints until the early eighth-century Islamic invasion were in Córdoba, Seville, Tarragona, and Toledo. The coins themselves in the sixth and seventh centuries were of relatively high value and used primarily for large-scale trade and government purposes; they were generally not used in local commerce, which contributed to the development of a barter economy at the local level.

The history of coinage in the Anglo-Saxon kingdoms of England followed a different path than that in the early continental Germanic kingdoms. In Roman Britain, coins were minted into the fourth century at London, but in the later fourth century the mint was closed down, and Britain depended upon mints in Gaul. In 395, the mints supplying Britain were closed, and no coins were imported for the next two centuries. By the seventh century, however, Merovingian coins began to appear in England and became the model for the *thrymas,* the Anglo-Saxon version of the triens. The solidus was also minted, but neither coin was minted in great number or had circulation beyond the kingdom of Kent. As the gold supply rapidly

dwindled, Anglo-Saxon kings turned to a thick silver coin, the *sceattas,* which was very similar to Frankish issues on the continent. Further reforms of the coinage were undertaken in the eighth and ninth centuries by various Anglo-Saxon kings. Inspired by the Carolingian coins of Pippin III the Short, Offa of Mercia produced a silver coin that became the basis of the later English penny. Brilliantly decorated in an innovative style, the penny bore the image of Offa and his wife, Cynethryth, and other patterns not dependent on Roman models. Offa's penny, which came to be valued at 12 to the shilling and 240 to the pound, was copied by the rulers of the other Anglo-Saxon kingdoms as well as the Viking conquerors of the ninth and tenth centuries.

In the Frankish lands, Merovingian and Carolingian kings issued a number of coins and introduced important reforms of the coin. Merovingian kings, beginning with Clovis (r. 481–511), minted coins based on late Roman and Byzantine models. Clovis and his successors issued both the solidus and triens; the former was the standard coin, but the latter was more common. Merovingian coins were mainly minted in gold, but issues in silver and copper existed in small numbers. The Salic law, for example, lists fines that describe a silver coin, the denarius, forty of which equaled a solidus. The coins were originally issued with the image of a current or previous emperor and the Byzantine symbol of victory, but by the mid-sixth century Merovingian kings had begun to impress their own names on their coins, rather than that of the emperor. Merovingian coinage increasingly diverged from late Roman imperial models after the mid-sixth century, and the coin itself was increasingly debased, in part because of the proliferation of mints and the lack of control over them exercised by the kings. By the end of the Merovingian dynasty in the eighth century, the gold coinage was virtually replaced by a silver coinage.

Frankish coinage underwent a major reform just as Frankish society did in the mid-eighth century, as a new dynasty, the Carolingian, took the throne. The first Carolingian king, Pippin the Short, reasserted royal control over the numerous mints in the kingdom, eliminated private mints, reduced the number of mints in the kingdom, and made the production of coinage solely a royal right. He also replaced the much debased gold coinage with a new silver coin, the *denarius,* and struck them with the king's name. Even greater and more influential reforms of the coinage were undertaken by Pippin's son, Charlemagne. In the 790s, Charlemagne reformed the coinage throughout the realm and increased the weight of the coin. The basic coin was the denarius, or penny; it was of pure silver and measured roughly three-quarters of an inch in diameter, with a weight of 1.7 grams. The coins were struck in some fifty mints in such towns as Aachen, Cologne, and Mainz and bore one of three designs: a stylized version of the king's name in Latin (Carolus), a temple, and, rarely, a portrait. Charlemagne also developed an accounting system for the coinage in which twelve pennies equaled a solidus or shilling and twenty shillings equaled a libra, or pound. His coin and accounting system remained the basis for European coinage until the thirteenth century.

Although it remained the standard, Charlemagne's coinage suffered somewhat during the ninth century. During the reign of Louis the Pious a small number of private mints appeared, and later Carolingian kings granted the right to mint to archbishops and other ecclesiastical leaders. And in Italy, even in Charlemagne's time, the coinage was not always consistent with Carolingian models. It was during the reign of Charlemagne's good friend, Pope Hadrian I, that the papacy began to strike coins. Papal coins followed Roman and Byzantine imperial models, but after Charlemagne's first visit to Rome included the Carolingian king or emperor's name along with the papal monogram. Papal and Carolingian symbols appeared together until 904, when only the name of the pope appeared on the coin.

See also Anglo-Saxons; Carolingian Dynasty; Charlemagne; Constantine; Leovigild; Lombards; Merovingian Dynasty; Odovacar; Offa of Mercia; Ostrogoths; Pippin III, Called Pippin the Short; Vandals; Visigoths

Bibliography

Blackburn, Mark A. S., ed. *Anglo-Saxon Monetary History: Essays in Memory of Michael Dolley.* Leicester, UK: Leicester University Press, 1986.

Bursche, Aleksander. *Later Roman-Barbarian Contacts in Central Europe: Numismatic Evidence.* Berlin: Gebr. Mann Verlag, 1996.

Dolley, Reginald H. Michael ed. *Anglo-Saxon Coins: Studies Presented to F. M. Stenton.* London: Methuen, 1961.

Grierson, Philip, and Mark Blackburn. *Medieval European Coinage.* Vol. 1, *The Early Middle Ages (5th–10th Centuries).* Cambridge: Cambridge University Press, 1986.

Herrin, Judith. *The Formation of Christendom.* Princeton: Princeton University Press, 1989.

Morrison, Karl F., and Henry Grunthal. *Carolingian Coinage.* New York: American Numismatic Society, 1967.

Pirenne, Henri. *Mohammed and Charlemagne.* Trans. Bernard Miall. New York: Barnes and Noble, 1992.

Columba, St. (c. 521–c. 597)

An Irish monk and missionary, Columba was an important force in the evangelization of the Picts in Scotland and the Angles in northern England. He may also have had followers from among the southern Anglo-Saxons, and thus have introduced Christianity to them before the arrival of St. Augustine of Canterbury. Bede notes that Columba was "distinguished by his monastic habit and life," and that "whatever type of man he may have been, we know for certain that he left successors distinguished for their purity of life, their love of God, and their loyalty to the monastic rule" (147).

Columba was an Irish monk born in circa 521 to the Ui Neill line, one of the most powerful ruling families in Ireland. He was raised fully in the Irish Celtic Christian tradition, which emphasized the role of the monastery and its abbot in the institutional structure and religious life of the church. He was also influenced by the missionary tradition, as was his younger contemporary St. Columban, and undertook a pilgrimage to spread the faith. In Ireland, he founded a monastery at Durrow or, as Bede notes, Dearmach, or Field of Oaks. He is best known, however, for his missionary activity in Scotland, where he converted the Picts to Celtic Christianity. He left Ireland with several companions in 563 and converted the people by his personal example of sanctity, his preaching, and his performance of numerous miracles. As thanks for his good work, Columba was granted the island of Iona, where he founded a monastery that was known for its piety and learning. It was the royal Scottish monastery and may have been the site of the Northumbrian king Oswald's conversion. At the very least, Oswald sought aid from Iona to reform the monasteries in Northumbria. The community at Iona was organized according to the Celtic, rather than the Roman Christian, model in which the abbot was the leading figure and all, including the bishop, were subject to his authority. And although he notes that Columba erred on the matter of Easter and other things, Bede clearly honored the piety and memory of St. Columba.

See also Anglo-Saxons; Augustine of Canterbury, St.; Bede; Columban, St.; Monasticism

Bibliography

Adomnan. *Adomnan's Life of Columba.* Ed. and trans. Alan O. Anderson and Marjorie O. Anderson. London: T. Nelson, 1961.

Bede. *Ecclesiastical History of the English People with Bede's Letter to Egbert and Cuthbert's Letter on the Death of Bede.* Trans. Leo Sherley-Price. Harmondsworth, UK: Penguin, 1991.

Blair, Peter Hunter. *The World of Bede.* Cambridge: Cambridge University Press, 1971.

Laistner, Max L. W. *Thought and Letters in Western Europe, A.D. 500 to 900.* 2d ed. Ithaca, NY: Cornell University Press, 1976.

Lawrence, C. H. *Medieval Monasticism: Forms of Religious Life in Western Europe in the Middle Ages,* 2d ed. London: Longman, 1989.

Stenton, Frank M. *Anglo-Saxon England.* 3d ed. Oxford: Clarendon, 1971.

Columban, St. (d. 615)

Irish monk and missionary of the late sixth and early seventh century who left an important legacy on the continent with his establishment of the monastery of Bobbio in Lombard Italy and of other monastic communities in the Merovingian kingdoms. His missionary activities were part of the Celtic tradition of *peregrinatio,* or pilgrimage, and foreshadowed the missionary activities on the continent of Anglo-Saxon monks like Boniface. A man of learning as well as piety, Columban is the earliest Irish monk who writings survive in any quantity, and whose piety and learning had a profound impact on the cultural and religious life of Merovingian Gaul.

Although his date of birth is uncertain, Columban may have been born around 560 in Leinster in Ireland. He received some education while young and later entered the monastic community at Bangor, where he acquired an excellent education and developed a command of Latin. He was introduced to a wide range of Christian authors, but probably few if any classical writers. As was true of all monastery students, Columban studied the Bible extensively and was introduced to the works of the great Christian fathers, including St. Augustine of Hippo, Eusebius of Caesarea, and Jerome, among others. He also was introduced to the rigorous practices of Irish monasticism, which included extreme mortification of the flesh, such as standing in the icy waters of the North Sea, hour after hour, arms outstretched in a cross, in prayer to God. He learned, accordingly, that humbling of the self was the key to salvation. He also absorbed the Irish tradition of missionary work—leaving home and family behind to spread the gospel in strange lands.

It was this tradition that led him to the continent in 590 with a group of disciples. And upon his arrival in Merovingian Gaul he began the work of a missionary, reforming the flawed practices of the Frankish church and establishing important new religious institutions to improve religious life. He was granted territory by the Merovingian king of Burgundy, Guntram, and used this grant to establish a famous monastery at Luxeuil, as well as monasteries at Annegray and Fontaines. These houses, especially Luxeuil, soon attracted numerous converts, particularly from the Frankish aristocracy, because of the rigor of the monastic life there. Columban's disciples were not all men, however, but included numerous Frankish aristocratic women, because the Irish monk cultivated friendships with women and recognized their spiritual equality. As a result, Frankish noble men and women supported his monastic reforms and founded monasteries, including so-called double monasteries of monks and nuns. He introduced Celtic Christian religious practices, including the practice of private penance.

His community was not just a center of disciplined religious life but also a center of learning, focusing on the study of the Scriptures and the church fathers. He reinvigorated a tradition of learning in the Frankish kingdom that had lain dormant and encouraged his monks to read and improve their rudimentary Latin skills. Although it is uncertain whether he encouraged the study of classical authors, his own writings show clear influence of Virgil and other Roman literary greats. Columban himself left an important literary legacy with his monasteries. Perhaps most important was his monastic rule, the earliest Irish monastic rule known to us. The rule instructs the monks on matters of silence, food and drink, religious duties, and monastic perfection, and it is infused with Columban's ethical teaching and religious rigor. His literary corpus also includes sermons, poems, and letters, including one to Pope Gregory I, called the Great, in which he defends the Irish means of determining the date of Easter.

Although well received by many Frankish nobles, Columban was not so well received by the Frankish clergy. His indictment of the lax ways of the Frankish church and his efforts at reform alienated a number of native church leaders. He also ran afoul of Frankish religious leaders for his continued endorsement of Irish practices that differed from those of the Roman church, including the Irish way to tonsure and way of reckoning Easter. Perhaps even worse, Columban refused to recognize the authority of the bishops, because in the Irish tradition the authority of the abbot was supreme over monks, priests, and bishops. His strict discipline also caused difficulties with the powerful queen Brunhilde. He frequently criticized her way of life. In 611, he visited the court of Brunhilde and her grandson Theuderic and refused to bless Theuderic's children because, Columban said, their mothers were prostitutes. Enraged, Brunhilde chased Columban from the kingdom.

After his expulsion from the Frankish kingdom, Columban wandered the continent for a while before settling in the Lombard kingdom in Italy. He received a grant of land from the Lombard king and founded another very important monastery at Bobbio in 614. Like Luxeuil, Bobbio was a center of learning and religious life and attracted converts from the local population as well as other Irish missionaries. Although Columban died in the following year, 615, he left an important legacy in Italy and the Frankish kingdom as a result of his learning and dedication to the monastic life, and his work prefigured the activities of later Irish and Anglo-Saxons missionaries on the continent.

See also Anglo-Saxons; Boniface, St.; Brunhilde; Gregory the Great; Lombards; Merovingian Dynasty; Monasticism

Bibliography

Bede. *Ecclesiastical History of the English People with Bede's Letter to Egbert and Cuthbert's Letter on the Death of Bede.* Trans. Leo Sherley-Price. Harmondsworth, UK: Penguin, 1991.

Blair, Peter Hunter. *The World of Bede.* Cambridge: Cambridge University Press, 1971.

Clarke, Howard B., and Mary Brennen, eds. *Columban and Merovingian Monasticism.* Oxford: British Archeological Reports, 1981.

Laistner, Max L. W. *Thought and Letters in Western Europe, A.D. 500 to 900.* 2d ed. Ithaca, NY: Cornell University Press, 1976.

Lawrence, Clifford H. *Medieval Monasticism: Forms of Religious Life in Western Europe in the Middle Ages,* 2d ed. London: Longman, 1989.

Riché, Pierre. *Education and Culture in the Barbarian West: From the Sixth through the Eighth Century.* Trans. John Contreni. Columbia: University of South Carolina Press, 1978.

Stenton, Frank M. *Anglo-Saxon England.* 3d ed. Oxford: Clarendon, 1971.

Wood, Ian. *The Merovingian Kingdoms. 450–751.* London: Longman, 1994.

Constantine (d. 337)

Roman emperor (r. 306–337) who, with Diocletian (r. 284–305), restored order to the Roman world and laid the foundation for the empire's success for centuries to come. His achievements were numerous, including the establishment of a new capital at Constantinople and reform of the coinage. He is important also for his military reforms and his introduction of many Germans into the Roman military, beginning a process known as the barbarization of the Roman army. He is particularly important for his conversion to Christianity and for becoming the first Christian emperor of the Roman Empire. Indeed, his activities as a Christian emperor had great consequences for the church and for the Germanic peoples who inherited the empire in the fifth and sixth centuries.

Constantine rose to power in the early fourth century in the wake of his father's death and the retirement of the leading Roman emperor, Diocletian, and his colleague Maximian. Diocletian had spent the preceding twenty years creating a delicate system of shared government that was designed to prevent the political and military collapse of the preceding half century. After he retired in 305, with the hope that his succession plan would succeed, he instead witnessed the rapid destruction of that system. It was in the civil wars that followed the retirement of Diocletian that Constantine rose to power.

One of the most critical moments in Constantine's struggle for power came in the year 312, when he fought his rival Maxentius, Maximian's son, for control of the Western Empire. The Battle of the Milvian Bridge, one of the bridges across the Tiber River to Rome, was won by Constantine, and it brought him possession of the ancient capital and the Western imperial title. His victory was preceded by a great vision that was the starting point, if not actual cause, of Constantine's conversion to Christianity. According to the church historian Eusebius in his biography of the emperor, Constantine told his biographer that he saw the sign of the cross in the heavens bearing the inscription "In this sign conquer." His victory confirmed the validity of the vision and led him to accept Christianity. And it was indeed in the following year that, with the Eastern emperor Galerius, Constantine issued the Edict of Milan, which legalized Christianity in the empire. He then ruled the empire with a colleague in the east, first Galerius and then Licinius, until 324, when he defeated Licinius in battle and reunited the empire. He founded a new capital, Constantinople (now Istanbul, Turkey) in 330 and ruled as sole emperor, although often with his sons as caesars, until his death in 337.

Constantine's reign had significant consequences for the Germanic successor kingdoms that emerged in the wake of the collapse of the Western Empire, as well as for much of early medieval Europe in general. As the first Christian emperor he established an important model for numerous kings and emperors, including the great Frankish rulers Clovis and Charlemagne, as well as for early medieval writers like Gregory of Tours. His relations with the church set an important precedent for later rulers in both the barbarian kingdoms and the Byzantine

Marble bust of Emperor Constantine (Araldo de Luca / Corbis)

Empire (as the Eastern Empire came to be called). On two occasions, both interestingly after military victories, one that brought him control over the western half of the empire and the other over the entire empire, Constantine convened church councils to decide major issues of the faith. The second of the councils, at Nicaea in 324, decided one of the fundamental tenets of the Christian faith, the relationship between God the Father and God the Son. Constantine presided over the council and participated in debate, and his presence may have influenced the outcome. At the very least, it set the model for the involvement of the emperor in the affairs of the church and asserted the right and responsibility of the emperor to convene church councils.

Constantine's involvement in the Council of Nicaea may also have led to the denunciation of the teachings of Arius and the declaration of Arianism as a heresy. Constantine, however, wavered in his support for orthodoxy and allowed the growth of Arianism in the empire. Consequently the Germanic tribes living along the imperial frontier were evangelized by Arian Christians, and many of the tribes that converted to Christianity accepted the Arian version. Constantine's religious legacy, therefore, was mixed. He provided a positive model of Christian rulership for later kings and emperors, but also contributed to the conversion of many barbarians to Arian Christianity, a process that later caused difficulties for Arian Christian kings, like Theodoric the Great, who ruled over Catholic Christian subjects in the post-Roman world.

Constantine's other legacy to the late Roman and early medieval world was his recruitment of Germans into the Roman army. It is one of the paradoxes of Constantine's reign that he was criticized by contemporaries and has been remembered by historians for the so-called barbarization of the army when he strove to identify himself as a conqueror of the barbarians and the "Triumpher over the barbarian races" (Triumfator, Debellator, Gentium barbararum). But, indeed, he both waged war against the Germans and other peoples along the frontier and expanded the existing policy of promoting Germans to high-ranking military posts.

His wars against the Germans were intended to stabilize a frontier that had proved particularly porous during the crisis the empire faced in third century and to provide Constantine a glorious military record to parallel his successes in the civil wars. Toward those ends, he waged wars against a number of Germanic peoples along the frontiers. He fought border wars with the Alemanni along the Rhine River in an attempt to preserve the integrity of that frontier, which

had been an important point of entry for the Germans in the third century. The emperor also faced the Visigoths along the Danubian border in the late 310s and early 320s. Here again he sought to restore the stability of the old frontier and even extend Roman power to the limits established by the emperor Trajan in the early second century. Constantine responded to Visigothic incursions into Roman territory with a series of battles that allowed the emperor to repel the invaders and extend Roman authority. Constantine's victories forced the Visigoths to surrender. The extent of his expansion beyond the Danube remains uncertain, however, and the Visigoths launched another attack in the mid-320s. Constantine sent his son against them, who successfully defeated them and extracted a treaty that required the Visigoths to defend the empire. Unfortunately for the empire, Constantine's successes were short–lived, and by the end of the fourth century, at the latest, his settlements had broken down, and various Germanic tribes had crossed into the empire.

Despite actively fighting the barbarians, Constantine also enrolled many of them in the army. Although this policy was not new, Constantine included larger numbers of Germans than any of his predecessors, which caused serious problems for the empire in the following century. The army itself had increased in size to meet internal and external threats, and in Constantine's time may have numbered as many as 600,000 men, a number that included traditional Roman legionnaires as well as auxiliary soldiers (auxiliae). The auxiliaries were more numerous in Constantine's army than they had traditionally been, in fact more numerous than the legionnaires. It was this contingent that was made up mostly of Germans, so that the army was nearly half immigrant. And the Germans found places at all levels of the Roman army. The highest-ranking officers were Germans, and Constantine's personal bodyguard was made up of Germans. Constantine also reorganized the army, dividing it into a frontier force and a central strike force, and German soldiers were in both units. Constantine's use of Germans thus did contribute to what has been called the barbarization of the army, a process that, in some ways, undermined Rome's ability to defend itself against other Germanic invaders. On the other hand, it allowed the barbarians to identify themselves with the empire and its values and thus become Romanized.

See also Arianism; Charlemagne; Clovis; Gregory of Tours; Theodoric the Great; Visigoths

Bibliography

Barnes, Timothy D. *Constantine and Eusebius.* Cambridge, MA: Harvard University Press, 1981.

Brown, Peter. *The World of Late Antiquity, A.D. 150–750.* London: Thames and Hudson, 1971.

Burckhardt, Jacob. *The Age of Constantine the Great.* Trans. Moses Hadas. Berkeley: University of California Press, 1983.

Grant, Michael. *Constantine the Great: The Man and His Times.* New York: Charles Scribner's Sons, 1994.

D

Dagobert (608–638/639)

The son of Chlotar II and grandson of Frede-gund, Dagobert was the last great and effective king of the Merovingian dynasty. Indeed, under Dagobert, the dynasty reached its high point, only to begin a gradual decline in the generation after his death. Despite the dynasty's misfortunes after his death, under Dagobert the kingdom enjoyed internal peace and prosperity and success against foreign foes. Like his father, Dagobert was active in the administration of law and may have promulgated two law codes for the Franks. He also, like Chlotar, maintained good relations with the church and its missionaries and also founded the important monastery of St. Denis in Paris, which came to serve as a royal tomb and the burial place of Dagobert himself.

Dagobert benefited from the successes of his father, Chlotar II, who had restored the unity and peace of the kingdom after years of civil strife involving Brunhilde and Frede-gund. Dagobert also played an important role in his father's efforts to preserve the authority of the dynasty over the entire kingdom. In 622, Dagobert was made subking of Austrasia, possibly as a concession to the local aristocracy and certainly at least to bind the Austrasian nobility closer to the ruling dynasty. Although it is slim, the evidence that exists suggests that Dagobert ruled the region well during his father's lifetime and was aided and greatly influenced by Chlotar's ally and mayor of the palace, Pippin of Landen, the ancestor of the Carolingian dynasty. At his father's death in 629, Dagobert assumed control of the entire kingdom. According to Fredegar, this was a poor time in Dagobert's reign, when the king sank into debauchery and avarice, exploiting particularly the resources of the church. It was Pippin, according to Fredegar, who reprimanded the king and turned him back on the proper path. Indeed, Pippin was one of Dagobert's most important and trusted advisors and joined the king when he moved his capital from Metz in Austrasia to Paris in Neustria. Dagobert moved in order to establish himself as the ruler of Neustria, and thus of the entire realm as well as Austrasia, which he had ruled since 622. Although he managed to secure his place in his father's kingdom in Neustria, Dagobert's move unsettled the nobility in Austrasia and forced Dagobert to address the concerns of the nobility, including perhaps the regionalism that may have motivated the nobles. As his father had done, Dagobert appointed his five- or six-year-old son Sigebert III (d. 656) as subking of Austrasia in 634. He also appointed his younger brother Charibert (d. 632) subking in Aquitaine, a very independent region that the Merovingians had yet to bring completely under their authority. Although he may have been making concessions to regionalism, Dagobert may also have intended the creation of subkings as a means to bind the kingdom more securely under his authority.

Whatever his goal, Dagobert seems to have succeeded in binding the kingdom more fully together under his authority; he was also, like his father before him, an active lawgiver. The king took tours throughout his kingdom—itinerancy was a key to the success of most early medieval rulers—dispensing justice. Fredegar notes that Dagobert "struck terror" into the hearts of the people of Burgundy when he toured that region in the late 620s. He also toured Austrasia with similar effect in 630. He resolved legal disputes on these tours and dispensed high justice from the royal court, and the proceedings were guided by specific ritual and written texts. After 631, however, it seems that Dagobert ceased taking judicial tours and dispensed justice from his capital in Paris, a testimony to the sophistication of Merovingian legal practices and the peace and order of Dagobert's reign. Moreover, the king may also have codified Frankish legal codes. His name is associated with several legal codes of the early seventh century, including the *Lex Ribuaria* (Law of the Ripuarian Franks) for the Austrasian kingdom. He also may have been involved in the codification of the laws of the Alemanni and the Bavarians. Like his father before him, Dagobert's activities as a lawgiver were intended to enhance his stature as king and to set him apart from the nobility, which needed the king all the more because he dispensed justice.

Dagobert also built upon his father's legacy of good relations with the church, an association important as a counterbalance to potential trouble from the nobility and as a support for his increasingly elevated conception of kingship. Like Chlotar, Dagobert consulted with the bishops and accepted their advice. He also, of course, oversaw the appointment of bishops and took steps to ensure the good quality of his appointments.

The king promoted the activities of missionaries and, in general, oversaw the administration and well-being of the church in his kingdom. His most important relationship, however, was with the monasteries of his kingdom, especially the monastery of St. Denis near Paris. Dagobert developed a special relationship with the community, which he founded in 624, and he often made lavish donations to it. According to a late, and probably unreliable tradition, Dagobert felt especially indebted to St. Denis because the saint had protected him from Chlotar's anger during a quarrel Dagobert and his father had. According to Fredegar, Dagobert embellished the church at the monastery with gold and many precious stones. The king also made numerous grants of land to the monastery and in a charter granted the abbey the right to hold a fair on the saint's feast day, October 5. The fair brought great economic benefit to the monastery and attracted increasingly larger crowds as the saint's popularity grew. St. Denis gradually became the patron of the dynasty, and Dagobert and many of his descendants were buried at the monastery.

At his death in 638/639, Dagobert was succeeded by his sons Sigebert III (d. 656), who had ruled as subking in Austrasia since 632, and Clovis II (d. 657). They inherited a kingdom that was at peace and enjoyed much prosperity, as well as close relations between the king and a very powerful church. The office of king had been greatly enhanced, and law and administration had been improved by Dagobert and Chlotar before him. Both Sigebert and Clovis enjoyed some success, and Clovis and his wife Balthild further strengthened ties with the church. But the growing power and ambition of the aristocracy was a bad omen, and signs of trouble began to emerge. Within a few generations of Dagobert's death, the dynasty began its irrevocable decline, and the so-called do-nothing kings (*rois fainéants*) began to assume the throne. Dagobert's reign, however, was the high point of the history of the Merovingian dynasty, and Dagobert was one of the greatest kings of the line.

See also Balthild, St.; Brunhilde; Carolingian
Dynasty; Chlotar II; Fredegund; Merovingian
Dynasty; Pippin of Landen; Rois Fainéants

Bibliography

Bachrach, Bernard S. *Merovingian Military
Organization, 481–751.* Minneapolis:
University of Minnesota Press, 1972.

Bachrach, Bernard S., trans. *Liber historiae
Francorum.* Lawrence, KS: Coronado, 1973.

Fouracre, Paul, and Richard A. Gerberding. *Late
Merovingian France: History and Hagiography,
640–720.* Manchester, UK: University of
Manchester Press, 1996.

Geary, Patrick. *Before France and Germany: The
Creation and Transformation of the Merovingian
World.* Oxford: Oxford University Press,
1988.

James, Edward. *The Franks.* Oxford: Blackwell,
1991.

Lasko, Peter. *The Kingdom of the Franks: North-West
Europe before Charlemagne.* New York: McGraw
Hill, 1971.

Wallace-Hadrill, J. M. *The Long-Haired Kings.*
Toronto: Toronto University Press, 1982.

———. *The Frankish Church.* Oxford: Clarendon,
1983.

Wallace-Hadrill, J. M., ed. and trans. *The Fourth
Book of the Chronicle of Fredegar with Its
Continuations.* London: Nelson, 1960.

Wemple, Suzanne. *Women in Frankish Society:
Marriage and the Cloister, 500 to 900.*
Philadelphia: University of Pennsylvania Press,
1985.

Wood, Ian. *The Merovingian Kingdoms, 450–751.*
London: Longman, 1994.

Desiderius (eighth century)

Successor of Aistulf and king from 757 to
774, Desiderius was the last of the kings of
the Lombards. His fate was linked with the
rise of the Carolingian dynasty and the complex diplomatic relations between the Carolingians, Lombards, and popes in Rome. He
pursued the traditional, aggressive policy of
Lombard kings and attempted, with some
success, to unify Italy under Lombard rule.
His threatening posture toward Rome and

the papal territories led to his conflict with
the popes, who sought aid from the Carolingian dynasty. Pippin the Short intervened
diplomatically on the pope's behalf, and his
son Charlemagne invaded in defense of the
papacy, absorbed the kingdom of the Lombards into the growing Carolingian Empire,
and deposed Desiderius as king and exiled
him to a Frankish monastery.

Although he eventually suffered defeat as a
result of his bad relations with Rome,
Desiderius began his reign as king in the good
graces of Rome. His election as king of the
Lombards on March 3 or 4, 757, in fact, was
supported by the pope, Stephen II (r.
752–757). The succession to Aistulf was a
complicated affair: Desiderius, a former official in Aistulf's government and duke of Tuscany, appears to have been a likely candidate,
but he faced strong opposition from another
Lombard noble, Ratchis. Desiderius, however, appealed to the pope for support in his
efforts to obtain the crown and met with representatives of the pope. In exchange for
promises to return papal cities seized by Aistulf, Desiderius received military backing
from the pope. Stephen also secured for
Desiderius the support of the Carolingian
king Pippin, who had already invaded Italy
twice in the 750s to punish Aistulf for harassing the pope. This important backing from
Rome secured the election of Desiderius and
the retirement of Ratchis.

The reign of the new king opened with the
promise of good relations between Rome and
the Lombards. In 758, Desiderius visited
Rome as a pilgrim and prayed at the tomb of
St. Peter, indicating his devotion to the Apostle and to his successor, the pope. But matters
changed quickly for the pope, now Paul (r.
757–767), as Desiderius returned to the aggressive and expansive policy of his predecessors. The new king imposed his will on the
southern Lombard duchies of Benevento and
Spoleto. Even worse, Desiderius refused to
return the papal cities as he had promised,
despite repeated requests from the pope, and
he even seized new territory near Rome. He

also negotiated with representatives of the Byzantine emperor in southern Italy, entering into an arrangement that would have seen the further erosion of papal authority in Italy and the further loss of papal territory. In response, Pope Paul sent numerous letters over the next several years to King Pippin for aid against Desiderius. Pippin was no longer interested in military involvement in Italy and was content to intervene diplomatically. In 760, Pippin's envoys convinced Desiderius to agree to return cities to the pope, but the Lombard king still did not follow through on the agreement, and the situation worsened for the pope.

During the reigns of Paul and his successor Stephen III (r. 767–772), the situation deteriorated for Rome, as Desiderius increased his power throughout Italy and benefited from a tumultuous papal election in 767. Moreover, Desiderius benefited from the turmoil in the Carolingian kingdom at the death of Pippin and succession of his sons Carloman and Charlemagne in 768. Charlemagne faced a revolt in part of his kingdom and received little help from his brother, and the two were on the point of civil war after Charlemagne suppressed the revolt. The tensions between the two brothers made intervention in Italy unlikely, but Desiderius, now at the height of his power, benefited further by the diplomatic initiative of Pippin's widow, Bertrada. In an attempt to resolve the crisis between her sons and improve their international standing, Bertrada negotiated a marriage alliance between her dynasty and the Lombard. Desiderata, the daughter of Desiderius, was married to Bertrada's son Charlemagne. The alliance bound the Carolingians with the Lombards and the powerful duke of Bavaria, Tassilo, who was married to another daughter of Desiderius. Clearly a coup for Desiderius, whose greatest rival, the pope, lost his most important ally, the king of the Franks. Although forced by the agreement to return territory to the pope, Desiderius surely gained more than he lost in the agreement. Indeed, the letters of complaint sent by the pope to the Carolingians reveal the great dissatisfaction Rome felt over the treaty.

Desiderius's triumph did not last long, as the alliance collapsed and an aggressive Carolingian king took sole control of the throne. In 771, Carloman died and his widow and sons fled to the Lombard capital of Pavia. Desiderius pressured the pope, now Hadrian (772–795) to recognize Carloman's heirs as king, but the pope felt less threatened by Desiderius because of other changes in the Carolingian kingdom. Charlemagne, now free of the threat of his brother, repudiated the marriage alliance and expressed greater support for the pope than even his father had. The new pope, mindful that Desiderius had not fulfilled his side of the agreement with Bertrada, was willing to strike at the king's allies in the papal administration and establish a stronger alliance with Charlemagne. Desiderius, with Carloman's sons at his side, marched on Rome, threatening a siege and demanding the coronation of the Carolingian princes. Hadrian threatened Desiderius with excommunication, which stopped his advance, and wrote to Charlemagne for aid.

The new king first attempted to negotiate a settlement with Desiderius, but the Lombard's refusal forced Charlemagne to invade in 773. His armies quickly broke the Lombard forces, which preferred flight to battle in the face of the powerful Carolingian army. Desiderius's kingdom quickly collapsed, as the southern duchies detached themselves from his authority and surrendered to the pope. Charlemagne laid siege to the capital of Pavia, where Desiderius had taken up residence, and captured the city in six months. The Carolingian king also took the city of Verona, Lombard Italy's second city, where Desiderius's son, Adelchis, had gone with Carloman's family. The invasion of Italy brought Carloman's family and Desiderius into Charlemagne's control. We hear little of either after 774; Desiderius was sent into exile in a monastery in Charlemagne's kingdom. Despite his many talents and early success, Desiderius overplayed his hand in the struggle with Charlemagne, who could not allow Desiderius to ensure the coronation of his nephews or to harass the pope. Desiderius's ambition brought about the end of the independent Lombard kingdom and the coronation of Charlemagne as king of the Lombards in 774.

See also Aistulf; Bertrada; Carloman, King of the Franks; Carolingian Dynasty; Charlemagne; Lombards; Pippin III, Called Pippin the Short; Tassilo

Bibliography

Christie, Neil. *The Lombards: The Ancient Langobards.* Oxford: Blackwell, 1998.

Davis, Raymond, trans. *The Lives of the Eighth-Century Popes* (Liber Pontificalis): *The Ancient Biographies of Nine Popes from* A.D. *715 to* A.D. *817.* Liverpool, UK: Liverpool University Press, 1992.

Einhard and Notker the Stammerer. *Two Lives of Charlemagne.* Trans. Lewis Thorpe. Harmondsworth, UK: Penguin, 1981.

Llewellyn, Peter. *Rome in the Dark Ages.* New York: Barnes and Noble, 1993.

Noble, Thomas F. X. *The Republic of St. Peter: The Birth of the Papal State, 680–825.* Philadelphia: University of Pennsylvania Press, 1984.

Riché, Pierre. *The Carolingians: A Family Who Forged Europe.* Trans. Michael Idomir Allen. Philadelphia: University of Pennsylvania Press, 1993.

Scholz, Bernhard Walter, trans. *Carolingian Chronicles: Royal Frankish Annals and Nithard's History.* Ann Arbor: University of Michigan Press, 1972.

Dhuoda (c. 803–c. 845)

Carolingian noble and wife of the powerful Bernard of Septimania, Dhuoda is best known for the *Liber manualis* (Handbook), which she wrote for her son William. The text is the only known work by a female Carolingian author and is an example of the mirror for princes, a literary genre defining the proper duties of the nobility. The *Liber* calls on William to do his duty to God and his father and country. It also reveals much about the character and desires of Dhuoda, as well as her deep longing for her son, who had been separated from her by her husband. Long discounted for its unconventional Latin, Dhuoda's work is now generally recognized for its emotional and spiritual content and is a held to be a great contribution to medieval women's literature.

Little is known of Dhuoda's life, other than what she reveals in the *Liber,* but other things can be discerned about her life from her husband's career. She was born, probably in 803, into the higher nobility, but the exact location is uncertain. It is generally assumed that she was born in the northern part of the Carolingian Empire, an area where her name is common. It is possible, however, that she was born in the south, where her husband later sent her to oversee his estates, something he would have been more likely to do if she was from the south and had relatives in the region, which would have increased her chances for success in administering her husband's possessions. She married Bernard, as she tells us, on June 29, 824, at the imperial palace at Aachen. Her husband was a high-ranking noble who was closely related to the Carolingian family and who was an important ally of the emperor Louis the Pious. Bernard was sent to oversee the Spanish March, a border region between Islamic Spain and Christian Europe. Dhuoda accompanied her husband on his travels until the birth of their first son, William, on November 29, 826. She was then sent to Uzès, where she remained apart from her husband and her son for most of the rest of their married life.

Dhuoda's stay in Uzès was lonely and troubled. Bernard was generally away, and was the focus of the rumor that he was involved in an affair with the emperor's wife, Judith. Although the rumor remained unsubstantiated, Dhuoda surely heard of it and was surely bothered by it. She was surely also discomfited by the civil wars of the 830s between the emperor and his sons, which also involved her husband. He did, however, survive the contest and rumors of the 820s and 830s, and he visited her in Uzès shortly after the death of Louis the Pious in 840. The visit was long enough to bring about the birth of their second child, Bernard, on March 22, 841. Her husband's participation on the losing side in the Battle of Fontenoy on June 25, 841, brought further heartbreak for Dhuoda. Her son William was sent to Charles the Bald as a hostage to secure Bernard's loyalty after the battle. Shortly thereafter, her other son, not yet baptized, was sent to her husband's side in Aquitaine.

In late 841, without either of her two beloved sons with her and abandoned by her husband yet again, Dhuoda began work on her *Liber,* which she completed on February 2, 843. She may have faced even more unhappiness after completion of the book. Her husband was executed by Charles the Bald for treason in 844, and her son William, joining with the rebels to avenge his father, was captured and executed in 849. It is likely that Dhuoda witnessed her husband's execution, but less likely that she lived to see her son's death, since she probably died within a year or so of the completion of the book for William. She mentions her illnesses throughout the book, and she left detailed information for her funeral, including the epitaph for her tomb.

Dhuoda's surviving son, Bernard, may have been an influential figure in the history of later Aquitaine as well as the father of the founder of the great monastery of Cluny. Although she had a most illustrious descendant, Dhuoda's own claim to fame is her *Liber manualis,* translated as *Handbook for William,* a work of seventy-three chapters plus introduction, prologue, and epitaph (Thiébaux 1994, 161–162). The work was intended as a guidebook for William at the royal court of Charles the Bald; it was clearly influenced in style and content by the Bible, the works of the church fathers, various Christian writers and poets (e.g., Venantius Fortunatus and Isidore of Seville), Roman grammarians, and the Roman poet Ovid. It is a deeply personal work that reveals Dhuoda's loneliness and longing and love for her son; the love is shown in the poem in the prologue, "Dhuoda greets

her beloved son William. Read." She hoped that her book would be one that William turned to often for advice and as a means to maintain a connection with his mother. Dhuoda outlined his duties as a prince, particularly his obligations to his lord. In a possible reference to the turmoil of the 830s, she tells her son not to show disloyalty to his lord. She also reminded him of his spiritual responsibilities and encouraged him to love God, pray, and accept the gifts of the Holy Spirit. For Dhuoda her son's worldly and spiritual duties were closely intertwined. Indeed, she saw a heavenly reward for her son if he fulfilled his duties as a virtuous prince in this world. She also stressed family obligations. William should honor and obey his father and look after his younger brother. Dhuoda also asks her son to pray for her and to honor the financial obligations she has incurred as a result of maintaining her husband's estates. With this most human and humble request, Dhuoda closes her book, and, despite the hardships of her life, seems at peace with the world and ready to find her heavenly reward.

See also Carolingian Dynasty; Charles the Bald; Fontenoy, Battle of; Isidore of Seville; Judith; Louis the Pious

Bibliography

Dhuoda. *Handbook for William: A Carolingian Woman's Counsel for Her Son.* Ed. and trans. Carol Neel. Washington, DC: Catholic University of America Press, 1999.

Dronke, Peter. *Women Writers of the Middle Ages: A Critical Study of Texts from Perpetua (d. 203) to Marguerite Porete (d. 1310).* Cambridge: Cambridge University Press, 1984.

Nelson, Janet. *Charles the Bald.* London: Longman, 1992.

Riché, Pierre. *The Carolingians: A Family Who Forged Europe.* Trans. Michael Idomir Allen. Philadelphia: University of Pennsylvania Press, 1993.

Scholz, Bernhard Walter, trans. *Carolingian Chronicles: Royal Frankish Annals and Nithard's History.* Ann Arbor: University of Michigan Press, 1972.

Thiébaux, Marcelle, ed. and trans. *The Writings of Medieval Women: An Anthology.* 2d ed. New York: Garland, 1994.

Wemple, Suzanne. *Women in Frankish Society: Marriage and the Cloister, 500 to 900.* Philadelphia: University of Pennsylvania Press, 1981.

Diet and Nutrition

The early medieval diet, particularly for the peasant class, was a notoriously poor one. Many of the fruits and vegetables popular in the modern world were unknown in the early Middle Ages, and some vegetables, such as celery, were known only for medicinal purposes. The majority of the calories in the early medieval diet was made up of carbohydrates, but there were occasions when meat, mostly chicken or pork, was eaten. The diet of the wealthy and powerful, of course, was much better than that of the peasants, who lived barely above the subsistence level.

The evidence for the diet can be found in a variety of written sources, but unfortunately not from any contemporary cookbooks, examples of which are known from ancient Roman and late medieval times. One valuable source for diet is the Rule of Benedict, which, although valuable only for understanding the restricted diet of monks, does provide examples of the things found on early medieval dinner tables. Benedict, who was more sympathetic to human weakness than some monastic regulators, allowed the monks two meals a day; at the "sixth and ninth hour" the monks were offered two cooked dishes. And, when available, a third dish was to be allowed that contained apples or vegetables. The monks could have a one-pound loaf of bread each day, but were not to eat "the flesh of quadrupeds" unless they were sick or weak. Benedict also allowed his monks roughly sixteen ounces of wine each day or twice that quantity of beer, but also cautioned against drinking too much. Other monastic diets could be more or less stringent than that in St. Benedict's rule. Some monks more as-

cetic than Benedict ate only gruel and vegetables. One saint ate only mushrooms, and the Carolingian monk Walafrid Strabo recommended a diet of "some salt, bread, leeks, fish, and wine." Other monasteries sometimes offered more extravagant fare, including quantities of chicken, geese, and cakes.

More extravagant than anything the monks could contemplate were the menus of early medieval kings and nobles. Unlike the monks or the peasants, meat was the mainstay of the diet of kings and aristocrats. In a passage from his life of Charlemagne, Einhard reveals that the preferred means of preparation was roasting, because the great emperor refused to follow doctor's orders to eat boiled meat. Pork, fresh or smoked or salted, was a popular meat, and beef and mutton were also part of the nobility's diet. Meats were prepared in a variety of ways, including in the form of bacon and sausages. The diet was further supplemented by meat brought in from the hunt, and included rabbit, which was also a domestic food animal. The dishes of the wealthy were highly seasoned with pepper, cumin, cloves, cinnamon, and other spices. Honey was also used for both food and drink, and both beer and wine were popular at the tables of the powerful. The *Capitulare de Villis* of the early ninth century, which regulated management of the royal estates, provides further information on the diet of the Carolingian nobility. Charlemagne ordered that his various estates should be stocked with a large quantity of chickens and geese, which would provide a ready supply of food as well as large quantities of eggs. Cheese, butter, a variety of fruits and vegetables, and fish were also found at the tables of the nobility, and fish was particularly important for seasons of religious fasting. Finally, bread was an important source of calories even for kings and nobles, but it was of the highest quality white bread rather than the coarser grains the peasantry often ate.

The diet of the peasants was clearly the least varied of all the diets of the early Middle Ages, and the diet most dependent on grains as a source of calories. The poor lived on a bare subsistence diet, and a significant portion of their income went to pay for food and drink. The diet of the peasants consisted of porridge or bread, the latter becoming more common as the use of mills increased in the early Middle Ages, made from barley, buckwheat, oats, rye, and several types of wheat. Another important source of calories was beer, the production of which underwent improvement in the Carolingian period with the introduction of hops, which acted as a preservative. Moreover, the beer or ale consumed in this period was quite thick, almost the consistency of soup and practically a meal itself. The diet was supplemented by vegetables that were grown in small gardens by the peasants' homes. Peasants often grew onions, leeks, and cabbages in these gardens. Peas and beans, important sources of protein, were also found in the peasants' gardens; they were grown more extensively after the ninth century as new agricultural techniques were introduced. These legumes improved the nutrition and health of the peasants greatly. The peasants also derived protein from various meats, although not to the same extent as the nobility did. Peasants had access to fish in some local ponds and rivers, and probably also ate some chicken and pork. Indeed, one of the most common images of early peasant life is that of the slaughtering of a pig in midwinter. Thus although it was not without some variety, the peasant's diet was a simple fare, generally involving a simple meal of bread, beer, and stewed vegetables.

See also Agriculture; Animals; Benedict of
    Nursia, St.; *Capitulare de Villis;* Carolingian
    Dynasty; Charlemagne; Einhard

Bibliography

Duby, Georges. *Rural Economy and Country Life in
    the Medieval West.* Trans. Cynthia Postan.
    Columbia: University of South Carolina Press,
    1968.
Riché, Pierre. *Daily Life in the World of
    Charlemagne.* Trans. Jo Ann McNamara.
    Philadelphia: University of Pennsylvania Press,
    1983.

Donation of Constantine

One of the most important and well-known forgeries of the early Middle Ages, this document presented itself as issued by the fourth-century emperor Constantine, conferring great power on the pope. The date of composition and the purpose of the *Constitutum Constantini,* or the Donation of Constantine, remain unclear. This uncertainty has led to a variety of interpretations, which often vary as a result of the date assigned to the document's creation. It has been described as a tool intended to support the efforts of the popes to improve ties with the new Carolingian dynasty after the deposition of the last Merovingian ruler, Childeric III, in 751 or following the coronation of Pippin in 754. It has also been seen as a document designed to undermine Byzantine territorial rights in Italy, particularly in light of Byzantine failures to protect the papacy from its enemies, the Lombards. The Donation, the great papal historian Walter Ullmann notes, may have been intended simply to free the papacy from the confines of an antiquated and ineffective Byzantine imperial government framework as part of its long-range program to establish a papal monarchy in Europe. Thomas Noble notes that the document may have served to establish an independent, papal territorial power in central Italy. The Donation, whatever its origin, enjoyed a long career, whether used in defense of or in opposition to papal authority, until proved a forgery by Lorenzo Valla in 1439.

There is a general consensus among historians that the Donation was written in the 750s, although some have dated it later in the eighth century and have interpreted its meaning in light of the history of Charlemagne. It was most likely written by a Lateran cleric, possibly with the knowledge of Pope Stephen II, and was associated with the coronation and Donation of Pippin, the first Carolingian king of the Franks. The forgery was based upon legends that had existed in some form or other since the fifth century, legends that told the story of the relations between the Roman emperor Constantine and Pope Sylvester I. The opening section of the false Donation outlines the events associated with Constantine's conversion in the early fourth century. This section of the forgery, which clearly borrows from the legend of Sylvester, includes the story of Constantine being cured of leprosy by Sylvester and then, grateful for this miracle, Constantine accepting instruction in the Christian faith from the pope. Also in this section, "Constantine" asserts the importance of Rome as the city of the apostles Peter and Paul and as such proclaims the place of its bishop as the ultimate authority in matters of orthodoxy. In the second part, "Constantine" makes his famed donation to the papacy. Before departing for his new capital in the east, Constantinople, he grants the pope supremacy over the episcopal sees of Antioch, Alexandria, Constantinople, Jerusalem, and all the churches of the world. He also grants temporal authority to the pope and his successors over "Judaea, Greece, Asia, Thrace, Africa, Italy, and various islands" (17). And, most importantly, Constantine bestows on the pope "our palace [the Lateran], the city of Rome and all the provinces, districts, and cities of Italy or of the western regions" (17). This final donation was clearly meant to imply that the imperial dignity in the Western Empire was being passed from Constantine to the pope and his successors and that the popes had the authority to appoint new temporal rulers over the lands of the Western Roman Empire.

Although its origins remain unclear, the later history of the Donation is more definite. The forgery was involved in the struggles between church and state and manipulated by advocates on both sides. In the late ninth century, Frankish bishops inserted the Donation into canon law collections as a means to secure ecclesiastical property rights. In the eleventh century emperors and popes passed judgment on the document according to their own political and religious agendas. It was denounced by ardent supporters of the papacy in the later German empire, including Otto III (d. 1003). Various popes pointed to it

to support for their territorial claims in Italy and rights to primacy in the ecclesiastical hierarchy. Indeed, the Donation of Constantine had perhaps even greater influence on political and religious affairs after its composition sometime in the eighth century than it did when it first appeared.

See also Carolingian Dynasty; Charlemagne; Childeric III; Donation of Pippin; Merovingian Dynasty; Pippin III, Called Pippin the Short

Bibliography
Dutton, Paul Edward, trans. *The Donation of Constantine.* In *Carolingian Civilization: A Reader.* Peterborough, Ont.: Broadview, 1993, pp. 13–19.
Henderson, E. F., trans. *Select Historical Documents of the Middle Ages.* Revised edition. London: George Bell and Sons, 1892, pp. 312–329.
Noble, Thomas X. F. *The Republic of St. Peter: The Birth of the Papal State, 680–825.* Philadelphia: University of Pennsylvania Press, 1984.
Ullmann, Walter. *The Growth of Papal Government in the Middle Ages.* 3d ed. London: Methuen, 1970.

Donation of Pippin

Traditional name of the oral or written promise made by the Carolingian king Pippin the Short to Pope Stephen II (r. 752–757). The Donation of Pippin was an important step in the establishment of the papal states and in the solidification of the alliance between the pope and the Carolingian kings. Later held to have confirmed the forged document in which Constantine supposedly granted great power to the papacy, Pippin's donation was a grant of land in central Italy, to which the king had no legal claim, to the pope. The promise was made in the context of the papacy's struggle with the Lombard king Aistulf, during which the pope declined support from the Byzantine Empire, and the elevation to the royal throne of the Carolingians. It appeared, therefore, at a critical time in the history of the early Middle Ages and had a significant impact on the history of the papal states.

The Donation of Pippin came into being in the context of the creation of the blossoming papal-Carolingian alliance and in the wake of the coronation of Pippin as king of the Franks. In the face of mounting pressure from the Lombard king Aistulf, Stephen was forced to find a new protector. Technically still a subject of the Byzantine Empire, the pope received little support from the emperor, who could do little even to protect Ravenna, the imperial capital in Italy. With the fall of Ravenna to Aistulf, the imperial presence in Italy was ended, as was any semblance of imperial protection for Rome. Aistulf's aggression led Stephen to seek aid from Pippin, whose elevation to the kingship owed something to Stephen's predecessor Pope Zachary. The Lombard king's reluctance to yield to Frankish and papal requests to return some of his conquests to Rome forced Stephen to take more drastic action. In January 754, therefore, the pope arrived at the royal palace at Ponthion in the Frankish kingdom, where he was warmly received by Pippin, and remained in the Frankish kingdom until the summer of that year.

In April, Stephen met Pippin at Quierzy (near Soissons, France) and received promises from the king for the restoration of lands in central Italy. This promise, which according to papal accounts included the Exarchate, imperial territory including Ravenna and the surrounding region, and Roman duchy, papal territory in central Italy, is often identified as the Donation of Pippin, but it does not exist in written form and may have been delivered only orally. Whatever the case may be, an alliance formed between the king and pope, which was strengthened in July of that year when Stephen anointed Pippin and his sons Charlemagne and Carloman and declared them the true kings of the Franks.

Although the promise at Quierzy is often seen as the Donation of Pippin, it has been suggested that a later document is the actual donation. This document, the Confession of St. Peter, is a list of cities that submitted to the pope; it was compiled by Pippin's representative following the king's campaigns in Italy. The Confession was made necessary by Aistulf's continued aggression in central Italy and Pippin's invasions in defense of the pope in 755 and 756. After defeating Aistulf a second time in 756 and imposing a peace on him, Pippin sent his supporter, the important abbot of St. Denis Fulrad, to collect the keys of the cities and territories in central Italy. The keys and the list of the cities were then placed on the altar of St. Peter in Rome and thus may constitute the true donation.

The donation, whether the promise of 754 or the document of 756, marked an important moment in the papal-Carolingian alliance and growth of the papal states. It confirmed the pact between Stephen and Pippin and either precipitated or concluded the king's forays into Italy. It was confirmed by Charlemagne in 778 and by Louis the Pious in 817, both of whom sought to strengthen their ties with the pope. The donation also, it should be noted, involved territories that were technically not Pippin's to give. The lands Pippin restored to the pope were imperial territories, and the empire's inability to control them further demonstrated the end of the imperial presence in central Italy. Clearly, the empire's loss benefited both the papacy and the Carolingian dynasty.

See also Aistulf; Carolingian Dynasty; Charlemagne; Donation of Constantine; Franks; Lombards; Louis the Pious; Pippin III, Called Pippin the Short; Zachary, St.

Bibliography

Davis, Raymond, trans. *The Lives of the Eighth-Century Popes (Liber Pontificalis): The Ancient Biographies of Nine Popes from A.D. 715 to A.D. 817.* Liverpool, UK: Liverpool University Press, 1992.

McKitterick, Rosamond. *The Frankish Kingdoms under the Carolingians, 751–987.* London: Longman, 1983.

Noble, Thomas F. X. *The Republic of St. Peter: The Birth of the Papal State, 680–825.* Philadelphia: University of Pennsylvania Press, 1984.

Riché, Pierre. *The Carolingians: A Family Who Forged Europe.* Trans Michael Idomir Allen.

Philadelphia: University of Pennsylvania Press, 1993.

Scholz, Bernhard Walter, trans. *Carolingian Chronicles: Royal Frankish Annals and Nithard's History.* Ann Arbor: University of Michigan Press, 1972.

Do-Nothing-Kings

See Rois Fainéants

E

Ebroin (d. 680)

Frankish mayor of the palace of the Neustrian kingdom of the Merovingians. Ebroin was a powerful figure who dominated politics in the Merovingian kingdom for much of the third quarter of the seventh century. Although deposed for a time in the 670s, Ebroin managed to recover his control of the office of mayor and dreamed of unifying the kingdoms of the Merovingians under his authority—a dream realized by the rival Carolingian dynasty and its leader Pippin of Herstal following the Battle of Tertry in 687. Before his period of disgrace, Ebroin engineered the retirement of Balthild, the Merovingian queen and saint, and, after his return to power, he appointed and controlled several Merovingian kings. His reign as mayor, however, was widely viewed as tyrannical, which led to a fierce rivalry with Pippin and his family, as well as his murder by a frightened noble in 680.

Ebroin rose to power in the wake of the overthrow of the Carolingian pretender Grimoald in the late 650s. Although of unknown family, Ebroin was the most dominant figure at the Merovingian royal court of Balthild and her son Chlotar III (d. 673), and he assumed the office of mayor of the palace for the Neustrian kingdom in 659. In 664 Balthild retired to the monastery she founded at Chelles, possibly because of a coup led against her by Ebroin, whose thirst for power outweighed his sense of loyalty. He then served as mayor, and the real power in Neustria, under King Chlotar until the king's death in 673.

After the death of Chlotar, the kingdom experienced a short period of crisis, which began with the fall of Ebroin and ended with his return to power. At the death of the king, Ebroin, without consulting the other nobles of the kingdom, raised Chlotar's brother, Theuderic III (d. 690/691) to the throne. Ebroin's high-handed act angered the other nobles of the kingdom, who offered the throne to the Merovingian king in Austrasia, Childeric II (d. 675). Ebroin and his king were overthrown, and both were tonsured and placed in a monastery—Ebroin received this punishment only after much pleading by several bishops, who thereby saved his life. But the reign of Childeric over both Austrasia and Neustria was a short and troubled one; not long after his elevation to the Neustrian throne a falling out with some of his key supporters occurred. Moreover, Childeric alienated the Neustrian nobility by his reliance on his loyal Austrasian supporters. He also developed a reputation as a brutal and tyrannical king who violated the rights and traditions of the nobility, actually beating one magnate. The Neustrian nobility, including many of

Ebroin's supporters, orchestrated an assassination plot against the king and his wife Bilichild in 675. Their death opened the door for the return of Ebroin and his king Theuderic III to power in Neustria.

Beginning in 675 Ebroin carefully and brutally established his control over the king and kingdom. Although outmaneuvered by a former ally, Bishop Leodegar, at first, Ebroin soon gained control of the king and took the office of mayor of the palace at the expense of his old ally. In fact, Leodegar was one of the many victims of Ebroin's ruthless quest to control all of the Merovingian kingdom. The bishop had his lips, eyes, and tongue cut out and was finally killed in 678 or 679 at Ebroin's order. Although he eliminated a powerful political rival, Ebroin gained little from his brutal treatment of the bishop, whose tomb became a center of miracles shortly after his death. But the bishop was only one of Ebroin's victims, who included other bishops and priests imprisoned or exiled because they had sided with the mayor's rivals. Many members of the nobility also suffered persecution in Ebroin's quest for power. Indeed, not only nobles and bishops in his own region of Neustria but also those in Austrasia were among Ebroin's victims. The most notable, of course, was the king, Dagobert II, who had been promoted in 675 to the Austrasian throne by Childeric's mayor of the palace, Wulfoald. In 679, the king was ambushed by Ebroin and killed, as Wulfoald may also have been, since he is no longer heard of after that time.

By the end of the 670s, Ebroin had made himself master of almost the entire Merovingian kingdom and had nearly reunited Austrasia, Neustria, and Burgundy, the three parts of the Merovingian realm, under the nominal authority of Theuderic. His success, together with the ruthless policies by which it was achieved, inspired great unrest in Austrasia and the opposition of noble families there, led by the early Carolingian Pippin of Herstal. Ebroin's power became even greater in 680, when he decisively defeated Pippin in battle

and treacherously murdered Pippin's brother Martin. But Ebroin's triumph was short-lived; not long afterward he was murdered by a royal official afraid of being Ebroin's next victim. And not long after the murder, Ebroin's dream of unifying the kingdom was realized by his rival Pippin.

> **See also** Balthild, St.; Carolingian Dynasty; Merovingian Dynasty; Pippin II, Called Pippin of Herstal; Tertry, Battle of

Bibliography

Bachrach, Bernard S. *Merovingian Military Organization, 481–751.* Minneapolis: University of Minnesota Press, 1972.

Fouracre, Paul, and Richard A. Gerberding. *Late Merovingian France: History and Hagiography, 640–720.* Manchester, UK: University of Manchester Press, 1996.

Riché, Pierre. *The Carolingians: A Family Who Forged Europe.* Trans. Michael Idomir Allen. Philadelphia: University of Pennsylvania Press, 1993.

Wood, Ian. *The Merovingian Kingdoms, 450–751.* London: Longman, 1994.

Education and Learning

Traditionally seen as the "Dark Ages," the early Middle Ages were not without their cultural and intellectual achievements. Although these achievements were modest in comparison with the great accomplishments of the ancient world as well as the later medieval world, education and learning did not disappear in barbarian Europe. Even in the worst of times, during the collapse of the Roman Empire and the invasion of various barbarian peoples, education continued, even if only in the monastery schools. Indeed, the monasteries remained the great centers of learning throughout the early Middle Ages and were responsible for preserving many of the great works of antiquity. Moreover, under Charlemagne's direction, a "renaissance" in learning and literature emerged in the late eighth and ninth centuries. Although once thought to have been a shining moment in an otherwise dark time, the Carolingian Renaissance was only the most dramatic example of cultural activity in the early Middle Ages.

The various barbarian peoples that entered the Roman world had their own traditions of education, of course, but these did not focus on the written word. Indeed, theirs was a practical education that emphasized those things necessary for success in tribal society. Many of their educational practices continued even after they settled in the Roman Empire and created their own kingdoms. Boys were taught how to ride, hunt, and use weapons. Girls were taught how to spin and weave wool and how to use the distaff and spindle. These customs continued, but the successors of the Romans also borrowed from the educational practices of the ancient world.

The practices of classical education had a long history in Greece and Rome before the arrival of the barbarians in late antiquity. Education was for boys only and involved the skills necessary for success in the public arena. Consequently, the focus of classical education was on grammar and rhetoric. Boys studied the various parts of speech, grammar and syntax, and rhetoric in order to speak eloquently and persuasively. Their models were Cicero, Caesar, Quintilian, Seneca, and others, some of whom continued to be the focus of learning after the end of Roman rule in the west. Although it suffered decay as a result of the entry into the empire of various Roman peoples, the classical tradition was preserved. And in the sixth century important transitional figures emerged who embodied the traditions of the past and laid the foundations for later learning. Among the more important figures were two from the early sixth century, Boethius, discussed in his entry, and, especially, Cassiodorus, who compiled two works on sacred and profane letters that encapsulated the best of the Roman and Christian tradition. His work on sacred letters remained at the heart of education for centuries after his death.

Although an important body of learning and pedagogical techniques survived the so-called fall of the Roman Empire, the ancient schools did not. As a result, a new center of education emerged in the early Middle Ages, the monastery. Even though the primary purpose of the monastery was spiritual, education and learning remained an important component of the religious life. Indeed, it was recognized that a good education in Christian letters was essential to the success of the religious life, and monks were required to select a book from the monastery library at least once a year. Consequently, monasteries were centers of book production, as the monks needed to copy the books so that members of the community could read. One of the greatest contributions of the monks was their preservation of many important ancient Christian and pagan classics. They also established schools in the monasteries, based on ancient patterns, to instruct the young boys who were enrolled in the various communities by their parents. It was not only Christian letters that were taught, but classical as well, since the greatest writers of Latin—the language of learning and the Church—were pagan Romans. The most important books of grammar, by the fourth-century grammarian Donatus and the early sixth-century grammarian Priscian, contained a fair sampling of the works of the great classical Roman poets. The traditions of education and learning, therefore, were preserved in the monastic communities of barbarian Europe, and some monasteries, such as Jarrow and Wearmouth in England, were recognized as great centers of learning.

Although he was not the only ruler to promote education and learning, Charlemagne, in the late eighth and early ninth centuries, is perhaps the most noteworthy and influential proponent of learning in the early Middle Ages. He himself, as his biographer Einhard notes, tried mightily to learn to read and write. Another biographer, Notker the Stammerer, noted that the great king would often visit the schools to watch over the progress of the students and would take time to encourage the studious and chastise those who were less than diligent. Moreover, he made learning the center of the reform and renewal of religious life in his great kingdom, issuing the capitulary *Admonitio Generalis* and the Letter to Baugulf to improve learning and the knowledge of Scripture throughout his kingdom. He mandated the construction of schools at monasteries and churches throughout his realm so that the bright young boys of the realm could learn to read and write. His legislation thus encouraged the monks and clergy of the kingdom to teach children who were not members of their religious communities. Charlemagne also encouraged the monasteries to continue their practice of copying important works of Christian and classical Roman literature. Although his renaissance was only marginally successful, his efforts to improve the standard of education and learning in his kingdom demonstrate the importance of education to early medieval rulers.

See also Admonitio Generalis; Boethius; Capitularies; Carolingian Dynasty; Carolingian Renaissance; Cassiodorus; Charlemagne; Letter to Baugulf

Bibliography

Dutton, Paul, ed. *Carolingian Civilization: A Reader.* Peterborough, Ont.: Broadview, 1993.

Einhard and Notker the Stammerer. *Two Lives of Charlemagne.* Trans. Lewis Thorpe. Harmondsworth, UK: Penguin, 1981.

Laistner, Max L. W. *Thought and Letters in Western Europe, A.D. 500 to 900.* 2d ed. Ithaca, NY: Cornell University Press, 1976.

McKitterick, Rosamond, ed. *Carolingian Culture: Emulation and Innovation.* Cambridge: Cambridge University Press, 1994.

Riché, Pierre. *Education and Culture in the Barbarian West: From the Sixth through the Eighth Century.* Trans. John Contreni. Columbia: University of South Carolina Press, 1976.

Edwin (c. 585–633)

Formidable Northumbrian king from 616 to 633; the first ruler of that kingdom to convert to Christianity. A successful warrior, who may have also possessed a substantial fleet, Edwin extended his authority over Britons and Saxons, according to Bede, and was recognized with the title bretwalda, or ruler over several kingdoms. His stature as a king in England made his conversion important and raised the concerns of other kings, including the pagan Penda and his Christian ally Cadwallon.

Edwin came to the throne in Northumbria after a long exile. The heir to the throne of Deira, Edwin took refuge at the court of a powerful king south of the Humber River. The reigning king in Northumbria, Æthelfrith, demanded his return, but the southern king, Raedwald, refused. The two came to war; Æthelfrith was defeated and killed, and his sons fled into exile. Edwin was welcomed as king of Deira and Bernicia, and eventually succeeded Raedwald as overlord south of the Humber. Indeed, by 626 he was the most powerful figure in England. He married a daughter of Aethelberht of Kent and had contacts with the Merovingian dynasty on the continent. He took possession of the Isle of Man, conquered sections of north Wales, and established a loose confederation, one that foreshadowed more stable and lasting unions. But his invasion of territory ruled by the Britons had dire consequences for his kingdom and his line. He threatened the kingdom of the Briton Cadwallon, the last great native British king. With his pagan ally, Penda of Mercia, Cadwallon launched a counterinvasion of Northumbria in 633. In October of 633, Edwin fought a great battle in Hatfield Chase against Cadwallon and Penda in which he was defeated and killed. Edwin's son Osfrid was killed during the battle while protecting his father. And another son, Eadrid, was forced to submit to Cadwallon and then was killed by him. Edwin's line was thus destroyed, as was his kingdom and political confederation.

Although he was a powerful king whose authority over much of England foreshadowed later English political organization, Edwin's real importance lies in his conversion to Christianity. Even though the faith did not survive in Northumbria in the generation after his death, Edwin established a significant precedent by his conversion. Edwin's conversion, according to Bede, was accompanied by the miraculous. His wife, Æthelberg, daughter of King Æthelberht of Kent, was a Christian, and when he proposed a marriage alliance, Edwin was told that she could not marry a non-Christian. He said that he would not interfere with her religion and would consider adopting it once he had had the opportunity to examine it. He delayed this conversion until several further events passed. He survived an assassination attempt sent by the king of the West Saxons, and witnessed the birth of a daughter, for which he thanked his pagan gods. Bishop Paulinus assured him that it was prayers to Christ that brought Edwin life and happiness. Edwin declared that only when he was victorious over his attempted murderer would he convert, and shortly thereafter he defeated the West Saxon king. He delayed baptism still, however.

Bede notes that it was a sign offered by Paulinus that finally persuaded the king to convert. While at the court of Raedwald, Edwin, knowing that he was about to be betrayed, had a vision in which he promised a stranger that he would submit to the stranger's teachings if his kingdom were restored to him. The stranger placed his hand on Edwin's head as a sign and shortly thereafter Raedwald was persuaded by his wife to protect Edwin. Later, Paulinus placed his right hand on Edwin's head and asked if he remembered his promise. The final sign convinced Edwin to convert, and on Easter, April 12, 627, he accepted baptism at the hands of Bishop Paulinus. At that moment, Edwin became the first of many later Northumbrian kings to accept Christianity.

See also Anglo-Saxons; Bede; Merovingian Dynasty; Penda

Bibliography

Bede. *Ecclesiastical History of the English People with Bede's Letter to Egbert and Cuthbert's Letter on the Death of Bede.* Trans. Leo Sherley-Price. Harmondsworth, UK: Penguin, 1991.

Blair, Peter Hunter. *The World of Bede.* Cambridge: Cambridge University Press, 1990.

Geoffrey of Monmouth. *The History of the Kings of Britain.* Trans. Lewis Thorpe. Harmondsworth, UK: Penguin, 1982.

Randers-Pehrson, Justine Davis. *Barbarians and Romans: The Birth Struggle of Europe,* A.D. *400–700.* Norman: University of Oklahoma Press, 198s.

Stenton, Frank M. *Anglo-Saxon England.* 3d ed. Oxford: Clarendon, 1971.

Whitelock, Dorothy, ed. *The Anglo-Saxon Chronicle.* Westport, CT: Greenwood, 1986.

Einhard (c. 770–840)

Frankish writer and biographer who was a member of Charlemagne's court school. One of the great success stories of Charlemagne's efforts to revive learning in his empire, Einhard is best know for his *Vita Karoli* (Life of Charlemagne), a biography of the great Carolingian emperor. The *Life* is the first biography of a major political figure since antiquity and reveals the debt of Carolingian writers to classical models. Despite its debt to ancient Roman biography, Einhard's work is one of the most important sources for the life of Charlemagne and one of the great works of medieval writing. It is not Einhard's only achievement, however, because he also wrote numerous letters, a theological tract, and an important work of hagiography. Highly interested in architecture, he most likely was the supervisor for the construction of Charlemagne's palace and church at Aachen, the grandeur of which Einhard mentions in his biography.

Born around 770 in the Main Valley to noble parents, Einhard was sent to receive his education at the monastery of Fulda, one of the great centers of learning in the Carolingian realm. In the early 790s, he joined Charlemagne's palace school at Aachen, where he was taught by the greatest of the Carolingian scholars, the Anglo-Saxon Alcuin.

Triumphal arch designed by Einhard from a seventeenth-century engraving (Paris, Bibliothèque Nationale)

He remained at court for a while and earned the friendship of his great hero, Charlemagne. In 806, the emperor sent Einhard to Rome as an ambassador and may have entrusted him with other missions. In 813, Einhard was the first to recommend that Charlemagne make his son, Louis the Pious, co-emperor and heir. In the years after Charlemagne's death in 814, Einhard remained at the court of Louis the Pious and was appointed advisor to Lothar, the oldest son of Louis. A lay abbot, Einhard retired from the court in 830 with his wife Imma to the monastery he founded on lands granted by Louis at Seligenstadt. He built a church there as well, where he deposited the relics of the saints Marcellinus and Peter, and he died there on March 1, 840.

Although Einhard had numerous accomplishments in his life, his greatest contribution to medieval Europe was the *Life of Charlemagne*. Despite his assertion that he lacked the skills necessary to write the biography, Einhard's work is one of the most important of the Carolingian Renaissance. His writing reveals the extent of his learning and bears clear echoes of many Roman and Christian Latin writers, including Cicero, Julius Caesar, Tacitus, Orosius, and Sulpicius Severus. His greatest debt, however, was to the great Roman biographer, Suetonius, whose *De vita Caesarum* (Lives of the Caesars), particularly his life of Augustus, provided the format and vocabulary for Einhard's work. But Einhard's work was no slavish copy of Suetonius; it was based also on Einhard's intimate knowledge of his subject. The work addresses the major wars of Charlemagne, his diplomatic activities, and building projects. Einhard provides information on the great ruler's family life, including the king's too strong love of his daughters (whom he would not allow to marry), personal appearance, and personality. Einhard also includes discussion of the imperial coronation of Charlemagne and makes the still controversial statement that had Charlemagne known what was going to happen that Christmas day he would have not gone to church. The life concludes with an extended discussion of Charlemagne's death and includes a copy of his will.

The purpose of the biography and its date of composition remain uncertain, and the former is surely conditioned by the latter. Einhard's life is clearly biased in favor of its subject. He notes in his preface that he must write so as not to allow "the most glorious life of this most excellent king, the greatest of all princes of this day, and his wonderful deeds, difficult for people of later times to imitate, to slip into the darkness of oblivion"(52). He offers only passing criticism of the king, and blames rebellions on the nobles or one of Charlemagne's wives rather than on any action of the king. The work is clearly intended to prove the greatness and virtue of its subject. Beyond Einhard's regard for Charlemagne and sense of obligation, it is likely that the work was intended as a commentary on political affairs in the Carolingian Empire after the death of Charlemagne. A letter of 830 establishes that date as the latest it could have been written. And if the biography were written in the late 820s, it was surely a commentary on the difficulties that Louis the Pious faced by that time, as his sons and the nobility began to stir against him. It has also been suggested that the biography was written early in the reign of Louis and within only a few years of Charlemagne's death. Certain internal evidence supports an early composition, and if the work were completed in the late 810s it was intended to support the claim of Louis as Charlemagne's divinely ordained heir to imperial power. The biography also helped define the nature of imperial power for the Carolingians, an issue Louis himself pursued. Whether the life was composed circa 817 or circa 830, it is one of the most important biographies of the Middle Ages, and one that provides an image of the ideal Christian ruler.

See also Alcuin of York; Anglo-Saxons; Carolingian Dynasty; Charlemagne; Lothar; Louis the Pious

Bibliography
Einhard and Notker the Stammerer. *Two Lives of Charlemagne.* Trans. Lewis Thorpe. Harmondsworth, UK: Penguin, 1981.
Einhard. *The Translation and Miracles of the Saints Marcellinus and Peter.* In *Carolingian Civilization: A Reader,* trans. Paul Edward Dutton. Peterborough, Ont.: Broadview, 1993, pp. 198–246.
Geary, Patrick. *Furta Sacra: Thefts of Relics in the Central Middle Ages.* Rev. ed. Princeton: Princeton University Press, 1990.
Innes, Matthew, and Rosamond McKitterick. "The Writing of History." In *Carolingian Culture: Emulation and Innovation,* edited by Rosamond McKitterick. Cambridge: Cambridge University Press, 1994, pp. 193–220.
Laistner, Max L. W. *Thought and Letters in Western Europe, A.D. 500 to 900.* 2d ed. Ithaca, NY: Cornell University Press, 1976.
McKitterick, Rosamond. *The Frankish Kingdoms under the Carolingians, 751–987.* London: Longman, 1983.
Riché, Pierre. *The Carolingians: A Family Who Forged Europe.* Trans Michael Idomir Allen. Philadelphia: University of Pennsylvania Press, 1993.

Euric (c. 420–c. 484)

Visigothic king who ruled over much of southern Gaul (now the south of France) and parts of Spain from his capital at Toulouse. Euric broke a long-standing alliance with the Romans and established an independent kingdom within the boundaries of the Western Empire that was one of the first and most successful successor kingdoms; it had a population of some ten million people and an area of some three hundred thousand square miles. A successful warrior, Euric commissioned a legal code, the *Codex Euricianus* (Code of Euric), with the aid of Roman jurist. He was also an Arian Christian and, unlike his predecessors as kings of Toulouse, pursued an anti-Catholic religious policy that alienated his Roman subjects.

Euric seized power over the Gothic kingdom of Toulouse, which had formed as a federate ally of the empire around 418, in 466 when he murdered his brother Theodoric II. The assassination was most likely not over political or religious policy, but rather was a simple power grab by Euric. His thirst for power was further revealed in his relations with the Romans and other barbarian peoples in the coming decades. In the opening years of his reign, Euric negotiated with other barbarians against the Romans and ended the treaty the Visigoths of Toulouse had with the Western Empire. In 468 and again in 472 and 473, Euric sent armies into Spain, where they had great success, capturing cities such as Pamplona and Tarragona to the west and along the coast, respectively.

Ultimately, Euric controlled nearly all of the Iberian peninsula, seizing it from both Roman and barbarian powers. In 469 he sent armies into northern Gaul, and from 471 to 475 he continued the conquest of much of Gaul. By 475, Euric had extended his power across a region that stretched from the Atlantic coast to the Loire and Rhone rivers. His wars to the north included struggles with the Franks, who had already made overtures toward expansion into that region. Euric's power was at its height, and he commanded both land and naval forces; this successful naval command was unique among the unseaworthy Visigoths and reveals the extent of Euric's success. Moreover, many former Roman military leaders had joined Euric's army, which only enhanced his power and reputation. A new treaty between the empire and the kingdom of Toulouse was signed in 475, which recognized the new state of affairs. When Roman government was ended in the Western Empire in 476, Euric waged war against Odovacar, then king in Italy, to force the new power to recognize the Goth's claim in Gaul. And despite aid from barbarian allies of the empire, Odovacar was forced to accept Euric's claims. After creating a great kingdom, Euric died quietly in late 484, and was succeeded by his son Alaric II (r. 484–507).

Along with the creation of a sizeable kingdom in the remnants of the Western Empire, Euric is best remembered for his legal code. Although uncertainty remains about whether the existing code is the one promulgated by Euric, it is certain that in 475 the king issued a series of laws. The code was written in Latin with the help of Roman lawyers, but did not adopt the Roman legal tradition, which was best represented by the codification of Justinian in the next century. Euric's codification did not involve only tribal law, however, but did include royal statutory law. Although not universal tribal law, the *Codex Euricianus,* was, most likely, universal in scope and applied equally to Euric's Visigothic and Roman subjects. The code itself addressed a wide variety of issues, including the use of charters, last wills, lending and borrowing, and other matters concerning relations between Romans and Visigoths. The law code also recognized, for the first time, the institution of private retainers.

In terms of religious policy, as with relations toward Rome, Euric's reign marked a change in Visigothic practice. Unlike his predecessors, who had adopted a policy of tolerating and cooperating with their Catholic Christian subjects, Euric took a harder, less tolerant line. Although to identify his policy as one of systematic persecution of Catholic Christians may be an exaggeration, his attitude toward the Catholic church in his kingdom was hostile. He prohibited the bishops of his realm from communicating with Rome. He prevented the appointment of new Catholic bishops to various sees in his kingdom and banished others, including the archbishop of Bourges. He took steps to restrict the ability of the Catholic church and its clergy to operate freely and was accused of keeping churches deserted. But his opposition to the church moderated somewhat after the empire recognized his territorial conquests. Euric's restrictions on the church were, in part, the result of his inability to incorporate it into the state. Once the political situation eased, so did his oppression of the church associated with the empire. That notwithstanding, his earlier hostility toward the church caused tension between him and his Roman subjects that undermined his ability to govern.

See also Alaric II; Arianism; Justinian; Odovacar; Visigoths

Bibliography

Bury, John B. *History of the Later Roman Empire: From the Death of Theodosius I to the Death of Justinian.* 2 vols. 1923. Reprint, New York: Dover, 1959.

Collins, Roger. *Early Medieval Spain: Unity in Diversity, 400–1000.* New York and London: Longman, 1983.

Heather, Peter. *The Goths.* Oxford: Blackwell, 1996.

Isidore of Seville. *Isidore of Seville's History of the Goths, Vandals, and Suevi.* 2d rev. ed. Trans. Guido Donini and Gordon B. Ford. Leiden: Brill, 1970.

Thompson, Edward A. *The Goths in Spain.* Oxford: Clarendon, 1969.

Wolfram, Herwig. *History of the Goths.* Trans. Thomas J. Dunlap. Berkeley: University of California Press, 1988.

———. *The Roman Empire and Its Germanic Peoples.* Trans. Thomas J. Dunlap. Berkeley: University of California Press, 1997.

F

Family

As in all societies throughout history, the family was the basic building block of late antique and early medieval society. The structure, definition, and size of families, however, evolved over time, as the nature of society itself changed. That notwithstanding, the family remained an important institution throughout the period, even when the ascetic and monastic movement emerged and challenged conventional family life. Indeed, during the fourth to eighth centuries the family became an even more stable and important institution, and the evolution of marriage customs in the same period further reinforced the structure of the family and its importance in society.

According to Tacitus (c. 56–c. 120), the Roman moralist and historian, the pre-migration Germanic family was a tight-knit unit. He notes that mothers nursed their own children, who often ran about naked and dirty, which allowed them to develop their bodies fully. Children were raised with minimal pampering and were only married once they had reached maturity. Adultery was rare, according to the Roman writer, and women caught in adultery were severely punished. The importance of the marriage vow and of family was taken very seriously, and women were expected to share in their husbands' labors in the field and even in war. Not only was the nuclear family bound closely together, but the extended family was as well. Members of the family were expected to participate in family feuds, and nieces "are as highly honored by their uncles as by their own fathers"(118). This idyllic picture, which may have more to do with Tacitus's desire to criticize contemporary Roman mores than any desire to reveal the reality of the Germanic situation, bears a grain of truth; the close bonds of the family in later barbarian Europe supports the portrayal in Tacitus of the pre-migration German family.

The family of the early Middle Ages was shaped not only by pre-migration Germanic tradition, but also by Roman and Christian traditions. Indeed, as the various Germanic peoples settled in the former Western Empire, they came into contact with Roman legal traditions and Christian views of the family. According to Roman law, the father was the *paterfamilias*, who had complete control over all his children as long as he lived. Although the life-and-death authority once exercised by the Roman father—according to legend, the founder of the Republic, Brutus, executed his own son for the son's betrayal of the city—no longer was in force by the fourth century of the Common Era, the father retained significant power in the family, which reinforced Germanic tendencies in that regard. Christian teachings emphasized friendship and charity within the family, and Christian theologians strove to define the importance of marriage, creating the monogamous traditions that shaped marriage and the family by the eighth century.

In the early Middle Ages, however, the family was in a somewhat fluid state owing to the various marriage customs of the Germanic peoples. Indeed, loose marital practices allowed for a much broader definition of family than that of a mother, father, and children. Polygyny was practiced, at least by kings and nobles, into the eighth century, and all children were welcomed by their father; illegitimate children even shared in the inheritance. Indeed, Charles Martel was born to an illicit union and rose to command the Frankish kingdom in the early eighth century. And the history of Gregory of Tours is filled with the multiple marriages of the Merovingian kings and their numerous concubines and children. This situation changed, however, under the Carolingian dynasty, which sought to promote monogamous marriages and thus stabilized family structure.

The family was also an economic unit. Marriages involved exchanges of often significant amounts of moveable wealth and property and were arranged to promote the economic interests of both sides. The family household was the center of much economic activity. It was there that the basic economic activities of the period took place. Cooking, brewing beer, baking, and spinning were done in the home. Women also prepared candles, soap, and other necessities for the family, and animal husbandry and farming were performed at this level. And all members of the family participated in the economic activity of the household. At the head of the household was the father, and all members of the family were subject to his authority.

It has been customary to maintain that children were raised with little sentimentality or affection. Indeed, it has been suggested that the chances for the survival of children were so slim that it is likely that little attention was paid to them before they were seven years old or so and that even then they were treated roughly. Corporal punishment, as contemporary legal codes reveal, was practiced, fathers could sell their children into slavery, and there is even some indication that infanticide was practiced, as it had been in ancient times. This view, however, has been challenged, and anecdotes from the histories of Einhard, Gregory of Tours, and others suggest that there was a great deal of family affection in the early Middle Ages. Charlemagne, for example, loved his daughters so dearly that he would not let them marry and always kept them by his side. He would go riding and hunting with them, and loved them and the illegitimate children they had with members of the royal court. Moreover, even the most ferocious Merovingian queens, Brunhilde and Fredegund, revealed their maternal sides quite clearly in the protection of their children. They struggled mightily against each other to promote the interests of their sons, and Brunhilde wrote the emperor tearfully seeking his aid in protecting her daughter, who had been lost in North Africa. The situation of children was also improved by the reforms of the Carolingian dynasty, which strengthened marital practices and family structure.

See also Brunhilde; Charlemagne; Charles Martel; Einhard; Franks; Fredegund; Gregory of Tours; Marriage; Merovingian Dynasty; Women

Bibliography

Einhard and Notker the Stammerer. *Two Lives of Charlemagne.* Trans. Lewis Thorpe. Harmondsworth, UK: Penguin, 1981.

Gies, Frances, and Joseph Gies. *Marriage and Family in the Middle Ages.* New York: Harper and Row, 1987.

Goody, Jack. *The Development of Family and Marriage in Europe.* Cambridge: Cambridge University Press, 1983.

Gregory of Tours. *The History of the Franks.* Trans. Lewis Thorpe. Harmondsworth, UK: Penguin, 1974.

Herlihy, David. *Medieval Households.* Cambridge, MA: Harvard University Press, 1985.

Riché, Pierre. *Daily Life in the World of Charlemagne.* Trans. Jo Ann McNamara. Philadelphia: University of Pennsylvania Press, 1983.

Tacitus. *The Agricola and the Germania.* Trans. Harold Mattingly. Revised trans. S. A. Hanford. Harmondsworth, UK: Penguin, 1982.

Wemple, Suzanne. *Women in Frankish Society: Marriage and the Cloister, 500 to 900.* Philadelphia: University of Pennsylvania Press, 1981.

Fastrada (d. 794)

The third wife of the great Carolingian king Charlemagne, Fastrada played a critical role in her husband's reign, according to the biographer Einhard. She was from the eastern part of the Frankish empire, and her marriage to Charlemagne demonstrates the position of women and marriage in the Carolingian kingdom in the eighth century. She also appears in a most negative light in Einhard's biography of Charlemagne.

After the death of Charlemagne's second wife, Hildegard, in 783, the great king married Fastrada. She was the daughter of a powerful east Frankish count, and the marriage between Charlemagne and Fastrada was an important political arrangement, one that reconciled the king to the powerful east Frankish nobility. The marriage produced two daughters, Theoderada and Hiltrude, of whom little else is known. Useful as the marriage may have been politically, Fastrada herself influenced political events, if Einhard is to be believed, less positively. He accused the queen of great cruelty and of influencing her husband to perpetrate actions "fundamentally opposed to his normal kindness and good nature"(76). As a result, Charlemagne faced two conspiracies during his marriage to Fastrada. The first revolt occurred in 785 and involved a number of nobles from the eastern part of the kingdom, and the second involved his favorite bastard, Pippin the Hunchback, in 792. Both re-

volts were suppressed, and Einhard blames the revolts on Fastrada and her negative influence on Charlemagne. Although Fastrada's exact role in the origins of the two revolts is unclear, it is likely that she had some influence on her husband and, at the very least, played an important role in the creation of marriage alliances in the Carolingian kingdom.

See also Carolingian Dynasty; Charlemagne; Einhard; Franks; Marriage; Women

Bibliography

Einhard and Notker the Stammerer. *Two Lives of Charlemagne.* Trans. Lewis Thorpe. Harmondsworth, UK: Penguin, 1981.

Collins, Roger. *Charlemagne.* Toronto: University of Toronto Press, 1998.

Halphen, Louis. *Charlemagne and the Carolingian Empire.* Trans. Giselle de Nie. Amsterdam: North-Holland, 1977.

McKitterick, Rosamond. *The Frankish Kingdoms under the Carolingians, 751–987.* London: Longman, 1983.

Riché, Pierre. *The Carolingians: A Family Who Forged Europe.* Trans. Michael Idomir Allen. Philadelphia: University of Pennsylvania Press, 1993.

Scholz, Bernhard Walter, trans. *Carolingian Chronicles: Royal Frankish Annals and Nithard's History.* Ann Arbor: University of Michigan Press, 1972.

Wemple, Suzanne. *Women in Frankish Society: Marriage and the Cloister, 500 to 900.* Philadelphia: University of Pennsylvania Press, 1985.

Fontenoy, Battle of (841)

A major engagement during the civil war between the surviving sons of Louis the Pious, the Battle of Fontenoy was a brutal and bloody struggle. The battle occurred on June 25, 841, and involved the emperor Lothar and his nephew Pippin II of Aquitaine (d. 864) against the kings Charles the Bald and Louis the German. Although the battle was terrible and resulted in the defeat of Lothar, it proved not to be decisive; Lothar continued to struggle against his brothers. However the outcome of the battle can be described, it was recognized as a significant contest by contemporaries and is memorialized in poetry and in the history of Nithard, a combatant in the battle.

According to Nithard, the battle was the result of fortuitous circumstances for Charles the Bald and Louis the German in late spring 841, as well as of the unwillingness of Lothar to agree to peace. Indeed, Lothar refused to make any concessions to his brothers concerning the government of the empire and refused to limit his powers as emperor. He was bolstered in his defiance by the arrival of his nephew Pippin II, whose troops and opposition to Charles strengthened Lothar's cause. Charles and Louis, however, also enjoyed good fortune when they were able to join their armies together, and Judith, Charles's mother and widow of Louis the Pious, had also recently arrived with a sizeable force.

The growth of the armies on both sides increased tensions between them and made battle between them more likely. Even though contemporary accounts make it seem that war was unavoidable, Charles and Louis attempted to negotiate a settlement and sent peace offers to Lothar on June 23. His refusal forced his brothers to prepare for battle on June 25. According to Nithard, they returned to camp to celebrate the feast day of St. John the Baptist (June 24). This was surely regarded as an omen by the two kings, who sought the judgment of God in battle and knew that the liturgy of the feast of St. John celebrated release and salvation. Charles and Louis then made ready for battle the next day, which they planned to begin at the eighth hour. As Nithard notes, the armies rose at dawn and established their positions, and two hours later the battle began. Both sides fought bitterly, and casualties were heavy. Both Louis and Charles enjoyed success during the battle, and Lothar and his army were forced from the field.

For Charles and Louis, divine judgment had been rendered. They had defeated their brother and secured their positions in the empire. The victory reinforced their alliance, which was confirmed in the Oath of Strasbourg in the next year. The battle also secured Charles's political survival and strengthened his hold on Aquitaine and the western Frankish kingdom, which he claimed as part of his legacy from Louis the Pious. But the battle was not the decisive victory for which Charles and Louis had hoped. Despite the overwhelming defeat he suffered, Lothar managed to continue the war against his brothers and insisted on his authority over the entire empire.

See also Carolingian Dynasty; Charles the Bald; Judith; Lothar; Louis the German; Louis the Pious; Nithard; Strasbourg, Oath of

Bibliography
McKitterick, Rosamond. *The Frankish Kingdoms under the Carolingians, 751–987.* London: Longman, 1983.
Nelson, Janet. *Charles the Bald.* London: Longman, 1992.
Riché, Pierre. *The Carolingians: A Family Who Forged Europe.* Trans. Michael Idomir Allen. Philadelphia: University of Pennsylvania Press, 1993.
Scholz, Bernhard Walter, trans. *Carolingian Chronicles: Royal Frankish Annals and Nithard's History.* Ann Arbor: University of Michigan Press, 1972.

Franks

A group of West Germanic peoples, the Franks became the most important of all the barbarians to establish a kingdom in the old Roman Empire. In two successive dynasties, the Merovingian and Carolingian, the Franks ruled large sections of Europe from the late fifth to the late tenth century and laid the foundation for medieval and modern France and Germany. They emerged along the Rhine River in two main groups: the Ripuarian Franks along the Middle Rhine, and the more important Salian Franks along the Lower Rhine. Their origins remain obscure, as demonstrated by the uncertain meaning of their name, which has been interpreted to mean "the brave," "the fierce," "the wild," and "the free." The last term may provide the key to the best understanding of their origins as small tribal groups of Germans living along the Rhine who had not been made subject to other barbarian peoples. Whatever their exact origins, the Franks went on to become the most important and influential of the successors of the Roman Empire and boasted a long line of illustrious kings and queens, including Clovis, Clothild, Brunhilde, Fredegund, Pippin the Short, Charlemagne, and Louis the Pious.

The Franks themselves developed the legend that their origins could be traced back to the Trojans, thus giving them an origin as impressive as that claimed by the Romans. This tale was as legendary as that of Rome's Trojan origins, and the Franks appear in history for the first time in the third century, when they exploited the weakness of the Roman Empire and invaded Gaul. They ravaged throughout much of Gaul in the later 250s and even reached the borders of modern Spain. They seized much booty before being defeated by Roman armies. The Franks continued to cause problems for the empire throughout the third century, until the empire managed to settle its own internal crisis. At that point, under the great emperor Diocletian (r. 284–305), the Franks, and many other Germanic invaders, were defeated and settled. The Franks themselves concluded a treaty with the empire that allowed them to settle as *foederati* (federated allies) of the empire.

During the fourth and fifth centuries the Franks maintained a mixed relationship with the Roman Empire. Many Franks served in the Roman armies and rose high in the military and civil ranks of the empire. They often supported the empire during invasions by other peoples and were instrumental in the defense of Gaul. Indeed, they joined with the Romans against the invasion of Attila the Hun and fought against the Huns in the Battle of the Catalaunian Plain in 451, a critical battle

in the history of the empire. In the fifth century, however, the Franks also struck back against the empire. In 406, when the Rhine frontier collapsed, the Franks and many other Germanic peoples crossed into the empire to begin carving out territories for themselves. At the same time, a group of Salian Franks located at Tournai began to rise to power. And it was this group of the Salian Franks, under the leadership of the ancestors of the Merovingian dynasty, that rose to predominance; the greatest king of the Merovingian line, Clovis, then gradually established a great kingdom across much of northern Europe.

The Merovingian dynasty lasted from the time of Clovis (r. 481–511) until the time of Childeric III (r. 743–751). The kingdom formed by the kings of this line extended from their traditional homeland across much of modern France. Their success was due, in part, to the conversion of their first king, Clovis, to Catholic Christianity rather than Arian Christianity, which most of the other barbarians chose and which differed from the Catholic Christianity of the Roman population. The dynasty was ultimately replaced by the Carolingian dynasty. The first Carolingian king, Pippin the Short, deposed the last of the Merovingian kings and assumed the throne in 751. He was succeeded by his son, Charlemagne, the greatest of the Carolingian line, who built a great empire, initiated a religious and cultural revival, and was crowned emperor by Pope Leo III on December 25, 800. The dynasty survived until 987.

The Franks, unlike many of their barbarian contemporaries like the Huns, were not horsemen, and their military was comprised mainly of foot soldiers. But like their contemporaries they were nonliterate—literacy and all that accompanies it came only with contact with the Romans. They did have law, or at least custom, which was first codified under Clovis in the Salic law. They also seem to have traded with the Romans, at least in the fifth century, because of the Roman glassware found in many Frankish graves of that period. Grave goods, especially those found at the royal tomb of Tournai, tell us other important things about the early Franks, not the least of which is that they remained devoted to their traditional gods into the late fifth century. Christians buried their dead without material goods, but the Franks buried a variety of goods, including weapons (swords and battle axes), horse heads with their full harness, gold and silver coins, and gold buckles and jewelry. The gold jewelry was typical of Germanic metalwork. There were cloisonné brooches that were made of gold and inlaid with garnets and precious gems. One tomb contained a large number of brooches in the shape of cicadas, which were symbols of eternal life. The buckles and other jewelry were also decorated with designs, often elongated animal designs know as the "ribbon animal style."

See also Brunhilde; Carolingian Dynasty; Charlemagne; Childeric III; Clothild; Clovis; Foederati; Fredegund; Jewelry and Gems; Gregory of Tours; Louis the Pious; Merovingian Dynasty; Pippin III, Called Pippin the Short; Tournai

Bibliography
Bachrach, Bernard S., trans. *Liber historiae Francorum.* Lawrence, KS: Coronado, 1973.
Fouracre, Paul, and Richard A. Gerberding. *Late Merovingian France: History and Hagiography, 640–720.* Manchester, UK: University of Manchester Press, 1996.
Gregory of Tours. *History of the Franks.* Trans. Lewis Thorpe. Harmondsworth, UK: Penguin, 1974.
James, Edward. *The Franks.* Oxford: Blackwell, 1988.
Lasko, Peter. *The Kingdom of the Franks: North-West Europe before Charlemagne.* New York: McGraw-Hill, 1971.
McKitterick, Rosamond. *The Frankish Kingdoms under the Carolingians, 751–987.* London: Longman, 1983.
Wallace-Hadrill. J. M. *The Long-Haired Kings.* Toronto: University of Toronto Press, 1982.
Wolfram, Herwig. *The Roman Empire and Its Germanic Peoples.* Trans. Thomas J. Dunlap. Berkeley: University of California Press, 1997.
Wood, Ian. *The Merovingian Kingdoms, 450–751.* London: Longman, 1994.

Fredegar (fl. c. 642)

Name associated with an anonymous Burgundian chronicler of the mid-seventh century, who is the most important source for Frankish history after Gregory of Tours. The chronicle attributed to Fredegar, traditionally divided into four books, is a composite of various other sources, including Gregory's history, compiled by as many as three authors. Most scholars, however, detect only two authors at work. The important and original section of the work is the fourth book, which chronicles events from 591 to 642. It thus provides important information on the Merovingian kings of the early seventh century as well as on the formative period of the Carolingian family. Sometime in the eighth century Fredegar's chronicle was taken up by another anonymous author, who continued the history to 768, the first year of the reign of Charlemagne.

Little is known of the author or authors of the work, and the name Fredegar is associated with manuscripts of the work only in the sixteenth century. From evidence in his chronicle, however, it is possible to suggest that Fredegar, or at least the author of the new material on the seventh century, was a Burgundian layman of some standing who was active in the 640s and may have died around 660. He clearly had access to royal archives and to ambassadors from Lombard, Visigoth, and Slavic lands. He also had access to church archives, even though his focus was not that of a cleric. His Latin, in Wallace-Hadrill's words, was "highly individual," and other commentators have said much worse. But the chronicle, especially the fourth book, remains a most important source of information for a pivotal point in Frankish history.

The work itself is mostly derivative, with the exception of the original fourth book. The first three books, or five chronicles depending upon the arrangement of the text, are drawn from a number of earlier chroniclers and historians, with occasional editorial remarks and interpolations by the chronicler. Fredegar included works of St. Jerome, Isidore of Seville, and Gregory of Tours, and other Frankish chroniclers, among others. The fourth book, or sixth chronicle, is Fredegar's own and shows a remarkable knowledge not only of Frankish political life, but also of affairs in the Byzantine Empire. Although haphazardly organized and not written on an annual basis as the chronicle format would suggest, the work nonetheless captures a vital moment in the history of the Merovingian dynasty. Fredegar's chronicle begins with the last years of Queen Brunhilde, whom Fredegar clearly dislikes; he must have recorded her grisly demise with some pleasure. His great heroes were Chlotar II, who overthrew Brunhilde, and his son Dagobert I, and it is thanks to Fredegar that we know a good deal about their reigns. It is also in the fourth book of Fredegar's chronicle that the famous legend of Frankish origins appears. According to Fredegar, the Franks were of Trojan origin, a legend that became very popular among the Franks and was probably well known in learned circles in Fredegar's time.

The work was continued in the eighth century, taking up where Fredegar left off and chronicling Frankish affairs in the early years of the Carolingian dynasty, and in the ninth century it became increasingly popular. It remains one of the most important sources of the history of the Frankish kingdoms in the seventh century.

See also Brunhilde; Carolingian Dynasty; Charlemagne; Chlotar II; Dagobert; Gregory of Tours; Merovingian Dynasty

Bibliography
Laistner, Max L. W. *Thought and Letters in Western Europe, A.D. 500 to 900.* 2d ed. Ithaca, NY: Cornell University Press, 1976.
Riché, Pierre. *The Carolingians: A Family Who Forged Europe.* Trans Michael Idomir Allen. Philadelphia: University Press, 1993.
Wallace-Hadrill, John M., ed. and trans. *The Fourth Book of the Chronicle of Fredegar with Its Continuations.* London: Nelson, 1960.

Fredegund (d. 597)

Wife and mother of the Merovingian kings Chilperic I and Chlotar II respectively, Fredegund was one of the great queens of the dynasty. She was also one of the most ruthless and ambitious Frankish queens, and her rise to power illustrates the flexibility of marriage customs among the Merovingian rulers and the opportunity these customs offered some women. She was probably a slave at court before becoming Chilperic's lover and, eventually, wife. Often motivated by the defense of her husband and children, she surely desired power for her own ends. She is best known, perhaps, for her long feud with a rival Merovingian queen, Brunhilde, and Brunhilde's husband Sigebert. This rivalry and Fredegund's ruthlessness are revealed in all their bloodthirstiness in the pages of the history of Gregory of Tours, whose great animosity toward Fredegund continues to shape historical estimates of the queen.

Fredegund rose to prominence in the Merovingian kingdom because of her relationship with King Chilperic. As a slave, Fredegund became the mistress and, possibly, wife of Chilperic around 566, before his marriage to the Visigothic Spanish princess, Galswintha. Although marriage to low-born women was not uncommon among Merovingian rulers, this custom was abrogated by Chilperic's brother, King Sigebert, who married Galswintha's sister Brunhilde. Jealous of his brother's success, Chilperic arranged a marriage with Galswintha and, according to Gregory of Tours, loved her dearly at first because she brought a large dowry with her. Apparently, Chilperic continued his relationship with Fredegund after his marriage to Galswintha, which led the Visigothic princess to complain bitterly to her husband about her treatment. Chilperic had Galswintha murdered, keeping the dowry, so that he could remain with Fredegund.

Although there is some dispute over the nature of the feud between Fredegund and Brunhilde, it is certain that Fredegund took great pains to protect herself and Chilperic from Brunhilde and her husband Sigebert. When it appeared that Sigebert was about to overwhelm Chilperic in battle and seize his kingdom, Fredegund had her husband's rival murdered. She also attempted to kill Brunhilde on numerous occasions, but repeatedly failed. For example, according to Gregory of Tours, at one point she sent a cleric to kill Brunhilde, but he was discovered and returned to Fredegund, who punished him by cutting off his hands and feet. Despite her best efforts, Fredegund could not strike down her rival, and in fact she was survived by Brunhilde. Of course, Fredegund could claim the satisfaction of causing the death of two of Brunhilde's husbands. Shortly after the murder of Sigebert, Brunhilde married Merovech, the son of Chilperic from an earlier marriage. Merovech and Brunhilde hoped that the marriage would advance their own political agendas, but that hope failed to materialize, as Fredegund and Chilperic hunted down Merovech, who ordered one of his servants to kill him.

Fredegund's murders, however, were not limited to Brunhilde's husbands and were not committed in defense of Chilperic alone. Indeed, according to one contemporary chronicler, Fredegund murdered Chilperic in 584 when the king learned that she was having an affair with one of his advisors. Fredegund also arranged the murder of Chilperic's sons by other wives. She caused the death of Merovech and also ordered the murder of her stepson Clovis, who was allegedly conspiring against his father. These murders were ostensibly committed to protect Chilperic against renegade sons, but they also promoted the interest of Fredegund's sons, especially Chlotar. Although she caused the death of two of his sons, Chilperic found Fredegund to be a useful ally. She not only plotted the murder of his major rival, Sigebert, but also struck against many bishops and nobles who were

deemed a threat to Chilperic's power. Ambitious and calculating for her own interests, Fredegund provided valuable services to her husband.

Although she sometimes seemed to promote her own interests beyond all others, Fredegund was nonetheless careful to protect her own children and could react in dramatic and emotional ways to their misfortune. When two of her sons, Chlodobert and Dagobert, were stricken with dysentery, she believed it was divine punishment for Chilperic's new taxation and destroyed the tax registers to save her sons. Their death drove her to great despair and an extended period of mourning. On another occasion, Fredegund tortured and murdered a large number of women in Paris, whom she accused of causing the death of her son Theuderic by witchcraft. To save her son Chlotar when he became seriously ill, Fredegund made a large donation to the church of St. Martin of Tours in the hope that the saint would intervene on behalf of her son. Chlotar, to her relief, survived. She also provided a large dowry for her daughter Rigunth before her daughter's departure for marriage in Spain, and she fell into a terrible rage when she learned that Rigunth had been despoiled of her wealth by her betrothed. Her maternal record, however, is not without blemish. After Rigunth returned from Spain, the two women quarreled constantly, and Fredegund tried to murder her daughter. And she rejected her newborn Samson. She feared she would die and refused to nurse her son, whom Chilperic baptized shortly before the infant died.

After the murder of Chilperic in 584, Fredegund's position was most insecure and she had to use all her talents to preserve her place and secure the succession for her son Chlotar. She took control of Chilperic's treasure, which aided her bid to maintain control for herself and her son. She also continued to attempt assassinations of her rivals, particularly Brunhilde, as well as various nobles and bishops. The most serious challenge came when the paternity of Chlotar was questioned. She managed to rally to her side a large number of nobles and three bishops, who supported the legitimacy of Chlotar and allowed her to assume the regency for her son. She also led armies in battle when her son's part of the kingdom was threatened by rival Merovingians. And despite her life of brutality and ruthlessness, Fredegund died peacefully in 597, reconciled with Guntram, the most important Merovingian king of the time. Her efforts to secure power for herself and her son proved successful, and she even triumphed over her rival posthumously, when Chlotar overthrew and executed Brunhilde in 613. Her career, thus, demonstrates the opportunities that Merovingian marriage customs offered ambitious women and also reveals the importance of family, especially of sons, to Merovingian queens.

See also Brunhilde; Chilperic I; Chlotar II; Columban, St.; Galswintha; Gregory of Tours; Merovingian Dynasty; Visigoths

Bibliography
Gregory of Tours, *The History of the Franks*. Trans. Lewis Thorpe. Harmondsworth, UK: Penguin, 1974.

James, Edward. *The Franks*. Oxford: Blackwell, 1988.

Lasko, Peter. *The Kingdom of the Franks: North-West Europe before Charlemagne*. London: Thames and Hudson, 1971.

Wallace-Hadrill, J. M. *The Long-Haired Kings*. Toronto: Toronto University Press, 1982.

Wemple, Suzanne. *Women in Frankish Society: Marriage and the Cloister, 500 to 900*. Philadelphia: University of Pennsylvania Press, 1985.

Wood, Ian. *The Merovingian Kingdoms, 450–751*. London: Longman, 1994.

Fritigern (fourth century)

Leader of the Gothic Tervingi (r. 376–380) and rival of Athanaric, Fritigern is best known as the commander of the Gothic armies that destroyed the Roman army led by the emperor Valens at the Battle of Hadrianople in 378. His opposition to Athanaric caused repeated problems for that Gothic judge, whose office, though royal, was of limited power, and led to a division of the Goths in 376. His victory over Valens was a serious, but not fatal, blow to the Roman Empire and caused important changes in the relationship between Rome and the barbarian peoples inside and outside the empire's boundaries.

During the struggles between the empire and Athanaric in the 360s and 370s, Fritigern emerged as a rival to Athanaric and an advocate of a pro-Roman policy. Fritigern, a figure of equal stature to Athanaric among the Goths, rose up against the Gothic ruler after a war with the Romans in the late 360s. Fritigern adopted a pro-Christian stance, and was perhaps supported by the famous missionary Ulfilas, during Athanaric's persecutions in the early 370s. Fritigern's support for the Christians may have been the result of a personal bond with the emperor Valens, who was an Arian Christian. The course of the rebellion remains unclear, it but was probably suppressed by the time of the arrival of the Huns in the mid-370s.

The Hunnish advance afforded Fritigern another opportunity to oppose the rule of Athanaric. The Gothic judge had some initial success against the invaders but was bested in battle by them. Athanaric also lost important territory to the Huns and had his supply lines cut off by them. The devastation caused by war with the Romans and Huns made things extremely difficult for the Goths. In the summer of 376, in response to the crisis brought on by the Huns, Fritigern proposed that the Goths turn to the Romans for help. He persuaded most of Athanaric's followers to abandon their leader and join Fritigern and enter into the empire. Athanaric's long struggle with the Romans made it difficult for him to seek the empire's support, and he withdrew to the Carpathian Mountains. But Fritigern successfully petitioned Valens for support and was allowed to settle in the empire as an ally (*foederatus*) in 376 with some 80,000 Goths.

Fritigern had successfully taken control of the Gothic Tervingi, and in the summer of 376 took the fateful step when he and his followers crossed the frontier into the empire.

Fritigern's welcome into the empire was less than enthusiastic, however, and almost immediately difficulties arose, difficulties that brought the Goths and Romans to war. These problems included the incompetence of local administrators to deal with the sudden influx of people and the great number of Goths involved. Although Rome had welcomed barbarian peoples into the empire as allies before, they had never brought so many in at one time. The Goths were expected to serve in the army, farm, and pay taxes, but the services necessary to accommodate them were lacking and for the next two years, Fritigern and his followers operated freely within imperial borders. In 378 Valens and the Western emperor Gratian sent an army of infantry and cavalry of between 30,000 and 40,000 troops to end the threat of Fritigern. Valens, however, seeking a victory without his imperial colleague, moved his troops forward against what he thought were 10,000 warriors, when instead there were roughly 30,000. Despite warnings from Gratian about Gothic battle tactics, despite Fritigern's efforts to reach a peaceful settlement, Valens marched his troops against the Goths near Adrianople in early August.

On August 9, Valens sent his troops forward without food or water in the boiling sun to meet the Goths, who had set fires along the Romans' path. Fritigern still sought to negotiate an agreement, but Roman soldiers, without orders, began a disorganized attack that proved fatal. The counterattack of the Gothic cavalry was rapid and forceful, and when other Goths returned from foraging, the assault on the Romans was made even more terrible. The Romans lost nearly two-thirds of their army at Hadrianople, and most of the casualties were from the infantry, the backbone of the Roman military. Among the dead were generals, unit officers, and the emperor Valens himself.

Fritigern had led his Goths to a smashing victory, but he was unable to exploit the situation and gradually disappeared from view. Although a tragedy for the empire, the Battle of Hadrianople was not the catastrophe it is often seen to be, and it had equally significant consequences for Fritigern. In the wake of the battle, the Gothic leader faced division within his own ranks, and he was unable to restrict the raids for plunder that followed the battle. The Romans, led now by Gratian and Theodosius the Great, took steps to limit the destruction the Goths could cause, steps that included the destruction of a force of Goths in the Roman army. Moreover, an important member of Athanaric's clan joined the Romans and led the opposition to Fritigern, even destroying a large raiding party allied to Fritigern. In response to these steps, the Goths increased Fritigern's royal powers, and he increased the pressure on the empire by extending his raids in Macedonia and northern Greece. He also engineered a plot against his former rival Athanaric that drove the Gothic leader into exile.

Despite these successes, Fritigern's cause was a lost one because of Roman military might and diplomatic skill. Although unable to stop Fritigern, the Romans could at least keep him in check militarily. Athanaric's welcome in Constantinople, together with the lavish funeral he was given there, was a means for the empire to display its compassionate side and identify itself as a friend to all Goths. By 382, when a treaty between Rome and the Goths was signed, Fritigern seems to have disappeared; no mention was made of him in the treaty. On the other hand, Fritigern's original goal for the Goths was achieved, since the Goths became imperial subjects by the terms of the treaty.

See also Athanaric; Hadrianople, Battle of; Huns; Theodosius; Ulfilas; Visigoths

Bibliography

Ammianus Marcellinus. *Ammianus Marcellinus.* Trans. John C. Rolfe. Cambridge, MA: Harvard University Press, 1971–1972.

Bury, John B. *The Invasion of Europe by the Barbarians.* New York: W. W. Norton, 1967.

Heather, Peter. *The Goths.* Oxford: Blackwell, 1996.

Wolfram, Herwig. *History of the Goths.* Trans. Thomas J. Dunlap. Berkeley: University of California Press, 1988.

———. *The Roman Empire and Its Germanic Peoples.* Trans. Thomas J. Dunlap. Berkeley: University of California Press, 1997.

G

Gaiseric (c. 390–477)

King of the Alans and Vandals from 428 to 477, Gaiseric was one of the more ambitious and cunning of the Germanic peoples who came into contact, or rivalry, with the Roman Empire. Indeed, Gaiseric, an Arian Christian, seemed less impressed with the empire and its traditions than did many of his contemporaries. He was ruthless in his dealings with imperial officials and exploited every opportunity he was offered. After signing a treaty with the empire, Gaiseric proceeded to violate it and took control of all of North Africa. His fleet controlled much of the western Mediterranean, which allowed him to accomplish his most famous, or infamous, feat—the capture and sacking of Rome in 455.

Writing in the sixth century, Jordanes provides a useful description of Gaiseric's physical appearance and personality: "Of medium height, lame from a fall off his horse, he had a deep mind and was sparing of speech"(Bury 1967, 246). Jordanes also notes that Gaiseric hated luxury, was covetous, and had an uncontrollable temper. Rounding out his description of Gaiseric, Jordanes notes, "He was far-sighted in inducing foreign peoples to act in his interests, and resourceful in sowing seeds of discord and stirring up hatred"(246–247). His many talents overshadowed his irregular birth—his mother was a slave, possibly of Roman descent—and enabled him to achieve great success in war. Indeed, he was a most formidable opponent, at least the rival of Attila, if not more dangerous than the king of the Huns. At the very least, Gaiseric carved a more lasting kingdom out of the Roman Empire than did Attila.

Gaiseric's rise to power in the Mediterranean was aided by the turmoil within the government of the Roman Empire. In the 420s the Roman general and military governor in Africa, Boniface, clearly sought to establish himself as ruler of the empire, or at least an independent ruler in Africa. He successfully defeated armies led by Roman commanders sent to bring him to heel. But an army sent under the leadership of the new count of Africa, the Goth Sigisvult, was almost more than Boniface could handle, and the Goth managed to seize the important cities of Hippo and Carthage. In order to secure his position against Sigisvult, Boniface may have sought an ally in the Vandal leader Gaiseric, and perhaps asked for aid against Sigisvult in exchange for a share of Africa, an exchange that the Vandal accepted. But the chronology of events and the cause of Gaiseric's migration to Africa remain unclear. There is another tradition that authorities in Constantinople invited Gaiseric to Africa to conquer Boniface. There is also a third version of events that holds that Gaiseric recognized an opportunity when he saw it and moved all the Vandals and Alans under his control, traditionally some 80,000, from their base in Spain to Africa in 429. Whatever the case, Gaiseric's subjects are traditionally held to have included roughly 15,000 warriors, whose swords Boniface or the imperial authorities hoped to use to their advantage but which were used instead against Boniface and Roman authority.

Although the numbers may be exaggerated, Gaiseric led a large enough population from Spain, where his people had been harassed by their traditional enemies the Visigoths as well as the Romans. He moved slowly across Africa and managed gradually, in the course of the 430s, to secure his position there. His first engagement was the siege of Hippo, in May or June of that year. St. Augustine, fearing for his city and near the end of his own life, may have called on Boniface to protect Hippo from the Vandals. But the Roman commander, now in the good graces of the empress Galla Placidia, had little success against Gaiseric, who laid siege to the city for fourteen months. Boniface received reinforcements from Constantinople, but they were of little help against Gaiseric, who maintained the siege and defeated imperial armies in engagements outside the city. Although he was forced to call off the siege before the city fell, Gaiseric demonstrated his abilities against Roman armies. Moreover, when Boniface was recalled to Italy, Gaiseric was left alone in Africa. In 435 he settled a treaty with the empire that granted Gaiseric and his Vandals much of North Africa and recognized them as *foederati* (federated allies). Four years later, in the face of continued turmoil, Gaiseric broke the treaty and marched against Carthage, which he took with little resistance.

Gaiseric retained control of his new kingdom until his death in 477 and expanded his authority into parts of the western Mediterranean. His conquests were recognized by a new treaty in 442, which was reinforced by the betrothal of his son Huneric to Emperor Valentinian III's daughter Eudocia. This gain was followed by Gaiseric's efforts to seize control of other parts of the rapidly deteriorated Western Empire and make a statement asserting his place in the western Mediterranean. He may have conspired with Attila and encouraged the Hun to invade Gaul to punish the Visigoths. In 455, Gaiseric invaded Italy and plundered the city of Rome. Although the pope, Leo the Great, sought to stop the attack on Rome, as he had two years earlier in negotiations with Attila, he managed only to extract the concessions that the Vandals would neither burn the city nor indulge in a massacre. Instead for two weeks Gaiseric and his followers plundered the city, taking thousands of prisoners and much treasure, including statues, gold, precious gems, and important ecclesiastical artifacts.

Gaiseric's assault on the former imperial capital was devastating; it was probably intended as a message that he was the most powerful ruler in the boundaries of the old Western Empire and that had to be taken into account. His conquests in the western Mediterranean included the Balearic Islands, Corsica, Sardinia, and Sicily. He faced repeated attempts to defeat him, including a massive naval attack of more than 1,000 ships that was launched by Emperor Leo I (457–474) in cooperation with the Western emperor in 468. The attack was a disaster for the empire. Gaiseric remained in control, and a peace treaty was finally settled between the Vandal king and the empire in 474. Indeed, over the course of his long reign, Gaiseric managed to create a powerful and impressive successor kingdom in part of the old Western Empire. His military skill and personal drive enabled him to create the most important new political unit in the western Mediterranean, one that lasted several generations before falling to the conquests of Justinian.

See also Alans; Augustine of Hippo, St.; Attila the Hun; Galla Placidia; Huns; Jordanes; Justinian; Vandals; Visigoths

Bibliography

Victor of Vita. *Victor of Vita: History of the Vandal Persecution.* Trans. John Moorhead. Liverpool, UK: Liverpool University Press, 1992.

Bury, John B. *The Invasion of Europe by the Barbarians.* New York: W. W. Norton, 1967.

Cameron, Averil. *The Mediterranean World in Late Antiquity,* A.D. *395–600.* New York: Routledge, 1993.

Clover, Frank M. *The Late Roman West and the Vandals.* London: Variorum, 1993.

Randers-Pehrson, Justine Davis. *Barbarians and Romans: The Birth Struggle of Europe,* A.D. *400–700.* Norman: University of Oklahoma Press, 1983.

Wolfram, Herwig. *The Roman Empire and Its Germanic Peoples.* Trans. Thomas J. Dunlap. Berkeley: University of California Press, 1997.

Galla Placidia (c. 388–450)

Daughter, sister, and mother of emperors, Galla Placidia played an important role in Roman politics in the first half of the fifth century. The daughter of Emperor Theodosius the Great and sister of Honorius, Galla Placidia is perhaps best known for her marriage to the Visigothic king Ataulf, the brother-in-law and successor of Alaric. Although the marriage was short-lived because of Ataulf's death, it offered the possibility of greater union between Ataulf and the empire. Galla Placidia returned to the empire after her husband's death, where she continued to play a role in political life and eventually assumed the regency for her son Valentinian III (425–455).

Galla Placidia was an important figure in the complicated relations between the Romans and Visigoths in the late fourth and fifth centuries. Held at bay by her father, Theodosius, and her brother Honorius's general Stilicho, the Visigoths exploited the emperor's weakness after his murder of Stilicho. In 410, the Visigothic king Alaric sacked the city of Rome, and Ataulf, according to contemporary accounts, captured Galla Placidia himself and took her as a hostage once the Visigoths withdrew from Rome. She remained with Ataulf as his people moved into southern Gaul after the death of Alaric and succession to the throne by Ataulf. The capture of Galla Placidia enraged Honorius and made the establishment of good relations between the two difficult. Even though Ataulf turned over to Honorius a pretender to the throne, Honorius refused to sign a treaty until Galla Placidia was returned. Ataulf, in response, laid waste to imperial territory in southern Gaul.

In 414, a significant step was taken by Ataulf and Galla Placidia that had the potential to change the relationship between the Romans and the Visigoths. In January of that year, in an elaborate ceremony, Ataulf and Galla Placidia were married. The wedding was conducted in the Roman fashion, and Ataulf dressed in the uniform of a Roman general. His wedding gifts to his bride included many of the spoils of the sack of Rome, such as fifty Roman youths dressed in silk each carrying gold and precious gems. According to a contemporary account, Ataulf is supposed to have declared a change of heart in regard to the empire. Rather than seeking to replace Romania with Gothia as he originally intended, Ataulf declared that the "unbridled license" of the Goths would not allow this and therefore he aspired "to the glory of restoring and increasing the Roman name with Gothic vigor" (Bury 1959, 197). This sudden change of attitude was most likely the result of the influence of Galla Placidia, who bore a son in 415, whom they named Theodosius, in honor of his maternal grandfather. The name was a declaration of the legitimacy of the child and staked his claim to inherit the imperial throne. Unfortunately, Theodosius died shortly after birth, and Ataulf was murdered in 416.

Galla Placidia continued to play an important role in Gothic and Roman affairs after the death of her first husband. Ataulf hoped to remain on good terms with the Romans and recommended to his brother that should anything happen to him, Galla Placidia be returned to the empire. Although the succession

to the throne after the death of Ataulf was tumultuous, Galla Placidia was returned to the imperial court on January 1, 417, even though Ataulf's eventual successor, Vallia, was hostile to Rome. On her return, and most likely much to her dismay, Galla Placidia was married to the military commander, Constantius, who was raised to the status of co-emperor by Honorius in 421. But the Eastern emperor refused to recognize the new emperor and empress in the west, and Constantius died that same year. Galla Placidia had two children by Constantius, including the future emperor Valentinian III. Her relations with Honorius, however, became strained after her second husband's death, and power struggles ensued between them. She retained the loyalty of her Gothic guard and used them against her brother. She was then banished to Constantinople in 425, where she and her son were welcomed by Emperor Theodosius II (408–450) who had two years earlier spurned her.

On the death of Honorius, Galla Placidia and her son returned to the Western Empire, where she ruled as regent for her young son. She faced numerous challenges during her years as regent, as well as the years following her son's majority, when she continued to exercise influence at court. She was troubled by both imperial politics, especially the rivalry with the powerful general Aëtius, and barbarian peoples, including the Vandals. In the early years of the regency of Valentinian, Galla Placidia's authority was unchallenged. But the successes that Aëtius enjoyed against the various barbarian peoples challenging the Western Empire allowed him to force Galla Placidia to make him her chief military commander in 429. When her son reached his majority, Aëtius's influence increased, even though Galla Placidia managed to replace him with a commander of her choice for a time. The empress's other great challenge came from Gaiseric and the Vandals. During her regency, Gaiseric took advantage of political unrest in Africa and moved there from Spain with his entire tribe of Vandals. Gaiseric managed to take control of much of imperial Africa, but did come to terms with Galla Placidia and signed a treaty in 435. Her last years were spent influencing affairs from behind the scenes and building churches and other public buildings in the imperial capital of Ravenna, Italy.

See also Aëtius; Alaric; Gaiseric; Honorius; Stilicho, Flavius; Vandals; Visigoths

Bibliography
Bury, John B. *History of the Later Roman Empire: From the Death of Theodosius I to the Death of Justinian.* 2 vols. 1923. Reprint, New York: Dover, 1959..
Hollum, Kenneth G. *Theodosian Empresses: Women and Imperial Dominion in Late Antiquity.* Berkeley: University of California Press, 1989.
Wolfram, Herwig. *History of the Goths.* Trans. Thomas J. Dunlap. Berkeley: University of California Press, 1988.
———. *The Roman Empire and Its Germanic Peoples.* Trans. Thomas J. Dunlap. Berkeley: University of California Press, 1997.

Galswintha (d. 567)

Spanish Visigothic princess, whose marriage with and subsequent murder by the Merovingian king, Chilperic I, may have caused a terrible blood feud between Galswintha's sister Brunhilde and Chilperic's new wife, Fredegund.

The daughter of King Athanagild (r. 550–568), Galswintha was sought after in marriage by Chilperic after his brother King Sigebert had married Brunhilde. Sigebert had broken recent Merovingian tradition by seeking marriage with a princess rather than a lowborn woman. His marriage to Brunhilde brought a woman of high status and also a sizeable dowry. Although already married to several women, according to Gregory of Tours, Chilperic sought marriage with Galswintha and promised the king that he would dismiss all his other wives if he were granted his request. Athanagild did so and sent Galswintha with a substantial dowry, just as he had with Brunhilde. Chilperic welcomed and honored his new wife greatly after her arrival at court. Gregory notes that Chilperic loved Galswintha dearly because "she had brought a large dowry with her"(222). To honor her new husband, Galswintha converted from the Arian Christianity practiced in her father's kingdom to the Catholic Christianity of the Merovingians.

Unfortunately the marriage was not to last; Chilperic still loved Fredegund, either a mistress or wife before Galswintha's arrival. He once again began to favor Fredegund, and Galswintha complained bitterly. She claimed that Chilperic showed her no respect and repeatedly asked to be allowed to return home, even if it meant leaving the dowry behind. Chilperic sought to placate her and denied his relationship with Fredegund. In the end, however, Chilperic had one of his servants murder Galswintha so that he could return to Fredegund. He kept the dowry after the murder and faced the rage of Sigebert and the other Merovingian kings.

The murder of Galswintha had serious repercussions for Chilperic and the Merovingian kingdom; civil war broke out shortly after the murder. It is possible that Sigebert was motivated by his wife's grief and anger to attack Chilperic. The bitter struggles between Brunhilde and Fredegund over the next several decades may also have been rooted in the murder of Galswintha. According to Gregory of Tours, God rendered judgment over Galswintha some time after her death by performing a miracle at her tomb. Whatever the exact consequences of the murder of Galswintha were, her life at the Merovingian court demonstrates the flexible nature of marriage among the Merovingians and the uncertain condition of women, no matter what their social rank.

See also Arianism; Brunhilde; Chilperic I; Chlotar II; Fredegund; Gregory of Tours; Marriage; Merovingian Dynasty; Visigoths

Bibliography
Gregory of Tours, *The History of the Franks.* Trans. Lewis Thorpe. Harmondsworth, UK: Penguin, 1974.
James, Edward. *The Franks.* Oxford: Blackwell, 1988.
Wallace-Hadrill, J. M. *The Long-Haired Kings.* Toronto: Toronto University Press, 1982.
Wemple, Suzanne. *Women in Frankish Society: Marriage and the Cloister, 500 to 900.* Philadelphia: University of Pennsylvania Press, 1985.
Wood, Ian. *The Merovingian Kingdoms, 450–751.* London: Longman, 1994

Geats
See Beowulf

Germanic Religion
A collection of beliefs, practices, and heroic tales about the gods, humankind, and nature, Germanic religion was at the core of barbarian culture prior to the conversion of the barbarians to Christianity. Current knowledge of Germanic religion is based on versions of these myths set down in writing long after their original creation; the myths are best preserved in Scandinavian literature because the barbarian peoples of northern Europe were the last to convert to Christianity. Information about Germanic religion is also found in the works of ancient Roman and medieval authors, most notably Julius Caesar, Tacitus, Jordanes, and the Venerable Bede. Evidence from ancient burial sites and other archeological artifacts also provides information concerning early Germanic religious beliefs. The myths and legends of Germanic religion often tell tales of heroic virtues, describe many different gods and their personalities, and outline the ultimate end of the universe. Although the various Germanic peoples that entered the Roman Empire and its successor kingdoms ultimately converted to one form of Christianity or another, it is likely that their understanding of their new faith was much shaped by their traditional beliefs.

According to the classical Roman writer Tacitus, the ancient Germans worshipped many gods who were similar to the gods of ancient Rome. Tacitus notes that the Germans worship Mercury "above all other gods," whom they honor with human sacrifices, probably captured prisoners of war, on high feast days. They also worshipped Hercules and Mars and sacrificed animals to them. These sacrifices to the gods took place, according to Tacitus and later literature, in sacred groves of trees or in wooden temples. Although influenced by his own society's beliefs and practices, Tacitus probably revealed the actual beliefs of the ancient Germans. Archeological evidence supports the widespread veneration of a fire god, and it is likely that Tacitus gave Roman names to deities honored by the early barbarians. His Mercury was probably the god Woden (or Odin) who was the chief of the gods, and Mars and Hercules probably represented the gods Tiwaz, a war god, and Thor, a god of thunder and champion of the gods.

The pantheon of the gods of Germanic religion, however, is much larger than the three main deities mentioned by Tacitus. Indeed, Tacitus himself in another section of his *Germania* describes Nerthus, the earth mother who rides a chariot among the people. She is worshipped in a sacred grove and, as Tacitus reports, is secretly bathed in a lake by slaves after a procession; the slaves are then drowned in the same lake. Tacitus also mentions the Alci, who are compared with the Roman equine gods Castor and Pollux, and Manus, who is the ancestor of all the Germanic peoples. Among other important deities is Balder, or Baldr, who is the subject of one of the great and moving tales of the gods. A son of the chief of the gods, Balder dreamt of his death; his mother tried to protect him by extracting an oath not to harm him from all creatures except the mistletoe. Balder's brother, Hoder, was persuaded to throw a mistletoe dart at his brother, which kills him. Hoder was led to do this by another important god, Loki, a trickster who could change shape and sex at will and who could both deceive the other gods and protect them from trouble. He is sometimes seen as the dark side of the chief of the gods.

Among the lesser gods, there is Heimdall, a rival of Loki; Ullr, an archer deity; and Bragi, a god of poetry and eloquence who has magic runes carved on his tongue. A number of female deities, such as Frigg, the mother of Balder who extracts the oath to protect her son, also appear in various tales, but they receive very little attention. The Vanir is another group of lesser gods, associated with fertility, health, and wealth. Finally, there are various spirits who appear in dreams or are thought to be ancestors who are protecting the family.

Among the many myths of Germanic religion are those that address the ultimate end of individual people as well as the origin and end of the universe. There are various conceptions of the afterlife in Germanic religion. It appears that some believed that life continued after death and was inseparable from the body. The dead lingered for a time, walking among the living and sometimes persecuting them, and sometimes needed to be killed again. There is also evidence from various Norse sagas and archeological finds that suggests the existence of a world of the dead. The practice of ship burials in which the body is placed in a boat, set out to sea, and burned suggests the belief in a world of the dead on the other side of the sea. Other burial sites that include weapons, horses, ships, and other tools of everyday life may indicate the belief in the necessity of these things in the afterlife. Some burial sites seem to be pointing north, which may have been the location of the world of the dead in Germanic beliefs. There was also the belief in an underworld, the hall of Hel, which is the name of both the place and its ruler. It is not a place of punishment but a place where all the dead go, which is surrounded by a great fence to keep out the living. In some texts, the lowest level of Hel is a dark and foreboding place reserved for the wicked. Another place for the dead is Val-

Wotan (seventh-century stele) (Bettmann/Corbis)

halla, which is the heavenly place for heroic warriors killed in battle. The warriors will live in this heavenly hall of 540 rooms until the end of time, feasting at great banquets, going into battle daily, and being restored to health by the next day.

Germanic religion also contains myths of the creation and destruction of the world. As written down in the thirteenth century, the creation myth was built upon a number of older traditions and is at times contradictory. In the beginning, according to Germanic belief, there was a great void filled with magic forces. Before the emergence of the earth, a number of cosmic rivers and separate worlds emerged, and from one of the rivers the primeval giant, Ymir, was created. He gave rise to a race of terrible giants by sweating them out from under his arms and legs. Ymir was nourished by the milk of a great cosmic cow, who also gave shape to another primeval being, Borr, the ancestor of the gods. Three of Borr's sons, Odin and his brothers, rose up and killed Ymir and created the earth out of his body. His flesh made up the earth, his blood formed the waters of the earth, his hair the trees, his bones the mountains, and his skull, supported by dwarves, was the sky. In the middle of the earth the gods created a land for the first humans, who were created by the gods from two dead tree trunks, and their descendants.

Germanic religion also had a myth concerning the end of the world that is contained in several epic tales from the Middle Ages. Ragnarok, which literally means "fate of the gods," though it is often translated "Twilight of the Gods," is the time of final destruction of the gods and of the world and everything in it. Although the primary account of the Ragnarök was written as the Germanic world was converting to Christianity and was clearly influenced by Christian eschatology, it does reveal important traditional Germanic attitudes toward the fate of the world. In this tale, the movement toward the end begins with the murder of Balder through the machinations of Loki. Although Loki is punished, his acts set in motion the chain of events that will bring about the final cataclysmic struggle. The great wolf, Fenris, breaks his fetters and leads forth the wolves who will devour the sun and moon. Loki too breaks loose and leads the giants and other evil forces against the gods, and a great battle ensues in which all the gods are killed. The sun will then burn out and the stars will sink into the sea as all of existence comes to an end. A new world, however, will rise from the ashes of the old world, new gods and humans will inhabit the world, and Balder and his brother Hoðr will rise again.

Germanic religion gradually faded away, to be preserved only in the later sagas, especially those of Scandinavia of the twelfth and thirteenth centuries. As a result of the efforts of Christian missionaries from the Roman Empire, the Anglo-Saxon missionary St. Boniface, the great Frankish emperor Charlemagne, and other rulers and missionaries, the barbarian peoples converted to Christianity during the early Middle Ages. The Ostrogoths and Visigoths converted in the fourth century, the Franks in the fifth, the Anglo-Saxons in the late sixth, and other peoples in the ninth and tenth. The last of the Germanic peoples to convert were those of Scandinavia and Iceland, those areas where most of the legends were preserved best.

See also Anglo-Saxons; Bede; Beowulf; Boniface, St.; Charlemagne; Franks; Ostrogoths; Visigoths

Bibliography

Bede. *Ecclesiastical History of the English People with Bede's Letter to Egbert and Cuthbert's Letter on the Death of Bede.* Trans. Leo Sherley-Price. Harmondsworth, UK: Penguin, 1991.

Dumézil, Georges. *Gods of the Ancient Northmen,* trans. Einer Haugen. Berkeley: University of California Press, 1973.

Grimm, Jakob. *Teutonic Mythology,* 4 vols. Trans. James Stevens Stallybrass. London: Routledge, 1999.

Heaney, Seamus, trans. *Beowulf: A New Verse Translation.* New York: Farrar Straus and Giroux, 2000.

Jordanes. *The Gothic History of Jordanes in English Version.* Trans. Charles C. Mierow. New York: Barnes and Noble, 1985.

Jolly, Karen Louise, *Popular Religion in Late Saxon England: Elf Charms in Context.* Chapel Hill: University of North Carolina Press, 1996.

Polomé, Edgar C. *Essays on Germanic Religion.* Washington, DC: Institute for the Study of Man, 1989.

Russell, James C. *The Germanization of Early Medieval Christianity: A Sociohistorical Approach to Religious Transformation.* Oxford: Oxford University Press, 1994.

Tacitus. *The Agricola and the Germania.* Trans. H.

Mattingly. Revised trans. S. A. Hanford. Harmondsworth, UK: Penguin, 1982.

Turville-Petre, Edward O. G. *Myth and Religion of the North: The Religion of Ancient Scandinavia.* London: Weidenfeld and Nicholson, 1964.

Gildas (c. 500–570)

A monk and Briton whose history of the Anglo-Saxon invasions of England is the only substantial contemporary account of the fall of late Roman Britain to the invading barbarians. His history is also the earliest source for the deeds that became the basis of the later Arthurian tales, even though Gildas never mentions a King Arthur in his work. Although it does not seem to have been frequently copied in the Middle Ages, his work is important also because it is one of the two sources the great Anglo-Saxon historian Bede used for his ecclesiastical history, and thanks to Bede the name of Gildas was remembered with honor by other historians in the Middle Ages.

Born around the year 500, the time of the great victory by the British over the invaders at Badon Hill, Gildas wrote his history in the middle of the sixth century, possibly in 547. Gildas's history of the conquest of England is not systematically organized, and includes a collection of quotations of scriptural citations and historical information. It is a bitter tale full of recrimination and reproach. The essential them of the work by Gildas, one borrowed by Bede in his discussion of the invasion and conquest of England, is that the coming of the Anglo-Saxons was the just punishment by God of people who claimed to be Christian but who indulged in wanton excess and luxury. The conquest of England, for Gildas, began with invasions of barbarians, probably Picts and Scots, and an appeal to the Roman general, Aëtius, for aid, which was not forthcoming. The Britons were able to expel the barbarians but then fell into civil war and further raids. A British ruler, traditionally Vortigern, invited Saxon war bands to aid against other barbarians, and those war bands were subsequently joined by other Saxons against the Britons. The invasions of the Saxons, according to Gildas, laid waste the towns of Briton and destroyed the way of life that had existed.

Gildas's account is not, however, without its heroes, and it is one of these who may have provided the first outlines for the figure of Arthur. Gildas fails to mention Arthur directly, but he only names kings directly who fit into his broader theme that the invasions are divine punishment for the Britons' failure to live as good Christians. Moreover, he does mention one leader on whom the legendary figure of Arthur may be based and a battle that is often listed among those of the legendary king. In 500, the year of Gildas's birth as he tells us, the Britons won a great victory over invading barbarian armies at Mount Badon, a victory that provided England a period of much needed peace that continued at least until the time that Gildas wrote his history. The victor at that battle was the Roman commander Ambrosius Aurelianus, who had reorganized the defense of the Britons, and whose victory was later associated with the deeds of King Arthur.

See also Aëtius; Anglo-Saxons; Bede; King Arthur; Vortigern

Bibliography

Barber, Richard. *The Figure of Arthur.* Totowa, NJ: Rowman and Littlefield, 1972.

Bede. *Ecclesiastical History of the English People with Bede's Letter to Egbert and Cuthbert's Letter on the Death of Bede.* Trans. Leo Sherley-Price. Harmondsworth, UK: Penguin, 1991.

Blair, Peter Hunter. *The World of Bede.* Cambridge: Cambridge University Press, 1970.

Gildas. *The Ruin of Britain and Other Works.* Ed. and trans. Michael Winterbottom. London: Phillimore, 1978.

Stenton, Frank M. *Anglo-Saxon England.* 3d ed. Oxford: Clarendon, 1971.

Goor

See Alans

Goths

See Ostrogoths; Visigoths

Gottschalk of Orbais (c. 803–c. 867/869)

Controversial Carolingian monk and theologian. Gottschalk was a talented theologian whose works provided important interpretations of the teachings of St. Augustine of Hippo. He was involved in two major controversies in his life. The first concerned the practice of child oblation, that is, placing a young child in a monastery before the child is old enough to make its own decision. The second was over his teachings concerning predestination, which were based on the works of Augustine but contrary to the orthodox teachings of the time. The predestination controversy involved a number of leading ecclesiastics in the Carolingian Empire and revealed the increasing intellectual confidence and sophistication of these Carolingian thinkers.

Gottschalk was born in Saxony in 803 and given to the monastery of Fulda as a child by his father. He spent his childhood at monasteries in Fulda and Reichenau under the direction of the abbot and bishop Rabanus Maurus. As an adult, Gottschalk requested that he be released from his monastic vows because he had not taken them personally and because there were no Saxon witnesses to the vow. A church council at Mainz in 829 granted his request, even though it refused to allow him to have the donation made by his father. Rabanus Maurus, however, appealed the decision at a separate church council, and Gottschalk was not released from his monastic vows. He was allowed to join another monastery, and for the next ten years was at monasteries in Corbie and Orbais, where he studied the writings of St. Augustine of Hippo. He also was ordained a priest some-

time in the 830s, but without the approval of the bishop in the diocese.

In the 840s he made a pilgrimage to Rome, where he began to preach the views on predestination he had learned from his study of Augustine. He taught that God had foreseen and in fact predestined the salvation or damnation of all people since before the beginning of time, which meant further that Jesus died only for the saved and that the sacraments were valid only for the saved. These views clearly challenged the authority of the church of his day, and the bishops who defended the church's tradition responded harshly to these ideas. Indeed, when word of his teaching reached the Carolingian Empire, his old rival Rabanus Maurus compelled Gottschalk to defend his views at a church council in Mainz in 848. His teaching was condemned at the council, and he was handed over to Archbishop Hincmar of Rheims. At a second council in the following year, Gottschalk was condemned again and was ordered whipped and imprisoned at the monastery of Hautvillers. His writings were burned, his ordination was overturned, and gradually his right to correspond with others was revoked. Despite the severity of his punishment, Gottschalk refused to renounce his ideas and continued to write on the matter and other theological topics until his death. His ideas were condemned at church councils throughout the 850s and 860s, and a number of other Carolingian ecclesiastics wrote treatises against Gottschalk's views. Indeed, the controversy was so great that it attracted the attention of the Carolingian king Charles the Bald, who requested the opinion of a number of ecclesiastics, including John Scotus Erigena.

Gottschalk was also a talented poet, and his surviving poetry confirms our understanding of him as an intelligent and pious man. Although few in number, Gottschalk's poems also reveal the quality and variety of poetry produced during the Carolingian Renaissance. His poetry was especially innovative in its use of rhyme. He wrote a number of religious poems, including poems on the canonical hours and predestination as well as one that was a prayer to Christ. His religious poems demonstrate an awareness of human sinfulness, but also a hope for God's mercy and the mediation of God's Son. He also wrote poems of a more personal nature, including one expressing personal melancholy, and another poem to a friend filled with expressions of love for this friend and praise of God. His poetry, as well as his other writings, reveal the success of Charlemagne's efforts to convert and educate the pagan Saxons.

See also Augustine of Hippo, St.; Carolingian Dynasty; Carolingian Renaissance; Charlemagne; Charles the Bald; Hincmar of Rheims

Bibliography

Duckett, Eleanor Shipley. *Carolingian Portraits: A Study in the Ninth Century.* Ann Arbor: University of Michigan Press, 1962.

Laistner, Max L. W. *Thought and Letters in Western Europe, A.D. 500 to 900.* 2d ed. Ithaca, NY: Cornell University Press, 1976.

Marenbon, John. "Carolingian Thought." In *Carolingian Culture: Emulation and Innovation* Ed. Rosamond McKitterick. Cambridge: Cambridge University Press, 1994, pp.171–192.

Riché, Pierre. *The Carolingians: A Family Who Forged Europe.* Trans Michael Idomir Allen. Philadelphia: University of Pennsylvania Press, 1993.

Gregory the Great (c. 540–604)

One of the greatest and most influential of the popes of the early Middle Ages, Gregory, pope from 590 to 604, is also recognized as one of the fathers of the church. Although not the powerful theologian that St. Augustine of Hippo was, Gregory made important contributions to the religious life of the early Middle Ages with his *Dialogues,* which includes a life of St. Benedict of Nursia; his *Pastoral Rule,* guidelines for the proper rule of bishops; and his sermons, many of which took the form of commentaries on books of Scripture. As

pope, he corresponded with the kings and queens of the Merovingian Franks; negotiated the difficult relationships between the papacy, the Lombard kings of Italy, and the Byzantine emperor in Constantinople; and reformed papal administration to make it a more effective power in central Italy. He is perhaps best known for the evangelical mission he sent to convert the Anglo-Saxons in England, which also signaled the importance of the barbarian kingdoms to the papacy.

Although little is known of his early life, Gregory was born sometime around 540 to good Christians of the senatorial class, and was the grandson of Pope Felix III. He most likely received a good education, although he knew no Greek and seems to have been little influenced by the classical literature he no doubt read. His learning and family background prepared him for a life of civil service, and in 572 or 573 he was appointed prefect of the city of Rome by the Senate. He held the post until about 574, when he experienced a religious conversion and retired to a monastery he founded on family property and dedicated to St. Andrew. His stay at the monastery was short because the pope, Pelagius II (579–590), called him out of retirement to papal service. He served as the papal representative in Constantinople until 585 or 586, when he returned to act as abbot of his monastery and secretary to the pope. On the death of Pelagius in 590, Gregory was acclaimed pope by the people of Rome, who acted without the consent of the Senate or emperor. He was chosen in large measure because of his administrative skills, which were needed to address the problems brought by excessive rain, flooding, and plague.

Gregory's fourteen-year pontificate, 590–614, was important for a number of reasons, including his administrative reforms and pastoral activities, which laid the foundation for traditions of the medieval papacy. He asserted the role of the papacy as the main power in Italy and in that role negotiated with Byzantines, Franks, and Lombards. He assumed the old imperial duty of charity and made numerous grants from his private wealth, making monthly donations of food to the poor, daily grants to the sick and infirm, and benefactions to monks and nuns. He assumed the responsibility of restoring public buildings such as aqueducts and churches, and took charge of the defense of the city by appointing military commanders and hiring soldiers. He reorganized papal lands to provide a more secure financial footing for the papacy.

Although an administrative genius, Gregory also established important pastoral practices that guided the papacy for generations to come. In his Pastoral Rule *(Regula pastoralis),* copies of which he sent to numerous bishops, Gregory offers guidelines for the bishop's office. He outlines the character traits needed to be a bishop, the spiritual obligations to a bishop's flock, the duties of teaching and preaching, and the responsibility to set a good personal example. Gregory himself lived by the rules he outlined, thus providing his own example for subsequent popes to follow. An active preacher, Gregory wrote numerous sermons and other works that promoted the cult of the saints, Catholic Christianity over paganism and Arian Christianity, and the monastic life, especially according to the Rule of St. Benedict of Nursia.

Active in church administration and religious life, Gregory faced numerous political challenges in his reign as pope, particularly as a result of the Lombard invasion of Italy in 568. In the generation before Gregory's ascension to the papal throne the Lombards had made great strides in the conquest of Italy and had undermined the ability of the emperor in Constantinople or his representative in Ravenna to defend the pope effectively. They also devastated the famous monastery of Benedict at Monte Cassino, thus demonstrating the weakness of the empire and the necessity for the pope finding alternate means of protection. The situation for Gregory worsened in 593 when the new Lombard king, Agilulf, came to power and resumed hostilities. He attempted to negotiate

a peace settlement with Agilulf, but was hampered by Constantinople's desire for war with the Lombard king. At one point, Gregory bought peace from Agilulf at the price of 500 pounds of gold and finally managed to secure peace in Italy, despite the Byzantines, in 598. Not only did Gregory work to secure peace with the Lombards, but he also sought to convert them from Arian to Catholic Christianity. He was a frequent correspondent of Theudelinda, the wife of Agilulf, who was a Catholic and was encouraged to convince her husband to convert. At the very least, Gregory's correspondence with Theudelinda brought the return of papal territories and numerous churches from Agilulf, even though the Lombards converted to Catholic Christianity only at the end of the seventh century.

Gregory also regularly corresponded with the Merovingian kings and queens during his reign, and his most important correspondent was the powerful queen Brunhilde. He wrote her because of his concern with improprieties in the Frankish church, particularly the practice of simony (the buying or selling of church offices). In order to obtain reform in the church, Gregory made concessions to Brunhilde; most importantly, he granted her request that the see of Vienne be elevated to the status of metropolitan bishopric. Little progress was made in the reform of the Frankish church, but an important relationship was established that foreshadowed the relationship of the Franks and the popes in the eighth century. Gregory's correspondence with Brunhilde had one significant result, however. According to Gregory, Brunhilde, whom the pope asked to support the missionary Augustine of Canterbury, was more responsible for the success of the mission to England than anyone but God.

Perhaps more than anything, Gregory is best known for that mission to convert the Anglo-Saxons of England in 596. According to the English historian Bede, Gregory had the idea of converting the English even before he became pope. One day while shopping in the market place Gregory saw a group of handsome boys for sale as slaves. He asked where they came from and was told from Britain. He inquired further if they were Christian and of what race they were. He was told that they were not and that they were Angles. He declared that it was appropriate that they were Angles because they had "angelic faces"(100) and that they must be rescued from the error of paganism. Gregory asked the pope to send him as a missionary to convert the English, but he was forbidden to go because he was needed in Rome.

Once he became pope, however, Gregory revived the idea of an evangelical mission to England, and sent St. Augustine and a number of missionaries to undertake the conversion of the English. To ensure the success of the mission, Gregory wrote to Brunhilde for support of the missionaries on their journey and to the English king Aelle to allow the establishment of the mission in England. Gregory continued to write to the English king, encouraging him to accept the faith, and also to Augustine, encouraging him in his mission. In the generation after Augustine the English converts fell back into paganism, but the mission to England did ultimately succeed, and an important relationship was established between England and Rome, one that had important consequences when Anglo-Saxon missionaries returned to preach on the continent.

Gregory's reign was important in the history of the papacy and in the history of early medieval Europe. His administrative reforms and pastoral regulations improved the standing of the papacy in Italy and set the standard for religious life and practice for popes and bishops. His correspondence with barbarian kings and queens left a great legacy and marked the beginnings of a shift in papal policy from east to west. Although Gregory remained a loyal subject of the emperor in Constantinople, he recognized the importance of the barbarian rulers of the west, and his contacts with them led to increasingly close ties between Rome and western rulers over the next century and a half, culminating in the formal alliance of the Franks and popes in the eighth century.

See also Anglo-Saxons; Augustine of Canterbury, St.; Augustine of Hippo, St.; Bede; Brunhilde; Lombards; Merovingian Dynasty

Bibliography
Bede. *Ecclesiastical History of the English People with Bede's Letter to Egbert and Cuthbert's Letter on the Death of Bede.* Trans. Leo Sherley-Price. Harmondsworth, UK: Penguin, 1991.

Colgrave, Bertram, ed. and trans. *The Earliest Life of Gregory the Great, by an Anonymous Monk of Whitby.* Lawrence: University of Kansas Press, 1968.

Evans, Gillian R. *The Thought of Gregory the Great.* Cambridge: Cambridge University Press, 1988.

Gregory the Great. *Saint Gregory the Great: Dialogues.* Trans. Odo John Zimmerman. New York: Fathers of the Church, 1959.

Herrin, Judith. *The Formation of Christendom.* Princeton: Princeton University Press, 1989.

Llewellyn, Peter. *Rome in the Dark Ages.* New York: Barnes and Noble, 1996.

Markus, Robert A. *Gregory the Great and His World.* Cambridge: Cambridge University Press, 1998.

Meyvaert, Paul. *Benedict, Gregory, Bede and Others.* London: Variorum Reprints, 1977.

Paul the Deacon. *History of the Lombards.* Trans. William Dudley Foulke. Philadelphia: University of Pennsylvania Press, 1974.

Richards, Jeffrey. *Consul of God: The Life and Times of Gregory the Great.* London: Routledge and Kegan Paul, 1980.

Straw, Carol. *Gregory the Great: Perfection in Imperfection.* Berkeley: University of California Press, 1991.

Gregory II, Pope (669–731)

One of two popes in the eighth century who were involved in a revolution in papal policy that led to the establishment of an alliance between the papacy and the Carolingian dynasty and the rupture of relations with the Byzantine Empire. Although it was his successor,

Pope Gregory III, who made formal overtures to the Carolingian mayor of the palace and effective ruler of the Franks Charles Martel and the later pope Stephen II who formalized the relationship, the conditions that required the diplomatic revolution were set in Gregory II's reign. His difficulties with both the Lombard king and the Byzantine emperor, as well as the papacy's growing connections with the Frankish kingdom, laid the foundation for a closer association in the coming generation.

Gregory's pontificate (715–731) revealed the growing tensions with the Byzantine Empire and growing connections with the barbarian kingdoms in a number of ways. One of the most important examples of the increasing ties with the west was Gregory's relationship to Boniface, an important Anglo-Saxon missionary with great influence among the Franks, who possessed the devotion to Rome shared by the English since their conversion to Christianity. Boniface's visits to Rome reinforced the Franks' interest in the papal city and brought Roman liturgical and administrative reforms to the Frankish church and newly converted areas of Saxony. In 719, Boniface visited Rome for the first time and swore allegiance to the pope before going to preach among the pagans of central Germany. Three years later in 722, Boniface returned to Rome to receive episcopal consecration from Gregory. He also swore an oath of allegiance to Gregory in preparation for his mission to convert the Saxons and reform the Frankish church. Gregory's own correspondence reveals that he saw the mission as an extension of the authority of the Roman church. Boniface's mission and dedication to Rome and Gregory's support of the mission was an important step in strengthening ties between Rome and the Frankish kingdom.

Gregory also faced serious challenges in Italy of the kind that ultimately led to a break between Rome and Constantinople. In 712 a new Lombard king, Liutprand, ascended the throne and renewed the Lombard effort to unify Italy. Although the Lombards had converted to Catholic Christianity at the end of the seventh century, they did not let spiritual concerns interfere with political ambitions and were thus still eager to take control of all of Italy, including territories controlled by the papacy. The papacy's traditional ally against the Lombards, the Byzantine Empire, was, however, powerless to assist Gregory in his struggles with Liutprand. Moreover, the emperor, Leo III, the Isaurian, had instituted a religious policy of iconoclasm (banning and eventual destruction of icons with images of Jesus, Mary, and the saints) without the approval of the pope. Leo further alienated the pope and people of Italy with his administrative reforms, which increased the burden of taxation on Italy.

Gregory was placed in an awkward position by the actions of the Lombard king and the Byzantine emperor. He attempted to restrain Liutprand and also remain loyal to Leo. In the 720s, for example, he negotiated successfully with Liutprand for the return of papal territory that had been seized by the Lombard king. Gregory also kept Liutprand from marching on Rome, and instead welcomed him into the city to pray at St. Peter's and make an offering of his cloak, sword, breastplate, and crown to the apostle Peter. The pope also sought to restrain the worst assaults on imperial rule by the people of Rome and refused to support a rival emperor. Gregory realized that his only support against the unreliable Liutprand was the emperor, but the pope's activities clearly established a new relationship between Rome and Constantinople. No longer was the pope a subject of the empire but an ally, and once the empire proved unable to help, later popes turned to a more reliable supporter in the kingdom of the Franks.

See also Boniface, St.; Carolingian Dynasty; Charles Martel; Gregory III; Leo III, the Isaurian; Liutprand; Lombards

Bibliography

Davis, Raymond, trans. *The Lives of the Eighth-Century Popes* (Liber Pontificalis): *The Ancient*

Biographies of Nine Popes from A.D. 715 to A.D. 817. Liverpool, UK: Liverpool University Press, 1992.

Herrin, Judith. *The Formation of Christendom.* Princeton: Princeton University Press, 1987.

Llewellyn, Peter. *Rome in the Dark Ages.* New York: Barnes and Noble, 1971.

Noble, Thomas F. X. *The Republic of St. Peter: The Birth of the Papal State, 680–825.* Philadelphia: University of Pennsylvania Press, 1984.

Paul the Deacon. *History of the Lombards.* Trans. William Dudley Foulke. Philadelphia: University of Pennsylvania Press, 1974.

Riché, Pierre. *The Carolingians: A Family Who Forged Europe.* Trans. Michael Idomir Allen. Philadelphia: University of Pennsylvania Press, 1993.

Gregory III, Pope (d. 741)

Mid-eighth-century pope (r. 731–741) who sought aid from the Carolingian mayor of the palace and effective ruler of the Franks, Charles Martel, in order to resolve the crisis brought on by the failure of Byzantine power in Italy and the continued encroachments on papal territory by the Lombards. Although Charles Martel was unable to aid the pope because of his long-standing friendship and political alliance with the Lombard king Liutprand, Gregory's diplomatic initiative marked a significant step in the history of the papacy and the Carolingian family. The pope's effort moved the papacy further into an alliance with the Frankish rulers of the west and further from the Byzantine emperor in Constantinople. It also laid the foundation for the alliance struck in the 750s between the popes and the Carolingian mayor of the palace and later king Pippin III the Short.

Gregory inherited a number of problems from his predecessor, Gregory II, including difficult relations with the Lombards and with the Byzantine emperor. In fact, the situation between Rome and Constantinople worsened in the opening year of Gregory III's reign as pope. In response to the emperor Leo III's policy of iconoclasm (the prohibition and eventual destruction of images of Jesus, Mary, and the saints) the new pope summoned a council in Rome to denounce the emperor's religious policy. The council asserted the growing independence of papal Rome from imperial Constantinople and was followed by Gregory's ambitious program of construction and renovation in Rome, a program that promoted the cult of images. Leo III's reaction is not altogether clear, but he did introduce a series of administrative reforms shortly after the council that may indicate his displeasure. He restructured taxation policy in Italy, reorganized the method of military recruitment, and withdrew a number of churches in Sicily from Roman jurisdiction.

Despite the increasing sense of alienation between Rome and Constantinople, Gregory continued to look to the emperor as his main source of protection against his enemies in Italy. The main rival of the popes was the Lombard king Liutprand, who had revived the traditional Lombard goal of unifying Italy. Liutprand, either because of illness or an agreement with Gregory II or probably both, had restrained his assault against Rome and papal territory in central Italy in the 730s. Unfortunately, several actions by Gregory III forced Liutprand back into action. During Liutprand's illness his nephew, Hildeprand, was made coregent, and Byzantine commanders in Italy struck against the Lombards. When Hildeprand counterattacked, the Byzantine commanders were supported by Gregory III. The pope also sought further support from Lombard powers in southern Italy, the dukes of Beneventum and Spoleto. This alliance and the attacks against the Lombards in the north roused Liutprand to action against the pope and his allies. Liutprand's offensive put the pope in very straitened circumstances. The Lombard king took several papal cities in central Italy and captured the duchies of Beneventum and Spoleto for a time. The pope was powerless to stop the king and was now without allies in southern Italy or in the Byzantine capital in Italy, Ravenna, which Liutprand had recaptured. And the emperor himself could not be relied on for help.

In the face of extreme crisis in 739–740, Gregory took the initiative and contacted Charles Martel. He in fact wrote to the Carolingian mayor of the palace twice during the years 739–740 seeking aid against the advances of Liutprand. It is likely that Gregory had little hope that anything positive would ensue from the correspondence, because the pope surely knew of the friendship that had existed between the two rulers since 725. If he was unaware of that personal tie, he could not have been unaware of Liutprand's military assistance to Charles in 739 against the Muslims. But that notwithstanding, the pope wrote to Charles. He was possibly persuaded to do so by the Anglo-Saxon missionary Boniface, who had received protection from the Carolingian mayor. Indeed, Charles's support for Boniface was highly regarded by Rome, and the activities of Boniface may have increased Rome's prestige among the Franks. Moreover, Gregory's second letter, in 740, was couched in language and combined with gifts—keys to the tomb of St. Peter, a link from St. Peter's chain—that were intended to gain the most favorable response possible from Charles Martel. The second letter and, especially, the gifts may have inspired Charles to aid the pope. Although there was no official reaction from Charles, who relied upon his alliance with Liutprand, it is possible that when he returned the ambassadors he sent his own ambassadors, who mediated between Gregory and Liutprand. Whatever the case, Liutprand made no attacks on Roman territory from 739–742, possibly as a result of a request by Charles Martel.

Although it is possible that Gregory's diplomatic initiative bore no immediate fruit, it was significant in itself. It marked a crucial step in the papacy's disengagement from its ancient alliance with the emperors in Constantinople and their representatives in Ravenna. It was also an important moment in the establishment of an independent papal power in central Italy and an important attempt to limit the Lombard advance. Gregory's effort also set the stage for the establishment of a formal alliance between the pope's successors and Charles Martel's son, Pippin III the Short in the 750s.

See also Boniface, St.; Carolingian Dynasty; Charles Martel; Gregory II, Pope; Leo III, the Isaurian; Liutprand; Lombards; Pippin III, Called Pippin the Short

Bibliography

Davis, Raymond, trans. *The Lives of the Eighth-Century Popes* (Liber Pontificalis): *The Ancient Biographies of Nine Popes from A.D. 715 to A.D. 817.* Liverpool, UK: Liverpool University Press, 1992.

Herrin, Judith. *The Formation of Christendom.* Princeton: Princeton University Press, 1987.

Llewellyn, Peter. *Rome in the Dark Ages.* New York: Barnes and Noble, 1971.

McKitterick, Rosamond. *The Frankish Kingdoms under the Carolingians, 751–987.* London: Longman, 1983.

Noble, Thomas F. X. *The Republic of St. Peter: The Birth of the Papal State, 680–825.* Philadelphia: University of Pennsylvania Press, 1984.

Paul the Deacon. *History of the Lombards.* Trans. William Dudley Foulke. Philadelphia: University of Pennsylvania Press, 1974.

Riché, Pierre. *The Carolingians: A Family Who Forged Europe.* Trans. Michael Idomir Allen. Philadelphia: University of Pennsylvania Press, 1993.

Gregory of Tours (c. 538–594)

Bishop of Tours from 573 until his death in 594, Gregory came from an illustrious Gallo-Roman family that included powerful political and religious figures. His father, Florentius, was a member of the senatorial class, and ancestors on both his paternal and maternal side were bishops of Clermont-Ferrand, Langres, and Tours. Gregory entered the priesthood at a young age, dedicated his life to the service of the church and the saints, and, despite weak connections with the town, became bishop of Tours in 573. Even though he had limited connections with

Tours, he was devoted to St. Martin, whose cult was centered in Tours. Gregory ruled as bishop for the last two decades of his life, during a time of great political strife between the grandsons and great-grandsons of the Merovingian king Clovis, including a violent feud between the queens Brunhilde and Fredegund and between their husbands. Although a successful bishop and staunch advocate of the cult of St. Martin of Tours, Gregory is best known as the author of the *Histories in Ten Books,* commonly known as *The History of the Franks.* The work contains a famous and influential portrait of Clovis, the founder of the Merovingian dynasty, and the tale of his descendants throughout the sixth century. This great work also includes extensive discussion of Gregory's time as bishop—seven of ten books of the *Histories* address this period—and reveals important information on the social, cultural, and, especially, religious life of the Frankish kingdoms in the sixth century. Gregory also wrote eight books on miracle stories, a life of the church fathers, lives of various saints and martyrs, *Commentary on the Psalms,* a preface for a collection of church masses, and a work on liturgical masses.

Gregory, originally Georgius Florentius, was born on November 30, 538, to Florentius, a Gallo-Roman senator, and his much younger wife, Armentaria, who also was of senatorial lineage, in the Auvergne in the town now called Clermont-Ferrand. Although quite expansive about the many dukes, senators, bishops, and saints in his ancestry, Gregory offers few details in his writings about his own life. It is likely that his father died while Gregory was still quite young, and certain that his education was taken over by his relatives, especially his maternal uncle Bishop Nicetius of Lyons and paternal uncle Bishop Gallus of Clermont-Ferrand. Like his uncles and many of the ancestors of whom he was so proud, Gregory was marked for the religious life. He became a priest in 543, entered a choir school in Lyons for further instruction, and became a

deacon in Lyons in 563. Moreover, his family connections introduced Gregory to many of the important saints of Gaul, including St. Julian of Brioude, whose relics once cured Gregory's brother Peter, and, most importantly, St. Martin of Tours, whose relics cured Nicetius of a terrible sore on his face. Devotion to the cult of the saints, especially St. Martin, remained an important aspect of Gregory's life.

Gregory himself benefited from saintly intervention. While on pilgrimage once, he was cured of a headache, and after his election as bishop of Tours in 573 the saints intervened to confirm his place as bishop. His election was controversial because the people of the town knew Gregory, who spent his time away from the region, only slightly. Shortly after arriving in Tours, Gregory placed the relics of St. Julian near those of St. Martin, an act that was followed by a brilliant flash of light. On the following day, he took the relics on procession, and a resident of the town declared that Martin had invited Julian to Tours, which was understood to mean that Martin wished Julian's spiritual son, Gregory, to be bishop. Although this event secured his place as bishop of Tours and the support of St. Martin, Gregory faced the challenge of surviving as a bishop despite the tumultuous politics of the Frankish kingdom.

Gregory faced numerous challenges as bishop from various Merovingian kings and queens, especially from Chilperic. Indeed, at the very outset of his tenure as bishop, Gregory tangled with Chilperic over rights of sanctuary and the marriage of the king's son, Merovech, to Brunhilde, the main rival to Chilperic and his wife Fredegund. At a council in Paris in 577, Gregory stood up to Chilperic and defended the fellow bishop who had performed the marriage ceremony for Merovech and Brunhilde. In 580, Chilperic nearly exiled him because of false allegations that Gregory intended to transfer authority to another Merovingian ruler. He also struggled with Chilperic over theological matters; he threatened the king with the wrath of God and the saints because Chilperic issued a charter denying the Catholic teaching that there were three persons in the Trinity. In the 580s, Gregory faced difficulties with Kings Guntram and Childebert. But his ability to weather these storms raised his prestige among the Merovingian kings and nobles as well as the people of his diocese. He became an important mediator between the various kings of the Franks, who indulged in civil war throughout much of Gregory's reign as bishop. At on point, he negotiated an important agreement between Childebert and Guntram. In 590 he received gifts from Fredegund, who was most likely hostile to Gregory because he assumed his position with the support of Brunhilde, and he was among those chosen to settle a dispute in the convent of St. Radegund, a member of the royal line, in Poitiers.

Although active in Merovingian politics and the religious life, Gregory wrote extensively; he is best known for his history, much of which is devoted to events in Gregory's own day. The work is divided into ten books; it begins as a chronicle of world history. The first book tells the story of Adam and Eve, and continues with the history of the ancient Jews, the birth of Christianity, and the introduction of Christianity into Gaul. The next two books cover the history of Christianity and the late Roman Empire in the third to the fifth centuries, and the rise of the Merovingian kingdom of the Franks and its greatest leader, Clovis. The third book takes the history of the kingdom into Gregory's time, and the remaining books are a detailed study of the kingdom in Gregory's lifetime.

Although somewhat episodic and chaotic, Gregory's history of his own time is a most valuable resource; it includes important portraits of the many kings and queens he knew and dealt with, including Chilperic, Fredegund, and Brunhilde. Drawing on the Bible and the works of Jerome, Eusebius, and other important Christian historians and writers, Gregory's work pays attention to the miraculous and is concerned with the moral and religious undertones of history. Its view of kingship is shaped by the teachings of the Hebrew Scriptures, and Gregory's famous portrait of Clovis as king reveals the notion that the king must do God's work. Along with his numerous writings on the saints and their miracles, Gregory's *Histories* provides important insights into the history of the late sixth century and, especially, the beliefs and practices of an influential, aristocratic bishop.

See also Brunhilde; Chilperic I; Clovis; Fredegund; Merovingian Dynasty; Martin of Tours, St.; Sigebert

Bibliography

Goffart, Walter. *The Narrators of Barbarian History (A.D. 550–800): Jordanes, Gregory of Tours, Bede, and Paul the Deacon.* Princeton: Princeton University Press, 1988.

Gregory of Tours. *The History of the Franks.* Trans. Lewis Thorpe. Harmondsworth, UK: Penguin, 1974.

———. *Gregory of Tours, Glory of the Martyrs.* Trans. Raymond Van Dam. Liverpool, UK: Liverpool University Press, 1988.

———. *Gregory of Tours, Glory of the Confessors.* Trans. Raymond Van Dam. Liverpool, UK: Liverpool University Press, 1988.

———. *Gregory of Tours: Life of the Fathers,* 2d ed. Trans. Edward James. Liverpool, UK: Liverpool University Press, 1991.

Laistner, Max L. W. *Thought and Letters in Western Europe, A.D. 500 to 900.* 2d ed. Ithaca, NY: Cornell University Press, 1976.

Nie, Giselle de. *Views from a Many-Windowed Tower: Studies of Imagination in the Works of Gregory of Tours.* Amsterdam: Rodopi, 1987.

Van Dam, Raymond. *Saints and Their Miracles in Late Antique Gaul.* Princeton: Princeton University Press, 1993.

Wallace-Hadrill, John M. *The Long-Haired Kings.* Toronto: University of Toronto Press, 1982.

Wood, Ian. *The Merovingian Kingdoms, 450–751.* London: Longman, 1994.

Grimoald (c. 615–c. 657)

Early leader of what became the Carolingian dynasty. Grimoald's ambition nearly destroyed the family and sent it to the political wilderness until its restoration to power by Grimoald's nephew, Pippin II of Herstal. The son of Pippin I of Landen—Pippin had established the family's early prominence through an alliance with Arnulf of Metz and their combined support of Chlothar's rebellion against Brunhilde—Grimoald assumed the office of mayor of the palace in Austrasia on his father's death in 640. But Grimoald dreamed of greater power than that of mayor and had his son adopted into the Merovingian family; his son actually assumed the throne for a time, but in the end Grimoald's plan failed and nearly ruined the family's fortunes.

Assuming leadership of the family at his father's death, Grimoald was a popular and ambitious figure. He sought the office of mayor of the palace, which his father had held, but which was now held by Otto, the tutor of King Sigebert III (d. c. 656). Grimoald's opportunity came during the revolt of Radulf, duke of Thuringia. Joining the king and other nobles in the battle, Grimoald displayed courage and ingenuity that won the king's favor. Sigebert's army was decisively defeated by Radulf, and the king himself survived only because he was rescued by Grimoald. Rising in royal favor, Grimoald took the opportunity to strike out against Otto, arranging his assassination and then taking his place as mayor of the palace in Austrasia. According to contemporary accounts, Grimoald held the region in tight control and was recognized as ruler of the realm. His success was due both to his own skill and the king's youth.

As mayor of the palace, Grimoald managed to accumulate great power and undertook a number of policies that continued to be pursued by later generations of the Carolingian family. As Pippin's son, Grimoald possessed numerous estates, an important source of wealth and power. His landed wealth allowed him to establish monasteries, which became sources of both political and spiritual support. By establishing monasteries, Grimoald could place political allies in positions of power with the ability to command even greater amounts of land and wealth that they could use on Grimoald's behalf. He continued to support these monasteries with his own wealth or that of the king after their foundation. Moreover, he persuaded his mother, Itta, to establish a monastery where she could retire. She established three churches on her property near the monastery and dedicated one of them to St. Peter. Her activities brought her into contact with St. Peter's successor, the pope in Rome; thus Grimoald and his mother laid the foundation for the relationship between the Carolingians and the pope that was so important to the family's success.

Grimoald also was an active supporter of Irish missionaries, who, along with the monks of the monasteries he founded, surely prayed for Grimoald and his family. He also benefited from another family connection. His residence as mayor was at Metz, where his father's ally and Grimoald's uncle Arnulf of Metz was buried. A powerful aristocrat and bishop, Arnulf was recognized as a saint shortly after his death. The spiritual power of the saint enhanced the reputation of Grimoald's family, and Grimoald's own ties to the church of Metz were strengthened when he successfully supported the appointment of his relative, Chlodulf, the son of Arnulf, as bishop of Metz.

His success as mayor of the palace, and the power he acquired in that role, may have inspired Grimoald to take an even more ambitious step at the death of King Sigebert in 656. The king, who died at the age of 26, owed his life to Grimoald, and because of his youth he was dominated by the powerful mayor. Although still young, Sigebert was most anxious to have a male heir, but he met at first with no success. According to some contemporary accounts, Grimoald took advantage of the king's anxiety to convince Sigebert to adopt Grimoald's own son, Childebert, as the king's heir. When the queen produced a male heir, Dagobert II (d. 679), it appeared that Grimoald's plans for the succession of Childebert the Adopted, as he is known, were ruined. Indeed, Sigebert changed his plans and entrusted Dagobert's education to his trusted ally Grimoald. But the mayor preferred the advancement of his family to loyalty to the Merovingian line, and he orchestrated the deposition of Dagobert and the promotion of Childebert as king.

After Sigebert's death, Grimoald had Dagobert tonsured as a monk and taken to Ireland. Childebert was made king in his place, and the moment of the triumph of the Carolingian family seemed to have arrived. But the nobles of Neustria and their king Clovis II (d. 657) were not willing to accept the usurpation and lured Grimoald into a trap. He was captured and executed, probably in 657. His son Childebert, however, survived the death of his father and reigned until 662. He may have survived because of the death of Clovis and the youth of Clovis's heir, Chlotar III (d. 673). In 662, Childebert's reign came to an end for reasons unknown, and he was replaced by Clovis's son Childeric II (d. 675). Grimoald's coup, therefore, was a terrible failure, and it pushed the family out of power until the time of Pippin of Herstal. Although the Carolingian family successfully usurped the throne in the eighth century, they were unable to do so in the time of Grimoald, whose attempt nearly destroyed the family.

See also Arnulf of Metz, St.; Balthild, St.; Brunhilde; Carolingian Dynasty; Chlotar II; Ebroin; Merovingian Dynasty; Pippin I, Called Pippin of Landen; Pippin II, Called Pippin of Herstal

Bibliography

Bachrach, Bernard S. *Merovingian Military Organization, 481–751*. Minneapolis: University of Minnesota Press, 1972.

Fouracre, Paul, and Richard A. Gerberding. *Late Merovingian France: History and Hagiography, 640–720*. Manchester, UK: University of Manchester Press, 1996.

Gerberding, Richard, A. *The Rise of the Carolingians and the "Liber Historiae Francorum."* Oxford: Clarendon, 1987.

James, Edward. *The Franks.* Oxford: Blackwell, 1991.

McKitterick, Rosamond. *The Frankish Kingdoms under the Carolingians, 751–987*. London: Longman, 1983.

Riché, Pierre. *The Carolingians: A Family Who Forged Europe.* Trans. Michael Idomir Allen. Philadelphia: University of Pennsylvania Press, 1993.

Wood, Ian. *The Merovingian Kingdoms, 450–751.* London: Longman, 1994.

Gundobad (d. 516)

Important king of the Burgundians (r. c. 480–516) and leading figure in the early post-Roman world, Gundobad was a lawgiver and frequently involved with the major kings of his day. He was the nephew of the Roman general and power behind the throne, Ricimer, and was involved in Roman service for a while. As king of the Burgundians, Gundobad was involved with the Franks and Ostrogoths, concluding marriage alliances with the kings of those peoples. He also, according to the sixth-century historian Gregory of Tours, considered converting from Arian Christianity to Catholic Christianity, and even if he did not convert, the Catholic faith was an important tradition in his family, as demonstrated by his niece Clothild.

One of several brothers of the royal family, Gundobad was also a high-ranking figure in the Roman military and a strong supporter of his uncle Ricimer, the leading figure in the Western Empire. He fought with his uncle against the Vandals and succeeded him as the chief military officer of the Western Empire from 472 to 474. He fell from favor when a new emperor took the throne in the west, and fled north to his family's homeland, where he became king by about 480 and shared rule with his three brothers for the next decade. By the early 490s, two of his brothers had died, and according to Gregory, Gundobad murdered one of his brothers,

Chilperic II, the father of Clothild. Although he may not have killed Chilperic, who may have died of natural causes, Gundobad was a leading power; he invaded Italy while Theodoric the Great was at war with Odovacar, the Germanic king who deposed the last Roman emporer in the West, in order to seize some territory. Theodoric was forced to expel the Burgundians and make territorial concessions to them. To improve their relationship, Theodoric and Gundobad forged a marriage alliance, in which one of Theodoric's daughters married Gundobad's son Sigismund in 496 or 497. Despite the marriage, the relationship between the two kings remained tense, in part because of the alliance that existed between the Burgundians and the Franks.

The relationship between the Burgundians and the Merovingian Franks, however, was also one that was often strained because of the ambitions of the two kings, Gundobad and Clovis. According to Gregory, a source of the tension between them came from Clothild, the wife of Clovis and niece of Gundobad. Gregory notes that Gundobad killed Clothild's father, but granted permission for her to marry the Frankish king, and she ultimately convinced her sons to avenge her father's death. Clovis himself made war on Gundobad. According to the historian of the Franks, Clovis was invited by Gundobad's brother Godigisel to join him against Gundobad about the year 500. When Clovis invaded, Gundobad called on his brother, who arrived but switched to Clovis's side during the battle, which forced Gundobad to flee. Unable to capture Gundobad, Clovis withdrew and left a detachment to support Godigisel, who was then defeated by an alliance of Gundobad and the Visigoths from Spain. Gundobad grew stronger and stopped payment of tribute to Clovis, who was forced to maintain his alliance with the Burgundian because of the threat of the Alemanni to the Franks. Indeed, Gundobad joined with Clovis against the Alemanni and the Visigoths when Clovis went to war against them and suffered

because of this alliance. In the settlement of these contests, which drew the attention of Theodoric, Gundobad lost territory and weakened the kingdom.

Although he was not the most successful military leader, Gundobad was an important lawgiver. Around the year 500, Gundobad codified the laws of the Burgundians in the *Lex Gundobada,* or *Liber constitutionem* (Book of Constitutions). The law was a compilation of traditional Burgundian tribal laws in Latin that applied to Gundobad's Burgundian subjects, issued in its final form by Gundobad's son Sigismund in 517. It included important sections on settlement patterns and distribution of land to the Burgundians and also contained a number of royal edicts. When issued by Sigismund it was joined by a collection of laws that concerned the Roman subjects of the Burgundian kings. The *Lex Gundobada* remained an important and influential legal code long after the destruction of the Burgundian kingdom, lasting into the ninth century, and is Gundobad's most important legacy.

See also Arianism; Clothild; Clovis; Franks; Gregory of Tours; Merovingian Dynasty; Law and Law Codes; Odovacar; Ricimer; Sigismund, St.; Theodoric the Great

Bibliography
Drew, Katherine Fisher, trans. *The Burgundian Code: The Book of Constitutions or Law of Gundobad and Additional Enactments.* Philadelphia: University of Pennsylvania Press, 1972.
Gregory of Tours. History of the Franks. Trans. Lewis Thorpe. Harmondsworth, UK: Penguin, 1974.
Randers-Pehrson, Justine Davis. *Barbarians and Romans: The Birth Struggle of Europe, A.D. 400–700.* Norman: University of Oklahoma Press, 1983.
Wolfram, Herwig. *The Roman Empire and Its Germanic Peoples.* Trans. Thomas J. Dunlap. Berkeley: University of California Press, 1997.
Wood, Ian. *The Merovingian Kingdoms, 450–751.* London: Longman, 1994.

Guntram (c. 535–592)

King of the Merovingian Franks, grandson of the great king Clovis, and favorite ruler of the bishop and historian Gregory of Tours, Guntram ruled over Burgundy, one of the kingdoms of the Franks, during a particularly tumultuous period in Merovingian history. Although at odds at times with his brothers, Guntram often sought to keep the peace and generally sought to promote unity and family interests rather than foment civil war and division. Despite differences with Fredegund, the wife of his brother Chilperic, he put personal interests aside to protect her son and his nephew, Chlothar II. He was also supportive of the church in his kingdom, and he was believed able to perform miracles by some of his contemporaries. Although he won the favor of church leaders because of his endorsement of religious reform, Guntram's piety could sometimes be a liability because it kept him from instilling fear in his subjects or rivals.

Guntram came to power on the death of his father, Chlotar I, in 561. He was joined by his brothers Charibert I, Chilperic, and Sigebert, with whom he came into conflict with over the division of Chlotar's kingdom. Traditionally, each of the sons of a Merovingian king would inherit part of the realm, a custom that in Guntram's generation caused great difficulty of the family. The conflict between the brothers was worsened, perhaps by the death of Charibert, certainly by the rivalry that also existed between Brunhilde, a Visigothic princess and the wife of Sigebert, and Fredegund, the wife of Chilperic. Guntram often found himself in the middle of the conflict between his brothers and between their wives, but he bore the brunt of his brothers' aggression. In 568, for example, Sigebert invaded Guntram's share of the kingdom and attempted to seize the city of Arles. Guntram and his armies were able to repel the invasion, and Sigebert lost many of his soldiers as they crossed the Rhone River after being turned away in their assault on Arles. In the 570s, the brothers once again came into conflict. In 573 a dispute broke out between Guntram and Sigebert that grew into a wider conflict involving all the brothers and their allies. Sigebert called on his allies among the Avars and faced an attack by Chilperic, who had formed an alliance with Guntram. Despite their combined might, Guntram and Chilperic were no match for Sigebert, and Guntram made peace with Sigebert in 575. Indeed, Sigebert seemed the most powerful of the three brothers and was on the point of eliminating Chilperic when Chilperic managed to assassinate his brother.

The death of Sigebert changed the landscape of the Merovingian kingdoms and altered the relationship of Guntram with the surviving members of his family. Chilperic once again became the aggressor in the family, and Guntram sought to protect his own interests and those of his nephew Childebert II (d. 596), successor of Sigebert. Chilperic struck quickly to seize cities belonging to Childebert, and Guntram took steps to protect his nephew and ensure his position as king. Although Guntram and Childebert had a falling out in the early 580s and Childebert joined with Chilperic, the two kings, Guntram and his nephew, remained on good terms after their falling out and remained allies against Chilperic until Chilperic's murder in 584. Once again the death of his brother altered Guntram's position in the kingdom. At first, Guntram was suspicious of the paternity of Chlotar II, Chilperic's son by Fredegund and his heir. Fredegund was reluctant to have the child baptized, which would have made Guntram the godfather, and she kept Chlotar from Guntram. As a result, Guntram became skeptical of Fredegund's claim that Chilperic was Chlotar's father. Ultimately, Fredegund and Guntram became reconciled, and Guntram remained Chlotar's defender until Guntram's death in 592. It should also be noted that Guntram's defense of family interests was not limited to the sons of his brothers. He was a staunch defender of his nieces, who were married or betrothed to Visigothic kings. He took a keen interest in the fate of Ingunde, who married the rebel

Hermenegild, and was active in the failed negotiations over the marriage between Reccared and Chlodosind. Indeed, in both cases Guntram attacked Visigothic territory, unsuccessfully, in defense of family interests.

Guntram's struggles with his brothers and in defense of family interests were complicated by turmoil in his own kingdom. The most dangerous episode for Guntram was the invasion of the pretender Gundovald (d. 585), who claimed that he was one of Chlotar I's sons and therefore had a right to the throne. Gundovald's claims were supported by other Merovingian kings, but failed to bring him a share in the kingdom, and so he departed for Constantinople until the early 580s. In 582 or 583 he made his first attempt to return to the kingdom. Although that attempt failed, he returned again in 584 and gathered much support. A number of important supporters of Guntram, including his chief military officer and nobles loyal to Guntram's ally and nephew Childebert II, supported Gundovald's attempt to claim the throne and joined his army. Guntram managed to suppress the attempt and capture or kill the disloyal followers as well as the pretender.

Although some members of the kingdom did not fear Guntram because of his piety, the king gained the respect and support of the church and its bishops in the Frankish kingdoms. He often corresponded and even dined with the bishops, especially Gregory of Tours. The king was well known for his acts of charity. He also helped end an outbreak of an epidemic by his actions, which were more like those of a bishop than a king. He called his subjects together in a church and ordered them to eat and drink only bread and water, and to keep prayer vigils. His prescription ended the outbreak, according to Gregory of Tours. Also, Gregory records the story of Guntram's miracle. As Gregory notes, a woman whose son was seriously ill with a fever "came up behind the King . . . [and]cut a few threads from his cloak"(510). She steeped the threads in water, which she then gave to her son who was immediately cured. Guntram was for Gregory the ideal Christian king; he was devoted to God, supported the interests of his family, and sought to keep the peace in the Merovingian kingdoms.

See also Brunhilde; Chilperic I; Chlotar II; Clovis; Franks; Fredegund; Gregory of Tours; Hermenegild; Merovingian Dynasty; Reccared I; Visigoths

Bibliography

Bachrach, Bernard S. *Merovingian Military Organization, 481–751.* Minneapolis: University of Minnesota Press, 1972.

Gregory of Tours. *History of the Franks.* Trans. Lewis Thorpe. Harmondsworth, UK: Penguin, 1974.

James, Edward. *The Franks.* Oxford: Blackwell, 1988.

Lasko, Peter. *The Kingdom of the Franks: North-West Europe before Charlemagne.* New York: McGraw-Hill, 1971.

Wallace-Hadrill, J. M. *The Long-Haired Kings.* Toronto: University of Toronto Press, 1982.

Wemple, Suzanne. *Women in Frankish Society: Marriage and the Cloister, 500 to 900.* Philadelphia: University of Pennsylvania Press, 1981.

Wood, Ian. *The Merovingian Kingdoms, 450–751.* London: Longman, 1994.

H

Hadrian I, Pope (d. 795)

Roman noble and pope (r. 772–795), Hadrian was an important figure in the birth of the Papal States and an important ally of the Carolingian ruler Charlemagne. The pope contributed to Charlemagne's renewal of church and society and supplied law and liturgical models that helped the king reform affairs in his realm. He also welcomed the king to Rome twice as a pilgrim. Moreover, Hadrian presided over the final separation of the papacy from the Byzantine Empire, its long-time protector, and strengthened the alliance with the Carolingians. The pope contributed also to the strengthening of the Papal States and the demise of the Lombard kingdom. His appeal to Charlemagne for aid against the Lombard king Desiderius led to the Carolingian king's invasion and destruction of the Lombard kingdom. Hadrian's invitation also led to the greater involvement of the Carolingian dynasty in Italian affairs.

According to the *Liber Pontificalis* (Book of the Popes), Hadrian was a "very distinguished man, sprung from noble ancestry and born to influential parents"(123). He was, the official biography notes further, "elegant and most decorous of manner, a resolute and strenuous defender of the orthodox faith, his homeland and the flock entrusted to him" (123). He was raised by his uncle Theodatus, a powerful fig-

ure in Roman lay and religious circles, because his parents died while Hadrian was still young. The *Liber Pontificalis* records that from his youth, Hadrian was a pious and devout person who spent much time in prayer and praise of God. He lived a chaste life and was generous to the poor. His piety was noticed by Pope Paul I (r. 757–767), who made him a cleric and gave him an important office in the Roman church. Hadrian also served Paul's successor, Stephen III (r. 768–772), who also employed Hadrian in important positions in the church of Rome. His service brought him the favor of the people of Rome and election to the office of pope on the death of Stephen III.

Along with a number of internal political difficulties, which he effectively resolved, Hadrian's greatest challenge upon his elevation to the papal throne was the protection of the Papal States from the lingering Lombard threat. Indeed, the internal tensions that existed at Rome were related to Italian political affairs, as some factions in Rome were still friendly to the Lombard king, Desiderius. The papacy, during the reign of Stephen II (752–757), had confirmed its alliance with the Frankish Carolingian dynasty, however, and Hadrian continued that policy and was supported by the pro-Frankish faction in Rome. The situation was complicated by affairs in the Frankish kingdom, as its rulers Charlemagne and Carloman found themselves on the point of civil war and Charlemagne himself married the daughter of Desiderius. The death of Carloman ended one crisis, but his widow and children fled to Italy and the protection of Desiderius, whose daughter was repudiated by Charlemagne in 771–772.

The situation only improved slightly for Hadrian with the death of Carloman; he still faced an aggressive Desiderius, who sought to expand Lombard control in Italy and see Carloman's sons elevated to the kingship. Hadrian sent emissaries to Desiderius noting the pope's willingness to negotiate matters with the Lombard king, but also demanding the return of several key cities that the king had recently conquered. Desiderius refused the pope's request and even threatened to invade Roman territory, but withdrew from the border when Hadrian threatened to excommunicate him. Desiderius's continued hostility to Rome led Hadrian to seek aid once and for all from the Frankish king. He petitioned Charlemagne, after first giving Desiderius one last chance, to fulfill the obligations his father, Pippin the Short, had undertaken toward Rome. The Carolingian king willingly invaded Italy at the pope's request in 773 and defeated his Lombard rival in 774, who was besieged in his capital of Pavia for six months before submitting.

While the siege was proceeding, Charlemagne journeyed to Rome as a pilgrim to celebrate Easter and was welcomed by the pope, who sent an official delegation to meet the king some thirty miles from the city. Indeed, Hadrian accorded Charlemagne full honors as patrician, the title that had been bestowed on his father Pippin. The pope also welcomed the king on the steps of St. Peter's, and the two established a personal friendship that lasted until Hadrian's death in 795, despite the occasional tension caused by their competing claims to authority in Italy. Not only did the two forge a lasting friendship at that time, but they also renewed the political alliance the papacy had established under Charlemagne's father. The exact terms of the political discussions that took place between Charlemagne and Hadrian at their first meeting, however, remain vague and uncertain. According to the *Liber Pontificalis,* Charlemagne confirmed the donation of his father, the so-called Donatron of Pippin which granted the papacy extensive lands in Italy, in full and deposited it on the altar of St. Peter. But this is a later and uncertain tradition and may not signal Charlemagne's exact intentions in regard to Italy and papal territory at that time. At the very least, Charlemagne did end the Lombard threat, with the exception of occasional raids on Roman territory from the Lombard duchies of the south, and established himself as king of the Lombards after his final victory over Desiderius.

Hadrian and Charlemagne remained close friends and important allies for the next two decades, and the pope provided further aid to the Carolingian ruler. In 780, Charlemagne made his second visit to Rome, where he was once again welcomed by Hadrian. On Easter, Charlemagne's son, Pippin (775/756–781), was baptized by the pope, who was also his baptismal sponsor. Hadrian, at Charlemagne's request, anointed the king's sons, Louis the Pious as king of Aquitaine and Pippin as king of Italy. Pippin established himself as king in Pavia, the old Lombard capital, and acted as his father's representative in Italy and did his will. Indeed, the establishment of Italy as part of the growing Carolingian Empire and the introduction of Carolingian authority in the peninsula remained a source of tension between Hadrian and Charlemagne. But the pope had little recourse, and his anointing strengthened the already powerful dynasty.

Although Charlemagne and Hadrian found themselves at odds at times over political and religious issues, they did find common cause in their opposition to the Spanish heresy of Adoptionism, which maintained that Christ was the son of God by adoption. Hadrian was also an important contributor to Charlemagne's religious reforms and sent him a copy of church law that the king could apply to the Frankish church. On the other hand, they found themselves in dispute over the second Council of Nicaea in 787. The empress Irene had invited representatives of the pope to attend the council, which repudiated Iconoclasm and restored the Byzantine tradition of the veneration of icons (religious images). Charlemagne and his advisors, as a result of a faulty translation of the decisions of the council, attacked the council. Despite religious and political differences, Charlemagne and Hadrian remained on good terms, and the king was greatly saddened at Hadrian's death and, according to Einhard, wept as if he had lost a brother. When he died in 795, Hadrian had presided over an important period in the history of the papacy and in relations between the Carolingians and Rome. He was succeed by Pope Leo III, who further developed the alliance with the Carolingians.

See also Carloman, King of the Franks; Carolingian Dynasty; Charlemagne; Desiderius; Donation of Pippin; Einhard; Franks; Irene; Leo III, Pope; Lombards; Louis the Pious; Pippin III, Called Pippin the Short

Bibliography

Einhard and Notker the Stammerer. *Two Lives of Charlemagne.* Trans. Lewis Thorpe. Harmondsworth, UK: Penguin, 1981.

Christie, Neil. *The Lombards: The Ancient Langobards.* Oxford: Blackwell, 1995.

Davis, Raymond, trans. *The Lives of the Eighth-Century Popes* (Liber Pontificalis): *The Ancient Biographies of Nine Popes from* A.D. *715 to* A.D. *817.* Liverpool, UK: Liverpool University Press, 1992.

Halphen, Louis. *Charlemagne and the Carolingian Empire.* Trans. Giselle de Nie. Amsterdam: North-Holland, 1977.

Llewellyn, Peter. *Rome in the Dark Ages.* New York: Barnes and Noble, 1993.

Noble, Thomas X. F. *The Republic of St. Peter: The Birth of the Papal State, 680–825.* Philadelphia: University of Pennsylvania Press, 1984.

Riché, Pierre. *The Carolingians: A Family Who Forged Europe.* Trans. Michael Idomir Allen. Philadelphia: University of Pennsylvania Press, 1993.

Scholz, Bernhard Walter, trans. *Carolingian Chronicles: Royal Frankish Annals and Nithard's History.* Ann Arbor: University of Michigan Press, 1972.

Hadrianople, Battle of (378)

Major battle between Roman imperial armies and rebellious Gothic armies; traditionally regarded as an important step in the "fall" of the Roman Empire. The battle was a dramatic victory for the Visigoths, who destroyed the imperial force and killed the emperor of the Eastern Roman Empire, Valens. Although they inflicted a catastrophic defeat on the Romans, the Visigoths were unable to take advantage of their victory and were forced to come to terms with the great Roman emperor, Theodosius. The victory of the Visigoths at Hadrianople did cause a change in the relationship between Rome and the barbarians, however, despite the Visigoths' inability to capitalize on their victory.

During the course of the migrations of peoples during the later fourth century, increasing pressure was placed on the Roman frontiers. This was due in part to the aggressive nature of the Huns, whose movement westward had either absorbed or displaced numerous settled peoples. Among these peoples was a group that later came to be known as the Visigoths. Their traditional homeland had been devastated and could no longer support them, and the Huns proved too great a threat to the Visigoths. A new leader, Fritigern, seized power and declared that he would save his people by fleeing into the Roman Empire. By the year 376, when Fritigern petitioned for entry, the absorption of foreign peoples was nothing new for Rome, which accepted them on the condition that they lay down their arms, submit to Roman authority, pay Roman taxes, work the land, and serve the Roman military. Other peoples had done this, and Fritigern's Goths were admitted on these conditions, but the number of people admitted, which Bury placed at 80,000 or more, and the incompetence of the local administration opened the way for disaster.

The Goths flooded across the border in numbers too large for the local military forces to keep order, and the Goths simply overran them. The emperor Valens was occupied with the Persian frontier and requested aid from his Western counterpart, Gratian. Over the next two years the Goths operated freely in the Balkans as the emperors prepared to march against them. In 378 both Valens and Gratian were ready to crush the Goths, and Valens assembled an army of infantry and cavalry of between 30,000 and 40,000 troops. Gratian too mobilized a sizeable force, but he faced a threat from the Alemanni, which he successfully overcame, that detained him from joining Valens. The Eastern emperor was all the more anxious to win a great victory over the barbarians after Gratian's victory over the Alemanni. He moved his troops forward to meet Fritigern's Goths, which reconnaissance numbered at 10,000 warriors, but which was actually three times that number. Despite warnings from Gratian, who had witnessed at first hand the new battle tactics of the Goths, Valens proceeded. In early August he marched his troops against the Goths near Hadrianople, and Fritigern sent messengers to treat with Valens. On August 5 and again on the day of battle, August 9, Fritigern sought to negotiate with the emperor, but without success. While Fritigern sent messengers, Valens sent his troops forward without food or water in the boiling sun to meet the Goths, who had set fires along the Romans' path. As negotiations were beginning, Roman soldiers, without orders, began the attack that proved fatal to the Roman force. The Roman attack was disorganized, and the counterattack of the Gothic cavalry was rapid and forceful. Units of Gothic cavalry returned from foraging to join the fray and made the assault on the Romans even more terrible. A cavalry unit then attacked the Roman left flank, and the Gothic foot soldiers made a ferocious push on the Roman center. The Roman cavalry fled, abandoning the Roman infantry, which was quickly surrounded and cut to pieces by superior Gothic forces. The Romans lost nearly two-thirds of the army at Hadrianople, and most of the casualties were from the infantry, the backbone of the Roman military. Among the dead were generals, unit officers, and the emperor Valens himself, who was either killed by an arrow or wounded and then burned to death when the building he was taken to was set on fire by the Goths.

Although Ammianus declared it the worst loss since Rome's defeat at Cannae and a tragic defeat for the empire, the Battle of Hadrianople was not a military turning point nor especially catastrophic for the empire. The Goths had a golden opportunity to do permanent harm to the empire after their victory, but they failed to follow it up with an aggressive assault on the empire's cities or armies. Moreover, the arrival of the new emperor, Theodosius, provided the empire with much needed support, and together with the Western emperor, Gratian, he was able to force the Goths to terms within a few years of the defeat in 378. Fritigern's victory, however, did force the Romans to come to terms with the Goths and settle them in Roman territory as subjects of the empire. And it was the descendants of these Goths, under the leadership of Alaric, who caused such great disturbance in the early fifth century. The Battle of Hadrianople also contributed to the triumph of Catholic Christianity, because the death of the Arian Christian Valens seemed to be God's judgment, and the new emperor Theodosius ultimately declared Catholic Christianity the official religion of the empire.

See also Alaric; Ammianus Marcellinus; Fritigern; Huns; Visigoths

Bibliography

Ammianus Marcellinus. *The Later Roman Empire (A.D. 354–378)*. Trans. Walter Hamilton. Harmondsworth, UK: Penguin, 1986.

Bury, John B. *The Invasion of Europe by the Barbarians.* New York: W. W. Norton, 1967.

Heather, Peter. *The Goths.* Oxford: Blackwell, 1996.

Wolfram, Herwig. *The Roman Empire and Its Germanic Peoples.* Trans. Thomas J. Dunlap. Berkeley: University of California Press, 1997.

Helena, St.

See Women

Hengist and Horsa (mid-fifth century)

Brothers who, according to the history of Bede and the *Anglo-Saxon Chronicle,* led a band of Anglo-Saxon mercenaries to England at the request of a British ruler. Rather than aiding the native Britons, they conquered them and established a kingdom. Bede also notes that they were descendants of Woden, "from whose stock sprang the royal house of many provinces"(56).

Following the Roman withdrawal from Britain in 410, the native British population faced raids from the Picts and Scots to their north. Unable to defend themselves from these invaders, the British, led by Vortigern, sought out mercenaries to help them. Vortigern invited a band of Angles and Saxons under the direction of Hengist and his brother Horsa to expel the invaders. In exchange for their assistance the mercenaries were promised the Isle of Thanet. In 449 Hengist and Horsa arrived with three shiploads of warriors to fight off the invaders from the north. Having successfully defeated the northerners, Hengist and Horsa turned their mercenaries against their employers and began their own invasion of Britain. In 455 Hengist and Horsa fought a battle against Vortigern. Horsa was killed in the battle, but Hengist defeated Vortigern and took over the kingdom of Kent. Hengist and his son Æsc fought several other battles against the Britons in the course of their conquest of Kent. In 465 they defeated the Britons and killed twelve British chieftains, and in 473 they fought another battle in which they overwhelmed the British and forced them to flee from the battlefield. Although the date of his death is unknown, Hengist may have ruled Kent for much of the next fifteen years. According to the *Anglo-Saxon Chronicle,* Æsc became king in 488 and reigned over Kent for the next twenty-four years.

See also Anglo-Saxons; *Anglo-Saxon Chronicle;* Bede; Vortigern

Bibliography

Bede. *Ecclesiastical History of the English People with Bede's Letter to Egbert and Cuthbert's Letter on the Death of Bede.* Trans. Leo Sherley-Price. Harmondsworth, UK: Penguin, 1991.

Blair, Peter Hunter. *The World of Bede.* Cambridge: Cambridge University Press, 1990.

Geoffrey of Monmouth. *The History of the Kings of Britain.* Trans. Lewis Thorpe. Harmondsworth, UK: Penguin, 1982.

Howe, Nicholas. *Migration and Mythmaking in Anglo-Saxon England.* New Haven: Yale University Press, 1989.

Stenton, Frank M. *Anglo-Saxon England.* 3d ed. Oxford: Clarendon, 1971.

Whitelock, Dorothy, ed. *The Anglo-Saxon Chronicle.* Westport, CT: Greenwood, 1986.

Heptarchy

A term, literally meaning seven kingdoms, used in Anglo-Saxon history to describe the political structure of early medieval England. The term is derived from remarks made by Bede concerning the nature of the political organization of England in the eighth century. It came into more general use among scholars in the sixteenth century. Although it became popular among scholars in the nineteenth century and still occasionally appears, it is generally not used by contemporary scholars.

The term heptarchy was used to describe a hypothetical confederacy of the Anglo-Saxon kingdoms of early medieval England, especially for the period from the sixth to the ninth centuries. It refers to the seven kingdoms that had been established by the Anglo-

Saxon invaders and their descendants: East Anglia, Essex, Kent, Mercia, Northumbria, Sussex, and Wessex. Although in some ways a useful designation because it reveals the basic structure of early English political organization, the term fails to convey the variety in political institutions, size, and importance of the various kingdoms. It implies an equality of status among the kingdoms that seldom if ever existed. The kingdoms of Mercia, Northumbria, and Wessex were certainly more powerful than the other kingdoms and at times exercised dominion over them. Essex often lost power in political struggles with the other kingdoms and may have disappeared before the coming of the Vikings, the time traditionally considered the end of the heptarchy. There were also subkingdoms, such as Deira (the region made famous by Pope Gregory the Great's encounter with Anglo-Saxon slaves in the Roman market), that were as powerful as some of the seven kingdoms of the heptarchy. The term also suggests a static relationship between the various kingdoms that fails to take into account the disappearance of some of the seven or the ebb and flow of political power among the various kingdoms. Although heptarchy is a convenient term to describe the political make-up of Anglo-Saxon England, it is a term that conveys a false impression of the Anglo-Saxon kingdoms of England and is best relegated to history's trash heap.

See also Æthelberht; Alfred the Great; Anglo-Saxons; Bede

Bibliography

Bede, *A History of the English Church and People.* Trans. Leo Sherley-Price. Harmondsworth, UK: Penguin, 1981.

Bassett, Steven, ed. *The Origins of Anglo-Saxon Kingdoms.* Leicester, UK: Leicester University Press, 1989.

Sawyer, Peter H. *From Roman Britain to Norman England,* 2d ed. London and New York: Routledge, 1998.

Stenton, Frank M. *Anglo-Saxon England.* 3d ed. Oxford: Clarendon, 1971.

Hermenegild (d. 585)

Spanish Visigothic prince and coregent with his father Leovigild and brother Reccared, Hermenegild led an unsuccessful revolt against his father. The rebellion may have been inspired by Hermenegild's conversion to Catholic Christianity from the Arian faith of his father. According to some accounts, his conversion and rebellion brought about his murder in 585, after the rebellion had been put down. Although his efforts ultimately failed, his conversion foreshadowed that of his brother, and with Reccared's conversion the Visigothic kingdom of Spain converted to Catholic Christianity.

Hermenegild played an important role in his father's reign before his rebellion in 579. The firstborn son of Leovigild, Heremenegild surely had a part to play in his father's conquests in Spain. In 573, Leovigild made his two sons coregents, thus granting them royal authority and marking them as eventual heirs to his power. Indeed, Hermenegild's elevation most likely reveals Leovigild's intention to establish a royal dynasty. Hermenegild also played a significant role his father's diplomacy. In 579 Hermenegild married the Merovingian princess Ingunde, the daughter of powerful Brunhilde, a Visigoth herself, and the Frankish king Sigebert. The marriage was surely a recognition of the importance of good relations between Leovigild's family and the Merovingian dynasty, as well as of the growing power of Leovigild. Of course, the marriage complicated relations between the two dynasties after the revolt and then murder of Leovigild.

Despite his earlier importance, Hermenegild rebelled in 579. The exact cause of the revolt, however, remains uncertain. The sources and chronology of events are a bit confused, and it remains unclear whether Hermenegild converted before or after his revolt began. According to some accounts, Hermenegild was driven to accept Catholic Christianity by his young—she was twelve at the time of the marriage—but determined wife. Hermenegild's stepmother and grandmother of Ingunde, Goiswinth, may have persecuted the young girl and pressured her to convert to Arian Christianity from the Catholic faith practiced by the Merovingians. In order to establish peace at court, Leovigild sent his son and daughter-in-law to southern Spain, which Hermenegild governed for his father. In southern Spain, Hermenegild came under the influence of Leander, the older brother of the famous encyclopedist Isidore of Seville. Leander is also identified as the agent of Hermenegild's conversion, and it is while he was in the south that Hermenegild both revolted and converted, in whatever order. What is of importance is that Hermenegild did convert and was probably influenced to do so by both his wife and Leander.

Whether he converted before or after the rebellion broke out, Hermenegild used his conversion as justification for the rebellion and declared that he had revolted because of religious persecution. To guarantee the success of his uprising, Hermenegild undertook furious diplomatic negotiations with a number of peoples. He forged alliances with those conquered by his father. He also found support from the Suevi, who committed to him for both political and religious reasons. The Suevi, a Germanic tribe who had established a kingdom in northwestern Spain and had been defeated by Leovigild in 576, had converted to Catholicism during the previous generation. He also found allies among the relatives of his wife, the Catholic Merovingians. He sought the support of the emperor in Constantinople and found a great friend and ally in Pope Gregory the Great. Although he found much support against Leovigild, the only effective aid came from the Suevi; both the Merovingians and the Byzantines were involved in internal and external military difficulties at the time.

The course of the revolt went poorly for Hermenegild. It broke out in 579, and the tide turned by 582 when Leovigild struck back hard at his son and his allies. The Suevi were defeated by Leovigild in 583 and forced to withdraw their support and recognize Leovigild's authority over them. Hermenegild withdrew to Seville, which fell after a lengthy siege in 584. Hermenegild then moved to Córdoba, where he was welcomed by the Byzantine commander of the town. But this support was not long lasting; the imperial commander quickly settled a treaty with Leovigild that returned the city to the Visigoth in exchange for 30,000 pieces of gold. Abandoned by the Byzantines, who withdrew with Ingunde and their son, Hermenegild sought refuge in a church in the hopes of negotiating with his father. Leovigild had mercy on his rebellious son. He demanded that Hermenegild renounce his royal title in exchange for his life and accept exile to Valencia. He moved in the next year, 585, to Tarragona, where he was murdered in the same year.

Hermenegild's conversion pointed the way of the future for the Visigoths in Spain, but it found him little support from Catholic Christians after his revolt failed. With the exception of Gregory the Great, most contemporary writers had little good to say about Hermenegild. The pope recognized Hermenegild as a martyr to the faith and implicated Leovigild in the murder, but this view finds little support from Gregory's contemporaries, and the Roman and Visigothic population of Spain seem to have held that the revolt was the result of Hermenegild's ambition and not his conversion. Some Merovingian kings sought revenge for the death of Hermenegild, and Guntram invaded Visigothic territory in defense of Ingunde. But Gregory of Tours found little good in the revolt, saying of Hermenegild, "Poor prince, he did not realize that the judgment of God hangs over anyone who makes such plans against his own father, even if that father be a heretic"(375). Notwithstanding this verdict on his revolt, his conversion was vindicated by the successful conversion of Visigothic Spain by Reccared.

See also Arianism; Brunhilde; Gregory the Great; Gregory of Tours; Isidore of Seville; Leovigild; Merovingian Dynasty; Reccared I; Visigoths

Bibliography

Bury, John B. *History of the Later Roman Empire: From the Death of Theodosius I to the Death of Justinian.* 2 vols. 1923. Reprint, New York: Dover, 1959.

Collins, Roger. *Early Medieval Spain: Unity in Diversity, 400–1000.* New York and London: Longman, 1983.

Gregory of Tours. *History of the Franks.* Trans. Lewis Thorpe. Harmondsworth, UK: Penguin, 1974.

Heather, Peter. *The Goths.* Oxford: Blackwell, 1996.

Isidore of Seville. *Isidore of Seville's History of the Goths, Vandals, and Suevi,* 2d rev. ed. Trans. Guido Donini and Gordon B. Ford. Leiden: Brill, 1970.

Thompson, Edward A. *The Goths in Spain.* Oxford: Clarendon, 1969.

Wolfram, Herwig. *History of the Goths.* Trans. Thomas J. Dunlap. Berkeley: University of California Press, 1988.

———. *The Roman Empire and Its Germanic Peoples.* Trans. Thomas J. Dunlap. Berkeley: University of California Press, 1997.

Honorius (384–423)

Son of the emperor Theodosius the Great and brother of the eastern emperor Arcadius, Honorius, in full Flavius Honorius, ruled the Western Empire in the early fifth century and presided over the beginning of the final demise of the empire in the west. His reign was troubled by uneasy relations with his own subordinates, especially Stilicho, and with Germanic leaders like the Visigoth Alaric. During Honorius's reign, the borders of the empire were breached on several occasions and Italy itself suffered invasion numerous times. His reign also witnessed the sacking of the city of Rome for the first time in 800 years, and even though it was no longer the capital, Rome's violation came as a profound and disturbing shock to the empire. His weakness and poor judgment were especially detrimental to the fate of the empire and worsened an already difficult situation.

The early years of his reign were marked by the guardianship of Stilicho, a Vandal-Roman general who had been his father's commander in chief, and the struggle with Alaric. Although occasionally allowing him to escape, Stilicho stood as the empire's firmest defense against the invasions of Alaric and his Visigoths. Sometimes caught in the competition between Honorius and his brother Arcadius, Stilicho remained loyal to the emperor and served him well. He benefited from this service by rapid promotion and close proximity to the imperial house, even marrying his daughter to Honorius. The emperor, however, came eventually to tire of Stilicho and became critical of his general's stewardship. To protect the imperial heartland against Alaric, Stilicho withdrew imperial troops from Britain and the frontiers. Even more serious, though, was the general's failure to defend the empire against the invasion of Italy by Radagaisus and his army of Ostrogoths during the first decade of the fifth century. Although Stilicho defeated the Ostrogoth, the devastation that Radagaisus caused in the north unsettled many. Moreover, Stilicho's efforts to secure the succession to the throne by the marriage of his son to Honorius's sister Galla Placidia alienated the emperor even more. In 408, when Arcadius died, Honorius was persuaded to allow Stilicho to go to Constantinople to guarantee the succession of Honorius's nephew. In Stilicho's absence, Honorius was persuaded that Stilicho had actually gone to place his own son on the throne. As a result, Honorius ordered the arrest and immediate execution of Stilicho, whose end came on August 22, 408.

Honorius had eliminated Stilicho, but he had only exacerbated the real problems of the empire. Indeed, Alaric, the greatest threat faced by the Western Empire, remained at large, but now Stilicho, who had had at least some success against Alaric, was no longer around to restrict Alaric's activities. Even worse, the wanton massacre of many of the German troops that had supported Stilicho provided Alaric another opportunity to invade Italy. In 408, Alaric marched into Italy and eventually reached Rome, no longer the capital but still a symbol of the empire. For the next two years, Honorius and his generals were involved in complicated negations with Alaric. Although making numerous concessions and ultimately demanding only settlement for his followers, Alaric was repeatedly rebuffed by Honorius. Indeed, Honorius refused the most favorable terms Alaric offered and suffered the consequences, the sack of the city of Rome. This event, which clearly shook the confidence of the empire, demonstrates the incompetence of Honorius. After their assault on Rome, the Visigoths most likely moved into southern Italy before heading north and settling in Gaul. The failures of Honorius thus contributed to the dismemberment of the Western Empire and the emergence of the first Germanic successor states.

Honorius also suffered a personal embarrassment in the sack of Rome; his sister, Galla Placidia, was kidnapped by Alaric's successor, Ataulf. She ultimately married her Visigothic captor, and both of them hoped to produce an heir to the imperial throne that would unite Visigoths and Romans. Ataulf's murder, however, ended this dream, and Honorius successfully negotiated for her return in 416, in exchange for his support of the Visigoths. Honorius then married his sister to one of his generals, a marriage that produced the heir, Valentinian, in 419.

In his remaining few years, Honorius remained relatively inactive and in so doing caused few problems for the empire. His death in 423 was the occasion for dispute over the succession, which ultimately fell to Valentinian under the regency of Galla Placidia. The reign of Honorius was clearly a low point for the empire. He presided over the withdrawal of troops from England and the frontiers, which allowed barbarian tribes to enter and begin to carve up the Western Empire. He eliminated his most important general, while not taking the steps necessary to get rid of his greatest enemy. He also presided over the sack of Rome, an event that heralded the imminent collapse of the Western Empire.

See also Alaric; Arbogast; Galla Placidia; Ostrogoths; Stilicho, Flavius; Vandals; Visigoths

Bibliography

Burns, Thomas S. *Barbarians within the Gates of Rome: A Study of Roman Military Policy and the Barbarians, ca. 375–425 A.D.* Bloomington: University of Indiana Press, 1994.

Bury, John B. *History of the Later Roman Empire: From the Death of Theodosius I to the Death of Justinian.* 2 vols. 1923. Reprint, New York: Dover, 1959.

———. *The Invasion of Europe by the Barbarians.* New York and London: W. W. Norton, 1967.

Claudian. *Claudian's Fourth Panegyric on the fourth consulate of Honorius.* Ed. and trans. William Barr. Liverpool, UK: Liverpool University Press, 1981.

Heather, Peter. *The Goths.* Oxford: Blackwell, 1996.

Wolfram, Herwig. *The Roman Empire and Its Germanic Peoples.* Trans. Thomas J. Dunlap. Berkeley: University of California Press, 1997.

Zosimus. *New History.* Trans. Ronald T. Ridley. Canberra: Australian Association for Byzantine Studies, 1982.

Huneric (d. 484)

The son and successor of the great Vandal king, Gaiseric. Huneric's rule (r. 477–484) is best known for its persecutions of Catholic Christians in his kingdom. But he also attempted to preserve his father's legacy and maintain the power and place of the Vandal kingdom in North Africa. Before his rule as king, Huneric was involved in his father's diplomacy and was betrothed to and eventually married an imperial princess. His reign, however, was relatively short, especially when compared with that of his father, and his efforts to solidify and unify the kingdom remained unfinished because of his death.

When Huneric came to the throne at his father's death in 477, he was already advanced in years. He was probably sixty-six years old, and although little is known of his life before he ascended the throne, Huneric probably was involved in the affairs of the kingdom during his father's reign. At the very least, it is known that Huneric was involved in diplomatic affairs. In 442, to guarantee a treaty with the Western Empire, Huneric was sent to Ravenna, the imperial capital, as a hostage and stayed there for three or four years. He was also betrothed to the Eudocia, the daughter of Emperor Valentinian III. She was quite young at the time of the engagement and the marriage had to wait some ten years. Moreover, Huneric was already married, but Gaiseric did not let such details interfere with diplomacy—he accused Huneric's Visigothic wife of attempting to poison him, cut off her nose and ears, and returned her to Visigothic Spain. The betrothal and eventual marriage with the imperial princess were clearly important concerns in Gaiseric's relations with the imperial government in Italy, which were obviously more significant than his relations with the Visigoths. These ties were unsettled, however, before Huneric actually married Eudocia. Before marrying Huneric, she married the son of her father's successor, which may have prompted Gaiseric's invasion and sack of Rome. Huneric captured his betrothed and married her in 456.

The marriage itself did not last, but it did produce one and possibly two sons. In 457, Eudocia bore Hilderic, and perhaps another son within the next few years. But Huneric and Eudocia were poorly matched, particularly in religion. There was, of course, the great difference in age, with Huneric probably some twenty-eight years older than his wife. Furthermore, she was a devout Catholic, and he was an aggressive Arian who persecuted Catholics. As a result she left her husband in 472 and fled to Jerusalem, where she spent the rest of her days.

Once on the throne in 477 Huneric paid far less attention to affairs with Rome and instead sought to unify the kingdom and ensure that his son would succeed him as king. To guarantee his son's succession he needed to eliminate rivals from within his own family, particularly the sons of Gaiseric's brothers. According to an agreement within the ruling family, the eldest son of any of Gaiseric's brothers or nephews was to inherit the throne, and Hilderic was the third oldest of that generation. In 481, Huneric launched a bloody purge of his brothers and nephews to secure his son's succession. The effort failed, however, because he failed to capture or kill the two nephews who were ahead of Hilderic, and it was those nephews who actually did take the throne from 523 to 530. Huneric's other domestic initiative was an equal failure. He attempted to unify the kingdom by imposing Arian Christianity on all his subjects. In 483 he passed an anti-Catholic edict, and in 484 issued a formal law against Catholic Christianity. He actively persecuted the Catholics in his kingdom and found support for this from the Arian bishop of Carthage. But to contemporaries his efforts seemed to inspire divine displeasure; his kingdom suffered famine in the summer of 484, and Huneric himself died of a mysterious and horrible disease in 484.

See also Alans; Arianism; Gaiseric; Jordanes; Justinian; Pope Leo I the Great; Vandals

Bibliography

Bury, John B. *The Invasion of Europe by the Barbarians.* New York: W. W. Norton, 1967.

Clover, Frank M. *The Late Roman West and the Vandals.* London: Variorum, 1993.

Randers-Pehrson, Justine Davis. *Barbarians and Romans: The Birth Struggle of Europe, A.D. 400–700.* Norman: University of Oklahoma Press, 1983.

Victor of Vita. *Victor of Vita: History of the Vandal Persecution.* Trans. John Moorhead. Liverpool, UK: Liverpool University Press, 1992.

Wolfram, Herwig. *The Roman Empire and Its Germanic Peoples.* Trans. Thomas J. Dunlap. Berkeley: University of California Press, 1997.

Huns

Nomadic steppe people who were skilled horsemen and great warriors and who challenged the power of the Roman Empire in the late fourth and fifth centuries. Although the Huns were never a direct threat to the existence of the empire, they did create great difficulties for Rome and won a number of battles against imperial armies. They both served in the Roman military against invaders and were themselves invaders. The Huns also may have caused such great terror among various Germanic tribes along Rome's periphery that their advance led to the Germanic migrations (or barbarian invasions) of the fourth and fifth centuries. They created a great empire under their greatest leader, Attila, which collapsed shortly after his death.

The origins and early history of the Huns remain obscure and uncertain. The ancients offer a number of views of their origins. The historian Ammianus Marcellinus said that they came from the "ice-bound north," suggesting, therefore, that they had Finno-Ugrian roots like the tenth-century invaders, the Magyars who settled in Hungary. Other sources describe them as a Turkic people, or as a new wave of Scythians, Iranian horsemen who disappeared in the second century. A popular modern view of the Huns places their origins on the frontiers of ancient China. According to this view, the Huns can be associated with the Hsiung-nu (the name Huns thus would be a corruption of the Chinese word for "common slaves"), northern neighbors of the Chinese until the second century A.D. The Hsiung-nu had long harassed the Chinese and inspired the erection of the Great Wall to protect the Chinese from their powerful neighbors. Kept in check by the great Han dynasty, the Hsiung-nu turned their attention elsewhere and eventually moved westward, with dire consequences for those in their way. As attractive as this last view is, it has met with increasing skepticism. It is likely that the Hunnish nation, like that of the other barbarian peoples, was not ethnically homogenous but made up of a number of peoples. At the very least, it is clear the Huns were a nomadic steppe people of Eurasia, who absorbed Alans, Goths, and other peoples as they swept into the Roman Empire.

The ancient sources also reveal certain physical and sociocultural characteristics of the Huns. According to the historian of the Goths, Jordanes notes that the Huns prepared their meat by placing it between the horse and saddle and "cooking" it as they rode. Moreover, up until the time of Attila, and to a lesser degree his predecessor Ruga, the Huns lacked a central ruling authority. As a nomadic people shepherding their flock from pasture to pasture, they were migratory and organized under tribal chieftains who were hierarchically ranked. The Huns themselves were organized by families and larger clan units, with families living together in one tent, six to ten tents forming a camp, and several camps forming a clan. Kinship, rather than kingship, was the most important institution among the Huns until the time of Attila, and even then it remained an important institution. Indeed, even Attila, the greatest ruler of the Huns was not recognized as a sacred king. The Huns were skilled horsemen and equally skilled in the use of the composite bow, a bow made of different materials that were glued together and reinforced by strips of sinew. The ancient sources also reveal the funeral rites, at least for exalted figures like Attila. His body was borne into an open field, where it was laid to rest in a tent of the finest Chinese silk. A ceremony called the *strava* then took place around the body, during which the Huns rode around the tent, chanting a dirge, tearing out their hair, and gashing their faces. He was then buried in a three-layer coffin of gold, silver, and iron and and much wealth was placed in the grave with him. The slaves who prepared Attila's tomb were killed so that its whereabouts would remain unknown.

The Huns, whatever their exact origins, first arrived in Europe in 375 and helped initiate the so-called migration of peoples. It should be noted, however, that although the arrival of the Huns and their allies among the Gepids, Rugians, and others caused great turmoil and forced the movement of the Goths, a generation passed before the Huns were politically mature enough to exploit the situation in the empire and along its frontiers. Nonetheless, the arrival of these terrifying warriors on horseback did destabilize the balance along Rome's frontier.

The Huns' advance included the conquest of the Alans along the Don River—and the Huns were ruthless overlords who kept their subject peoples from seceding—which brought them and their allies from among the subject Alans into contact with the Ostrogothic kingdom of Ermanaric. The exact size of the army of the Huns remains in doubt, but it is likely that they fought a series of successful battles against Ermanaric. The Gothic king then took his own life, a sacrifice to the gods for the safety of his people that proved ineffective. The failure of Ermanaric and his successor led to the absorption of much of Ermanaric's nation by the Huns. Some Goths, however, escaped subjugation by seeking the protection of the emperor, Valens, and requesting admission to the empire as *foederati* (federated allies). This was perhaps the most serious consequence of the Huns' first contact with the Germanic peoples living along Rome's frontier. The settlement of the Goths in the empire had disastrous consequences; in 376 the Goths fought a major battle at Hadrianople that resulted in the death of the emperor and the weakening of the empire.

A generation passed, however, before the Huns themselves raised the banner of war and conquest again. In the last decade of the fourth century, Hunnish raiders once again began striking at the frontiers of the empire and at the Germans living on either side of that frontier. During the winter of 394–395, the Huns simultaneously attacked the Balkan provinces of the empire and, moving across the Caucasus, Asia Minor. The advance was stopped by a Visigothic count, Tribigild, whose success inspired his demands for reward from the imperial government. When

the emperor refused, Tribigild rebelled, in 399, and another Visigoth in the service of the empire, Gainas, was sent to put down the rebellion. Gainas quickly rallied the large number of Visigoths in the Roman army to his side, and then he too rebelled. His campaign was much more serious than that of Tribigild; he aimed to establish himself as the power behind the throne in Constantinople. Gainas met success early and even occupied the city of Constantinople for a time. He was, however, expelled from the capital, and as many as 7,000 of his followers were massacred during the withdrawal. But Gainas, remaining undaunted, attempted to establish a kingdom north of the Danube and sacrificed the Roman soldiers in his control to the god of the Danube to ensure success. At this point the Huns, led by the first known Hunnish king, Uldin, met the Visigoth and his army. The two armies fought several battles. Uldin ultimately triumphed; Gainas died in battle on December 23, 400, and the Hunnish king sent his rival's head to Constantinople. The imperial government lavished gifts on Uldin and established a treaty with him.

The treaty proved a great benefit to the empire when a wave of Goths and other peoples spread into the empire in 405, possibly the result of increasing pressure from the Huns themselves. Uldin, however, honored the treaty with Rome when the Gothic leader Radagaisus invaded the empire. Although it was the Roman military commander Stilicho who defeated Radagaisus, he was able to secure his victory because of the support of Uldin's Huns. Although he was only one of several Hunnish rulers at the time, Uldin's association with Rome set the stage for Roman-Hunnish relations for much of the next generation. Roman military commanders, such as Stilicho and Aëtius, employed Hunnish soldiers, and made alliances toward that end with other Hunnish kings, such as Charaton. The Huns aided Roman generals against invading barbarians and against internal rebels during this period, and also solidified their position along the Roman frontier, possibly in the Carpathian mountain region.

During the opening decades of the fifth century, the Huns underwent a process of transformation. As they moved into the Carpathians and also across Illyria, the Huns shed some of their earlier social and political structures. They became less pastoral and migratory and more dependent upon the agricultural produce of their subject peoples. They also undertook raids to acquire the livestock they no longer husbanded themselves. With settlement came changes in their political organization, as the old tribal structure of hierarchically ranked chieftains was gradually replaced by a smaller number of kings and, eventually, a sole king who ruled the Hunnish peoples and their subject folk.

In the 420s Attila's uncles Octar and Ruga ruled the Huns as kings and shaped them into a more unified people. Ruga, the senior partner, was particularly important to the formation of the Huns and helped establish the foundation for his nephew's success. As king, Ruga oversaw important changes in the relationship of the Huns and the Roman Empire. In 433, the leading general of the West, Aëtius, feared for his position and life and turned to the Huns for assistance. He negotiated a treaty with Ruga and returned to the Western Empire with strong Hunnish military support that enabled him to reestablish his power and, in fact, increase his authority. The relationship with Aëtius was surely an aid to Ruga and his Huns, who also were involved with the Eastern Empire. Ruga staged raids on the Eastern Empire and threatened the capital of Constantinople. He was the first leader of the Huns to extract tribute from the Eastern Empire, imposing a treaty on Constantinople involving annual payments of 350 pounds of gold. Although this was not a significant amount, it did suggest a changing balance of power and the increasing self-confidence of the Huns and their king. Ruga also demanded the return of Hunnish soldiers who had deserted to imperial armies, and failure to return them, Ruga declared, would

be a violation of the treaty between the empire and the Huns.

Ruga's death occurred before he could resolve the disagreement over the return of Hunnish soldiers, which would be addressed by his successors, his nephews Attila and Bleda. The Huns continued to enjoy success against the empire under Attila and Bleda. In 435, they negotiated a new treaty with Rome that doubled the annual tribute and required the return or ransom of Hunnish deserters. In the early and mid-440s, Hunnish power continued to expand at Rome's expense. The violation of the treaty Attila had signed led to an invasion of the empire that involved the razing of a number of cities by the Huns, who also threatened the city of Constantinople. Attila's invasion led to another treaty with the empire that increased the annual tribute to 2,100 pounds of gold and a one-time payment of 6,000 pounds of gold. At this point, fortunes turned for the Huns, who no longer appeared so fearsome to their enemies. Bleda was blamed for this and was assassinated by his brother, who now became the sole ruler of the Huns.

Attila quickly resumed hostilities against the empire, ravaging the Balkans, and reestablishing his position. In 450 he turned his attention to the Western Empire, perhaps because of a marriage proposal from the emperor's sister, Honoria. He invaded with a huge force, numbering between 300,000 and 700,000 soldiers according to contemporary sources, made up of Huns and various subject peoples and allies. Despite a sizeable force, Attila met several setbacks at the hands of Aëtius and his equally mixed army of Romans and Germans, setbacks that included the failure to take the critical city of Orleans. Aëtius and Attila fought a terrible and bloody battle on the Catalaunian Plains. At one point things were going so badly for the Huns that Attila prepared to commit suicide. But the Huns rallied and left the battlefield in orderly fashion, and they were not pursued by the Roman armies—wounded, the Huns would have fought on ferociously, and Aëtius needed the

Huns too much to destroy them. Attila pressed on and invaded Italy in 452 for a second time. The invasion began more favorably for the Huns, until they met Pope Leo the Great, who persuaded Attila to withdraw, which he did. According to sacred tradition, Saints Peter and Paul and a host of angels and saints supported Leo and forced Attila's departure. Another explanation for Attila's withdrawal is that his army was being decimated by plague. Attila refused to relent and planned a great invasion of the Eastern Empire in 453, but his death on his wedding night put an end to those plans.

With the death of Attila, the Roman Empire breathed more easily. Although he never threatened the empire's existence, Attila posed a great challenge that did serious damage to the empire and its allies. Unfortunately for the Huns, but fortunately for everyone else, Attila had no successor that was his equal. His numerous sons failed to provide a united front and were unable to overcome the challenge raised by the various subject peoples, particularly the Gepids. In 454 the Huns and their allies were decisively defeated by an ethnically diverse army, similar to those that had fought for and against Attila, at the Battle of Nedao. Attila's oldest son, Ellac, died at Nedao, but other sons continued the struggle and were defeated and killed by 469. The empire of the Huns collapsed, and rival Germanic peoples carved out new kingdoms in its place. The Western Roman Empire, too, did not long survive the death of Attila and the collapse of his empire. Within a generation of his death and the disappearance of his empire, various Germanic peoples had moved into the Western Empire and brought about its fall.

See also Aëtius; Alans; Ammianus Marcellinus; Attila the Hun; Hadrianople, Battle of; Jordanes; Ostrogoths; Visigoths

Bibliography

Bury, John B. *History of the Later Roman Empire: From the Death of Theodosius I to the Death of Justinian.* Vol. 1. 1923. Reprint, New York: Dover, 1959.

Heather, Peter. "Goths and Huns, c. 320–425." In *The Late Empire, A.D. 337–425,* vol. 13, The Cambridge Ancient History, ed. Averil Cameron and Peter Garnsey. Cambridge: Cambridge University Press, 1998, pp. 487–537.

Lot, Ferdinand. *The End of the Ancient World and the Beginnings of the Middle Ages.* Trans. Philip and Mariette Leon. New York: Harper Torchbooks, 1961.

Reynolds, Susan. "Our Forefathers? Tribes, Peoples, and Nations in the Historiography of the Age of Migrations." In *After Rome's Fall: Narrators and Sources of Early Medieval History,* ed. Alexander Callander Murray. Toronto: University of Toronto Press, 1999, pp. 17–36.

Thompson, Edward A. *A History of Attila and the Huns.* Oxford: Clarendon, 1948.

———. *The Huns.* Oxford: Blackwell, 1995.

Wolfram, Herwig. *The Roman Empire and Its Germanic Peoples.* Trans. Thomas J. Dunlap. Berkeley: University of California Press, 1997.

I

Irene (c. 752–802)

Empress, imperial regent, and even emperor herself (r. 797–802), Irene was an important and powerful figure at the Byzantine court in the late eighth and early ninth century. Irene was able to exercise great influence, in part because of the premature death of her husband, Leo IV (r. 775–780), but also because of her own talents and ambition. Like all emperors, Irene was active in religious, political, and military policy. She was in diplomatic contact with the great Carolingian ruler Charlemagne and even attempted to arrange a marriage alliance with the Carolingian. Her involvement in religious policy seriously strained relations with the church of Charlemagne. Her political ambitions also had serious repercussions in the Frankish world, particularly when she usurped the imperial throne from her son and gave Charlemagne's advisors a further justification for encouraging Charlemagne to take the imperial title.

At the death of the iconoclastic emperor, Constantine V in 775, Leo IV succeeded to throne with his wife, Irene. With the early and unexpected death of Leo, Irene was thrust into great prominence in the Byzantine Empire as the regent for her young son Constantine VI (r. 780–797). Throughout the 780s, Irene was the guiding force in the empire and introduced important new policies that were often contrary to those of her predecessors, the most dramatic of which was overturning the policy of iconoclasm. Unlike Leo III, Constantine IV, and, to a lesser degree, Leo IV, Irene favored the veneration of icons as an integral part of religious life and practice in the Byzantine Church. Consequently in 787, with her son, Irene presided over the Second Council of Nicaea. This council officially reversed the iconoclastic policies of the previous three generations and restored icons to a respected place in the church. The council was ecumenical—its decisions were binding on all Christians—and was attended by a large number of bishops, monks, and priests from the Byzantine Empire. It also boasted two representatives of the pope, Hadrian I (772–795), whose presence confirmed the universal nature of the council. The pope's legates returned to Italy with the decisions of the council, which were to be accepted by the churches under Hadrian's authority. Indeed, the Council of Nicaea achieved two goals that undermined recent imperial policy: the abolition of iconoclasm and improvement in relations with the west.

Irene's good relations with the pope established at the council were part of a broader effort on her part to improve relations with the leaders of western Europe. Her efforts to improve relations with western leaders, however, achieved only partial success, and the council at Nicaea was both a high point and a low point in her efforts to secure better relations with western leaders. Although she gained the good graces of the pope, Irene lost the good relations she had secured earlier in the decade with the most important leader in western Europe, Charlemagne. At the outset of her regency, in 781, Irene sought to arrange a marriage alliance with the great Carolingian ruler. Charlemagne was clearly pleased by the proposed marriage between his daughter, Rotrude (d. 839), and Irene's son and the future emperor, Constantine. The children were quite young at the time, ages six or seven and eleven respectively, but this would have been a marriage alliance of great importance, at least to the Carolingian ruler, who saw the prestige of the association with the imperial throne in Constantinople. The marriage, however, never came to be, and relations between Charlemagne and Irene worsened before the end of the 780s.

Irene's support of the Lombard duke Arichis, whom she promised to grant the rank of patrician in return for his obedience, surely angered the great Carolingian, who sought to establish his authority over much of Italy. Even more serious damage was done to Carolingian-Byzantine relations by the council in 787. Although representatives of the pope were invited, no representatives of the Carolingian church, the largest church in western Europe, were invited. This slight enraged the great king and gravely harmed relations between Charlemagne and Irene. Indeed, in response to the council, Charlemagne commissioned an answer to the perceived errors of Irene's council. The Caroline Books (*Libri Carolini*) were written by Theodulf of Orléans, with some possible aid from Alcuin, to denounce the veneration of icons promoted by Irene. Based on faulty translations of the acts of the council, the Caroline Books were a bitter denunciation of Irene's policy as heresy and a statement of the orthodoxy of the Carolingian church.

Although Irene's relationship with the greatest power of western Europe was seriously damaged by the late 780s, she spent most of the decade strengthening the empire. She had success quieting the unrest brought on by Leo the Isaurian's religious policy, as well as some success defending the frontiers of the empire. In 790, however, she faced a serious internal rival—her own son. In that year, Constantine, in full manhood by now and recently married to a Byzantine noble's daughter, sought to end his mother's excessive influence and assert his own authority. Irene was sent into internal exile from 790 to 797, and Constantine ruled as sole emperor. His reign was not the most successful, however; he faced military setbacks against Arab and Bulgarian armies on the empire's eastern and northern frontiers. He also divorced his wife to marry a woman at court, which caused great scandal in Byzantine society. His military failures and personal scandals undermined confidence in him and allowed for the return of his mother. On August 15, 797, she launched a successful coup, and she had Constantine arrested and blinded in the very room of his birth. Even though he probably survived the blinding, he was now rendered unfit to rule, and Irene ruled as emperor until 802, when she was overthrown.

Although she did not rule as emperor for long, her usurpation was not without significant consequence, at least in western Europe. Indeed, her impact in the Byzantine Empire during her sole reign was not great, but her usurpation had important repercussions for Charlemagne and his court scholars. Already in the 790s Charlemagne's advisors had spoken of him in imperial terms, noting that he was a great conqueror who ruled over much of the old Western Roman Empire. Many of Charlemagne's advisors denounced Irene's actions, declaring that a woman could not rightfully hold the office of emperor. In a famous letter in 799, Alcuin noted that "the governor of that empire has been deposed by his own circle and citizens." For Alcuin, therefore, as for others around Charlemagne, the imperial throne was vacant because a woman claimed to hold it. Irene's deposition of her son and usurpation of the throne was used as a further justification for Charlemagne himself to claim the title of emperor. And, although the exact meaning for all involved remain unclear, Charlemagne was crowned emperor of the Romans by Pope Leo III on December 25, 800. Irene's ambition and failure in relations with western Europe played some role in that great event.

See also Alcuin of York; Carolingian Dynasty; Charlemagne; Hadrian I, Pope; Leo III, the Isaurian; Leo III, Pope; Theodulf of Orléans

Bibliography

Davis, Raymond, trans. *The Lives of the Eighth-Century Popes* (Liber Pontificalis): *The Ancient Biographies of Nine Popes from* A.D. *715 to* A.D. *817*. Liverpool, UK: Liverpool University Press, 1992.

Herrin, Judith. *The Formation of Christendom.* Princeton: Princeton University Press, 1989.

McKitterick, Rosamond. *The Frankish Kingdoms under the Carolingians.* Longman: London, 1983.

Obolensky, Dmitri. *The Byzantine Commonwealth: Eastern Europe, 500–1543.* New York: Praeger, 1971.

Riché, Pierre. *The Carolingians: A Family Who Forged Europe.* Trans. Michael Idomir Allen. Philadelphia: University of Pennsylvania Press, 1993.

Sullivan, Richard. *Heirs of the Roman Empire.* Ithaca, NY: Cornell University Press, 1974.

Isidore of Seville (c. 560–636)

Spanish bishop and author of numerous works, Isidore was one of the greatest scholars of the early Middle Ages; his work was influential and popular, both in Spain and the rest of Europe. Only the work of Augustine of Hippo, among authors before 800, was copied more often than the work of Isidore. His most important work, the *Etymologies,* was an encyclopedia of all knowledge at the time and was an important reference work for scholars for generations to come. He also wrote works of history and biography as well as a commentary on the Bible and works on Christian doctrine. His work of history was highly nationalistic and portrayed the Visigothic kingdom of Spain in most glorious light as a great Christian kingdom and as the rival and worthy successor of the Roman Empire.

Little is known of his life outside of his great literary output. He was probably born at Carthagena, which was in Byzantine hands at the time, before his family moved to Seville. His older brother, who was a great influence on him, St. Leander (d. 599 or 600), was an active figure in Visigothic religion and politics. Leander influenced the conversion of Hermenegild, a Visigothic prince who led an unsuccessful revolt against his father, and then Reccared I from Arian Christianity to Catholic Christianity. Leander was also bishop of Seville and an advocate of the monastic life. Considering Leander's support for monasticism, it is possible that Isidore himself was a monk. Although Isidore himself did write a rule for monastic life, it is uncertain whether he was a monk. He was most likely put on the path of the religious life while he was young, whether or not he became a monk. He probably was made a deacon and priest as soon as legally possible and eventually succeeded his brother as bishop of Seville at Leander's death in 599 or 600.

As bishop, Isidore was elevated to the national stage and most likely influenced affairs in the Visigothic kingdom, even if this influence was not as great as that of his brother. Although he performed the normal daily duties as bishop, he also corresponded with the Visigothic kings and seems to have been quite close to King Sisebut (612–621), who was an active supporter of intellectual and cultural life in Spain. In his correspondence with kings, bishops, and other clergy, Isidore cultivated a new model of kingship, promoted the concept of the Visigothic kingdom as the ideal Christian state, denigrated the Byzantine Empire, and denounced the Visigothic kings' attempts to convert the Jews of Spain to Christianity. He also presided over two important church councils in Seville in 619 and at the Fourth Council of Toledo in 633. The council at Toledo especially was of great significance and reinforced the values of Isidore by defining the proper behavior of the clergy, the proper teachings of the Catholic faith, and the ideals concerning the Visigothic kings and kingdom.

Although most likely an important figure in Spain, Isidore is best known for his literary works. His most important and influential work was the *Etymologies* (*Etymologiarum sive originum libri XX*), which is extant in over 1,000 manuscripts and was probably found in most monastic libraries in the Middle Ages. Unfinished at his death and completed by one of his disciples, the *Etymologies* was a compendium of all knowledge of the ancient world. Isidore drew from Augustine of Hippo, Jerome, Cassiodorus, Pope Gregory the Great, and Virgil, among other classical and Christian authors, in the preparation of his great encyclopedia. His approach was linguistic, and he opened each entry with the derivation of the word being treated. These derivations were often quite fanciful, so much so that these explanations have often prevented recognition of the value of the material included. The *Etymologies* covered a wide range of topics, including the seven liberal arts (grammar, rhetoric, dialectic, arithmetic, geometry, music, and astronomy), medicine, law, books of the Bible, angels, saints, men, animals, fabulous monsters, the universe, agriculture, war, ships, dress, food, drink, and furniture. The *Etymologies* thus treated all branches of knowledge, and it was intended as a tool for scholars to use; the rise of scholarship in Spain following Isidore's death suggests that it was successful in that regard.

Isidore wrote a number of other secular works. He wrote a second learned treatise, *De natura rerum* (On the Nature of Things), which was widely popular; it discusses the sun, moon, and planets, as well as earthly natural phenomena, including the Nile River, earthquakes, and the sea. Its purpose was to provide an explanation of nature to rival that offered by popular astrology. He also wrote several works of history, including a world history *(Chronica mundi),* a biographical guide of illustrious people *(De viris illustribus),* and the very important *History of the Goths, Vandals, and Suevi.* His works of history are for us important sources for the understanding of the history of the Visigoths; for his own time, they were also a means to glorify the Visigoths. In his *History of the Goths,* he praises the Goths of Spain, and portrays the Gothic kingdom as the true successor of the Roman Empire, which is now subject to the Goths. He also criticizes the Byzantine Empire and declared its greatest emperor, Justinian, a heretic. Like his other works, all Isidore's historical writings were very popular in Spain, and the *Chronica* and *De viris* were found in libraries throughout Europe.

Along with his numerous secular works of literature, Isidore wrote a number of religious works. His work borrows from many important church fathers, most important among whom for Isidore were Augustine and Gregory the Great. He wrote a rule for monastic life that borrowed from Augustine and Gregory and, probably, from St. Benedict of Nursia. A practical guide, the Rule of Isidore, among other things, encouraged the monks to read Christian works and to take books out of the library, read them, and return them each day. He also wrote the *Sententiae,* a moral and pastoral guide for clergy that was very influential, exists in hundreds of manuscripts, and provided a source book for many later collections of church law. He was the author of a commentary on the books of the Hebrew Scriptures, as well as a polemical treatise against the Jews (*De fide catholica contra fide Iudaeos*). This treatise, which was influenced by Augustine, reveals one of the darker aspects of medieval Christian civilization. The work is hostile to the Jews and encourages the conversion of Jews to Christianity as a means to bring about the final age of humankind. Conversion of the Jews would also contribute to the complete integration of Visigothic Spain and enable it to reach its most glorious potential. Despite his hostility to the Jews, Isidore's legacy includes an important body of written work that had a generally positive influence on the development of culture and society.

See also Arianism; Augustine of Hippo, St.; Gregory the Great; Hermenegild; Justinian; Reccared I; Visigoths

Bibliography

Cohen, Jeremy. *Living Letters of the Law: Ideas of the Jew in Medieval Christianity.* Berkeley: University of California Press, 1999.

Curtius, Ernst Robert. *European Literature and the Latin Middle Ages.* Trans. Willard R. Trask. 1953. Reprint, with a new epilogue by Peter Goodman, Princeton: Princeton University Press, 1990.

Herrin, Judith. *The Formation of Christendom.* Princeton: Princeton University Press, 1987.

Isidore of Seville. *History of the Goths, Vandals, and Suevi.* 2d rev. ed. Trans. Guido Donini and Gordon B. Ford. Leiden: Brill, 1970.

King, P. D. *Law and Society in the Visigothic Kingdom.* Cambridge: Cambridge University Press, 1972.

Laistner, Max L. W. *Thought and Letters in Western Europe, A.D. 500 to 900.* 2d ed. Ithaca, NY: Cornell University Press, 1976.

Riché, Pierre. *Education and Culture in the Barbarian West: From the Sixth through the Eighth Century.* Trans. John Contreni. Columbia: University of South Carolina Press, 1976.

Thompson, E. A. *The Goths in Spain.* Oxford: Clarendon, 1969.

Wolfram, Herwig. *History of the Goths.* Trans. Thomas J. Dunlap. Berkeley: University of California Press, 1988.

Ivories

Ivory was a popular and important medium in early medieval art; carved ivories served a variety of artistic purposes. Ivory was frequently used for liturgical objects and also for book covers and reliquaries. Ivory was also used for more secular objects, including small boxes and combs. Early medieval artists borrowed from classical models for their works and often created beautiful and high-quality pieces. The material for the ivories varied between England and the Continent. Continental artisans had access, even though restricted and limited in quantity, to elephant ivory from Africa, although they also used animal bones and teeth and whalebone. Anglo-Saxon artisans, however, had no access to elephant ivory, and their "ivories" are often made of whalebone or walrus tusk.

Ivory was a popular material for artists in the Roman Empire, and elephant ivory could be obtained by artists with little difficulty. But after the fall of the empire in the west, this commodity became harder to come by until the ninth century, when the Carolingians expanded trade. Despite the scarcity of ivory, even under the Carolingians, the art form continued to be popular, and imperial models continued to influence artists. Ivories continued to appear throughout the post-Roman world and are found among the treasures of the Merovingians. Ivory carving was frequently used to produce religious items, and ivory carvers employed simple tools similar to those of the woodworker. The ivories were often polished or painted and were often placed with metalwork and jewels in the finished product.

Under the Carolingians ivory carving flourished again and reflected the Carolingian interest in Roman imperial models. Carolingian ivory workers created small boxes and combs, but more frequently produced book covers, which borrowed from classical models or were patterned after contemporary manuscript illuminations. They were often used to adorn psalters, the Gospels, and other books of Scripture and therefore often depict scenes from the life of Christ, including his birth, Crucifixion, and Resurrection. One example from Metz that was commissioned by the bishop Drogo (d. 855), Charlemagne's son, depicts the Temptation of Christ along with a number of episcopal rites. The

Tenth-century ivory and metal book cover depicting Christ as Pantocrater (Elio Ciol/Corbis)

borders of the ivory covers are sometimes decorated with a geometric design or leaf pattern.

Anglo-Saxon artists, although forced to find an alternate source of "ivory," produced high quality works made of whalebone and, particularly from the tenth century, morse teeth (walrus tusk). Some early examples of whalebone ivory carving include a writing tablet that was decorated with carved interlace design and carved panels of winged beasts, and eighth-century Northumbrian crosses, which have similar carved animals. There are also examples of small boxes or caskets of carved whalebone, but, as with all whalebone items, there are not very many of these items because of the limited durability of the whalebone. There are more numerous examples of Anglo-Saxon carvings in morse. Like the Carolingian artists, Anglo-Saxon ivory carvers often created book covers that included designs from the life of Jesus or other religious images.

See also Anglo-Saxons; Barbarian Art; Charlemagne; Carolingian Dynasty; Carolingian Renaissance; Merovingian Dynasty

Bibliography
Beckwith, John. *Ivory Carvings in Early Medieval England.* London: Harvey Miller, 1972.

Hubert, Jean, Jean Porcher, and Wolfgang Fritz Volbach. *The Carolingian Renaissance.* New York: George Braziller, 1970.

Lasko, Peter. *The Kingdom of the Franks: North-West Europe before Charlemagne.* New York: McGraw Hill, 1971.

———. *Ars Sacra, 800–1200.* 2d ed. New Haven, CT: Yale University Press, 1994.

Neese, Lawrence. *Justinian to Charlemagne: European Art, 565–787: An Annotated Bibliography.* Boston: Hall, 1987.

Randall, Richard H., Jr. *Masterpieces of Ivory from the Walters Art Gallery.* New York: Hudson Hills, 1985.

J

Jarrow

See Benedict Biscop

Jewelry and Gems

In the early Middle Ages the various barbarian peoples that settled in the remnants of the Western Roman Empire left an important artistic legacy in the metalwork they created. Sophisticated and attractive works in gold and silver were created for both secular and religious purposes. Originally employed for personal adornment, the techniques for creating jewelry and metalwork were later employed to create sacred and liturgical objects. These creations were so highly valued that the fine for the murder of a metalworker was three times that of a peasant and twice that of a blacksmith. The discovery of numerous artifacts at archeological sites like Tournai demonstrates the creativity and talent of these early medieval artisans and the quality of their creations.

As the various Germanic tribes made contact with the Roman Empire, they brought their own traditions with them, which merged with those of the empire. During the migration period, the barbarian peoples were already forging jewelry and other metalwork. The practice of jewelry-making predates contact between Romans and barbarians, but came to be influenced by contacts with the empire. The Visigoths and Lombards especially were influenced by imperial models of jewelry. Close contact with the empire shaped metalworking patterns, and Visigoths and Lombards imitated Byzantine models and received gifts of jewelry and metalwork from Constantinople. A third people, the Franks, particularly under the Merovingian dynasty, showed less influence from Rome and a greater reflection of traditional Germanic models.

Early medieval artisans crafted a variety of types of jewelry and metalwork for their noble patrons. There was a wide range of jewelry made of silver and gold and encrusted with precious gems that was worn by the barbarian peoples of early medieval Europe. Rings and earrings were commonly worn, as were buckles, pins, necklaces, bracelets, arm bands, and brooches. The jewelry of gold and silver was often decorated with amethyst, pearls, emeralds, garnets, and other precious stones. Cameos were also popular among the barbarian peoples. One of the most popular pieces of jewelry was the fibula, a type of brooch used to hold a cloak or other article of clothing together. The fibula came in a variety of styles, including the gold disk fibula developed by the Merovingians in the seventh century, which remained an essential part of

Square-headed brooch, from Darenth Park, Dartford, Kent, early Anglo-Saxon, early sixth century (British Museum)

clothing until the thirteenth century. Fibulae in the shape of birds or eagles, often worn in pairs, constituted another popular design. The various techniques used to create personal jewelry were employed for religious purposes as well, in the creation of chalices, reliquaries, crosses, and related items. The skills used to design gold and gem jewelry were also applied to the creation of book covers for the important manuscripts in monastic or royal libraries.

The jewelry and other metal items used for personal adornment or for religious purposes were created by highly skilled artisans. The designs of the jewelry fell into one of several categories. The patterns of some pieces were simply abstract and geometric in design. Other pieces used an animal pattern in the decoration of the metalwork and jewelry. The animal style is generally classified as Style I or Style II. Style I placed animal parts and compact animals in an abstract or deco-

rative pattern in the metalwork; it is recognized as a northern European style that spread into France in the sixth century. Style II, or the ribbon animal style, originated in Lombard Italy and spread northward. It employed animal figures in elongated, intertwined, continuous, and symmetrical patterns. Also popular was the use of cloisonné, the practice of setting garnets or other jewels or glass in gold compartments or bands that were then soldered to a metal base.

Many of these practices and styles continued into the Carolingian period. But as the research of Genevra Kornbluth shows, the Carolingian period was also one of innovation, especially in the handling of gemstones. A number of quality gems were produced by Carolingian artists, demonstrating the great variety in Carolingian art; they were produced as a result of royal and noble patronage. Carolingian artists also introduced a new technique in the production of gems. They did not use the carving tools of the Roman and Byzantine Empires; instead, they used a round drill that was fitted with a rotating ball or wheel. The gems they produced were of high quality and unique in that they were not influenced by Roman imperial precedents.

See also Barbarian Art; Carolingian Dynasty; Clothing; Clovis; Lombards; Merovingian Dynasty; Tournai; Visigoths

Bibliography
Hubert, Jean, Jean Porcher, and Wolfgang Fritz Volbach. *Europe in the Dark Ages.* London: Thames and Hudson, 1969.
Kornbluth, Genevra A. *Engraved Gems of the Carolingian Empire.* University Park: Pennsylvania State University Press, 1995.
Lasko, Peter. *The Kingdom of the Franks: North-West Europe before Charlemagne.* New York: McGraw Hill, 1971.
Neese, Lawrence. *Justinian to Charlemagne: European Art, 565–787: An Annotated Bibliography.* Boston: Hall, 1987.
Ross, Marvin, and Philippe Verdier. *Arts of the Migration Period in the Walters Art Gallery.* Baltimore: Walters Art Gallery, 1961.

John Scottus Erigena (fl. 845–879)

The most original and perhaps greatest of all Carolingian Renaissance scholars, John Scotus Erigena was a highly controversial thinker whose influence lasted long after his death and whose thought aroused opposition into the twelfth century. John Scottus was actively involved in a theological controversy during his stay in the Carolingian Empire, but remained a close friend and advisor of the West Frankish king Charles the Bald. He was also the only Carolingian scholar with more than superficial knowledge of Greek, and this knowledge contributed to his production of a number of highly original works.

Little is known of his life, including the dates of his birth and death, although there is some indication that he was born around 810 and lived into the 870s. It is certain, though, that he was from Ireland, as his name implies,

and left his homeland for the Carolingian realm at some point in the 830s. At some point after his arrival in the Frankish kingdoms, John Scottus came to the attention of the western Carolingian king Charles the Bald. He is mentioned as being at the court of Charles, who came to appreciate the Irishman's genius, in the year 843, but may have been known before that. John was recognized by contemporaries in the Carolingian kingdom as a holy man even though he was never consecrated as a priest or monk. He was also noted for his knowledge of Greek, which he most surely acquired before his arrival in the kingdom of Charles the Bald. His learning attracted the attention, not only of the king, but also the archbishop of Rheims, Hincmar.

It was Hincmar who invited John to participate in the controversy that had recently erupted over the teaching of Gottschalk of Orbais concerning predestination, which had already attracted the attention of Carolingian bishops like Hincmar and Rabanus Maurus. John's response, however, *De divina praedestinatione* (On Divine Predestination) was as controversial as the original teachings of Gottschalk. The Irish scholar rejected Gottschalk's double predestination and argued that souls were predestined to salvation, suggesting that evil, sin, and Hell were not real. His position was judged heretical by his contemporaries and condemned, but John Scottus survived because Charles the Bald remained his loyal supporter. He remained at the royal court until his death and while there wrote a great deal of poetry, in Greek and Latin, that celebrated the victories of the king and honored religious holy days. He also was commissioned by Charles to translate the works of Pseudo-Dionysius the Areopagite, an unknown author who wrote influential works of mystical theology around the year 500, from Greek into Latin; he was working on a commentary on the Gospel of John at the time of his death.

The most important and influential of John Scottus's works was the *Periphyseon,* or *De divisione naturae* (On the Division of Nature).

Drawing on his knowledge of the Latin and Greek fathers of the church and Christian Neoplatonic thought, John Scottus created a highly sophisticated theology, which developed some of the ideas of his earlier works. In his discussion of the nature of God and his creation, John divided and classified all of creation but argued that God was incomprehensible and could not be put into any category. His work posed a serious challenge to his contemporaries, who had difficulty understanding it and thought it heretical. But the work survives in numerous manuscripts, attesting to its popularity, and exercised great influence on theologians in the tenth century and beyond.

See also Carolingian Renaissance; Charles the Bald; Gottschalk of Orbais; Hincmar of Rheims

Bibliography

Laistner, Max L. W. *Thought and Letters in Western Europe, A.D. 500 to 900.* 2d ed. Ithaca, NY: Cornell University Press, 1976.

Marenbon, John. "Carolingian Thought." In *Carolingian Culture: Emulation and Innovation,* edited by Rosamond McKitterick. Cambridge: Cambridge University Press, 1994, pp. 171–192.

Nelson, Janet. *Charles the Bald.* London: Longman, 1992.

Van Riel, Gerd, Carlos Steel, and James McEvoy, eds. *Iohannes Scottus Eriugena: The Bible and Hermeneutics.* Leuven: Leuven University Press, 1996.

Jordanes (sixth century)

Historian of the Goths, Jordanes has left the primary record for the early history of the Gothic people. Although probably less reliable and less complete than the now lost history of the Goths by Cassiodorus, Jordanes's history, *De origine actibusque Getarum* (On the Origins and Deeds of the Getae), is the earliest narrative source for the history of the Goths. Like the history of the later polymath, Isidore of Seville, Jordanes's work was intended to glorify the Goths and justify their authority over the Romans.

Little is precisely known of the life of Jordanes, including the exact dates of his birth and death. His movements remain uncertain, but a few matters about his life can be pieced together from his surviving writings. He identifies himself as being of Gothic descent, and in the early sixth century he served as a notary to the Ostrogothic king of Italy, Theodoric the Great, who became one of the great heroes of his history. An Arian Christian, as most Goths were, Jordanes converted to Catholic Christianity at some point in his life, and some scholars have identified him with a contemporary bishop of the same name. This identification, as with most things, remains uncertain. It is generally held that he wrote his history in Constantinople around 550, but he may also have lived in one of the empire's provinces along the Danube River.

His most important work, commonly known as the *Getica,* has long shaped our understanding of the origins of the Goths. The *Getica* itself chronicles the history of the Goths from the origins of the people until Jordanes's day. It is a distillation of the much larger history of the Goths by Cassiodorus, but Jordanes also drew upon oral traditions, thus involving the Goths in the composition of his history. The work is divided into four main sections: a geographical introduction, the history of the united Goths, the Ostrogoths, and the Visigoths and separate histories of the united Goths, etc. The work covers the reign of Theodoric the Great and other matters treated by contemporary Latin and Greek sources, but it alone treats the earliest history of the Goths. Indeed, it is this material that is the most important and controversial.

The model of Gothic history established by Jordanes that has long been a point of debate among historians. According to Jordanes, the Goths originated in Scandinavia and then moved south and east, where they eventually divided into two main groups, Ostrogoths and Visigoths. Since much of this material has been proved wrong yet some supported by archeological research, most scholars treat it cautiously, neither completely rejecting it nor accepting it without reservation. The *Getica* also contains information on the movements of other barbarian peoples, including the Huns and Vandals. It describes the great Battle of the Catalaunian Plains and the funeral of Attila the Hun.

Jordanes wrote a second work on the history of the Roman people, commonly known as the *Romana*. This too was a compilation based on another lost history and was probably written in Constantinople at around the same time as the *Getica*. It surveys the history of Rome from its legendary founding by Romulus to the age of the emperor Justinian. It is generally a less valuable and less interesting survey.

See also Arianism; Attila the Hun; Cassiodorus; Catalaunian Plains, Battle of the; Huns; Justinian; Ostrogoths; Theodoric the Great; Vandals; Visigoths

Bibliography

Goffart, Walter A. *The Narrators of Barbarian History (A.D. 500–800): Jordanes, Gregory of Tours, and Paul the Deacon.* Princeton: Princeton University Press, 1988.

Jordanes. *The Gothic History of Jordanes in English Version.* Trans. Charles C. Mierow. New York: Barnes and Noble, 1985.

Laistner, Max L. W. *Thought and Letters in Western Europe, A.D. 500 to 900.* 2d ed. Ithaca, NY: Cornell University Press, 1976.

Riché, Pierre. *Education and Culture in the Barbarian West: From the Sixth through the Eighth Century.* Trans. John Contreni. Columbia: University of South Carolina Press, 1976.

Wolfram, Herwig. *The Roman Empire and Its Germanic Peoples.* Trans. Thomas J. Dunlap. Berkeley: University of California Press, 1997.

Judith (c. 800–843)

The second wife of Louis the Pious and the mother of Charles the Bald, Judith was an important figure in Carolingian political affairs in the early ninth century. She was her husband's trusted advisor, especially after the death of Benedict of Aniane in 821. The birth of her son Charles and her strenuous efforts on his behalf have traditionally been seen as contributing to the collapse of the Carolingian Empire. At the very least, she was accused a variety of crimes by her husband's enemies and suffered a number of indignities at the hands of her stepsons, especially Lothar. She survived these insults to see her husband and son triumph over their enemies, as well as seeing her son succeed to the throne, along with his half brothers Lothar and Louis the German, after the death of Louis. She also developed a reputation as a patron of letters and learning.

After the death of his first wife in 818, Louis the Pious was encouraged, despite his reputation, to marry again to save himself from the temptations of the flesh. According to the *Royal Frankish Annals,* he married Judith "after looking over many daughters of the nobility"(Scholz 1972, 105). She was a member of a powerful and important noble family, whose alliance seemed likely to benefit Louis, and she was also recognized by contemporaries for her beauty and intelligence. She and Louis were married in February 819, and two years later they had their first child, Gisela. She bore Louis a son on June 13, 823, the future king and emperor, Charles the Bald. At the time Louis had three sons from his first marriage and had also already established a plan of succession in which his oldest son, Lothar, was to share the imperial title with him and succeed as sole emperor on his father's death. Louis's two other sons shared in the inheritance as subordinate kings of parts of the Carolingian Empire. The birth of Charles and the need to find a place in the succession for him eventually led to some difficulty.

From the time of her son's birth until 829, Judith worked to find a share in the succession plan for Charles. At first Louis found help from Lothar, who agreed to protect his young stepbrother. But this situation did not last, and Judith herself found little comfort in the promises of Lothar. According to Nithard,

Lothar consistently sought to undermine the agreement with his father. Judith and Louis were not unaware of this and found an able ally in Louis's trusted supporter Bernard of Septimania, an association that later came back to haunt Judith. Bernard proved a capable ally for both Louis and Judith, and he helped stabilize the southeastern frontier of the empire. Louis felt secure enough with the support of Bernard and Judith to alter the plan of succession in 829 to include Charles.

The change in the succession proved almost fatal for Judith and Louis; Louis faced two major revolts in the 830s that nearly ended his reign. His older sons, led by Lothar, rebelled against Louis in 830 and 833–834. In reaction to the changed settlement of 829, and with the support of the so-called imperial party of bishops, the older sons of Louis revolted against their father, with Lothar eventually taking charge. Numerous allegations were made against Judith, including sorcery and adultery with Bernard of Septimania, who was himself married to Dhuoda, a noblewoman and the author of a famous manual on the duties of a prince addressed to her son. Judith was forced to take the veil, and Louis and Charles were held by Lothar. But Louis quickly recovered, and the rebellion was put down. Judith was recalled from the convent and swore a solemn oath of purgation, thereby establishing her innocence before a great council of the nobles and bishops of the realm. Judith and her husband, however, had not seen the last of their troubles; a second and more serious revolt broke out in 833. Once again, Louis's older sons revolted, in part because of the new division of the empire forged after the first revolt. Judith again was dispatched to a convent, and Louis was forced to resign his office. Again, Louis was able to restore himself to power, and again Judith was called to his side and restored in a great ceremony.

For most of the remaining decade of her life, Judith witnessed the triumph of her husband and son, bittersweet as those victories may have been for her. She ruled with Louis until his death in 840. In 837 she persuaded Louis to restructure the succession to power in order that Charles might receive an inheritance, and Louis granted his son a kingdom that included much of modern France. She also helped restore good relations between Lothar and his father and stepbrother. In 839, Lothar returned from Italy, was brought back into the good graces of his father, and granted a sizeable portion of the empire as his legacy. Lothar also agreed to aid and support his godson Charles, who promised aid and support in return. Not only did Judith consolidate her position and that of her son, she also, according to some accounts, exacted vengeance on her enemies. Despite these successes, Judith also witnessed the outbreak of civil war after her husband's death. Although she helped her son secure his position in his part of the empire and witnessed the marriage of her son, Judith was sent into retirement at Tours by that same son, who also seized her lands from her. She, no doubt, was consoled by her son's successes, and died on April 19, 843, shortly after her "retirement."

Best known for her important role in her husband's reign, Judith was also a patron of the arts and education. She sponsored several works by important Carolingian scholars, including a work of history and biblical commentaries. Among those who received her patronage was Rabanus Maurus, who dedicated biblical commentaries on the books of Judith and Esther to her and praised her learning, wit, and desire to imitate holy women. Walafrid Strabo, who was made tutor for Charles the Bald from 829 to 838 by Judith, described Judith as pious, loving, and clever. She may also have been responsible for the establishment and expansion of her husband's court library.

See also Benedict of Aniane; Carolingian Dynasty; Charles the Bald; Dhuoda; Lothar; Louis the German; Louis the Pious; *Royal Frankish Annals*

Bibliography
Ferrante, Joan M. "Women's Role in Latin Letters from the Fourth to the Early Twelfth Century."

In *The Cultural Patronage of Medieval Women*, ed. June Hall McCash. Athens: University of Georgia Press, 1996, pp. 73–105.

Halphen, Louis. *Charlemagne and the Carolingian Empire.* Trans. Giselle de Nie. Amsterdam: North-Holland, 1977.

McKitterick, Rosamond. *The Frankish Kingdoms under the Carolingians, 751–987.* London: Longman, 1983.

Nelson, Janet. *Charles the Bald.* London: Longman, 1992.

Riché, Pierre. *The Carolingians: A Family Who Forged Europe.* Trans. Michael Idomir Allen. Philadelphia: University of Pennsylvania Press, 1993.

Scholz, Bernhard Walter, trans. *Carolingian Chronicles: Royal Frankish Annals and Nithard's History.* Ann Arbor: University of Michigan Press, 1972.

Ward, Elizabeth. "Caesar's Wife: The Career of the Empress Judith, 819–829." In *Charlemagne's Heir: New Perspectives on the Reign of Louis the Pious,* ed. Peter Godman and Roger Collins. Oxford: Clarendon, 1990, pp. 205–227.

Wemple, Suzanne. *Women in Frankish Society: Marriage and the Cloister, 500 to 900.* Philadelphia: University of Pennsylvania Press, 1981.

Julian the Apostate
See Ammianus Marcellinus

Justinian (c. 482–565)

One of the greatest emperors in Byzantine history, Justinian made profound and lasting imprint on the course of the empire's subsequent development. Famed for his marriage to the actress and courtesan, Theodora, whose reputation has been permanently darkened by the sixth-century Byzantine historian Procopius, Justinian influenced much of Byzantine law, religion, and art and architecture. His codification of the law, involvement in religious disputes, rebuilding of Constantinople, and building programs elsewhere in the empire provided the foundation for later intellectual, legal, and cultural development. Many of his achievements were accomplished with the support of Theodora, whose strength helped Justinian at times of crisis and whose death left the emperor less effective than he had been earlier in his reign. His most ambitious effort, however, was the reconquest of the west and reunification of the empire under his authority. His wars in Italy, more destructive than any of the barbarian invasions of the peninsula, led to the successful restoration of Byzantine power in Italy and the destruction of the kingdom of the Ostrogoths, but at a great cost. And the success was only short-lived; three years after Justinian's death, Italy was overrun by the Lombards. Byzantine influence lasted for several generations, but the effort was ultimately a failure, and Justinian's overall legacy is marked by great successes and failures.

Rising to power as the nephew of the reigning emperor Justin (r. 518–527), Justinian—originally Petrus Sabbatius and later Flavius Petrus Sabbatius Justinianus—first reached Constantinople in 495 to receive an education. Later, when his uncle took power, he joined Justin in the capital and played an important role in government during his uncle's reign. He was rewarded by promotion as well as with a special dispensation to marry Theodora, needed because members of the senatorial aristocracy could by law not marry anyone who appeared on the stage. Justin made his nephew caesar in 525 and co-emperor in 527. Hard-working, dedicated, with a limited ability to delegate authority, Justinian dominated affairs in Constantinople for the next forty years.

Justinian reached a major turning point early in his reign when he faced the Nika Revolt in 532. Although a number of Justinian's initiatives had already been started before that date, they were only completed after the revolt, and therefore his survival of the rebellion was critical. The revolt broke out over the arrest of the leaders of two rival factions in Constantinople—factions often in conflict with each other that led to rioting; this arrest brought the factions together against the government of Justinian. The rebellion was so severe that it nearly toppled the emperor, who was on the verge of fleeing the city with members of the imperial court. Theodora, however, gave an impassioned speech that persuaded her husband to stand his ground. He then gave the order for a detachment of barbarian mercenaries to enter the city and put down the revolt. According to contemporary accounts, the barbarians entered the hippodrome, the arena in which the rebels concentrated, and massacred 30,000 people. The leaders of the rebellion were also executed, and Justinian remained in firm control of the empire.

There were two immediate consequences of Justinian's suppression of the revolt: the completion of the reform and codification of Roman law and the rebuilding of the city of Constantinople. Indeed, one of the most pressing needs the emperor faced after the Nika Revolt was the restoration of the city after the great destruction caused by the rebellion. Along with aqueducts and number of public buildings, Justinian built a great new church, the Hagia Sophia. This became the imperial church, standing as the head of all churches in the empire and binding all Christians in the empire together. It was also a repository and model for late imperial art and asserted the close association between politics and religious belief in the empire. Its lavish decoration, including mosaics and different colored marble, and massive structure inspired Justinian to declare "Solomon, I have outdone thee!" when he first saw the completed church. Like a new Solomon, Justinian also was a great lawgiver, and he was able to complete the codification of the law he began in 529. The *Corpus Iuris Civilis* (Body of the Civil Law) was compiled by the jurist Tribonian and several commissions organized by Justinian or Tribonian; upon completion it was organized in four main sections: the Code of Justinian, the Digest, the Institutes, and the Novels. The codification of the law was intended not only to organize the law,

which had been in a confused state, but also to create a bond of unity in the empire in the same way that the Hagia Sophia was designed to do.

Justinian's activities in law and building were those of the traditional Roman emperor, and indeed he was himself in that tradition. As a result, he also saw it as his duty to rule over a united empire that included the old Roman heartland of Italy and Rome, the ancient capital. Therefore, beginning in the 530s and continuing for some two decades, Justinian's armies undertook the reconquest of parts of the old Western Empire. The first step came with the invasion and rapid conquest of Vandal North Africa. Justinian had originally hoped to secure the aid of the Vandal king, Hilderic, but his overthrow and replacement by Gelimer forced the emperor to change plans. In 533–534, Justinian's loyal and talented general, Belisarius, led Byzantine armies into North Africa, where he managed to defeat Gelimer and the Vandals. The kingdom was quickly restored to Roman rule, and Belisarius was granted a triumph— the ancient Roman ceremonial parade accorded to victorious generals—through the streets of Constantinople. Gelimer was displayed during the triumph, as were many captive Vandals. The Vandal king was settled on an estate far from the kingdom, and many of the most able Vandal soldiers were enrolled in the Byzantine army and dispatched to the Persian frontier.

Justinian next turned his eyes to Italy, where the great king Theodoric had ruled an Ostrogothic kingdom from the 490s until his death in 526. Theodoric's successors, however, were not his equal, and the kingdom itself was rent by conflict between those who supported an alliance with the empire and those who rejected any ties to the empire or its traditions. Justinian exploited these divisions, especially as they involved Theodoric's daughter and regent, Amalaswintha. According to Procopius, Justinian had more than a diplomatic interest in the beautiful and intelligent princess, and may have desired a marriage alliance as a means to claim Italy. Procopius also alleges that Theodora, deeply jealous of Amalaswintha, secretly plotted against her and encouraged the Gothic opposition to kill the princess. Her murder, after Justinian had declared that he would defend the Gothic princess and promised swift punishment should anything happen to her, gave the emperor a pretext to invade Italy. If Procopius is to be believed, the murder came as the result of a letter from Theodora, which assured the Gothic nobles that Justinian would do nothing if they acted against Amalaswintha. It is possible that Justinian and Theodora indulged in a dangerous diplomatic game that led to the death of Amalaswintha, but also provided them the opportunity to restore imperial control over Italy. Whatever the case, Amalaswintha was deposed and murdered, and Justinian used this as a pretext for his invasion of Italy.

The war began with a feint into Sicily in 535, which Belisarius quickly conquered. The rapidity of the general's success inspired Justinian to proceed more aggressively in 536, when Byzantine armies marched onto the Italian mainland. Although Belisarius enjoyed early success, the war dragged on for nearly twenty-five years and caused great destruction to the Italian peninsula. The Goths put up a great struggle under different leaders and over two generations, and the Romans of Italy, though they at first welcomed the invaders, proved less open to the restoration of Roman rule and its taxation.

The war proceeded in several phases, at first involving Belisarius, who enjoyed success against Witigis, the successor to Amalaswintha and her son Athalaric. In the 540s, however, Justinian and Belisarius faced a greater challenge from the king Totila, who won a series of victories and benefited from Justinian's difficulties on the Persian frontier. Justinian was also fearful of granting Belisarius too many troops because the Goths had offered Belisarius ruling authority in Italy. The general had refused the offer, but Justinian remained distrustful and eventually recalled his old friend. The Gothic Wars went on until 561, and the final defeat of the Goths was inflicted by Narses, who began a major campaign in 552. In late June or early July of that year, Narses met Totila in battle at Busta Gallorum, a plain in the northern Apennines. Narses, with a second army of invasion, overwhelmed Totila and his forces. The Goths left 6,000 dead on the field, and Totila was mortally wounded. Repeated efforts over the next few years to push back the Byzantines proved unsuccessful, and from 559 to 560, Narses gradually restored Byzantine authority throughout all of Italy. One final effort was launched in 561, but again the Goths failed, and with that failure, the Ostrogoths passed into extinction. The Italian conquest, however, did not long survive Justinian's death; the Lombards began their conquest of Italy in 568.

Justinian's reign was thus a pivotal one for both the Eastern and Western Empire. He oversaw the codification of the law, which actually ended by having greater influence on later medieval and modern Europe than on the Byzantine Empire, and a massive building program in Constantinople and Italy that laid the foundation for later Byzantine and medieval European art. His conquest of Italy restored imperial rule to the peninsula, destroyed the Ostrogothic kingdom, and brought the existence of the Ostrogothic nation to an end. The conquest, however, failed, and direct Byzantine rule ended with the Lombard invasion. A Byzantine presence continued for several generations in Italy, however, and the competition between the Byzantines and Lombards caused Italy further difficulties. The conquest also came at great cost for the empire, as did all of Justinian's activities, and his successors proved less suited to the challenges at hand than did Justinian.

See also Amalaswintha; Belisarius; Gothic Wars; Lombards; Narses; Ostrogoths; Procopius; Theodora; Theodoric the Great; Vandals

Bibliography

Barker. John W. *Justinian and the Later Roman Empire.* Madison: University of Wisconsin Press, 1960.

Cassiodorus. *The Variae of Magnus Aurelius Cassiodorus.* Trans. S. J. B. Barnish. Liverpool, UK: Liverpool University Press, 1992.

Browning, Robert. *Justinian and Theodora.* London: Thames and Hudson, 1987.

Burns, Thomas S. *A History of the Ostrogoths.* Bloomington: Indiana University Press, 1984.

Bury, John B. *History of the Later Roman Empire: From the Death of Theodosius I to the Death of Justinian.* 2 vols. 1923. Reprint, New York: Dover, 1959.

Heather, Peter. *The Goths.* Oxford: Blackwell, 1996.

Llewellyn, Peter. *Rome in the Dark Ages.* New York: Barnes and Noble, 1993.

Procopius. *The History of the Wars; Secret History,* 4 vols. Trans. H. B. Dewing. Cambridge, MA: Harvard University Press, 1914–1924.

Treadgold, Warren. *The History of the Byzantine State and Society.* Stanford, CA: Stanford University Press, 1997.

Ure, Percy N. *Justinian and His Age.* Harmondsworth, UK: Penguin, 1951.

Watson, Alan. *The Digest of Justinian.* Philadelphia: University of Pennsylvania Press, 1997.

Wickham, Chris. *Early Medieval Italy: Central Power and Local Society, 400–1000.* Ann Arbor: University of Michigan Press, 1981.

K

King Arthur

Semilegendary hero and king of the Britons who defended England from Anglo-Saxon invaders in the fifth or sixth century and who traditionally fought twelve battles, including the great Battle of Badon Hill *(Mons Badonicus)* in 516. The legendary figure of Arthur is possibly based on a historical person, who has been identified as one of a broad range of figures, including a professional mercenary, a late Roman military commander, a Welsh duke, and an Irish king in Scotland. He is best known, however, through the tales of romance composed on the basis of the old legends in the high and late Middle Ages by Geoffrey of Monmouth, Thomas Malory, and others that describe the adventures of Arthur and Merlin, Lancelot and Guinevere, and their home, the fabled Camelot.

The origins of the legend can be found in the descriptions of invasion-era England by Gildas in the sixth century and Nennius in the ninth century, as well as in the comment of an anonymous early medieval Welsh poet who says of a certain warrior that he "was not Arthur." Although Gildas does not name his hero, he seldom does name names in his history, and he does describe the victory at Badon Hill and the brief recovery of the fortunes of the Britons after the battle—key elements in the later fame of Arthur. Nennius identifies his hero as Arthur and lists twelve battles, including Badon Hill and Camlann where Arthur died, that the great hero fought against invading Saxon armies. Although two of the battles have been located geographically and probably did occur, the other ten battles have not been located and may not have occurred, or least as Nennius described them. It is from these simple beginnings that the full-scale legend evolved in Welsh and later English sources. It was a legend of great popularity that, at the same time, made any English prince named Arthur suspect in the eyes of the ruling monarch.

Some scholars claim to have identified Camelot, the most famous landmark of the legend of Arthur. As early as the fifteenth and sixteenth centuries, Cadbury Castle in South Cadbury, Somerset, was recognized as Camelot. In the 1960s excavations discovered early fortifications that could be associated with a historical Arthur and also unearthed foundations of a church and numerous objects of everyday use of high quality. Although some scholars accept this as Arthur's castle, others reject it and argue that the documentary record of an active warrior does not support his association with the structures found at Cadbury.

See also Anglo-Saxons; Gildas; Nennius

Bibliography

Alcock, Leslie. *Arthur's Britain: History and Archeology, A.D. 367–634.* Harmondsworth, UK: Penguin, 1971.

Barber, Richard. *The Figure of Arthur.* Totowa, NJ: Rowman and Littlefield, 1972.

Geoffrey of Monmouth. *The History of the Kings of Britain.* Trans. Lewis Thorpe. Harmondsworth, UK: Penguin, 1996.

Gildas. *The Ruin of Britain and Other Works.* Ed. and trans. Michael Winterbottom. London: Phillimore, 1978.

Malory, Sir Thomas. *Le Morte d'Arthur.* Ed. Norma Lorre Goodrich. New York: Washington Square Press, 1966.

L

Law and Law Codes

Prior to their contacts with the Roman Empire in the migration period, the Germanic, or barbarian, peoples of Europe had no written laws or legal codes. The nature of the law was customary. Law was remembered and passed along through an oral tradition that stretched back for generations. Although customary, the law was not simplistic; it included a well-defined set of procedures, such as the use of the oath. Although the extent of influence varied, depending upon when and where the invaders made contact, contact with the Romans, who had a great legal tradition and had prepared important legal codes already in the third century, profoundly altered the nature of the laws of the various barbarian tribes. The Germanic peoples who entered the empire learned the tradition of written law and the practice of codifying the law, and kings of the Franks, Visigoths, and other peoples issued laws and law codes as their kingdoms were established. Exposure to the Romans and other barbarian peoples also led to the emergence of the principle of the law, a development that remained important long after the initial contact with the empire. According to this principle, each person was bound by the laws of his own group.

Like the conquest of the Roman territories on the Continent by various barbarian peoples, the conquest of England by the Anglo-Saxons in the fifth century introduced important challenges for the tradition of the law. The Anglo-Saxon accomplishment, however, is unique among the various peoples that created kingdoms in the former Western Empire because Roman contact and influence had been on the wane even before the arrival of the invaders, and in the fifth century little of the Roman legacy survived. There were no Roman jurists, and there was no Roman legal inheritance to speak of. As a result, Anglo-Saxon laws were issued in the vernacular, were little influenced by Roman traditions, and reflected long-standing Germanic customary law. Furthermore, the Anglo-Saxon kings of England issued no special laws for the Romans, as did their contemporaries on the continent. Æthelberht of Kent was one of the early kings to issue important laws in the vernacular, and his laws were recognized as statements of his royal authority. They were the king's laws and were to be followed as such. The early laws dealt with such matters as the wergeld, feud, personal injury, and payment of fines to keep the peace. They also addressed the nature of royal and local courts and instituted the necessary regulations that emerged from the conversion to Christianity. Beginning with Alfred the Great, however, Anglo-Saxon kings showed Roman influence

Illustration from Alaric's Breviary (Paris, Bibliothèque Nationale)

issue written laws, called *belagines* (although these are sometimes thought to have been Ostrogothic laws only).

As the Visigoths became more settled and expanded into Spain, creating the kingdom of Toulouse (418–507), a more sophisticated legal code became necessary, in part to regulate the relationship between the Goths and the Romans living in the kingdom. There is some evidence to suggest that the legal code took shape by the mid-fifth century, when the king, Theodoric II (d. 466), issued written legal statutes. Although once associated with the Ostrogothic king Theodoric the Great, the *Edictum Theodorici* (Edict of Theodoric) now is believed to have been issued around 458 by the Visigothic king. The edict was intended to resolve various issues between Romans and Goths, but was in no sense a complete code of laws. It was under Theodoric's brother and successor, Euric, that the legal code now known as the *Codex Euricianus* (Code of Euric) most likely appeared. Sometime around the year 475 and possibly as late as 483, Euric, or perhaps his son Alaric II a generation later, issued this code of laws, which remained influential into the eighth century. The code, written in Latin, became the personal law of the Visigoths thus establishing the principle of personality, and it dealt with disputes between Romans and Goths that arose out of their cohabitation in the same kingdom. It addressed such matters as loans, gifts, purchases, wills, interest payments, and charters.

The *Codex Euricianus* was not, however, a universal legal instrument that was territorial like the Code of Justinian, nor was it a complete compilation of all Gothic law, but rather a collection of royal statutes. Consequently, a second legal document was necessary and was issued by Alaric, probably in 506, to be applied to his Roman subjects. The *Breviarium Alaricianum* (Breviary of Alaric), or the *Lex Romana Visigothorum* (Roman Law of the Visigoths), was compiled by a number of jurists commissioned by Alaric who borrowed from the imperial Theodosian Code of 438. These two codes were in effect throughout the Visigothic realm by the early sixth century and were replaced only in the mid-seventh century, when King Recceswinth issued a unified code for Romans and Visigoths. Nonetheless, the *Codex Euricianus* and the *Breviarium Alaricianum* are the most important and influential of the early Germanic legal codes and are in many ways as significant an achievement as the Bible of Ulfilas, the translation of the scriptures into Gothic that laid the foundation for the written language.

Less influential but still important laws and legal codes were issued by the Burgundians, Ostrogoths, and Vandals. The Burgundians entered the Roman Empire and settled for a time along the Rhine River, and then for a much longer period along the Rhone River, where they were heavily exposed to Roman influence. Like the Visigoths, the Burgundians had followed the tradition of customary law and were now faced with the need to provide a legal tradition for a mixed population of Burgundians and Romans. In the late fifth and early sixth centuries, two Burgundian kings, Gundobad and his son Sigismund, issued legal codes intended to resolve that problem. Gundobad, around the year 500 or slightly before, issued the *Lex Gundobada* (Law of Gundobad), or *Liber constitutionem* (Book of Constitutions), which applied to the Burgundian peoples of the kingdom and was further refined by Sigismund. In 517 or 518, Sigismund issued the *Lex Romana Burgundionum* (Roman Law of the Burgundians), which, following Visigothic precedent, applied to the king's Roman subjects and was most likely drawn up by Roman legal scholars. The existence of these two codes thus confirmed the principle of personality.

The codes had a mixed fate once the Burgundians were conquered by the Frankish king Clovis (r. 481–511). The *Lex Gundobada* remained the personal law of the Burgundian peoples under Frankish rule for centuries, but the Roman law was quickly replaced by the Breviary of Alaric. In similar fashion, the laws and legal compilations that had been issued in Ostrogothic Italy and Vandal Africa were replaced by their conquerors. In Italy, Theodoric the Great preserved what he could of Roman administration and law, and in Africa, the Vandals faced the problem of ruling a mixed barbarian and Roman population. In each case, however, the conquests of Justinian eradicated whatever legal reforms took place in the kingdoms. With the exception of the personal law of the Burgundians, the laws of the Burgundians, Ostrogoths, and Vandals had a lesser impact than did the laws of the Visigoths.

Despite their important legacy in many areas, the Ostrogoths had a much less significant impact on the history of law in Italy than the Lombards, who entered Italy not long after the end of the wars between the Goths and Byzantines. Like the Visigoths and other peoples who established themselves in former imperial territory, the Lombards were

faced with the challenge of ruling over a diverse population. The solution the Lombards seem to have adopted, like that of their predecessors throughout the former Western Empire, followed the principle of personality; the Roman population followed Roman law and the Lombards followed Lombard customary law. The king remained the source of new law and continued to produce new laws and legal traditions. In the seventh century, however, the Lombards went beyond what other peoples had done. Lombard law was codified by King Rothari; and he produced the most complete set of laws of any of the barbarian kings, including nearly all of the royal law and codifying Lombard legal principles nearly in full. In 643, Rothari published, with the help of Roman jurists, the *Edictus Rothari* (Edict of Rothari), which addressed family and property law and civil laws concerning personal injury and property damage. Rothari's code was clearly influenced by Roman law, and many of the prologues of the laws followed the formula of imperial legal preambles.

The *Edictus Rothari* remained the fundamental legal code of the Lombard kingdom until the kingdom was conquered by Charlemagne, and Rothari's successors preserved the code and added new laws to it as needs arose. These new laws too show the influence of Roman law, as well as the growing influence of the Catholic church on the Lombards and their legal tradition. Moreover, even after Charlemagne's conquest of the kingdom, Lombard law continued to be the law for most of the population of Italy and was only supplemented by Carolingian law. The laws of the Lombards remained an important legal tradition even after the collapse of the Carolingian Empire, and became one of the important traditions studied by lawyers in the High Middle Ages.

As in many other areas, the Franks left a lasting impact on medieval law and law codes. The most famous of Frankish law codes is the Salic law, which was compiled by the first great Merovingian king, Clovis, in the early sixth century; it is a collection of the laws of the Salian Franks, although it does not include all the laws of the Franks. Like the laws of the Visigoths and others, the Salic law was most likely codified by a team of Frankish officials and Roman lawyers; it included Frankish custom and the royal edicts of Clovis. The Salic law is not an orderly codification of the law, but a collection of important laws and customs that was intended, among other things, to preserve the peace in the Merovingian kingdom. The law also concerns royal rights and prerogatives and imposes higher fines for crimes against the king, his property, and agents. Moreover, although designed to cover all those living in the Merovingian kingdom, the Salic law, like the laws of the Visigoths and others, recognizes the principle of personality. The code imposes different penalties for crimes, depending on whether they are committed by Franks or by Romans and provides a legal distinction between Romans and barbarians. Originally compiled before 511, the Salic law was revised and expanded by later Merovingian kings, including Chlotar I and Chilperic I, in the later sixth and seventh centuries, and a prologue and epilogue were added in later versions. It was also revised by the Carolingians and was much studied in the eighth and ninth centuries.

The Carolingians inherited the Salic law, just as they inherited the kingdom from the Merovingian kings. The first Carolingian king, Pippin the Short, was also the first Carolingian to reform the law. In 763–764, Pippin produced a law book of 100 titles—and often called the 100-Title Text—that included all Frankish law. Charlemagne too produced a shorter version of the code, in 70 titles, in 798, and ordered, according to a contemporary source, a revision of all the laws of the empire made in 802, two years after his imperial coronation. The Carolingian version of the Salic law seems to have lost its personal character, no longer to have been based on the principle of personality; rather it had assumed territorial status; that is, the law was now over all peoples living in the empire and not just the Franks, presenting itself as applying equally to all peoples in the empire and making no distinction between Franks and others. It continued to be concerned with peace and order and assessing fines and wergelds, but it gave much greater weight to the authority of the king than earlier revisions had. It also expressed a number of Roman legal ideas, including the idea that royal land belonged to the office, not the person, of the king.

Charlemagne's legal reforms were not limited to revisions of the Salic law; he also oversaw the codification of the laws of the Alemanni and the Bavarians, probably in 788, after they had been conquered by the great Carolingian king. Charlemagne, and his successors Louis the Pious and Charles the Bald, also issued new laws in the capitularies, which contained the word of the law as expressed by the king. The capitularies were often stated at royal councils and then written down and disseminated throughout the kingdom.

See also Æthelberht of Kent; Alemanni; Alaric II; Alfred the Great; Anglo-Saxons; Capitularies; Carolingian Dynasty; Charles the Bald; Clovis; Charlemagne; Euric; Gundobad; Justinian; Lombards; Louis the Pious; Merovingian Dynasty; Ostrogoths; Pippin III, Called the Short; Rothari; Salic Law; Sigismund, St.; Ulfilas; Vandals; Visigoths

Bibliography

Attenborough, Frederick L. ed. and trans. *The Laws of the Earliest English Kings.* Cambridge: Cambridge University Press, 1922.

Drew, Katherine Fisher, trans. *The Burgundian Code: The Book of Constitutions or Law of Gundobad and Additional Enactments.* Philadelphia: University of Pennsylvania Press, 1972.

———. *The Lombard Laws.* Philadelphia: University of Pennsylvania Press, 1973.

Ganshof, François Louis. *Frankish Institutions under Charlemagne.* Trans. Bryce Lyon and Mary Lyon. Providence, RI: Brown University Press, 1968.

Heather, Peter. *The Goths.* Oxford: Blackwell, 1996.

King, Peter D. *Law and Society in the Visigothic Kingdom.* Cambridge: Cambridge University Press, 1972.

McKitterick, Rosamond. *The Carolingians and the Written Word.* Cambridge: Cambridge University Press, 1989.

Pollock, Frederick, and Frederic W. Maitland. *The History of English Law before the Time of Edward I.* 2d ed. 2 vols. London: Cambridge University Press, 1968.

Rivers, Theodore J., trans. *Laws of the Alamans and Bavarians.* Philadelphia: University of Pennsylvania Press, 1977.

———. *The Laws of the Salian and Ripuarian Franks.* New York: AMS, 1986.

Wallace-Hadrill, J. M. *The Long-Haired Kings.* Toronto: Toronto University Press, 1982.

Wood, Ian. *The Merovingian Kingdoms, 450–751.* London: Longman, 1994.

Wolfram, Herwig. *The Roman Empire and Its Barbarian Peoples.* Trans. Thomas J. Dunlap. Berkeley: University of California Press, 1997.

Wormald, Patrick. "*Lex Scripta* and *Verbum Regis:* Legislation and Germanic Kingship from Euric to Cnut." In *Early Medieval Kingship,* ed. Peter Sawyer and Ian N. Wood. Leeds, UK: University of Leeds Press, 1977, pp. 105–138.

Leander, St.

See Isidore of Seville

Leo III, the Isaurian (c. 680–741)

Byzantine emperor (r. 717–741) and founder of a dynasty whose religious policy caused great dissension in the empire. His policy, known as iconoclasm, contributed to a growing schism between the church in Rome and the church in the Byzantine Empire. The antagonism that existed between the popes and Leo III, who also increased the burden of taxation in Italy without improving his defense of the papacy against the Lombards, reinforced the tendency of the popes to look to western European leaders for protection. Indeed, Leo's iconoclastic policy drove Pope Gregory III to appeal to the Carolingian mayor of the palace, the power behind the throne in the kingdom of the Franks, for aid. The ongoing iconoclastic controversy after Leo's death attracted the attention of Charlemagne and his court scholars, especially Theodulf of Orléans.

Leo took the throne in 717 in a bloody coup that eliminated the last of the Heraclian dynasty, which had been established a century earlier. Although he managed to take the throne, Leo was immediately faced with a great crisis—Muslim soldiers were besieging the great capital of the Eastern Empire, Constantinople. By a combination of luck, skill, and superior technology, including Greek fire, a type of napalm that destroyed the attackers' ships, Leo managed to save the city by 718. Over much of the next decade, Leo continued to expel Muslim invaders from Byzantine territory. Indeed, his efforts were critical to the long-term survival of the empire, which did not fall to the Muslims until 1453, and to the preservation of three distinct cultural regions around the medieval Mediterranean—a Latin Christian, a Greek Christian, and a Muslim region. For many of his subjects, however, Leo's efforts at defending the empire were only secondary to the more important efforts of the monks and priests of the realm. During the assault on Constantinople, the patriarch marched around the city walls bearing a religious image, or icon, of Mary, which many believed saved the city. Faith in the icon was something that Leo did not share, and the widespread belief in them may have offended the religious sensibilities of the emperor, who most likely recalled the Mosaic prohibition against graven images. Although Leo introduced a number of governmental, military, and administrative reforms that would greatly strengthen the empire, he is remembered mostly for the almost disastrous religious policy that arose out of his hostility to icon worship.

Leo, either because of religious conviction or animosity toward the priests who promoted veneration of images, instituted a policy of iconoclasm in 727. The policy may have also been motivated by a terrible volcanic eruption in the Aegean Sea, which Leo interpreted as divine disfavor caused by the use of icons. Whatever his motive, Leo pronounced an imperial decree against the use of icons in the Byzantine church and also began to attack the monasteries. Leo was exercising what he thought was his divine right as emperor to intervene in religious matters, but the monks had traditionally criticized religious policy making by the emperors. His efforts were at first modest, but they became increasingly harsh, and as early as 730 there are records of the destruction of icons. Defenders of the use of icons, mostly monks, were harshly treated and sometimes martyred, which only hardened the determination of those opposed to the new policy. Leo's son and successor, Constantine V (r. 741–775), took an even harder line against icons. Ultimately, the iconoclastic policy was overturned, but not before contributing to increased tensions between the church in the east and the west.

Leo's foray into religious policy making was not well received at Rome by Pope Gregory II or Gregory III. Whatever the merits of the policy were, and there alone Leo's actions would have received condemnation from Rome, the popes would have opposed Leo purely on the grounds of principle. It was not the responsibility of the emperor to determine matters of the faith; rather he was to protect the church and its ministers. In many ways, the emperors in Constantinople had failed to protect the church in Italy—a responsibility many centuries old by Leo's time. Moreover, not only did Leo fail to protect the pope and his church in Italy, especially from the Lombards who had been seeking to conquer the peninsula since 568, but he had increased the administrative demands on the popes and had significantly increased taxation in Italy. As a result, relations between Rome and Constantinople worsened to the point that Gregory III turned for help to the great rising power in the north, the Carolingian Franks and their leader Charles Martel, for aid against the Lombards. Charles needed his alliance with the Lombards and was unable to help, but an important precedent was set for both the Carolingians and the papacy. Over the next generation an alliance between the two was established, and a break between Rome and Constantinople occurred. Indeed, Leo's intervention in religious policy and reorganization of administration in Italy drove the popes into an alliance with the Carolingians, an alliance that contributed to the Carolingian usurpation of the royal power from the last of the Merovingian kings in 751.

Thus Leo's iconoclastic policy continued to have repercussions into the late eighth and even early ninth century, long after the emperor's death. Moreover, it was the reaction against his policy of iconoclasm in the Byzantine Empire that led to further troubles between Constantinople and the kingdom of the Franks. Although Leo's son Constantine V was an ardent iconoclast, his son, Leo IV (775–780), and his son's wife, Irene, were not. And it was Irene who overturned the policies of Constantine V and Leo the Isaurian. In 787, she and her son, the emperor Constantine VI, presided over the second Council of Nicaea, which restored the veneration of icons in the empire. Although the council received papal blessing and was attended by two representatives of the pope, Nicaea's decisions were not welcomed by the leader of the largest church in Europe. Representatives of Charlemagne's Frankish church were not invited to the council, and its decisions were repudiated by the Carolingian church. In the Caroline Books (*Libri Carolini*), Theodulf of Orléans, with the possible help of the great Anglo-Saxon scholar and missionary Alcuin of York, and working from a flawed copy of the decrees of the council, provided the official response of the Carolingian church to Irene's Council of Nicaea. Theodulf offered a sophisticated view of art in his work, even though it failed to accurately address the defense of images announced at Nicaea. Moreover, the controversy over icons begun by Leo continued to plague the Byzantine Empire into the ninth century. And in one of history's ironies, leaders of the Byzantine church sought advice from the court of Louis the Pious, the son of Charlemagne, whose representatives had not been invited to Nicaea.

See also Alcuin of York; Carolingian Dynasty; Charlemagne; Charles Martel; Gregory II, Pope; Gregory III, Pope; Irene; Lombards; Louis the Pious; Merovingian Dynasty; Theodulf of Orléans

Bibliography

Davis, Raymond, trans. *The Lives of the Eighth-Century Popes* (Liber Pontificalis): *The Ancient Biographies of Nine Popes from A.D. 715 to A.D. 817.* Liverpool, UK: Liverpool University Press, 1992.

Herrin, Judith. *The Formation of Christendom.* Princeton: Princeton University Press, 1989.

Llewellyn, Peter. *Rome in the Dark Ages.* New York: Barnes and Noble, 1993.

McKitterick, Rosamond. *The Frankish Kingdoms under the Carolingians.* Longman: London, 1983.

Obolensky, Dmitri. *The Byzantine Commonwealth: Eastern Europe, 500–1543.* New York: Praeger, 1971.

Riché, Pierre. *The Carolingians: A Family Who Forged Europe.* Trans. Michael Idomir Allen. Philadelphia: University of Pennsylvania Press, 1993.

Sullivan, Richard. *Heirs of the Roman Empire.* Ithaca, NY: Cornell University Press, 1974.

Leo III, Pope (d. 816)

Important pope whose long reign (r. 795–816) witnessed a number of significant developments in papal policy and diplomatic relations. He was an active builder and restorer of churches and public structures such as aqueducts and a great benefactor of the city. He negotiated a difficult theological issue between the churches of Jerusalem and the east and the western, especially Frankish, churches. He also faced and suppressed two serious revolts in Rome during his reign. Despite his numerous accomplishments, Leo is best known for the imperial coronation of Charlemagne on Christmas Day, 800.

Although lacking the family connections of his predecessor, Hadrian I (r. 772–795), Leo III had long been known to the papal establishment and the people of Rome when he was made pope. He was raised and educated in the papal administration, served as a high-level bureaucrat, and was the cardinal priest of the church of St. Susanna in Rome before his election on December 27, 795, the day after the death of Hadrian. The *Book of the Popes (Liber Pontificalis)* describes him as "chaste, eloquent and of resolute mind" (Davis 1992, 179). He is also described as a "defender of the church,"(179) and as a papal administrator he took active care of the poor and the sick. His rapid election demonstrates the high regard the clergy and people of Rome had for Leo. But faithful servant of the people and church of Rome though he was, Leo's lack of important family connections caused him difficulty throughout his reign as pope.

Perhaps aware of his weak position in Rome, Leo immediately sought to strengthen the papacy's ties to the Carolingian king Charlemagne. Indeed, unlike his predecessor, Leo had no desire to pursue the alliance with the papacy's traditional protector in Constantinople, and in 796 he sent the keys of St. Peter and the banner of the city of Rome to Charlemagne. The great king called for a new treaty between himself and the pope, in which the king would defend the church against internal and external enemies and the pope would, like Moses, stand with arms upheld in prayer for victory. Leo began to date his official documents from the time of Charlemagne's conquest of the Lombards in 774, and he also promoted the see of Salzburg to metropolitan status at the king's request in 798. Leo clearly tied the papacy to the great power to the north.

Although he secured a protector and diplomatic ally, Leo still faced problems in

St. Peter with Pope Leo III and Charlemagne (Rome, Vatican Library)

Rome from a rival faction, an aristocratic one that included relatives of Pope Hadrian. On April 25, 799, the turmoil in Rome reached a crisis. On that day Leo left the Lateran palace to lead a major religious procession throughout the city of Rome and was attacked in front of the monastery of Saints Sylvester and Stephen by two nephews and a former ally of Hadrian. Although the accounts vary, it is clear that Leo was roughly handled by his attackers and may have been blinded and had his tongue cut out by them. The *Book of the Popes* notes also that his attackers "left him half-dead and drenched in blood." He was then placed under a sort of house arrest, being put into a monastery by his enemies, but he was rescued by his chamberlain, who lowered him from the monastery walls by a rope. The pope was then safely returned to St. Peter's, where his enemies would not harm him. He was then escorted to Charlemagne's court at Paderborn (now in Germany) by the king's ally Winichis, duke of Spoleto.

At Charlemagne's court, according to some accounts, Leo miraculously regained the powers of sight and speech and defended himself against the accusations of his attackers. Leo was accused of adultery, perjury, and simony (the buying and selling of church offices), serious crimes that would have rendered him unfit for office. Uncertain of how to proceed, Charlemagne kept Leo at court until the situation at Rome quieted down before returning him to the city. In November 799, Leo was returned with a Frankish escort to protect him and was enthusiastically welcomed back by the people of Rome. On the day after his arrival, his attackers were tried before Leo and his Frankish escort and found guilty, but sentencing was deferred until the arrival of Charlemagne.

Despite the importance of the situation, or perhaps because of it, Charlemagne did not arrive in Rome for a year after Leo's return, an indication of continued uncertainty among the king and his advisors of how to proceed. Charlemagne left his kingdom in August 800 and, according to the *Royal Frankish Annals,* was met by the pope and his entourage twelve miles from the city of Rome. King and pope dined together and entered Rome the following day, November 24, 800. Charlemagne was welcomed by enthusiastic crowds and was led by the pope to the basilica of St. Peter, where they prayed together. On December 23, before Charlemagne and an assembly of Frankish and Roman secular and religious nobles, Leo swore an oath of purgation and declared his innocence of the crimes of which he was accused. Leo's oath was accepted as proof of innocence because no one

at the assembly could prove otherwise. Leo was restored to his place. The fate of the rebels against him was also decided. They were condemned to death, but the sentence was reduced to exile for life on the request of the pope himself.

Two days after his trial, Leo performed the most famous act of his reign. On Christmas Day, 800, at the shrine of St. Peter, Leo crowned Charlemagne emperor. According to the *Royal Frankish Annals,* when Charlemagne rose from prayer Leo "placed a crown on his head, and he was hailed by the whole Roman people: To august Charles, crowned by God, the great and peaceful emperor of the Romans, life and victory!"(Scholz 1972, 81). The *Book of Pontiffs* adds that the acclamation was repeated three times and that Leo then anointed Charles emperor. Although the exact meaning of the coronation to the various participants in the act will probably never be known, we need not accept Einhard's remark that Charlemagne would have avoided mass had he known what was going to happen. It is likely that the new emperor was not at all pleased by the way the coronation—which he surely knew about—had taken place, and may have thought that Leo sought to put him in the pope's debt. Indeed, it is possible that Leo sought to reassert his authority after his rescue by Charlemagne, or he may have intended to bind the Carolingian ruler even more closely to himself. It may also be that Leo had less self-serving motives and sought to reward the king with the imperial crown as thanks for all his efforts on behalf of the papacy and church. Whatever the case, the imperial coronation on December 25, 800, was Leo's most important act and one that shaped political thought and practice for the next thousand years.

The remainder of Leo's reign was relatively secure, no doubt as a result of Charlemagne's support. He was an able administrator and active builder, which benefited the city greatly. He did find himself at cross-purposes with his benefactor in 809, however, over a matter of liturgical practice in which the Western church differed from the church in the Holy Lands. Although Leo supported Frankish practice, he recommended that the Frankish version not be publicly recited. And in 808, Leo complained to the emperor about Charlemagne's representatives in Italy.

Leo did face one final crisis after the death of Charlemagne; long-simmering resentments that had not been eradicated in 800 boiled over, and the Roman aristocracy revolted for a second time in 814. the pope acted promptly and had the leaders of the rebellion executed. Charlemagne's successor, Louis the Pious, was concerned by Leo's harsh response and ordered his nephew, King Bernard of Italy, to investigate the situation. Leo's explanation proved satisfactory to the Carolingian emperor, but not to the Roman nobles who in 815 sought to take lands away from the papacy. Once again Louis, through his nephew Bernard, intervened, and this time on behalf of the pope. The situation in Rome remained unsettled, but it was Leo's successor as pope who addressed the situation. Leo died June 12, 816, after a long reign in which he drew the papacy closer to the Carolingians and, most importantly, crowned Charlemagne emperor.

See also Carolingian Dynasty; Charlemagne; Lombards; Louis the Pious; *Royal Frankish Annals*

Bibliography

Davis, Raymond, trans. *The Lives of the Eighth-Century Popes* (Liber Pontificalis): *The Ancient Biographies of Nine Popes from* A.D. *715 to* A.D. *817.* Liverpool, UK: Liverpool University Press, 1992.

Einhard and Notker the Stammerer. *Two Lives of Charlemagne.* Trans. Lewis Thorpe. Harmondsworth, UK: Penguin, 1981.

Halphen, Louis. *Charlemagne and the Carolingian Empire.* Trans. Giselle de Nie. Amsterdam: North-Holland, 1977.

Herrin, Judith. *The Formation of Christendom.* Princeton: Princeton University Press, 1987.

Llewellyn, Peter. *Rome in the Dark Ages.* New York: Barnes and Noble, 1971.

McKitterick, Rosamond. *The Frankish Kingdoms under the Carolingians, 751–987.* London: Longman, 1983.

Noble, Thomas F. X. *The Republic of St. Peter: The Birth of the Papal State, 680–825.* Philadelphia: University of Pennsylvania Press, 1984.

Riché, Pierre. *The Carolingians: A Family Who Forged Europe.* Trans Michael Idomir Allen. Philadelphia: University of Pennsylvania Press, 1993.

Scholz, Bernhard Walter, trans. *Carolingian Chronicles: Royal Frankish Annals and Nithard's History.* Ann Arbor: University of Michigan Press, 1972.

Leovigild (r. 568/569–586)

Visigothic king of Spain (r. 568/569–586), Leovigild enjoyed great military success against a variety of rivals, including the Byzantine Empire as well as other barbarian peoples. His power was recognized by other kings in Europe, and his son Hermenegild married a Merovingian princess. But Hermenegild also sought to overthrow his father and rebelled. Hermenegild's revolt and marriage also revealed one of the fundamental tensions of Leovigild's reign, the tension between Catholic and Arian Christians. Although Leovigild took great steps to unify the kingdom religiously as well as politically, the great religious dilemma was resolved only during the reign of his other son, Reccared. Leovigild did attempt to establish common ground between his Arian beliefs and those of the Catholic majority in Spain, but ultimately failed in his efforts. Both Hermenegild and Reccared converted to Catholic Christianity, and it was Reccared who provided the solution of the great religious question that Leovigild tried so hard to answer.

Raised to the status of coruler and given charge of Spain by his brother Liuva I (r. 568/569–573), Leovigild was one of the great kings of the sixth century. He sought to unify Spain, both politically and religiously, under his authority. To secure that end, he modeled royal ceremonial rites more closely after the practices of the Eastern Empire and abolished the law forbidding intermarriage between Goths and Romans. He also undertook frequent campaigns to suppress rebels and rivals for power. As one contemporary chronicler noted, Leovigild restored Gothic territory in Spain to its traditional boundaries. He led his armies in annual campaigns against a variety of foes including Byzantines, Basques, and other barbarian peoples. The king also suppressed a number of independent cities, including Córdoba, and extended his kingdom into the northeast. He thus incorporated most of the peninsula into his kingdom. As a sign of his growing power and self-confidence, Leovigild founded the city Reccopolis, an action usually reserved for Roman emperors, and in 573 made his sons Hermenegild and Reccared coregents to help administer the kingdom. Moreover, his efforts brought him recognition outside the kingdom, including an important marriage between his son Hermenegild and the Merovingian princess Ingunde in 579. Of course, his military success also generated dissension within the kingdom, and Hermenegild's marriage to the Catholic Ingunde, as well as his close relationship with Leander, leader of the Catholic church and brother of the important author Isidore of Seville, eventually led the young king to convert to Catholicism from his father's Arianism.

Despite the marriage alliance between his son and the Catholic Merovingian princess, Leovigild was committed to the Arian faith and sought to unify his kingdom under the Arian banner. He took a number of steps to ensure the success of his version of the Christian faith at the expense of the Catholic church in Spain, including banishing a number of bishops. His efforts, however, did not turn to persecution; instead he promoted conversion. To accomplish that end and the triumph of Arianism in Spain, he held a council at Toledo in 580. The council promoted the Arian faith of Leovigild but also sought to convert Catholic Christians in Spain, passing several decrees that were intended to make conversion more likely. The council introduced theological changes that brought Spanish Arianism closer to Catholic teaching by recognizing that the Son of God was equal (aequalis) to the Father, not just similar (similis), as the Arian church in Spain had taught. The council also recognized the Catholic sacrament of baptism and abolished the law mandating rebaptism for converts, thus eliminating an impediment to conversion. Leovigild's council also adopted a more conciliatory policy toward the veneration of relics, which was unknown to Arian Christians. The more tolerant and open attitude of Leovigild's church enjoyed some success, and at least one bishop, Vincent of Saragossa, converted. His effort failed nonetheless, because of the strength of the Catholic faith among his Roman subjects and because of the intellectual weakness of the Arian church.

The failure of Leovigild's religious policy is no better illustrated than in the actions of his two sons Hermenegild and Reccared, both of whom converted to Catholic Christianity. The more serious conversion for Leovigild was that of Hermenegild, which was accompanied by a revolt against his father. In 579, Hermenegild made his conversion and broke with his father. He actively sought allies against Leovigild and found them in Constantinople and among the people his father had conquered. He also found a friend and supporter in Pope Gregory I the Great, who later promoted Hermenegild as a martyr to the faith. Indeed, Hermenegild portrayed himself as a victim of persecution and used that as justification for rebellion against his father. His efforts ultimately failed, and his rebellion was put down by 584. Leovigild exiled his son to Valencia in 584 and then to Tarragona, where Hermenegild was murdered in 585. Despite Gregory's support of Hermenegild, most contemporary Catholic writers, including Isidore of Seville and the Frankish historian Gregory of Tours, had little sympathy for him or his revolt.

Reccared too converted to Catholic Christianity, but only after his father's death, and in other ways he shared in the important legacy Leovigild left. Although not successful in his religious policy, Leovigild left his successor with a powerful and unified kingdom. Leovigild had conquered much of the peninsula and had reformed the royal administration in a way that borrowed from Roman imperial practices, including celebrating his victories on the coins he minted. He also elevated the status of the king above his noble and non-noble subjects and introduced a number of new officials to the royal administration. These reforms benefited Leovigild's successor, as did his efforts to unify the kingdom religiously. Though Leovigild's attempts failed in that regard, the notion of unifying the kingdom religiously was a powerful one and needed only Reccared's recognition that it could only be unified by the Catholic Christian faith.

See also Arianism; Gregory the Great, Pope; Gregory of Tours; Hermenegild; Merovingian Dynasty; Reccared I; Visigoths

Bibliography

Bury, John B. *History of the Later Roman Empire: From the Death of Theodosius I to the Death of Justinian.* 2 vols. 1923. Reprint, New York: Dover, 1959.

Collins, Roger. *Early Medieval Spain: Unity in Diversity, 400–1000.* New York: St. Martin's Press, 1983.

Gregory of Tours. *History of the Franks.* Trans. Lewis Thorpe. Harmondsworth, UK: Penguin, 1974.

Heather, Peter. *The Goths.* Oxford: Blackwell, 1996.

Isidore of Seville. *Isidore of Seville's History of the Goths, Vandals, and Suevi,* 2d rev. ed. Trans. Guido Donini and Gordon B. Ford. Leiden: Brill, 1970.

Thompson, Edward A. *The Goths in Spain.* Oxford: Clarendon, 1969.

Wolfram, Herwig. *History of the Goths.* Trans. Thomas J. Dunlap. Berkeley: University of California Press, 1988.

———. *The Roman Empire and Its Germanic Peoples.* Trans. Thomas J. Dunlap. Berkeley: University of California Press, 1997.

Letter to Baugulf

The circular letter on learning to the abbot Baugulf of Fulda, or *De litteris colendis,* was, with the capitulary *Admonitio Generalis* of 789, the cornerstone of Charlemagne's program of intellectual and cultural reform. Although he addressed it only to the abbot Baugulf, Charlemagne ordered that the letter be circulated among various Carolingian ecclesiastics, and it thus contributed to the development of the Carolingian Renaissance. The letter outlines Charlemagne's desire to provide basic education for the boys of his kingdom and reveals his notion that providing a basic Christian education was essential to his duty as king.

Despite its importance, the exact date of the letter remains uncertain, and modern knowledge of it is the result of mere chance. The composition of the letter, probably at Charlemagne's own dictation, is traditionally dated to the period 780 to 800. Some scholars have proposed a more specific dating to the years 781 to 791 or even to 794 to 796, but the broadest range remains the most generally accepted of the dates of the document. The letter itself is known only from two manuscripts. One manuscript from the twelfth century was destroyed in a bombing raid during World War II, and the other one, which was discovered only in 1927, is from the eighth century. Although only one copy of the letter is still extant, it was most likely copied and sent some time later with some additions to many monasteries by Baugulf.

The letter includes Charlemagne's desire that the monks and secular clergy of his realm should devote themselves to follow the "life set out in their rule and their practice of holy religion"(279). But more than that, they "ought also to be zealous in the cultivation of learning and in teaching those who by the gift of God are able to learn"(279). He encourages learning and education so that his subjects can better follow the will of God and praise God without error in speech or practice. He notes in the document that although he has received many letters with expressions of good pious belief, he has noticed many errors of speech in them. Charlemagne, therefore, encourages Baugulf and the clergy to study the Scriptures and literature in general so that they may better know God's message and better do God's will. The king's appeal to the monks and clergy of the realm to devote themselves to study and teaching was an important stimulus to the growth of the Carolingian Renaissance.

See also Admonitio Generalis; Capitularies; Carolingian Renaissance; Charlemagne

Bibliography

Charlemagne. "A Letter of Charles on the Cultivation of Learning, 780–800." In *Carolingian Civilization: A Reader,* ed. Paul Edward Dutton. Peterborough, Ont.: Broadview, 1993, pp. 79–80.

Brown, Giles. "Introduction: The Carolingian Renaissance." In *Carolingian Culture: Emulation and Innovation,* ed. Rosamond McKitterick. Cambridge: Cambridge University Press, 1994, pp. 1–51.

Laistner, Max L. W. *Thought and Letters in Western Europe, A.D. 500 to 900.* 2d ed. Ithaca, NY: Cornell University Press, 1976.

McKitterick, Rosamond. *The Frankish Kingdoms under the Carolingians, 751–987.* London: Longman, 1983.

Liutprand (d. 744)

The greatest of the Lombard kings of Italy, Liutprand ruled during a time of great prosperity and growth for the Lombard kingdom (r. 712–744). He expanded the boundaries of the kingdom in Italy and sought to bring the entire peninsula under his authority. The Lombard duchies of the south were brought to heel by Liutprand, and he conquered many of the possessions of the Byzantine Empire in Italy. He also enjoyed success against the papacy, which owned extensive estates in central Italy coveted by Liutprand. His advances in central Italy were watched closely by the popes of his age, and his successes in Italy, paradoxically, laid the foundation for the later

invasions of the Carolingian king Pippin and the conquest of the kingdom by Charlemagne. Although Carolingian rulers ultimately brought about the demise of the Lombard kingdom, Liutprand was a trusted ally of the Franks. He was also a skilled ruler who introduced important legal and administrative reforms in the kingdom.

Although vilified in the *Liber Pontificalis* (The Book of the Popes), Liutprand was most likely a devout Christian, who came to the throne after the Lombards had converted from Arian Christianity to Catholic Christianity. He took the throne in 712, following a period of disarray in the Lombard kingdom, and shortly thereafter pursued the traditional Lombard policy of striving to unite Italy. His efforts led him into conflict with the popes of his day—Gregory II, Gregory III, and Zachary—but he did attempt to maintain good relations with the popes and, as Paul the Deacon notes, made pious donations to the church in his kingdom. He defended the Italian peninsula against attacks from Saracen pirates and declared himself the defender of the church and orthodoxy in response to the policy of iconoclasm instituted by the Byzantine emperor Leo III, the Isaurian. Indeed, he took the opportunity to combine his desires to unify Italy under his authority and to establish himself as defender of the church when he seized imperial territory in Italy during the turmoil of the iconoclastic controversy. He also reached a diplomatic settlement with Pope Zachary shortly after the pope ascended the throne, as part of which he returned four towns previously seized from papal territory. It seems, then, that Liutprand was not the enemy of the papacy he is sometimes styled by hostile sources, and he clearly was not the threat to the papacy that his predecessors were.

Although not an open enemy of the institution of the papacy, Liutprand did threaten papal territories, just as he threatened the rest of the peninsula. During his long reign as king, Liutprand gradually extended the boundaries of the kingdom and the extent of

Lombard power. In the 720s, in coordination with the Frankish mayor of the palace Charles Martel, Liutprand secured his northern border at the expense of the duchy of Bavaria. He also exploited Byzantine weakness in the 720s when he seized several cities in Italy, an action that unsettled Pope Gregory II, with whom Liutprand had previously had good relations. The pope in turn arranged an alliance with the Lombard duchies in the south, Spoleto and Benevento, which angered the king and may have forced him to attack papal territory in defense of Lombard interests. Although a treaty was negotiated between Rome and the king, the attack led to ill feelings, as well as Liutprand's subjugation of the southern duchies to his authority. After a period of quiet in the 730s, Liutprand was once again forced into action against the pope, now Gregory III, who had supported rebellion in the duchy of Spoleto and had called for the defense of Ravenna against Lombard aggression and conquest.

It was during the hostilities at the end of the late 730s that Pope Gregory III laid the foundation for the later destruction of the Lombard kingdom. After Liutprand's renewed aggression and conquest of papal territories, Gregory sent a note to the Carolingian mayor Charles Martel, seeking aid against the Lombard king. This appeal by the pope proved fruitless for several reasons. The Lombards and Franks had long been allies, and Paul the Deacon tells the story of Charles sending his son Pippin to Liutprand to receive the traditional gift of the king's hair. Liutprand sent both his hair and many gifts to confirm the friendship between the two rulers and their peoples. It was also important at that time for Charles to preserve the alliance with Liutprand because Muslim armies from Spain continued to threaten the Frankish kingdom. Despite the failure of this attempt by Gregory, later popes did seek and receive aid from the Carolingians against the Lombards. Hostility between the pope and the king survived Gregory's reign, but it was eased during the early years of Pope Zachary,

who personally met with Liutprand and negotiated the return of several papal towns. Indeed, it was Liutprand's devotion to the Catholic faith and respect for the holy see that contributed to Zachary's success.

Although Liutprand's dream of uniting all of Italy ultimately was not realized, he exercised great influence over events on the peninsula and greatly enhanced Lombard royal authority in Italy. He also strengthened royal power within the Lombard kingdom. He strengthened his ties with the dukes and other nobles throughout the kingdom. He also enhanced his ties with all free people in the kingdom by imposing an oath that bound them all to him. He improved royal bureaucracy and the administration of justice. He also cultivated a more sophisticated concept of power. Finally, Liutprand revised the Lombard code of law. Although his struggles with the papacy led in the end to an alliance that brought about the end of the Lombard kingdom, Liutprand clearly presided over a highly successful period in Lombard history and left his successors, both Lombard and Frankish, an important legacy.

See also Arianism; Carolingian Dynasty; Charles Martel; Franks; Gregory II, Pope; Gregory III, Pope; Lombards; Paul the Deacon; Zachary, St.

Bibliography

Christie, Neil. *The Lombards: The Ancient Langobards.* Oxford: Blackwell, 1998.

Davis, Raymond, trans. *The Lives of the Eighth-Century Popes* (Liber Pontificalis): *The Ancient Biographies of Nine Popes from A.D. 715 to A.D. 817.* Liverpool, UK: Liverpool University Press, 1992.

Herrin, Judith. *The Formation of Christendom.* Princeton: Princeton University Press, 1989.

Llewellyn, Peter. *Rome in the Dark Ages.* New York: Barnes and Noble, 1993.

Noble, Thomas X. F. *The Republic of St. Peter: The Birth of the Papal State, 680–825.* Philadelphia: University of Pennsylvania Press, 1984.

Paul the Deacon. *History of the Lombards.* Trans. William Dudley Foulke. Philadelphia: University of Pennsylvania Press, 1974.

Riché, Pierre. *The Carolingians: A Family Who Forged Europe.* Trans. Michael Idomir Allen. Philadelphia: University of Pennsylvania Press, 1993.

Lombards

A Germanic people who first appear in the sources in the first century A.D., settling along the Elbe River, the Lombards, or Langobardi (Long Beards), developed a reputation for being an especially fierce people. Although they suffered occasional setbacks, they won numerous victories over other barbarian peoples, and at the same time were skilled diplomats, able to maintain good relations with the Avars, Byzantines, and Franks. They are best known, however, for their invasion and conquest of much of Italy, which undermined the efforts of the emperor Justinian to reestablish imperial power in Italy. Although pagan or Arian at the time of the invasion, the Lombards were able to establish good relations with the bishops of Italy and eventually converted to Catholic Christianity. Their efforts to unify the Italian peninsula under a Lombard king caused the popes in Rome great anxiety. The Lombard struggle with the papacy contributed to the formation of the papal states and the destruction of the Lombard kingdom in 774 by Charlemagne, whose aid had been sought by the pope.

The origins of the Lombards remain obscure, and the early Roman and medieval texts add little to our knowledge of the earliest period. The first mention of the Lombards was made by Tacitus (c. 56–c. 120) in the *Germania,* who placed them along the lower Elbe River. Later Roman and early medieval writers placed them in lower Austria by the fifth century and then south of the Danube River in Pannonia (modern western Hungary and eastern Austria) in the sixth century. Paul the Deacon, the eighth-century historian of the Lombards, placed their origins in Scandinavia and then traced their migrations into Pannonia. His version of the history, however, follows the standard pattern of migration that most late Roman and early medieval historians ascribed to various barbarian tribes. The period between the first appearance of the Lombards and their settlement in Pannonia is uncertain; the archeological records suggest that theirs was a pastoral existence. They also seem to have developed a fairly well-organized tribal structure and a reputation for fierceness that was later justified in their contacts with Rome and other barbarian peoples.

However that may be, by the end of the fifth century it is most likely that the Lombards had moved into Pannonia; in the next century they were led by the vigorous king Audoin (r. 546–560/1). By the time of Audoin, the Lombards had become a force to be reckoned with and had defeated the Heruls and Gepids in battle. Audoin had gained such renown that he was able to arrange his marriage to a grand-niece of Theodoric the Great, the Ostrogothic king of Italy, a marriage that may have been the inspiration for the Lombard invasion of Italy. Indeed, it was Audoin's son, Alboin, who led the Lombards into Italy.

After distinguishing himself in battle against the Gepids during his father's lifetime, Alboin continued to wage war as king in his own name. Although defeated by the Gepids in 565, Alboin rejoined battle two years later after forming an alliance with the Avars. His victory led to the destruction of the Gepids and death of their king at the hand of Alboin, who made a goblet of his rival's skull and and then married his rival's daughter. After his victory over the Gepids, according to tradition, Alboin entered Italy at the invitation of the disgruntled Byzantine general Narses. Although Narses's invitation may have played a part in the invasion, Lombard awareness of the weakened state of Italy, brought about by the Gothic Wars and divisions in the church, as well as possible family connections, surely also played a role. After settling affairs in Pannonia, Alboin entered the peninsula in 568 with up to 150,000 followers; he quickly conquered much of northern Italy and may have even threatened

Mounted soldier in cast bronze (The Art Archive / Bargello Museum Florence / Dagli Orti)

Rome. Alboin's success in Italy, however, was cut short by an assassination plot involving his wife, who had grown tired of seeing her husband drink from her father's skull.

The death of Alboin reveals two of the weaknesses of the Lombard system, the tradition of elective kingship and a powerful noble class. A new king did emerge immediately in the wake of the assassination; Cleph (r. 572–574) was elected, but he was then assassinated in his turn. This was followed by a ten-year period in which no king was elected and the dukes ruled throughout Lombard Italy. The dukes also continued the subjugation of Italy, spreading south into Tuscany, Beneventum, and Spoleto,. There was, however, little effort to intermingle with the Italian population, and the Lombards both kept themselves separate from and continued to oppress the native population. Their warlike tendencies also led them north in an attempt to conquer Burgundy, an almost fatal mistake. The Lombard dukes faced the might of the Merovingian Franks in Burgundy, a might enhanced by an alliance with the Byzantine Empire. The Lombards paid dearly for their expedition north and were nearly destroyed by the Merovingians. It was this experience, at least in part, that led to a restoration of the kingship, as the dukes joined together to elect Cleph's son Authari (r. 584–590) king. His reign was noteworthy for his marriage to Theudelinde, a Bavarian Catholic princess, recovery of much of the territory lost to the Franks and Byzantines, and efforts to strengthen the Lombard kingship.

During the seventh century, Authari's successors built on his legacy, continuing to strengthen the monarchy and to preserve their ethnic identity. They also expanded

Lombard control in Italy, but introduced important changes in the government and religion of the Lombards. Both developments are evident already during the reign of Authari's immediate successor, Agilulf (r. 590–616), whom Authari's widow, Theudelinde, chose to be king and her new husband. Agilulf stabilized the Lombard frontiers in Italy, limiting imperial territory in the process. He also introduced the practice of early designation of royal successors, identifying his son, Aldoald (616–626), as the heir while the boy was still young. Although an Arian Christian, Agilulf had his son baptized a Catholic and allowed his Lombard subjects to baptize their children as Catholics.

This concession was surely made in deference to Theudelinde, who exercised great power and influence, was courted by Pope Gregory I, and was a patron of the Irish Catholic missionary, St. Columban. Indeed, it was during the reign of Theudelinde and Agilulf that Columban established the famous monastery of Bobbio. Theudelinde's efforts on behalf of the Catholic faith failed, however, and when, according to Paul the Deacon, her son went insane, the new king, Ariald (r. 626–636), was an Arian Christian. Indeed, the reaction against Theudelinde, which may have been motivated by the Lombards' desire to maintain their own identity, lasted two generations and continued into the following reign. The reign of Rothari was characterized not only by the promotion of Arian Christianity, but also—and more importantly—by the codification of the Lombard laws. The laws revealed both Germanic tradition and Roman legal practice and show the ambivalent attitude the Lombards had toward the Romans.

Although indebted to both their Ostrogothic and Roman predecessors in ruling Italy, the Lombards introduced their own customs and social and political arrangements in Italy, as Rothari's laws demonstrate. The most significant aspect of the Lombards' rule in Italy was their effort to retain their ethnic identity, which led to their limited intermingling with the native Italian population as well as their preference for Arian Christianity. Their political system was organized around a king, whose capital was, eventually, established in the city of Pavia. The king came increasingly to rely on taxes and revenues from his royal estates and remained the leading figure in the kingdom, assisted at court by a growing bureaucracy and a number of officials appointed by the king. The dukes were the next most important power in the kingdom and numbered as many as thirty-five during the kingdom's existence. They were sometimes independent of the king, as were the dukes of Spoleto and Beneventum, and were great powers in their own right, who were often elected to the kingship. At the bottom of the social hierarchy were half-free peasants, slaves, and freedmen, but the most important class was that of the *arimmani* (Lombard word for soldiers). The *arimmani* were free men who were responsible for serving in the Lombard military and were essential to the success of the Lombard kings.

Despite the successes of Rothari and other early seventh-century kings, the Lombards faced turmoil during the latter part of the century. They suffered from internal dissent brought on by religious differences and the ambition of the dukes. Moreover, the Lombards faced foreign invasion by the Merovingians and by the Byzantines during the reign of King Grimoald (r. 662–671), who also had to evict invading Avars from part of Lombard Italy. There was a major rebellion in the north during the reign of King Cuncipert (r. 680–700), which the king suppressed, enabling him to bring a group of northern bishops under his control. It was also during this period, that the Lombards, under King Aripert I (r. 653–661), converted to Catholic Christianity from the Arian faith of Rothari and some earlier Lombard kings.

The turmoil of the late seventh century gave way to the high point of Lombard history in the eighth, under the great kings Liutprand, Aistulf, and Desiderius, whose very success led paradoxically to the demise of the

Lombard kingdom. The first of these kings, Liutprand, exploited the turmoil in Italy brought on by the Iconoclastic Controversy in the Byzantine Empire. The controversy emerged because of the decision of Leo III, the Isaurian, to eliminate the use of icons in worship, alienating the papacy, which was already disenchanted with the empire for its failure to protect Italy. Liutprand moved quickly to improve his control of the kingdom and expand its boundaries at the expense of the empire. Although an aggressive and expansionist king, Liutprand strove to maintain good relations with the pope. A Catholic Christian, the king tried to cooperate with Rome even though the popes felt threatened by his efforts to control Italy. His mixed success is demonstrated by the efforts of Pope Gregory III to forge an alliance with the Carolingian mayor, Charles Martel, against the Lombards—Charles was reluctant because of his own ties with Liutprand—and the treaty Liutprand signed with Pope Zachary, who nonetheless promoted ties with the Carolingians.

Liutprand's successor, Aistulf, was the most aggressive and bloodthirsty of the Lombard kings. According to one contemporary source, Aistulf was a "shameless Lombard king" who possessed "pernicious savagery" and cruelty (Davis 1992, 55). In keeping with Lombard tradition, he sought to unify the peninsula under his authority, and therefore posed a great threat to papal territories in central Italy. He seized Ravenna, the imperial stronghold in Italy, from the Byzantines and ended the imperial presence there. The victory over the empire, however, forced the popes to find a new protector and brought about the beginning of the end of the Lombard kingdom. Pippin the Short, recently crowned king of the Franks, agreed to come to the aid of the pope and invaded Italy twice in the 750s to restrain Aistulf. Although Aistulf signed treaties guaranteeing the safety of the pope and his lands, the Lombard king nonetheless frequently broke them. He surely would have violated his last agreement with Pippin had Aistulf not died in a hunting accident in 756.

Aistulf was succeeded by Desiderius, the final Lombard king of Italy. His reign began well and was supported by the pope himself. Moreover, Desiderius enjoyed good relations with the Carolingians, who formed an alliance with the Lombard king against the duke of Bavaria. Benefiting from the unrest in the Frankish kingdom at the death of Pippin, Desiderius forged a marriage alliance with the Carolingians, joining his daughter to Charlemagne. But the marriage was repudiated by the great king shortly after, and the growing threat posed by Desiderius to the papacy led Pope Hadrian I to seek aid from Charlemagne, who invaded Italy in 773 and by the next year had conquered the kingdom. Charlemagne assumed the iron crown of the Lombard kingdom and incorporated Lombard Italy into his growing empire. Although the Lombard kingdom came to an end in 774, its memory is preserved in the region of Italy that still bears the name Lombardy.

See also Aistulf; Alboin; Arianism; Avars; Carolingian Dynasty; Charlemagne; Charles Martel; Desiderius; Franks; Gregory the Great, Pope; Gregory III, Pope; Hadrian I, Pope; Justinian; Liutprand; Merovingian Dynasty; Narses; Ostrogoths; Paul the Deacon; Pippin III, Called the Short; Rothari; Theodoric the Great; Theudelinde; Zachary, St.

Bibliography

Christie, Neil. *The Lombards: The Ancient Langobards.* Oxford: Blackwell, 1998.

Davis, Raymond, trans. *The Lives of the Eighth-Century Popes* (Liber Pontificalis): *The Ancient Biographies of Nine Popes from A.D. 715 to A.D. 817.* Liverpool, UK: Liverpool University Press, 1992.

Drew, Katherine Fisher, trans. *The Lombard Laws.* Philadelphia: University of Pennsylvania Press, 1973.

Goffart, Walter. *Barbarians and Romans, A.D. 418–584: The Techniques of Accommodation.* 1980.

Hallenback, Jan T. *Pavia and Rome: The Lombard Monarchy and the Papacy in the Eighth Century.* Philadelphia: American Philosophical Society, 1982.

Herrin, Judith. *The Formation of Christendom.*
Princeton: Princeton University Press, 1987.

Llewellyn, Peter. *Rome in the Dark Ages.* New York:
Barnes and Noble, 1996.

Paul the Deacon. *History of the Lombards.* Trans.
William Dudley Foulke. Philadelphia:
University of Pennsylvania Press, 1974.

Riché, Pierre. *The Carolingians: A Family Who Forged
Europe.* Trans. Michael Idomir Allen.
Philadelphia: University of Pennsylvania Press,
1993.

Scholz, Bernhard Walter, trans. *Carolingian
Chronicles: Royal Frankish Annals and Nithard's
History.* Ann Arbor: University of Michigan
Press, 1972.

Wallace-Hadrill, J. M. *The Barbarian West, A.D.
400–1000.* New York: Harper and Row, 1962.

Wickham, Chris. *Early Medieval Italy: Central Power
and Local Society, 400–1000.* Ann Arbor:
University of Michigan Press, 1981.

Wolfram, Herwig. *The Roman Empire and Its
Germanic Peoples.* Trans. Thomas J. Dunlap.
Berkeley: University of California Press, 1997.

Lothar (795–855)

Carolingian king and emperor, Lothar was the son and successor of Louis the Pious and brother of Charles the Bald and Louis the German. As the oldest son of Louis the Pious, Lothar was recognized early in his father's reign as the heir designate and was associated with his father as emperor in 817. In the 820s he played an important role in Italy as his father's representative and formalized a long-standing relationship between the Carolingian dynasty and the papacy. The remarriage of Louis to Judith and the birth of Charles the Bald complicated the relationship between Lothar and his father. In the 830s Lothar led two revolts against his father, both of which failed, leaving Lothar in disgrace. He ultimately was restored to his father's good graces, but after the death of Louis the Pious the empire was torn apart by civil war. Lothar, although bested by his brothers, came to terms with them and ruled as emperor until his death in 855.

The firstborn son of Louis the Pious and his wife Irmengard (d. 818), Lothar had reached adulthood in 814 when his grandfather Charlemagne died, and Louis assumed the throne. His maturity benefited Louis by making Lothar an important associate in government, but it also plagued Louis, because Lothar became the focus of opposition to the new emperor. In the opening years of his reign, however, Louis was well served by Lothar, who ruled in Bavaria from 814 to 817. In 817, when Louis implemented the *Ordinatio imperii,* his plan of succession for the empire, Lothar was made co-emperor and recognized as Louis's successor, while Lothar's brothers, Louis the German and Pippin, were made sub-kings, subject to the authority of Louis and Lothar. Lothar was given the responsibility of ruling Italy, which led to the revolt of his cousin, Bernard, king of Italy. The revolt was brutally suppressed by Louis, and Lothar assumed his responsibilities in Italy.

In the 820s, Lothar played an important role in Italy and in the relations of the Carolingian Empire and the papacy in Rome. He exercised a number of royal, or imperial, functions in Italy by calling councils and issuing capitularies. Aware that Judith, his father's second wife, was about to give birth, Lothar called on the pope, Paschal I, to crown him emperor in 823. In this way he was able to assert his place in the empire and confirm his title of emperor, because papal coronation was becoming the official means to assume the imperial title. Although this action may have been an effort to counter any efforts by Louis the Pious to limit his authority, Lothar remained an important figure in the family and the state. He had previously stood as godfather to Judith and Louis's first child, Gisele, and now stood as godfather for his new half-brother, later known as Charles the Bald. Indeed, godparentage had become a very significant responsibility in Carolingian society.

Lothar also played an important role in regularizing relations between the papacy and the Carolingian dynasty. In 824, Lothar issued the *Constitutio Romana* (Roman Constitution)

Frankish Emperor from his psalter, ninth century (The Art Archive/British Library)

on his father's behalf. This constitution was issued after a period of turmoil in the city of Rome and confirmed Carolingian rights in Rome and papal territories. The constitution legislated that the Frankish rulers were to be notified upon the election of a new pope and that the people of Rome were to swear an oath of loyalty to the Carolingian emperor. The Carolingians also enforced loyalty to the pope and promised to protect papal territories in central Italy.

Although he remained an important figure in government, Lothar, along with his brothers Pippin and Louis the German, became increasingly concerned about the place of their newest brother Charles, a concern that eventually led them into rebellion against their father. Their concerns were found to be justified in 827, when their father reorganized the succession plan to include Charles. For many ecclesiastics, the *Ordinatio* of 817 was sacred, and consequently any violation of it was regarded as an act against God. For others in the empire, especially members of the nobility, its sacred character was less of an issue, but nevertheless the restructuring of the succession plan provided an excuse to revolt. And in the late 820s and early 830s, Lothar and his brothers did revolt against their father and Charles. Lothar was motivated by his desire to rule as well as by the encouragement of ambitious members of the nobility. He was also supported by leaders in the church who believed in the sacred nature of government and the *Ordinatio,* ideas that they often reminded Lothar about.

Lothar was involved in two rebellions against his father Louis. The first revolt occurred in 830; it was initiated by his brother Pippin who had the most to lose in the new succession plan. Lothar quickly joined the rebellion from Italy, entering it because of his dissatisfaction over his father's promotion of Bernard of Septimania to high rank at the court, a move that threatened Lothar's own position. Lothar quickly took charge of the situation and placed Louis and Charles under house arrest. His efforts at ruling, however,

met with little success, and, as the chronicler Nithard noted, "the state of the empire grew worse from day to day, since all were driven by greed and sought only their own advantage" (Scholz 1972, 131). Lothar's position was undermined by Louis, who secretly negotiated with both Pippin and Louis the German. By Easter 831, Louis had been restored to the throne. Lothar was returned to Italy in disgrace, and his supporters were jailed, but he was permitted to remain as king in Italy. Louis also restructured the plan of succession once again and created four equal kingdoms out of the empire for his four sons.

Louis, however, failed to keep his bargain with his sons and faced a revolt again, one that was much more serious than the revolt of 830. In 833 Lothar and Louis and Pippin formed an alliance against their father. The four and their armies met on the so-called Field of Lies, where Louis the Pious's armies abandoned him for Lothar, who took his father into custody. Judith was sent to Italy, Charles was sent off to a monastery, and in October, Lothar forced his father to perform an act of penance and abdicate at a great council. Lothar's rough treatment of his father, however, alienated his brothers, especially Louis, who came to the aid of the older Louis. By February 834 the tide had turned, and Louis the Pious was restored to the throne. The emperor and his allies defeated Lothar's army, and Lothar surrendered and was once again returned to Italy.

Turmoil in the Carolingian Empire, however, continued during Louis's last years and into the early 840s. Lothar remained quietly in Italy for several years while his father secured his position once again. On the death of Pippin, Louis restructured the succession yet again, establishing a large kingdom for his son Charles. Lothar was restored to his father's good graces, largely thanks to the efforts of Judith who desired a good relationship between Charles and Lothar, shortly before the older Louis's death. Lothar and Charles were to share the empire, and, although placed on equal footing with Charles, Lothar inherited the imperial title. His claims to this title, as well as his claims to territory drove his efforts in the following years. Indeed, almost immediately after Louis's death, his sons once again fell into civil war, as in various combinations they struggled to enforce their claims to power and territory. Although he reconciled with his godson Charles, Lothar soon turned against him and was then faced by a hostile alliance from his two brothers. Open warfare took place, which culminated in the bloody Battle of Fontenoy in 841, which was marked by massive losses for all combatants. Although weakened, Lothar struggled on, but his brothers reaffirmed their alliance against him with the famous Oath of Strasbourg in 842, and in 843 Lothar agreed to a division of the empire in the Treaty of Verdun.

From the end of the civil war in 843 until his death in 855, Lothar ruled as emperor over the central portion of the empire, which included the imperial capital of Aix-la-Chapelle (modern Aachen, in Germany) and Italy. Although tensions remained and Lothar was constantly attempting to assert his position in the realm, the brothers did manage to rule peacefully during Lothar's lifetime. They held an important council in 844 that sought to reorganize the church, as well as councils in 847 and 851 that emphasized brotherly rule and the unity of the empire. At the same time, however, Lothar attempted to keep his two brothers apart and sought to forge alliances with one against the other. He found little success in that until his reconciliation with Charles in 849, which was commemorated by the commissioning of a new illuminated Gospel from Tours and a magnificent gem, the Lothar Crystal, which told the story of Susannah and the Elders. On September 22, 855, Lothar retired to a monastery, where he died six days later. He was succeeded in the northern section of his territory by his son Lothar II (d. 869), and in Italy by his son Louis (d. 875), who assumed the title of emperor. Although he successfully maintained his position in the empire during his life, Lothar's middle kingdom, especially

the inheritance of Lothar II, remained a source of contention for many years to come.

See also Capitularies; Carolingian Dynasty; Charlemagne; Charles the Bald; Fontenoy, Battle of; Franks; Judith; Louis the German; Louis the Pious; Nithard; Strasbourg, Oath of; Verdun, Treaty of

Bibliography
Godman, Peter, and Roger Collins, eds. *Charlemagne's Heir: New Perspectives on the Reign of Louis the Pious.* Oxford: Clarendon, 1990.
Llewellyn, Peter. *Rome in the Dark Ages.* New York: Barnes and Noble, 1993.
McKitterick, Rosamond. *The Frankish Kingdoms under the Carolingians, 751–987.* London: Longman, 1983.
Nelson, Janet. *Charles the Bald.* London: Longman, 1992.
Reuter, Timothy. *Germany in the Early Middle Ages, c. 800–1056.* London: Longman, 1991.
Riché, Pierre. *The Carolingians: A Family Who Forged Europe.* Trans Michael Idomir Allen. Philadelphia: University of Pennsylvania Press, 1993.
Scholz, Bernhard Walter, trans. *Carolingian Chronicles: Royal Frankish Annals and Nithard's History.* Ann Arbor: University of Michigan Press, 1972.

Louis the German (d. 876)

Third son of Louis the Pious, who inherited the eastern portion of the Carolingian Empire on his father's death. A participant in the civil wars against his father, Louis the German also supported his father at key moments when his older brother, Lothar, seemed too harsh in his treatment of the elder Louis. After his father's death, Louis the German was involved in fratricidal warfare with Lothar and Charles the Bald that led to the fragmentation of the empire of Charlemagne. Although there was at least nominal cooperation between the brothers and nominal recognition of the imperial authority, the empire was essentially divided into three separate kingdoms ruled by Louis and his brothers. The kingdoms created by the sons of Louis the Pious established the outlines of later medieval and even modern France and Germany, and Louis the German himself set important precedents for later rulers of medieval Germany.

Born probably in Aquitaine circa 804, Louis was raised to prominence in Louis the Pious's reorganization of the empire in 817. In that division of the realm, which made Lothar co-emperor and heir to the imperial throne, Louis was made king of Bavaria, the base of power for Louis that lasted throughout his entire life. In the 820s Louis served his father in his assigned region of Bavaria, but in the 830s, perhaps in response to his father's efforts to create a region in the kingdom for Charles the Bald, the son of his second wife, Louis took part in two rebellions against Louis the Pious. Indeed, Louis the German, with his brother Pippin, initiated the revolt of 830, intending to "liberate" his father from the pernicious influence of his stepmother Judith and his father's close advisor Bernard of Septimania. After the initial success of the revolt, Lothar took control of it and alienated his younger brothers. Louis the Pious, under house arrest, secretly sent messengers to Louis and Pippin, encouraging their support in exchange for greater territories in the empire. The younger Louis readily accepted, and his support for his father was essential to the collapse of the rebellion of 830.

The empire continued to face turmoil over the next several years, and once again Louis the German took an active role in revolt against his father. In 833, Louis and his brothers Lothar and Pippin revolted against the elder Louis, deposing him and placing him, Judith, and Charles the Bald in monasteries. Lothar's bad treatment of his father, however, and his efforts to gain greater control of the empire angered Louis. As he had in 830, Louis the German played a key role in restoring his father to the imperial throne. His efforts were rewarded in 839 when, after the death of Pippin, Louis the Pious sought to restrict his son Louis to Bavaria and favored

both Charles the Bald and the rehabilitated Lothar. The younger Louis quite naturally struggled to maintain his authority in the eastern part of the Carolingian Empire.

On the death of Louis the Pious in 840, the difficult situation in the empire exploded into open civil war between his three surviving sons. Lothar sought to gain control of the entire empire, and his ambition drove his younger brothers Louis and Charles into an alliance against him. The two brothers formed an alliance in the spring of 841 and fought a terrible, bloody battle against Lothar at Fontenoy on June 25, 841. Louis and Charles triumphed over Lothar and remained firm in their alliance, despite Lothar's efforts to divide them. In the following year, Louis and Charles confirmed their alliance in the famed Oath of Strasbourg, which was sworn and recorded in early forms of the Romance and German languages. Lothar was gradually worn down by his younger brothers and came to terms with them in 843 with the Treaty of Verdun, which assigned Lothar the imperial title and central kingdom of the empire. Charles was assigned the western kingdom, and Louis received the eastern kingdom, including territories that extended east of the Rhine River and north of the Alps.

Although the three brothers had come to terms and continued to meet and to appear on the surface to cooperate with each other, none of the three were content with the settlement, and each conspired to enlarge his share at his brothers' expense. As king of East Francia, Louis was the sole binding force in a newly created territory and sought to solidify his authority throughout his kingdom, in part by establishing or favoring monasteries—a policy used effectively by his successors in the tenth century. As ever, Bavaria remained his power base and the starting point for his expansionist tendencies to the east and west. His efforts to expand his eastern frontier met with little success, but he did send forth missionaries in an effort to extend both religious and political authority. He also made several attempts to seize West Francia from his half brother and former ally, Charles the Bald. In 853 a group of west Frankish nobles sought his aid, and in 854 he sent his son to Aquitaine. In 858, Louis himself invaded his half brother's kingdom, but on neither occasion was he able to unseat his brother, in part because Charles the Bald received the full support of the bishops of his realm.

Louis also cast covetous eyes on the kingdom of his older brother Lothar, or least that of Lothar's heirs. When Lothar died in 855, his kingdom was divided among his sons, with his son Louis inheriting the imperial crown. The other son, Lothar, inherited much of the northern part of his father's kingdom, Lotharingia, but died without heir. Louis the German and Charles each sought to acquire the territory. Louis invaded in 870, and he and his brother came to terms in the treaty of Meerssen in that year. They divided the realm of Lotharingia between themselves, with both brothers gaining important territory and Louis obtaining the capital, Aachen. Louis also attempted to seize the imperial title after the death of his nephew Louis in 875, but was outmaneuvered by Charles the Bald, who was crowned emperor.

Along with his struggles against his brothers, Louis the German faced challenges to his power from his sons, Carloman (d. 880) and Louis the Younger (d. 882), but not Charles the Fat (d. 888). As early as 856 he faced rebellion from his son Carloman, who built up his power in Bavaria at his father's expense. In 860 Louis sought to curtail his son's advances, and in 863 an open power struggle developed between the two. By 865 the two had been reconciled, but Carloman's brother, Louis the Younger, suspicious of his older brother, revolted. The revolt was brought to a close by 866, thanks in part to the efforts of Charles the Bald to reconcile his brother and his nephew. Although Louis the Younger quarreled with his father on occasion after 866 and continued to be mistrustful of his brother, Louis the German never faced the kinds of revolt that his brother Lothar or his father Louis the Pious had faced. In part, this

was due to his ability to reconcile with his sons after disputes broke out. It was also due to his willingness, perhaps as a result of his awareness of potential problems from his sons, to bestow power on his sons. In the late 850s and early 860s, Louis granted land and authority to his sons—they were given power to rule that was less than that of a king but more than that of a noble. They were granted important territorial regions, and in that way they were the precursors of the territorial dukes of the later Middle Ages.

At his death, Louis's three sons divided the realm among themselves. One of them, Charles the Fat, went on to assume the imperial title that his father had at times pursued, only to lose it when deposed in 887.

Louis the German's reign was marked by relative stability in his own kingdom and efforts, not always successful, to expand his western and eastern frontiers. In a good Carolingian fashion, he promoted missionary activity among the pagan folk on his eastern frontier. His efforts to convert the pagan and expand his border prefigured the activities of tenth-century rulers, and his arrangement with his sons also foreshadowed later medieval developments. Although in many ways a traditional Carolingian ruler, Louis laid the foundation for developments in later medieval Germany.

See also Carolingian Dynasty; Charlemagne; Charles the Bald; Fontenoy, Battle of; Franks; Judith; Lothar; Louis the Pious; Nithard; Strasbourg, Oath of; Verdun, Treaty of

Bibliography
Fichtenau, Heinrich. *The Carolingian Empire*. Trans. Peter Munz. Toronto: University of Toronto Press, 1979.
Ganshof, François L. *The Carolingians and the Frankish Monarchy: Studies in Carolingian History*. Trans. Janet L. Sondheimer. London: Longman, 1971.
Halphen, Louis. *Charlemagne and the Carolingian Empire*. Trans. Giselle de Nie. Amsterdam: North-Holland, 1977.
McKitterick, Rosamond. *The Frankish Kingdoms*

under the Carolingians, 751–987. London: Longman, 1983.

Nelson, Janet. *Charles the Bald*. London: Longman, 1992.

Reuter, Timothy. *Germany in the Early Middle Ages, c. 800–1056*. London: Longman, 1991.

Riché, Pierre. *The Carolingians: A Family Who Forged Europe*. Trans. Michael Idomir Allen. Philadelphia: University of Pennsylvania Press, 1993.

Scholz, Bernhard Walter, trans. *Carolingian Chronicles: Royal Frankish Annals and Nithard's History*. Ann Arbor: University of Michigan Press, 1972.

Louis the Pious (778–840)

The only surviving son and heir of the great Carolingian king, Charlemagne, Louis the Pious ruled the empire from 814 until his death in 840. As emperor he introduced important reforms of the structure and organization of the empire and continued the religious and cultural reforms associated with the Carolingian Renaissance. Traditionally accused of causing the collapse of the Carolingian Empire because of his excessive devotion to the church and his domination by his wife and other advisors, Louis is no longer blamed for the empire's collapse. Instead his reign and his understanding of his office are seen in a more positive light, especially the first decade, when he instituted a number of far-reaching political and religious reforms. Although the empire did not fall because of Louis but because of fundamental flaws in its structure that had already emerged in Charlemagne's last years, its fortunes did suffer during Louis's reign because of the revolts his sons waged against him.

Louis's youth was marked by his early introduction to power. In 781, when not quite three years old, Louis was crowned and anointed king of Aquitaine by Pope Hadrian I. This crowning has traditionally been seen as Charlemagne's concession to demands for independence in Aquitaine, a territory incorporated into the empire by Pippin the Short, but more likely he intended it as an effective means to govern the province and provide practical experience for Louis. Aquitaine did provide important lessons for Louis, who faced revolts from native Gascons and repeated raids from Muslim Spain. Louis effectively responded to both these threats during his reign as king and even undertook counteroffensives into Spain. Although he frequently communicated with his father, Louis ruled Aquitaine on his own and was never visited by Charlemagne in the subkingdom. He also participated in military campaigns outside Aquitaine, including campaigns in Italy and Saxony. Moreover, while king of Aquitaine, Louis had a number of experiences that shaped his later life. In 794, Louis married Irmengard, the daughter of a powerful noble, who bore him three sons and two daughters. He also initiated a program of church reform with Benedict of Aniane. Finally, Louis's future was shaped by his father's ordering of the succession. In 806, Charlemagne implemented a plan of succession that divided the realm among his sons, a long-standing Frankish tradition, in which Louis would continue to be king of Aquitaine. On September 11, 813, after his other brothers had died, Louis was crowned emperor by his father at a great assembly in Aachen.

In 814, following his father's death, Louis succeeded to the throne as the sole emperor of the Frankish realm and brought a more profound understanding of the office of Christian king or emperor than his father had had. Like his father, Louis was filled with the sense of Christian mission that his position entailed, perhaps best demonstrated by his expulsion of prostitutes and actors from the imperial court and his dismissal of his sisters, none of whom had been allowed by his father to marry, to religious communities. Unlike his father, however, Louis understood his position strictly in imperial terms, an understanding reflected in his official title: "Louis, by Order of Divine Providence, Emperor and Augustus." Unlike his father who made reference to his royal dignities in his official impe-

Emperor Louis the Pious in the dress of a Christian Roman ruler from Hrabanus Maurusis (Rome, Vatican Library)

rial title, Louis dispensed with royal dignities in his official title from the beginning of his reign and provided a solid foundation for the empire in 817. In that year, following a serious accident while crossing a bridge in which several were injured, Louis held a council at Aachen. At the council, Louis established a new framework for the Frankish empire, whose territorial integrity would remain inviolate. In the *Ordinatio imperii,* Louis instituted a plan that would have allowed the empire to continue as a political and spiritual unit forever. His eldest son, Lothar, was associated with Louis and would ultimately succeed him as emperor over the entire Frankish realm. Louis's younger sons, Louis the German and Pippin of Aquitaine, would receive subkingdoms—a concession to Frankish tradition—but would be subject to their father and then their brother. This bold new design was rooted in Louis's firm convictions that God had bestowed upon him the burden of government and that the empire itself was a divinely ordained unit.

Equally important steps were taken by Louis to reorganize and strengthen relations with the pope in Rome. In 816 he was crowned by Pope Stephen IV in the city of Rheims, a coronation that has traditionally been seen as a concession to papal authority and an abdication of sovereignty. Louis, in fact, gave nothing up by accepting coronation from Stephen, but merely solidified relations between the pope and emperor and confirmed what was implicit in the coronation of 813. Furthermore, because the pope was the highest spiritual power and the representative of Peter, the great patron saint of the Carolingians, it was only logical that Louis should receive papal blessing. But more important than the coronation was the new constitutional and legal settlement that Louis imposed on Rome in two stages, in 816/817 and 824. Starting with the unwritten rules that had guided relations between the Carolingians and the pope for the previous two generations, Louis issued the *Pactum Ludovicianum* in 816 and confirmed it the following

year with the new pope, Paschal I. This document identified the territories under papal control and precisely defined the relationship between Rome and the Frankish rulers. Although recognizing papal autonomy, the pact proclaimed the duty of Carolingian rulers to protect Rome. This agreement provided a written basis for the relationship between the pope and the Carolingian emperors and regularized the relationship between them by incorporating it into traditional Carolingian governmental structures.

An even greater step in the development of the relationship between Louis and Rome occurred with the publication of the *Constitutio Romana* in 824. In 823, following a period of turmoil in Rome involving the pope and high-ranking officials of the city's administration, Lothar, acting as his father's representative, issued the *Constitutio,* which confirmed the long-standing relationship between the Carolingian rulers and the popes. The *Constitutio* was intended to protect the pope and people of Rome and to provide a clear written framework for the place of Rome in the empire. The *Constitutio* stated the obligation of the pope to swear on oath of friendship to the emperor after his election as pope but before his consecration. The people living in the papal territories were also to swear an oath of loyalty to the emperor. The Carolingians claimed the right to establish courts in Rome to hear appeals against papal administrators. The *Constitutio* summarized, in writing, the customary rights and obligations of three generations of Frankish rulers, providing a more solid foundation for the exercise of Carolingian power in Italy.

Louis also instituted important reforms of the church in his empire during his reign as emperor, building upon reforms that were begun while he was still king of Aquitaine. With his close friend and advisor, Benedict of Aniane, Louis implemented monastic reforms that attempted to standardize monastic life in the empire. The reforms were intended to establish a uniform monastic practice in an empire in which a variety of monastic rules were followed. The reforms, implemented in 816–817, introduced the Rule of Benedict of Nursia, or at least Benedict of Aniane's understanding of it, as the standard rule of the empire. Louis's reform legislation also sought to improve further the morality and education of the clergy.

Louis's political and religious reforms were not uniformly popular in the empire, and in 817 a revolt broke out that affected the shape of the emperor's reign. His nephew, Bernard, king of Italy, with the support of bishops and nobles, revolted against the settlement of 817. Louis quickly, and ruthlessly, suppressed the revolt. Bernard was sentenced to death. His sentence was commuted to blinding—a particularly unpleasant punishment that led to Bernard's death soon after it occurred. The nobles were exiled, and the bishops, including Theodulf of Orléans, were deposed from their sees. Four years after the revolt, in 821, Louis issued a general amnesty, recalling and restoring the exiles and bishops. As part of this reconciliation, Louis underwent voluntary penance for the death of Bernard. Although the act, undertaken from a position of strength, was regarded as meritorious at the time, it set a bad precedent for later in Louis's reign.

Louis clearly made substantial improvements on the organization of the empire and on Carolingian relations with Rome in the first half of his reign, but in the second half he suffered from the revolts of his sons and the near collapse of the empire. The difficulties Louis faced were the result, in part, of his second marriage to Judith, a member of the Welf family, which had extensive holdings in Bavaria and other parts of Germany. The birth of a son on June 13, 823, the future Charles the Bald, and the promotion of Bernard of Septimania further complicated matters for Louis. He also suffered from the death of his closest advisor, Benedict of Aniane, in 821. These problems were made more serious by the ambitions of Louis's older sons, especially Lothar, as well as those of the nobility, who could no longer count on the spoils of foreign

wars of conquest to enrich themselves or their reputations. In fact, the end of Carolingian expansion, with the exception of missionary activity among the Danes and other peoples along the eastern frontier, limited the beneficence of the Carolingian rulers and allowed the warrior aristocracy to exploit the tensions within the ruling family for their own gain.

The situation came to a head in the late 820s and early 830s and led to almost ten years of civil strife throughout the empire. A revolt broke out in 830 after Louis had promoted Bernard of Septimania to the office of chamberlain and granted territory to Charles in the previous year. With the support of various noble factions, the older sons of Louis rebelled against their father in April and accused Bernard and Judith of adultery, sorcery, and conspiracy against the emperor. Lothar, although not originally involved, joined the rebellion from Italy and quickly asserted his authority over his younger brothers. Lothar took his father and half-brother into custody, deposed Bernard, who fled, and sent Judith to a convent. But his own greed disturbed his brothers, who were secretly reconciled with their father. At a council in October, Louis rallied his supporters and took control of the kingdom back from Lothar. Judith took an oath that she was innocent. Louis reorganized the empire, dividing it into three kingdoms and Italy, which Lothar ruled. The sons of Louis would rule independently after their father's death, and no mention of empire was made in this settlement.

Although Louis was restored, the situation was not resolved in 830, and problems remained that caused a more serious revolt in 833–834. Along with the question of how to provide for Charles, the problem of the ambitions of Lothar and his brothers remained, as did that of an acquisitive nobility. Furthermore, certain leading ecclesiastics, including Agobard of Lyons and Ebbo of Rheims, argued that Louis had violated God's will by overturning the settlement of 817 when he restructured the plan of succession in 830.

The older sons formed a conspiracy against their father that led to a general revolt in 833. Meeting his sons and Pope Gregory IV (r. 827–844) at the so-called Field of Lies, Louis was betrayed and abandoned by his army and captured by his sons. Once again, the emperor was subjected to humiliating treatment at the hands of Lothar. Judith was sent to Rome with the pope, and both Charles and Louis were sent to monasteries. In October Lothar held a council of nobles and bishops at which Louis was declared a tyrant, and then Lothar visited his father in the monastery of St. Médard in Soissons and compelled Louis to "voluntarily" confess to a wide variety of crimes, including murder and sacrilege, to renounce his imperial title, and to accept perpetual penance. Lothar's actions, however, alienated his brothers Louis and Pippin, who rallied to their father's side. In early 834 Louis the German and Pippin revolted against their brother and were joined by their father, who had regained his freedom. Lothar was forced to submit and returned in disgrace to Italy. In 835 Louis made a triumphant return. He was once again crowned emperor, by his half-brother Bishop Drogo of Metz, and he restored Judith and Charles to their rightful places by his side. The bishops who had joined the revolt against Louis were deposed from their offices by Louis at this time.

Louis remained in power until his death, but his remaining years were not peaceful ones; familial tensions remained. It was important to Louis, and especially to Judith, that Charles be included in the succession, but Louis recognized at the same time that it was necessary not to alienate his other sons too completely in the process. And, of course, Lothar's ambitions remained even though he remained out of favor for several years after 834. Louis faced further revolts from Louis the German as well as the son of Pippin; after Pippin died in 838, his portion of the realm was bestowed on Charles rather than Pippin's own heirs. One of Louis's last important acts was his reconciliation with Lothar, who pledged his support for Charles and was rewarded with the imperial title. Louis also divided most of the empire between Lothar and Charles, an act that almost certainly guaranteed further civil war after Louis's death on June 20, 840.

Despite the very real break-up of the empire in the generation after his death, Louis should not be blamed for the collapse of the Carolingian Empire, which had revealed its flaws already in the last years of Charlemagne's life. Louis's reign, particularly the first part before 830, was a period of growth for the empire, or at least the idea of empire. In fact, his elevation of the idea of empire as the ultimate political entity and his own understanding that the empire was established by God was a significant advancement in political thought and remained an important political idea for his own line and for the line of his successors. His codification of Carolingian relations with Rome was equally important, creating a written document that strengthened and defined imperial-papal ties for the ninth and tenth centuries. Although he faced difficulties in the last decade of his life that prefigured the break-up of the empire in the next generation, Louis was a farsighted ruler, whose reign provided many important and lasting contributions to early medieval government and society.

See also Benedict of Aniane; Carolingian Dynasty; Carolingian Renaissance; Charlemagne; Charles the Bald; Louis the German; *Ordinatio Imperii;* Pippin III, Called the Short

Bibliography

Cabaniss, Allen, trans. *Son of Charlemagne: A Contemporary Life of Louis the Pious.* Syracuse, NY: Syracuse University Press, 1961.

Ganshof, François Louis. *The Carolingians and the Frankish Monarchy.* Trans. Janet Sondheimer. London: Longman, 1971.

Godman, Peter, and Roger Collins, eds. *Charlemagne's Heir: New Perspectives on the Reign of Louis the Pious.* Oxford: Clarendon, 1990.

Halphen, Louis. *Charlemagne and the Carolingian Empire.* Trans. Giselle de Nie. Amsterdam: North-Holland, 1977.

McKitterick, Rosamond. *The Frankish Kingdoms under the Carolingians, 751–987.* London: Longman, 1983.

Noble, Thomas X. F. *The Republic of St. Peter: The Birth of the Papal State, 680–825.* Philadelphia: University of Pennsylvania Press, 1984.

Scholz, Bernhard Walter, trans. *Carolingian Chronicles: Royal Frankish Annals and Nithard's History.* Ann Arbor: University of Michigan Press, 1972.

M

Marriage

One of the most important and central institutions in any society, marriage was a custom that underwent profound and lasting change during late antiquity and the early Middle Ages. Traditions common among the Germanic peoples, including polygyny and concubinage, were gradually worn away by the influence of Roman civilization, and especially Christianity. Certain Germanic customs continued, but the institution of marriage came to be defined as an indissoluble union between two people. Although women lost a degree of social mobility as a consequence of the new practice of marriage, they gained greater security and a more important role in the family.

Perhaps the earliest account of the marriage practices of the Germanic peoples is to be found in the *Germania* of the great first-century Roman historian, Tacitus. He explains that the German peoples possess a very strict marriage code that is most worthy of praise. The barbarians, as he calls them, each take only one wife, with the exception of those whose status brings them many offers of marriage. The dowry, he says, is brought to the wife from the husband and not, as it in Rome, to the husband from the wife. The gifts presented are quite revealing of the attitudes of the barbarians, according to Tacitus.

The dowry generally consists of oxen, a horse and bridle, or a shield, spear, and sword. The bride bestows gifts of arms on her husband, thus establishing a bond between the two in which they willingly share hardships and good times. The new bride joins her husband's household and shares in all its labors.

Tacitus explains that the marriage is a permanent bond, and that secret love letters are unknown. Adultery, he says, is seldom practiced and severely punished. And women generally remain committed to one man; Tacitus does not mention the fidelity of men, making it likely that men were less faithful than women. Tacitus's view of Germanic marriage, however, must be accepted only with extreme caution; he was, after all, as much a moralist as a historian. For Tacitus, the Germanic people were noble savages, whose moral and ethical behavior stood in stark contrast to the immorality of the Romans of the first century. His moralistic agenda notwithstanding, Tacitus's depiction of marriage among the Germanic tribes on Rome's frontiers offers at least a glimpse into early Germanic marital customs.

It is generally held that the early Germans recognized two forms of legitimate marriage, one that involved parental participation and one that did not. The latter form has been traditionally known as *Friedelehe,* a practice in which a free woman entered a relationship with a free man. (Marriage between slaves was not recognized as legitimate and marriage between the free and unfree was strictly forbidden in law.) Although the romantic nature of this form of marriage has been rightly questioned, it most likely existed as a form of quasi-marriage, in which the rights and economic security of the woman involved were relatively unprotected. Of course, this marriage custom was not approved, and the man involved could be forced to pay heavy fines if the bride's family pressed charges. Another form of marriage that occurred without parental involvement was *Raubehe,* marriage by abduction. The most famous example of this type of marriage was the kidnapping of the Thuringian princess, Radegund, whose hand in marriage was fought over by the sons of the great Frankish king Clovis (r. 481–511). The legal codes of the various Germanic peoples, however, came to punish this practice severely—at least when it took place within the individual kingdoms.

Although there were exceptions, the most common type of marriage was a formal arrangement between a suitor and the prospective bride's parents. Marriages were contracted when the couple involved reached the *legitima aetas* (legitimate age) or *perfecta aetas* (perfect age). This age varied among the various Germanic peoples: twenty for the Burgundians, twelve or fifteen for the Franks, and twenty-five for the Visigoths. First marriages are believed to have taken place generally when couples were in their middle teens, although some scholars suggest that first marriages took place when the couple involved was as old as their middle twenties.

The arrangement of the marriage of a daughter involved three specific steps: the *petitio* (formal marriage proposal), the *desponsatio* (betrothal), and the *nuptiae* (wedding ceremony). The suitor offered a formal pledge, the *arrha,* which could include payment to the parents. If the pledge was accepted, then the suitor and the woman's parents entered a legally binding contract, followed by the exchange of rings before witnesses. Penalties for breaking the contract were quite severe for the woman and her family but less severe for the man, if he broke the contract. Betrothed women could be executed if they married someone else, and parents could be fined heavily. Penalties for the groom were modest; at worst they involved payment of the dowry. Following the betrothal, the bride was delivered to her spouse's household, which symbolized the transfer of legal authority from the father to the husband.

Marriages were also important economic transactions, especially for the woman. The bride was entitled to two significant monetary grants from her new husband, which were granted to guarantee her financial security now that she was released from her father's legal custody. The bride, as Tacitus notes, received the *dos* (dowry, bridegift). The dowry could be quite substantial, particularly among the elite of Germanic society. Visigothic law set the maximum dowry at one-tenth of the husband's property, but it could include up to twenty slaves and twenty horses. Among the Franks and Lombards the dowry was even larger, one-third of the husband's property among the Franks and one-quarter of the property among the Lombards. The bride was also entitled to the *morgengabe* (morning gift). This gift was customarily given by the husband to his wife following the consummation of the marriage and was generally less substantial than the dowry. Although it could be as extravagant as the five cities Chilperic gave to Galswintha, the *morgengabe* was usually more modest in value and involved money, jewelry, and clothing. The bride, however, did not come empty-handed to the marriage but contributed her trousseau, which included personal items (dresses, bracelets, earrings, and other jewelry) and household items (linens, a bed, benches, and stools). The bride's contribution to the marriage could be quite substantial, as was that of Rigunth, a Frankish princess, whose trousseau amounted to fifty wagonloads of goods. And Galswintha's was so great that Chilperic murdered her rather than divorce her and return it.

The institution of marriage from the fifth to eighth centuries was relatively unstable and marked by ease of divorce, polygyny, and concubinage among the German peoples who took over the Roman Empire. Divorce was a fairly simple affair, at least for the man. A wife could be repudiated for a variety of things, including adultery, inability to bear children, and "bad" behavior. She could also be divorced for no reason, provided the husband was willing to give up control of her property. The woman had to endure the worst behavior; she could not even divorce her husband for adultery. Moreover, as Tacitus notes, the wealthier Germans practiced polygyny, and this practice became increasingly popular among the Germanic peoples who took over the Western Roman Empire. Although not practiced by all Germanic peoples in the post-Roman world, polygyny was quite common among the Franks. Ingunde, the wife of Chlotar I, asked her husband to find a husband for her sister and, liking his sister-in-law so well, Chlotar married her himself. And he may have married others as well while still married to Ingunde. Chilperic was expected to renounce Fredegund and his other wives in order to marry Galswintha, and Dagobert I had many wives and concubines. There is evidence that even the early Carolingians practiced polygyny before they implemented the rule of monogamy. Along with multiple wives, Frankish rulers possessed concubines, and they were emulated in this practice by members of the nobility.

The instability of marriage among the Germanic peoples, especially the Franks, was particularly disadvantageous to women. Women were particularly vulnerable to divorce and had an insecure position in the marriage. But the instability of marriage did offer some women the opportunity of social advancement, particularly lower-class or slave women like Fredegund. Women did have rights to the property they brought into the marriage, and a wife could keep this property if she were divorced through no fault of her own. Unlike their ancient Roman counterparts, Germanic women had greater economic and legal independence from their husbands, and like Roman women they were released from paternal authority when they married.

Marriage customs, however, underwent dramatic change during the eighth and ninth centuries as a result of reforms implemented by the Carolingian dynasty. The church had long struggled to limit multiple marriages, concubinage, and divorce among the Franks and other Germans, with only marginal success. Beginning with Pippin and, with greater force, his son Charlemagne, Frankish law came to conform to church law. The Carolingians instituted a reform of marriage laws and custom that established marriage as an indissoluble bond between two people. The Carolingian rulers continued the practice of concubinage, but they practiced serial marriage instead of multiple marriage. Charlemagne himself had several concubines and a series of wives, but he remained with each until her death. His personal example of monogamous marriage was translated into law. In his *Admonitio Generalis* he forbade remarriage after divorce, and in a law passed in 796 eliminated adultery as a reason for divorce. A man could separate from an adulterous spouse according to this law, but he could not remarry while his wife lived. Although Carolingian legislation limited the social mobility open to some women, it made marriage a more stable and secure institution and strengthened the role of the woman in the family.

See also Admonitio Generalis; Carolingian Dynasty; Charlemagne; Chilperic I; Clovis; Dagobert; Fredegund; Galswintha; Merovingian Dynasty; Radegund

Bibliography

Gies, Frances, and Joseph Gies. *Marriage and Family in the Middle Ages.* 2d. Edition. New York: Harper and Row, 1987.

Herlihy, David. *Medieval Households.* Cambridge, MA: Harvard University Press, 1985.

Reynolds, Philip L. *Marriage in the Western Church: The Christianization of Marriage.* Leiden: Brill, 1994.

Tacitus. *The Agricola and the Germania.* Trans. H. Mattingly. Trans. Rev. S. A. Handford. Harmondsworth, UK: Penguin, 1970.

Wemple, Suzanne. *Women in Frankish Society: Marriage and the Cloister, 500–900.* Philadelphia: University of Pennsylvania Press, 1985.

Merovingian Dynasty (450–751)

Ruling family of Frankish Gaul from the mid-fifth to the mid-eighth century, when it was replaced by Pippin the Short and the Carolingian dynasty. Creators of the most effective and longest lasting successor state to emerge in the post-Roman world, the Merovingians rose to prominence under their greatest king, Clovis (r. 481–511), who first forged various Frankish peoples into a unified kingdom. Although his successors were generally not his equals, they managed to expand the boundaries of the realm and strengthen the dynasty's hold on the kingdom. For most of the two centuries after the death of Clovis, the Merovingian kings were the among the most powerful and important of the rulers who came to power in Europe after the fall of the Western Roman Empire. They were plagued, however, by internal strife, as each of the various descendants of Clovis strove to seize control of the kingdom under his own authority and at the expense of his brothers or other male relatives. Indeed, the central weakness of the dynasty was the tradition of dividing the realm among all legitimate, and sometimes illegitimate, male heirs. This often led to civil war, including the truly bitter competition between the Merovingian queens Brunhilde and Fredegund in the late sixth century. Despite this underlying structural weakness, the dynasty prospered in the seventh century under the kings Chlotar and Dagobert. By the late seventh century, however, the dynasty faced internal discord, early death and weakness of several kings, and an increasingly acquisitive nobility. Although certainly not the "do-nothing kings" *(rois fainéants)* of popular tradition, the late Merovingians became increasingly irrelevant in the kingdom by the late seventh and early eighth centuries. Their authority was severely curtailed by the rising power of the Carolingian mayors of the palace, who deposed the last Merovingian king, Childeric III, in 750.

The dynasty traditionally traced its origins to a certain Merovech, the son of a sea god, but the first historical king of note was Childeric I (d. 481), the father of Clovis. Little is known of Childeric's reign other than what Gregory of Tours reported in his history and what appears in the later chronicle of Fredegar. According to Gregory, Childeric was a successful warlord from northeastern Gaul and Germany—modern Belgium and the Rhineland—who fought battles at Orléans and Angers, and also seized several islands from the Saxons when they fought the Romans. Childeric also negotiated a treaty with the Saxon leader Odovacar, possibly the same leader who deposed Romulus Augustulus in 476. Although a great warrior and successful conqueror, Childeric, according to Fredegar, was deposed for profligacy. Childeric, however, made an arrangement with one of his faithful followers, who was to agitate for Childeric's return and then send the king half of a coin they had divided when it was safe to return. While in exile, Childeric stayed with a Thuringian king, whose wife Basina followed Childeric back to the Franks and became his queen because she saw in him a ruler of great power.

Two other sources, the king's tomb at Tournai and a letter from Bishop Remigius of Rheims, provide information on Childeric's reign. The burial site provides important information on the cultural sophistication and Romanization of the Franks already in the mid-fifth century. Although there is ample evidence of the "barbarian" nature of the Franks in the tomb, there is also evidence of Roman influence. The tomb was built near a Roman cemetery and Roman road and contains a

Dagobert I, 605–639 Merovingian Frankish king, receiving the kingdom of France, folio 73R of the fourteenth-century French manuscript Great Chronicles of France, *Northern School (The Art Archive / Bibliothèque Municipale Castres / Dagli Orti)*

brooch and Byzantine coins that suggest contacts with the imperial capital at Constantinople. Moreover, there was other jewelry of high quality. The bishop's letter to Childeric's son Clovis reveals the extent of Childeric's domain and suggests that Childeric was in contact with the Catholic Christian bishops of Gaul.

On the death of Childeric in 481, his son Clovis ascended the throne, and it is with Clovis that the history of the Merovingian dynasty truly begins. Although well known from the pages of the history of Gregory of Tours, Clovis must remain a shadowy figure; the portrait offered by Gregory is very much the creation of the bishop of Tours himself.

Gregory's king is depicted as having been in many ways God's instrument, one that punished the wicked; expelled God's enemies, the Arians, from Gaul; protected the saints, bishops, and church; and converted directly to Catholic Christianity from paganism. Indeed, one of the most famous tales of Clovis's reign involves his conversion. His wife Clothilda, a Burgundian Catholic, sought to convert her husband to her faith, but with little success. Her efforts were hindered when their first son died after she had him baptized; Clovis questioned the power of the Christian God and preferred the power of the traditional gods of the Franks. Ultimately, Clovis converted, as Gregory tells us, during a battle that he was losing. He offered to convert to his wife's faith if he should win the battle, which he did. Gregory then describes how Clovis accepted baptism, like a new Constantine, from the hands of Bishop Remigius, and with him 3,000 of his followers converted as well.

Gregory also describes the great conquests of Clovis over rival Franks, Romans, Visigoths (an almost crusade-like battle against Arian Christians), Burgundians (to avenge injuries against his wife), and others. Clovis occasionally employed great trickery to defeat his rivals, but all, in Gregory's eyes, in a good cause. Perhaps the best illustration of the character of Clovis is given in Gregory's tale of the ewer of Soissons. After defeating the Roman "king" Syagrius of Soissons, Clovis came into possession of great booty, part of which was a sacred vessel of importance to the bishop of Soissons. Honoring a request from the bishop, Clovis asked if the follower to whom he had given the vessel would return it. But the follower refused and cut the vessel in half, offering the king only his share. Later, Clovis cut his follower in half with a great blow with his broadsword, declaring that this was what the warrior had done to his cup at Soissons. The tale was designed to demonstrate Clovis's authority and, more importantly, his devotion to the Catholic bishops even before his conversion.

Although a marvelous and memorable portrait, the image presented by Gregory of Tours is most likely not a portrait of the historic Clovis. Rather, Gregory's portrait was intended for Clovis's descendants, who failed to obey the bishops and the church and divided the kingdom in civil war. The historic Clovis was rather different from Gregory's portrait. Although he was a good friend of the bishops, Clovis most likely did not convert directly to Catholic Christianity; at the very least he leaned toward Arianism before receiving baptism from the Catholic Remigius. Moreover, he was most likely not the ruthless barbarian Gregory made him out to be. He was most certainly a successful warrior king, but he also seems to have been influenced by Roman culture. Most notably, his codification of Frankish law in the *Lex Salica* (Salic law), a written Latin version of Frankish custom, suggests the influence of Roman legal traditions. Clovis also borrowed Roman administrative techniques, particularly those involving collecting taxes. In 511, Clovis divided his kingdom among his sons, which traditionally has been understood as an example of the personal nature of Merovingian kingship (so that division of the kingdom would simply be the division of his personal property among his heirs). This division, however, followed Roman administrative boundaries, with each region having a Roman city as capital, and may have been influenced as much by Roman as Frankish traditions.

The legacy of Clovis was undoubtedly a mixed one, however. Although he had established a great kingdom and forged important connections with the bishops of Gaul, he also established the tradition of the division of the realm—traditionally recognized as the fatal flaw in the history of the Merovingian dynasty. The division practically guaranteed that civil war between the descendants of Clovis would occur regularly, and within a decade of his death civil war had indeed broken out. The sixth century was particularly plagued by this problem, which was exacerbated by the Merovingian practice of polygyny and serial marriage. As a result of royal marriage practices, only little influenced by the increasing Christianization of the Merovingians and their kingdom, there were numerous claimants to the throne, especially since both legitimate and illegitimate sons could succeed their fathers. Moreover, heirs to the throne had to be recognized by all other Merovingian kings, and often war was the only means to enforce a claim or depose a pretender. Although certainly a problem, civil war did have the benefit of eliminating those with weak claims to the throne and strengthening the ties between the Merovingian kings and the Frankish aristocracy and episcopacy.

The most famous example of a civil war, or blood feud, among the Merovingians was that of the queens Fredegund and Brunhilde, the wives of Chilperic I (r. 561–584) and Sigebert (r. 561–575) respectively. The traditional competition between rival Merovingian kings may have been worsened by the hatred that existed between their queens, who were motivated by a thirst for power, the concern to protect their families, and possibly, in Brunhilde's case, the desire for revenge. Although the Merovingian kings had been in the habit of marrying lowborn women, Sigebert married a Visigothic princess, Brunhilde, which inspired Chilperic to do the same. Perhaps already married to Fredegund, who was at least an important concubine, Chilperic married Brunhilde's sister, Galswintha, whom he murdered, possibly at Fredegund's instigation, shortly after the marriage. This led to the promotion of Fredegund and the beginning of several decades of assassinations and attempted assassinations of bishops, kings, and queens. Fredegund engineered the murder of Sigebert, Chilperic, and several bishops, and attempted to murder Brunhilde. Despite her best efforts, Fredegund was survived by Brunhilde—often just as ruthless as her rival in promoting the interests of her male heirs—who ruled the Merovingian kingdom through her sons and grandsons during the last decade of the sixth century and the first decade of the seventh. In 613, however, the nobility of Austrasia—one of the three subkingdoms that emerged in the sixth century, along with Neustria and Burgundy—rallied behind Fredegund's son Chlotar to depose Brunhilde, try and condemn her for numerous crimes, and execute her in the most brutal fashion.

The two generations following the fall of Brunhilde, from 613 to 638, were a time of the resurgence of the dynasty and in many ways its high point, as well as the moment of the first appearance of members of the family that became the Carolingian dynasty. In gratitude for his support, Chlotar II (r. 613–629) made Pippin of Landen, an early Carolingian, mayor of the palace and granted other concessions to his family and that of Arnulf of Metz, who had formed a marriage alliance with Pippin. Balancing the interests of the major aristocratic families of the realm would be one of the chief concerns of Chlotar and his son Dagobert (r. 629–638/639). They did this by promoting the status of the monarchy as a sacral institution against the nobility, and also by legislating actively. Chlotar issued numerous diplomas and charters; he passed the Edict of Paris in 614, which has often been seen as a surrender of royal power but may be better understood as a means by the king to force the aristocracy to ensure law and order throughout the kingdom. Clearly the king was successful in this; Fredegar notes that Chlotar reigned happily *(feliciter),* suggesting a time of peace and order. Chlotar, and Dagobert after him, laid the foundations for a chancery—an essential tool for the diplomatic activities of the kings—and built up a sort of school at the royal palace, to which the sons of nobles were invited to be educated, strengthening ties between the monarchs and the nobles. Moreover, to further their hold on the kingdom and to establish a counterweight to the power of the nobles, Chlotar and, especially, Dagobert drew closer to the church. Dagobert, for example, strengthened the dynasty's ties with the powerful abbey of St. Denis near Paris.

Despite the successes of Chlotar and Dagobert, the Merovingians suffered a period of decline after Dagobert's death. Although the dynasty suffered over the course of the next century, the decline was not as precipitous as is traditionally held. Indeed, the dynasty kept a firm hold on the throne until the usurpation of Pippin the Short in 751, and even then the first Carolingian king faced opposition and took very cautious steps to secure the throne. An earlier attempt at usurpation by the Carolingian mayor Grimoald in the 650s failed, a failure that demonstrates the continued authority of the Merovingian line. In the 650s and 660s, Clovis II and his wife Balthild had a successful reign, and

Balthild after her husband's death was an effective regent who refashioned the dynasty's relations with the church and reformed the church in the kingdom. At the same time, however, the Merovingians faced increasing competition from various factions of the nobility, particularly from the later Carolingian line. The nobility of the subkingdoms came more and more to compete for access to and control of the monarchs, many of whom were weakened by youth or incompetence. The office of mayor of the palace became increasingly important in the late seventh century, and the mayors of the two main subkingdoms, Austrasia and Neustria, competed for control of the kingdom. In 687, Pippin of Herstal confirmed the ascendancy of his family and reunified the kingdom when he defeated his rival mayor at the Battle of Tertry.

By the late seventh and early eighth century, the Merovingian dynasty was being gradually replaced by the Carolingian dynasty. Effective control of the kingdom had been taken by Pippin and his successor Charles Martel, even though the Merovingians continued to issue charters and remained on the throne. During Charles Martel's reign as mayor of the palace, the various Merovingian kings who held the throne were increasingly marginalized, even if not to the extent portrayed by Einhard in his description of the last of the line (who owned only one estate, were maintained by the Carolingians, and trotted out once a year in a donkey cart to appear at a council of state). In fact, the Merovingians had become so irrelevant to Martel's ability to rule that during the last four years of his life he ruled without a king on the throne and divided the realm between his two sons, Pippin the Short and Carloman, just as the Merovingian kings had done. His successors were forced to restore a Merovingian, Childeric III, to the throne in 743 because of political unrest in the kingdom, but he was little more than a figurehead. In 750, Pippin felt secure enough to depose Childeric and usurp the throne. He petitioned the pope for support in his deposition, perhaps feeling

it necessary to substitute the sanction of the church and the Christian God for the divine aura that Childeric could claim as the descendant of a sea god.

> **See also** Balthild, St.; Brunhilde; Carloman, Mayor of the Palace; Carolingian Dynasty; Charles Martel; Childeric III; Chlotar II; Clothilda; Clovis; Dagobert; Fredegar; Fredegund; Gregory of Tours; Odovacar; Pippin of Herstal; Pippin of Landen; Pippin III, Called the Short; Poitiers, Battle of; Rois Fainéants; Romulus Augustulus; Tertry, Battle of; Tournai; Visigoths

Bibliography

Dill, Samuel. *Roman Society in Gaul in the Merovingian Age.* 1926. Reprint, London: Allen and Unwin, 1966.

Fouracre, Paul, and Richard A. Gerberding. *Late Merovingian France: History and Hagiography, 640–720.* Manchester, UK: University of Manchester Press, 1996.

Geary, Patrick. *Before France and Germany: The Creation and Transformation of the Merovingian World.* Oxford: Oxford University Press, 1988.

Gregory of Tours. *History of the Franks.* Trans. Lewis Thorpe. Harmondsworth, UK: Penguin, 1974.

Harmondsworth, UK: Bachrach, Bernard S. *Merovingian Military Organization, 481–751.* Minneapolis: University of Minnesota Press, 1972.

James, Edward. *The Franks.* Oxford: Blackwell, 1991.

Lasko, Peter. *The Kingdom of the Franks: North-West Europe before Charlemagne.* New York: McGraw Hill, 1971.

Wallace-Hadrill, J. M. *The Long-Haired Kings.* Toronto: Toronto University Press, 1982.

———. *The Frankish Church.* Oxford: Clarendon, 1983.

Wallace-Hadrill, J. M., ed. and trans. *The Fourth Book of the Chronicle of Fredegar with Its Continuations.* London: Nelson, 1960.

Wemple, Suzanne. *Women in Frankish Society: Marriage and the Cloister, 500–900.* Philadelphia: University of Pennsylvania Press, 1985.

Wood, Ian. *The Merovingian Kingdoms, 450–751.* London: Longman, 1994.

Missi Dominici

Carolingian royal officials who represented the king's interests in specified regions. The *missi dominici* (singular: *missus dominici*), or messengers of the lord king, were responsible for announcing the king's will on the local level and for ensuring that justice was done throughout the realm. The missi dominici were specially chosen by the king, and the office was used as a means to establish royal control in a large and growing empire.

Although missi dominici seem to have been used by the kings of the Merovingian dynasty as well as by the early Carolingian mayors of the palace, the office was only fully exploited by Charlemagne, who turned it into a regular and important part of his administration. At first even Charlemagne used the office on an occasional basis, but as his reign progressed the missi dominici became a more formal and regular tool of government. By 802, at the latest, the missi dominici had become a normal tool of Charlemagne's government and were sent out to all parts of the empire on an annual basis to perform their various services for the king. But there is evidence to suggest that they were used much earlier; they were probably used to disseminate the capitulary of Herstal in 779 and were also most likely used to administer oaths of fidelity to Charlemagne in 789 and 792–793. The missi dominici remained an important part of Carolingian government, at least through the reigns of Louis the Pious and Charles the Bald.

There were two categories of missi dominici: the *missi ad hoc,* or "special" *missi,* and the "ordinary" *missi.* The powers of the two were not different, but the special missi were used for specific missions to examine particular circumstances or injustices. The more important office, however, was that of the "ordinary" missi dominici. Although early in Charlemagne's reign they were chosen from among many of the king's retainers, regardless of social rank, after 802, they were chosen only from among the secular and ecclesiastical nobility, to reduce the possibility of corruption. Indeed, the classic format of the missi dominici included a lay aristocrat, such as a count, and an ecclesiastical noble, such as an abbot or bishop. They were given responsibility for exercising royal authority in a specific geographic area within the kingdom known as a *missaticum.*

The missi dominici held numerous responsibilities as the king's official representatives. Their primary duty was to enforce the royal will. They were charged with transmitting new capitularies throughout the kingdom, enforcing the new laws laid out in those capitularies, investigating the conduct of counts and other royal agents, and collecting revenues. They were to ensure that justice was done properly in the royal and local courts, and they could hear judicial appeals. They were also employed to administer oaths of fidelity to the king and to prepare the army for military campaigns. The counts throughout the realm were expected to provide food and lodging for the missi dominici, and legislation was enacted to ensure they were properly received when they reached their *missaticum.* Although an often effective tool of government, the missi dominici were not above corruption themselves, as the reforms of 802 suggest. And Theodulf of Orléans noted the difficulties faced by the missi dominici, who were frequently offered bribes. The missi dominici were, nonetheless, an important element of Carolingian administration.

See also Capitularies; Carolingian Dynasty; Charlemagne; Charles the Bald; Louis the Pious; Merovingian Dynasty

Bibliography
Fichtenau, Heinrich. *The Carolingian Empire.* Trans. Peter Munz. Toronto: University of Toronto Press, 1979.
Ganshof, François Louis. *Frankish Institutions under Charlemagne.* Trans. Bryce Lyon and Mary Lyon. Providence, RI: Brown University Press, 1968.

Halphen, Louis. *Charlemagne and the Carolingian Empire*. Trans. Giselle de Nie. Amsterdam: North-Holland, 1977.

McKitterick, Rosamond. *The Frankish Kingdoms under the Carolingian, 751–987*. London: Longman 1983.

———. *The Carolingians and the Written Word*. Cambridge: Cambridge University Press, 1989.

Monte Cassino

See Benedict of Nursia, St.

N

Narses (c. 480–574)

Byzantine general and eunuch, Narses was an important figure in the administration of the emperor Justinian (r. 527–565) and his wife Theodora. A highly loyal member of the court, who may have shared Theodora's faith, Narses played a key role in support of the emperor during the Nika Revolt of 532. He later took charge of Byzantine forces during the reconquest of Italy. Taking over from Belisarius, Narses brought the Gothic Wars to a close and achieved final victory for Justinian. He also played a key role in the reorganization of the administration of the peninsula after the conquest and then struggled against the Lombards as they advanced into Italy.

Narses was probably already in his forties when he arrived at court at the beginning of Justinian's reign. He came from Armenia, a slave eunuch who entered imperial service and by the later 520s was commander of the emperor's bodyguard. He was probably close to Justinian as a result, and his loyalty to the emperor brought him into the confidence of Theodora. Although not an educated man, Narses could unravel a problem quickly and was noted for his humanity and dignity in all situations. Indeed, he was a man of such decency that the fifth-century Byzantine historian Procopius never mentions him in his *Secret History*. His loyalty and many talents were displayed most clearly during the Nika Revolt in 532, when he joined with Belisarius and others to bring an end to the revolt. His role as the commander of the imperial bodyguard was of particular importance, and he and his guard helped in the massacre that brought an end to the rebellion.

His service in the Nika Revolt led to advancement for Narses, and, in 538, he was sent to Italy to determine whether the war could be ended more quickly. His appointment essentially made him Belisarius's commander, and the two fell into repeated conflict. These disagreements, along with Belisarius's prominence, led to the appointment of Narses as commander of the armies in Italy and the recall of Belisarius. Narses, having witnessed the troubles of Belisarius, insisted that he himself be granted the tools necessary to complete the job. In 551, Narses was given command of the war in Italy, and in 552 he invaded with a large force that included a substantial number of Lombards as mercenaries. Although opposed by the armies of the Ostrogothic king Totila, Narses proceeded along the coast to Ravenna. He was joined by a second Byzantine army and then met the Gothic king at a decisive battle in late June or early July. The Battle of Busta Gallorum, on a plain in the northern Apennines, was a complete disaster for the Goths, who left 6,000 dead on the battlefield and withdrew with their king mortally wounded. In October, Narses again met in battle with the Goths and again defeated them. This time, however, an armistice was settled between the two sides. But the war was still not at an end, and Narses and various Gothic leaders met in battle several more times in 554 and 555. For the next several years, Narses was able to restore imperial authority over Italy. In 561, the Ostrogoths once again rose up and once again were defeated by Narses, and this time it was the final defeat of the Goths, who disappeared from history at that point.

Narses remained in Italy after the final defeat of the Ostrogoths and after the death of Justinian. As conquering general, Narses remained in authority for the next several years, but he was deposed from office, after enriching himself greatly, because the Italian population complained that his rule was worse than that of the Goths. His position might have remained secure had he not lost the favor of Justinian's successor, Justin II (r. 565–578), who sacked the old general. After losing his military command, Narses retired from imperial service. The invasion of the Lombards in 568 under their king, Alboin, led to the recall of Narses, even though, according to the Lombard historian Paul the Deacon, the general himself had invited the Lombards in because of the treatment he received from Justin. Whatever the case, the Lombards proved too powerful even for Narses, who had little success against them; he once again retired from public life and died a few years later, after a career of long and effective service to the empire.

See also Alboin; Belisarius; Justinian; Lombards; Ostrogoths; Theodora

Bibliography
Barker. J. W. *Justinian and the Later Roman Empire.* Madison: University of Wisconsin Press, 1960.

Browning, Robert. *Justinian and Theodora.* London: Thames and Hudson, 1987.

Burns, Thomas S. *A History of the Ostrogoths.* Bloomington: Indiana University Press, 1984.

Bury, John B. *History of the Later Roman Empire: From the Death of Theodosius I to the Death of Justinian.* 2 vols. 1923. Reprint, New York: Dover, 1959.

Christie, Neil. *The Lombards: The Ancient Langobards.* Oxford: Blackwell, 1998.

Heather, Peter. *The Goths.* Oxford: Blackwell, 1996.

Llewellyn, Peter. *Rome in the Dark Ages.* New York: Barnes and Noble, 1993.

Paul the Deacon. *History of the Lombards.* Trans. William Dudley Foulke. Philadelphia: University of Pennsylvania Press, 1974.

Procopius. *The History of the Wars; Secret History,* 4 vols. Trans. H. B. Dewing. Cambridge, MA: Harvard University Press, 1914–1924.

Wickham, Chris. *Early Medieval Italy: Central Power and Local Society, 400–1000.* Ann Arbor: University of Michigan Press, 1981.

Nennius (fl. early ninth century)

Along with the sixth-century monk Gildas, Nennius was one of the most important early contributors to the legend of King Arthur. His work, the *Historia Brittonum* (History of the Britons), contains the earliest mention of the figure King Arthur and greatly influenced the twelfth-century writer Geoffrey of Monmouth, who elaborated on the earlier Arthurian tales.

Nennius was a Welsh historian and antiquary who wrote at the end of the eighth or the beginning of the ninth century. His famous *Historia Brittonum* is traditionally dated between circa 800 and 829/830 and appeared originally in Wales. It remains uncertain, however, whether Nennius wrote the *Historia* himself or merely copied it from an earlier source or sources. Although best known for its treatment of the legendary Arthur, the *Historia* is not without reliable historical information; it includes details on the early residents and Anglo-Saxon invaders of the island, material on the kingdom of Bernicia, and topographical information. The descriptions of the struggles in Bernicia accord well with the tradition recorded by Bede and appear to follow Gildas, who noted that victory sometimes went to the invaders and sometimes to the Britons. Nennius's work is most famous for his account of the Britons' struggle against the Anglo-Saxon invaders, particularly his description of the one great leader, whom he named Arthur. Most significantly, the history of Nennius includes a list of the twelve great victories, culminating with the Battle of Badon Hill, that Arthur won against the invaders. The *Historia* also contains the history of the world in six ages, tales of miracles and prodigies in England, and details of the life of St. Patrick. The work exists in some thirty-five manuscripts from the tenth to the thirteenth century and was a popular and influential work.

See also Anglo-Saxons; Bede; Gildas; King Arthur

Bibliography

Alcock, Leslie. *Arthur's Britain: History and Archeology, A.D. 367–634.* Harmondsworth, UK: Penguin, 1971.

Barber, Richard. *The Figure of Arthur.* Totowa, NJ: Rowman and Littlefield, 1972.

Nennius. *Nennius: British History and the Welsh Annals.* Ed. John Morris. Totowa, NJ: Rowan and Littlefield, 1980.

Stenton, Frank M. *Anglo-Saxon England.* 3d ed. Oxford: Clarendon, 1971.

Nithard (c. 800–844)

Carolingian count and historian, Nithard was an active figure in the affairs of his day. A lay abbot, grandson of the great king and emperor Charlemagne, and participant in the civil wars between the sons of Louis the Pious, Nithard is best known as the chronicler of the wars of Lothar, Louis the German, and Charles the Bald. His account provides our best account of the wars and important insights into the character of his hero, Charles the Bald, as well as into the nature and ideal of Carolingian kingship.

Little is known of Nithard's life, other than what he reveals in his work of history, and even the date of his death is uncertain. He is traditionally thought to have died on June 14, 844, in battle against Pippin II of Aquitaine (d. 864), but it has been suggested that he died fighting the Vikings on May 15, 845. In either case, his death occurred in battle, and it followed a life active in public affairs and close to the great powers of the day. He was the son of Charlemagne's daughter Bertha (779/780–after 823) and her lover, the court scholar Angilbert. He was raised at court, where he received an excellent education, as indicated in his observations on the movement of a comet in 841–842 and his ability to quote Scripture and Virgil. Later in life he became a partisan of Charles the Bald and joined the king in the fratricidal struggles of the early 840s. Nithard served as an envoy to Lothar for Charles in 840, seeking unsuccessfully to make peace with the emperor. In 841, he fought on Charles's side in the Battle of Fontenoy, and in 842 Nithard served on a commission to determine the division of the empire between Charles and Louis the German. In 843, in return for his faithful service, Nithard was made lay abbot of St. Riquier by Charles the Bald. He was buried in the monastery after his death in battle in 844 or 845, and was memorialized in an epitaph that celebrates his wisdom and mourns his death and the brevity of his term as abbot.

Nithard was also the court historian of Charles the Bald, at whose request he wrote his famous work, *Four Books of Histories* (*Historiarum Libri VI*). Although clearly partisan, Nithard's work provides the best view of the events of the 830s and 840s. It begins with an introduction to the wars that outlines events from the death of Charlemagne through the death of Louis the Pious. This book describes the civil turmoil in the 830s, which set the stage of the wars of the early 840s, and in it Nithard, as he does throughout the work, sides with Charles and portrays Lothar in the worst possible light. Books two through four describe the wars of Charles, Louis, and Lothar. These books contain valuable information about the partisans in the wars, the various battles, and related material, including two versions of the Oath of Strasbourg (842), one in an early form of Romance, the other in an early form of German. The *Histories* also contain a sympathetic portrait of Charles the Bald, commentary on ideal Christian kingship, and an eyewitness perspective on the events Nithard describes. Although not elegantly written, the *Histories* remain compelling reading; Nithard could capture scenes effectively and often wrote passionately. The fourth book, which Nithard wrote reluctantly because of his shame over the course of the civil war, ends rather abruptly; it may have been left unfinished by the author.

See also Angilbert; Carolingian Dynasty; Charlemagne; Charles the Bald; Fontenoy, Battle of; Lothar; Louis the German; Louis the Pious; Strasbourg, Oath of

Bibliography

Laistner, Max L. W. *Thought and Letters in Western Europe, A.D. 500 to 900.* 2d ed. Ithaca, NY: Cornell University Press, 1976.

McKitterick, Rosamond. *The Frankish Kingdoms under the Carolingians, 751–987.* London: Longman, 1983.

Nelson, Janet. *Charles the Bald.* London: Longman, 1992.

Scholz, Bernhard Walter, trans. *Carolingian Chronicles: Royal Frankish Annals and Nithard's History.* Ann Arbor: University of Michigan Press, 1972.

O

Odovacar (c. 433–493)

Germanic warrior of the Scirian tribe who rebelled against the last western Roman emperor, Romulus Augustulus, and Romulus's father, the master of the soldiers, Orestes. Odovacar deposed Romulus and is thus traditionally said to have ended the line of emperors ruling the Western Empire. Unlike earlier rebellious military commanders, he neither declared himself emperor nor promoted someone else as emperor. Instead, he recognized the authority of the emperor in Constantinople, Zeno, and established himself as king in Italy. His reign of seventeen years was plagued by a long war with his eventual successor, Theodoric the Great, who murdered Odovacar but benefited from the traditions of Odovacar's monarchy.

Odovacar was born probably in 433, and was the son of Edica-Edikon, a servant of the great Hunnish ruler, Attila. Edica-Edikon prospered greatly under Attila, and created an independent Germanic kingdom after the death of the Hun and collapse of his empire. The kingdom did not last long, however, as Edica-Edikon was killed in battle in 469. Odovacar and his brother Hunnulf both fled the kingdom, with Odovacar going to Italy, followed by many of his father's supporters. In Italy, Odovacar entered the service of the western emperor as a member of the impe-rial guard, but sided with the emperor's powerful general, Ricimer, when civil war broke out between them in 472. His support for Ricimer was crucial to Ricimer's victory, and Odovacar learned much from his example, even though Ricimer died shortly after his victory.

In 476, Odovacar led a revolt of Germanic soldiers against the emperor, Romulus Augustulus, the son and puppet of Orestes. Orestes had earlier forced the emperor Julius Nepos into exile and declared his son emperor. The claim was not recognized in Constantinople, but Orestes strove to make it effective in Italy. He faced the rebellion led by Odovacar because he was unwilling to grant Germanic soldiers in the army equal status with Roman soldiers. Odovacar defeated Orestes and executed him on August 28, 476. Odovacar deposed and exiled Romulus rather than execute him because, according to a contemporary, of his youth and beauty. But Odovacar compelled Romulus to send a delegation of senators to Zeno, the emperor in Constantinople, declaring that no new emperor was needed and that they welcomed the rule of Odovacar. The Germanic warrior was willing to give up the title king for patrician and authority to rule in Italy. Zeno was in an awkward position, since the legitimate western emperor still lived, but he addressed

Odovacar as patrician nonetheless. Odovacar sought accommodation with the emperor during his reign, and as a sign of good faith executed the murderer of Julius Nepos. Despite his best efforts, and willingness to recognize the sovereignty of the emperor in the east, Odovacar was not able to sign a treaty with the emperor. He did, however, establish peace in Italy and an important and effective royal administration that was built on cooperation with the senatorial aristocracy.

Although somewhat eased by the death of Julius Nepos in 480, relations between Zeno and Odovacar remained tense; they became highly strained in 486. The emperor faced a rebellion, and Odovacar, if not openly supporting the rebel, seems at least to have been in negotiations with him. In response, Zeno encouraged the Rugians, who had settled just north of Italy, to attack Odovacar. In 487, however, Odovacar struck first and destroyed the kingdom, thus ending the possibility of the establishment of a rival kingdom in Italy. His victory, however, had very negative consequences for Odovacar; the king's wife was an Ostrogoth, and her death and the flight of her children came to the attention of Theodoric the Great.

In 488, Theodoric negotiated a secret treaty with Zeno that granted Theodoric the right to rule Italy in the emperor's place if he defeated Odovacar. In the following year, Theodoric's armies reached Italy, and Odovacar, sensing treachery on Zeno's part, took steps to break formally with the emperor. He established his son as caesar and hoped that the break would be welcomed by the aristocracy, which had become increasingly alienated from the emperor over religious issues. Odovacar and Theodoric fought two bloody battles, in 489 and 490, which cost both sides numerous casualties but which were both won by Theodoric. The second victory was, in some ways, a worse defeat for Odovacar, because the senatorial aristocracy shifted its support to Theodoric. But the invader's victory was not sealed; Odovacar made a stand in Ravenna, a near

impregnable stronghold. Theodoric besieged the city, and Odovacar held fast from August 490 until February 493. In July 491, Odovacar launched a ferocious but unsuccessful assault on the besiegers. Finally, the bishop of Ravenna negotiated a treaty between the two rulers that would allow the two to rule Italy together. Odovacar submitted, and Theodoric entered Ravenna on March 5, 493. A few days later, Theodoric murdered Odovacar, claiming that his rival was plotting against him. On that same day, according to a contemporary chronicler, "all Odovacar's soldiers were slain wherever they could be found, and all his kin"(Bury 1959, 426). Odovacar and his family and people were thus annihilated by Theodoric, but Odovacar left his murderer an important foundation for the establishment of a great kingdom in Italy.

See also Attila the Hun; Huns; Orestes; Ostrogoths; Ricimer; Romulus Augustulus; Theodoric the Great; Zeno

Bibliography

Bury, John B. *History of the Later Roman Empire: From the Death of Theodosius I to the Death of Justinian.* 2 vols. 1923. Reprint, New York: Dover, 1959.

Lot, Ferdinand. *The End of the Ancient World and the Beginning of the Middle Ages.* 1931. Reprint, New York: Harper and Row, 1961.

Randers-Pehrson, Justine Davis. *Barbarians and Romans: The Birth Struggle of Europe,* A.D. *400–700.* Norman: University of Oklahoma Press, 1983.

Wolfram, Herwig. *History of the Goths.* Trans. Thomas J. Dunlap. Los Angeles: University of California Press, 1988.

———. *The Roman Empire and Its Germanic Peoples.* Trans. Thomas J. Dunlap. Berkeley: University of California Press, 1997.

Offa of Mercia (d. 796)

One of the greatest and longest ruling kings of Anglo-Saxon England, Offa (r. 757–796) is also the great king about whom the least is known. The only information about Offa and his reigns come from outside the kingdom of Mercia; it includes charters and chronicles written in Northumbria, Wessex, and elsewhere in England. Although possibly as great a ruler as Alfred, who clearly respected Offa, the Mercian king lacks a contemporary Mercian biographer to announce and record his greatness. Despite this lack of information, it is clear that Offa had a profound impact on England during his long reign, and his power and organizational ability are demonstrated by the famed earthwork he built, Offa's Dyke, along the Welsh frontier. Alfred himself praised Offa as a king and adopted laws, now lost, from Offa. And the pope and the greatest king of the early Middle Ages, Charlemagne, treated Offa with respect and recognized his power.

Offa came to power in 757 by driving his rival Beornred into exile by force of arms. His military success at the beginning characterized the rest of his long reign; it was the key to his success, but it was also the key to the demise of the kingdom in the following generation. Indeed, the great Anglo-Saxon scholar and friend of Charlemagne, Alcuin of York, recognized that it was Offa's ruthlessness that secured not only his success but also his untimely death. It was this ruthlessness that secured his power inside and outside of Mercia, restoring the kingdom of Mercia to a position of preeminence in England. After conquering Mercia by the sword, Offa extended his authority over other kingdoms in England. The first to fall victim to Offa was Kent, in the 760s. The struggle to control the kingdom of Kent was long lasting and brought Offa the bitter enmity of the archbishop of Canterbury. The Kentish kings were able to restore their independence for nearly a decade after 776, but they were finally suppressed in 785.

In the 770s Offa brought the kingdom of Sussex under his control by defeating, according to a Northumbrian chronicle, the "men of Hastings" in battle. In the 780s he asserted his authority over Wessex, when that

kingdom fell into civil war after a prolonged period of peace under one of its kings. Offa was able to exploit the situation when a usurper revolted and both he and the king died in battle. Further claimants to the throne of Wessex rose up, including Beorhtric, who received support from Offa and married one of Offa's daughters. The Mercian king's support was essential for Beorhtric's victory, and this support allowed Offa to extend his influence and authority over Wessex. His influence was also felt in Northumbria, and his political authority extended far to the south, where several lesser kingdoms also succumbed to his advance. He also extended his authority westward at the expense of the Welsh, and an expansion borne witness to by Offa's greatest extant legacy, Offa's Dyke, an engineering and organizational marvel of the eighth century that extends some 150 miles over mountainous terrain. Indeed, this fortification may have been part of a military system of fortified towns of the kind later made famous by Alfred the Great. By the 780s Offa could claim to be king of the English, a title recognized in the charters of contemporaries. Perhaps in recognition of his power and in emulation of the Carolingian dynasty, Offa had his son consecrated as king in 787.

Offa's political power was recognized and respected on the continent. He corresponded with Pope Hadrian (r. 772–795) and received legates in the mid-780s from the pope. He also convinced Hadrian to establish a new archiepiscopal see in his kingdom at Lichfield in 787. The new archbishop proved a counterbalance to the hostile archbishop of Canterbury, but he did not last long after the death of Offa. Nonetheless, Offa sought to establish the ecclesiastical independence of the church in his kingdom and empowered it by the foundation of monasteries, including St. Albans. His representatives also participated in church councils in England and on the continent, including the Council of Frankfurt in 794.

It was not only the pope who recognized Offa; the great Frankish king, Charlemagne, also corresponded with Offa and respected his power. Always courteous in correspondence with Offa, Charlemagne wrote seeking advice or mercy from Offa in regard to exiles from Mercia in the Frankish kingdom. Charlemagne's opinion of Offa was most likely influenced by the Mercian king's participation through his clergy at the Council of Frankfurt and by the active trade that existed between the two kingdoms. In 796 a trade agreement was forged between the two kings, in which merchants from both kingdoms were to be protected by both kings. The extent of trade is demonstrated by the improvement in English coinage under Offa, who was likely influenced by the coinage of his Carolingian contemporary. Offa's coin, the penny, remained the basis of English coinage until the thirteenth century and surpassed all other coins in England in his day. The coins also demonstrate further the political shrewdness of the king; they often bore Offa's image or that of his wife, Cynethryth, in imitation of Byzantine or late Roman practice.

Offa was clearly a king of wide-ranging influence in England and the continent. He was also a brutal king, who managed to rule much of England by suppressing or eliminating the sovereigns of the other English kingdoms. It was this brutality that proved the undoing of his kingdom in the generations following his death on July 26, 795, and that ended the revival of the power of Wessex. Although the political power of his kingdom was short-lived, his influence lasted well beyond his death in the coinage he introduced to England, his military construction, and the laws he implemented that were adopted by Alfred.

See also Alcuin of York; Alfred the Great; Anglo-Saxons; Carolingian Dynasty; Charlemagne; Hadrian I, Pope

Bibliography
Keynes, Simon. "The British Isles: England, 700–900." In *The New Cambridge Medieval History*, vol. 2, ed. Rosamond McKitterick. Cambridge: Cambridge University Press, 1995, pp. 18–42.
Levison, Wilhelm. *England and the Continent in the Eighth Century.* Oxford: Clarendon, 1946.
Stenton, Frank M. *Anglo-Saxon England.* 3d ed. Oxford: Clarendon, 1971.

Ordinatio Imperii

Succession plan designed by Louis the Pious in 817. The *Ordinatio Imperii* (Disposition for the Empire) was intended to establish a unified empire, while still recognizing the long Frankish tradition of dividing the realm between the king's heirs. It was thought to be divinely inspired by contemporaries, especially the members of the church. It shaped Louis's policies for much of the next decade, but it was gradually undermined by the birth of another son to Louis and his second wife, Judith. Violation of the *Ordinatio* then became a justification for rebellion for Louis's opponents.

In 817, Louis the Pious met with the leaders of the realm to determine the empire's fate. He may have been inspired to do this because of an accident he had near Easter. As he was leaving the church he had attended for services on Maundy Thursday, the arcade through which he walked collapsed and injured the emperor and several of his companions. Shortly thereafter, Louis held a great assembly at his capital, Aix-la-Chapelle (modern Aachen, in Germany), at which he established a succession plan, the *Ordinatio Imperii,* based upon the idea of the empire's unity. Louis sought divine inspiration, holding a three-day vigil of prayer and fasting before promulgating the *Ordinatio.* At the assembly, he bestowed the imperial title upon his eldest son, Lothar, made him co-emperor, and granted him the duty of ruling Italy. He granted his other sons, Louis the German and Pippin, royal authority over subkingdoms in the eastern and western parts of the empire. Sovereign in their own territory, the younger sons would be subject to the authority of Lothar once Louis died.

This attempt at establishing the empire's unity was not met with uniform support. Although Louis made an attempt to recognize

Frankish tradition, his settlement was met by passive resistance from the Franks, whose tradition favored divided succession. He also faced opposition from his nephew Bernard, king in Italy, who was ignored in the settlement and in fact was essentially stripped of his authority by the appointment of Lothar to rule in Italy. Bernard rose up in rebellion against his uncle, a rebellion that was quickly suppressed by Louis. Bernard was blinded for his rebellion and died from the punishment. The *Ordinatio*'s later history was troubling for Louis, who revised the plan of succession to include a fourth son, Charles the Bald, and was accused of violating the document, and thus violating God's will. Having provided this justification for rebellion, Louis found himself the target of revolts in 830 and 833–834, as members of the nobility and the church supported the uprisings of Louis's older sons.

> **See also** Carolingian Dynasty; Charles the Bald;
> Judith; Lothar; Louis the German; Louis the
> Pious

Bibliography
Dutton, Paul Edward, trans. "The Ordinatio
Imperii of 817." In *Carolingian Civilization: A
Reader*. Trans. Paul Edward Dutton.
Peterborough, Ont.: Broadview, 1993, pp.
176–79.
Ganshof, François Louis. *The Carolingians and the
Frankish Monarchy*. Trans. Janet Sondheimer.
London: Longman, 1971.
Pullan, Brian, trans. *Sources of Medieval Europe from
the Mid-Eighth to the Mid-Thirteenth Century*.
New York: Barnes & Noble, 1966.
Riché, Pierre. *The Carolingians: A Family Who Forged
Europe*. Trans. Michael Idomir Allen.
Philadelphia: University of Pennsylvania Press,
1993.
Scholz, Bernhard Walter, trans. *Carolingian
Chronicles: Royal Frankish Annals and Nithard's
History*. Ann Arbor: University of Michigan
Press, 1972.

Orestes (d. 476)

Roman military commander and father of Romulus Augustulus, who is traditionally recognized as the last western Roman emperor. Orestes, whose son was still a boy when he was promoted to the imperial dignity, was the real power behind the throne, as Ricimer had been before him. His efforts to seize power failed, however, because of the unwillingness of Zeno, the emperor in Constantinople, to recognize Romulus, and because of the opposition of Odovacar.

Orestes, a Roman but a subject of the Huns, rose to prominence in the service of the greatest Hunnish king, Attila. He was the Latin secretary of Attila, and sometime rival of another of Attila's aides, Edica-Edikon, the father of Odovacar. According to some accounts, the rivalry between the two nearly brought about Edica-Edikon's demise, and surely created tensions between Orestes and Odovacar. After the collapse of the empire of Attila, Orestes offered his services elsewhere and was raised to the rank of master of soldiers and given the rank of patrician by the emperor Julius Nepos. The emperor saw in Orestes a Roman with connections with leading aristocratic families and also with important experience and contacts with the barbarians, who served in Rome's army in great numbers or settled along Rome's frontiers as friend or foe.

The emperor ordered Orestes to Gaul to protect the province from the threat of various German tribes, but the new master of soldiers had other plans. Instead of going to Gaul, Orestes marched on the capital of the Western Empire at Ravenna. In the face of the advance, Julius Nepos fled to Dalmatia on August 28, 475. In control of Italy and the capital, Orestes chose not to assume the imperial dignity himself, but instead conferred it on his young son Romulus Augustulus on October 31, 475. Orestes, however, remained the real power in Italy, ruling through his son.

Although he successfully seized control, Orestes's usurpation was not recognized by the emperor Zeno in Constantinople, who maintained that the legitimate emperor of the Western Empire was the exile Julius Nepos and not Romulus Augustulus. Despite this lack of recognition, Orestes kept control of Italy for a year after his rebellion against Julius Nepos. His downfall was the result, not of the refusal of Zeno to recognize Romulus but of Orestes's inability to preserve the loyalty of his troops. The vast majority of his army was made up of German soldiers of various tribes. They demanded grants of land in Italy as reward for their service in the Roman army. Grants of land had been a traditional reward for military service, and other barbarian peoples had received these grants, but never in Italy. True to his Roman roots, Orestes refused to grant his Germanic soldiers land in Italy, and as a consequence, he faced a revolt led by Odovacar, who declared that he would make this concession if he ever obtained power. Orestes was quickly overwhelmed by Odovacar and the Germans in the imperial army. Orestes was executed on Odovacar's orders on August 28, 476, and shortly thereafter Odovacar forced Romulus Augustulus to abdicate, but allowed him to retire and did not kill him. Odovacar did not resurrect the system established by Orestes; instead he refused to establish a new puppet emperor in the west and ruled over Italy under the sovereignty of the emperor in Constantinople. The death of Orestes and deposition of his son Romulus is thus traditionally seen as the end of the Roman Empire in the west, even though much that was Roman survived long after their deaths.

See also Attila the Hun; Huns; Odovacar; Ricimer; Romulus Augustulus; Zeno

Bibliography

Bury, John B. *History of the Later Roman Empire: From the Death of Theodosius I to the Death of Justinian.* 2 vols. 1923. Reprint, New York: Dover, 1959.

———. *The Invasion of Europe by the Barbarians.* New York: W. W. Norton, 1967.

Lot, Ferdinand. *The End of the Ancient World and the Beginning of the Middle Ages.* 1931. Reprint, New York: Harper and Row, 1961.

Randers-Pehrson, Justine Davis. *Barbarians and Romans: The Birth Struggle of Europe, A.D. 400–700.* Norman: University of Oklahoma Press, 1983.

Wolfram, Herwig. *The Roman Empire and Its Germanic Peoples.* Trans. Thomas J. Dunlap. Berkeley: University of California Press, 1997.

Ostrogoths

A barbarian people whose name means "Goths of the rising sun," or "Goths glorified by the rising sun," or simply "East Goths," the Ostrogoths played an important role in the history of the later Roman Empire. Identified as early as the first century by Roman writers, the Ostrogoths were at first part of a larger population of Goths that included the Visigoths. During the third century, the larger Gothic population came into contact, often violent, with the Roman Empire. Defeated by the empire, with which they then cultivated better relations, the Goths divided into eastern and western groups, the Ostrogoths and the Visigoths, and their subsequent histories diverged. For the Ostrogoths, as well as the Visigoths, history in the fourth and fifth centuries was shaped by the movements of the Huns and the rise and fall of the great Hunnish empire of Attila. In the fifth century, a reconstituted Ostrogothic tribe formed into a powerful group led by kings. The most famous and important of these kings, Theodoric the Great, participated in political life in the Eastern Roman Empire and created a successor kingdom in Italy in the late fifth and early sixth century. Despite the qualities of Theodoric and the strength of his kingdom, the Ostrogothic kingdom of Italy did not long survive the death of Theodoric. In the 530s, the great emperor Justinian sought to conquer the Western Empire, which had fallen under barbarian control in 476. For some twenty years, Justinian's soldiers and generals fought Ostrogothic armies before finally defeating them, destroying Theodoric's creation, and essentially elimi-

Theodoric's Mausoleum, Ravenna (Angelo Hornak/Corbis)

nating the Ostrogoths as a people and a force in history.

Ancient accounts record that Gothic history began in 1490 B.C., when a Gothic king led his people in three boats from Scandinavia to the mouth of the Vistula River. Eventually the Goths moved to the area between the Don and Danube Rivers, before being forced out in the mid-third century A.D. by the Huns. The traditional accounts of the origins of the Goths by ancient historians like Jordanes, however, are not generally accepted. The origins of the Goths are no longer traced to Scandinavia but rather to Poland, where archeological discoveries place a sophisticated, but nonliterate, culture. It was from there that the Goths moved, after which move they made contact with the Roman Empire. In the third century the Goths had repeated clashes with the empire, winning some and putting the empire, already in serious straits, into even greater jeopardy. Roman emperors gradually turned the tide and nearly destroyed the Goths. In the wake of these defeats, however, tradition holds that a great king emerged, Ostrogotha, in circa 290, who founded the kingdom of the Ostrogoths. Although it is unlikely that Ostrogotha existed, it is at that point that the division of the Goths into two groups occurred.

In the fourth century the two groups, the Tervingi, or Visigoths, and Greuthingi, or Ostrogoths, had more or less come to terms with the empire. By the 370s, however, the relationship between the various Gothic groups and the empire changed as they faced the threat of the Huns. Prior to the arrival of the Huns, King Ermanaric, a member of the Amal clan, had created a substantial kingdom in eastern Europe. He led the struggle against the Huns but was defeated by them, and in 375 he sacrificed himself to the gods in the hopes of saving his people from the Huns. His successor and some of the Goths continued the struggle against the Huns for another year before they were conquered and absorbed by them. From the end of the fourth to the middle of the fifth century, the Greuthingi/Ostrogoths remained part of the Hunnish empire and fought in the armies of the greatest Hun, Attila.

After the death of Attila, however, the fortune and composition of the Ostrogoths underwent a change. Most scholars believe that the Ostrogoths of this period are unrelated to earlier groups identified as Ostrogoths. Whatever the relationship is, in the mid-fifth century under the king Valamir, an Amal, the Ostrogoths emerged from domination by the Huns. Valamir exploited the confused situation in the empire of the Huns after Attila's death in 453 and the defeat of Attila's successor at the Battle of Nedao in 454. Although Valamir and his Goths most likely fought with the Huns against other subject peoples, the Ostrogoths emerged as an independent people because of the collapse of the Huns not long after the battle. Valamir then faced other rivals and endured further attacks by the Huns before their ultimate demise; he died in battle against the Gepids in 468/469.

Valamir was succeeded by his brother Thiudimer, who moved his followers into Roman territory, where they became *foederati* (federated allies) of the empire and came into contact with another group led by the Ostrogothic king Theodoric Strabo, or the Squinter. The two groups struggled against each other for preeminence and for preference before the emperor. The empire itself, however, underwent important changes during this period. In the 470s a new emperor, Zeno, came to power in Constantinople, and the emperor in Italy was deposed and the imperial line ended by the barbarian Odovacar in 476. These changes among the Ostrogoths and within the empire had an important bearing on the future of the Ostrogothic people.

In 473 Thiudimer died and was succeeded by his son Theodoric the Amal, or later known as the Great, who had been named successor in 471. Prior to his nomination, Theodoric had spent ten years in Constantinople as a hostage of the emperor. During that period Theodoric learned a great deal about the empire and its customs and culture, even though it appears that he did not learn to write. Upon assuming power, he found himself in competition with the other Theodoric, whose followers had revolted against the emperor in 471 and again in 474. The later revolt was part of a palace coup against the new emperor, Zeno, who turned to the Amal for support. In order to ensure that neither group of Ostrogoths or their leaders became too powerful, Zeno also began to negotiate with Theodoric Strabo and settled a treaty with him in 478. But Zeno's duplicity backfired and angered Theodoric the Amal, who rose against the emperor and settled a treaty with Theodoric Strabo in 479. The hostilities between the two Theodorics were settled for a time, too, as the two closed ranks against the emperor. In 481, Strabo attacked Constantinople but failed to take it or depose the emperor. Shortly thereafter he was killed when his horse reared and threw him onto a rack of spears. Theodoric the Amal was the beneficiary of his occasional ally and rival's death. Although Strabo was succeeded by Rechitach, his followers gradually joined with Theodoric the Amal, who had Rechitach murdered in 484.

Theodoric the Amal, or the Great, to give him his more familiar name, was able to create a great Ostrogothic power that quickly threatened the power of Emperor Zeno. The Ostrogothic king continued the struggle with Zeno, which was resolved for a time in 483, with the emperor making great concessions to the king. Indeed, Theodoric was made a Roman citizen, given the title of patrician, and awarded a consulship for the next year. The Ostrogoths were given a grant of land within the empire. But it occurred to Zeno that he could not trust the rising power of Theodoric, and he replaced him as consul, an event followed by renewed hostilities between the Ostrogoths and the empire. Theodoric's revolt in 485 put further pressure on Zeno, who responded by offering Theodoric the opportunity to lead the assault on Odovacar, the barbarian king in Italy since 476. This assignment, which Theodoric himself had first suggested in 479, was beneficial to both king and emperor and one that Theodoric quickly accepted.

In 488–489 Theodoric led his Ostrogoths, probably numbering some 100,000 people, against Odovacar in Italy. The struggle between the two leaders lasted until 493; it was a hard fought war, with Theodoric winning the battles but unable to take his rival's capital of Ravenna. Indeed, after losing two battles Odovacar established himself in the capital, from which he ventured out to meet Theodoric on the field of battle. Odovacar's hand was strengthened by one of his generals,

who joined Theodoric but then rejoined Odovacar, slaying the Gothic warriors who were with him. As a result Odovacar was able to take the offensive, but only for a short while, until Theodoric was reinforced by a Visigothic army. In the early 490s Theodoric gradually took control of Italy and forced Odovacar to come to terms. On February 25, 493, the two leaders agreed to terms that were to be celebrated at a great banquet. Theodoric apparently agreed to share power with his rival, but at the banquet he killed Odovacar, and Theodoric's followers killed the followers of Odovacar in a bloody massacre that ended the war and brought control of Italy to Theodoric.

After his victory, Theodoric was hailed king of Italy, but at first he had to refuse the title in favor of patrician of Italy. The new emperor Anastasius I (r. 491–518) refused to recognize the title of king, with its implications of Theodoric's independence, reminding him that he held power at the discretion of the emperor. Ultimately, however, Theodoric was recognized as king in Constantinople and ruled Italy until his death in 526. His reign was highly beneficial for Italy, and his relationship with the native Roman population was generally good, despite his Arianism and the Romans' Catholicism. He preserved much of the traditional Roman administration, as had Odovacar, and cooperated with the Senate. He ensured the food supply to Italy and patronized Boethius and Cassiodorus as part of a cultural revival. He was also an active builder throughout Italy, erecting public monuments and churches as well as his famous palace and mausoleum in Ravenna. His activities were not limited to Italy, however, but included an ambitious foreign policy that saw him establish hegemony over the Vandals in Africa and the Visigoths in Spain. In competition with Clovis in northern Europe, Theodosius was able to limit the Merovingian king's expansion into southern Gaul. Although in name only a king, Theodoric, as contemporaries admitted, ruled as effectively as any emperor.

Theodoric's later years and the years following his death were marked by increasing turmoil, leading to the eventual fall of the Ostrogothic kingdom. This situation was due in part to changes in the Eastern Empire, as well as to mistakes on his own part. In 518 a new emperor, Justin, assumed the throne and brought an end to a period of doctrinal uncertainty in the empire. He was a Catholic Christian who promoted traditional orthodox teaching, and in 523 he prohibited Arianism in the empire. The support for orthodox teaching and stability in doctrine restored the Italian population's faith in imperial leadership. Moreover, Theodoric was further challenged in matters of religion by the success of the Catholic Clovis against the Visigoths. His concerns were heightened by an alleged plot involving a number of senators, including his advisor Boethius. He ordered Boethius executed and at the same time imprisoned the pope, who had just returned from an embassy to Constantinople. These actions strained relations with his Roman subjects and darkened an otherwise enlightened reign.

Theodoric's situation was worsened by his lack of a male heir, and just prior to his death he encouraged his followers to accept his widowed daughter, Amalswintha, as regent for his grandson Athalaric. At first Theodoric's wishes were accepted, but gradually the Ostrogothic nobility turned against Amalswintha. Although she was praised for her intelligence and courage, the nobility were divided over her guidance of Athalaric and her pro-Roman foreign policy. When Athalaric reached his majority in 533, a number of nobles sought to persuade him to turn on his mother. The rebellion was nearly successful. Amalswintha requested a ship from Emperor Justinian to take her to Constantinople, but ultimately stayed and triumphed over her rivals. She married a cousin, Theodohad, in 534 to stabilize the throne, but her husband failed to remain loyal to her, and Athalaric died that same year. Her arrest and murder, which was inspired, according to the fifth-century Byzantine historian Procopius, by Justinian's

wife Theodora out of jealousy, provided the emperor with the pretext for his invasion of Italy.

Justinian's invasion of Italy, led at first by Belisarius and later Narses, opened the final chapter of the history of the Ostrogoths. The Gothic Wars, which lasted from 534 to 552, were devastating for both Italy and the Ostrogoths. The opening phase of the war saw rapid victories and much success for the invading armies, in part because of the weakness of Theodohad. Belisarius reached Rome in 536, and Theodohad was deposed in favor of Witigis. The rise of Witigis and the arrival of a second Byzantine general, Narses, slowed imperial progress. When Narses was recalled, Belisarius went on the offensive again and may have forced Witigis to take desperate measures, which possibly included Belisarius's acceptance of the imperial title. Although this remains uncertain, Belisarius was recalled in 540 and took the Ostrogothic king with him. In 541, Witigis was replaced as king by Totila.

Under Totila's leadership, the Ostrogoths fought back successfully and prolonged the war for another eleven years. Totila was able to win back territory in Italy from Byzantine armies and forced the return of Belisarius in 544. In 545 Totila began a siege of Rome; he occupied it in 546, laying waste to the city in the process. Control of the city swung back and forth between the two sides for the rest of the war, which Belisarius was unable to conclude, despite putting great pressure on his rival, because of inadequate supplies and soldiers. Belisarius was recalled in 548, at his own request, and replaced by Narses two years later. Narses demanded sufficient resources to bring the war to a swift conclusion and got them. In 552 Narses won the Battle of Busta Gallorum, at which Totila was killed and organized Gothic resistance was ended. Although Totila had a successor as king and pockets of Ostrogoths resisted until 562, the Ostrogothic kingdom in Italy was crushed by the Byzantine invasion. The Ostrogoths ceased to be an independent people, and the last of the Ostrogoths were probably absorbed by the Lombards during their invasion of Italy in 568.

See also Amalaswintha; Arianism; Attila the Hun; Belisarius; Boethius; Clovis; Foederati; Huns; Justinian; Lombards; Merovingian Dynasty; Narses; Odovacar; Theodora; Theodoric the Great; Totila; Vandals; Visigoths; Zeno

Bibliography

Amory, Patrick. *People and Identity in Ostrogothic Italy, 489–554.* Cambridge: Cambridge University Press, 1997.

Browning, Robert. *Justinian and Theodora.* Rev. ed. London: Thames and Hudson, 1987.

Burns, Thomas. *The Ostrogoths: Kingship and Society.* Bloomington: Indiana University Press, 1980.

———. *A History of the Ostrogoths.* Bloomington: University of Indiana Press, 1984.

Bury, John B. *History of the Later Roman Empire: From the Death of Theodosius I to the Death of Justinian.* 2 vols. 1923. Reprint, New York: Dover, 1959.

Goffart, Walter. *Barbarians and Romans* A.D. *418–584: The Techniques of Accommodation.* Princeton: Princeton University Press, 1980.

Heather, Peter. *The Goths.* Oxford: Blackwell, 1996.

Jordanes. *The Gothic History of Jordanes.* Trans. Charles C. Mierow. New York: Barnes and Noble, 1985.

Moorhead, John. *Theodoric in Italy.* Oxford: Clarendon, 1992.

Procopius. *History of the Wars.* Trans H. B. Dewing. Cambridge, MA: Harvard University Press, 1969–1993.

Wolfram, Herwig. *History of the Goths.* Trans. Thomas J. Dunlap. Berkeley: University of California Press, 1988.

———. *The Roman Empire and Its Germanic Peoples.* Trans. Thomas J. Dunlap. Berkeley: University of California Press, 1997.

Wood, Ian. *The Merovingian Kingdoms, 450–751.* London: Longman, 1994.

P

Paul the Deacon (c. 720–c. 799)

Best known for his important work of history, *Historia Langobardorum* (The History of the Lombards), Paul the Deacon was also a teacher and monk who wrote a life of Pope Gregory the Great, poetry, and works on pedagogy and monastic life. He was an influential figure at two royal courts, that of his own Lombard people and that of the great Carolingian king, Charlemagne. As a Lombard he benefited from the support of learning and culture initiated by King Liutprand, but also suffered from the collapse of the Lombard kingdom in Italy under the advance of Charlemagne. His learning, however, attracted the attention of the great and powerful, and his history of his people was very popular and influential in the Middle Ages; it remains the best source for the history of the Lombards from their origins to the mid-eighth century.

Paul was born about 720 to a noble Lombard family. His father, Warnefrid, and mother, Theodolinda, were of sufficient wealth and prominence that they were able to send their son to a fashionable court for his education. It is unclear whether he was sent to the royal court at Pavia of King Ratchis (r. 744–749), or possibly that of his famous predecessor Liutprand, or to Cividale, the court of the duke of Friuli. In any case, he was most likely taught by a leading scholar of his day, one who was able to teach the young Paul some Greek and Hebrew as well as the curriculum of traditional Christian and Roman Latin authors. By 770, Paul had come to the attention of the Lombard King Desiderius and was made the tutor of the king's daughter, Adelperga. In 774, when the Lombard kingdom in Italy fell to Charlemagne, Paul retired to the community of Monte Cassino and, perhaps unwillingly, became a monk. He remained there until 783, when he journeyed to the court of Charlemagne to plead for the release of his brother, who had been involved in a conspiracy against the great Frankish king, and for the return of his property. The mission ultimately proved successful, and Paul remained at court as an honored guest for the next several years, where he joined other leading scholars such as the Anglo-Saxon Alcuin of York and tutored one of the king's daughters. He returned to Monte Cassino in 785, perhaps with greater commitment to the monastic life thanks to his experience at Charlemagne's court, and remained there until his death in 799.

Paul wrote a wide variety of works during his career. His earliest composition may have been a poem composed for Adelperga around 770. He wrote other poems during his life, although their number was not great. He

wrote a poem in praise of St. Benedict of
Nursia and verses in his correspondence with
other members of Charlemagne's court. His
finest poems include one that is a delight-
ful description of Lake Como and another
that is a moving plea to Charlemagne for
his brother's freedom. He edited a fourth-
century history of Rome and continued it
down to the age of Justinian, and wrote a life
of Pope Gregory I and a history of the bishops
of Metz. His writings also included more religious works, among them a collection of
homilies that Charlemagne recommended for
use by the clergy in his kingdom and a commentary on the Rule of Benedict that influenced the monastic reforms of the early ninth
century.

His most famous and important work,
however, was the *Historia Langobardorum,*
which traces the history of the Lombards
from their origins to the death of King Liutprand in 744. The work exists in over one
hundred manuscripts and was imitated and
used by writers down to the fifteenth century. Paul borrowed from earlier historians,
including Gregory of Tours, Isidore of Seville,
and Bede, but his most important sources—
the anonymous *Origo Gentis Langobardorum*
(The Origin of the Lombard People) and the
chronicle of Secundus—are now lost. Although relatively weak on exact chronology,
the *History* is a simple but powerful narrative
of the Lombard people. Paul describes the
Lombards' origin and their entry into Italy, as
well as the many invasions the Lombards
were forced to fight off. He writes of the
great kings and dukes of the Lombards and
tells of the exciting escape of the young king
Grimoald from the Avars. He discusses the affairs of popes, bishops, and monks, as well as
supernatural events and miracles. His work is
a source of great value, and it is regrettable
that death kept him from including in his *History* the tale of the defeat of his people by
Charlemagne, whom he admired.

See also Alcuin of York; Avars; Bede; Benedict of
Nursia, St.; Carolingian Dynasty; Carolingian
Renaissance; Charlemagne; Desiderius; Franks;
Gregory the Great, Pope; Gregory of Tours;
Isidore of Seville; Liutprand; Lombards

Bibliography
Christie, Neil. *The Lombards.* Oxford: Blackwell,
1998.
Laistner, Max L. W. *Thought and Letters in Western
Europe, A.D. 500 to 900.* 2d ed. Ithaca, NY:
Cornell University Press, 1976.
McKitterick, Rosamond. *The Frankish Kingdoms
under the Carolingians, 951–987.* London:
Longman, 1983.
Paul the Deacon. *History of the Lombards.* Trans.
William Dudley Foulke. Ed. Edward Peters.
Philadelphia: University of Pennsylvania Press,
1974.
Riché, Pierre. *Education and Culture in the Barbarian
West: From the Sixth through the Eighth Century.*
Trans. John Contreni. Columbia: University of
South Carolina Press, 1976.

Peasants

Throughout late antiquity and the early Middle Ages, society was divided into a number
of legal and social classes. Society was ruled
by kings and powerful landed nobles and was
served by slaves; between the ranks of the
great free and the unfree were the peasants.
The peasants, descendants of the ancient
coloni (plural of *colonus,* Latin for farmer), remained essentially legally free until after the
year 1000 and were the most important figures in the economic life of the period. The
peasants, or *coloni* as they are often called in
contemporary sources, were also the most
numerous members of society. Although they
were the largest part of the population, it is
impossible to get a complete picture of the
peasants because they figure in so few contemporary documents, and those that do por-
tray them often present a misleading picture.
The most famous of the sources for early medieval peasant life are the polyptychs of
Charlemagne and the Carolingian dynasty.

In all likelihood, the great majority of residents in the countryside of barbarian Europe
were free, landholding peasants, but the

terms on which the land was held and the economic wealth of the peasants varied greatly. Most peasants and their families lived on small properties, of one *mansus,* or Anglo-Saxon hide, which were large enough to support a family. These properties could be freely disposed of by the peasants, who could buy and sell their lots and pass them along to their children. Of course, as small proprietors, the peasants were constantly under the pressure of wealthy and powerful figures who sought to acquire the *mansi* of the peasants. As a defense, peasants sometimes made a grant of their holding or part of it to a local church or monastery, which then allowed the peasant to receive it back and work it for his family's benefit. Peasants were also sometimes forced to squeeze several families on a parcel of land designed for one family. Moreover, rural families sometimes held land in tenancy and were obligated to offer payment or service to the landowner. Their tenant holdings were part of a large estate and were often not contiguous but scattered across the estate. The size and number of holdings varied as well, and some tenants had quite extensive lots to work. Both tenant farmers and small freeholders often hired themselves out to other landowners in order to supplement their incomes. Some peasants, however, were able to acquire several *mansi* of their own and teams of animals to work the fields, and thus became relatively comfortable. The owners of four or *mansi* were expected to do service at the lord's court.

The *mansus* was made up of a number of parts, and the peasants were members of a large community, the village. The individual holding, whether free or tenant in whatever form, included, among other things, a simple hut of stone, wood, or clay where the peasant family lived. Although some were larger and more elaborate, these homes generally had a single room divided into sections, a dirt floor, a bed, benches, and tables. Around the hut were fields for farming, forests, meadows, vineyards, and mills and other buildings necessary for the agricultural economy of the peasant. The peasants spent most of their lives working the farms, raising wheat, oats, and other grains, as well as livestock, including chickens, cows, sheep, and pigs. Beyond the individual landholdings of the peasants was the village. This larger community provided some relief from the more onerous burdens of peasant life and tenant farming. Members of the village often worked together, and the more successful free peasants often regulated the daily affairs of the members of the community and arbitrated their disputes. Decisions affecting the village, such as when to plant and to harvest or how to manage the wastelands, were made by the community as a whole.

See also Agriculture; Anglo-Saxons; Animals; Carolingian Dynasty; Charlemagne; Slaves and Slavery

Bibliography
Bloch, Marc. *French Rural History: An Essay on Its Basic Characteristics.* Trans. Janet Sondheimer. Berkeley: University of California Press, 1966.
Duby, Georges. *The Early Growth of the European Economy: Warriors and Peasants from the Seventh to the Twelfth Century.* Trans. Howard B. Clarke. Ithaca, NY: Cornell University Press, 1979.
Riché, Pierre. *Daily Life in the World of Charlemagne.* Trans. Jo Ann McNamara. Philadelphia: University of Pennsylvania Press, 1983.
Wolfram, Herwig. *The Roman Empire and Its Germanic Peoples.* Trans. Thomas J. Dunlap. Berkeley: University of California Press, 1997.
Wood, Ian. *The Merovingian Kingdoms, 450–751.* London: Longman, 1994.

Penda (d. 654)

Mercian king (r. 632/633–654) who transformed his kingdom into a significant power during his lifetime. Penda was a mighty king, who extended his overlordship over much of southern England. Although not a Christian himself, Penda allowed his son, Paeda, to introduce Christianity into the kingdom.

Penda is first mentioned in a passage from the *Anglo-Saxon Chronicle* in the year 628 after the Battle of Cirencester. The passage notes that he made an agreement with the West Saxons in which the Mercians annexed territory along the river Severn. At that time Penda was most likely not yet king but a powerful noble of royal lineage. He assumed the kingship after the defeat and death of Edwin, king of Northumbria, in 632. In an alliance with Cadwallon of Gwynedd, a native Briton, Penda invaded Deira, devastated the countryside, and slew Edwin, who had extended his authority over Mercia and other regions. Although now king, Penda was forced to recognize the authority of the new Northumbrian king, Oswald of Bernicia, in 633. For the next eight years Penda was not strong enough to challenge Oswald, but in 641 he rose up against the Northumbrian king and defeated and killed him at the Battle of Maserfelth. Oswald himself was almost immediately recognized as a saint and martyr because of his death at the hands of the pagan Penda.

Following the victory over Oswald, Penda was the greatest king of the English, but he did not attempt to establish himself as overlord of the other kingdoms. He did, however, drive the West Saxon king into exile in 645, following the Saxon king's repudiation of his wife, Penda's sister. He also subjugated the kingdom of East Anglia, and made his son subking of Middle Anglia in 653. And he was recognized as a great power by the other kings, some of whom served in his army. His sole rival was the king of Northumbria, Oswy, though even he respected the power of Penda. Oswy, despite being deemed a personal enemy by Penda, married one of his daughters to Penda's son Paeda and sent a son as a hostage to Penda's court. Despite cordial diplomatic arrangements and the marriage tie, Penda and Oswy did eventually go to war. The cause and course of the war remains unclear, but it was likely the result of border struggles between the two kings. According to Bede, Penda marched against Oswy with some thirty legions in an effort to destroy him. In the army, as a testimony of Penda's power, were soldiers and kings of Mercia's

neighboring kingdoms. It is likely that Penda enjoyed some success against Oswy, besieging him in a castle and nearly destroying the king and his army. Penda himself demanded and received a significant amount of treasure from Oswy. But at the Battle of Winwaed, near Leeds, on November of 654, Penda was defeated and killed by Oswy, who, according to Bede, had promised God before the battle that if he were victorious, he would consecrate his daughter to the religious life and build monasteries on twelve estates. Following Penda's death, Mercia was subjugated by Oswy, who remained overlord until Penda's son Wulfhere retook the throne.

Penda's reign was important in the history of early Anglo-Saxon England. He established Mercia as a significant power and extended his influence throughout southern England. Although Mercia succumbed to Northumbria after his death, Penda's kingdom remained an important power in the coming generations. Although not a Christian himself, he did allow the introduction of Christianity into kingdoms under his control.

See also Anglo-Saxons; *Anglo-Saxon Chronicle;* Bede

Bibliography

Blair, Peter Hunter. *The World of Bede.* Cambridge: Cambridge University Press, 1990.

Randers-Pehrson, Justine Davis. *Barbarians and Romans: The Birth Struggle of Europe,* A.D. *400–700.* Norman: University of Oklahoma Press, 1983.

Stenton, Frank M. *Anglo-Saxon England.* 3d ed. Oxford: Clarendon, 1971.

Whitelock, Dorothy, ed. *The Anglo-Saxon Chronicle.* Westport, CT: Greenwood, 1986.

Pippin I, Called Pippin of Landen (d. 640)

A leading noble in the Merovingian subkingdom of Austrasia, Pippin rose to prominence in the revolt against the queen, Brunhilde, in 613. He was rewarded for his role with the office of mayor of the palace and exercised great influence on the kingdom during the reigns of Chlotar II and his son Dagobert. With St. Arnulf of Metz, with whom he was joined by the marriage of his daughter and Arnulf's son, Pippin was one of the founders of the Carolingian dynasty. He built up substantial wealth and family connections and laid the groundwork for the later success of the family. Although his efforts were later undermined by the failed coup of his nephew Grimoald, Pippin's achievements did provide the necessary foundation for the family's ultimate triumph. His namesakes, Pippin II and III, restored the family to the office of mayor of the palace, from which they rose to the office of king of the Franks.

Pippin's rise to power was aided by birth and wise marriage alliances. He was from an economically prosperous area of Austrasia, the Meuse River basin, where his family held extensive lands. His position was enhanced by his marriage to Itta, who was the sister of the future bishop of Trier and, according to a contemporary text, was celebrated because of her virtues and wealth. The marriage alliance he forged with Arnulf of Metz, however, proved of even greater value to Pippin and his family. The marriage of his daughter Begga (d. 693) to Arnulf's son Ansegisel (d. 676) drew two powerful families closer together, and the lands of Pippin and Arnulf provided the territorial and economic foundation for the Carolingian family whose rise to prominence began with Pippin.

Already a wealthy and influential landowner, Pippin's status in the kingdom improved dramatically in 613 when he and Arnulf joined with the Merovingian king Chlotar II to overthrow Queen Brunhilde, who had been the effective ruler of Neustria and the bitter rival of Chlotar's mother Fredegund. Successful in his revolt and in reuniting the kingdom, Chlotar rewarded his supporters. Arnulf was made bishop of Metz, and Pippin was made mayor of the palace in Austrasia, where he became the virtual ruler. Pippin's appointment came shortly after Chlotar appointed his young son Dagobert

king in Austrasia. Pippin assumed a heavy share of the burden of government and held an office that enabled him to exercise great power in the king's name. Dagobert benefited from the tutelage of Pippin as well. Moreover, Pippin continued to serve the Merovingian dynasty after Chlotar's death in 629. When Dagobert assumed control of the entire Merovingian kingdom, Pippin continued in his position as mayor. According to the seventh-century chronicle of Fredegar, Pippin provided a steadying hand in the early years of Dagobert's reign. The new king, who had ruled so well in Austrasia during his father's lifetime, now became debauched and greedy. Responding to the complaints of the nobles from the subkingdom of Neustria, Pippin reprimanded the young king and restored him to the virtues he exhibited during Chlotar's life.

Although Fredegar recognized Pippin as a wise counselor who loved justice, rival nobles in Austrasia were not so enamored of the mayor and sought to create a break between Pippin and Dagobert. Their efforts were not immediately successful, but Dagobert did gradually move away from his former mentor, and in 633 removed him from the position of mayor. Pippin's loss of office and the efforts to separate him from Dagobert reveal the nature of Merovingian politics in the seventh century. Although still firmly in charge of the kingdom, the Merovingians ruled over a number of aristocratic families that were involved in frequently shifting alliances. For much of his life, however, Pippin had been able to manage these alliances, as his marriage ties suggest, and even after his fall from office he remained a vital force in Austrasia.

After the death of Dagobert in 639, Pippin moved quickly to retake his position as mayor of the palace. According to Fredegar, he ruled prudently and through friendly tips with his vassals. He also strove to have the nobility recognize the new king in Austrasia, Sigebert III, the ten-year old son of Dagobert. Despite his ability to restore his authority quickly after the death of Dagobert, Pippin did not rule long; he died suddenly in 640. Although he did not long survive Dagobert, Pippin had provided a secure base for his family's future.

See also Arnulf of Metz, St.; Brunhilde; Carolingian Dynasty; Chlotar II; Dagobert; Fredegar; Fredegund; Grimoald; Merovingian Dynasty; Pippin II, Called Pippin of Herstal; Pippin III, Called the Short

Bibliography
Fouracre, Paul, and Richard A. Gerberding. *Late Merovingian France: History and Hagiography, 640–720.* Manchester, UK: University of Manchester Press, 1996.
James, Edward. *The Franks.* Oxford: Blackwell, 1991.
Riché, Pierre. *The Carolingians: A Family Who Forged Europe.* Trans Michael Idomir Allen. Philadelphia: University of Pennsylvania Press, 1993.
Wallace-Hadrill, J. M., ed. and trans. *The Fourth Book of the Chronicle of Fredegar with Its Continuations.* London: Nelson, 1960.
Wood, Ian. *The Merovingian Kingdoms, 450–751.* London: Longman, 1994.

Pippin II, Called Pippin of Herstal (d. 714)

Frankish mayor of the palace and virtual leader of the Merovingian kingdom in the late seventh and early eighth century. His reign as mayor witnessed the further growth in power of the Carolingian family, and contributed to the ultimate triumph of the dynasty in the time of his descendants Pippin III the Short and Charlemagne. His victory at the Battle of Tertry in 687 solidified his hold on power and reunited the kingdom under the Merovingian king he supported, Theuderic III (d. 691). He held the office of mayor and remained the main authority in the kingdom until his death in 714; he was ultimately succeeded by his son Charles Martel.

Although Pippin was noted, according to the annals written circa 800, for "the strength of his justice, the unconquerable solidity of his bravery and the guidance of his modera-

tion,"(Fouracre 1996, 351) his path to power was not an easy one. Despite the success of his grandfathers, Pippin I of Landen and Arnulf of Metz, the second Pippin was faced by powerful opponents and forced to deal with the failed coup of the family's previous leader, Grimoald, who had sought to replace the ruling Merovingian dynasty with a member of his own family. Pippin was also forced to deal with the murder of his father, Ansegisel, who was killed by a rival family after emerging as the leader of the family after Grimoald's failure. Moreover, in his first contests with the Neustrian mayors of the palace, Pippin, who was an Austrasian noble, was defeated. In 680, he fought a battle against the Neustrian mayor Ebroin and was decisively defeated. The family suffered more than military defeat; Ebroin ordered the murder of Pippin's brother, Martin, who had sought refuge in Laon. A later battle with Ebroin's successor Waratto ended in another defeat for Pippin.

Although he endured some serious defeats early in his career, Pippin ultimately triumphed over his Neustrian rivals. For one thing, the near tyrannical rule of the Neustrian mayors alienated a large portion of the nobility, which turned to Pippin for help. In 687, war again broke out between the Neustrian mayor, now Berchar, and the Austrasians, led by Pippin. At the request of the Neustrian nobility, Pippin led a campaign against Berchar and his king, Theuderic III, and fought a major battle at Tertry. Pippin's victory secured his position, along with that of his family, in the kingdom. He took control of the king and the royal treasury and reunited the kingdom under his authority as mayor of the palace. Pippin and his descendants ruled the Frankish kingdom for the next three centuries, and after 751 they ruled as kings.

From 687 until his death in 714, Pippin was the real power in the Frankish kingdom, even though a member of the Merovingian dynasty continued to reside on the throne. As mayor of the palace, Pippin directed both the internal and external affairs of the realm. To strengthen his own position after the Battle of Tertry, Pippin promoted family members and loyal supporters to key positions in the kingdom. He made one supporter mayor in Neustria, and then later replaced this supporter with his own son, Grimoald. He placed other allies in places of power in Neustria and made other sons, including Drogo who was duke of the Burgundians, officials in other parts of the kingdom. He also arranged marriages between his family and the families of important nobles throughout the kingdom, the most successful of the marriages he arranged being his own earlier marriage to Plectrude, who came from an important family in the area of modern Cologne.

Pippin extended his family's control of the kingdom, but he did not attempt to usurp the Merovingian throne as his uncle Grimoald had. Perhaps learning the lessons of his uncle's failed coup, Pippin continued to install Merovingians on the throne. He ruled first with Theuderic III, and then with Clovis IV (r. 691–695), Childebert III (r. 695–711), and finally Dagobert III (r. 711–715). Although not the *rois fainéants* (do-nothing kings) of popular legend, these kings were clearly the junior partners in the government of the kingdom. Indeed, as the *Annals of Metz* notes, Pippin called the annual meeting of the nobles of the realm and presided over it, after allowing the kings to ask for peace, call for the protection of widows and orphans, and the like.

Among Pippin's many duties was the prosecution of war against external foes and rebellious elements within the kingdom. Although Pippin led the armies, the *Annals of Metz* report that the king "ordered the army to be ready for departure on the appointed day" (356), which suggests that the Merovingian kings, with the exception of the infant Clovis, had greater authority than the pro-Carolingian annals allow. Whatever the case, Pippin led a campaign into Aquitaine, the first of many Carolingian forays into that rich region, which had traditionally resisted Frankish authority. Of greater concern to Pippin,

however, were affairs on the northern and eastern frontiers of the kingdom. He marched against the Frisians to the north, who had raided Frankish territory and had extensive trade contacts with England. Pippin's success against the Frisians was followed by the colonization of the region by Austrasian nobles and by the construction of churches. Pippin also appointed the Anglo-Saxon missionary Willibrord bishop of the newly conquered region. Although relations between Rome and the Carolingians were formalized only in the reign of Pippin's grandson, the connection with Willibrord, who had close ties to Rome, laid the foundation for the later alliance. Just as his descendants later expanded on ties to Rome, so too they adopted his policy of conquest and conversion of pagan peoples along their eastern frontier.

Pippin also exploited his relationship with the church in the kingdom. His relations with the bishops were sometimes difficult, and he exiled bishops and replaced them with personal allies or family members. Pippin not only appointed bishops to important sees in the kingdom, but also appointed abbots to prominent monasteries. He also endowed monasteries and churches, and established proprietary family churches. His ecclesiastical policy mirrored his political one and was intended to further strengthen his and his family's hold on power. Appointments to office and charitable donations to religious communities were designed to bring the support of the church to Pippin. Toward this end as well, Pippin put churches and monasteries, and their significant wealth, under the control of close allies, and sometimes took territories from the churches and granted the land to his supporters.

By the time of his death on December 16, 714, Pippin had successfully established himself and, to a lesser degree, his family as the most important power in the Frankish kingdom. His death, however, led the kingdom into turmoil, as his wife and children struggled for control of his legacy. Despite the best efforts of his widow, Plectrude, to promote the interests of her grandson, it was the son of one of Pippin's concubines, Charles Martel, who eventually took over his father's legacy and continued the growth of the family's power.

See also Arnulf of Metz, St.; Carolingian Dynasty; Charlemagne; Charles Martel; Grimoald; Merovingian Dynasty; Pippin of Landen; Pippin III, Called the Short; Plectrude; Rois Fainéants; Tertry, Battle of

Bibliography

Fouracre, Paul, and Richard A. Gerberding. *Late Merovingian France: History and Hagiography, 640–720.* Manchester, UK: University of Manchester Press, 1996.

Gerberding, Richard, A. *The Rise of the Carolingians and the "Liber Historiae Francorum."* Oxford: Clarendon, 1987.

Halphen, Louis. *Charlemagne and the Carolingian Empire.* Trans. Giselle de Nie. Amsterdam: North-Holland, 1977.

McKitterick, Rosamond. *The Frankish Kingdoms under the Carolingians, 751–987.* London: Longman, 1983.

Riché, Pierre. *The Carolingians: A Family Who Forged Europe.* Trans. Michael Idomir Allen. Philadelphia: University of Pennsylvania Press, 1993.

Wallace-Hadrill, J. M., ed. and trans. *The Fourth Book of the Chronicle of Fredegar with Its Continuations.* London: Nelson, 1960.

Wood, Ian. *The Merovingian Kingdoms, 450–751.* London: Longman, 1994.

Pippin III, Called the Short (d. 768)

Mayor of the palace and founder of the Carolingian royal dynasty, Pippin laid the foundation for much of Carolingian royal policy and success. Although often overshadowed by his more illustrious son, Charlemagne, Pippin was a great military, political, and religious reformer in his own right. As mayor and king, he imposed his authority on the kingdom and expanded its boundaries. He formalized the alliance with the pope in Rome that had first been attempted during the reign of Pippin's father, Charles Martel. In fact, the alliance was essential for Pippin's elevation to the kingship, as well as for the long-term growth of the Papal States. Both before and after his usurpation of the throne, Pippin was actively involved in the reform of the church. In many ways, Pippin left a lasting and important legacy for Charlemagne and the Carolingian line.

On the death of his father, Charles Martel, in 741, Pippin and his brother Carloman inherited control of the kingdom. Although officially only mayor of the palace, Charles Martel divided control of the kingdom between his two sons as any Frankish king would, having ruled without a Merovingian king during the last three years of his life. Pippin and Carloman inherited the office of mayor and authority over the entire realm. Their succession to power, however, was not achieved without strife. In the opening years of their joint reign, Pippin and Carloman faced widespread opposition, including the revolt of their half brother, Grifo, who had been excluded from the inheritance. Although Grifo failed to gain power, he remained a problem until his death in 753. But Grifo was not the only source of trouble for Pippin and Carloman at the outset of their reign. They faced unrest and rebellion in Aquitaine and Bavaria, as well as from other Frankish noble families who regarded the Carolingians as equals.

In 743, Pippin and Carloman discovered the heir to the Merovingian throne in a monastery and restored him, as Childeric III, to his rightful place as king. The restoration, possibly initiated by Carloman, may have been done to suppress rebellious partisans of the Merovingian dynasty or to establish legitimacy for the Carolingians' position. Whatever the purpose, the restoration of Childeric proved to be only a short-term solution. In 747, after undertaking military campaigns and religious reform with his brother, Carloman retired to the monastery of Mount Soracte near Rome. Pippin moved quickly to restrict Carloman's sons' claims to power and to consolidate his position as mayor. He was now the sole mayor in the kingdom and king in everything but name.

In 750 Pippin took the first of several steps that brought about a revolution in the Frankish kingdom. He sent two of his most trusted advisors, Archbishop Burchard of Würzburg and Abbot Fulrad of St. Denis, to Pope Zachary (r. 741–752) in Rome to ask whether the person with the power or the person with the title should be king. Zachary answered as Pippin had hoped. By turning to the pope, Pippin hoped to gain a higher spiritual sanction than that possessed by the Merovingians, who claimed descent from a sea god. In 751, at an assembly of the leaders of the realm in Soissons, Childeric was deposed and sent to a monastery. At the same time, Pippin was elected king by the nobility and crowned and anointed king by the bishops of the realm, including possibly, Boniface, the papal representative in the kingdom. The ceremony of anointing, of unction, was borrowed from the Hebrew Scriptures and was intended to establish the Carolingians as kings of the new children of Israel.

In 753, Pope Stephen II (r. 752–757) traveled north to meet with Pippin. Fleeing from the advances of the Lombard king Aistulf, Stephen hoped to secure the aid of the Frankish king. The two met at the royal residence of Ponthion to discuss the issue and other things during the winter of 753–754. Stephen received the promise of aid from Pippin, who also supported the pope's claims to various estates in central Italy. The following spring, Pippin met with various nobles to gain support for a campaign against the Lombards to protect the pope. Because of earlier alliances with the Lombards, many nobles were reluctant to agree to the invasion of Italy, but the appearance of Carloman, who had been sent to argue against the pope's request by Aistulf, helped Pippin's cause. In July 754, Stephen upheld his side of the bargain, crowning and anointing Pippin king. Stephen not only crowned Pippin but also crowned and anointed his sons, Charles and Carloman,

granted them the imperial title of patrician, and declared that only descendants of Pippin could legitimately rule the Franks. The revolution was now complete. The Carolingians had become the kings of the Franks and, perhaps more importantly, had become close allies of the pope.

Although at first opposed to the invasion of Italy, the nobles agreed at a second council in 755, after Aistulf had refused Pippin's request to honor the pope. Pippin invaded at the head of a large army and defeated the Lombards at Susa before laying siege to the capital of Pavia. Aistulf relented, gave hostages, and agreed to return territory to the pope. Once Pippin had withdrawn, however, Aistulf broke the treaty. In 756, Pippin again invaded, with the enthusiastic support of the nobles, and again laid siege to Pavia and forced Aistulf to submit. Pippin, determined to enforce the agreement, sent Abbot Fulrad to each of the cities Aistulf was to return to the pope to collect keys from them. A list was compiled by Fulrad, which has come to be known as the Donation of Pippin, and deposited on the altar of St. Peter's in Rome. Aistulf's death in 756 and the Lombard political situation thereafter made any return to Italy on Pippin's part unnecessary. But his two invasions strengthened the alliance between Rome and the Carolingians and helped establish the Papal States.

Pippin's campaigns in Italy were not his only foreign military ventures. In fact, he learned of Stephen's journey to the Frankish kingdom in 753 while returning from a campaign in Saxony. He raided Saxony to enforce a treaty that permitted the free movement of Christian missionaries in that region. More important than the Saxon campaign, however, was the reconquest of the duchy of Aquitaine, a region that had been part of the Frankish kingdom in the seventh century. A region of great agricultural wealth, Aquitaine was also the center of opposition to Carolingian power before and after 750. Moreover, Pippin claimed that the duke, Waifar, had violated the integrity of the church. Defense of ecclesiastical and political interests led Pippin to invade the duchy numerous times, including annual campaigns from 760 to 768. In 761, Pippin led a major expedition that saw his triumph over the duke as well as the assassination of Waifar by some of his own men, probably in the pay of Pippin. Although victorious over Waifar in 761, Pippin's conquest of Aquitaine was a painstaking process, in which the king gradually conquered forts and cities and gradually won over Waifar's vassals. To secure his hold on the duchy, Pippin placed his supporters in positions of political power and installed loyal ecclesiastics as abbots of the monasteries in the duchy. Although a revolt occurred shortly after his death, Pippin had restored Frankish control over Aquitaine and was able to include the duchy in his legacy to his sons.

Along with his usurpation and military campaigns, Pippin carried out a number of political and religious reforms. One crucial policy was not a reform: Pippin acquired extensive estates throughout the realm as a means to bolster his power. In fact, the establishment of landed wealth and power was as important for his elevation to the kingship as the coronation by the bishops. The accumulation of land and loyal vassals on that land provided the justification for the usurpation of the throne. Pippin acquired further power through the establishment of control over monasteries throughout the realm, which he used to curtail the power of the aristocratic bishops. One of the most important monasteries of the kingdom and a former Merovingian royal monastery, St. Denis near Paris, became an important supporter of Pippin and his new dynasty, and was important in Pippin's elevation to the kingship. He also reformed royal administration by increasing the use of writing in government and by employing churchmen as administrators. Finally, he commissioned a new edition of the Salic law that exalted the virtues of the Franks and their new royal dynasty.

Pippin was also an active religious reformer both before and after the retirement of his brother in 747. In the early years of his rule as mayor, Pippin recognized the value of reform of the church, which had suffered during the civil wars of the previous generations. Although not as enthusiastic a supporter of the missionary and reform work of Boniface as was his brother Carloman, Pippin nonetheless supported efforts to reform the church in the Frankish kingdom and certainly recognized the value of the devotion to Rome that Boniface preached. After the retirement of Carloman and death of Boniface in 754, Pippin relied increasingly on Chrodegang, bishop and then archbishop of Metz. Although the king promoted the role of the monastery in the Frankish church, especially to limit the power of the bishops, he found an important ally in Chrodegang, who presided over numerous councils with the king during Pippin's reign.

Councils were held at Ver in 755, at Verberie in 756, at Attigny in 760, and at Gentilly in 767, and were intended to reform religious life and organization in the kingdom. Chrodegang encouraged a closer alliance with Rome for the church, incorporating Roman liturgical traditions in the church, and improved ecclesiastical discipline among the clergy, who had been derided by Boniface for their ignorance and immorality. The clergy, according to Boniface, indulged in battle and committed adultery, and one priest could not offer the blessing properly, blessing "in the name of the country and of the daughter." The councils sought to combat these problems, and passed legislation prohibiting clergy from going to war and demanding that monks and nuns renounce wealth and accept stability. The councils of Pippin also sought to improve church organization by prohibiting the establishment of monasteries on private land by lay nobles.

By his death in 768, Pippin had taken control of the kingdom of the Franks, and he was able to pass the kingship on to his two sons, Charles and Carloman. In good Frankish tradition, Pippin divided the kingdom between his two sons. As a counterbalance to that potentially disruptive tradition, however, Pippin had established the traditions in government, the church, and military that his son Charles, or Charlemagne as he came to be known, exploited to such great end. Although he did not adopt all the policies of his father, Charles was nonetheless greatly indebted to his father for the legacy he left behind. Indeed, if Pippin's achievements had been limited to the founding of the Carolingian royal dynasty, he would certainly still be an important figure. But his reform of the Frankish church and government, which also paved the way for the Carolingian Renaissance emerging under Charlemagne, were important for the long-term success of his dynasty. His association with the pope set a precedent for church-state relations that lasted until at least the end of the Middle Ages, and his conquests created a powerful kingdom that his son was able to transform into an empire. Truly, Pippin was a great king.

See also Aistulf; Boniface, St.; Carolingian Dynasty; Carolingian Renaissance; Charlemagne; Charles Martel; Childeric III; Chrodegang of Metz; Clovis; Donation of Pippin; Merovingian Dynasty; Salic Law

Bibliography

Davis, Raymond, trans. *The Lives of the Eighth-Century Popes* (Liber Pontificalis): *The Ancient Biographies of Nine Popes from* A.D. *715 to* A.D. *817.* Liverpool, UK: Liverpool University Press, 1992.

Ganshof, François Louis. *The Carolingians and the Frankish Monarchy.* Trans. Janet Sondheimer. London: Longman, 1971.

James, Edward. *The Franks.* Oxford: Basil Blackwell, 1988.

Llewellyn, Peter. *Rome in the Dark Ages.* New York: Barnes and Noble, 1996.

McKitterick, Rosamond. *The Frankish Kingdoms under the Carolingians, 751–987.* London: Longman, 1983.

Noble, Thomas X. F. *The Republic of St. Peter: The Birth of the Papal State, 680–825.* Philadelphia: University of Pennsylvania Press, 1984.

Riché, Pierre. *The Carolingians: A Family who Forged Europe.* Trans. Michael Idomir Allen.

Philadelphia: University of Pennsylvania Press, 1993.

Scholz, Bernhard Walter, trans. *Carolingian Chronicles: Royal Frankish Annals and Nithard's History.* Ann Arbor: University of Michigan Press, 1972.

Wallace-Hadrill, J. M. *The Frankish Church.* Oxford: Clarendon, 1983.

Plectrude (d. after 721)

Wife of the Carolingian mayor of the palace Pippin II of Herstal (d. 714) and, after her husband's death, rival for control of the Frankish kingdom and the Merovingian king with Charles Martel (d. 741), who was Pippin's son by another woman. A member of an important noble family, Plectrude offered Pippin a good marriage alliance and sought to keep control of her power after her husband's death and promote her own heirs to the office of mayor.

Plectrude was from an important noble family that had extensive domains in the area between the Rhine, Meuse, and Moselle rivers. Her father, Hugobert, was a powerful palace official whose connections and wealth made marriage to Plectrude an attractive proposition. Moreover, she had no brothers, only sisters, and was sure to inherit many of the vast estates of her family, thus making her an even more coveted bride. In 670, Pippin married Plectrude and increased his own power in the north and northwest of the Frankish kingdom as a result. She bore him two sons, Drogo (d. 708) and Grimoald (d. 714), whose marriages further enhanced their father's power. Pippin married the mother of Charles Martel while his first wife still lived, but Plectrude remained the favored and politically prominent wife. She continued by Pippin's side during the rest of his life, signed official documents as his wife, and supported various monasteries in the kingdom, especially Echternach, which was associated with her mother.

Plectrude remained at her husband's side during his life, and she attempted to keep power after his death in 714. Both of her sons had predeceased their father, Grimoald having died only a few months before Pippin, and after her husband's death she promoted Grimoald's son Theodoald to the office of mayor of the palace to the Merovingian king Dagobert III (d. 715). She also took control of Pippin's treasure and imprisoned her stepson Charles Martel to secure Theodoald's position and prevent Charles from seizing power. Her efforts on her grandson's behalf were met with hostility by the part of the nobility opposed to Pippin and his family. According to a contemporary chronicler, Plectrude kept "Charles from the legitimate governance of his father's authority and she herself, with the infant, in a womanly plan, presumed to control the reins of so great a kingdom" (Fouracre 1996, 365). This hostile chronicler continues that because "she had decided to rule with feminine cunning more cruelly than was necessary, she quickly turned the wrath of the Neustrian Franks to the destruction of her grandson"(365). She faced a revolt that ended with Theodoald in flight and a new mayor, Ragamfred, elected in his stead. The new mayor later marched against her in Cologne and seized part of Pippin's legacy. Not only did she face opposition from outside the family, but her stepson, Charles, also rose against her, seized the rest of his father's wealth, and ultimately took control of the kingdom.

See also Carolingian Dynasty; Charles Martel; Marriage; Merovingian Dynasty; Pippin II, Called Pippin of Herstal

Bibliography

Fouracre, Paul, and Richard A. Gerberding. *Late Merovingian France: History and Hagiography, 640–720.* Manchester, UK: University of Manchester Press, 1996.

Fouracre, Paul. *The Age of Charles Martel.* New York: Longman, 2000.

Riché, Pierre. *The Carolingians: A Family Who Forged Europe.* Trans. Michael Idomir Allen. Philadelphia: University of Pennsylvania Press, 1993.

Wallace-Hadrill, J. M., ed. and trans. *The Fourth Book of the Chronicle of Fredegar with Its Continuations.* London: Nelson, 1960.

Wemple, Suzanne. *Women in Frankish Society: Marriage and the Cloister, 500–900.* Philadelphia: University of Pennsylvania Press, 1985.

Poitiers, Battle of (732)

Battle fought by the Frankish mayor of the palace, Charles Martel, against invading Muslims from Spain on October 25, 732, somewhere between Tours and Poitiers. Although the military importance and technological impact of the battle has been questioned, it was regarded as a major victory for Charles by contemporaries and by the chroniclers of the ninth century who termed Charles "the Hammer" *(Martellus)*.

As a result of the Muslim conquest of Spain in the early eighth century, southern Gaul was plagued by frequent Muslim raids into its territory. Although conquest of the territory by the Muslims was unlikely, their raids into Aquitaine and surrounding areas were a serious problem. In the 720s when the Muslims attacked Autun and towns along the Rhone River, the brunt of the fighting was born by the duke of Aquitaine, Odo. In 732 a more serious raid was launched by the emir of Spain, Abd al-Rahman, that swept through Aquitaine and reached Bordeaux and Poitiers. Odo, who suffered defeat at the hands of the invaders, had requested aid from Charles Martel. After sacking the monastery of St. Hilary in Poitiers, the Muslim party moved toward the wealthy monastery of St. Martin of Tours. It was on the way to Tours that Charles Martel met Abd al-Rahman, and after a week of minor skirmishes, Charles and Odo defeated the invaders.

The battle has acquired much fame, but generally for the wrong reasons. It has often been held that the victory at Tours "saved" Christian Europe from Muslim conquest in the eighth century. But conquest of Gaul and the larger Frankish kingdom by Muslim raiders from Spain was most unlikely to occur. The invasions were attempts to gain plunder but posed no long-term threat. The victory at Tours did end the raids by Muslims from Spain, and helped Charles Martel strengthen his hold on the kingdom. The battle also demonstrated the weakness of Odo, which Charles exploited after the duke's death in 735.

The Battle of Tours is also supposed to have marked a great turning point in the history of military technology. According to the thesis of Lynn White, Jr., the battle marked the introduction of the stirrup to western Europe, and the use of the stirrup and the mounted shock troop guaranteed the victory of the Franks over the Muslims. This view, however, has been shown to be wrong; there is neither written nor archeological evidence to support White's conclusions.

Although the military and technological importance of the Battle of Tours is often overstated, the battle remains an important moment in Carolingian history. Charles Martel's victory, recognized as a great achievement by those in the eighth and ninth centuries, was significant. The victory at Tours ended Muslim raids from Spain, and later Carolingian rulers were to extend the frontier into Muslim territory. The victory also further demonstrated the talents of Charles Martel as a military leader and allowed him to gain greater authority over the Frankish kingdom and the duchy of Aquitaine.

See also Carolingian Dynasty; Charles Martel

Bibliography

Bachrach, Bernard S. "Charles Martel, Mounted Shock Combat, the Stirrup, and Feudalism." *Studies in Medieval and Renaissance History* 7 (1970): 47–75.

Contamine, Philippe. *War in the Middle Ages.* Trans. Michael Jones. Oxford: Basil Blackwell, 1984.

Riché, Pierre. *The Carolingians: A Family Who Forged Europe.* Trans. Michael Idomir Allen. Philadelphia: University of Pennsylvania Press, 1993.

White, Lynn, Jr. *Medieval Technology and Social Change.* Oxford: Oxford University Press, 1964.

Procopius (c. 490/507–c. 560)

Author of the most important histories of the reign of Justinian and Theodora, Procopius was an eyewitness and participant in the events he describes. Although he was also the author of official histories of Justinian's reign, Procopius is known best for his scandalous and unrelentingly hostile work *The Secret History* (*Anecdota,* or Unpublished Things), which portrayed nearly everyone associated with Justinian in a most negative light. Indeed, his invective against Theodora was so harsh, and nearly pornographic, that the great historian Edward Gibbon wrote that "her arts must be veiled in the obscurity of a learned language," and J. B. Bury described the *Secret History* as an "orgy of hatred." At the same time, Procopius did write very important official histories, including *History of the Wars* (*Polemon,* or *De bellis*) and *On Buildings* (*Peri Ktismaton,* or *De aedificiis*).

Procopius was probably born around 500, as early as 490 and as late as 507, in Caesarea in ancient Palestine (modern Israel). Little is known of his early life, but he probably received an education according to ancient traditions and was learned in the Greek classics. Indeed, as his later works clearly show, he knew the writings of the great historians Herodotus (c. 484–430/420 B.C.) and Thucydides (460–after 404 B.C.). He later became a *rhetor,* or attorney, and in 527 joined the staff of the great general Belisarius as a legal advisor. He remained with Belisarius until 540 and joined him on his campaigns against the Persians (527–531), the Vandals (533–534), and the Goths (535–540). He may well have lost the general's favor in 540 and returned to Constantinople after Belisarius captured Ravenna and remained in the imperial capital until his death, although his exact movements are uncertain. He did witness the plague in Constantinople in 542, received the title *illustris* in 560, and may have been prefect of Constantinople in 562–563. Although much remains uncertain about his movements after 542, and even the date of his death is not definitely known, it was after his return from the Gothic campaign that Procopius began to write. He published his great official histories in the 550s and 560s; the *Secret History* was published after his death. Although much is uncertain concerning his life, his literary record remains as a significant and lasting achievement.

Procopius's works provide important accounts of the political and military affairs of the day as well as bitterly personal insights into the major figures of his day. Written in Greek, his works draw on Herodotus, Thucydides, and possibly Arrian (d. 180 A.D.) and reveal his growing disenchantment with Justinian and the members of his court, including Belisarius and, especially, Theodora. His first work, *History of the Wars,* was published in 551 or 552, with an addition in 554 or 557, and covers the emperor Justinian's wars from the 530s to 554. Divided into eight books, the *History* addresses the wars with the Persian Empire (Books 1–2); wars against the Vandals (Books 3–4); and the Gothic Wars (Books 5–7). The eighth book surveys all theaters of war from 550 to 554. The accounts focus on military and political affairs and often include speeches from the participants and other digressions from the main narrative. The work also reveals his belief in Christianity and opposition to doctrinal disputes and, more importantly, his growing disenchantment with Justinian. Despite that developing hostility, Procopius did also write a panegyric to Justinian, possibly commissioned by the emperor, on the emperor's building program.

Published in 560 or 561, although possibly unfinished, *On Buildings* may have been written several years earlier, possibly before the collapse of the dome of the Hagia Sophia in 558. The work describes in important details Justinian's building program throughout the empire. Procopius discusses the numerous fortifications and churches—including the Hagia Sophia, the greatest of all—and supports the ideology of Byzantine imperialism, stressing that Justinian served and was inspired by God. In stark contrast to the portrayal of the emperor in *Buildings, The Secret History* offers a vicious and vindictive portrait of Justinian and Theodora and others. It purports to offer the "true" reasons for the actions of the emperor and empress, who were motivated by greed and a desire for evildoing, and describes them both as demons, a term he meant literally and not as a figure of speech. *The Secret History* does offer some substantial criticisms of Justinian's policies, but it is best known for its purple prose and scurrilous attacks on the empire's leaders. Although written as early as 550, *The Secret History* was not published until after Procopius's death and was lost for centuries, being discovered in the Vatican Library and published in 1632.

See also Belisarius; Justinian; Ostrogoths; Theodora; Vandals

Bibliography

Browning, Robert. *Justinian and Theodora,* rev. ed. London: Thames and Hudson, 1987.

Bury, John B. *History of the Later Roman Empire: From the Death of Theodosius I to the Death of Justinian.* 2 vols. 1923. Reprint, New York: Dover, 1959.

Cameron, Averil. *The Mediterranean World in Late Antiquity, A.D. 395–600.* New York: Routledge, 1993.

———. *Procopius and the Sixth Century.* London and New York: Routledge, 1996.

Evans, James A. S., *Procopius.* New York: Twayne, 1972.

Gibbon, Edward. *The Decline and Fall of the Roman Empire.* New York: Modern Library, 1983.

Procopius. *The History of the Wars; Secret History,* 4 vols. Trans. H. B. Dewing. Cambridge, MA: Harvard University Press, 1914–1924.

R

Radagaisus

See Stilicho

Radegund (c. 525–587)

Merovingian queen and abbess, Radegund stands in stark contrast to other famous sixth-century Merovingian queens such as Brunhilde and Fredegund, who were known for their bloody quest for power and defense of family interests. Unlike them, Radegund renounced the worldly life and rejected an earthly family for a heavenly one. Although married to a Merovingian king, she lived a celibate life and was eventually allowed to leave her husband and found a convent. Her community, in which Radegund accepted a lowly position rather than that of abbess, was well known for its piety, but also for its internal turmoil, brought on by the competition between noble and non-noble members of the convent. Even though she renounced the world, Radegund did not remain completely separate from it, corresponding with bishops, kings, and emperors. She was held in such great esteem by her contemporaries that they wrote two biographies of her, and the sixth-century historian Gregory of Tours included much information about her in his *History of the Franks,* as well as the letter of the foundation of her monastery.

Born to the royal family of the barbarian kingdom of Thuringia in about 525, Radegund was brought into the Merovingian kingdom in 531 when the sons of the first Merovingian king, Clovis, Theuderic I (r. 511–533) and Chlotar I (r. 511–561), destroyed her family's kingdom. Radegund herself described the destruction of the kingdom in an epic poem she wrote, which reveals her sadness over the kingdom's fate and the death of her brother, who was killed by Chlotar sometime after he captured the brother and sister and took them back to his kingdom. Although he already had at least one wife and as many as seven, Chlotar married Radegund in 540 in order to legitimize his authority in Thuringia. According to one of her biographers, the sixth-century poet Venantius Fortunatus, who was her chaplain, Radegund spent her youth in preparation for her eventual marriage and was well educated, studying the works of St. Augustine of Hippo, St. Jerome, and Pope Gregory the Great, among others. During her marriage to Chlotar, Radegund remained celibate, much to her husband's dismay, but was able to exploit her position for the benefit of others nonetheless. She actively sought to free captives, often paying the ransoms for their release. She also spent lavishly on the poor.

Her marriage to Chlotar, however, was clearly not meant to last, and in about 550

Radegund and King Chlotar (The Art Archive/Bibiothèque Municipale Poitiers/Dagli Orti)

she left him to found the monastery of the Holy Cross in Poitiers. The accounts of her separation from her husband are contradictory. According to Venantius Fortunatus, Radegund was allowed to leave her husband because of the murder of her brother. Chlotar, after killing her brother, not only allowed the separation but sent her to the bishop of Soissons, who was to consecrate her in the religious life in order to calm the situation politically with the bishops of his own kingdom. Her other biographer and disciple, Baudonivia, writing in the early seventh century, portrayed the whole affair differently. She wrote that after Radegund had left the king, Chlotar fell into a fit of despair and desired that his wife return to him. Indeed, he even went to Poitiers with one of his sons, Sigebert, to take his wife back, but relented in the end and allowed her to take up the religious life. This decision was influenced by Radegund's connections with numerous bishops of the kingdom, who helped persuade Chlotar to allow her to live as a nun. Moreover, not only did Chlotar allow her to take the veil but he also provided a substantial endowment so that she could establish her new community in Poitiers.

Although the founder of the new religious community, Radegund was not its abbess. As noted in the letter of foundation, preserved by Gregory of Tours, Radegund appointed Lady Agnes as mother superior. Radegund writes, "I submitted myself to her in regular obedience to her authority, after God" (535). Indeed, despite her royal standing, Radegund lived her life at the monastery of the Holy Cross as a regular nun and set the example in pious living for the other nuns in the community to follow. Baudonivia wrote in her biography that Radegund "did not impose a chore unless she had performed it first herself"(Thiébaux 1994, 113). She was also zealous in the performance of her religious duties and was frequently at prayer. Even while resting, Radegund had someone read passages from the Scriptures to her. She also performed acts of extreme self-mortification,

and, according to Venantius Fortunatus, sealed herself up in a wall in her monastery near the end of her life and lived there as a hermit until her death.

Radegund lived her life as a simple nun in her community, but she was still royalty; she continued to participate in the life of the kingdom and used her status for the benefit of the community she established. In her foundation letter, she secured the protection of her monastery from the leading bishops of the realm as well as from various Merovingian kings. She also cultivated her relationship with the bishops of the realm, including her biographer, Venantius Fortunatus, and Gregory of Tours, after the initial contacts at the foundation. Her royal status enabled her to acquire a piece of the True Cross (believed to be the cross on which Christ was crucified) from the emperor in Constantinople. This act, which benefited her community, may also have had political overtones. Her correspondence with the emperor and his delivery of the holy relic may have been intended to improve diplomatic ties between the Merovingian dynasty and Byzantine emperors. She also prayed for the various Merovingian kings and often sent them letters of advice, partly in an effort to preserve the peace within the Merovingian kingdom. She also prohibited the marriage of a Merovingian princess, a nun at the convent in Poitiers, to the Visigothic prince Reccared. Indeed, even though she lived the life of a simple nun, Radegund played an important role in the kingdom because of her status as a former Merovingian queen.

See also Augustine of Hippo, St.; Brunhilde; Fredegund; Gregory of Tours; Gregory the Great, Pope; Merovingian Dynasty; Monasticism; Reccared I; Visigoths; Women

Bibliography
Gregory of Tours. *The History of the Franks.* Trans. Lewis Thorpe. Harmondsworth, UK: Penguin, 1974.
Schulenburg, Jane Tibbetts. *Forgetful of Their Sex: Female Sanctity and Society, ca. 500–1100.*

Chicago: University of Chicago Press, 1998.

Thiébaux, Marcelle, trans. *The Writings of Medieval Women: An Anthology.* New York: Garland, 1994.

Wemple, Suzanne. *Women in Frankish Society: Marriage and the Cloister, 500–900.* Philadelphia: University of Pennsylvania Press, 1985.

Wood, Ian. *The Merovingian Kingdoms, 450–751.* London: Longman, 1994.

Reccared I (d. 601)

Son of the last Visigothic Arian king of Spain, Leovigild, and brother of the rebellious Hermenegild, Reccared was the first Catholic Christian king of Spain (r. 573/586–601). Although he broke from his father's religion, Reccared built upon Leovigild's efforts to unify the kingdom under one religious faith. He held an important church council to confirm the place of the new faith in the kingdom and promoted the ideal of sanctified kingship, with the support of the church. He also took great strides to enforce his authority over the Visigothic nobility in Spain and to extend the power of the Visigothic kingdom in Europe through marriage alliances and warfare.

During the reign of Leovigild, both Reccared and his brother Hermenegild played important roles at court. Their father was a successful king who enjoyed victories over other peoples in Spain, including the Byzantines. He also cultivated an almost imperial ideal of kingship in Spain, a legacy Reccared later enjoyed. Reccared and his brother were made coregents with Leovigild in 573, a step designed to strengthen Leovigild's hold in the kingdom and to establish a royal dynasty in Spain. In 578, Leovigild, in imitation of the Roman emperors, founded a new city, now Toledo, which he named Reccopolis after his younger son. Perhaps because of the favoritism shown him by his father, Reccared remained loyal to Leovigild and did not join the rebellion of Hermenegild in 579. Under the influence of his Catholic Merovingian wife, Ingunde, and Leander of Seville, arch-bishop and older brother of Isidore, Hermenegild converted to Catholic Christianity. Conflict between father and son continued until 584, when the dispute was resolved. The murder of Hermenegild in 585 paved the way for the eventual succession of Reccared to the throne on his father's death in 586.

As king in his own name, Reccared built on the legacy of his father. Even in terms of religion, Reccared can be seen to have continued his father's policies, with the exception that the unifying religion in Visigothic Spain was Catholic Christianity, not Arian Christianity as his father had hoped. In 587 Reccared converted to Catholic Christianity, which brought him and the kingdom in line with the Hispano-Roman population as well as with his sometime rival the Franks. His conversion also found support from the established Catholic church and the pope, Gregory the Great, with whom Reccared began to correspond. Although generally accepted in Spain, Reccared's conversion did meet some opposition from the Arian bishops, who were supported by the king's stepmother, Gosvintha. This opposition notwithstanding, Reccared converted the Visigoths to Catholic Christianity, and to celebrate and confirm his conversion Reccared held a great church council, the Third Council of Toledo, in 589. The council was attended by the five archbishops of Spain, some fifty Catholic bishops, eight former Arian bishops, and many Arian priests and secular nobles. All participants at the council confessed the Nicene Creed, confirming their acceptance of Catholic Christianity, and the council passed a series of laws for the church in Spain. The former Arian bishops were welcomed into the Catholic church and confirmed in their sees. Reccared had successfully unified the kingdom under the banner of religion and was recognized by contemporaries for his great accomplishment.

Reccared's successes were not limited to the sphere of religion. He built on his father's policy of bringing the nobility to heel and asserting royal authority over them. At one point, he uncovered a conspiracy against him led by a leading noble. The rebel was captured and forced to endure the *decalvatio* (which was either the shaving of his head or scalping; the meaning is uncertain), had his right hand chopped off, and was led through Toledo on a donkey to send a warning to other possible rebels. The king also maintained good relations with the papacy and generally prospered in the international arena, especially in his dealings with the Merovingian Franks. His father had arranged a marriage for him with Rigund, the daughter of Chilperic I. But Chilperic's death ended the possibility of the marriage, and the revolt and death of Hermenegild further complicated relations with the Merovingians. Despite concerns over the fate of Hermenegild's wife and the enmity of Guntram, the most important Merovingian king of the day, Reccared arranged to marry a Merovingian princess. The marriage in fact failed to take place, and Reccared married a Visigothic woman, Baddo. Nevertheless, his ability to arrange the marriage in the first place demonstrates his stature in Merovingian eyes. Moreover, although Guntram approved the marriage, he later attacked Visigothic territory but was easily defeated by Reccared.

Reccared also furthered his father's policy of enhancing the stature of Visigothic kingship, elevating it to almost imperial rank. Indeed, he clearly ruled as an emperor in his kingdom, as had Leovigild. Reccared also organized larger administrative units in the kingdom as subdivisions of an empire. His relationship with the church in Spain also resembled that of a Roman emperor with the church in the empire. Building upon the precedents of his father, Reccared left an important legacy to the Visigothic kingdom in Spain, a legacy that survived the murder of his son and successor, Liuva II, and the end of the dynasty in 603.

See also Arianism; Chilperic I; Franks; Gregory the Great; Guntram; Hermenegild; Isidore of Seville; Leovigild; Merovingian Dynasty; Visigoths

Bibliography

Bury, John B. *History of the Later Roman Empire: From the Death of Theodosius I to the Death of Justinian.* 2 vols. 1923. Reprint, New York: Dover, 1959.

Collins, Roger. *Early Medieval Spain: Unity in Diversity, 400–1000.* London: Longman, 1983.

Gregory of Tours. *History of the Franks.* Trans. Lewis Thorpe. Harmondsworth, UK: Penguin, 1974.

Heather, Peter. *The Goths.* Oxford: Blackwell, 1996.

Isidore of Seville. *Isidore of Seville's History of the Goths, Vandals, and Suevi.* 2d rev. ed. Trans. Guido Donini and Gordon B. Ford. Leiden: Brill, 1970.

Thompson, E. A. *The Goths in Spain.* Oxford: Clarendon, 1969.

Wolfram, Herwig. *History of the Goths.* Trans. Thomas J. Dunlap. Berkeley: University of California Press, 1988.

———. *The Roman Empire and Its Germanic Peoples.* Trans. Thomas J. Dunlap. Berkeley: University of California Press, 1997.

Reihengräber

See Row-Grave Cemeteries

Religion, Germanic

See Germanic Religion

Ricimer (d. 472)

Roman military leader of Germanic descent, Ricimer (in full, Flavius Ricimer) was the power behind the throne in the Western Empire from 456 until his death in 472. Although an Arian Christian and a barbarian and therefore constitutionally unable to hold imperial office, Ricimer, like Stilicho before him, was the real ruler in the Western Empire. He appointed and deposed emperors and struggled against various rivals and usurpers. He also kept Italy safe from attacks by Alans, Ostrogoths, and Vandals. Indeed, his success in the defense of Italy is best illustrated by its fall to the Germanic general Odovacar only four years after Ricimer's death.

The son of parents of royal Suevi and Visig-othic descent, Ricimer rose to prominence, as did many Germans of his day, through military service to Rome. Early on in his military career, while in the service of Aëtius, he befriended the future emperor Marjorian. He became a great hero to the Romans in 456, when he successfully defended Italy from a Vandal attack off Sicily and Corsica. His exploits earned him promotion to the office of master of the soldiers. In the same year, Ricimer joined with his friend Marjorian to depose the reigning emperor in the west, Avitus. Marjorian demonstrated the potential to be an effective emperor and suppressed a near revolt in southern Gaul shortly after his ascension. He also enjoyed a victory over the Visigoths in Gaul in 460, but suffered a disastrous defeat at the hands of Gaiseric and the Vandals. Unfortunately, his early display of ability and initiative inspired the enmity of his friend Ricimer. Upon Marjorian's return to Italy from Gaul after his defeat at the hands of the Vandals, Ricimer captured him and executed him in August 461.

Ricimer then became the undisputed master of Italy and parts of the Western Empire. He then promoted a puppet emperor, whom he dominated until 465. The greatest threat to his power came from a general in Gaul, Aegidius, who refused to recognize Ricimer's authority. To counter Aegidius, Ricimer denounced him as a usurper and used barbarian kings in the north against him; his death by poisoning in 464 strengthened Ricimer's hand. The next great threat to his power came in 467 with the arrival of a new emperor, Anthemius, who had been appointed by the Eastern emperor, Leo I. But any possibility of competition was eliminated by the marriage of Ricimer to Anthemius's daughter. The good relations, however, did not last; and the two became rivals fairly quickly, and civil war broke out in 472 after Anthemius's failure in a campaign against Vandal Africa. Ricimer appointed Olybrius emperor and defeated his rival in battle on July 11, 472. Ricimer, however, did not long survive his rival and died on August 18, 472. His death paved the way for further unrest and the establishment of a Germanic kingdom in Italy, but his virtual reign preserved the integrity of imperial Italy from the attacks of Vandals, Visigoths, and other barbarians.

See also Aëtius; Alans; Arianism; Gundobad; Odovacar; Ostrogoths; Stilicho, Flavius; Vandals; Visigoths

Bibliography

Bury, John B. *History of the Later Roman Empire: From the Death of Theodosius I to the Death of Justinian.* Vol. 1. 1923. Reprint, New York: Dover, 1959.

Dill, Samuel. *Roman Society in Gaul in the Merovingian Age.* 1926. Reprint, London: Allen and Unwin, 1966.

Randers-Pehrson, Justine Davis. *Barbarians and Romans: The Birth Struggle of Europe, A.D. 400–700.* Norman: University of Oklahoma Press, 1983.

Rois Fainéants (Do-Nothing Kings)

Name traditionally applied to the last of the kings of the Merovingian dynasty. The so-called *rois fainéants,* or do-nothing kings, held the throne from the death of Dagobert in 638 to the deposition of the final Merovingian king, Childeric III, in 751 by Pippin III the Short. Although a fairly common designation, it is a misleading one; the decline of the Merovingian dynasty was neither as dramatic nor as rapid as the name implies. In fact, the Merovingians remained important figures in the Frankish kingdoms until the time of Charles Martel in the early eighth century.

The impression of sudden and extreme Merovingian weakness is primarily the result of the eighth and ninth century sources that tell the tale of the last century of Merovingian rule. Most of these sources were written by those who supported the Carolingian dynasty that replaced the Merovingians in 751. These sources all portrayed the Carolingian kings in the most favorable light and the last of the descendants of the first great Frankish king, Clovis (r. 481–511), in the worst light. The most important of these sources is the life of Charlemagne written by Einhard, a member of Charlemagne's court. According to Einhard the last Merovingian king, Childeric, was a pathetic figure indeed. Childeric possessed little but the title of king, according to Einhard, and sat on the throne playing the role of king with his long hair and flowing beard. He had little wealth, only the income of a small estate and whatever the Carolingian mayors of the palace provided to support him. He would ride in an oxcart to attend the general assembly of the kingdom, at which whatever answers he gave to questions of state or to visiting ambassadors were initiated by the mayor of the palace. Although the real power of Childeric was quite limited, this portrayal clearly exaggerates the relative power of the Merovingian and Carolingian families, and it has cast an inaccurate shadow over the Merovingian kings of the previous century. Einhard and other pro-Carolingian writers developed this image to buttress the claims to the throne of a dynasty that only a generation or so before usurped royal power.

Although the Carolingians exploited their power as mayors of the palace during the late seventh and early eighth centuries, they were not the sole aristocratic family seeking power, and the Merovingian dynasty remained an important part of the power structure in the Frankish kingdoms. The continued strength of the descendants of Clovis is demonstrated by a number of things. The failure of the coup of Grimoald, a Carolingian mayor, in the 650s shows that the Franks were not yet ready for a new royal dynasty. The various aristocratic factions in the three Frankish kingdoms—Austrasia, Burgundy, and Neustria—competed for control of the kingdoms and for access to the kings. The murders of the Merovingian kings Childeric II and Dagobert II in the 670s were due not to their weakness but rather to their strength and the opposition to their policies. As late as

the 720s Merovingian kings issued charters and other royal enactments for the kingdoms that were effectively implemented. In fact, in the early eighth century, when the Carolingians were clearly in the ascendancy, Merovingian kings competed for the support of important monasteries. Perhaps the best example of the lingering prestige of the dynasty as late as the 740s is the appointment by Pippin and Carloman of Childeric III as king. Thus, although the later Merovingian kings were not the equals of Clovis, the founder of the dynasty, they were not the weak and ineffective kings of tradition.

> *See also* Carolingian Dynasty; Charlemagne; Charles Martel; Childeric III; Clovis; Dagobert; Einhard; Merovingian Dynasty; Pippin III, Called the Short

Bibliography
Einhard and Notker the Stammerer. *Two Lives of Charlemagne*. Trans. Lewis Thorpe. Harmondsworth, UK: Penguin, 1981.

Romulus Augustulus (fifth century)

Last of the Roman emperors of the western part of the empire, Romulus Augustulus, or in full Flavius Momyllus Romulus Augustus, assumed the imperial throne while still a boy and reigned from October 31, 475, until August 28, 476. He was placed on the throne by his father, Orestes, the master of soldiers, who ruled in his name. His reign was cut short by the Germanic warrior, Odovacar. His deposition traditionally has marked the "fall of the Roman Empire"; no emperor reigned over the Western Empire after his fall.

Romulus Augustus, known as Augustulus (little Augustus) because of his youth, was placed on the throne by his father, the powerful and ambitious general Orestes, after Orestes rebelled against the reigning emperor in Italy, Julius Nepos (d. 480). Orestes ruled for nearly a year in the name of his son, but the emperor in Constantinople, Zeno, refused to recognize Romulus as the legitimate emperor in the west. An even more serious problem for Orestes and Romulus arose among the Germanic soldiers who made up such a large part of the Roman army. They demanded equal status with Roman soldiers, which Orestes refused to grant. Odovacar, a leading Germanic prince, did agree to raise the barbarian soldiers' status should he gain power, and a rebellion then broke out against Orestes. He was quickly overpowered and executed at Odovacar's order on August 28, 476. Romulus, however, was spared. A contemporary chronicler noted that Odovacar spared him because of his youth and fair looks and sent him to live out his days in Campania. And it was with his relatives that Romulus Augustulus lived out his life in anonymity.

After deposing Romulus Augustulus, Odovacar returned the imperial seal and other trappings of the imperial office to the emperor Zeno and did not appoint an emperor to rule in the west. The year 476, therefore, has traditionally been seen as the "end" of the Roman Empire. Of course, this view fails to consider several things about the empire. It continued until 1453 in the east with its capital Constantinople. Moreover, although the line of western Roman emperors came to an end in 476, a number of other Roman traditions continued for some time to come. The language of the former Western Empire, Latin, continued to be the language of learning and government until the end of the Middle Ages. Christianity remained the predominant religion of the west and was gradually made the official religion of the Germanic rulers who rose to power in the old empire. The majority of the population were Roman or descended from Roman citizens, and many vestiges of the old Roman administration were preserved by the barbarian successors of the emperors. Although the deposition of Romulus Augustulus brought an end to the line of emperors in the west, it did not "end" the empire or its influence.

See also Odovacar; Orestes; Zeno

Bibliography
Bury, John B. *History of the Later Roman Empire:*
From the Death of Theodosius I to the Death of Justinian. 2 vols. 1923. Reprint, New York: Dover, 1959.
Randers-Pehrson, Justine Davis. *Barbarians and Romans: The Birth Struggle of Europe, A.D. 400–700.* Norman: University of Oklahoma Press, 1983.
Wolfram, Herwig. *The Roman Empire and Its Germanic Peoples.* Trans. Thomas Dunlap. Los Angeles: University of California Press, 1997.

Rothari (d. 652)

A Lombard king (r. 636–652) and lawgiver, Rothari was a successful warrior and the last of the Arian Lombard kings. His reign continued the anti-Catholic reaction begun by his predecessor, Ariold (626–636), but was noted most for Rothari's codification of the Lombard laws. His reforms of the law reveal the sometimes ambivalent attitude of the Lombards toward the Romans. The law code he created used Roman models, even as Rothari made major assaults on the last section of imperial Italy governed by the Byzantine Empire.

Rothari, according to the Lombard historian Paul the Deacon, was "brave and strong, and followed the path of justice; he did not however, hold the right line of Christian belief, but was stained by the infidelity of the Arian heresy" (193–194). Indeed, like his predecessor, Ariold, Rothari restored the traditional Lombard support for Arianism and continued the reaction against the pro-Catholic policy of Theudelinde. His support for Arian Christianity was intended, as it had been for Ariold, as a means to preserve the identity of the Lombards and distinguish them from the native population of Italy, which was Catholic. The Lombards had long been kept apart from the Italo-Roman population and often took a hard line against the empire. And on these matters Rothari was a traditional Lombard.

The new king followed the model of Ariold in one other significant way, if we are to trust the Frankish historian Fredegar. According to

Fredegar, on the death of Ariold, his widow, Gundeberga, was invited by the Lombard nobility to choose a new king and husband, just as her mother, Theudelinde, had done at the death of her first husband, Authari (r. 584–590). Gundeberga asked Rothari to put away his wife and to become her husband and king of the Lombards. Fredegar notes that Rothari married Gundeberga, but kept her locked away in a little room and lived with concubines for several years, until he restored her to her place at the suggestion of the Merovingian king Clovis II (r. 639–657). The similarity with Paul the Deacon's tale of Theudelinde renders this tale suspect, but Rothari did, in fact, marry Gundeberga, probably in order to preserve the continuity of the monarchy and the stability of the kingdom.

As king, Rothari made two major contributions to the history of the Lombard kingdom. He launched a highly successful assault against imperial Italy in 643, undertaken in concert with attacks on imperial territory by the independent Lombard duke of Beneventum. He conquered parts of the Italian coast as well as the Italian imperial capital of Ravenna in 643, a conquest that seriously hindered Constantinople's ability to influence Italian affairs and, in the long run, forced the papacy to find another protector. Rothari's success against the empire also led to a treaty between the two in 652. The king's second great accomplishment also occurred in 643, when he codified the laws of the Lombards. Known as Rothari's Edict *(Edictus Rothari),* the code of Lombard laws and customs was arranged in 388 chapters and, like the other barbarian law codes of the time, was written in Latin. Among other things, the Edict emphasized the cooperation between the king and the people, as represented in the army and council of nobles. Rothari dealt with manumission of slaves, inheritance, division of property, marriage customs, and the place of women in society in the code. He also sought to eliminate or at least reduce the practice of the vendetta in Lombard society and thereby guarantee peace. Indeed, preservation of the peace was an impor-

tant goal of the Edict, which legislated on manslaughter and personal injury. Rothari, therefore, was a great king, conqueror, and lawgiver of the Lombards.

> *See also* Arianism; Franks; Fredegar; Law and Law Codes; Merovingian Dynasty; Paul the Deacon; Theudelinde

Bibliography
Christie, Neil. *The Lombards: The Ancient Langobards.* Oxford: Blackwell, 1998.
Drew, Katherine Fisher, trans. *The Lombard Laws.* Philadelphia: University of Pennsylvania Press, 1973.
Herrin, Judith. *The Formation of Christendom.* Princeton: Princeton University Press, 1987.
Llewellyn, Peter. *Rome in the Dark Ages.* New York: Barnes and Noble, 1996.
Paul the Deacon. *History of the Lombards.* Trans. William Dudley Foulke. Philadelphia: University of Pennsylvania Press, 1974.
Wallace-Hadrill, J. M. *The Barbarian West, A.D. 400–1000.* New York: Harper and Row, 1962.
Wallace-Hadrill, J. M., ed. and trans. *The Fourth Book of the Chronicle of Fredegar with Its Continuations.* London: Nelson, 1960.
Wolfram, Herwig. *The Roman Empire and Its Germanic Peoples.* Trans. Thomas J. Dunlap. Berkeley: University of California Press, 1997.

Row-Grave Cemeteries

A traditional Germanic burial practice, the row-grave cemeteries *(Reihengräber)* are important archeological finds because of the wealth of material found in them. There are numerous sites in the Rhine River area and northern France from the migration period and in north central Spain dating from the arrival of the Visigoths. The appearance of these cemeteries in Spain is particularly important; they were once thought to provide evidence of settlement patterns for the Spanish Visigoths. Although no longer thought to reveal such patterns, the row-grave cemeteries are important nonetheless, in part because they are not found in Visigothic France or even Ostrogothic Italy.

Numerous row-grave cemeteries have been found in Spain, and they contain important evidence of Visigothic material culture. Roughly seventy of these cemeteries have been found in Spain, including a very large one of 666 burials with about 1,000 bodies in Duraton. Of particular importance are the burials of women, roughly one fifth of whom were buried in traditional Gothic dress. Another important site, at El Carpio de Tajo, has some 285 graves that stretch over several generations for a village of about 50 or 60 people, and about 90 of the sites contain grave goods. The evidence from these sites presents an uncertain picture about burial practices in the fifth and sixth centuries. It has been suggested that either the graves represent the native Hispano-Roman population emulating the conquerors and including the types of burial goods the Goths would or that the graves containing grave goods are those of the Visigothic lords, who buried their dead with their wealth as a sign of status.

The graves contain important examples of Visigothic dress in the fifth and sixth centuries. The finds at Duraton contain traditional female clothing, which included a cloak attached at the shoulder with a brooch as well as a belt with a large buckle around the waist. The brooches were of fine quality. An especially important pattern was the eagle brooch found in various graves. The eagle may have become popular as a symbol of power that the Visigoths adopted from the Huns and Romans. Although the source of this style for a brooch is unclear, it became popular, and brooches following it were fashioned out of gold and inlaid with precious stones. Also, combs were frequently included among the grave goods and seem to have been an important manufacture among the Goths.

See also Huns; Ostrogoths; Visigoths

Bibliography

Collins, Roger. *Early Medieval Spain: Unity in Diversity, 400–1000.* New York: St. Martin's, 1995.

Heather, Peter. *The Goths.* Oxford: Blackwell, 1996.

Thompson, E. A. *The Goths in Spain.* Oxford: Clarendon, 1969.

Wolfram, Herwig. *History of the Goths.* Trans. Thomas J. Dunlap. Berkeley: University of California Press, 1988.

Royal Frankish Annals

One of a number of chronicles of the Carolingian period that describe events in the kingdom or in a particular monastery or bishopric, the *Royal Frankish Annals* (in Latin, *Annales regni Francorum,* as they have been called since the nineteenth century) are the most important record of events in the early generations of the Carolingian dynasty. The *Royal Frankish Annals* are an official, or at least semi-official, account of the major political, military, and religious events of Carolingian history from 741 to 829. The *Royal Frankish Annals* thus cover events during the reigns of Pippin the Short, Charlemagne, and Louis the Pious, the later part of whose reign is surveyed also in the history of Nithard. The chronicle includes the official Carolingian version of such significant moments as the replacement of the Merovingian line by Pippin and his coronation in 751, the wars and imperial coronation of Charlemagne, and the early and successful years in the reign of Louis the Pious. The *Royal Frankish Annals* were divided after 829 and continued in the Annals of St. Bertin, which surveyed events in the Western Frankish kingdom until 882 and were written in part by Hincmar of Rheims, and the Annals of Fulda, which covered the Eastern Frankish kingdom until 887.

The *Royal Frankish Annals* were most likely composed by a number of different authors over a prolonged period. First written in 787 or 788 as part of the general revival of letters, especially history, under Charlemagne, the *Royal Frankish Annals* were written by several distinct hands and can be divided into three or four sections. Like the minor annals of the period, the *Royal Frankish Annals* were divided into year-by-year entries, with short discussions of the major events of each year.

The first section of the work, from 787/788 to 793, begins with an entry on the year 741, noting the death of Charles Martel and the elevation of his sons Pippin and Carloman. The entries for the year 741 to 787/788 were drawn largely from the continuation of the chronicle of Fredegar and the minor annals composed in the various monasteries of the empire, but from 788 on the authors were contemporary with the events they described. The next section covers the period from 793 to 809, and again its author or authors recorded events that they lived through. The final section before the division into two main annals covers the period from 809 to 829; it can be subdivided even further, with a break at 820.

The style of the final section seems to have improved over the earlier sections, and it has been suggested that the author of part of it was the archchaplain of Louis the Pious. But the identity of any of the annalists remains uncertain, although it is likely that the archchaplain of the royal palace had a hand in the composition of the *Royal Frankish Annals* and equally as likely that Einhard did not. Although he is no longer held to be responsible, Einhard was traditionally associated with the revision of the *Royal Frankish Annals* ordered by Louis the Pious. The entries for the years 741 to 812 were revised to improve the style and were expanded with information from other sources, with the entries for several years being completely or almost completely rewritten. Although written from the Carolingian perspective, the *Royal Frankish Annals* remain one of the most important sources for the events of the Carolingian period.

See also Carloman, Mayor of the Palace; Carolingian Dynasty; Charlemagne; Charles Martel; Einhard; Fredegar; Hincmar of Rheims; Louis the Pious; Nithard; Pippin III, Called the Short

Bibliography

Innes, Matthew, and Rosamond McKitterick. "The Writing of History." In *Carolingian Culture: Emulation and Innovation,* ed. Rosamond McKitterick. Cambridge: Cambridge University Press, 1994, pp. 193–220.

Laistner, Max L. W. *Thought and Letters in Western Europe, A.D. 500 to 900.* 2d ed. Ithaca, NY: Cornell University Press, 1976.

McKitterick, Rosamond. *The Frankish Kingdoms under the Carolingians, 751–987.* London: Longman 1983.

Nelson, Janet, trans. *The Annals of St. Bertin: Ninth Century Histories.* Manchester, UK: University of Manchester Press, 1991.

Reuter, Timothy, trans. *The Annals of Fulda : Ninth Century Histories.* Manchester, UK: University of Manchester Press, 1992.

Riché, Pierre. *The Carolingians: A Family Who Forged Europe.* Trans. Michael Idomir Allen. Philadelphia: University of Pennsylvania Press, 1993.

Scholz, Bernhard Walter, trans. *Carolingian Chronicles: Royal Frankish Annals and Nithard's History.* Ann Arbor: University of Michigan Press, 1972.

S

Salic Law

Legal code traditionally thought to have been compiled under the great Merovingian king Clovis (r. 481–511), the Salic law *(Lex Salica)* is one of the most important of early medieval legal compilations. The importance of the code is the result, in part, of the preeminence of the Franks in the post-Roman world. It remained an important legal source throughout the Merovingian period and was compiled again by the Carolingians. Sections of the law dealing with the right to succession were of great importance in the fourteenth and fifteenth centuries. The code in its earliest version contains sixty-five titles that address a wide variety of legal and social matters, making it a valuable source for early Merovingian history.

The code was, according to the prologue of a later version, originally compiled during the reign of the first Merovingian king. Known as the *Pactus Lex Salicae* to distinguish it from the many later revisions, it is traditionally thought to have been compiled late in the reign of Clovis, possibly between 507 and 511. Although attribution to Clovis comes from a later version, it is likely that the law appeared early in Merovingian history, surely before the death of Clovis, and it was probably commissioned by him. It is a collection of the laws of the Salian Franks, although it does not include all the laws of the Franks. The *Pactus* is the written version of the traditional customs of the Franks, and the codification of these laws in Latin reflects the growing sophistication and stability of the Franks under Clovis and important Frankish contacts with late Roman culture and government. Indeed, this collection of custom and royal edict was most likely codified by a team of Frankish officials and Roman lawyers. Originally compiled before 511, the Salic law was revised and expanded by later Merovingian kings in the later sixth and seventh centuries, and a prologue and epilogue were added in later versions. It was also revised by the Carolingians and was much studied in the eighth and ninth centuries.

The Salic law is not an orderly codification of the law, but a collection of important laws and customs that provide important insights into Merovingian society. One of the most important concerns of the Salic law is the preservation of peace in the Merovingian kingdom, and a number of chapters address social relations. One section addresses the inheritance of private property, and an earlier section specifies the fines to be paid for the theft of a bull. Penalties are imposed for wrongly calling a woman a "harlot" and for calling someone a "hare" or "fox." Another important section concerns the payment of the wergeld (payment made in compensation for taking a life) to the family of deceased. Other parts of the code deal with lesser offences and injuries and routinely impose a fine for these crimes. The penalties are often quite specific, such as a fine of 2500 denars for attempting to poison someone with an arrow, or 1200 denars for striking someone so hard on the head that the brain appears. Rape, murder of women and children, assault and robbery, and housebreaking are other crimes regulated in the Salic law. The law also concerns royal rights and prerogatives and imposes higher fines for crimes against the king, his property, and his agents.

The Salic law also provides insight into the social structures of Merovingian society. One of the most notable things revealed in the code is the social stratification of Frankish society in the sixth and seventh centuries. The penalties vary according to the social rank of the perpetrator and victim, with harsher fines imposed on the lower orders. The code reveals the continued practice of slavery, and a class of freemen and peasants, as well as one of nobles and kings. Moreover, although designed to cover all those living in the Merovingian kingdom, the Salic law originally observed the principle of personality, according to which each person was bound by the laws of his own group. Thus it imposed different penalties for crimes by Franks and crimes by Romans and provided a legal distinction between Romans and barbarians. Under the Carolingians the law came to apply to all the people of the realm equally, bearing witness to the integration of Franks and Romans into one society.

See also Carolingian Dynasty; Clovis; Franks; Law and Law Codes; Merovingian Dynasty

Bibliography
Geary, Patrick J. *Before France and Germany: The Creation and Transformation of the Merovingian World.* Oxford: Oxford University Press, 1988.
Rivers, Theodore John, trans. *The Laws of the Salian and Ripuarian Franks.* New York: AMS, 1986.
Wallace-Hadrill, J. M. *The Long-Haired Kings.* Toronto: Toronto University Press, 1982.
Wood, Ian. *The Merovingian Kingdoms, 450–751.* London: Longman, 1994.
Wormald, Patrick. "*Lex Scripta* and *Verbum Regis:* Legislation and Early Germanic Kingship from Euric to Cnut." In *Early Medieval Kingship,* ed. Peter H. Sawyer and Ian N. Wood. Leeds, UK: School of History, University of Leeds 1977, pp. 105–138.

Saxon Capitularies

Two laws issued by Charlemagne during his prolonged conquest of Saxony, 772–804, the Saxon Capitularies were intended to promote the conversion of the Saxons to Christianity, which was an essential component of Charlemagne's conquest. The two capitularies, issued about twelve years apart, reveal two different approaches to conversion of the Saxons, approaches determined, in part, by the progress of the conquest of Saxony.

The first capitulary, the *Capitulatio de partibus Saxoniae* (Capitulary concerning the parts of Saxony), was issued by Charlemagne at an assembly at the palace at Paderborn in 785. It was issued shortly after the suppression of the revolt of the Saxon leader Widukind, during a period in which extreme acts of violence and brutality were committed by both sides. Beyond the revolt against Carolingian authority, the Saxons attacked and destroyed churches and harmed and killed priests and monks who had been engaged in missionary activity. In his turn, Charlemagne not only put down the revolt but also massacred some 4,500 Saxons at Verdun and forcibly moved a large number of Saxons into Frankish territory. Consequently, the Saxon capitulary of 785 was a draconian law that sought to impose Christianity on the Saxons by the same force that Charlemagne applied in imposing Carolingian political authority. The various decrees in the first Saxon capitulary included penalties of death for forced entry into a church, stealing from a church, eating meat during Lent, killing a priest or bishop, and refusing baptism. Death was also imposed on those who follow pagan burial rites, perform human sacrifice, or burn anyone believed to be a witch. Charlemagne also enacted a number of heavy fines in the capitulary, including fines for contracting an unlawful marriage, refusing to baptize an infant, and praying in groves of trees or at springs. The capitulary further demanded payment of the tithe to the church and forbade meetings other than church services on Sundays. Finally, the capitulary of 785 included a number of chapters establishing Carolingian government and administration.

The second capitulary, the *Capitulare Saxonicum* (Capitulary concerning the Saxons), was issued at the new imperial capital of Aachen in 797. This capitulary was also conditioned by events in the conquest of Saxony and also followed a revolt of the Saxons that was mercilessly suppressed by the great king. But the revolt and enactment of the capitulary followed a long missionary and military campaign in Saxony. Indeed, following the first publication of the first Saxon capitulary, Charlemagne continued to engage in the process of evangelization in Saxony that followed the harsh conditions set out in the ruling of 785. His treatment of the Saxons was so harsh that his closest advisor, Alcuin, complained to the king about it. By 797, Charlemagne contended that the conversion of Saxony had been completed, even though the military campaigns continued for several more years. The *Capitulare Saxonicum,* therefore, was shaped to fit the new conditions and was, therefore, a much less harsh law. It offered the milk and honey of the faith rather than the iron of the sword. Although there is no indication that the earlier capitulary was no longer in effect, the capitulary of 797 abandoned the rigid regime of death sentences and instead proposed various fines for any failure to live as a good Christian. Charlemagne's efforts ultimately bore fruit; the region eventually accepted Carolingian rule and the Christian faith, and in the tenth century Saxony was one of the great centers of

medieval Christianity as well as of a resurgence of Carolingian political ideas.

See also Alcuin of York; Capitularies; Carolingian Dynasty; Charlemagne; Franks; Widukind

Bibliography
"Paderborn, 785 (Capitulary concerning the parts of Saxony)" and "Concerning the Saxons, 797," in *Readings in Medieval History,* ed. Patrick J. Geary. Peterborough, Ont.: Broadview, 1989, pp. 316–320.

Ganshof, François Louis. *Frankish Institutions under Charlemagne.* Trans. Bryce Lyon and Mary Lyon. Providence, RI: Brown University Press, 1968.

Halphen, Louis. *Charlemagne and the Carolingian Empire.* Trans. Giselle de Nie. Amsterdam: North-Holland, 1977.

Loyn, Henry R. and John Percival, trans. *The Reign of Charlemagne.* New York: St. Martin's Press, 1975.

McKitterick, Rosamond. *The Carolingians and the Written Word.* Cambridge: Cambridge University Press, 1989.

Riché, Pierre. *The Carolingians: A Family Who Forged Europe.* Trans. Michael Idomir Allen. Philadelphia: University of Pennsylvania Press, 1993.

Sigebert
See Brunhilde

Sigismund, St. (d. 524)
Burgundian king (r. 516–523) and saint, whose reign was marked by the introduction of important legal codes and strained relations with the Franks and Ostrogoths. The son of Gundobad and son-in-law of Theodoric the Great, Sigismund was nonetheless a convert from Arian to Catholic Christianity, like his cousin, Clotilda, the wife of the Merovingian king Clovis. Despite his conversion, Sigismund, according to the sixth-century historian of the Franks Gregory of Tours, was the victim of Clotilda's vengeance because Gundobad had allegedly killed Chi-

lperic, her father and Gundobad's brother. Although that remains uncertain, Sigismund was clearly caught between aggressive Frankish and Ostrogothic powers and struggled to preserve his kingdom, in part by styling himself a traditional ally of the Roman Empire and seeking an alliance with the Eastern Empire. He was eventually overthrown and killed.

Although he became king in his own name in 516, Sigismund was an important figure in the kingdom even before that time. He was made coregent by his father Gundobad in 501 and ruled with him until Gundobad's death in 516. Sigismund also played an important role in his father's diplomacy when he married the daughter of the great Ostrogothic king of Italy, Theodoric. His significance extended to religious affairs as well; he converted to Catholic Christianity, from Arian Christianity, by the year 515. His conversion, like that of Clovis not long before, allowed him to cultivate better relations with the Roman people in the kingdom, especially with the bishops. Indeed, Sigismund had very good relations with the Catholic hierarchy in his kingdom, especially with the powerful and influential bishop Avitus, who wrote a number of letters for the king. Sigismund further improved his relationship with the Catholic hierarchy in 515 by his foundation of the monastery of St. Maurice at Agaune, which became one of the more important communities in the Middle Ages. The monks at the house participated in the *laus perennis* (perpetual prayer) so that God would be praised unceasingly.

As king, Sigismund's greatest achievement was the codification and publication of Burgundian and Roman law in 517. Following the traditions of the barbarian successors to the Roman Empire, the Burgundian kingdom followed the legal principle of personality, according to which each person was bound by the laws of his own group. Like the Visigoths before him, Sigismund issued two separate legal codes, one that applied to his people and another that applied to his Roman subjects. The *Lex Gundobad* (Law of Gundobad), or *Liber constitutionem* (Book of Constitutions), was issued in its final form, although it was most likely originally prepared during the reign of Sigismund's father. This was a very important legal code, whose influence would last for several centuries. The king also issued the *Lex Romana Burgundionum* (Roman Law of the Burgundians), which was the personal law of his Roman subjects. Although a significant legal code, Sigismund's Roman law did not survive the fall of the kingdom; it was replaced once the kingdom fell to the Merovingian Franks.

Although Sigismund introduced a number of major reforms in the kingdom, he was less successful in international relations. Upon succeeding his father in 516, Sigismund was faced with the challenge posed by the Franks and Ostrogoths. He was fortunate that his marriage to Theodoric's daughter enabled him to at least keep Theodoric from advancing against him. Even though Theodoric was surely displeased by Sigismund's conversion to Christianity, he maintained good relations with the Burgundian king and allowed him to make a pilgrimage to Rome. To improve his situation, though, Sigismund cultivated relations with the Byzantine Empire as a balance to potential threats from the Franks and, especially, the Ostrogoths, whose relations with Constantinople were strained. When he succeeded to the throne, Sigismund also inherited the Roman title of patrician, which his father had held. But good ties with Constantinople were insufficient to save Sigismund from his closer neighbors.

In 522, Theodoric's daughter died, which removed any impediment to Theodoric's invasion of the kingdom. Moreover, relations with the Franks were long difficult, even though his relative, Clotilda, had married Clovis and, according to tradition, converted him to Christianity. Indeed, according to Gregory of Tours, Clotilda encouraged her sons to invade the Burgundian kingdom to avenge the murder of her father by Gundobad. In 522 or 523, Sigismund faced an invasion of both Franks and Ostrogoths, which he could not stop. He was defeated in battle and handed over to the Franks by his own people, who had abandoned him. In 524, he was murdered by the Frankish king, who ordered that Sigismund be thrown in a well. The kingdom preserved its independence for another ten years before it was finally absorbed by the Franks in 534.

See also Arianism; Clotilda, St.; Clovis; Franks; Gundobad; Gregory of Tours; Merovingian Dynasty; Law and Law Codes; Ostrogoths; Theodoric the Great

Bibliography

Drew, Katherine Fisher, trans. The Burgundian Code: The Book of Constitutions or Law of Gundobad and Additional Enactments. 1972.

Gregory of Tours. History of the Franks. Trans. Lewis Thorpe. Harmondsworth, UK: Penguin, 1974.

Randers-Pehrson, Justine Davis. Barbarians and Romans: The Birth Struggle of Europe, A. D. 400–700. Norman: University of Oklahoma Press, 1983.

Wolfram, Herwig. The Roman Empire and Its Germanic Peoples. Trans. Thomas J. Dunlap. Berkeley: University of California Press, 1997.

Wood, Ian. The Merovingian Kingdoms, 450–751. London: Longman, 1994.

Slaves and Slavery

One of the most pernicious and persistent practices throughout human history, slavery was found everywhere in the ancient Mediterranean and continued in some form into the Middle Ages. Indeed, some scholars have suggested that the continuance of the practice of slavery and holding of slaves was an essential part of ancient society and that only when slavery was ended, and ultimately transformed into serfdom, did the ancient world truly end. Although slavery persisted into late antiquity and the early Middle Ages, it differed from the traditional Roman practice of holding large gangs of agricultural slave laborers. Still, slaves were found performing agricultural labor in late antiquity and the early Middle Ages in significant numbers, even if they were sometimes hard to distinguish from the local free peasants; they were also found at a number of other tasks, including military. Slavery existed among all the peoples that created kingdoms in the former Western Roman Empire, including Franks, Goths, Lombards, and Vandals.

Slavery had been a fundamental component of economy of the Mediterranean in the classical age; in late antiquity, its practice continued to be supported as a natural part of life. Indeed, the great church father, St. Augustine of Hippo, justified slavery's practice in the fifth century by noting that it was the consequence of sin. Although some deeply pious Christians freed their slaves—for example, the sixth-century pope Gregory the Great who, according to the seventh-century Anglo-Saxon historian Bede, purchased a number of Anglo-Saxon slaves to free them and join them to the church—there was no great push by the church for the manumission of slaves. Augustine also provides evidence for its ubiquity in the late fourth and fifth centuries, observing that nearly every household possessed slaves. Indeed, the household slave remained an important functionary, and each soldier generally had at least one or two slaves at his service. In the Roman Empire of the fourth and fifth centuries, slaves continued to be used in a number of other places, including mines, quarries, foundries, and weaving factories. They were, or course, also used as laborers on the farms of the empire, but not in great gangs housed in barracks, as they had been during the early days of the empire. They were often given small plots of land to work to encourage their productivity and also to preserve the land as taxable property. In fact, it was forbidden by law to sell a slave without his property. As a result of this, the slave and free peasant became increasingly difficult to distinguish, with the slave better off in some ways than the peasant. In one of his letters, Augustine voiced the concern that the peasant would abandon his place and join the ranks of the slaves.

Despite their many uses, slaves amounted to no more than 10 or 12 percent of the population. Nevertheless, there still existed a lucrative slave trade, which involved commerce in slaves gathered mainly from the frontier areas of the empire in modern western Hungary and Morocco. Slaves were obtained through inheritance, but more by conquest or trade. Indeed, as the various barbarian peoples entered the empire they sold their compatriots or, more often, the people they had conquered. The invasions themselves led to the continued slave trade, as many Roman citizens fell into slavery. Alaric, during the Visigothic invasion of Italy and sack of Rome, captured many slaves. The invasion of Attila and the Huns also led to the capture of many slaves, as did the invasions of the Vandals, Odovacar, and Theodoric the Great.

In the immediate post-Roman world, slavery existed in various forms among the various successor kingdoms established by the Germanic peoples who had moved into the empire. Among the Visigoths, slaves were found working the royal estates in Spain and as skilled laborers in the household. Slaves also served in the Visigothic army, although their rank and treatment was little improved by their military service. A noblewoman would be flogged and burned alive for having sexual relations with a slave. The same fate awaited the slave, but a free nobleman could father as many slave children as he wished. In the Ostrogothic kingdom of Italy a slave's life was a harsh one, and slavery was primarily rural. Slaves were chattel with very few rights or privileges, who could be killed by their owners or burned alive for having sexual relations with a widow or causing a fire. Slaves could not legally marry and could be transferred at will from one estate to another. They could even be assigned to a peasant, whose treatment could be worse in practice than that of some distant owner.

The practice of slavery continued in Italy after its conquest by the Lombards in the sixth century, and their invasion of the peninsula brought them many slaves, which provided them a larger slave workforce than that of the Goths or Romans before them. Testimony to the size of the slave population in the Lombard kingdom is found in the numerous references to them in Lombard law. A seventh-century law code, the *Leges Rothari* ("Laws of King Rothari") identifies the existence of slaves of Germanic and Roman descent. The Roman slaves were often skilled and so valued more highly than their Germanic counterparts, who generally worked the fields as agricultural labor, though both Roman and Germanic slaves did serve as farmhands. Slaves were used for household and agricultural labor, and there was a monastery that owned a large number of female slaves who wove cloth. The life of the slave improved by the time of King Liutprand, in part because of the influence of the church after the conversion of the Lombards to Catholic Christianity. The marriage of slaves was now recognized as legitimate, part of the fine for killing a slave was given to the slave's family, and slaves could be freed to join the clergy.

In the Frankish kingdoms slavery in some form or other existed into the ninth and tenth centuries, but the distinction between a slave and serf became increasingly blurred. There is evidence that slavery existed from the earliest days of the Merovingian dynasty. The Salic law describes certain legal processes involving slaves, and the sixth-century Frankish historian Gregory of Tours tells of the brutal treatment of slaves, including the burying of two alive, by the Frankish noble Rauching. Of course, Gregory held Rauching up as an example of the worst treatment of slaves, and not all slaves endured such debased conditions. Indeed, the sixth-century queen Fredegund may have been a slave, or at least a servant at the royal court, and the seventh-century queen (and later saint) Balthild was a slave, even though of royal birth. The extent of slavery during the Merovingian period remains uncertain, however, because of uncertainties in the sources themselves and vagueness in terminology. It is likely, though, that slavery was not that extensive under the Merovingian dynasty, as records from the early days and as well as the later period of the dynasty indicate. The records of bishops at either end of Merovingian history reveal a small percentage of slaves on episcopal estates. Slavery was most likely hereditary, but there are records of frequent manumission of slaves. Aside from Gregory's tale of Rauching, the evidence suggests that slaves were not poorly treated, in part because of a labor shortage the kingdom suffered, so that both the free peasantry in the countryside and the slaves were most likely well treated.

Slavery surely continued under the Carolingian dynasty, though in a much changed form from classical slavery; there is evidence revealing the transformation of slaves into serfs. The morality of slavery was much discussed by Carolingian scholars, who often borrowed from Augustine and the other church fathers. The most important of the Carolingian scholars, the Anglo-Saxon Alcuin of York, justified slavery in the very terms used by St. Augustine, and others recognized it as a natural part of the divine order of things. There is also much evidence of an active slave trade in the Carolingian Empire, and the trade was carried on by both Jewish and Christian merchants. Slaves came from the border regions of the empire, including Saxony and the Slavic lands, but it was not uncommon for an unfortunate to be captured while traveling the highways and sold into slavery. The conquests of Charlemagne and other Carolingian rulers were another source of slaves, as captives of war who were not ransomed were kept as slaves. The number of slaves was most likely not that great, seldom more than 10 percent on records from the great estates, but there were concentrations of slaves on the estates employed in a variety of occupations. Alcuin, for example, appears to have had large numbers of slaves at work on the monasteries under his control, and records from a number of other great estates indicate that about 10 percent of the workforce was made up of slaves. Carolingian slaves served as traders and bodyguards, but their most important duty was as agricultural laborers. In their role as farmers, the slaves of the Carolingian era show signs of becoming the serfs of the later Middle Ages.

See also Alaric; Alcuin of York; Anglo-Saxons; Augustine of Hippo, St.; Balthild, St.; Carolingian Dynasty; Franks; Fredegund; Gregory the Great, Pope; Gregory of Tours; Liutprand; Lombards; Merovingian Dynasty; Odovacar; Ostrogoths; Salic Law; Theodoric the Great; Vandals; Visigoths

Bibliography

Bede. *Ecclesiastical History of the English People with Bede's Letter to Egbert and Cuthbert's Letter on the Death of Bede.* Trans. Leo Sherley-Price. Harmondsworth, UK: Penguin, 1991.

Bloch, Marc. *French Rural History: An Essay on Its Basic Characteristics.* Trans. Janet Sondheimer. Berkeley: University of California Press, 1966.

———. *Slavery and Serfdom in the Middle Ages.* Trans. William R. Beer. Berkeley: University of California Press, 1975.

Bonnassie, Pierre. *From Slavery to Feudalism in South-Western Europe.* Trans. Jean Birrell. Cambridge: Cambridge University Press, 1991.

Cameron, Averil. *The Mediterranean World in Late Antiquity,* A.D. *395–600.* New York: Routledge, 1993.

Dockès, Pierre. *Medieval Slavery and Liberation.* Trans. Arthur Goldhammer. Chicago: University of Chicago Press, 1982.

Duby, Georges. *The Early Growth of the European Economy: Warriors and Peasants from the Seventh to the Twelfth Century.* Trans. Howard B. Clarke. Ithaca, NY: Cornell University Press, 1974.

Gregory of Tours. *The History of the Franks.* Trans. Lewis Thorpe. Harmondsworth, UK: Penguin, 1974.

Wallace-Hadrill, J. M. *The Barbarian West,* A.D. *400–1000.* New York: Harper and Row, 1962.

———. *The Long-Haired Kings.* Toronto: University of Toronto Press, 1982.

Wood, Ian. *The Merovingian Kingdoms, 450–751.* London: Longman, 1994.

Solidus

See Coins and Coinage

Stilicho, Flavius (c. 360–408)

Roman military commander and regent whose career stood in the tradition of Arbogast, the fourth century German soldier who was the power behind the throne, and in contrast to that of the Gothic king Alaric. The son of a Vandal cavalry officer in the service of Rome and a Roman noblewoman, Stilicho fully embraced the empire and its customs, including Catholic Christianity. He had a successful career and was a loyal follower of the emperor Theodosius the Great. As regent for Theodosius's son Honorius, Stilicho faced the increasing pressure of the barbarians on the empire and invasions by Goths led by Alaric and Radagaisus. Although not wholly successful against either king, Stilicho struggled valiantly to preserve the integrity of the Western Empire, even at the cost of nearly losing Britain. His talent for managing his rivals is perhaps best illustrated in the failure of Honorius to prevent the successful invasion of Italy and sack of Rome by Alaric in the years following Stilicho's execution.

The son of a Vandal father and Roman mother, whose marriage required imperial dispensation, Stilicho was marked early on for advancement in the service of the empire. His parents placed him on the roster of the guards of the court as a small boy, where he may have made contact with the future emperor Theodosius. In 383, Stilicho served on an imperial delegation to the Persian king Shapur III (r. 383–388). Upon his return from the embassy to Shapur, Stilicho married Theodosius's favorite niece, Serena, and was raised to the office of master of the stable. By 385, he was made a general and given promotion to the rank of chief of the guard. In 391, the year he first faced Alaric, Stilicho was promoted to a high-ranking post in the Eastern Empire, and in 393 he was made master of both services, the commander in chief of the army.

Stilicho's rapid rise, together with the clear favor of the emperor, brought him to the top of the Roman military hierarchy before the death of his patron. His debt to the emperor did not, however, go unpaid; although little is known of his early military career, it is certain that Stilicho played an important, if not decisive, role in the victory over the pretender to the Western Empire Eugenius and his military commander Arbogast in 394. Indeed, Stilicho probably led the attack on the second day of the battle that turned the tide and brought about the defeat of Eugenius and his general. Stilicho was of such importance to the emperor that he set off for the Eastern Empire before Theodosius, who died suddenly on January 17, 395, while on his way there. Stilicho was favored by the emperor one last time when Theodosius on his deathbed entrusted his sons, Honorius and Arcadius, to the care of the Vandal general.

The death of Theodosius left Stilicho the most powerful figure in the empire, even though he was not without rivals and subject to Theodosius's heirs, Honorius in the Western Empire and Arcadius in the Eastern Empire. Indeed, his greatest rival, and personal enemy of long standing, Rufinus, was the commander in chief for Arcadius. And, under Rufinus's direction, Arcadius restricted Stilicho's field of action and ordered that Stilicho, who preparing to challenge Alaric in part of the Eastern Empire, send some of his troops to defend Constantinople against their mutual enemy Alaric and his followers. Ever loyal to the house of Theodosius and the empire, Stilicho yielded to Arcadius's demands, but the troops he sent murdered Rufinus, perhaps at their general's initiative. Stilicho next faced Eutropius, who assumed the position of chief advisor to Arcadius until late 399. The two negotiated control of important border regions between the two halves of the empire and struggled to contain Alaric. At the same time, of course, they struggled for power in the empire, which Eutropius lost in a plot that included an ally of Stilicho in the Eastern Empire.

As the leading military commander in the

empire, Stilicho took on the responsibility of protecting it from various barbarian groups and spent much of his career in a complex game of cat and mouse with Alaric. They had served together when Theodosius crushed the usurpation of Eugenius, but they had become rivals as Alaric's demands went unmet by the imperial governments. In 397, Stilicho had the opportunity to destroy Alaric and his army but negotiated a settlement with him, which allowed the Gothic king to trouble the Eastern Empire and Stilicho's rival at the time, Eutropius. Although Alaric abandoned his claims to western territory over the next four years—during which time Stilicho reached the pinnacle of power, assumed the office of consul, and married his daughter, Maria, to Honorius—he invaded Italy in late 401 while Stilicho was engaged with other barbarians. Quickly turning his attention to Alaric by early 402, Stilicho called for reinforcements from Britain and the Rhine frontier to protect Italy. He also gave command to a pagan Alan, who attacked while Alaric and the Goths were celebrating Easter, thus inflicting a severe defeat on him. This was followed by an even more crushing defeat by Stilicho by late summer 402, but Stilicho once again allowed Alaric to survive and receive a military commission from Arcadius. Alaric launched one more assault on the Western Empire in 407, again at a time of crisis for Stilicho, who sought to reach an agreement with his long-term enemy; the attempt failed because of Stilicho's fall.

Stilicho faced other challenges during his career leading the Roman military. In 397–398, he faced the revolt of the Roman count of Africa, which cut off the grain supply to Italy. Stilicho overcame this challenge by importing grain from elsewhere and by sending a powerful army to suppress the unruly governor. The victorious general of that army mysteriously died not long after his victory, and many blamed Stilicho for the death. He made new treaties with the Alemanni and the Franks, and deposed a Frankish king he disliked. More serious than his difficulties in Africa or Gaul was

the invasion by the barbarian Radagaisus and a large band of Ostrogoths in 405. This serious breach of the Rhine frontier, perhaps the result of Stilicho's efforts to protect Italy at the expense of the rest of the empire, would lead to Stilicho's downfall. Although he imposed a punishing defeat on Radagaisus near Florence in the summer of 406, Stilicho could not decisively defeat him. Radagaisus remained a threat to Italy for the next several years, to the dismay of Honorius and Stilicho.

The return of Alaric and death of Arcadius further complicated matters for Stilicho. Indeed, competition over the succession to the throne of Arcadius between Stilicho and Honorius, as well as the death of Maria and Stilicho's loss of important imperial territory and failure to inflict final defeats on Alaric and Radagaisus led to his downfall. No longer confident in his general, Honorius ordered the arrest and execution of Stilicho on August 22, 408. Two years later, Alaric sacked the city of Rome.

See also Alaric; Arbogast; Honorius; Ostrogoths; Theodosius the Great; Vandals; Visigoths

Bibliography
Burns, Thomas S. *Barbarians within the Gates of Rome: A Study of Roman Military Policy and the Barbarians, ca. 375–425 A.D.* Bloomington: University of Indiana Press, 1994.
Bury, John B. *History of the Later Roman Empire: From the Death of Theodosius I to the Death of Justinian.* 2 vols. 1923. Reprint, New York: Dover, 1959.
———. *The Invasion of Europe by the Barbarians.* New York: W. W. Norton, 1967.
Claudian. *Claudian's Fourth Panegyric on the fourth consulate of Honorius.* Ed. and trans. William Barr. Liverpool, UK: Liverpool University Press, 1981.
Heather, Peter. *The Goths.* Oxford: Blackwell, 1996.
Wolfram, Herwig. *The Roman Empire and Its Germanic Peoples.* Trans. Thomas J. Dunlap. Berkeley: University of California Press, 1997.
Zosimus. *New History.* Trans. Ronald T. Ridley. Canberra: Australian Association for Byzantine Studies, 1982.

Strasbourg, Oath of (842)

An agreement between Charles the Bald and Louis the German, the Oath of Strasbourg solidified an alliance between the two kings during the civil wars following the death of Louis the Pious. Subscribed to by the two kings and their followers, the oath marked an important turning point in the struggles with the emperor Lothar. The oath, preserved by the historian Nithard, is also an important linguistic milestone because it was pronounced and recorded in early versions of the Romance and Germanic languages.

Following their victory over their brother Lothar at the Battle of Fontenoy in 841, Charles the Bald and Louis the German met to forge a pact confirming their continued cooperation because Lothar refused to accept peace after his defeat. They met at the city of Strasbourg on February 12, 842, to exchange oaths of loyalty and mutual assistance, declaring also that if they should violate the oath, their followers were released from their oaths to the kings. Louis, as the elder brother, spoke first in Romance, the language of Charles's followers, and swore to aid his brother and treat him as one should his brother on the condition that Charles treat him in the same way. Charles in turn, speaking in the Germanic language *(lingua teudisca)* of his brother's soldiers, made the same oath, and each brother swore not to enter into any agreement with Lothar that might harm the other's interests. The followers of the two kings then swore in their own languages that they would not give any aid to their king if the king violated the oath. The Oath of Strasbourg thus confirmed the pact of friendship and cooperation between Charles and Louis and enabled them to bring Lothar to a settlement in the Treaty of Verdun in 843.

See also Carolingian Dynasty; Charles the Bald; Fontenoy, Battle of; Lothar; Louis the German; Louis the Pious; Nithard; Verdun, Treaty of

Bibliography

Dutton, Paul Edward. *Carolingian Civilization: A Reader.* Peterborough, Ont.: Broadview, 1993.

McKitterick, Rosamond. *The Frankish Kingdoms under the Carolingians, 751–987.* London: Longman, 1983.

Nelson, Janet. *Charles the Bald.* London: Longman, 1992.

Riché, Pierre. *The Carolingians: A Family Who Forged Europe.* Trans Michael Idomir Allen. Philadelphia: University of Pennsylvania Press, 1993.

Scholz, Bernhard Walter, trans. *Carolingian Chronicles: Royal Frankish Annals and Nithard's History.* Ann Arbor: University of Michigan Press, 1972.

Sutton Hoo

Site (in England's Somerset region) of one of the most important archeological discoveries for the history of the Anglo-Saxon kingdoms. In 1939 a burial mound was discovered at Sutton Hoo by Basil Brown that revolutionized modern understanding of pre-Christian Anglo-Saxon civilization. The discovery of a burial ship and its possessions from the first quarter or first half of the seventh century transformed the prevalent perception of early East Anglian courts, and Anglo-Saxon royal courts in general, as impoverished and backward centers with few contacts outside England; it revealed a dynamic court life with wide-ranging contacts with the European continent.

The burial site, noted for its extraordinary richness, is without human remains and may have been a site intended as a memorial rather than a place of interment. Whatever the case, the question of whose burial mound it was remains unanswered. Its close proximity to Rendlesham, the residence of the kings of East Anglia, and its contents have led to the theory that it was a royal burial site. Among those considered to have been buried in the 90-foot open rowing boat at Sutton Hoo are the seventh-century East Anglian kings Raedwald, Earpwald, and Sigeberht.

The mound is remarkable for the number and variety of domestic and imported goods found inside. Among its numerous and luxurious possessions are the traditional burial goods of pre-Christian warriors, including spearheads, a wooden shield covered in leather, two

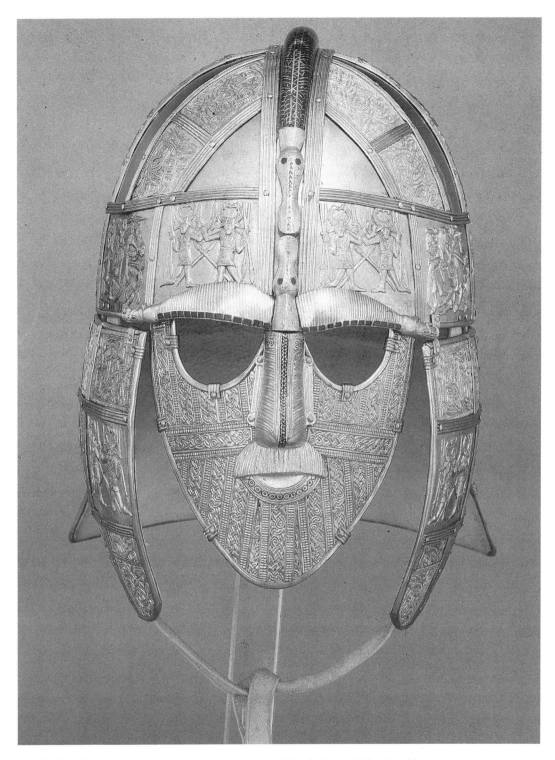

A gold helmet found at the Sutton Hoo burial site (Art Archive / British Museum / Eileen Tweedy)

Golden buckle from an Anglo-Saxon king from Sutton Hoo (British Museum)

large drinking horns, and a helmet. A sword decorated with gold and garnets is noteworthy for the skilled craftsmanship used in its creation. There is also an extensive cache of jewelry of great quality. Some of the jewelry is also decorated with gold and garnets, thus linking it with workshops in Kent and on the Continent. A gold buckle with interlacing snakes and small animals is both exquisite in design and typical of contemporary Germanic art. The mound also contains a huge whetstone, wooden buckets with silver mounts, a five-stringed musical instrument, fragments of chain mail and textiles of great quality, and an iron battle standard with bulls' heads. Products of foreign provenance in the find include a purse with thirty-seven gold coins from the Continent, a Byzantine salver with four stamps of the emperor Anastasius I (441–518), and a bronze bowl from the eastern Mediterranean.

Although the original find was spectacular, it was not the end of the excavations at Sutton Hoo. Subsequent work has uncovered another twenty burial mounds and forty-four burial sites without mounds. The burial sites without mounds reveal that both inhumation and cremation were practiced, and they also contain possible evidence for the practice of human sacrifice. Whatever else is discovered at Sutton Hoo, the original find has contributed greatly to our understanding of this period and demonstrated the extensive contacts that England had with both the Frankish and Byzantine worlds, although more with the former than latter. Sutton Hoo also revealed the wealth and quality craftsmanship of this period of early medieval English history.

See also Anglo-Saxons

Bibliography

Bruce-Mitford, Rupert L. S. *The Sutton Hoo Ship Burial.* 3 vols. London: British Museum, 1975–1983.

Carver, Martin. *The Age of Sutton Hoo.* Woodbridge, UK: Boydell, 1992.

———. *Sutton Hoo: Burial Ground of Kings?* Philadelphia: University of Pennsylvania Press, 1998.

Evans, Angela Care. *The Sutton Hoo Ship Burial.* London: British Museum, 1986.

Stenton, Frank M. *Anglo-Saxon England.* 3d ed. Oxford: Clarendon, 1971.

Synod of Whitby (664)

One of the most important church councils of early English history, the synod held at Streanaeschalch, or Bay of the Beacon (identified with Whitby since the eleventh century), determined the shape of Christianity in the Anglo-Saxon kingdoms. The council, held by Oswy, king of Northumbria (r. 655–670), met in 664 (although some prefer the year 663) to resolve the debate over the calculation of Easter initiated by the contact between missionaries from the Celtic church of Ireland and those from the Roman church of southern England.

After the restoration of Roman Catholic Christianity to England by St. Augustine of Canterbury, conflict occurred between the advocates of the Roman faith and those of the Celtic Christian faith. Missionaries of both churches were especially active in the kingdom of Northumbria, whose king, Oswy, accepted the Celtic tradition, whereas his wife, Eanfled, a princess from Kent, was raised in the Roman tradition. Among the various differences between the practices of the two churches was a difference in the method of calculating the date of Easter, with the Celtic church celebrating the feast a week earlier than the Roman church. As a result, Eanfled would continue fasting while her husband was feasting and celebrating the resurrection of Jesus Christ. The divergence in practice in the royal household, which paralleled the divergence in the kingdom, inspired Oswy to hold a council at Streanaeschalch, the monastery of his cousin Abbess Hilda, to resolve the debate.

The council's main focus was to determine the proper means to calculate the date of Easter, but it also was to decide issues concerning liturgy, organization, the tonsure, and other matters of church discipline. Oswy opened the council by observing that all believers in one God should follow one rule and should celebrate the sacraments of heaven in the same way. The spokesman for the Celtic church, St. Colman (c. 605–676), began the debate by arguing that the saintly and pious fathers of his church, including the widely respected St. Columba (c. 521–597), had long determined the date of Easter in the Celtic way, and that these same fathers had learned their method of calculation from John the Apostle. Although the visiting bishop of the West Saxons, Agilbert, had been appointed to defend the Roman cause, he yielded to Wilfrid (634–709), the abbot of Ripon, who spoke the Anglo-Saxon language better. Wilfrid argued that his church's custom came from Rome, the city of the apostles St. Peter and St. Paul. He said also that these customs are followed in Italy, Gaul, Africa, Asia, and Greece—everywhere but Ireland and Scotland. Colman responded by defending the many Irish saints who had followed the Celtic practice, but Wilfrid argued that no matter how saintly the Celtic fathers were they could not take precedence over St. Peter, who had been given the keys to the kingdom of heaven. Hearing this Oswy asked Colman if this were true and if he could make an equal boast about Columba. Learning that Colman could not, Oswy declared, "Then, I tell you, Peter is guardian of the gates of heaven, and I shall not contradict him" (Bede 1981, 192). The king thus accepted the Roman tradition and ensured the ultimate triumph of Roman Catholic Christianity in England.

See also Anglo-Saxons; Augustine of Canterbury, St.; Bede; Columba, St.; Oswy; Wilfrid

Bibliography

Bede. *Ecclesiastical History of the English People with Bede's Letter to Egbert and Cuthbert's Letter on the Death of Bede.* Trans. Leo Sherley-Price. Harmondsworth, UK: Penguin, 1991.

Blair, Peter Hunter. *The World of Bede.* Cambridge: Cambridge University Press, 1991.

Mayr-Harting, Henry. *The Coming of Christianity to Anglo-Saxon England.* 3d ed. University Park: Pennsylvania State University Press, 1991.

Stenton, Frank M. *Anglo-Saxon England.* 3d ed. Oxford: Clarendon, 1971.

T

Tassilo (742–794)

The last semi-independent duke of Bavaria (r. 749–788), Tassilo was a member of the powerful Agilolfing family, which had once been rivals of the Carolingian family for control in the Frankish kingdoms. He claimed a long tradition of successful rule in Bavaria, and he and his family had established good relations with the church in the duchy and endowed numerous monasteries. He had also established important alliances with other peoples, including the Lombards. His downfall came at the hands of his relative Charlemagne, whose expansionistic policies led him to absorb the Bavarian duchy and force Tassilo into retirement at a monastery.

The son of Odilo, duke of Bavaria, Tassilo enjoyed an important political and religious inheritance. The family had long supported the church in Bavaria and could claim the support of the monasteries they had so richly endowed. Tassilo was also the daughter of Chiltrude (d. 754), Charles Martel's daughter and sister of Pippin; even though his mother married Tassilo's father against her brother's wishes, through her Tassilo had some claim to the Carolingian legacy. On his father's death, however, the duchy was seized by Grifo, one of Charles Martel's sons, who raised an unsuccessful rebellion against Martel's heirs, Pippin and Carloman. On the sup-

pression of the revolt, Pippin installed his young Tassilo on the ducal throne of Bavaria, which he held until 788.

As duke, Tassilo maintained an uneasy relationship with Pippin and strove to preserve as much of Bavarian independence as possible in his relations with his powerful uncle. Tassilo actively promoted the church in his duchy and welcomed the advice of the ecclesiastical nobles of the Bavarian church. He also lavished the church with numerous donations and was especially generous to the monasteries of his duchy, including the monasteries of Kremsmünster and Mondsee. His support of the church also included the promotion of missionary activity in neighboring Carinthia, and the successful conversion of the region led to increased political influence for Tassilo in Carinthia. Tassilo also pursued a foreign policy calculated to strengthen his position in relation to the Carolingians. To that end, he formed a marriage alliance with the Lombard king Desiderius. Despite his best efforts at independent action, however, Tassilo remained tied to Pippin. He accompanied the Carolingian king on one of his trips to Italy in support of the pope, and in 757 he swore an oath of allegiance to Pippin and became his vassal.

After the death of Pippin, Tassilo faced the new challenge of dealing with the new

Carolingian ruler, Charlemagne. Although Charlemagne's accession was troubled, he quickly took control of the kingdom. Like Tassilo, Charlemagne first married a daughter of Desiderius, but the arrangement fell apart shortly after the death of Charlemagne's brother Carloman. Tassilo wisely chose not to involve himself in the struggle between Charlemagne and Desiderius, but this did little to ease the Carolingian's concerns about the duke of Bavaria. In 781, Charlemagne forced Tassilo to renew the pledge of vassalage he had sworn to Pippin in 757. In 787, concerned at the state of affairs, Tassilo sought the aid of the pope, Hadrian I, who had previously been favorable to the Bavarian duke. But at this point, the pope sided with the king of the Franks rather than the duke of the Bavarians. Failing to gain the support of the pope, Tassilo was forced to renew his oath of allegiance in 787, but, possibly at the urgings of his wife, he continued to intrigue against Charlemagne and began negotiations with the Avars. Informed of this by loyal Bavarian nobles, Charlemagne summoned the duke to the royal court, where Tassilo admitted to acts of treason. He was condemned to death, but in 788 his sentence was commuted to a life of penance in the monastery of Jumièges. With the fall of Tassilo, the duchy of Bavaria was absorbed into the empire of the Franks, becoming a stepping-stone for the Carolingian advance against the Avars in the 790s.

See also Avars; Carolingian Dynasty; Charlemagne; Charles Martel; Desiderius; Hadrian I, Pope; Lombards; Pippin III, Called the Short

Bibliography
Einhard and Notker the Stammerer. *Two Lives of Charlemagne.* Trans. Lewis Thorpe. Harmondsworth, UK: Penguin, 1981.
Halphen, Louis. *Charlemagne and the Carolingian Empire.* Trans. Giselle de Nie. Amsterdam: North-Holland, 1977.
McKitterick, Rosamond. *The Frankish Kingdoms under the Carolingians, 751–987.* London: Longman, 1983.
Odegaard, Charles E. *Vassi et Fideles in the Carolingian Empire.* Cambridge, MA: Harvard University Press, 1945.
Riché, Pierre. *The Carolingians: A Family Who Forged Europe.* Trans. Michael Idomir Allen. Philadelphia: University of Pennsylvania Press, 1993.
Scholz, Bernhard Walter, trans. *Carolingian Chronicles: Royal Frankish Annals and Nithard's History.* Ann Arbor: University of Michigan Press, 1972.

Tertry, Battle of (687)

Important battle in the rise of the Carolingian dynasty that helped secure the place of the Carolingians in Austrasia and the Frankish kingdom as a whole. Although a decisive victory for Pippin II of Herstal, it was not the decisive turning point in Carolingian history that it is often made out to be. The battle did strengthen Pippin's position as mayor of the palace, but it was two generations before another Carolingian, Pippin III the Short, claimed the kingship of the Franks.

During the seventh century, as the fortunes of the Merovingian dynasty declined and the kingdom was once again divided among the later descendants of the first great Merovingian king, Clovis (r. 481–511), into the regions of Austrasia, Neustria, and Burgundy, rival aristocratic factions competed for power against each other and against the Merovingian do-nothing kings *(rois fainéants),* as they have traditionally been called. In the region of Austrasia the descendants of Arnulf of Metz, the sainted bishop and ancestor of the family, had once again taken control of the office of mayor of the palace. In Neustria, the Arnulfing Pippin faced the powerful Ebroin and the Merovingian king Theuderic III. Pippin had been defeated by Ebroin in 680, but he survived his rival, who was assassinated and whose murderers gained asylum at Pippin's court. Ebroin's successor made peace with Pippin but was deposed by his own son, Ghislemar. Both Ghislemar and his successor, Berchar, remained on bad terms with Pippin, and war once again broke out between the mayors of Austrasia and Neustria.

The war broke out as a result of the long-standing hostility between the Austrasian and Neustrian leaders and the civil strife in Neustria. Berchar had alienated many Neustrian nobles, who joined Pippin and invited him to become involved in the struggle in Neustria. According to one near-contemporary, pro-Carolingian account, Pippin asked his followers to join him in war against the Neustrians. Pippin sought war, according to this account, because Theuderic and Berchar rejected his appeals on behalf of the clergy, the Neustrian nobility asked for aid, and he desired to punish the proud king and his mayor. Pippin's followers agreed to join in the war, and after marshalling his troops, Pippin moved along the Meuse River to meet his rival. Theuderic, learning of the advance of Pippin, levied his own troops, and he rejected, on Berchar's advice, any offers of a peaceful settlement from Pippin. Having been rebuffed, Pippin prepared for battle and at dawn on the day of battle at Tertry quietly moved his troops across the river. Theuderic and Berchar, learning that Pippin's camp was empty, moved in to plunder it and were ambushed by Pippin's army. The king and his mayor fled while their troops were massacred. Berchar too was killed while wandering, and Pippin captured Theuderic, along with the royal treasury. The victor at Tertry, Pippin took control of the king and his wealth and united the three kingdoms of Austrasia, Burgundy, and Neustria under his authority. The Battle of Tertry was a significant victory for Pippin and his descendants, but it was only under his son, Charles Martel, and grandson, Pippin the Short, that power was consolidated in Carolingian hands.

See also Arnulf of Metz, St.; Carolingian Dynasty; Charles Martel; Clovis Merovingian Dynasty; Pippin II, Called Pippin of Herstal; Pippin III, Called the Short

Bibliography
Bachrach, Bernard S. *Merovingian Military Organization, 481–751*. Minneapolis: University of Minnesota Press, 1972.
McKitterick, Rosamond. *The Frankish Kingdoms under the Carolingians, 751–987*. London: Longman, 1983.
Riché, Pierre. *The Carolingians: A Family Who Forged Europe*. Trans. Michael Idomir Allen. Philadelphia: University of Pennsylvania Press, 1993.

Thane
See Thegn

Thegn
Anglo-Saxon term that evolved from the verb *thegnian,* to serve, *thegn* acquired a more precise definition from the age of Alfred the Great in the ninth century to the end of Anglo-Saxon history in England with the Battle of Hastings in 1066. A thegn was primarily one of the king's retainers, but the term was also used for a servant of the more powerful counts of Anglo-Saxon England, who at times caused difficulties of the Anglo-Saxon kings. In either case, service was rewarded with higher status and territory for the thegn.

Although the term *thegn* appeared only once in Anglo-Saxon laws before the tenth century, it appeared in the *Anglo-Saxon Chronicle* and *Beowulf* and replaced the early Anglo-Saxon term *gesith* (noble) at some point during the early Middle Ages. And whatever term was used, the function of royal servant was one of honor and prestige and was a duty that eventually became hereditary. Indeed, in exchange for service the kings began to grant thegns hereditary rights to lands that had been granted as reward for the services rendered. In this way, the thegns were transformed into a landed nobility, even though the king retained rights over the thegn and his land. Moreover, proximity to the king and the special relationship between the two brought the thegn greater prestige in society. This heightened status was recognized as early as the sixth century by the higher wergeld given the thegn, which was six times or more that of an ordinary peasant. Thegns were relatively numerous and could be wealthy in their own right or dependent on maintenance from the king.

The basic duty of the thegn was that of service. One of the primary duties, of course, was military service. The thegn was personally called to serve in the king's host as mounted infantry, and refusal to do so could lead to the loss of the thegn's lands. The thegn's other military duties included bringing a certain number of his own men into military service to the king, and building and repairing roads and fortifications. They also had civil obligations, such as standing as witness to the king's charters. Thegns also oversaw administration of the kingdom at the local level and were the king's representatives in the shires, keeping him in touch with local affairs. As the king's men, the thegns also played a role in royal justice on a panel that was a sort of precursor to the modern grand jury.

See also Alfred the Great; *Anglo-Saxon Chronicle;* Anglo-Saxons; *Beowulf;* Witenagemot

Bibliography
Loyn, Henry R. *Anglo-Saxon England and the Norman Conquest.* 2d ed. London: Longmans, 1991.
Sawyer, Peter H. *From Roman Britain to Norman England.* 2d ed. London and New York: Routledge, 1998.
Stenton, Frank M. *Anglo-Saxon England.* 3d ed. Oxford: Clarendon, 1971.

Theoda (fl. 847/848)

Religious prophetess who appeared in the Carolingian Empire from the country of the Alemanni in the mid-ninth century, Theoda (also spelled Theuda or Thiota) preached the coming of the end of the world. She attracted a large following, which was quickly suppressed by the bishop of Mainz. Her appearance, however, challenged Carolingian ideas about the nature of the ministry in the church.

In the year 847 or 848, according to a contemporary chronicler, Theoda appeared in the city of Mainz, arriving from somewhere in Germany. According to the chronicler, Theoda claimed to know many divine mysteries. She preached the coming of the end of the world and declared that it would arrive on the last day of the year. Apparently she was a skilled preacher, because many men and women began to follow her. They offered her gifts and asked her to pray for them. She also inspired many priests, according to the chronicler, to give up their vows and follow her as though she had been sent from heaven. She was quickly brought before a council of bishops of Mainz, who interrogated her about her teachings. When asked about them she admitted that she learned those things from a certain priest and then began to teach them herself. The council denounced her teachings and had her publicly flogged. She accepted the verdict of the council, admitted that she had "irrationally seized" upon the right of preaching, and gave up her ministry in shame. After the council, Theoda disappears from all records, and her ultimate end is unknown.

See also Alemanni; Carolingian Dynasty; Franks

Bibliography
McKitterick, Rosamond. *The Frankish Kingdoms under the Carolingians, 751–987.* London: Longman, 1983.
Russell, Jeffery Burton. *Dissent and Reform in the Early Middle Ages.* Berkeley: University of California Press, 1965.
Wemple, Suzanne. *Women in Frankish Society: Marriage and the Cloister, 500–900.* Philadelphia: University of Pennsylvania Press, 1985.

Theodora (d. 548)

Wife and inspiration of the Byzantine emperor Justinian (r. 527–565), who shared his rule and was an important source of strength for him until her death in 548. Although her background was not the usual one for an empress, Theodora rose from humble circumstances to

Mosaic of Theodora from the Church of San Vitale, Ravenna (Hulton Archive)

play a critical role in Justinian's reign. She helped him survive the most difficult moment in his reign and played an important role in his religious and military programs. Her death from cancer on June 28, 548, was a terrible blow to the emperor, who was never the same after the loss of his beloved.

Theodora is not only an important figure but, at least in her own time, also a controversial one. She was from most humble beginnings; her father was the animal trainer for the imperial arena, and she herself performed on the stage. In the late Roman and early Byzantine world, acting on the stage was deemed a most inglorious profession and a bar from marriage to a person of senatorial rank. Moreover, she was forced into prostitution on occasion to support her family, and, according to the sixth-century Byzantine historian and general Procopius, she was an ex-

cellent and insatiable prostitute. He notes in his *Secret History* that Theodora, while still a young and underdeveloped girl, acted as a sort of male prostitute and resided in a brothel. When she was older she continued life as a courtesan and would exhibit herself publicly. Procopius says that she would attend parties with ten men and lie with them in turn, then proceed to lie with the other partygoers, and then lie with their servants. Not only, Procopius tells us, was she incredibly promiscuous but she was also without shame. She would perform a special act in the theater where she would lie almost completely naked, have servants sprinkle barley grains over her private parts, and have geese come along and pick the grains up with their bills.

Procopius's account clearly is an exaggeration and was included in a work not intended for public consumption. Although *The Secret*

History offers a gross caricature of the empress, it does contain a kernel of truth—Theodora was an actor and, probably, a prostitute. Her family history was an unfortunate one. Her father, Akakios, the bear keeper for the Green faction—one of two factions in Constantinople that provided charioteers and other performers for the games in the arena and that had extensive support networks throughout the city—died while Theodora was still a girl. Her mother remarried in the hopes that her new husband would be awarded the position. Unfortunately for Theodora, her two sisters, and her mother this did not happen, and only after public pleading by her mother or Theodora and her sisters did their stepfather receive the position. But the award was made by the Blues, the rival faction to the Greens, an action that Theodora never forgot. Life, however, remained difficult, and Theodora performed on the stage, where her sharp wit and talent won her popularity.

Unwilling to settle for the difficult life of the stage, Theodora aimed higher and became the mistress of Hecebolus, a high government minister and governor of a minor province in Africa. Her relationship with Hecebolus brought great changes to her life. She accompanied him to Africa, but their relationship soon soured, as Theodora's biting wit proved too much for the older and duller Hecebolus to endure. She was sent away after a terrible fight and left to her own resources. Procopius says that she turned to prostitution, but again caution should be exercised in accepting his bitter commentary. It is certain that Theodora spent time in Alexandria, where she met a number of leading Monophysite clergy. At this point, under the influence of the pious Monophysites, Theodora underwent a religious conversion and renounced her former way of life. She managed to find her way back to Constantinople, where she established herself in a small house, practicing the honorable and very traditional profession of sewing.

It was at this point that she met Justinian, nephew of the emperor Justin and heir apparent. Despite her rather checkered past, Theodora possessed a number of qualities that attracted Justinian. Not the least of these qualities was her physical beauty. Contemporary accounts comment on her attractiveness, and mosaics and sculpture confirms this. She was petite and had an oval face with large black eyes—features that served her on the stage and before the emperor. But her qualities went far beyond physical beauty; it was her personal qualities that inspired such great love and devotion from Justinian. Even her harshest critic, Procopius, noted that she was very clever and had a biting wit. Indeed, in his *History of the Wars* Procopius presents a most favorable portrait of Theodora that is in stark contrast to the portrait in *The Secret History.* And another contemporary, John Lydus, noted that she was more intelligent than anyone in the world. She also possessed some learning and culture that enabled her to fit in Justinian's world. But more than learning and intelligence, Theodora possessed great self-confidence and nerves of steel. Justinian himself was a man capable of prodigious amounts of work, but he sometimes lacked resolve, and it was Theodora who provided that strength of will.

Justinian, fifteen years her senior, was deeply smitten by Theodora and made her his mistress and shortly thereafter planned to marry her. There were several obstacles to the marriage: Theodora's humble birth, the legal barrier against an actor marrying a senator, and the reigning empress, Euphemia, who absolutely forbade the relationship. Theodora was elevated to the patriciate by Justin, Justinian's uncle and the emperor. Euphemia's death in 524 eliminated another of the obstacles to marriage. Justin, lastly, issued a law allowing actors who had renounced their previous lifestyle, had lived honorably, and had received high dignity to marry members of the senatorial aristocracy. In 525 Justinian and Theodora married, and in 527, at the death of Justin, they ascended to the imperial dignity.

In many ways Theodora exercised great influence over her husband and his reign. Her most important moment, however, came during the Nika Revolt in 532, which nearly toppled Justinian's government. The revolt broke out in January on the heels of yet another riot between the Greens and Blues. Violence between the two factions was not uncommon in Constantinople, but this riot took on more serious implications because leaders of the two factions were arrested and condemned to death. The factions were united by the desire to save their leaders and also by dissatisfaction with taxes, bread distribution, and government agents. The government's failure to respond effectively to the demands of the Blues and Greens and unwillingness to release the leaders led to great violence. The factions stormed the City Prefect's palace, killing police and releasing prisoners as they went. Shouting "Nika the Blues! Nika the Greens!" (Nika meaning win or conquer), the rioters destroyed much of the city. The revolt was so serious that the crowds, directed in part by ambitious senators who sought to exploit the situation, proclaimed a rival emperor, the senator Hypatius.

Justinian's efforts to suppress the revolt were half-hearted and ineffective, but more deliberate attempts depended upon palace guards whose loyalty was uncertain. Justinian's personal appearance before the crowd did little but alienate them further. At that crucial moment Justinian seems to have lost his nerve and ordered flight. Theodora stood before her husband's council and made, according to Procopius, the following speech:

Whether or not a woman should give an example of courage to men, is neither here nor there. At a moment of desperate danger one must do what one can. I think that flight, even if it brings us to safety, is not in our interest. Every man born to see the light of day must die. But that one who has been emperor should become an exile I cannot bear. May I never be without the purple I wear, nor live to see the day when men do not call me "Your Majesty." If you wish safety, my Lord, that is an easy matter. We are rich, and there is the

sea, and yonder our ships. But consider whether if you reach safety you may not desire to exchange that safety for death. As for me, I like the old saying, that the purple is the nobles shroud. (Procopius, *History of the Wars* I.24.33–37, cited in Robert Browning, *Justinian and Theodora,* p. 72.)

Theodora's strength gave Justinian the resolve he needed, and a plan was hatched by Justinian and his loyal generals. Using German mercenaries, the generals infiltrated the crowd of rebels in the Hippodrome and successfully massacred 30,000 people. The revolt was suppressed. The rival emperor was captured and brought before Justinian, who was about to commute the death sentence of his old friend to permanent exile when Theodora convinced her husband to execute his rival. The revolt had ended, and Justinian survived, thanks to his loyal generals and, most especially, Theodora.

Theodora's most dramatic impact on Justinian's reign occurred during the Nika Revolt, but she influenced Justinian's domestic and foreign policy throughout their lives together. She clearly had her favorites among Justinian's civil and military staff, and those whom she disliked suffered. She orchestrated the fall of two of his ministers whom she despised. Priscus, an imperial secretary who had enriched himself at public expense, was tonsured and packed away to a monastery by the empress. John of Cappadocia, an imperial financial minister who had risen from humble beginnings, was another victim. Although he was an honorable minister, his methods were brutal, and his deposition was demanded during the Nika Revolt. He was implicated in a plot against Justinian and accused of the murder of a bishop. His methods and possible betrayal of the emperor made him an enemy of Theodora, who forced Justinian to believe the worst about John. Although Theodora struck out ruthlessly against those she thought unfaithful to Justinian and those who, like Hypatius, openly opposed him, Theodora was also an important benefactor. She was a staunch ally of the general Narses, who earned her favor by his defense of Justinian in 532. She protected him and promoted his cause during the wars in Italy. Theodora not only influenced personnel decisions but also presented a more human face to the imperial dignity by her largesse. With Justinian she indulged in acts of charity that were functions of both imperial responsibility and Christian duty. On numerous occasions, Theodora, with and without her husband, made lavish charitable donations. Following the devastating earthquake in Antioch in 528, Justinian and Theodora, all contemporary records attest, sent great amounts of money to help rebuild the city. On a trip to northwestern Asia Minor, Theodora offered large donations to churches along her route. She also took special care of poor young women who had been sold into a life of prostitution. On one occasion she called the owners of the brothels to the court, reprimanded them for their activities, and purchased the girls from them out of her own purse. She returned them to their parents and also established a convent where they could retire.

The empress also played a critical role in religious affairs in the empire. It was her favorite Vigilius who succeeded to the papal throne in 537, although not simply because he was her favorite. She conspired in the elevation of Vigilius to the office of the papacy above all because she thought he would be a more pliable pope on religious matters important to her and the emperor. But more than that she offered protection to an important religious minority in the empire. As the emperor, Justinian was the protector of the faith and defender of orthodoxy. Consequently, he enforced orthodox Christian belief and ordered the persecution of heretics, including the execution of many Manichaeans of high social rank. The empire, however, faced a serious division over the nature of Jesus Christ that threatened imperial unity and relations with Rome. The largest minority sect in the empire was that of the Monophysites, who were particularly numerous in the wealthy and populous region of Syria.

Theodora, a devout Monophysite Christian, defended and protected her co-religionists. She encouraged the promotion of Monophysites or their sympathizers to positions of ecclesiastical importance and protected Monophysites in her private chapel. She also may have influenced Justinian's publication of a profession of faith that sought a common ground between orthodox Catholic doctrine and Monophysite doctrine.

Theodora's impact may also have been felt on Justinian's foreign policy. One of the emperor's great dreams was to restore Italy to imperial control, and the situation on the peninsula after the death of the great Gothic king Theodoric in 526 afforded him an opportunity. Theodoric was succeeded by his eight-year-old grandson, Athalaric, under the regency of his mother and Theodoric's daughter, Amalaswintha. The regent was a cultured, educated, and ambitious woman who found herself at odds with much of the Gothic nobility. Facing conspiracy from the nobility, especially after the death of her son, Amalaswintha found an ally in Justinian, whom she nearly visited in Constantinople in 532. For the emperor, a close alliance with Amalaswintha provided an entry into Italian affairs and the possible extension of imperial control. Her talent and royal blood made her an attractive marriage candidate, a fact not lost on anyone in the imperial capital—especially Theodora. The Gothic queen, however, never made the trip east and was eventually imprisoned by her rivals in Italy. It is at this point that the possible influence of Theodora can be seen.

Justinian sent an envoy to protest the imprisonment, threatening war if anything should happen to the queen. According to Procopius, the envoy received a second message from Theodora, instructing him to inform the Gothic king, Theodohad, that Justinian would do nothing should anything happen to Amalaswintha. And not long after Amalaswintha was murdered. Justinian had his pretext to invade Italy. Theodora provided this pretext, Procopius tells us, out of jealousy, but it is likely that Justinian was aware of the second letter and approved of it. Whether he did or not is conjecture, but clearly he benefited from the letter, just as he benefited from Theodora's inner strength and good political sense throughout their lives together.

See also Amalaswintha; Belisarius; Gothic Wars; Justinian; Procopius; Theodoric

Bibliography

Browning, Robert. *Justinian and Theodora.* Rev. ed. London: Thames and Hudson, 1987.

Bury, John B. *History of the Later Roman Empire: From the Death of Theodosius I to the Death of Justinian.* Vol. 2. 1923. Reprint, New York: Dover, 1959.

Clark, Gillian. *Women in Late Antiquity: Pagan and Christian Lifestyles.* Oxford: Clarendon, 1993.

Obolensky, Dmitri. *The Byzantine Commonwealth: Eastern Europe, 500–1453.* New York: Praeger, 1971.

Theodoric the Great (c. 451 or 453/454–526)

One of the greatest of the barbarian kings and the greatest of the Gothic kings, Theodoric the Great, or the Amal as he was originally known, reigned over the Ostrogoths from 471 to 526 and ruled an independent Gothic kingdom in Italy from 493 to 526. He assumed power in Italy by defeating a rival barbarian king, Odovacar, and Theodoric's reign was generally recognized for its effectiveness and tolerance. He skillfully managed the relations between his people and the native Roman population and also maintained good relations with the emperors in Constantinople. Theodoric was able to keep the peace in Italy between Ostrogoths and Romans despite important differences in religion—Theodoric and his people were Arian Christians and the native Italians were Catholic Christians. He preserved the best aspects of the administrations of Odovacar and the Romans and worked well with the Senate and Roman nobles. He was an active builder, promoted culture, and patronized the great scholars Boethius and Cassiodorus. His reign, however, was marred in its later years by increasing tension between Goths and Romans, as Catholic Christianity found important new leaders. The situation was worsened by Theodoric's execution of Boethius and his father-in-law, Symmachus, leading Roman senators. Despite the difficulties of his later years, complicated further by the lack of a male heir, Theodoric was one of the greatest kings to rule in the years after the fall of the Western Empire.

The early life of Theodoric is important for his later years, though modern knowledge of it is marked with confusion. One particularly vexing problem about his early years is the date of his birth, which is traditionally given as 456. According to the tradition, Theodoric was born on the day that his family learned the news that his uncle Valamir had been attacked by and had defeated a large band of Huns. But this date is unlikely because it would make Theodoric quite young—indeed, perhaps too young—when he was sent to Constantinople as a hostage and still quite young when he later took control of the kingdom. More recent scholarship has suggested dates of birth as early as 451, which would correspond to the victory of the Ostrogoths and their Roman allies over the Huns at the Battle of the Catalaunian Plains, a date that would make Theodoric a more mature, and politically useful, boy when he was sent to Constantinople. Whatever his exact date of birth, he was born to the royal Amal family and was sent as a hostage in 459/460 as surety for a treaty between the Ostrogoths and Eastern Empire. While at the imperial court, Theodoric learned a great deal and had experiences that shaped his later life. He became aware of rivalries among the Gothic people, and most likely came to fear and hate rival Ostrogothic families who gained preferment at the imperial court. He also witnessed the sophisticated governmental practices of the empire, which he used when he became king of the Ostrogoths and then later ruler in Italy. He also gained a solid, if unspectacular, education, most likely learning to do arithmetic and to read and write.

Theodoric, wrongly identified as Justinian (Ancient Art and Architecture Collection)

Theodoric was released from his service as a hostage in the late 460s, after which, in about 469, he returned to his homeland, received control of a subkingdom, and began his ascent to power among the Ostrogoths. Already in 470 he launched campaigns, sometimes in the name of the empire, against his political rivals or to expand his territory. His success in 470 revealed his ambition; the campaign probably took place without his father's permission, and marked, for Theodoric, the start of his independent authority. In the 470s he became an increasingly powerful and important figure in the military and political life of the Eastern Empire. His main Gothic rival, Theodoric Strabo, or the Squinter, rose in the imperial ranks in the 470s and took a prominent part in a revolt against Emperor Zeno. Having fled from the capital in 475, Zeno was able to return thanks to the support from Theodoric of the Amal clan and strike against Strabo, who quickly fell from grace, though he remained a powerful rival to both Theodoric and Zeno. Theodoric the Amal received numerous honors from Zeno and was made commander of East Roman troops. Theodoric's people were made *foederati* (federated allies) of the empire and were given an annual subsidy from the emperor. Despite these achievements, Theodoric still faced a challenge from Strabo, who sometimes was supported by Zeno for fear of an over mighty Theodoric the Amal. Strabo's sudden death in 481 freed his rival's hand. Theodoric was now sole king of the Ostrogoths and a dangerous friend of the empire.

The 470s and early 480s saw important changes in the life of Theodoric and the Roman Empire. Theodoric had become one of the most powerful figures in the Eastern Empire. In 482–483 Theodoric waged a terrible offensive in the empire to force Zeno to come to terms, which the emperor did. Theodoric was rewarded with a consulship for 484, but his term in office was cut short by Zeno's fears that the Ostrogoth had turned against him. Despite his own strength,

Theodoric knew that he was no match for the full power of the empire, and events in the Western Empire offered both Theodoric and Zeno a solution to their problematic relationship. In 476 the last of the Western Roman emperors, Romulus Augustulus, and his general, Orestes, were defeated by the German general Odovacar. After defeating his rivals, Odovacar executed Orestes and deposed Romulus and sent him into internal exile. Odovacar also declared the end of the imperial line in Italy and, although recognizing the sovereignty of the emperor in Constantinople, ruled as an independent king in Italy. In 488, following another revolt by Theodoric, Zeno requested that the Ostrogoth invade Italy and restore it to imperial control.

Theodoric's march to Italy was not unimpeded, as other barbarian peoples struggled against him, but he reached Italy by the summer of 489. His rival Odovacar was waiting for him with his army. Theodoric won two victories against Odovacar in August and September of 489. He also welcomed Tufa, one of Odovacar's leading generals, and it seemed that Theodoric would quickly triumph over his enemy. But Odovacar was able to secure himself behind the walls and swamps of Ravenna, and Tufa rejoined Odovacar shortly after leaving, taking with him the Ostrogothic soldiers he commanded on the way to Ravenna. Odovacar then took the offensive and forced Theodoric to withdraw to the city of Pavia. Theodoric, however, managed to break the siege and defeat Odovacar once again, on August 11, 490, with the aid of a large number of Visigoths. Odovacar returned to Ravenna, where Theodoric besieged him. But Ravenna could not be taken, and Theodoric was forced to negotiate with Odovacar. Agreement was reached on February, 493, and Theodoric entered Ravenna on March 5. Apparently he had agreed to share power with Odovacar. On March 15, he welcomed Odovacar at a great banquet, at which Theodoric himself killed Odovacar. The murder of Odovacar was followed by the massacre of his family and supporters. Theodoric had eliminated his rival and then proceeded to take control of Italy.

Theodoric's position remained uncertain for some time, in part because of his desire to be recognized as the ruler in Italy by the emperor in Constantinople. He was anxious to be recognized in the capital of the empire because he portrayed his kingdom as the legitimate successor of the Roman Empire in Italy. He did this for a number of reasons. He certainly had some sentimental attachment to all things Roman as a result of his time as a hostage in Constantinople. He also recognized the importance of being "Roman." That identity meant civilization and defined relations with the nobility in Italy, as well as with the church, a very powerful force. It was also a means to secure support for his kingdom from the population of Italy, the birthplace of the Roman Empire. He could also use it in his relations with Constantinople, as an instrument to remind the emperor that any violation of the peace between them was a violation of the empire and an offense against God.

Theodoric's status was resolved gradually over the first two decades of his rule in Italy, and in two stages, in 497/498 and in 508, the Ostrogoth gained recognition from the emperor for his independent status as king in Italy. His rule in Italy, from 497 until his death in 526, was a time of peace and prosperity for the peninsula. Moreover, his kingdom became the center of the greatest power in western Europe, as Theodoric established his authority not only over Italy but also over other parts of the old Western Empire. His closest rival, the Merovingian king Clovis, managed some success against Theodoric in southwestern France, but he never really attempted to unseat Theodoric, to whom he was related by marriage. (His sister, Audofleda, married Theodoric and bore the daughter Amalaswintha.) Indeed, marriage alliances constituted one of the tools Theodoric used to enhance his power in the old Western Empire. Another instrument in the extension of his power, of course, was his great ability as a general. His defense of the Visigothic kingdom in Spain and subsequent acquisition of the kingdom in 511 revealed his talents as a military leader, as did his campaigns for and against the emperor and against Odovacar.

Although king of Visigothic Spain, Theodoric is best known for his rule of Italy. As the independent ruler of Italy, Theodoric presided over a cultural and economic revival in the peninsula. He worked effectively with the Roman nobility, who enjoyed the peace brought by Theodoric and managed to revive the productivity of their estates. Theodoric's equitable distribution of land, which did not overly burden the Roman population of Italy, also stimulated an economic revival. He not only worked well with the nobles but respected and honored the Senate, and in many ways preserved Roman imperial governmental practices. Despite his Arianism, Theodoric remained on good terms with the pope and Catholic church in Italy. Indeed, at one point he was invited to resolve a disputed papal election, and his good relations with the church were critical to his acceptance as the ruler in Italy. He also supported the traditions of Roman law and education in his kingdom. He helped maintain the infrastructure in Italy, restoring many roads and public buildings. He was also a great builder in his own right, most notably of the magnificent mausoleum that still stands in Ravenna today. Finally, Theodoric was a patron of arts and letters. His personal secretary was the prominent Christian writer Cassiodorus, and Theodoric also had close relations with the great intellectual and author, Boethius.

Despite his long and prosperous reign, Theodoric's end was not a happy one, and his great kingdom did not long survive his death. Several events conspired to bring Theodoric's reign to an unfortunate end. His failure to have a male heir made the establishment of a dynasty difficult and caused tensions among the Ostrogoths, which worsened other internal problems. It also undermined his foreign policy and the extension of his power over Spain. Furthermore, his good relations with the church came to an end for two reasons. The election of a new pope, John I (523–526), ended Theodoric's good relations with the papacy, in part because of John's hostility toward Arianism. His relations with the church also worsened because the tensions that existed within the church, between its eastern and western halves, were eased, as the new emperor, Justin (518–527), outlawed Arianism and supported Catholic orthodoxy. Theodoric's Arianism was made to appear even more at odds with the Catholic population by the conversion of Clovis and the Merovingian dynasty to Catholic Christianity. Finally, his good relations with the Senate and Roman nobility were poisoned by an alleged conspiracy of senators in 522. Boethius's defense of his fellow senators implicated him in the plot in the eyes of Theodoric, and as a result, Boethius fell from favor and was executed in 524.

Theodoric died in August of 526. According to the fifth-century Byzantine historian Procopius, Theodoric died of typhoid brought on by remorse for the deaths of Boethius and his father-in-law, Symmachus, who was also implicated in the plot against Theodoric. Procopius notes that Theodoric was served fish for dinner one evening and saw in it the face of Symmachus. Theodoric fled to his room frightened by the vision, and then called for a doctor, to whom he disclosed his great dismay over the execution of Symmachus and Boethius.

Theodoric was succeeded by his grandson, Athalaric, whose mother, Amalaswintha, served as a regent during the first part of her son's reign. The problems of Theodoric's last years continued to plague his successor and Amalaswintha. Dissension among the Goths led to her death and the eventual invasion and destruction of the Gothic kingdom by Justinian. A brilliant, tolerant, and effective ruler in many ways, Theodoric could not provide for a lasting settlement in the kingdom he created.

See also Amalaswintha; Arianism; Boethius; Catalaunian Plains, Battle of the; Clovis; Huns; Justinian; Merovingian Dynasty; Odovacar; Orestes; Ostrogoths; Romulus Augustulus; Visigoths; Zeno

Bibliography

Amory, Patrick. *People and Identity in Ostrogothic Italy, 489–554.* Cambridge: Cambridge University Press, 1997.

Burns, Thomas. *A History of the Ostrogoths.* Bloomington: University of Indiana Press, 1984.

Bury, John B. *History of the Later Roman Empire: From the Death of Theodosius I to the Death of Justinian.* 2 vols. 1923. Reprint, New York: Dover, 1959.

Cassiodorus. *The Variae of Magnus Aurelius Cassiodorus.* Trans. S. J. B. Barnish. Liverpool, UK: Liverpool University Press, 1992.

Heather, Peter. *The Goths.* Oxford: Blackwell, 1996.

Hodgkin, Thomas. *Theodoric the Goth: the Barbarian Champion of Civilization.* New York: G. P. Putnam, 1983.

Jordanes. *The Gothic History of Jordanes.* Trans. Charles C. Mierow. New York: Barnes and Noble, 1985.

Moorhead, John. *Theodoric in Italy.* Oxford: Clarendon, 1992.

Procopius. *Procopius, with an English Translation by H. B. Dewing.* Cambridge, MA: Harvard University Press, 1962.

Wolfram, Herwig. *The Roman Empire and Its Germanic Peoples.* Trans. Thomas J. Dunlap. Berkeley: University of California Press, 1997.

Wood, Ian. *The Merovingian Kingdoms, 450–751.* London: Longman, 1994.

Theodulf of Orléans (c. 760–820/821)

Court scholar, abbot, and bishop, Theodulf of Orléans was a leading figure in the Carolingian Renaissance during the reign of Charlemagne. Theodulf was perhaps the finest poet and most gifted theologian among Charlemagne's court scholars. He was also the primary author of the *Libri Carolini* (Caroline Books), a *missus dominicus* (emissary) for the king, and a dedicated preacher. During his term in office as bishop of Orléans, he sought to implement the reforms spelled out in Charlemagne's *Admonitio Generalis.*

Theodulf was born in Spain to Visigothic parents in circa 760 and entered Charlemagne's service after the great ruler's extension of his territory into Spain. He became a devoted supporter of the king and his religious and educational reforms. He benefited from his service, being made abbot of two important monasteries and, some time before 798, bishop of Orléans by Charlemagne. Theodulf partook fully in the reform program of Charlemagne, both as bishop and royal agent.

As *missus dominicus* to southern France in 798, Theodulf performed in exemplary fashion, judging cases of law and executing the royal will. He also learned firsthand of the corruption that such officials perpetrated when he was offered gifts by the litigants whose cases he was to arbitrate. Although he did not accept these gifts, Theodulf recognized that others did and worked to eliminate such abuses of power. In similar fashion, as bishop of Orléans he sought to reform ecclesiastical life and discipline, issuing a number of edicts designed to improve religious life in his diocese. He also established schools to educate young boys in his diocese. In the 790s he was called on to write the Carolingian response to the Second Council of Nicaea (787), at which the veneration of icons forbidden under the iconoclastic emperors was restored, and he accordingly prepared the *Libri Carolini,* which contained the Carolingian denunciation of the veneration of icons and a sophisticated philosophy of art. Although authorship was traditionally given to Alcuin, it is now recognized that Theodulf was the author, but with some role held by Alcuin in the production. Theodulf was also probably present at Charlemagne's coronation as emperor on Christmas Day, 800. His service to the Carolingian dynasty continued during the reign of Charlemagne's successor, Louis the Pious. But in 817 Theodulf was im-

plicated in a rebellion against the emperor, although there is little evidence to confirm or deny any role. Louis deposed Theodulf from his office of bishop and exiled him to Angers, where he died in 820 or 821.

Theodulf was, above all, a theologian and poet of great skill. Along with the *Libri Carolini* Theodulf produced treatises, at Charlemagne's invitation, on baptism and the Holy Spirit. He also produced a new edition of the Bible. Even more celebrated than his theological works is his poetry. Theodulf was the finest and most original poet of all the court scholars of Charlemagne's age. His poetry was characterized by elegant Latin and abundant references to classical literature, especially Ovid (43 B.C.–A.D. 17), and his poem *Ad Carolum regem* (To Charles the King) is a charming and often satirical portrait of Charlemagne and his scholars. His religious poetry was often pessimistic, however, reflecting on the poor mores of those around him. He revealed his deep appreciation of art in his poetry, an appreciation that is also reflected in the manuscripts illuminated at his scriptorium and in the beautiful mosaics decorating the church he had built at St. Germigny-des-Prés.

See also Admonitio Generalis; Alcuin of York; Carolingian Renaissance; Charlemagne; Louis the Pious; Missi Dominici; Visigoths

Bibliography

Dutton, Paul Edward, ed. *Carolingian Civilization: A Reader.* Peterborough, Ont.: Broadview, 1993.

Freeman, Ann. "Theodulf of Orléans and the *Libri Carolini.*" *Speculum* 32 (1957): 664–705.

Laistner, Max L. W. *Thought and Letters in Western Europe, A.D. 500 to 900.* 2d ed. Ithaca, NY: Cornell University Press, 1976.

McKitterick, Rosamond. *The Frankish Kingdoms under the Carolingians, 751–987.* London: Longman, 1983.

Riché, Pierre. *The Carolingians: A Family Who Forged Europe.* Trans. Michael Idomir Allen. Philadelphia: University of Pennsylvania Press, 1993.

Theodulf of Orleans. *The Poetry of Theodulf of Orleans: A Translation and Critical Study.* Ed. and trans. Nikolai A. Alexandro. Ann Arbor: University Microfilms, 1970.

Theudelinde (d. 628)

Bavarian princess, Theudelinde (also spelled Theodelinda) was the wife of two Lombard kings, Authari (r. 584–590) and Agilulf (r. 590–616), and the mother of a third, Adaloald (r. 616–626). A powerful figure in the Lombard kingdom, Theudelinde exercised her influence in the realm for nearly thirty years. She effectively chose the successor to her first husband, Authari, and acted as regent for her son, Adaloald. In frequent correspondence with Pope Gregory the Great, some of which is found in the history of the eighth-century historian Paul the Deacon, she sought to convert the Lombards from Arian Christianity to Catholic Christianity and welcomed Catholic missionaries into the kingdom. Although ultimately the Lombards did adopt Catholic Christianity, her efforts inspired an Arian reaction during the reigns of Ariold (r. 626–636) and Rothari (r. 626–652).

Paul the Deacon recorded a romantic tale of the courtship of Theudelinde by Authari, which involved Authari's anonymous visit to the Bavarian court. The marriage having been arranged between the Lombard and Bavarian kings, Theudelinde was sent to the Lombard kingdom. She wed King Authari at Verona on May 15, 589. Although Authari was a committed Arian, and welcomed few non-Arians to his court, he chose to marry the Catholic Theudelinde. He did so because of long-standing ties between the Lombards and the Bavarians and because of their mutual hostility toward the Franks, who had the Bavarians on the defensive at that time. Theudelinde was also of the ancient Lombard royal line and thus a suitable match for the Lombard king and former duke. Indeed, the marriage benefited both sides, strengthening the Lombard-Bavarian alliance, which successfully halted a Frankish advance in 590 and established a lasting peace with the Franks in 591.

During her marriage to Authari, Theudelinde established herself as a major figure in the kingdom, and she remained so until her death in 628. According to Paul the Deacon, Theudelinde was so highly esteemed by the Lombards that at the death of Authari they allowed her to remain queen and asked her to choose the successor to Authari as her husband and king. In consultation with the Lombard leaders, she chose Agilulf, duke of Turin. During his reign, Theudelinde continued to exercise her influence and corresponded with Pope Gregory. Under her guidance, Agilulf forged a treaty with the pope, one of the greatest landowners in Italy as well as the spiritual leader of Catholic Christians. She also supported the activity of the Irish missionary St. Columban, which not only improved the religious life of the kingdom but also established a connection with lands to the north of Italy. At her husband's death in 616, she was made regent for their son Adaloald, and she remained his coruler even when he reached his majority. His reign and life, however, ended abruptly in 626 amid allegations that he had gone mad. Theudelinde's support for Catholicism may have been the real reason for the sudden end of Adaloald's reign, but even though an Arian reaction set in after 626, her influence continued with the marriage of her daughter to the new king, Ariold.

Theudelinde was a major political force throughout her life in the Lombard kingdom, but is perhaps best known for her missionary efforts in support of Catholic Christianity. Although somewhat independent minded in her faith and support for the northern Italian bishops against the pope in a doctrinal dispute, Theudelinde was on good terms with the pope. She actively supported the religious life in her kingdom and built a church dedicated to St. John the Baptist at Monza, near Milan, which she richly endowed. She also received lavish gifts from Pope Gregory to be bestowed on the new church. Her support for new religious foundations did not end with Monza, but included the establishment of monasteries at Bobbio and elsewhere. The foundation at Bobbio, one of the most important and influential monasteries of the early Middle Ages, came as the result of her support for the Irish missionary St. Columban. Although in the short run her support for Catholic Christianity failed to counter Lombard Arianism, Theudelinde's efforts in support of the Catholic church were vindicated when the Lombards converted to Catholic Christianity later in the seventh century.

See also Arianism; Columban, St.; Franks; Gregory the Great, Pope; Merovingian Dynasty; Paul the Deacon; Rothari

Bibliography

Christie, Neil. *The Lombards: The Ancient Langobards.* Oxford: Blackwell, 1998.

Herrin, Judith. *The Formation of Christendom.* Princeton: Princeton University Press, 1987.

Llewellyn, Peter. *Rome in the Dark Ages.* New York: Barnes and Noble, 1996.

Paul the Deacon. *History of the Lombards.* Trans. William Dudley Foulke. Philadelphia: University of Pennsylvania Press, 1974.

Wallace-Hadrill, J. M. *The Barbarian West, A.D. 400–1000.* New York: Harper and Row, 1962.

Wolfram, Herwig. *The Roman Empire and Its Germanic Peoples.* Trans. Thomas J. Dunlap. Berkeley: University of California Press, 1997.

Three-Field System

See Agriculture

Tolbiac, Battle of (496)

Battle fought between the Merovingian king of the Franks, Clovis, and the Alemanni about the year 496. According to the sixth-century Frankish historian Gregory of Tours, the battle was the turning point in the reign of Clovis, who converted to Catholic Christianity following the victory. The traditional chronology of the conversion, however, is now questioned, and it is considered most likely that Clovis did not convert directly to Catholic Christianity from paganism. Although the battle may not have occurred as Gregory described it and may have become confused with the battle at Zülpich some ten years later, it may still be recognized as an example of the broader policy of conquest and expansion pursued by the greatest Merovingian king.

As recorded in the history of Gregory of Tours, the Battle of Tolbiac involved the Franks and Alemanni; it has generally been dated to around 496. The battle was critical in the religious formation of Clovis and the Merovingian kingdom. As Gregory reported, Clothild, Clovis's Catholic wife, had pleaded with him for several years to accept her faith. She even baptized their first two sons in the Catholic faith, the first dying shortly after baptism and the second surviving only as a result of Clothild's prayers. Despite his wife's missionary efforts, Clovis was not persuaded and preferred to follow the traditional gods of the Franks, who had served him so well until that point. During the Battle of Tolbiac, however, Gregory wrote that Clovis experienced a change of heart. His army was on the point of annihilation when he appealed to his wife's God and swore that if God gave him victory over his enemies he would convert. The tide of battle suddenly turned, and Clovis emerged victorious. Not long after, according to Gregory, Clovis accepted baptism at the hands of St. Remigius, the archbishop of Rheims.

The exact chronology of Clovis's reign and the date of the battle remain uncertain, although the events of his reign most likely did not follow the pattern set by Gregory of Tours. Nevertheless, Gregory's image is still important, because it remained the predominant view of this great king until recent times. Gregory's depiction of the Battle of Tolbiac portrays Clovis as a Christian king, whose conversion in battle resembles the conversion of the Roman emperor Constantine in the fourth century, as recorded by Eusebius of Caesarea. Clovis was, therefore, first and foremost a Christian king whose conversion was effected by the power of God. Although it is likely that the events of Clovis's life did not unfold the way Gregory described them, the description of the Battle of Tolbiac and the broader image established by Gregory provided later kings and ecclesiastics an important precedent to follow.

See also Alemanni; Clovis; Constantine; Franks; Gregory of Tours; Merovingian Dynasty

Bibliography

Bachrach, Bernard S. *Merovingian Military Organization, 481–751.* Minneapolis: University of Minnesota Press, 1972.

Daly, William M. "Clovis: How Barbaric, How Pagan?" *Speculum* 69 (1994): 619–664.

Geary, Patrick J. *Before France and Germany: The Creation and Transformation of the Merovingian World.* Oxford: Oxford University Press, 1988.

Gregory of Tours. *The History of the Franks.* Trans. Lewis Thorpe. Harmondsworth, UK: Penguin, 1974.

Wallace-Hadrill, John M. *The Long-Haired Kings.* Toronto: Toronto University Press, 1982.

Wood, Ian. *The Merovingian Kingdoms, 450–751.* London: Longman, 1994.

Totila (d. 552)

Eventual successor of Witigis as king of the Ostrogoths in Italy and the greatest Gothic military commander since Theodoric the Great, Totila (r. 541–552) led his people for eleven years and mounted a major challenge to Justinian's efforts to conquer Italy and restore it to imperial control. His early and dramatic military victories restored Gothic confidence and rallied them against the Byzantine general Belisarius. Although unable to inflict a total defeat on the Byzantines, Totila effectively wore down imperial resistance until his defeat by Narses and death in battle. His strategy to make the conquest of Italy so bloody and difficult that Justinian would abandon his effort nearly succeeded, but at great cost to the people, cities, and countryside of Italy. Totila's successor, Teja, did not survive long after Totila's death, and the

Goths themselves fell to the armies of Justinian in 555.

After the failure of Witigis against the Byzantine armies in Italy, along with the failure of the Goths' efforts to promote Belisarius, the commander of the Byzantine troops in Italy, to the office of western emperor, the Goths fell into a short period of political turmoil, as two Gothic leaders rose to prominence only to fall to political murders. Totila was the nephew of one of these murdered leaders; he was elected king in the fall of 541 with the duty of restoring Gothic authority in Italy. Totila was a skilled commander who was also blessed with some good fortune, which aided him throughout the 540s. The efforts that the Goths had made to promote Belisarius to the imperial dignity made him suspect in Constantinople, and Persian efforts on the empire's eastern frontier limited the number of troops and resources that could be committed to the war in Italy. Moreover, in the spring of 542 Totila won a major battle at Faenza, rallying the Goths to his side. He once again raised a rebellion against the invaders, and imperial armies moved north to contain him and lay siege to Verona. With some 5,000 troops, Totila moved against an imperial force of some 12,000 troops, and in a brilliant tactical move defeated them. His smaller force managed to catch its rival in a pincer movement, and a reserve of 300 Gothic lancers fell on the imperial army's rear at a crucial moment. His ranks swelling to some 20,000 troops, Totila followed this victory with another major success over the imperial army near Florence and a rapid move to southern Italy to lay claim to the entire peninsula.

Totila's fortunes improved even more in 543 as he moved into the south. He managed to enter Naples and treated both the civilian population and the imperial garrison leniently—a clever strategy that gained the support and respect of many in Italy. He repeated this policy of leniency when he took the city of Rome after a siege that lasted from late 545 until December 546. Even the return of Belisarius, who had been recalled to Constantinople after the defeat of Witigis, could not stop the advance of Totila, who hoped that his military victories would force the emperor to negotiate. Although Justinian was unwilling to come to the table, Totila was not without diplomatic successes; he managed to remove the Frankish threat by ceding part of northern Italy to the Merovingian king Theudebert. Totila's next move, however, was not as successful. He led his army north in the spring of 547 against Ravenna, an imperial stronghold, and lost Rome to Belisarius, a loss that undermined confidence in Totila. His failure to retake the city diminished his prestige even more and led to a breakdown in marriage negotiations with the Merovingian Franks. He did, however, manage to retake the city in 549, seize a number of fortresses in 549 and 550, and take the offensive in Dalmatia and Sicily.

Although enjoying a measure of success and forcing the recall of the great Belisarius, Totila was not able to overcome the Byzantine advantage in wealth and soldiers. Justinian refused to negotiate with the Gothic king and would not even meet with the envoys Totila sent to Constantinople. Instead, Justinian responded to Totila's efforts with total war in Italy. His first replacement for Belisarius died, but this only delayed the inevitable, as the emperor sent the great general Narses to prosecute the war with renewed vigor. After a successful march into Italy, Narses secured Ravenna and proceeded on to Rome. In July 552, the armies of Totila and Narses clashed at Busta Gallorum, the decisive battle of the war. Although outnumbered, Totila decided to accept battle, hoping that late reinforcements or an unexpected attack would bring him victory. A cavalry charge at the center of the larger imperial force was the main act of the battle. The Gothic cavalry was broken in the assault, the Gothic armies fled from the field, and some 6,000 Gothic soldiers were killed in the rout. Totila died in battle, as did the hopes of any success for the Goths. Although Totila's

nephew continued the struggle, the Goths were essentially broken on the field of Busta Gallorum, and the Gothic people disappeared from history by 555, the date of the final Byzantine victory.

See also Belisarius; Franks; Justinian; Lombards; Merovingian Dynasty; Narses; Ostrogoths; Theodoric the Great; Witigis

Bibliography

Browning, Robert. *Justinian and Theodora,* rev. ed. London: Thames and Hudson, 1987.

Burns, Thomas. *A History of the Ostrogoths.* Bloomington: University of Indiana Press, 1984.

Bury, John B. *History of the Later Roman Empire: From the Death of Theodosius I to the Death of Justinian.* 2 vols. 1923. Reprint, New York: Dover, 1959.

Cassiodorus. *The Variae of Magnus Aurelius Cassiodorus.* Trans. S. J. B. Barnish. Liverpool, UK: Liverpool University Press, 1992.

Heather, Peter. *The Goths.* Oxford: Blackwell, 1996.

Procopius. *History of the Wars.* Trans H. B. Dewing. 1962.

Wolfram, Herwig. *History of the Goths.* Trans. Thomas J. Dunlap. Berkeley: University of California Press, 1988.

———. *The Roman Empire and Its Germanic Peoples.* Trans. Thomas J. Dunlap. Berkeley: University of California Press, 1997.

Tournai

Important early burial site that, like the site at Sutton Hoo for the Anglo-Saxons, offers important evidence for the early Frankish dynasty of the Merovingians. The tomb is that of the second king of the dynasty, Childeric (d. 481), the father of the dynasty's greatest king, Clovis (r. 481–511).

The tomb was discovered in 1653 and given complete and careful descriptions and illustrations by Jean-Jacques Chifflet, an Antwerp doctor. It is most fortunate that Chifflet took such great care to document the artifacts of this discovery; most of them were

Childeric's signet ring, cast, and impression (Ashmoleon Museum, Oxford)

stolen from the Cabinet des Medailles in Paris in 1831. A few pieces remain but the astonishing collection can only be appreciated by the account by Chifflet. The tomb contained a wide range of burial goods and was clearly identified as Childeric's by a gold signet ring bearing the king's name and his image showing him wearing his hair long (a tradition of the dynasty to come). The find also contained war goods including a spear, his horse's head with its harness, a battleaxe, and two swords exquisitely inlaid with gold and garnets. There was also a hoard of one hundred gold coins and two hundred silver coins. The burial site contained numerous other items such as a crystal globe, gold buckles, gold belt mounts, and a magnificent cloak embroidered with three hundred bees or cicadas of gold and garnet.

Chifflet's discovery is important because of the light it shines on the first Merovingian kings; it suggests something of the contacts and wealth they had. The use of garnets, for example, suggests Gothic influence; it became traditional in Frankish metalwork. The coin hoard and various decorative ornaments suggest contacts with Constantinople and the Eastern Empire. The coins also demonstrate the growing wealth of the emerging dynasty. The grave goods, furthermore, reveal something of the character of Childeric's court. Burial of the horse's head along with certain other goods clearly reveals the pagan character of the king and his court. But he was no wandering Germanic king searching for a livelihood. Instead, he was most likely a settled warrior king who had become an ally of the late Roman Empire. As recent archeological work around the area has shown, the grave at Tournai was close to a Roman cemetery and a Roman road, which suggests the influence of late Roman culture on this early Frankish king.

See also Anglo-Saxons; Clovis; Merovingian Dynasty; Sutton Hoo

Bibliography

Geary, Patrick. *Before France and Germany: The Creation and Transformation of the Merovingian World.* New York: Oxford University Press, 1988.

Lasko, Peter. *The Kingdom of the Franks: North-West Europe before Charlemagne.* London: Thames and Hudson, 1971.

Wallace-Hadrill, J. M. *The Long-Haired Kings and Other Studies in Frankish History.* Toronto: University of Toronto Press, 1982.

Wood, Ian. *The Merovingian Kingdoms, 450–751.* London: Longman, 1994.

U

Ulfilas (c. 311–382/383)

Gothic bishop, missionary, and translator, Ulfilas, which means "little wolf" in the Gothic language, was a key figure in the ongoing Christianization of the Goths. He was hailed as the Moses of his age by the emperor Constantius II, and was compared with the prophet Elijah by others. His reputation came from his missionary activity among Goths who remained loyal to their traditional faith, as well as from his standing as tribal leader of the Goths. He also earned this praise because, like Moses, he brought the word of God to his people with his translation of the Bible into the Gothic language. Like the much later translation of the Bible by Martin Luther, that of Ulfilas had an important influence on the development of a language and culture.

Born around 311, Ulfilas was a third-generation Danubian Goth whose ancestors on his mother's side, at least, may have come from Cappadocia. But he was a true Goth from birth and, despite his name, was probably not of low social origins. Indeed, his apparent education and later career suggest otherwise. From his early years, Ulfilas seems to have been trilingual, learning Greek and Latin along with his native language. He also probably studied rhetoric; at least his later theological and exegetical works suggest such training. His upper-class social origins are suggested also by his membership in a delegation to Constantinople between 332 and 337 representing the Goths before the imperial government. He may have even lived in Constantinople for a while at that time before returning to his homeland.

On a second trip into imperial territory, to Antioch in 341, Ulfilas was consecrated "bishop of the Christians in the Getic land" by Eusebius the bishop of Constantinople. It is likely that his ordination was part of a broader Roman initiative to convert all the Goths, but it also suggests recognition of the minority population of Goths and their need for spiritual leadership. His promotion to bishop also suggests the esteem in which the Romans held Ulfilas, who advanced to the episcopal office after holding only the minor church office of lector. As bishop in the 340s, Ulfilas sought to fulfill the task bestowed on him at his consecration; as a result, he was an active missionary. He not only ministered to his flock effectively, but also reached out to non-Christian Goths. His Christianity was the mainstream Christianity of the empire and was influenced by the Arianism of the ruling emperors of the time. Although Ulfilas may not have accepted fully all the tenets of Arianism, he rejected the Nicene Creed and generally held a centrist position between the two extremes. Whatever the exact nature of his belief, Ulfilas was an effective missionary, and his activities among his fellow Goths may have alienated those who maintained belief in the traditional gods. In the first Gothic persecution of Christians in 348, Ulfilas was expelled, perhaps because of his evangelical zeal, and as a result of his expulsion has been known by the honorary title *confessor*.

He and his followers, for whom he was both a spiritual and secular leader, were settled within the Roman Empire by the emperor, and Ulfilas again assumed his duties as bishop. As bishop in exile from his native land, Ulfilas sought to continue his evangelical and pastoral work, and even indulged in writing theological treatises. He preached in Gothic, Greek, and Latin, and participated in the council of 360, which supported the Arian faith in the empire. His greatest achievement, however, was his translation of the Bible into the Gothic language, probably after 350. He was faced, first, with the challenge of preparing an alphabet for the Gothic tongue, and only after that could he translate Scripture. He most probably translated his Bible from the Greek version commonly used in the fourth century. His translation and missionary activity were a great inspiration to other Goths who carried on his work, and his Bible provided a single source to unify the Goths in language and faith.

In his later years it is likely that Ulfilas opposed Athanaric, who persecuted Christians, and supported his fellow Arian and pro-Roman Goth, Fritigern. But when Fritigern revolted against the empire, Ulfilas was more inclined toward Rome than Fritigern. Indeed, Ulfilas spent his last days in the imperial capital at Constantinople, preparing for the start of a church council on the Arian question. Ulfilas remained committed to his Arian faith, declaring on his deathbed: "There is one eternal, unbegotten, and invisible God, who before time existed alone. Within time he created the Son, the only-begotten God."(Wolfram 1997, 84–85) Although the empire was moving toward Catholic Christianity, it allowed the barbarian peoples to follow the Christianity of their ancestors. Ulfilas had inspired numerous disciples who spread his Arianism to other barbarian peoples, including the Ostrogoths, the Vandals, and possibly the Franks.

See also Arianism; Athanaric; Fritigern; Visigoths

Bibliography

Heather, Peter. *The Goths.* Oxford: Blackwell, 1996.

Thompson, Edward A. *The Visigoths in the Time of Ulfila.* Oxford: Clarendon, 1966.

Wolfram, Herwig. *History of the Goths.* Trans. Thomas J. Dunlap. Berkeley: University of California Press, 1988.

———. *The Roman Empire and Its Germanic Peoples.* Trans. Thomas J. Dunlap. Berkeley: University of California Press, 1997.

V

Valens (328?–378)

Arian Christian Roman emperor (r. 364–378), whose career is noteworthy for his disastrous defeat by the Visigoths at the Battle of Hadrianople, Valens was co-emperor with his brother Valentinian I (r. 364–375); Valens ruled in the eastern capital of Constantinople. His reign was marked by successes against the Visigoths and Persians as well as against pretenders to the throne before his final, tragic defeat.

Valens was promoted to the imperial throne on March 28, 364, when he was elevated to the dignity by his brother Valentinian following the death of Emperor Jovian (r. 363–364). He was faced almost immediately by a rebellion, but managed to suppress it and execute its leaders. After defeating his rival for the throne, Valens turned his attention to the defense of the imperial frontiers against pressures from the Goths. In 367 and again in 369, Valens crossed the Danube River, leaving imperial territory, to attack the Goths. He successfully laid waste to Gothic territories and then returned to Constantinople to celebrate his victory and assume the title *Gothicus*. Although the raids did not yield any long-term benefits, they did promote the status of the emperor and force the Goths to come to terms. Valens and the Gothic leader Athanaric agreed to a treaty in September 369, meeting on boats in the middle of the Danube. As part of the agreement, the Romans sealed off the border from Gothic trade with the empire. Valens may also have sought to exploit the intratribal struggles that existed between the Gothic leaders Athanaric and Fritigern by forging a treaty with Fritigern.

Valens's early success against the Visigoths was not, however, repeated later in his reign. With the arrival of the Huns, new pressures were placed on the Roman frontiers and the barbarian peoples living along those frontiers. The Huns were recognized as a major threat by the Visigoths and seriously undermined the authority of Athanaric, who had previously struggled with the Romans and persecuted the Christians in his midst. The weakness of Athanaric and the enormity of the threat of the Huns inspired a large faction of the Goths, led by Fritigern, to petition Valens for entry into the empire as *foederati* (federated allies) in 376. The request was not unprecedented, but the size of the population involved, some 80,000, was. Despite the great number of people involved, Valens agreed to allow the Goths to cross the boundary and settle in Roman territory, a fateful decision that had a great influence on the subsequent course of events.

Valens had allowed the Goths to enter, and he made promises of food, territory, and administrative help. But none of this came, and in fact the Goths were harassed by local Roman administrators rather than helped. The poor treatment and general suffering caused the Goths to revolt against the Romans, and Valens himself decided to lead the army against the rebels. After some negotiation and poor decision making by Valens, the battle was fought on August 9, 378, at Hadrianople (in modern Turkey). The Romans were overwhelmed and annihilated by the Goths, and Valens died during the battle. The Goths were allowed to settle in the empire by Valens's successor, Theodosius the Great.

See also Alaric; Arianism; Athanaric; Battle of Hadrianople; Fritigern; Huns; Visigoths

Bibliography

Ammianus Marcellinus. *The Later Roman Empire (A.D. 354–378).* Trans. Walter Hamilton. Harmondsworth, UK: Penguin, 1986.

Bury, John B. *The Invasion of Europe by the Barbarians.* New York: W. W. Norton, 1967.

Cameron, Averil. *The Later Roman Empire, A.D. 284–430.* Cambridge, MA: Harvard University Press, 1993.

Ferrill, Arthur. *The Fall of the Roman Empire: The Military Explanation.* New York: Thames and Hudson, 1986.

Heather, Peter. *The Goths.* Oxford: Blackwell, 1996.

Wolfram, Herwig. *The Roman Empire and Its Germanic Peoples.* Trans. Thomas J. Dunlap. Berkeley: University of California Press, 1997.

Vandals

One of the barbarian peoples who established successor kingdoms in the deteriorating remnants of the Western Empire in the fifth century. Although active from the early fourth century, the Vandals only established a kingdom of any consequence in the fifth century under their greatest king, Gaiseric, who carved out a kingdom of his own in North Africa. His son and other descendants preserved this kingdom into the sixth century and created one of the more powerful entities

in the newly forming post-Roman Mediterranean. The Vandal kingdom ultimately fell to the armies of Justinian in the 530s, as he attempted to reunite the eastern and western parts of the Roman Empire under his authority. The Vandals are perhaps best known for Gaiseric's sack of the city of Rome in 455, and have, since the eighteenth century, been associated with the term *vandalism*. They acquired a reputation for senseless destruction and violence that is reflected in the modern term, but one that is undeserved and inaccurate.

The early history of the Vandals before their entry into the empire in the fifth century remains a bit unclear. They probably originated in the region of the Baltic Sea or in Scandinavia, and in the first century of the Common Era they moved south and divided into two groups, the Silings and the Hasdings. By the year 300, at the latest, the Vandals seem to have settled in central Europe where they gradually began to make contact with the Roman Empire and other barbarian peoples. These relationships, however, before too long became increasingly complicated, as the Vandals, like other peoples living outside the empire's frontiers, faced increasing pressure from westward-moving Huns or the peoples they displaced. The two groups of Vandals reunited and joined with other barbarian peoples, then were forced from their homeland after losing a struggle against a confederation of Goths. According to one tradition, the Vandals petitioned the emperor Constantine for admittance into the empire as a people. But this version of events is quite unlikely, even though some individual Vandals may have been settled within the empire at that time. They most likely remained somewhere in central Europe, perhaps reaching parts of modern Hungary in the course of the fourth century. As the pressure from the Huns continued to increase, the necessity of moving the tribe increased. By the late fourth and early fifth century, the Vandals had become *foederati* (federated allies), and had joined with the Roman military commander Stilicho against Alaric and the Goths.

This connection with Stilicho, along with competition and cooperation with other barbarian peoples, led to the entry of the Vandals into the empire when they crossed the Rhine River in 406. After an initial setback following the crossing, the Vandals inflicted a crushing defeat on the Frankish allies of Rome who defended the frontier. Following this victory, the Vandals, along with their Alan allies, went from one end of Gaul to the other and caused serious devastation. Thanks to the decline in the power of the Western Empire, the Vandals, like other barbarian peoples, roamed freely in the empire. After two and a half years in Gaul, they marched into Spain, where they divided again in two and attempted to establish themselves.

The period in Spain was pivotal in the history of the Vandals and witnessed the first appearance of their greatest king, Gaiseric. Before the rise of Gaiseric, however, the Vandals enjoyed a measure of success and endured serious setbacks in Spain. By 422, a confederation of Vandals and Alans had conquered southern Spain, but only after being forced south by Visigothic armies sent by Rome. Indeed, a Visigothic army marched into Spain on Rome's behalf, nearly obliterating the Siling Vandal tribe and forcing the Alans and Hasding Vandals together in 418. Forced by the pressure of the Visigoths, the Vandals moved into the south. By 428, the Vandal king Gunderic (r. 406–428) had captured the Roman cities of Cartagena and Seville. But the sack of Seville did not come without great cost, as Gunderic died while the city was being plundered by the Vandals.

At the death of Gunderic, Gaiseric (c. 390–477) assumed the throne, even though Gunderic had male heirs; Gaiseric regularized this succession plan later by establishing that the oldest Hasding male of the royal family should take the throne. Gaiseric was the son of a Vandal king and an unfree woman, possibly a Roman captured in a raid. At the time of succession he was nearly forty, and had a mature son, Huneric, who may have himself been married to a Visigothic princess.

Gaiseric was the greatest of the Vandal kings and one of the ablest barbarian kings of his age, equal to the more famous Attila the Hun. Indeed, Gaiseric had great vision; he created a kingdom in Africa that lasted several generations, before falling in the end to Byzantine armies led by Justinian's general Belisarius.

Gaiseric's vision is best revealed by his movement into Africa, which was embroiled in great turmoil at that time. Recognizing the difficulties the imperial government faced because of the ambitions of its general Boniface, in 429 Gaiseric moved all his people, some 80,000 according to tradition, to Africa in a fleet of ships. Once there, Gaiseric moved gradually across the region and threatened Roman authority. According to one account, Boniface had invited Gaiseric to Africa to help against a Gothic army sent to suppress his revolt, but then faced a hostile Gaiseric. Whatever the cause of his movement, Gaiseric reached St. Augustine's city of Hippo in 430 and laid siege to the city that lasted fourteen months. Although the town held out against Gaiseric and the siege was lifted, Roman efforts to rescue it failed when Gaiseric defeated an army led by Boniface, who was now back in Rome's good graces. Gaiseric occupied the town after the siege and settled a treaty with the empire in 435 that recognized Vandal control over the territory. Four years later, in 439, Gaiseric violated the treaty by seizing the great capital of Carthage. He was now clearly in control of important parts of Africa, and the empire was forced to deal with that reality.

Gaiseric had established his kingdom in North Africa, and he remained in control there until his death in 477, despite Roman efforts to dislodge him. It must be noted, however, that relations between Gaiseric and the empire were not always hostile. In 442 Gaiseric agreed to a treaty with the Western Empire in which his authority in Africa was recognized by the empire. And he remained on good terms with the western emperor, Valentinian III (d. 455). But when Valentinian was murdered and his daughter Eudocia, who had already been betrothed to Huneric, was forced to marry the new emperor's son, Gaiseric reacted violently. He led his fleet to Italy and sacked Rome, although at the request of Pope Leo I, known as Leo the Great, he did not massacre the population or burn the city down. He later conquered several islands in the western Mediterranean, and in 456 he defeated a fleet sent against him by the eastern emperor. In 474 he settled a treaty with Constantinople recognizing his authority, and in 476 negotiated rights over Sicily with the western emperor, an agreement that was accepted by the emperor's successor, Odovacar. At his death on January 24, 477, Gaiseric was clearly the greatest power in the western Mediterranean. He transformed the tribal group that followed him into a settled people and was the founder of a kingdom that seemed likely to last for a long time to come.

Gaiseric was succeeded by his son Huneric, who had lived a long life and was probably sixty-six at the time of succession. Little is known of Huneric's early life other than his role as hostage at the imperial court and his marriages. He was married early on, perhaps before his father took the throne, and was betrothed to Eudocia to confirm the treaty of 442. His first wife was accused of attempting to poison Gaiseric and sent back to Visigothic Spain after being mutilated. The marriage of Eudocia to the new emperor's son was an excuse for the sacking of Rome; the two were married the following year. But Huneric's aggressive Arianism alienated his wife, a devout Catholic, who left him for Jerusalem in 472. As king Huneric is perhaps known for his persecution of Catholics in his kingdom, which became quite serious in the last year of his reign. His death in 484 prevented the persecution from doing serious damage to the church in Africa.

Despite the purge of family members that he had earlier carried out, Huneric was succeeded by his nephew Gunthamund (r. 484–496) rather than his own son. And it was at this point that the kingdom began to suffer from serious internal and external difficul-ties. Indeed, already under Huneric the attempt to keep the succession in one line of the family demonstrated the problems of Gaiseric's succession plan, according to which the oldest of the sons of the male members of the royal family was to inherit the crown. Gunthamund in his turn faced a series of difficulties. Although he did end Huneric's persecution of Catholics, Gunthamund remained a committed Arian, who made little accommodation with the Catholic church, which increasingly alienated the majority Catholic population from the ruling dynasty. He also felt increasing pressure from the native Berbers, who had formerly served Gaiseric. The Vandal king also faced a challenge from Theodoric the Great, who pushed the Vandals out of Sicily. These difficulties continued under Gunthamund's successor Thrasamund (r. 496–523), whose unrelenting Arianism further alienated the Vandals from the Roman population. He also faced the further erosion of Berber support and even threatened war with Theodoric. But good relations prevailed between the Ostrogoths and Vandals, both because of Thrasamund's earlier marriage to Theodoric's daughter and because of the Vandal's realization of Theodoric's power. Hilderic (r. 523–530), the mature son of Huneric, was the next to rule, and unlike his predecessors he took a tolerant line with the Catholics, despite his own continued Arianism. This act endeared him to the Roman population, as did his diplomatic turn toward the empire and away from the Ostrogoths. He was a personal friend of the great emperor Justinian. His diplomatic shift, however, brought him to the brink of war with Theodoric, a war prevented only by Theodoric's death, and his closeness to the empire led to a revolt, which deposed him.

The final Vandal king was Gelimer (r. 530–534), who assumed the throne by a palace coup, which violated Gaiseric's succession plan and the peace treaty with the empire in existence since 474. Indeed, the deposition of Justinian's friend Hilderic angered the emperor on a personal as well as political level. In 533, Justinian sent his great general Belisarius against the Vandals. A combination of Belisarius's military brilliance and Gelimer's miscalculation and willingness to concede battle led to the rapid defeat of the Vandals by a relatively small imperial army. After a series of defeats, Gelimer capitulated in March or April of 534 and was settled in the empire away from his former kingdom. Justinian, thanks to Belisarius, was able to restore Africa to imperial control and also able to take his first step toward reuniting the empire. The Vandal kingdom, although one of the most powerful under Gaiseric, was destroyed, and the Vandal people absorbed by the empire.

The Vandals had little physical impact on the African countryside, or at least left little evidence of it. They did seize land from the Roman provincials in an effort to secure their own economic base and weaken Roman power. They built little in the way of fortifications and did not establish urban bases from which they could have defended themselves against the Romans. Their lack of building fortifications may have been the result of the Vandals' pride in their navy, which was quite powerful and allowed them to control much of the western Mediterranean and sack Rome in 455. They also left little in terms of a written record of their time in Africa. Unlike other barbarian peoples, the Vandals did not compile a law code, although there was a collection of laws that reveals Roman influence. And all accounts of the Vandals were written by writers from the Eastern Empire, who generally left an unfavorable portrait.

Vandal life in Africa is best captured by the Byzantine writer, the fifth-century Byzantine historian Procopius, in his history of the Vandal wars. He noted that the Vandals spent all their time in the baths or attended the theater. They wore much gold and dressed in elaborate clothes and were entertained by dancers and mimes. Procopius notes also that they indulged in great banquets, with a wide variety of meat, fish, and other foods. They

pursued a number of pleasures, including hunting. Finally, it should be noted that the Vandals were committed Arians, who persecuted the native Catholic population. But here too, their stay in Africa had little long-term impact.

See also Alans; Alaric; Arianism; Augustine of Hippo, St.; Attila the Hun; Belisarius; Huneric; Huns; Gaiseric; Galla Placidia; Jordanes; Justinian; Law and Law Codes; Odovacar; Ostrogoths; Theodoric the Great; Visigoths

Bibliography
Bury, John B. The *Invasion of Europe by the Barbarians.* New York: W. W. Norton, 1967.
Cameron, Averil. *The Mediterranean World in Late Antiquity,* A.D. *395–600.* New York: Routledge, 1993.
Clover, Frank M. *The Late Roman West and the Vandals.* London: Variorum, 1993.
Randers-Pehrson, Justine Davis. *Barbarians and Romans: The Birth Struggle of Europe,* A.D. *400–700.* Norman: University of Oklahoma Press, 1983.
Todd, Malcolm. *Everyday Life of the Barbarians: Goths, Franks, and Vandals.* London and New York: G. P. Putnam's' Sons, 1972.
Victor of Vita. *Victor of Vita: History of the Vandal Persecution.* Trans. John Moorhead. Liverpool, UK: Liverpool University Press, 1992.
Wolfram, Herwig. *The Roman Empire and Its Germanic Peoples.* Trans. Thomas J. Dunlap. Berkeley: University of California Press, 1997.

Verdun, Treaty of (843)

Major treaty between the surviving sons of Louis the Pious—Charles the Bald, Lothar, Louis the German—in the breakup of the empire forged by Charlemagne. The treaty brought to a close the civil war that had raged since the time of the death of Louis the Pious. It divided the Carolingian Empire between Charles, Louis, and Lothar, and established the outlines for the later French kingdom and German empire. Although the treaty divided the empire into three administrative realms, it did not necessarily destroy the empire; the brothers worked together for a time, and each of the brothers attempted to establish his authority over the entire realm during the next several decades.

At his death in 840, Louis the Pious was succeeded by his three sons, Charles, Lothar, and Louis the German, and Pippin II, an adult grandson, the son of his deceased son Pippin. The oldest son, Lothar, had lived in relative disgrace in Italy during Louis's later years because of his part in the revolts against his father in the early 830s, but he was reconciled to his father shortly before Louis's death. Lothar was assigned authority over the eastern section of the Frankish kingdom, with the exception of Bavaria, which Louis the German administered. The other surviving son, Charles, was assigned authority over the western part of the Frankish kingdoms, and Pippin laid claim to his father's territory in Aquitaine. Lothar, who held the imperial title along with his rights over the eastern part of the kingdom, rushed north from Italy to establish his authority over the entire realm and worked to undermine the authority of Charles. Charles, in turn, joined with his other half brother, Louis, in an alliance against the ambitious Lothar. The alliance was followed, in 841, by a terrible and bloody battle between the three brothers at Fontenoy near Auxerre in Burgundy, at which Lothar was defeated and forced to flee to Aachen. Louis and Charles sealed the victory over their elder brother by swearing oaths of mutual support at Strasbourg in 842, a compact that was followed by their assault on Lothar in Aachen. With the capture of Aachen, Lothar realized that he was beaten, and thus the three brothers came together to negotiate the organization of the realm.

Negotiations began in June 842, and lasted over a year before a settlement was reached with the Treaty of Verdun, the text of which no longer exists. The discussions between the brothers began near Mâcon in an atmosphere of distrust and demands by Lothar for a fair and equitable partition of the realm. As part of the negotiations, which included some 120 participants along with the three kings, a survey of all the lands and possessions of the empire was taken. Lothar's demands, however, backfired, and he ultimately ended with the least defensible section of the realm. The treaty most likely began with a call for divine support, and the final settlement centered around the core realms of Aquitaine, Lombardy, and Bavaria for Charles, Lothar, and Louis respectively. Along with Aquitaine, Charles received the western kingdom, whose boundary followed a line along several rivers, the Scheldt, Meuse, Saône, and Rhone. Louis received Bavaria and lands east of the Rhine and also some important cities and wine-producing regions on the west bank of the Rhine. Lothar received a middle kingdom, stretching in the north from the traditional Carolingian heartland down into Italy in the south.

Lothar was granted the imperial title but had only nominal authority over his brothers. His most important imperial responsibilities involved obligations in relation to Italy and the pope. Charles and Louis had real power and freedom of action in their own kingdoms, and Charles received an added bonus with the exclusion of Pippin II, his nephew and heir to lands in Aquitaine. The treaty brought an end to terrible fraternal conflict in the Carolingian Empire, and, in the following year, Charles, Louis, and Lothar swore to maintain good fraternal relations and help preserve the peace in each others' kingdoms. The treaty, however, may have been intended only as a short-term solution and a framework to allow for the formation and reformation of the empire.

The rationale for the agreement remains poorly understood, and there are numerous explanations concerning the purpose and meaning of the treaty and its division of the empire. It has been suggested that an effort was made in forging the treaty and configuring the creation of the three kingdoms to appeal to national instincts in the various parts of the empire. Arguing that neither France nor Germany had yet emerged, other scholars have noted the importance of economic considerations, and have cited Lothar's concerns for a fair and equitable division that led to the land survey as support for their view. But already in the ninth century, the historian and member of the royal family Nithard noted that the primary concern of the three brothers was for the welfare of their vassals, a group that was essential to the long-term success of the kings of each region. Whatever the intentions of the three participants in the treaty, the settlement at Verdun set the boundaries of the later medieval kingdoms of France and Germany and provided a framework for the ultimate permanent division of the Carolingian Empire.

See also Carolingian Dynasty; Charlemagne; Charles the Bald; Fontenoy, Battle of; Lothar; Louis the German; Louis the Pious; Nithard; Strasbourg, Oath of

Bibliography

McKitterick, Rosamond. *The Frankish Kingdoms under the Carolingians, 751–987.* London: Longman, 1983.

Nelson, Janet. *Charles the Bald.* London: Longman, 1992.

Riché, Pierre. *The Carolingians: A Family Who Forged Europe.* Trans. Michael Idomir Allen. Philadelphia: University of Pennsylvania Press, 1993.

Scholz, Bernhard Walter, trans. *Carolingian Chronicles: Royal Frankish Annals and Nithard's History.* Ann Arbor: University of Michigan Press, 1972.

Visigoths

Barbarian people whose migration played an important role in the decline and fall of the Western Roman Empire. The contacts of the Visigoths (literally "west men"; also known as the West Goths or Tervingi) with the Roman Empire may have started as early as the first century, but clearly occurred in the third century when a powerful Gothic kingdom formed along the imperial frontier by the Danube River. These early contacts between the Visigoths and the Romans were often violent and foreshadowed things to come for both Romans and Goths. The Romans were able to smash the Visigothic threat in the third century, only to face a greater one in the fourth and fifth centuries. From their settlements outside the empire, the Visigoths entered the empire as a result of the advance of the Huns. Once inside the empire, the Visigoths became both its defender and attacker. They inflicted a stunning defeat on imperial armies in 378 and pillaged parts of the Eastern Empire before coming to terms with Emperor Theodosius the Great. After the emperor's death, and under the aggressive leadership of Alaric, the Visigoths moved again and sacked Rome in 410. They then moved out of Italy and eventually settled in southwestern France and Spain, where they established one of the most successful kingdoms to form out of the dissolving Western Empire. Although chased from France by the Merovingian king Clovis (r. 481–511), they remained in Spain and established a dynamic civilization that boasted, among other things, the works of the important early seventh-century scholar Isidore of Seville. They also converted to Catholic Christianity from the Arian Christianity that the missionary Ulfilas had disseminated among them in the fourth century. Despite its advanced political and cultural institutions, the kingdom fell in the early eighth century when Muslim invaders conquered most of Spain. But Visigothic civilization continued to influence Christian Europe even after the kingdom's conquest by Islam.

The people who came to be identified as the Visigoths are traditionally thought to have emerged in Scandinavia and then to have moved further south, where they came into contact with the Roman Empire. According to the sixth-century historian Jordanes, "from this island of Scandza, as from a hive of races of a womb of nations, the Goths are said to have come forth long ago under their king, Berig by name" (104). Historians have long accepted this tale of Gothic origins as essentially true, but recent archeological investiga-

Votive crowns of King Reccenswith (Owen Franken/Corbis)

tion has challenged this view, suggesting instead origin along the Vistula River in Poland. Although the record is uncertain, in part because the Goths were a nonliterate people and left no written records, it is possible that the Goths were involved with hostilities between Romans and barbarians in the first and second centuries. Their distance from the frontier, however, guaranteed that they were not the focus of imperial concerns. The Visigoths, however, eventually moved from their original homeland southward along the Roman frontier along the Danube and caused the Romans increasing difficulty, especially in the dark years of the third century.

In 238 the first Gothic attack on Roman territory occurred, which was followed by further hostilities between the two powers. Over the next several decades, Gothic attacks became an ever greater problem for the empire, and in 251 the Goths defeated a Roman army and killed Emperor Decius. In the next generation, however, Roman emperors Aurelian and Claudius were able to turn the tide, inflicting severe defeats on the Visigoths that nearly wiped them out as a people.

The Visigoths then settled in the region between the Danubian border and the Black Sea and remained good neighbors to the empire for over a century. During this time, the Visigoths had much better relations with the empire. There were frequent trade contacts between the two, as a variety of goods were exchanged, including cattle, clothing, grain, slaves, and wine. It was during this period as well that the Gothic missionary bishop Ulfilas spread Arian Christianity among the Gothic people and converted some of them, despite a fierce reaction against his missionary work by Gothic leaders. Settled life also brought increasing social sophistication and wealth. New social elites emerged, including specialized armed warriors who served Gothic chieftains. The warriors, as revealed from burial sites in modern Denmark, were well armed and carried knives, spears, lances, and other specialized weaponry. Along with the warrior elite there emerged a new ruling elite, as well as a peasant class that was dedicated to farming. Indeed, agriculture became an important economic activity in this period, as did metalworking; a number of brooches worked in a way characteristic of the Goths began appearing at this time.

For much of the fourth century relations between the empire and the Goths were relatively peaceful, but efforts by the empire to extend its influence into Gothic territory strained relations. This situation was worsened by the westward movement of the Huns, who had conquered Ostrogothic territory and were increasing their pressure on the Visigoths. In 376, the pressure from the Huns was so severe that the Visigoths divided into two camps, one led by Athanaric, who had failed to prevent the Huns' advance, and a larger contingent, led by Fritigern, that petitioned Emperor Valens for entry into the empire. The Romans had welcomed barbarian peoples into the empire as *foederati* (federated allies) previously, but not in such great numbers. Traditionally, the number of Goths to cross into the empire in 376 was about 80,000—an overwhelming number that the local administrators could not handle. Indeed, the sheer number was only one of the difficulties that was faced by the Visigoths and the Romans. The Goths' Arianism increased tensions with the predominately Catholic Roman population, and Roman officials failed to provide the food and other materials necessary for survival that had been promised by the emperor. The Goths rose in rebellion and in 378 fought a great battle against Roman armies at Hadrianople, during which Valens was killed and the imperial force was destroyed. For the next several years the Goths had free rein in Roman territory.

In 382, Emperor Theodosius the Great, who had been made eastern emperor in 379 and given command in the Gothic Wars, brought an end to the pillaging of the Goths. He forged a treaty with the Visigoths that granted them land to farm in exchange for service in the Roman military. This treaty held until Theodosius's death in 395 and proved beneficial to the emperor, who employed large numbers of Goths to put down pretenders to the throne, even though he was forced to subdue rebellious Goths on occasion. The death of Theodosius in 395, however, brought about a significant change in the relationship between the two people and the fortunes of both Romans and Visigoths.

The rise of Alaric as leader of the Visigoths in the late 390s resulted in the increasing hostility of the Goths toward the Romans. Alaric himself had received a high-ranking imperial military post but nevertheless launched raids into Italy in the early fifth century; he was stopped by Emperor Honorius's chief military officer, Stilicho. But the murder of Stilicho in 408 at the emperor's order removed this impediment to Alaric's ambitions. Moreover, the emperor refused to grant Alaric further concessions or to honor previous financial obligations, which pushed the Gothic leader to launch another attack on Italy in 410. In August of that year, Alaric sacked the city of Rome—the first time the city had suffered such treatment in 800 years—plundering and pillaging it for three days. The event profoundly shocked the people of the empire and inspired St. Augustine of Hippo's writing of his great work *The City of God*. After sacking the city, Alaric led his followers south with the intention of invading Africa. But his efforts failed, and he died shortly thereafter, replaced by Ataulf, who led the Visigoths into Gaul.

During the fifth century the Visigoths regularized their position in Gaul and eventually expanded into Spain. Ataulf's claim to rule in Gaul was uncertain, and relations with the empire took an interesting turn because of his abduction of the emperor's sister Galla Placidia, whom Ataulf married in 414. But Ataulf's death in 415 ended any possibility of one his heirs ascending the imperial throne. His successors returned his widow to the emperor and signed a treaty in 418 in which the Romans recognized Visigothic claims to reside in Gaul between Toulouse and Bordeaux. The treaty was signed by Theodoric I (r. 418–451), who was elected king in 418 and led the Visigoths during their period of settlement and expansion in Gaul. Although probably not recognized as an independent ruler, Theodoric exercised important power over his people and strove to improve its position in the empire. On the one hand, Theodoric remained a loyal ally of the Romans and often led his Visigoths in battle on behalf of the empire. They actively campaigned on behalf of the empire in Spain to prevent other barbarian peoples from conquering that region. They also participated in the great battle fought in 451 against Attila and the Huns on the Catalaunian Plains, where Roman success depended largely on the Visigoths and their king Theodoric, who died in battle. But Theodoric also sought to use any imperial crisis to his advantage and rallied his people on behalf of Galla Placidia in her struggles against the general Aëtius in the 430s. Theodoric also led numerous campaigns in southern Gaul to expand Visigothic control in that part of the empire and attacked its capital, Arles, on several occasions.

Theodoric had laid the foundation for later Visigothic expansion under his sons, who succeeded him in turn after his death in 451. The increasing weakness of the Western Empire also enabled the Visigoths to increase the size of their kingdom, although it should be noted that the Visigothic kingdom was not the picture of governmental stability. Theodoric's first two successors, his sons Thorismund and Theodoric II, were assassinated in 453 and 466 respectively. His third son Euric, however, did reign for some eighteen years, and he built upon his father's legacy and Roman weakness to create a great kingdom in southern France and Spain. Breaking the long-standing agreement with the empire, Euric initiated a series of campaigns lasting from 471 to 476 in which he captured most of southern Gaul. At the same time, Euric's armies were extending Visigothic control over all of Spain, and as a result Euric created the most significant successor kingdom of the age.

The kingdom, which Euric passed on to his son Alaric II when he died a natural death in 484, inherited a number of Roman institutions that both Euric and Alaric exploited effectively. A number of administrative and bureaucratic techniques were adopted by these kings for their realm, most importantly Roman tax-gathering practices. They also were influenced by Roman legal traditions. Euric issued a set of laws, possibly the *Code of Euric,* in 473, and Alaric issued the *Breviary of Alaric* in 506. These legal codes, which were influenced by Roman legal traditions and incorporated Roman laws, addressed a wide range of issues, including loans, use of charters, wills, and other matters concerning relations between Romans and Visigoths under their authority. These kings also shaped church history in their kingdom, promoting the Arian faith that the majority of the Visigoths now professed but being careful not to offend their Catholic Roman subjects by persecuting the Catholic church in their realm. Under Euric and Alaric the Visigoths enjoyed their greatest success, but also suffered a significant setback in 507 when Alaric suffered a crushing defeat at the hands of the Merovingian king Clovis at the Battle of Vouillé. This battle, which the sixth-century Frankish historian Gregory of Tours portrays as something of a crusade, forced the Visigoths out of most of Gaul and limited their kingdom to the lands in Spain. But despite this loss and the death of Alaric II, the Visigoths enjoyed nearly another two centuries of success in Spain.

Although the defeat by Clovis was a serious one, it did not end Visigothic power even in all of Gaul. This was due in part to the Visigoths' own king, but also to support from the powerful Ostrogothic king in Italy, Theodoric the Great. Indeed, Ostrogothic armies in 508 helped push Clovis's armies out of Visigothic territory and allowed Alaric's heirs to preserve part of their former possession in Gaul. But Theodoric's support was not wholly altruistic and formed part of his plan for a greater Gothic kingdom. He extended his authority over Spain and deposed Alaric's heir in favor of a prefect who administered Spain as part of a broader province. Theo-

doric also transferred the Visigothic treasury to his own capital at Ravenna. This situation was bound to cause dissatisfaction among the Goths in Spain, and after Theodoric's death in 526 the Visigothic royal line was restored when Amalaric, Alaric's son, took the throne.

Amalaric's rule was a short and unhappy one, which involved further military losses to the Merovingian kings and ended with his murder in 531. This abrupt end to his reign was followed by an extended political crisis in the kingdom, despite the lengthy rule of Amalaric's murderer Theudis (r. 531–548). The kingdom was plagued by internal instability brought about by the competition of the nobility for greater power and by the attempts of several nobles to usurp the throne or establish themselves as independent of the king. This situation began to change in the 560s, as the Visigothic kings gradually took back control of the kingdom, and it was Leovigild (r. 568–586) who successfully ended the turmoil and restored royal authority fully during his reign.

Leovigild's reign is noteworthy for several reasons, not the least of which was his restoration of royal power. For much of the first decade of his reign, Leovigild led or sent out military campaigns to suppress rebellious nobles or to conquer rival barbarian or Byzantine powers in Spain. To celebrate his triumph and signal his claims to powers similar to those of the emperors, he founded a city, which he named after his son Reccared. He also forged a marriage alliance with the Merovingians when his son Hermenegild married a Merovingian princess, perhaps building on the marriages of the Visigothic princesses Galswintha and Brunhilde to Merovingian kings. Moreover, Leovigild sought to establish religious uniformity in his kingdom. He promoted the Arian faith, but rather than persecuting Catholic Christians, he sought to convert them by incorporating Catholic practices into the Arian church and moderating Arian theology. His efforts were not that successful; they may even have contributed to Hermenegild's conversion to

Catholic Christianity and failed revolt. The religious dilemma, however, was resolved after Leovigild's death by his son Reccared (r. 586–601), who converted to Catholic Christianity and declared it the official faith of the kingdom in 589.

The church Reccared founded was extremely independent and zealous in defense of the faith. Indeed, Reccared himself aggressively promoted the new faith against elements in the kingdom that supported the traditional Arianism of the Visigoths. The church remained independent of Rome and was hostile toward the Jews, an attitude supported by royal legislation against the Jews that cost the kings vital support at the time of the Muslim invasions. On the other hand, the Visigothic church was highly sophisticated, and church and king presided over a flourishing cultural life in Spain in the late sixth and seventh centuries. The most notable contribution was that of Isidore of Seville, but Spain was also characterized by a vigorous monastic life, a high level of ecclesiastical culture, and widespread literacy in Latin (unique at a time when inhabitants of the other barbarian kingdoms were only beginning to learn the language). Remarkable too were the churches built in Visigothic Spain, with their characteristic horseshoe arches and lavish decoration.

Despite the apparent strength of the Visigothic kingdom, the seventh century witnessed the beginning of the end of this dynamic realm. The monarchy continued to be successful and developed an increasingly sophisticated political theory, revealed in the first royal anointing and coronation after Old Testament models among the barbarian peoples, which took place as early as 631, or at least by the time of King Wamba (r. 672–680). But even before Wamba, Visigothic kings had taken steps to strengthen the monarchy and improve relations between barbarians and Romans. King Chindaswinth (r. 642–653) and his son and successor Recceswinth (r. 653–672) reformed Visigothic law and issued new legal codes that superseded earlier versions, eliminated all distinctions between Romans and Goths, and permitted marriage between the two peoples. Visigothic kings also eliminated the last of their rivals for control of all of Spain. They also continued, however, to pass anti-Semitic legislation, which alienated an important sector of the population. Finally, in the opening decades of the eighth century the Visigoths faced their greatest challenge—Muslim invasion from Africa. In 711, a force of Muslim Berbers led by Tarik defeated a Visigothic army led by King Roderick (r. 710–711) and killed the king. Visigothic resistance continued, but the kingdom was conquered by the Muslims by 725. Although conquered by the Muslims, the influence of the Visigothic kingdom lasted long beyond its disappearance.

See also Aëtius; Agriculture; Alaric; Arianism; Attila the Hun; Augustine of Hippo, St.; Brunhilde; Clovis; Galla Placidia; Galswintha; Gregory of Tours; Hadrianople, Battle of; Hermenegild; Huns; Isidore of Seville; Jordanes; Law and Law Codes: Leovigild; Merovingian Dynasty; Ostrogoths; Reccared I; Stilicho, Flavius; Theodoric the Great; Ulfilas

Bibliography

Bonnassie, Pierre. "Society and Mentalities in Visigothic Spain." In *From Slavery to Feudalism in South-Western Europe,* trans. Jean Birrell. Cambridge: Cambridge University Press, 1991, pp. 60–103.

Bury, John B. *The Invasions of Europe by the Barbarians.* New York: W. W. Norton, 1967.

Goffart, Walter. *Barbarians and Romans* A.D. *418–584: The Techniques of Accommodation.* Princeton: Princeton University Press, 1980.

Heather, Peter. *The Goths.* Oxford: Blackwell, 1996.

Isidore of Seville. *History of the Goths, Vandals, and Suevi.* Trans. Kenneth B. Wolf. 1990.

James, Edward, ed. *Visigothic Spain: New Approaches.* Oxford: Clarendon, 1980.

Jordanes. *The Gothic History of Jordanes.* Trans. Charles C. Mierow. New York: Barnes and Noble, 1985.

King, Peter D. *Law and Society in the Visigothic Kingdom.* Cambridge: Cambridge University

Press 1972.

Thompson, Edward A. *The Visigoths in the Time of Ulfila.* Oxford: Clarendon, 1966.

———. *The Goths in Spain.* Oxford: Clarendon, 1969.

Wolfram, Herwig. *History of the Goths.* Trans. Thomas J. Dunlap. Berkeley: University of California Press, 1988.

———. *The Roman Empire and Its Germanic Peoples.* Trans. Thomas J. Dunlap. Berkeley: University of California Press, 1997.

Wood, Ian. *The Merovingian Kingdoms, 450–751.* London: Longman, 1994.

Vortigern (fl. 425–455)

King of the Britons, who assumed power after the Roman withdrawal from the island. According to an early tradition recorded by the *Anglo-Saxon Chronicle,* Bede, and Gildas, Vortigern invited the Saxon kings Hengist and Horsa to England as mercenaries. His invitation led to the eventual conquest of Britons by the Anglo-Saxons, even though the king of the Britons had invited the two leaders to aid the Britons against the Picts and Scots. According to the sixth-century historian Gildas, a great hero arose in the wake of these invasions; that hero was later believed to be King Arthur.

After the last of the Roman armies left the island of England in the early fifth century, the people of the island were forced to find a means to defend themselves from the attacks of the less civilized Picts and Scots to the north. They sought aid from the emperor Honorius in 410, but got little more than the approval to organize their own defense. In about 425, a leader of the Roman-British aristocracy, Vortigern, arose to take control of part of the country and provide for its defense. Called a tyrant or king by Gildas and other early sources, Vortigern acted as a traditional Roman military governor and struggled to protect the Britons from the invaders. He may have attempted to secure aid from the western emperor by writing a letter to the general Aëtius, but any efforts in that re-

gard failed. He did find allies in the Saxon leaders Hengist and Horsa, who, according to the *Anglo-Saxon Chronicle,* were invited during the reigns of the emperors Marcian and Valentinian III, probably between 449 and 456. According to the early sources, the Saxons arrived in three longboats on the eastern side of the island, at a place called Ipwinesfleet according to the *Anglo-Saxon Chronicle,* and they immediately waged war against the Picts and Scots.

Vortigern's plan at first seemed a good one; the Saxons enjoyed great success against the northern invaders at the British king's direction. But Hengist and Horsa soon sent word back to their homeland of their victories and need for help to secure further victory over their enemies. They also informed their kin that "the country was fertile and the Britons cowardly" (Bede 1981, 56). The Saxons were soon joined by large numbers of Germans, including more Saxons and Angles and Jutes. They then turned against the Britons and Vortigern and proceeded to conquer the Britons. According to the *Anglo-Saxon Chronicle,* Vortigern took up the sword against his former allies, and in a battle in 455 Horsa was killed. But despite this loss and continued wars with Vortigern, the Saxons took control of much of the kingdom.

Vortigern's fate is uncertain, but his legacy, according to the early sources, is certain. The king was blamed for the conquest of England by the Anglo-Saxons. For Gildas, the king was a proud tyrant whose unwise rule welcomed the conquerors in. Bede developed the earlier accounts of the progress of the Angles, Saxons, and Jutes, noting that it was the sinfulness of the Britons that brought on God's judgment in the conquest by the mercenaries hired by Vortigern.

See also Aëtius; *Anglo-Saxon Chronicle;* Anglo-Saxons; Bede; Gildas; Hengist and Horsa; Honorius; King Arthur

Bibliography
Bede. *Ecclesiastical History of the English People with Bede's Letter to Egbert and Cuthbert's Letter on the*

Death of Bede. Trans. Leo Sherley-Price. Harmondsworth, UK: Penguin, 1991.

Blair, Peter Hunter. *The World of Bede.* Cambridge: Cambridge University Press, 1990.

Gildas. *The Ruin of Britain and Other Works.* Ed. and trans. Michael Winterbottom. London: Phillimore, 1978.

Howe, Nicholas. *Migration and Mythmaking in Anglo-Saxon England.* New Haven: Yale University Press, 1989.

Sawyer, Peter H. *From Roman Britain to Norman England.* 2d ed. London and New York: Routledge, 1998.

Stenton, Frank M. *Anglo-Saxon England.* 3d ed. Oxford: Clarendon, 1971.

Whitelock, Dorothy, ed. *The Anglo-Saxon Chronicle.* Westport, CT: Greenwood, 1986.

Vouillé, Battle of (507)

Major battle between the Merovingian king of the Franks, Clovis, and the Visigothic king in Spain, Alaric II, in 507. According to the tradition recorded by the sixth-century Frankish historian Gregory of Tours, Clovis waged the war as a sort of crusade to expel the Arian Visigoths from Gaul, and the battle came well after the conversion of Clovis to Catholic Christianity. Although the relationship between the time of Clovis's conversion and the battle is now open to question, it is certain that Clovis gained the victory over Alaric, who died in the battle, and that it was a key battle in one of the Frankish king's wars of expansion and conquest.

As recorded by Gregory of Tours in his history, Clovis desired to remove the Visigoths from Gaul because of their Arianism. He declared to his ministers that he could not bear the existence of the Visigoths in Gaul. He said further that the Franks should invade the region and that with God's help he would defeat the Visigoths and take over their territory. His followers agreed with the proposal, and the army marched toward Poitiers to meet the forces of Alaric II. Along the way, one of Clovis's soldiers took hay from the monastery of St. Martin of Tours, which the

king had expressly forbidden. Upon learning of this, Clovis killed the soldier in order to maintain the support of the powerful saint. The battle itself took place some ten miles from Poitiers, according to Gregory. The fighting included hand-to-hand combat and the exchange of volleys of javelins. The Visigoths fled the attack, and, Gregory wrote, "Clovis was the victor, for God was on his side" (153). Clovis killed Alaric while the Goths fled, but two Goths attacked and struck Clovis with their spears on each side. He was saved by his leather corselet; after the battle, he captured several cities and forced the Visigoths from Gaul.

Modern research, however, shows that both the events leading up to the battle and the battle itself were not so simple and clear-cut as Gregory portrayed them. At the very least, it has been argued that Clovis himself converted to Catholic Christianity only late in his life, or at least after the traditional date of 496, and that he was motivated by a number of factors other than crusading zeal when he attacked Alaric II. The two kings had long been in negotiations over a variety of issues, and previous battles had left the Franks defeated. Clovis had also been successful at times against the Visigoths, and he may have attacked in 507 to exact the payment of tribute he was owed by Alaric. There is clear indication that economic issues inspired Clovis. Moreover, there is no hint in Gregory of the international diplomacy that was involved, which was intended to keep Clovis out of southwestern Gaul. The Ostrogothic king of Italy and greatest power in the west, Theodoric the Great, had supported Alaric and threatened to intervene on his side should Clovis attack. Byzantine warships, however, limited Theodoric's ability to maneuver.

The battle itself probably involved a large Frankish infantry, with the king and his retainers mounted, and a Visigothic cavalry of inferior numbers. Rather than fleeing outright as Gregory reports, the skilled cavalry probably made several feigned retreats to trick the Franks, who were too stubborn and well trained to fall for the trick. Whether or not Clovis was responsible for the death of Alaric, at any rate the Visigothic king did die in the battle. Clovis may well have accepted baptism as a Catholic Christian following the victory, and religious motives should not be totally discounted; most likely they did play a role in Clovis's planning, even though not in the way that Gregory portrayed them.

See also Alaric II; Arianism; Clovis; Franks; Gregory of Tours; Merovingian Dynasty; Ostrogoths; Visigoths; Theodoric the Great

Bibliography

Geary, Patrick J. *Before France and Germany: The Creation and Transformation of the Merovingian World.* Oxford: Oxford University Press, 1988.

Gregory of Tours. *The History of the Franks.* Trans. Lewis Thorpe. Harmondsworth, UK: Penguin, 1974.

Wallace-Hadrill, J. M. *The Long-Haired Kings.* Toronto: Toronto University Press, 1982.

Wood, Ian. *The Merovingian Kingdoms, 450–751.* London: Longman, 1994.

Wolfram, Herwig. *History of the Goths.* Trans. Thomas J. Dunlap. Berkeley: University of California Press, 1988.

W

Weapons and Armor

One of the more important functions of late antique and early medieval nobles, kings, and emperors was as warriors or war leaders. As a result it was necessary for them to be properly outfitted for battle, and a certain standard in weapons and armor developed. The basic nature of military technology in barbarian Europe was established already in the pre-migration period among the barbarians themselves, as well as by the ancient Romans and others, and involved both offensive and defensive tools. Included in the armory of the barbarian warrior was some form of armor, a shield, thrusting weapons like spears and swords, axes, and bows and arrows. There was also a degree of specialization among the various peoples who invaded the empire.

The weapons used by the early medieval warrior were the descendants of the pre-migration Germanic warrior and his ancient Roman counterpart. Although the tactics employed by Germans and Romans in the use of their weapons differed, the basic outlines of the armaments of the ancient Roman and barbarian soldier were essentially the same. Of course, there was some diversity in the armories of the Romans and of the various Germanic peoples. In fact, it is sometimes suggested that some of the peoples who invaded the Roman Empire were given their names

from the weapons that were unique to them. The Saxons were so called because of the long knife, the *saxo* or *seax,* that they used, and the Angles were known for their barbed spear, or *ango.* Similarly, the Huns were known for the *hunnica,* a type of whip, and the Franks for their throwing axe, the *frankisca.*

Along with the various "national" weapons, noble warriors carried a basic complement of implements of destruction, including a sword or a long knife, a spear, an axe, and a bow and arrows. The poorer foot soldiers carried a lesser complement of weapons, which included a spear, shield, and bow and arrows. The difference in weaponry carried by the noble, usually cavalry, warriors and the infantrymen was due in part to expense. Indeed, outfitting a typical noble warrior was quite a costly proposition. The average cost of a helmet was six solidi, and the cost for a sword and scabbard was about seven solidi, the equivalent of six or seven months' wages for the average soldier, or six or seven cows. Clearly, the fully armed and armored warrior in barbarian Europe was usually a wealthy and powerful figure.

The sword was usually one of two kinds: a blade of some three feet, rather than the shorter Roman sword, which measured roughly two feet in length, or the shorter *saxo.* The long sword, or *spata,* was a double-edged blade suitable for thrusting and slashing and general destruction, and the *saxo* was a single-edged blade that was lighter, more easily wielded, and could even be thrown. In the Carolingian age, however, these two types of sword were merged into one, as the *spata* was transformed from a blade of parallel edges that ended in a short point to a blade that gradually tapered to a point. Carolingian swords were also engraved and decorated with gold, silver, or ivory handles, and were so highly prized for their quality that Charlemagne and other Carolingian rulers sought to restrict their export.

The spear or lance was another popular and important weapon; it was such a valuable part of a soldier's armory that Carolingian legislation required monasteries to provide lances as an annual gift to the king. The least expensive weapon in the early medieval armory, it could be used in various ways by either the infantry or cavalry soldier. This weapon, made of ash and sometimes fitted with a metal point, could be used as either a throwing or a thrusting weapon, and contemporary illustrations depict its use in both ways. Throwing spears continued to be used by soldiers as the early Middle Ages progressed, but the lance gradually became primarily a thrusting weapon used by both cavalry and infantry. As a thrusting weapon, the lance could be thrust downward in a stabbing motion or could be thrust upward to knock an opponent off his horse. It was once argued that during the Carolingian period the lance was held under the arm of the mounted warrior who, held in place by a stirrup, could use the full power of the horse against his enemy, creating a force of mounted shock troops. Although the idea is attractive, there is little evidence, either from contemporary illustrations or from archeological discoveries, to support this theory.

Warriors in barbarian Europe were equipped with two other important weapons. The axe was used during this period as a throwing weapon or a slashing weapon, and it was often double-edged and appeared with either a short or long handle. Bows and arrows were also used and were an essential component of the foot soldiers' armory. Carolingian legislation required that infantry troops carry an extra string and twelve arrows as part of their equipment. Throughout the early Middle Ages the bow was a necessary part of the infantry's weaponry, and arrows have been found in the graves of the Merovingian Franks and other barbarian peoples. The Lombards were noted for their use of a composite reflex bow made of wood, horn, and sinew that was glued together to form a more flexible bow, which gave the string more pull. Even though a short, simple bow was commonly used by the Merovingians and Carolingians archers, it was gradually replaced, beginning in the ninth century, by the composite bow.

Along with a wide range of weapons, barbarian warriors of late antiquity and the early Middle Ages had an extensive complement of body armor. Indeed, Charlemagne appeared as the "iron Charles" to his opponents because of his strong will and body armor. The early medieval soldier used a mixture of body armor, helmet, and shield, with the noble warrior possessing more elaborate and expensive defensive armament. Perhaps the most important piece of protective gear was body armor, which appeared in a variety of styles, but was usually called either *brunia* or *lorica* in contemporary sources. One style, generally preferred by the poorer soldiers, was the so-called *lorica squamata*. This was a cloth-covered suit that was popular because it offered protection to the soldier and was relatively affordable for the common foot soldier. Better known was the *lorica hamata,* a suit of mail that offered better protections but was fabulously expensive and therefore affordable only to the wealthier nobles in the army. A shirt of mail was made of interlocking iron rings of the same size and provided its owner great protection in battle. There are also examples of leg armor made of iron, and the hands and arms were protected by armored gloves and armguards. After about

800, the hauberk, or *halsbergen* (German: neck guard) became a common piece of body armor. This was a caped hood that was worn over the head, under the helmet, and either over or under the mail shirt to provide protection for the neck.

Along with armor to protect the body, early medieval combatants wore helmets, which were usually conical and made of several possible materials, to protect their heads and faces. The most common helmet was the *spangenhelm,* so called because its design involved six or more metal strips *(spangen)* that joined the headband to a plate of metal. The framework strips of the helmet were usually of bronze or iron, but a fully iron helmet was rare. The framework was then filled with metal or horn plates. The spangenhelm common in the early Middle Ages was most likely based on an original model used by the Huns, and the Ostrogoths designed a distinctive spangenhelm, used by the Ostrogothic kings as a diplomatic gift for other rulers.

The final piece of equipment used for protection by all soldiers in barbarian Europe was the shield, which was also probably the least expensive of all offensive and defensive weapons possessed by cavalry and infantry soldiers. Despite its low cost, the shield was a very important piece of equipment, as Carolingian legislation reveals. Charlemagne required that shield makers live in all regions of the empire, and Louis the Pious and Louis the German required that some monasteries include shields in their annual gifts to the ruler. And makers and merchants of shields often accompanied armies when they campaigned. The shield itself was used to protect the soldier from his enemy's blows, and according to contemporary records, it could even protect a soldier from a javelin. The shield was usually made of a sturdy wood and covered with leather, which would keep the shield in one piece even after the wood split under the force of heavy blows. The shield was reinforced with iron or other metal strips and rivets, and it measured roughly three feet in diameter and offered protection from the thigh to the shoulder. Shields might be round or oval; the shield was always concave and had a grip along one side so that it could be held. Some shields had a pointed boss, which allowed the shield to be used as an offensive weapon and thrust against an attacker.

See also Anglo-Saxons; Carolingian Dynasty; Charlemagne; Franks; Huns; Lombards; Louis the German; Louis the Pious; Merovingian Dynasty; Ostrogoths; Poitiers, Battle of

Bibliography

Bachrach, Bernard S. "Charles Martel, Mounted Shock Combat, the Stirrup, and Feudalism." *Studies in Medieval and Renaissance History* 7 (1970): 47–75.

———. *Merovingian Military Organization, 481–751.* Minneapolis: University of Minnesota Press, 1972.

———. *Early Carolingian Warfare: Prelude to Empire.* Philadelphia: University of Pennsylvania Press, 2001.

Contamine, Philippe. *War in the Middle Ages.* Trans. Michael Jones. Oxford: Basil Blackwell, 1984.

Coupland, Simon. "Carolingian Arms and Armor in the Ninth Century." *Viator: Medieval and Renaissance Studies* 21 (1990): 29–50.

DeVries, Kelly. *Medieval Military Technology.* Peterborough, Ont.: Broadview, 1992.

Ganshof, François Louis. *Frankish Institutions under Charlemagne.* Trans. Bryce Lyon and Mary Lyon. Providence, RI: Brown University Press, 1968.

Martin, Paul. *Arms and Armour from the 9th to the 17th Century.* Trans. René North. Rutland: Tuttle, 1968.

Verbruggen, Jan F. *The Art of Warfare in Western Europe during the Middle Ages: From the Eighth Century to 1340.* 2d ed. Trans. Sumner Willard and S. C. M. Southern. Woodbridge, UK: Boydell, 1997.

White, Lynn, Jr. *Medieval Technology and Social Change.* Oxford: Oxford University Press, 1964.

Wearmouth

See Benedict Biscop

Widukind (d. c. 807)

Westphalian nobleman who led a serious rebellion against Charlemagne. Widukind managed to rally the pagan Saxons against Carolingian religious and political expansion. The severity of his rebellion threatened Carolingian efforts and caused great difficulties for Charlemagne. Widukind's eventual conversion to Christianity was a key moment in the long Carolingian struggle to conquer and convert the Saxon people.

Shortly after his rise to power as king and the death of his brother, Charlemagne began the conquest of Saxony. Although it began as a response to cross-border raiding by the Saxons, the campaign in Saxony quickly turned into a more serious venture. Indeed, Charlemagne began to look upon the conquest and conversion to Christianity of the pagan Saxons as part of his responsibility as king. The conquest of Saxony ended by taking some thirty years to complete (772–804) and involving some of Charlemagne's most terrible actions, including the deportation of large numbers of Saxons from their homeland to the heart of Frankish territory. The Saxons themselves were poorly organized and lacked any unifying institutions, which made the process all the more difficult, especially since they were intent on preserving their independence and religious traditions.

The Saxons struggled to prevent Charlemagne from conquering them, and the most effective leader against Carolingian incursion into Saxony was Widukind. In 778 Widukind, taking advantage of Charlemagne's absence from Saxony to campaign in Spain, led a massive revolt against Carolingian authority. Unifying the Saxons for the moment, Widukind managed to retake important territory along the Rhine River and even planned to attack the important Carolingian monastery of Fulda. Responding with great urgency, Charlemagne returned from Spain to restore order in the region. His generals waged two further campaigns in 779 and 780 to quell the rebellion. In 782, Charlemagne held a great assembly to organize the region and establish religious institutions there. According to the *Royal Frankish Annals,* many Saxons participated in this assembly, but Widukind did not participate because he remained in rebellion.

After Charlemagne's return to his kingdom, Widukind led the Saxons in revolt again and routed the armies established by Charlemagne in Saxony. The churches and monasteries established by the Carolingian king were destroyed, and the priests and monks were attacked and killed. In a great rage, Charlemagne returned and massacred 4,500 Saxons at Verdun in an effort to suppress the rebellion. His efforts failed, and Widukind and his followers struggled on. Charlemagne also issued his first Saxon Capitulary at that time, which sought to impose Christianity on the Saxons by force. Charlemagne's continued pressure on the Saxons in the mid-780s, however, wore Widukind down, and in 785 he submitted to his Carolingian rival. In 785, Widukind and his son accepted baptism. Although the conquest of Saxony took another twenty years to complete, the submission and conversion of Widukind was a significant step in the process and ended the most serious challenge to Charlemagne's conquest.

See also Carolingian Dynasty; Charlemagne; Franks; Saxon Capitularies

Bibliography

Collins, Roger. *Charlemagne.* Toronto: University of Toronto Press, 1998.

Einhard and Notker the Stammerer. *Two Lives of Charlemagne.* Trans. Lewis Thorpe. Harmondsworth, UK: Penguin, 1981.

Fichtenau, Heinrich. *The Carolingian Empire.* Trans. Peter Munz. Toronto: University of Toronto Press, 1979.

Halphen, Louis. *Charlemagne and the Carolingian Empire.* Trans. Giselle de Nie. Amsterdam: North-Holland, 1977.

McKitterick, Rosamond. *The Frankish Kingdoms under the Carolingians, 751–987.* London: Longman 1983.

Riché, Pierre. *The Carolingians: A Family Who Forged Europe.* Trans. Michael Idomir Allen.

Philadelphia: University of Pennsylvania Press, 1993.

Scholz, Bernhard Walter, trans. *Carolingian Chronicles: Royal Frankish Annals and Nithard's History*. Ann Arbor: University of Michigan Press, 1972.

Witenagemot

General council of the Anglo-Saxon kings, also known as the *Witan* (Anglo-Saxon: wise men), that met to witness royal charters and other enactments of the king. The witenagemot (meeting of wise men) was made up of the leading nobles of the realm along with the leading bishops, abbots, and priests of the kingdom. The members of the council, however, were a relatively fluid group who came when called by the king.

Although it was clearly an important institution in Anglo-Saxon England, the witenagemot's origins remain unclear and are known primarily from charter evidence, which becomes less available after the reign of Alfred the Great. No longer identified as the descendant of a Germanic institution or the precursor of the English Parliament, the witenagemot most likely evolved out of the king's need for advice and was based on his ability to call nobles and ecclesiastics to court. The witenagemot was a mobile assembly that came together before the king as he traveled throughout the kingdom. Members of the assembly were generally high-ranking clergy and nobility; thegns also participated, but only when the king's court was in the thegn's territory. When meeting in the council, the nobles and churchmen came not as representatives of any specific group, but as advisors to the king who knew the law and needs of the land. They worked together with the king to ensure that law and justice was executed throughout the realm. Although he could rule without the members of the witenagemot, the wise king considered consulting with them valuable and was careful to call the council to advise with him. The council did not meet at specific intervals, but was called to meet when the need arose, when the king needed its help to resolve some problem at hand.

See also Alfred the Great; Anglo-Saxons; Thegn

Bibliography
Loyn, Henry R. *Anglo-Saxon England and the Norman Conquest*. 2d ed. London: Longmans, 1991.
———. *The Governance of Anglo-Saxon England, 500–1087*. London: Edward Arnold, 1984.
Lyon, Bryce. *A Constitutional and Legal History of Medieval England*. 2d ed. Palo Alto, CA: Stanford University Press, 1980.
Stenton, Frank M. *Anglo-Saxon England*. 3d ed. Oxford: Clarendon, 1971.

Witigis (fl. 536–540)

Ostrogothic king in Italy from 536 to 540 who led his people against the Byzantine armies sent by Justinian to conquer the peninsula and restore imperial rule there. Although not of the royal line of Theodoric the Great, Witigis was a successful general, whose prominence led to his election as king. He adopted an aggressive strategy against the Byzantine armies led by Belisarius and took the offensive against Byzantine territory outside of Italy. He also pursued diplomatic ties with the Merovingian Franks and the Lombards. His efforts, however, proved fruitless, and he eventually succumbed to Belisarius, whom the Goths hoped to elect as emperor.

On the death of Theodoric's last heir, Theodohad, in 536, the Goths turned to Witigis, who had enjoyed some success in the campaigns against the armies of the Eastern Empire. Theodohad's failure to save the city of Rome led to his death, and the Goths hoped to have someone worthy of Theodoric to take the throne. Witigis, not of the royal line, proclaimed himself a member of Theodoric's family because the deeds he and the great king performed were of similar stature. To confirm his position on the throne, however, Witigis married Amalaswintha's daughter Matasuntha. His own propaganda to the Goths never stressed this marriage, but he did inform Emperor Justinian of the marriage. The new king also suggested that Justinian's purpose in the war, avenging the murder of Amalaswintha, had been fulfilled by the murder of Theodohad and the marriage, which restored Amalaswintha's line to the throne. His argument, however, did not persuade Justinian, and both the emperor and the new Gothic king were fully committed to war.

Shortly after his election as king in late 536, Witigis moved his Gothic armies south to meet Belisarius, who had recently taken possession of the city of Rome. Along with his march on Rome, Witigis secured a peace treaty with the Merovingian king of the Franks that guaranteed that the Franks would not invade Italy and take advantage of the uncertain situation. He also launched a campaign against the Byzantines in Dalmatia. Indeed, Witigis took the initiative in the hopes of ending the invasion of the Byzantines. Upon reaching Rome, Witigis began a siege of the city that lasted almost a year in the hopes of capturing it outright or forcing Belisarius into open battle. Over the next year, the Goths launched repeated assaults on the city walls, often leading to numerous casualties on their side. The Byzantine forces suffered as well, although not only from Gothic attacks but also from shortage of food and the spread of disease. Attempts to find a diplomatic solution failed, and the arrival of Eastern Roman armies forced Witigis to accept a truce in late 537.

Despite his aggressive efforts, Witigis was doomed to failure, and events began to turn against him by early 538. The Dalmatian campaign failed, and Belisarius, no longer hampered by the siege, decided to take the initiative and ordered a cavalry force to attack a nearby town where the families of the Gothic soldiers resided. His plan succeeded; Witigis was forced to break off the siege and returned to the royal city of Ravenna. He then faced a series of attacks by Belisarius and other forces. The Byzantine general began a march north from Rome to defeat his rival. The Alemanni raided northern Italy, and the devastation contributed to famine conditions on the peninsula. Even worse, an imperial army under the command of Narses arrived to aid Belisarius and counter Gothic numeric superiority. But the arrival of Narses offered the Gothic king a glimmer of hope because of the rivalry that existed between Narses and Belisarius, which often paralyzed the Byzantine war effort.

Witigis in 538 and 539 came to the realization that he would not overcome the Byzantines militarily and sought to win through diplomatic negotiations. Here too, however, Witigis was unsuccessful. Indeed, his earlier treaty with the Franks did not prevent the Merovingian king Theudebert from raiding northern Italy in 539. The Goths no longer trusted the Franks and refused further offers of assistance from them. Witigis's efforts to establish an alliance with the Lombards also proved a failure. And as his diplomatic initiatives came to nothing, Witigis faced a resurgent Belisarius, who managed to unite the Roman armies in 539 and lay siege to Ravenna. By 540, the end of Witigis was near, as the Goths started to abandon him. But Ravenna was nearly impregnable, and so the king began negotiations, at first with other barbarian peoples and with the Persians, and then finally with Constantinople. He hoped for a settlement and was willing to accept terms from Justinian. But Belisarius seemed unwilling to come to terms and may have given the Goths the impression that he was willing to accept the imperial dignity from them. The Goths were willing to elevate him to the rank of emperor, and there is some possibility that he seriously considered it. Ultimately, however, Belisarius remained loyal to Justinian, and accepted the surrender of Witigis, entering Ravenna in May 540. The reign of Witigis had come to an end, but the Goths continued the struggle against the Byzantine invaders under the next Gothic king, Totila.

See also Alemanni; Amalaswintha; Belisarius; Franks; Justinian; Lombards; Merovingian Dynasty; Narses; Ostrogoths; Theodoric the Great; Totila

Bibliography

Browning, Robert. *Justinian and Theodora*. Rev. ed. London: Thames and Hudson, 1987.

Burns, Thomas. *A History of the Ostrogoths*. Bloomington: University of Indiana Press, 1984.

Bury, John B. *History of the Later Roman Empire: From the Death of Theodosius I to the Death of Justinian*. 2 vols. 1923. Reprint, New York: Dover, 1959.

Cassiodorus. *The Variae of Magnus Aurelius Cassiodorus*. Trans. S. J. B. Barnish. Liverpool, UK: Liverpool University Press, 1992.

Heather, Peter. *The Goths*. Oxford: Blackwell, 1996.

Procopius. *History of the Wars*. Trans H. B. Dewing. 1979.

Wolfram, Herwig. *History of the Goths*. Trans. Thomas J. Dunlap. Berkeley: University of California Press, 1988.

———. *The Roman Empire and Its Germanic Peoples*. Trans. Thomas J. Dunlap. Berkeley: University of California Press, 1997.

Women

The place of women in late antique and early medieval society was a complex one; women used a variety of strategies to negotiate their way at a time when their legal status was often low. Modern understanding of these strategies and the place of women in barbarian Europe is made difficult by the nature of the sources, which are often limited to the more traditional histories of government and battles. That notwithstanding, a variety of sources—collections of laws, contemporary literature, religious documents, histories—properly approached can provide insights into the lives of women of the time. The vast majority of women, it can safely be said, simply labored. They worked the fields with their peasant brothers, fathers, and husbands, raised children, and tended the family. The small minority, about whom most can be known, also tended to the family, one of the primary duties of all the women of barbarian Europe, but these women also had the opportunity to exercise power as queens and nobles. Furthermore, they could have recourse to a life of religion and often founded or headed communities of religious men and women. Although their history can sometimes be difficult to discern, women in the late antiquity and the early Middle Ages played an important role in society.

The earliest literary record of barbarian women was provided by the Roman historian and moralist, Tacitus (c. 56–c. 120), whose *Germania* provides an account of the status and duties of barbarian women prior to the migration period and its extensive contacts with the Roman Empire. According to Tacitus, Germanic women were especially esteemed and respected in society. They were thought to possess special holiness and powers of prophecy, and were often asked their advice, which was often heeded, on a wide range of matters. Tacitus also notes that women rallied their warrior husbands and fathers in battle by baring their breasts and "making them realize the imminent prospect of enslavement" (108). The Roman historian also provides details concerning the domestic life of women among the pre-migration Germanic tribes. He notes that their dress differs from that of men in two important ways. Women wear sleeveless outer garments of linen decorated in purple, which expose their arms and shoulders. Tacitus also notes the important role that women play in marriage and family among the Germans. Marital customs were well defined, according to Tacitus, and involved a specific exchange of gifts between husband and wife that defined their relationship as one of partnership and mutual labor. Indeed, as noted in the *Germania,* the gifts included oxen and weapons, indicating that women were involved in farming and warfare. Marriages were strictly monogamous, and women were severely punished for adultery. Women also were responsible for nursing and raising children, and thus played a central role in all aspects of family life.

Unfortunately, Tacitus's description is as much an indictment of Roman values and decadent family life as it is a picture of the status of Germanic women. Consequently, his assessment must be treated cautiously and is perhaps best understood as commentary on Roman social life. Nevertheless, although his view is colored by his attitudes toward Roman society, it is not without merit and at the very least provides a rough outline of the areas in which women did play a role. In work, family, politics and war, and religious life, women in late antiquity and the early Middle Ages exercised some, often considerable, influence.

The fundamental role for women in barbarian Europe was that of wife and mother, which was true no matter what social rank they held. Their importance in marriage and family was clearly outlined in the numerous legal codes that were compiled throughout the early Middle Ages. Notably, the Salic law defined the value of men and women in society and established different values for women depending upon their age and ability to bear children. One section noted that if a pregnant woman was struck, the fine was 28,000 denars; if a woman of childbearing age was struck, the fine was 24,000 denars; and if a woman past the age childbearing was struck, the fine was only 8,000 denars. In the laws of King Alfred the Great, a fine was assessed for both mother and child if a pregnant woman was killed, and in earlier Anglo-Saxons laws the amount of inheritance a woman was owed from her husband's family was determined by the bearing of children. Moreover, during the Merovingian and early Carolingian dynasties women used childbearing as a means to power. Women of lower status at times married and bore children to powerful figures in the kingdom. And some women, who were not married but still bore children, enjoyed the prestige of having children with nobles and kings. Merovingian queens especially were empowered by the birth of sons, and the their prestige as mothers of kings was even greater than their status as wives of kings. Indeed, as late as the age of Charlemagne, the children from illegitimate unions were given

rank and status, which enhanced the prestige of their mothers. Clearly, the most important duty of women was to produce children; in the higher social ranks, bearing children was essential for preserving the dynasty and for use later in marriage alliances.

Although the primary duties of women in late antiquity and the early Middle Ages involved the family, high-ranking women could, and often did, exploit their position. In all the successor kingdoms, women played an important political role. Indeed, even in the Roman and Byzantine Empires, women exercised great influence and direct political authority. Constantine's mother, St. Helena, was an important figure in the church during her son's reign and was an influential pilgrim to Jerusalem, where she discovered the True Cross (believed to be the cross on which Christ was crucified). Theodora, Justinian's wife, was the emperor's partner throughout their marriage. She encouraged Justinian to stand his ground during the Nika Revolt in 532, played a key role in Justinian's plans to reconquer Italy, and helped her husband manage the divided church in the empire. Her contemporary, and some would say victim, Amalaswintha, daughter of the Ostrogothic king Theodoric the Great, assumed the regency for her son and continued to be a powerful figure in Ostrogothic Italy until her murder by rival Gothic nobles who opposed her pro-Roman policy. In Lombard Italy, Queen Theudelinde was the real power in the kingdom for three generations, marrying two successive kings and acting as regent for her son. She introduced Catholic Christianity to the kingdom and was a close friend of Pope Gregory I, called the Great.

In the Frankish kingdoms of the Merovingian and Carolingian dynasties, queens also influenced politics. From the very beginning of the Merovingian dynasty, women played a key role in the direction the kingdom took. Clotilda, a Burgundian Catholic princess, according to the sixth-century historian of the Franks Gregory of Tours, convinced her husband Clovis (r. 481–511), the great Merovingian king of the Franks, to convert to Catholic Christianity. Also, according to Gregory, she persuaded one of her sons to invade and conquer the Burgundians in revenge for the reigning king's murder of her father. In subsequent generations, queens continued to play a central role in the political life of the kingdom, and perhaps the two greatest figures were Brunhilde and Fredegund. The career of Fredegund reveals the fluid nature of marriage and rank in the Merovingian kingdom. She may have been a slave woman, and was surely lowborn, yet she married a king and bore him an heir, Chlotar II, who went on to reign in the early seventh century, restoring the dynasty's greatness. Both Brunhilde and Fredegund, furthermore, employed ruthless measures to guarantee their own power and that of their husbands and especially their sons. They indulged in a terrible blood feud during which each sought to kill the other or the husbands, sons, and supporters of her opponent. During the last decade of the sixth and first decade of the seventh century, Brunhilde was the real power in the kingdom.

In the Carolingian period, marriage customs changed, and women had fewer opportunities to rule as Brunhilde and Fredegund did. Nonetheless, leading Carolingian women managed to influence affairs of state. The widow of Pippin II, Plectrude, seized control of her husband's treasury and nearly managed to take control of the kingdom before being defeated by Pippin's son Charles Martel. Bertrada, the widow of Pippin III, called the Short, exercised great influence after her husband's death and remained an esteemed figure during her son's reign. She negotiated a marriage alliance with the Lombards for her son Charlemagne and struggled to keep the peace between her sons Charlemagne and Carloman. Charlemagne married Fastrada, the daughter of a powerful east Frankish count, in order to gain political influence in the eastern part of the kingdom; he may have kept his daughters close by his side, refusing to let them marry, so that their husbands would not use their connections to the royal line as justification for revolt. The wife of Louis the Pious, Judith, actively promoted her son, Charles the Bald, and was identified by Louis's sons by his first wife as the cause for disruption in the empire. And the noblewoman, Dhuoda, wrote an important manual for her son to teach him the proper behavior at court and as a Christian nobleman. Although women did not often have formal, legal powers, their close proximity to kings, emperors, and other powerful figures provided them the opportunity to influence affairs and even rule themselves.

As Tacitus noted, pre-migration Germanic women were esteemed for their powers of prophecy. In the mid-ninth century, the prophet Theoda gained a significant following when she preached the coming of the end of the world and called for religious reform. She was quickly suppressed by the authorities, and there were few true female prophets in late antiquity and the early Middle Ages. Women did, however, play a key role in religious life, just as they often did in political life. Indeed, many of the same women who influenced politics shaped religious affairs in their kingdoms. Theodora sponsored and protected Monophysite monks and priests and even established a special chapel in the imperial palace where they officiated for her. Theudelinde warmed relations between the Arian Lombards and the Catholic church in Italy, and laid the foundation for the ultimate triumph of Catholic Christianity in the kingdom. According to Gregory of Tours, Clotilda not only convinced Clovis to accept Catholic Christianity, and with him 3,000 of his followers, but also entered a convent after her husband's death.

Brunhilde, despite her violent struggle with Fregedund and hostility toward the Irish saint Columban, supported the mission to England of Augustine of Canterbury and encouraged reforms in the church at the suggestion of Gregory the Great. Moreover, other royal women, including Balthild, wife of the seventh-century Merovingian king Clovis II, and Radegund, a sixth-century

Merovingian queen, founded or led communities of religious women. Indeed, one way that queens and aristocratic women could exercise power and influence was through the foundation or endowment of monasteries, for men or women. And the religious life was highly esteemed even by the most ruthless of kings. In their communities, royal women could wield great power over the other nuns, and they also gained power in the wider world because of the economic strength of their house. Moreover, religious women throughout the early Middle Ages ruled over the unique institution of the double monastery—a community of monks and nuns ruled over by an abbess. Although often without much legal authority, women nonetheless played an important role in the political, religious, and social life of late antiquity and the early Middle Ages.

See also Alfred the Great; Amalaswintha; Anglo-Saxons; Augustine of Canterbury, St.; Bertrada; Brunhilde; Carolingian Dynasty; Charlemagne; Charles the Bald; Charles Martel; Clotilda, St.; Columban, St.; Dhuoda; Fredegund; Gregory I the Great, Pope; Gregory of Tours; Judith; Justinian; Lombards; Louis the Pious; Marriage; Merovingian Dynasty; Ostrogoths; Plectrude; Radegund; Salic Law; Theodora; Theodoric the Great; Theudelinde

Bibliography

Cameron, Averil. *The Mediterranean World in Late Antiquity*, A.D. *395–600*. New York: Routledge, 1993.

Clark, Gillian. *Women in Late Antiquity: Pagan and Christian Lifestyles.* Oxford: Clarendon, 1993.

Gies, Frances, and Joseph Gies. *Marriage and Family in the Middle Ages.* New York: Harper and Row, 1987.

Gregory of Tours. *History of the Franks.* Trans. Lewis Thorpe. Harmondsworth, UK: Penguin, 1974.

Kirshner, Julius, and Suzanne Wemple, eds. *Women of the Medieval World.* Oxford: Basil Blackwell, 1985.

Leyser, Henrietta. *Medieval Women: A Social History of Women in England, 450–1500.* New York: St. Martin's, 1995.

Schulenburg, Jane Tibbetts. *Forgetful of Their Sex: Female Sanctity and Society, ca. 500–1100.* Chicago: University of Chicago Press, 1998.

Shahar, Shulamith. *The Fourth Estate: A History of Women in the Middle Ages.* New York: Routledge, 1990.

Tacitus. *The Agricola and the Germania.* Trans. H. Mattingly, rev. trans. S. A. Handford. Harmondsworth, UK: Penguin, 1982.

Thiébaux, Marcelle, trans. *The Writings of Medieval Women: An Anthology.* New York: Garland, 1994.

Wemple, Suzanne. *Women in Frankish Society: Marriage and the Cloister, 500 to 900.* Philadelphia: University of Pennsylvania Press, 1981.

Wulfstan

See Anglo-Saxons

Z

Zachary, St. (d. 752)

A central figure in the political revolution in the Frankish kingdom, Zachary, or Zacharias, was pope during an important period in the development of the papacy (r. 741–752). He was actively involved with diplomatic affairs during his reign, frequently attending to negotiations with representatives of the Byzantine Empire, the Franks, and the Lombards. He sought to limit Lombard aggression during his reign, but is remembered most for his relations with the powerful Carolingian family. Indeed, it was Zachary's response to a famous question from Pippin that provided the Carolingian with the justification to depose the last of the Merovingian kings. Zachary was also in close correspondence with the great Anglo-Saxon missionary St. Boniface and made an important translation into Greek of the Dialogues of Gregory the Great that was well known in the Byzantine Empire.

Born to a Greek family living in Calabria, possibly in 679, Zachary was eventually ordained a deacon and priest and may have participated in an important church council in Rome in 732 held by his predecessor Gregory III. A portrait in Rome portrays him as a thin and small person, balding and with a reserved air. According to his official biographer, Zachary was "gentle and gracious, adorned with all kindness, a lover of the clergy and all the Roman people" (Davis 1992, 35). He was also "slow to anger and quick to have pity, repaying no one evil for evil, nor taking even merited vengeance, but dutiful and compassionate to everyone" (35). Clearly these virtues, even if they are only the standard traits attributed to all popes by their biographers, would serve the pope well in his often difficult relations with the Lombard rulers of Italy.

Although no longer a threat to Rome because of their Arianism, the now Catholic Lombard kings in Italy still pursued the dream of unifying the peninsula under their authority. Zachary faced this problem almost immediately upon ascending the papal throne, but did not feel bound to follow the policies of Pope Gregory III, who sought an alliance with the Carolingian Franks, and instead found new solutions to the problem. Indeed, he sought to establish a policy of conciliation with King Liutprand (r. 712–744). Liutprand had advanced on the independent southern Lombard duchy of Spoleto. Zachary broke with the duke, who had refused to return Roman territory to the pope. Liutprand quickly brought the duke to heel, but he too was slow to return the territory to Rome. Zachary then went to the Lombard capital, Pavia, where he met the king and made his demands known. Liutprand was so taken by the courage and prestige of the pope that he returned several cities and other important territories to the papacy. He also provided an escort of his nobles to return Zachary to Rome. Although this worked out well for the pope, difficulties with Liutprand continued because the king did not feel bound to respect imperial territory in Italy. His attacks on Ravenna initiated a second papal visit, and again Liutprand made concessions to the pope.

The policy of conciliation toward the Lombards seemed to have born fruit for the papacy, and Zachary was able to continue the policy during the reign of Liutprand's successor, Ratchis (r. 744–749). Indeed, so impressed was Ratchis with the pope that he abandoned efforts to bring all of Italy under his authority and then abdicated and retired to a monastery. Unfortunately, Ratchis's successor, Aistulf (r. 749–756), was perhaps the most bloodthirsty and expansionistic of all the Lombard kings and was less open to Zachary. The pope's death in 752, however, meant that a resolution of the Lombard question would have to wait until the time of his successor. Zachary's relationship with the Lombards did bring a period of peace and stability for Italy and, especially, papal territories on the peninsula.

Zachary was also actively involved in affairs in the north, where important religious reforms and political change benefited from his rule. The great missionary, Boniface, was in frequent correspondence with Zachary, who guided and encouraged the missionary's activities in the Frankish kingdom and Saxony. Shortly after the pope ascended the throne, Boniface wrote Zachary professing his loyalty and submission to Rome. Boniface also organized the Frankish church and brought it more fully under the influence and authority of Rome. Zachary approved of Boniface's activities, confirmed three new bishoprics Boniface founded, and made Boniface the papal legate in the Frankish realm. The pope also adopted some of the reform initiatives of Boniface, and was in correspondence with the Carolingian mayors, Pippin and Carloman, concerning church councils and church reform in the kingdom.

The correspondence with Boniface and the Carolingian leaders led to the most famous moment of Zachary's reign. Pippin and Carloman, mayors of the palace, were the real powers in the kingdom, and the Merovingian king, Childeric III, served mainly as a figurehead. In 747, Zachary welcomed Carloman to the monastery of Monte Cassino, just north of Rome, after the Carolingian mayor had abdicated and taken monastic vows. Three years later, Pippin, as the sole real power in the Frankish kingdom, sent two high-ranking representatives to the pope with an important message. As the *Royal Frankish Annals* note, Pippin asked the pope "whether it was good or not that the kings of the Franks should wield no power" (Scholz 1972, 39). The pope responded that "it was better to call him king who had royal power than the one who did not" (39), and ordered that Pippin be made king. Having gained the answer he desired, Pippin deposed the last of the Merovingian kings and assumed the throne as the first Carolingian king. Zachary had provided Pippin with the justification and higher sanction that he needed to usurp the throne, thus surely strengthening the Carolingian's support for the papacy.

See also Aistulf; Anglo-Saxons; Arianism; Boniface, St.; Carloman, Mayor of the Palace; Carolingian Dynasty; Childeric III; Franks; Gregory I the Great, Pope; Gregory III, Pope; Liutprand; Lombards; Merovingian Dynasty; Pippin III, Called the Short; *Royal Frankish Annals*

Bibliography
Christie, Neil. *The Lombards.* Oxford: Blackwell, 1998.
Davis, Raymond, trans. *The Lives of the Eighth-Century Popes* (Liber Pontificalis): *The Ancient Biographies of Nine Popes from* A.D. *715 to* A.D. *817.* Liverpool, UK: Liverpool University Press, 1992.
Llewellyn, Peter. *Rome in the Dark Ages.* New York: Barnes and Noble, 1993.

McKitterick, Rosamond. *The Frankish Kingdoms under the Carolingians, 751–987*. London: Longman, 1983.

Noble, Thomas F. X. *The Republic of St. Peter: The Birth of the Papal State, 680–825*. Philadelphia: University of Pennsylvania Press, 1984.

Riché, Pierre. *The Carolingians: A Family Who Forged Europe*. Trans. Michael Idomir Allen. Philadelphia: University of Pennsylvania Press, 1993.

Scholz, Bernhard Walter, trans. *Carolingian Chronicles: Royal Frankish Annals and Nithard's History*. Ann Arbor: University of Michigan Press, 1972.

Ullmann, Walter. *A Short History of the Papacy in the Middle Ages*. London: Methuen, 1972.

Zeno (d. 491)

Eastern Roman emperor (r. 474–491) whose reign witnessed the so-called fall of the Roman Empire in 476. His own reign demonstrates the flaw in the traditional argument about the "fall of Rome," and his continued interest in the affairs of Italy after 476 reveals the importance of the entire empire to the emperors in Constantinople. Zeno's reign was marked by the ambitions of a number of generals, both Roman and barbarian, who sought control of Italy. It was also marked by his own efforts to strengthen the position of the Eastern Empire in the face of the advance of various Germanic peoples, and the conclusion of a treaty with the Vandals that was the first of its kind for Rome and the barbarians.

Since 395 the Roman Empire had been ruled by two emperors in two capitals, one in Constantinople and the other in one of several cities in Italy. In the 470s that situation continued, but it was threatened by the powerful and ambitious generals in Italy. In 475, Orestes, the highest ranking officer in the Western Empire, rose up against the emperor Julius Nepos, who fled into exile. Orestes made his son, Romulus Augustulus, emperor, but Zeno rejected this claim and continued to support Julius Nepos as his legitimate colleague in the west. The situation was complicated for Zeno in the following year when Orestes and Romulus Augustulus were overthrown by Odovacar, a German tribal leader who was serving in the Roman army, who led a revolt of German soldiers against the western emperor. Odovacar executed Orestes but merely deposed Romulus and allowed him to retire with his family. Odovacar also sent word of his actions to Zeno and requested that Zeno grant him the title Patricius (patrician) so that he could rule Italy legitimately. Zeno was told by Odovacar's representatives, who returned the imperial insignia to Zeno, that there should be only one emperor—Zeno—and that Odovacar would rule as his representative. But Zeno stood by his exiled colleague, Julius Nepos, and informed Odovacar that the legitimate authority in the Western Empire was Julius. Nevertheless, Zeno did confer the office of Patricius on Odovacar, and thus began a long period of uncertain relations between the two rulers. The situation was clarified somewhat by the murder of Julius Nepos in 480, but no formal treaty was ever signed by Zeno and Odovacar.

While Odovacar ruled as the imperial representative in Italy, Zeno faced another powerful and ambitious barbarian general, Theodoric the Great, king of the Ostrogoths. Indeed, Zeno was particularly in Theodoric's debt because the Goth rescued the emperor at a critical period in his reign. In 475, the Gothic commander, Theodoric Strabo, forced Zeno from the throne, and with the aid of Theodoric the Great Zeno was able to seize back the imperial throne. Theodoric was richly rewarded for his efforts and promoted in the ranks of the Roman military. But Theodoric also used his position to improve the position of his Gothic peoples and threatened the stability of Zeno's control of the Eastern Empire in the mid-480s. Zeno's resources as emperor, however, turned out to be too great for Theodoric to overwhelm, even though his rebellion was quite serious. Instead, Zeno offered Theodoric the opportunity to march against Odovacar in Italy as the emperor's representative in Italy. Zeno intended to ease the pressures in his own part of the empire and use Theodoric to correct the uncertain situation in Italy. Although the exact nature of the political establishment Theodoric was to create and the relations of Italy and Constantinople that were to follow remain unclear, it is certain that Zeno intended to use Theodoric to end Odovacar's reign in Italy. In fact Theodoric claimed the title of king once he had established himself in Italy, but the murder of Odovacar and the creation of a new Gothic kingdom in Italy took place after Zeno's death. The emperor was, however, responsible for guiding the empire through uncertain times and establishing new and innovative relations with various barbarian peoples.

See also Odovacar; Orestes; Romulus Augustulus; Ostrogoths; Theodoric the Great; Vandals

Bibliography

Bury, John B. *History of the Later Roman Empire: From the Death of Theodosius I to the Death of Justinian.* 2 vols. 1923. Reprint, New York: Dover, 1959.

———. *The Invasion of Europe by the Barbarians.* New York: W. W. Norton, 1967.

Lot, Ferdinand. *The End of the Ancient World and the Beginning of the Middle Ages.* 1931. Reprint, New York: Harper and Row, 1961.

Randers-Pehrson, Justine Davis. *Barbarians and Romans: The Birth Struggle of Europe, A.D. 400–700.* Norman: University of Oklahoma Press, 1983.

Wolfram, Herwig. *The Roman Empire and Its Germanic Peoples.* Trans. Thomas J. Dunlap. Los Angeles: University of California Press, 1997.

Rulers of Barbarian Europe

Anglo-Saxon Kings of Wessex and England

Cerdic (519–534)
Cynric (534–560)
Ceawlin (560–592)
Ceol (591–597)
Ceolwulf (597–611)
Cynegils (611–643)
Cenwelh (643–674)
Seaxburh (674–676)
Centwine (676–685)
Caedwalla (685–688)
Ine (688–726)
Aethelherd (726–740)
Cuthred (740–756)
Sigeberht (756–757)
Cynewulf (757–786)
Brihtric (786–802)
Egbert (802–839)
Æthelwulf (839–860)
Æthelbald (855–860)
Æthelberht (860–865)
Æthelred (865–871)
Alfred the Great (871–899)
Edward the Elder (899–924)
Æthelstan (924–939, first king of England)
Edmund I (939–946)
Eadred (946–955)
Eadwig (955–959)
Edgar (959–975)
Edward the Martyr (975–978)
Æthelred the Unready (978–1013)

Byzantine Emperors

Zeno (474–491)
Anastasius I (491–518)
Justin I (518–527)
Justinian I (527–565)
Justin II (565–578)
Tiberius II (578–582)
Maurice (582–602)
Phocas (602–610)
Heraclius (610–641)
Constantine III (641)
Constans II (641–668)
Constantine IV (668–685)
Justinian II (685–695, banished)
Leontius (695–698)
Tiberius III (698–705)
Justinian II (restored, 705–711)
Philippicus Bardanes (711–713)
Anastasius II (713–716)
Theodosius III (716–717)
Leo III, the Isaurian (717–741)
Constantine V Copronymus (741–775)
Leo IV (775–780)
Constantine VI (780–797)
Irene (797–802)
Nicephorus I (802–811)
Stauracius (811)
Michael I Rhangabe (811–813)
Leo V (813–820)

Michael II (820–829)
Theophilus (829–842)
Michael III (842–867)
Basil I (867–886)
Leo VI (886–912
Alexander (912–913)
Constantine VII Porphyrogenitus (913–959)
Romanus I Lecapenus (919–944)
Romanus II (959–963)
Nicephorus II Phocas (963–969)
John I Tzimisces (969–976)
Basil II, the Bulgar-slayer (976–1025)

Carolingian Rulers of the Franks
Pippin I (614–628, 640)
Grimoald (640–657)
Pippin II (mayor of the palace, 680–714)
Charles Martel (mayor of the palace,
    714–741)
Carloman (mayor of the palace 741–747)
Pippin (mayor of the palace, 741–751; king,
    751–768)
Carloman (king, 768–771)
Charlemagne (king, 771–800; emperor,
    800–814)
Louis the Pious (emperor, 814–840)
Lothar (emperor, 840–855)
Louis II (emperor, 855–875)

West Frankish Kingdom	East Frankish Kingdom
Charles the Bald (840–875; emperor, 875–877)	Louis the German (840–876)
	Charles the Fat (876–887; emperor, 884–887)
Louis the Stammerer (877–879	Arnulf (887–899)
Louis III (879–882)	Louis the Child (899–911)

Carloman (879–884)
Charles the Fat (884–887, deposed)
Odo (not a Carolingian, 888–898)
Charles the Simple (898–922)
Robert I (brother of Odo, 922–923)
Ralph (son-in-law of Robert I, 923–936)
Louis IV, called d'Outremer (936–954)
Lothar (954–986)

Louis V (986–987)

Lombard Kings of Italy
Alboin (560/561–572)
Cleph (572–574)
Interregnum (574–584)
Authari (584–590)
Agilulf (590–616)
Adaloald (616–626)
Ariold (626–636)
Rothari (626–652)
Aripert I (653–661)
Grimoald (662–671)
Perctarit (671–688)
Cuncipert (680–688 co-ruler, 688–700)
Aripert II (700–712)
Liutprand (712–744)
Ratchis (744–749)
Aistulf (749–756)
Desiderius (757–774)

Merovingian Rulers of the Franks
Merovech (d. 456)
Childeric I (456–481)
Clovis (481–511)
Chlothar I (511–561)
Chlodomer (511–524)
Theuderic (511–533)
Childebert I (511–558)
Theodebert (533–548)
Chilperic I (561–584, Soissons [later, Neustria])
Sigebert I (561–575, Austrasia)
Childebert II (575–595)
Theodebert II (595–612)
Theuderic II (612–613)
Sigebert II (613)
Chlothar II (584–613, Neustria; 613–629, entire kingdom)
Dagobert (629–639)
Clovis II (637–657, Neustria) Sigebert III (632–656)
Chlothar III (655–673)
Childeric II (662–675)
Theuderic III (673–690/91, Neustria)
Dagobert (675–679, Austrasia)
Clovis III (691–694)
Childebert III (694–711)

Dagobert III (711–715)
Chilperic II (715–721, Neustria)
Chlothar IV (717–719, Austrasia)
Theuderic IV (721–737)
Interregnum (737–743)
Childeric III (743–751)

Popes and Antipopes
Sylvester I (314–335)
Mark (336)
Julius I (337–352)
Liberius (352–366)
Felix II (antipope, 355–358)
Damasus I (366–384)
Ursinus (antipope, 366–367)
Siricius (384–399)
Anastasius I (399–401)
Innocent I (401–417)
Zosimus (417–418)
Boniface I (418–422)
Eulalius (antipope, 418–419)
Celestine I (422–432)
Sixtus III (432–440)
Leo I (440–461)
Hilary (461–468)
Simplicius (468–483)
Felix III (II) (483–492)
Gelasius I (492–496)
Anastasius II (496–498)
Symmachus (498–514)
Lawrence (antipope, 498, 501–506, died 507 or 508)
Hormisdas (514–523)
John I (523–526)
Felix IV (III) (526–530)
Dioscorus (antipope, 530)
Boniface II (530–532)
John II (533–535)
Agapetus I (535–536)
Silverius (536–537)
Vigilius (537–555)
Pelagius I (556–561)
John III (561–574)
Benedict I (575–579)
Pelagius II (579–590)
Gregory I (590–604)
Sabinian (604–606)
Boniface III (607)

Boniface IV (608–615)
Deusdedit, later Adeodatus I (615–618)
Boniface V (619–625)
Honorius I (625–638)
Severinus (640)
John IV (640–642)
Theodore I (642–649)
Martin I (649–653)
Eugenius I (654–657)
Vitalian (657–672)
Adeodatus II (672–676)
Donus (676–678)
Agatho (678–681)
Leo II (682–683)
Benedict II (684–685)
John V (685–686)
Conon (686–687)
Theodore (687)
Paschal (687)
Sergius I (687–701)
John VI (701–705)
John VII (705–707)
Sisinnius (708)
Constantine (708–715)
Gregory II (715–731)
Gregory III (731–741)
Zachary (741–752)
Stephen (II) (752)
Stephen II (III) (752–757)
Paul I (757–767)
Constantine (antipope, 767–768)
Philip (antipope, 768)
Stephen III (IV) (768–772)
Hadrian I (772–795)
Leo III (795–816)
Stephen IV (V) (816–817)
Paschal I (817–824)
Eugenius II (824–827)
Valentine (827)
Gregory IV (827–844)
John (antipope, 844)
Sergius II (844–847
Leo IV (847–855)
Benedict III (855–858)
Anastasius the Librarian (antipope, 855)
Nicholas I (858–867)
Hadrian II (867–872)
John VIII (872–882)

Marinus I (882–884)
Adrian III (884–885)
Stephen V (VI) (885–891)
Formosus (891–896)
Boniface VI (896)
Stephen VI (VII) (896–897)
Romanus (897)
Theodore II (897)
John IX (898–900)
Benedict IV (900–903)
Leo V (903–904)
Christopher (antipope, 903–904)
Sergius III (904–911)
Anastasius III (911–913)
Lando (913–914)
John X (914–928, died 929)
Leo VI (928)
Stephen VII (VIII) (929–931)

John XI (931–935)
Leo VII (936–939)
Stephen VIII (IX) (939–942)
Marinus II (942–946)
Agapetus II ((946–955)
John XII (955–964)
Leo VIII (963–965)
Benedict V (964, died 966)
John XIII (965–972)
Benedict VI (973–974)
Boniface VII (antipope, 974)
Benedict VII (974–983)
John XIV (983–984)
John XV (985–996)
Gregory V (996–999)
John XVI (antipope, 997–998)
Sylvester II (999–1003)

Subject Index to Entries

Subject Bibliography

Primary Sources in Translation

Adomnan. *Adomnan's Life of Columba.* Ed. and trans. Alan O. Anderson and Marjorie O. Anderson. London: T. Nelson, 1961.

Ammianus Marcellinus. *Ammianus Marcellinus.* Trans. John C. Rolfe. Cambridge, MA: Harvard University Press, 1971–1972.

Alexander, Michael, trans. *Beowulf.* Harmondsworth, UK: Penguin, 1983.

Amt, Emilie, ed. *Women's Lives in Medieval Europe.* New York: Routledge, 1993.

Attenborough, Frederick L., ed. and trans. *The Laws of the Earliest English Kings.* Cambridge: Cambridge University Press, 1922.

Augustine. *Confessions: Books I–XIII.* Trans. Francis J. Sheed. Indianapolis: Hackett, 1993.

———. *Concerning the City of God against the Pagans.* Trans. Henry Bettenson. Harmondsworth, UK: Penguin, 1981.

———. *On Christian Doctrine.* Trans. Donald W. Robertson, Jr. New York: Macmillan, 1958.

Bachrach, Bernard S., trans. *Liber historiae Francorum.* Lawrence, KS: Coronado, 1973.

Bede. *Commentary on the Acts of the Apostles.* Trans. Lawrence Martin. Kalamazoo, MI: Cistercian Publications, 1989.

———. *Ecclesiastical History of the English Church and People,* trans. Leo Sherley-Price. Revised edition. London: Penguin Classics, 1968.

Boethius. *The Consolation of Philosophy.* Trans. Richard Green. New York: Bobbs-Merrill, 1962.

Caesarius of Arles. *Caesarius of Arles: Sermons.* Trans. Mary Magdeleine Mueller. 3 vols. New York: Fathers of the Church, 1956–1973.

Cassiodorus. *The Variae of Magnus Aurelius Cassiodorus.* Trans. S. J. B. Barnish. Liverpool, UK: Liverpool University Press, 1992.

Claudian. *Claudian's Fourth Panegyric on the fourth consulate of Honorius.* Ed. and trans. William Barr. Liverpool, UK: Liverpool University Press, 1981.

Colgrave, Bertram, ed. and trans. *The Earliest Life of Gregory the Great, by an Anonymous Monk of Whitby.* Lawrence: University of Kansas Press, 1968.

Davis, Raymond, trans. *The Lives of the Eighth-Century Popes* (Liber Pontificalis): *The Ancient Biographies of Nine Popes from A.D. 715 to A.D. 817.* Liverpool, UK: Liverpool University Press, 1992.

Dhuoda. *Handbook for William: A Carolingian Woman's Counsel for Her Son.* Ed. and trans. Carol Neel. Washington, DC: Catholic University of America Press, 1999.

Drew, Katherine Fisher, trans. *The Burgundian Code: The Book of Constitutions or Law of Gundobad and Additional Enactments.* Philadelphia: University of Pennsylvania Press, 1972.

————. *The Lombard Laws.* Philadelphia: University of Pennsylvania Press, 1973.

Dutton, Paul Edward, ed. *Carolingian Civilization: A Reader.* Peterborough, Ont.: Broadview, 1993.

Einhard. *The Translation and Miracles of the Saints Marcellinus and Peter.* In *Carolingian Civilization: A Reader,* trans. Paul Edward Dutton. Peterborough, Ont.: Broadview, 1993, pp. 198–246.

Einhard and Notker the Stammerer. *Two Lives of Charlemagne.* Trans. Lewis Thorpe. Harmondsworth, UK: Penguin, 1981.

Emerton, Ephraim, ed. and trans. *The Letters of Saint Boniface.* New York: Columbia University Press, 2000.

Fouracre, Paul, and Richard A. Gerberding. *Late Merovingian France: History and Hagiography, 640–720.* Manchester, UK: University of Manchester Press, 1996.

Fry, Timothy, ed. and trans. *RB 1980: The Rule of Benedict in Latin and English with Notes.* Collegeville, MN: Liturgical Press, 1981.

Geoffrey of Monmouth. *The History of the Kings of Britain.* Trans. Lewis Thorpe. Harmondsworth, UK: Penguin, 1982.

Gildas. *The Ruin of Britain and Other Works.* Ed. and trans. Michael Winterbottom. London: Phillimore, 1978.

Gregory of Tours. *The History of the Franks.* Trans. Lewis Thorpe. Harmondsworth, UK: Penguin, 1974.

————. *Gregory of Tours, Glory of the Martyrs.* Trans. Raymond Van Dam. Liverpool, UK: Liverpool University Press, 1988.

————. *Gregory of Tours, Glory of the Confessors.* Trans. Raymond Van Dam. Liverpool, UK: Liverpool University Press, 1988.

————. *Gregory of Tours: Life of the Fathers,* 2d ed. Trans. Edward James. Liverpool, UK: Liverpool University Press, 1991.

Gregory the Great. *Life and Miracles of St. Benedict (Book Two of the Dialogues).* Trans. Odo J. Zimmerman and Benedict Avery. Collegeville, MN: St. John's Abbey Press, 1949.

Head, Thomas, ed. *Medieval Hagiography: An Anthology.* New York: Garland Publishing, Inc., 2000.

Heaney, Seamus, trans. *Beowulf: A New Verse Translation.* New York: Farrar Straus and Giroux, 2000.

Isidore of Seville. *Isidore of Seville's History of the Goths, Vandals, and Suevi.* 2d rev. ed. Trans. Guido Donini and Gordon B. Ford. Leiden: Brill, 1970.

Jordanes. *The Gothic History of Jordanes in English Version.* Trans. Charles C. Mierow. New York: Barnes and Noble, 1985.

Keynes, Simon, and Michael Lapidge, trans. *Alfred the Great: Asser's Life of King Alfred and Other Contemporary Sources.* Harmondsworth, UK: Penguin, 1983.

Larrington, Carolyne. *Women and Writing in Medieval Europe: A Sourcebook.* New York: Routledge, 1995.

Loyn, Henry R., and John Percival. *The Reign of Charlemagne: Documents on Carolingian Government and Administration.* New York: St. Martin's Press, 1975.

Malory, Sir Thomas. *Le Morte d'Arthur.* Ed. Norma Lorre Goodrich. New York: Washington Square Press, 1966.

McCarthy, Maria Caritas. *The Rule for Nuns of St. Caesarius of Arles: A Translation with Critical Introduction.* Washington, DC: Catholic University of America Press, 1960.

Nelson, Janet, trans. *The Annals of St. Bertin: Ninth Century Histories.* Manchester, UK: University of Manchester Press, 1991.

Nennius. *Nennius: British History and the Welsh Annals.* Ed. John Morris. Totowa, NJ: Rowman and Littlefield, 1980.

Noble, Thomas F. X. and Thomas Head, eds. *Soldiers of Christ: Saints and Saints' Lives from Late Antiquity to the Early Middle Ages.* University Park: Pennsylvania State University Press, 1995.

Paul the Deacon. *History of the Lombards.* Trans William Dudley Foulke. Philadelphia: University of Pennsylvania Press, 1974.

Procopius. *The History of the Wars; Secret History,* 4 vols. Ed. and trans. Henry B. Dewing. Cambridge, MA: Harvard University Press, 1914–1940.

————. *Secret History,* Ed. and trans. Henry B.

Dewing. Cambridge, MA: Harvard University Press, 1914–1940

Reuter, Timothy, trans. *The Annals of Fulda: Ninth Century Histories.* Manchester, UK: University of Manchester Press, 1992.

Rivers, Theodore J., trans. *Laws of the Alamans and Bavarians.* Philadelphia: University of Pennsylvania Press, 1977.

———. *The Laws of the Salian and Ripuarian Franks.* New York: AMS, 1986.

Scholz, Bernhard Walter, trans. *Carolingian Chronicles: Royal Frankish Annals and Nithard's History.* Ann Arbor: University of Michigan Press, 1972.

Tacitus. *The Agricola and the Germania.* Trans. H. Mattingly, rev. trans. S. A. Handford. Harmondsworth, UK: Penguin, 1982.

Theodulf of Orleans. *The Poetry of Theodulf of Orleans: A Translation and Critical Study.* Ed. and trans. Nikolai A. Alexandro. Ann Arbor: University Microfilms, 1970.

Thiébaux, Marcelle, ed. and trans. *The Writings of Medieval Women: An Anthology.* 2d ed. New York: Garland, 1994.

Victor of Vita. *Victor of Vita: History of the Vandal Persecution.* Trans. John Moorhead. Liverpool, UK: Liverpool University Press, 1992.

Wallace-Hadrill, John M., ed. and trans. *The Fourth Book of the Chronicle of Fredegar with Its Continuations.* London: Nelson, 1960.

Watson, Alan. *The Digest of Justinian.* Philadelphia: University of Pennsylvania Press, 1997.

Whitelock, Dorothy, ed. *The Anglo-Saxon Chronicle.* Westport, CT: Greenwood, 1986.

Zosimus. *New History.* Trans. Ronald T. Ridley. Canberra: Australian Association for Byzantine Studies, 1982.

Art and Culture

Baker, Peter S., ed. *Beowulf: Basic Readings.* New York: Garland, 1995.

Beckwith, John. *Early Medieval Art.* London: Thames and Hudson, 1969.

———. *Ivory Carvings in Early Medieval England.* London: Harvey Miller, 1972.

Bjork, Robert E., and John D. Niles, eds. *A Beowulf Handbook.* Lincoln: University of Nebraska Press, 1997.

Brown, George Hardin. *Bede the Venerable.* Boston: Twayne, 1987.

Brown, Giles. "Introduction: the Carolingian Renaissance." In *Carolingian Culture: Emulation and Innovation,* ed. Rosamond McKitterick. Cambridge: Cambridge University Press, 1994. Pp. 1–51.

Brown, Peter. *Augustine of Hippo: A Biography.* Berkeley: University of California Press, 1967.

Cameron, Averil. *Procopius and the Sixth Century.* London and New York: Routledge, 1996.

Chadwick, Henry. *Boethius: The Consolations of Music, Logic, Theology, and Philosophy.* Oxford: Clarendon, 1981.

Chambers, Raymond. W. *Beowulf: An Introduction to the Study of the Poem with a Discussion of the Stories of Offa and Finn.* 3d ed., supplement by C. L. Wrenn. Cambridge: Cambridge University Press, 1959.

Contreni, John J. "The Carolingian Renaissance: Education and Literary Culture." In *The New Cambridge Medieval History,* vol. 2, ed. Rosamond McKitterick. Cambridge: Cambridge University Press, 1995. Pp. 709–757

Curtius, Ernst Robert. *European Literature and the Latin Middle Ages.* Trans. Willard R. Trask. 1953. Reprint, with a new epilogue by Peter Goodman, Princeton: Princeton University Press, 1990.

Davis-Weyer, Caecilia. *Early Medieval Art, 300–1150.* Toronto: Toronto University Press, 1986.

Deane, Herbert. *The Political and Social Ideas of Saint Augustine.* New York: Columbia University Press, 1964.

Duckett, Eleanor Shipley. *Anglo-Saxon Saints and Scholars.* New York: Macmillan, 1947.

Evans, James A. S. *Procopius.* New York: Twayne, 1972.

Freeman, Ann. "Theodulf of Orléans and the *Libri Carolini.*" *Speculum* 32 (1957): 664–705.

Gibson, Margaret, ed. *Boethius: His Life, Thought, and Influence.* Oxford: Blackwell, 1981.

Hasenfratz, Robert J. *Beowulf Scholarship: An*

Annotated Bibliography, 1979–1990. New York: Garland, 1993.

Henderson, George. "Emulation and Invention in Carolingian Art." In *The New Cambridge Medieval History,* vol. 2, edited by Rosamond McKitterick. Cambridge: Cambridge University Press, 1995. Pp. 248–273.

Hubert, Jean, Jean Porcher, and Wolfgang Fritz Volbach. *The Carolingian Renaissance.* New York: George Braziller, 1970.

Hubert, Jean, Jean Porcher, and Wolfgang Fritz Volbach. *Europe in the Dark Ages.* London: Thames and Hudson, 1969.

Hunt, David, and Jan Willem Drijvers, eds. *The Late Roman World and its Historian: Interpreting Ammianus Marcellinus.* London: Routledge, 1999.

Innes, Matthew, and Rosamond McKitterick. "The Writing of History." In *Carolingian Culture: Emulation and Innovation,* edited by Rosamond McKitterick. Cambridge: Cambridge University Press, 1994, pp. 193–220.

Kornbluth, Genevra A. *Engraved Gems of the Carolingian Empire.* University Park: Pennsylvania State University Press, 1995.

Lasko, Peter. *Ars Sacra 800–1200.* 2d ed. New Haven: Yale University Press, 1994.

———. *The Kingdom of the Franks: Northwest Europe before Charlemagne.* London: Thames and Hudson, 1971.

Marenbon, John. "Carolingian Thought." In *Carolingian Culture: Emulation and Innovation.* Ed. Rosamond McKitterick. Cambridge: Cambridge University Press, 1994, pp.171–192.

Mayvaert, Paul. "The Authorship of the 'Libri Carolini': Observations Prompted by a Recent Book." *Revue bénédictine* 89 (1979): 29–57.

McKitterick, Rosamond, ed. *Carolingian Culture: Emulation and Innovation.* Cambridge: Cambridge University Press, 1994.

———. *The Carolingians and the Written Word.* Cambridge: Cambridge University Press, 1989.

Mütherich, Florentine, and Joachim E. Gaehde. *Carolingian Painting.* New York: George Braziller, 1976.

Nie, Giselle de. *Views from a Many-Windowed Tower: Studies of Imagination in the Works of Gregory of Tours.* Amsterdam: Rodopi, 1987.

Neese, Lawrence. *Justinian to Charlemagne: European Art, 565–787: An Annotated Bibliography.* Boston: Hall, 1987.

O'Donnell, James J. *Augustine.* Boston: Twayne, 1985.

———. *Cassiodorus.* Berkeley: University of California Press, 1979.

Randall, Richard H., Jr. *Masterpieces of Ivory from the Walters Art Gallery.* New York: Hudson Hills, 1985.

Riché, Pierre. *Education and Culture in the Barbarian West: From the Sixth to the Eighth Century.* Trans. John Contreni. Columbia: University of South Carolina Press, 1978.

Ross, Marvin, and Philippe Verdier. *Arts of the Migration Period in the Walters Art Gallery.* Baltimore: Walters Art Gallery, 1961.

Snyder, James. *Medieval Art: Painting, Sculpture, Architecture, 4th–14th Century.* New York: Harry Abrams, 1989.

Tolkien, J. R. R. "*Beowulf:* The Monsters and the Critics." *Proceedings of the British Academy* 22 (1936): 245–295. Grabar, André. *Early Medieval Painting from the Fourth to the Eleventh Century.* Lausanne: Skira, 1957.

Van Riel, Gerd, Carlos Steel, and James McEvoy, eds. *Iohannes Scottus Eriugena: The Bible and Hermeneutics.* Leuven: Leuven University Press, 1996.

Wallach, Luitpold, *Alcuin and Charlemagne: Studies in Carolingian History and Literature.* Ithaca, NY: Cornell University Press, 1959.

Wills, Gary. *Saint Augustine.* New York: Penguin, 1999.

England and the Continent in the Early Middle Ages

Arnold, Christopher J. *Roman Britain to Saxon Shore.* Bloomington: Indiana University Press, 1984.

Bassett, Steven, ed. *The Origins of Anglo-Saxon Kingdoms.* Leicester, UK: Leicester University Press, 1989.

Blair, Peter Hunter. *The World of Bede.* Cambridge: Cambridge University Press, 1990.

Blumenthal, Uta-Renata, ed. *Carolingian Essays: Andrew W. Mellon Lectures in Early Christian Studies.* Washington, D.C.: The Catholic University of America Press, 1983.

Boussard, Jacques. *The Civilization of Charlemagne.* Trans. Frances Partridge. New York: McGraw-Hill Book Company, 1968.

Brown, Peter. *The Rise of Western Christendom: Triumph and Diversity.* Cambridge, MA: Blackwell, 1996.

Bullough, Donald. "*Europae Pater:* Charlemagne and His Achievement in the Light of Recent Scholarship." *English Historical Review* 75 (1970): 59–105.

Cabaniss, Allen. *Agobard of Lyons: Churchman and Critic.* Syracuse, NY: Syracuse University Press, 1953.

Christie, Neil. *The Lombards: The Ancient Langobards.* Oxford: Blackwell, 1998.

Collins, Roger. *Charlemagne.* Toronto: University of Toronto Press, 1998.

———. *Early Medieval Spain: Unity in Diversity, 400–1000.* New York and London: Longman, 1983.

Daly, William M. "Clovis: How Barbaric, How Pagan?" *Speculum* 69 (1994): 619–664.

Hallenback, Jan T. *Pavia and Rome: The Lombard Monarchy and the Papacy in the Eighth Century.* Philadelphia: American Philosophical Society, 1982.

Dill, Samuel. *Roman Society in Gaul in the Merovingian Age.* 1926. Reprint, London: Allen and Unwin, 1966.

Duckett, Eleanor Shipley. *Alcuin, Friend of Charlemagne: His World and His Work.* New York: Macmillan, 1951.

———. *Carolingian Portraits: A Study in the Ninth Century.* Ann Arbor: University of Michigan Press, 1962.

Farmer, David H. *The Age of Bede.* Harmondsworth, UK: Penguin, 1998.

Fichtenau, Heinrich. *The Carolingian Empire.* Trans. Peter Munz. Toronto: University of Toronto Press, 1979.

Fouracre, Paul. *The Age of Charles Martel.* New York: Longman, 2000.

Ganshof, François L. *The Carolingians and the Frankish Monarchy: Studies in Carolingian*

History. Trans. Janet L. Sondheimer. London: Longman, 1971.

Geary, Patrick. *Before France and Germany: The Creation and Transformation of the Merovingian World.* Oxford: 1988.

Gerberding, Richard, A. *The Rise of the Carolingians and the "Liber Historiae Francorum."* Oxford: Clarendon, 1987.

Godman, Peter, and Roger Collins, eds. *Charlemagne's Heir: New Perspectives on the Reign of Louis the Pious.* Oxford: Clarendon, 1990.

Halphen, Louis. *Charlemagne and the Carolingian Empire.* Trans. Giselle de Nie. Amsterdam and New York: North-Holland, 1977.

James, Edward. *The Franks.* Oxford: Blackwell, 1991.

James, Edward, ed. *Visigothic Spain: New Approaches.* Oxford: Clarendon, 1980.

Keynes, Simon. "The British Isles: England, 700–900." In *The New Cambridge Medieval History,* vol. 2, ed. Rosamond McKitterick. Cambridge: Cambridge University Press, 1995. Pp. 18–42.

Kirby, David P. *The Earliest English Kings.* London: Unwin Hyman, 1991.

Lapidge, Michael. *Bede and His World: The Jarrow Lectures, 1958–1993.* 2 vols. Aldershot, UK: Variorum, 1994.

Levison, Wilhelm. *England and the Continent in the Eighth Century.* New York: Oxford University Press, 1998.

Llewellyn, Peter. *Rome in the Dark Ages.* New York: Barnes and Noble, 1993.

Loyn, Henry R. *Anglo-Saxon England and the Norman Conquest,* 2d ed. London: Longmans, 1991.

McKitterick, Rosamond. *The Frankish Kingdoms under the Carolingians, 751–987.* London: Longman, 1983.

Myres, John. N. L. *The English Settlements.* Oxford: Clarendon, 1986.

Nelson, Janet. *Charles the Bald.* London: Longman, 1992.

Noble, Thomas F. X. *The Republic of St. Peter: The Birth of the Papal State, 680–825.* Philadelphia: University of Pennsylvania Press, 1984.

Reuter, Timothy. *Germany in the Early Middle Ages, c. 800–1056.* London: Longman, 1991.

Riché, Pierre, *The Carolingians: A Family Who Forged Europe.* Trans. Michael Idomir Allen. Philadelphia: University of Pennsylvania Press, 1993.

Sawyer, Peter. H. *From Roman Britain to Norman England.* 2d ed. London and New York, 1998.

Smyth, Alfred P. *King Alfred the Great.* Oxford: Oxford University Press, 1995.

Stenton, Frank M. *Anglo-Saxon England.* 3d ed. Oxford: Clarendon, 1971.

Sturdy, David J. *Alfred the Great.* London: Constable, 1995.

Sullivan, Richard. *Aix-La-Chapelle in the Age of Charlemagne.* Norman: University of Oklahoma Press, 1974.

Sullivan, Richard E. "The Carolingian Age: Reflections on Its Place in the History of the Middle Ages." *Speculum* 64 (1989): 257–306.

Wallace-Hadrill, John. M. *The Long-Haired Kings.* Toronto: Toronto University Press, 1982.

Wickham, Chris. *Early Medieval Italy: Central Power and Local Society, 400–1000.* Ann Arbor: University of Michigan Press, 1981.

Wood, Ian. *The Merovingian Kingdoms, 450–751.* London: Longman, 1994.

Yorke, Barbara. *Kings and Kingdoms of Early Anglo-Saxon England.* London: Seaby, 1990.

Late Antiquity and the Migration Period

Alcock, Leslie. *Arthur's Britain: History and Archeology, A.D. 367–634.* Harmondsworth, UK: Penguin, 1971.

Amory, Patrick. *People and Identity in Ostrogothic Italy, 489–554.* Cambridge: Cambridge University Press, 1997.

Bachrach, Bernard S. "The Alans in Gaul." *Traditio* 23 (1967): 476–89.

———. *A History of the Alans in the West, from Their First Appearance in the Sources of Classical Antiquity through the Early Middle Ages.* Minneapolis: University of Minnesota Press, 1973.

Barber, Richard. *The Figure of Arthur.* Totowa, NJ: Rowman and Littlefield, 1972.

Barker. John. W. *Justinian and the Later Roman Empire.* Madison: University of Wisconsin Press, 1960.

Barnes, Timothy. D. *Ammianus Marcellinus and the Representation of Historical Reality.* Ithaca, NY: Cornell University Press, 1998.

———. *Constantine and Eusebius.* Cambridge, MA: Harvard University Press, 1981.

Bassett, Steven, ed. *The Origins of Anglo-Saxon Kingdoms.* Leicester, UK: Leicester University Press, 1989.

Baüml, Franz. H., and Marianna. Birnbaum. *Attila: The Man and His Image.* Budapest: Corvina, 1993.

Brown, Peter. *Late Antiquity.* Cambridge, MA: Harvard University Press, 1998.

———. *Society and the Holy in Late Antiquity.* Berkeley and Los Angeles: University of California Press, 1982.

———. *The World of Late Antiquity, A.D. 150–750.* London: Thames and Hudson, 1971.

Browning, Robert. *Justinian and Theodora.* London: Thames and Hudson, 1987.

Burns, Thomas S. *A History of the Ostrogoths.* Bloomington: Indiana University Press, 1984.

Burckhardt, Jacob. *The Age of Constantine the Great.* Trans. Moses Hadas. Berkeley: University of California Press, 1983.

Burns, Thomas S. *Barbarians within the Gates of Rome: A Study of Roman Military Policy and the Barbarians, ca. 375–425 A.D.* Bloomington: University of Indiana Press, 1994.

Bursche, Aleksander. *Later Roman-Barbarian Contacts in Central Europe: Numismatic Evidence.* Berlin: Gebr. Mann Verlag, 1996.

Bury, John B. *History of the Later Roman Empire: From the Death of Theodosius I to the Death of Justinian.* Vol. 1. 1923. Reprint, New York: Dover, 1959.

———. Bury, John B. *The Invasions of Europe by the Barbarians.* New York: W. W. Norton, 1967.

Cameron, Averil. *The Mediterranean World in Late Antiquity, A.D. 395–600.* New York: Routledge, 1993.

Cameron, Averil, and Peter Garnsey, eds. *The Late Empire, A.D. 337–425. Cambridge Ancient History,* vol. 13. Cambridge: Cambridge University Press, 1998.

Clover, Frank. M. *The Late Roman West and the Vandals.* London: Variorum, 1993.

Goffart, Walter. *Barbarians and Romans, A.D.*

418–584: The Techniques of Accommodation. 1980.

Grant, Michael. *Constantine the Great: The Man and His Times.* New York: Charles Scribner's Sons, 1994.

Heather, Peter. *The Goths.* Oxford: Blackwell, 1996.

———. "Goths and Huns, c. 320–425." In *The Late Empire, A.D. 337–425,* vol. 13, The Cambridge Ancient History, ed. Averil Cameron and Peter Garnsey. Cambridge: Cambridge University Press, 1998. Pp. 487–537.

Herrin, Judith. *The Formation of Christendom.* Princeton: Princeton University Press, 1987.

Hodgkin, Thomas. *Theodoric the Goth: The Barbarian Champion of Civilization.* New York: G. P. Putnam, 1983.

Howe, Nicholas. *Migration and Mythmaking in Anglo-Saxon England.* New Haven: Yale University Press, 1989.

Jones, Arnold H. M. *The Later Roman Empire, 284–602: A Social Economic and Administrative Survey.* Baltimore: Johns Hopkins University Press, 1986.

King, Peter. D. *Law and Society in the Visigothic Kingdom.* Cambridge: Cambridge University Press, 1972.

Klingshirn, William E. *Caesarius of Arles: The Making of a Christian Community in Late Antique Gaul.* Cambridge: Cambridge University Press, 1994.

Lot, Ferdinand. *The End of the Ancient World and the Beginnings of the Middle Ages.* New York: Harper and Row, 1961.

Matthews, John. *Western Aristocracies and Imperial Court, A.D. 364–425.* Oxford: Clarendon, 1998.

Matthews, John. *The Roman Empire of Ammianus Marcellinus.* Baltimore: Johns Hopkins University Press, 1989.

Moorhead, John. *Theodoric in Italy.* Oxford: Clarendon, 1992.

Murray, Alexander, ed. *After Rome's Fall: Narrators and Sources of Early Medieval History.* Toronto: University of Toronto Press, 1998.

Obolensky, Dmitri. *The Byzantine Commonwealth: Eastern Europe, 500–1543.* New York: Praeger, 1971.

Randers-Pehrson, Justine Davis. *Barbarians and Romans: The Birth Struggle of Europe, A.D. 400–700.* Norman: University of Oklahoma Press, 1983.

Reynolds, Susan. "Our Forefathers? Tribes, Peoples, and Nations in the Historiography of the Age of Migrations." In *After Rome's Fall: Narrators and Sources of Early Medieval History,* ed. Alexander Callander Murray. Toronto: University of Toronto Press, 1999, pp. 17–36.

Sullivan, Richard. *Heirs of the Roman Empire.* Ithaca, NY: Cornell University Press, 1974.

Thompson, Edward. A. *A History of Attila and the Huns.* Oxford: Clarendon, 1948.

———. *The Huns.* Oxford: Blackwell, 1995.

Treadgold, Warren. *The History of the Byzantine State and Society.* Stanford, CA: Stanford University Press, 1997.

Ure, Percy. N. *Justinian and His Age.* Harmondsworth, UK: Penguin, 1951.

Wallace-Hadrill, John. M. *The Barbarian West, A.D. 400–1000.* New York: Harper and Row, 1962.

Wolfram, Herwig. *History of the Goths.* Trans. Thomas J. Dunlap. Berkeley: University of California Press, 1988.

———. *The Roman Empire and Its Germanic Peoples.* Trans. Thomas J. Dunlap. Berkeley: University of California Press, 1997.

Van Dam, Raymond. *Leadership and Community in Late Antique Gaul.* Berkeley and Los Angeles: University of California Press, 1985.

Military History

Bachrach, Bernard S. "Charles Martel, Mounted Shock Combat, the Stirrup, and Feudalism." *Studies in Medieval and Renaissance History* 7 (1970): 47–75.

———. *Early Carolingian Warfare: Prelude to Empire.* Philadelphia: University of Pennsylvania Press, 2001.

———. *Merovingian Military Organization, 481–751.* Minneapolis: University of Minnesota Press, 1972.

Contamine, Philippe. *War in the Middle Ages.* Trans. Michael Jones. Oxford: Basil Blackwell, 1984.

Coupland, Simon. "Carolingian Arms and Armor in the Ninth Century." *Viator: Medieval and Renaissance Studies* 21 (1990): 29–50.

DeVries, Kelly. *Medieval Military Technology.* Peterborough, Ont.: Broadview, 1992.

Ferrill, Arthur. *The Fall of the Roman Empire: The Military Explanation.* New York: Thames and Hudson, 1986.

Le Bohec, Yann. *The Imperial Roman Army.* Trans. Raphael Bate. New York: Routledge, 2000.

Luttwak, Edward. *The Grand Strategy of the Roman Empire.* Baltimore: Johns Hopkins University Press, 1974.

Martin, Paul. *Arms and Armour from the 9th to the 17th Century.* Trans. René North. Rutland: Tuttle, 1968.

Verbruggen, Jan. F. *The Art of Warfare in Western Europe during the Middle Ages: From the Eighth Century to 1340.* 2d ed. Trans. Sumner Willard and S. C. M. Southern. Woodbridge, UK: Boydell, 1997.

Religion

Bullough, Donald. "Alcuin and the Kingdom of Heaven: Liturgy, Theology, and the Carolingian Age." In *Carolingian Essays,* ed. Uta-Renate Blumenthal. Washington, DC: Catholic University Press, 1983, pp. 1–69.

Brown, Peter. *Relics and Social Status in the Age of Gregory of Tours.* Readiing, UK: University of Reading, 1977.

———. *Religion and Society in the Age of Augustine.* New York: Harper and Row, 1972.

Clarke, Howard B., and Mary Brennen, eds. *Columban and Merovingian Monasticism.* Oxford: British Archeological Reports, 1981.

Cohen, Jeremy. *Living Letters of the Law: Ideas of the Jew in Medieval Christianity.* Berkeley: University of California Press, 1999.

Dumézil, Georges. *Gods of the Ancient Northmen.* Trans. Einer Haugen. Berkeley: University of California Press, 1973.

Evans, Gillian. R. *The Thought of Gregory the Great.* Cambridge: Cambridge University Press, 1988.

Farmer, David Hugh, ed., *Benedict's Disciples.* Leominster, UK: Fowler Wright, 1980.

Fox, Robin Lane. *Pagans and Christians.* New York: Knopf, 1987.

Geary, Patrick. *Furta Sacra: Thefts of Relics in the Central Middle Ages.* Rev. ed. Princeton: Princeton University Press, 1990.

Grimm, Jakob. *Teutonic Mythology,* 4 vols. Trans. James Stevens Stallybrass. London: Routledge, 1999.

Hanson, Richard. P. C. *The Search for the Christian Doctrine of God: The Arian Controversy, 318–381.* Edinburgh: 1988.

Higham, Nicholas. J. *The Convert Kings: Power and Religious Affiliation in Early Anglo-Saxon England.* Manchester, UK: Manchester University Press, 1997.

Jolly, Karen Louise, *Popular Religion in Late Saxon England: Elf Charms in Context.* Chapel Hill: University of North Carolina Press, 1996.

Knowles, David. *Christian Monasticism.* New York: McGraw Hill, 1969.

Lawrence, Clifford H. *Medieval Monasticism: Forms of Religious Life in Western Europe in the Middle Ages,* 2d ed. London: Longman, 1989.

Markus, Robert A. *Gregory the Great and His World.* Cambridge: Cambridge University Press, 1998.

Mayr-Harting, Henry. *The Coming of Christianity to Anglo-Saxon England,* 3d ed. University Park: Pennsylvania State University Press, 1991.

McKitterick, Rosamond. *The Frankish Church and the Carolingian Reforms, 789–895.* London: Longman, 1977.

Meyvaert, Paul. *Benedict, Gregory, Bede and Others.* London: Variorum Reprints, 1977.

Pelikan, Jaroslav. *The Emergence of the Catholic Tradition.* Vol. 2 of *The Christian Tradition: A History of the Development of Doctrine.* Chicago: University of Chicago Press, 1978.

———. *The Growth of Medieval Theology (600–1300).* Vol. 3 of *The Christian Tradition: A History of the Development of Doctrine.* Chicago: University of Chicago Press, 1978.

Polomé, Edgar C. *Essays on Germanic Religion.* Washington, DC: Institute for the Study of Man, 1989.

Reuter, Timothy, ed. *The Greatest Englishman:*

Essays on St. Boniface and the Church at Crediton. Exeter: Paternoster Press, 1980.

Richards, Jeffrey. *Consul of God: The Life and Times of Gregory the Great.* London: Routledge and Kegan Paul, 1980.

Russell, James C. *The Germanization of Early Medieval Christianity: A Sociohistorical Approach to Religious Transformation.* Oxford: Oxford University Press, 1994.

Russell, Jeffery Burton. *Dissent and Reform in the Early Middle Ages.* Berkeley: University of California Press, 1965.

Straw, Carol. *Gregory the Great: Perfection in Imperfection.* Berkeley: University of California Press, 1991.

Sullivan, Richard. "What Was Carolingian Monasticism? The Plan of St. Gall and the History of Monasticism." In *After Rome's Fall: Narrators and Sources of Early Medieval History,* ed. Alexander Callander Murray. Toronto: University of Toronto Press, 1998, pp. 251–287.

Turville-Petre, Edward O. G. *Myth and Religion of the North: The Religion of Ancient Scandinavia.* London: Weidenfeld and Nicholson, 1964.

Ullmann, Walter. *A Short History of the Papacy in the Middle Ages.* London: Methuen, 1972.

Van Dam, Raymond. *Saints and Their Miracles in Late Antique Gaul.* Princeton: Princeton University Press, 1993.

Wallace-Hadrill, John M. *The Frankish Church.* Oxford: Clarendon, 1983.

Social and Economic History

Blackburn, Mark A. S., ed. *Anglo-Saxon Monetary History: Essays in Memory of Michael Dolley.* Leicester, UK: Leicester University Press, 1986.

Bloch, Marc. *French Rural History: An Essay on Its Basic Characteristics.* Trans. Janet Sondheimer. Berkeley: University of California Press, 1966.

———. *Slavery and Serfdom in the Middle Ages.* Trans. William R. Beer. Berkeley: University of California Press, 1975.

Bonnassie, Pierre. *From Slavery to Feudalism in South-Western Europe.* Trans. Jean Birrell. Cambridge: Cambridge University Press, 1991.

Bruce-Mitford, Rupert L. S. *The Sutton Hoo Ship Burial.* 3 vols. London: British Museum, 1975–1983.

Carver, Martin. *The Age of Sutton Hoo.* Woodbridge, UK: Boydell, 1992.

———. *Sutton Hoo: Burial Ground of Kings?* Philadelphia: University of Pennsylvania Press, 1998.

Dockès, Pierre. *Medieval Slavery and Liberation.* Trans. Arthur Goldhammer. Chicago: University of Chicago Press, 1982.

Dolley, Reginald H. Michael ed. *Anglo-Saxon Coins: Studies Presented to F. M. Stenton.* London: Methuen, 1961.

Duby, Georges, ed. *A History of Private Life.* Vol. 2, *Revelations of the Medieval World.* Trans. Arthur Goldhammer. Cambridge, MA: Harvard University Press, 1988.

———. *Rural Economy and Country Life in the Medieval West.* Trans. Cynthia Postan. Columbia: University of South Carolina Press, 1968.

———. *The Early Growth of the European Economy: Warriors and Peasants from the Seventh to the Twelfth Century.* Ithaca, NY: Cornell University Press, 1979.

Evans, Angela Care. *The Sutton Hoo Ship Burial.* London: British Museum, 1986.

Finberg, Herbert P. R., ed. *Agrarian History of England and Wales.* Vol. 1. Cambridge: Cambridge University Press, 1972.

Ganshof, François Louis. *Frankish Institutions under Charlemagne.* Trans. Bryce Lyon and Mary Lyon. Providence, RI: Brown University Press, 1968.

Gies, Frances, and Joseph Gies. *Marriage and Family in the Middle Ages.* New York: Harper and Row, 1987.

Gladitz, Charles. *Horse Breeding in the Medieval World.* Dublin: Four Courts Press, 1997.

Goody, Jack. *The Development of Family and Marriage in Europe.* Cambridge: Cambridge University Press, 1983.

Grierson, Philip, and Mark Blackburn. *Medieval European Coinage.* Vol. 1, *The Early Middle Ages (5th–10th Centuries).* Cambridge: Cambridge University Press, 1986.

Harvey, John. *Mediaeval Gardens.* Beaverton, OR: Timber, 1981.

Herlihy, David. *Medieval Households.* Cambridge, MA: Harvard University Press, 1985.

Hodges, Richard. *The Anglo-Saxon Achievement: Archeology and the Beginnings of English Society.* London: Duckworth, 1989.

King, Peter D. *Law and Society in the Visigothic Kingdom.* Cambridge: Cambridge University Press 1972.

Lewit, Tamara. *Agricultural Production in the Roman Economy, A.D. 200–400.* Oxford: Tempus Reparatum, 1991.

Lyon, Bryce. *A Constitutional and Legal History of Medieval England.* 2d ed. New York: Norton, 1980.

Morrison, Karl F., and Henry Grunthal. *Carolingian Coinage.* New York: American Numismatic Society, 1967.

Munz, Peter. *Life in the Age of Charlemagne.* New York: G. P. Putnam's Sons, 1971.

Odegaard, Charles E. *Vassi et Fideles in the Carolingian Empire.* Cambridge, MA: Harvard University Press, 1945.

Pirenne, Henri. *Mohammed and Charlemagne.* Trans. Bernard Miall. New York: Barnes and Noble, 1992.

Pollock, Frederick, and Frederic W. Maitland. *The History of English Law before the Time of Edward I.* 2d ed. 2 vols. London: Cambridge University Press, 1968.

Reynolds, Philip. L. *Marriage in the Western Church: The Christianization of Marriage.* Leiden: Brill, 1994.

Riché, Pierre. *Daily Life in the World of Charlemagne.* Trans. Jo Ann McNamara. Philadelphia: University of Pennsylvania Press, 1983.

Shahar, Shulamith. *Growing Old in the Middle Ages: 'Winter clothes us in shadow and pain'.* Trans. Yael Lotan. New York: Routledge, 1995.

Slicher van Bath, Bernard H. *The Agrarian History of Western Europe: A.D. 500–1850.* Trans. Olive Ordish. London: Arnold, 1963.

Todd, Malcolm. *Everyday Life of the Barbarians: Goths, Franks, and Vandals.* London and New York: G. P. Putnam's' Sons, 1972.

Veyne, Paul. *A History of Private Life.* Vol. 1, *From Pagan Rome to Byzantium.* Trans. Arthur Goldhammer. Cambridge, MA: Harvard University Press, 1987.

White, Lynn, Jr. *Medieval Technology and Social Change.* Oxford: Oxford University Press, 1964.

Wormald, Patrick. "*Lex Scripta* and *Verbum Regis:* Legislation and Germanic Kingship from Euric to Cnut." In *Early Medieval Kingship,* ed. Peter Sawyer and Ian N. Wood. Leeds, UK: University of Leeds Press, 1977, pp. 105–138.

Women

Blamires, Alcuin. *Women Defamed, Women Defended.* Oxford: Oxford University Press, 1990.

Clark, Gillian. *Women in Late Antiquity: Pagan and Christian Lifestyles.* Oxford: Clarendon, 1993.

Damico, Helen and A. Hennessy, eds. *New Readings on Women in Old English Literature.* Bloomington, IN: Indiana University Press, 1990.

Dronke, Peter. *Women Writers of the Middle Ages: A Critical Study of Texts from Perpetua (d. 203) to Marguerite Porete (d. 1310).* Cambridge: Cambridge University Press, 1984.

Ferrante, Joan M. "Women's Role in Latin Letters from the Fourth to the Early Twelfth Century." In *The Cultural Patronage of Medieval Women,* ed. June Hall McCash. Athens: University of Georgia Press, 1996, pp. 73–105.

Hollum, Kenneth G. *Theodosian Empresses: Women and Imperial Dominion in Late Antiquity.* Berkeley: University of California Press, 1989.

Jewell, Helen. *Women in Medieval England.* Manchester and New York: Manchester University Press, 1996.

Kirshner, Julius, and Suzanne Wemple, eds. *Women of the Medieval World.* Oxford: Basil Blackwell, 1985.

Leyser, Henrietta. *Medieval Women: A Social History of Women in England, 450–1500.* New York: St. Martin's, 1995.

McCash, June Hall, ed. *The Cultural Patronage of Medieval Women.* Athens, GA: University of Georgia Press, 1996.

Nelson, Janet L. "Queens as Jezebels: The Careers of Brunhild and Balthild in Merovingian History." In *Medieval Women,* ed. Derek Baker. Oxford: Blackwell, 1978, pp. 31–77.

Schulenburg, Jane Tibbetts. *Forgetful of their Sex: Female Sanctity and Society, ca. 500–1100.* Chicago: University of Chicago Press, 1998.

Shahar, Shulamith. *The Fourth Estate: A History of Women in the Middle Ages.* New York: Routledge, 1990.

Stafford, Pauline. *Queens, Concubines, and Dowagers: The King's Wife in the Early Middle Ages.* Athens: University of Georgia Press, 1983.

Stuard, Susan Mosher, ed. *Women in Medieval Society.* Philadelphia: University of Pennsylvania Press, 1976.

Ward, Elizabeth. "Caesar's Wife: The Career of the Empress Judith, 819–829." In *Charlemagne's Heir: New Perspectives on the Reign of Louis the Pious,* ed. Peter Godman and Roger Collins. Oxford: Clarendon, 1990, pp. 205–227.

Wemple, Suzanne. *Women in Frankish Society: Marriage and the Cloister, 500 to 900.* Philadelphia: University of Pennsylvania Press, 1981.

Index

Skulls, deformed, 23
Slaves and slavery, 288, **317–319**
    Angle slave boys as inspiration to
        Gregory the Great, 2, 50,
        184–185, 202
    children and, 162
    Franks and, 314
    Germanic religion and, 178
    laws and, 309, 314
    marriage and, 262
    slaves killed after Attila's burial, 207
Slavs, 54, 97
Sofia. *See* Serdica
Soissons, chalice of, 126, 128, 266
Solidus (coin), xv, 129, 130
Soliloquies (Augustine), 28
Song of Roland, 108
Spain
    Alans and, 15, 349
    Charlemagne's invasion of, 108
    coinage and, 130
    Euric and, 157–158, 358–359
    Gaiseric and, 174
    Hermenegild and, 202–203
    Isidore of Seville and, 213
    Jews in, 213, 214–215
    legal codes, 232
    Leovigild and, 240–242
    Muslims and. *See* Muslims
    Reccared I and. *See* Reccared I
    Roman Catholicism and, 42, 202,
        240–242, 304
    row-grave cemeteries, 309–310
    Theodoric the Great and, 283, 338
    Vandals and, 351
    Visigothic church in, 358
    Visigoths and, 42, 202–203, 355,
        358
    See also Visigoths; *specific places and
        rulers*
Spangelhelm, 367
Spanish March, 95, 108, 143
Spata, 365–366
Spears, 365, 366
Spices, 145
Spoleto, 187, 244, 246, 247, 375
St. Albans, monastery at, 277
St. Denis, monastery of, 94, 95, 139,

140, 267, 296
St. Hilary, monastery of, 298
St. Martin, monastery of, 298
St. Maurice, monastery of, 316
St. Paul's Cathedral, 2
St. Peter, Confession of, 148
Stephen II, Pope
    Aistulf and, 11–13, 91, 295
    Bertrada and, 75–76
    Carloman and, 89
    Chrodegang of Metz and, 123
    Desiderius and, 141
    Donation of Constantine and, 147
    Donation of Pippin and, 95,
        147–148, 295
    Pippin III (the Short) and, 94, 114,
        295
Stephen III, Pope, 142, 197
Stephen IV, Pope, 257
Stilicho, Flavius, xvi, 175, **320–321**
    Alans and, 14, 321
    Alaric I and, 15, 16–17, 320, 321,
        356
    Arbogast and, 40
    Arcadius and, 320, 321
    execution of, 204, 320, 321
    Honorius and, 204, 320
    Radagaisus and, 208, 321
    Vandals and, 348–349
Stirrups, 38, 55, 299, 366
Strasbourg, 48
Strasbourg, Oath of, 116, 252, 253,
        274, **322**, 354
Strava ceremony, 207
Suetonius, 156
Suevi, 48, 203, 306
Sulpicius Severus, 156
Sussex, 34, 35, 202, 277
Sutton Hoo, **322–324**
Swords, 363–364
Syagrius, 18, 126, 128
Sylvester I, Pope, 147
Symmachus, 77, 335, 339
Synod of Whitby (664), 36, 66, **325**

Tacitus, xiii, 177
    on clothing, 124
    on families, 161

influence on Einhard, 156
    on Lombards, 245
    on marriage customs, 261–263
    on women, 369
    writings preserved by Carolingians,
        100
Tarik, 358
Tassilo, 76, 95, 107, 142, 327–328
Taxes, xv, 168, 187, 235, 266
Tertry, Battle of, 93, 151, 268, 292,
        328–329
Tervingi. *See* Visigoths
Thane. *See* Thegn
Thegn, **329–330**
Theoda, **330**, 371
Theodatus, 197
Theoderada, 163
Theodoald, 112, 298
Theodohad, 30, 284, 334, 369, 370
Theodolinda, 287
Theodora, 225–226, **330–335**, 372
    Amalaswintha and, 29–30, 65, 227,
        284
    Nika Revolt and, 333
    Procopius on, 225, 299, 300,
        331–333
Theodore of Tarsus, 38, 67
Theodoric the Great, xviii, 226, 265
        (figure), 280, 282–284,
        335–339, 337 (figure), 358
    Alaric II and, 18
    Arianism and, 42, 77, 136, 335,
        339
    Attila the Hun and, 358
    Boethius and, 77–78, 335
    Caesarius of Arles and, 86
    Cassiodorus and, 103, 335, 338
    Clovis and, 128, 283, 338, 359
    death of, 104, 339
    descendents of. *See* Amalaswintha;
        Athalaric
    Gundobad and, 193
    Jordanes and, 222
    legal codes, 233
    mausoleum at Ravenna, 281
        (photo), 338
    Odovacar and, 18, 275, 276, 283,
        335

About the Author

Michael Frassetto earned his Ph.D. in history at the University of Delaware and was awarded a Fulbright Scholarship to research his dissertation in Berlin in 1989–1990. He is an associate editor at the Encyclopaedia Britannica and an adjunct instructor at the University College of Benedictine University. He is the author of numerous articles on medieval history. He is also the editor of *Medieval Purity and Piety: Essays on Medieval Clerical Celibacy and Religious Reform, Western Views of Islam in Medieval and Early Modern Europe: Perception of Other* (with David Blanks), and *The Year 1000: Social and Religious Response to the Turning of the First Millennium.*